CONTEMPORARY

Marketing

Sixth Edition

CONTEMPORARY

Marketing

Sixth Edition

Louis E. Boone
*Ernest G. Cleverdon
Chair of Business and
Management
University of South Alabama*

David L. Kurtz
*The R. A. and Vivian Young
Chair of Business
Administration
and Head, Department of
Marketing and Transportation
University of Arkansas*

The Dryden Press
Chicago   New York   San Francisco   Philadelphia
Montreal   Toronto   London   Sydney   Tokyo

Acquisitions Editor: Rob Zwettler
Developmental Editor: Jan Richardson
Project Editor: Karen Steib
Design Director: Alan Wendt
Production Manager: Barb Bahnsen
Permissions Editor: Doris Milligan
Director of Editing, Design, and Production: Jane Perkins

Copy Editor: Nancy Maybloom
Indexer: Sheila Ary
Compositor: The Clarinda Company
Text Type: 9½/12 Helvetica

Library of Congress Cataloging-in-Publication Data

Boone, Louis E.
    Contemporary marketing.

    Bibliography: p.
    Includes index.
    1. Marketing.   I. Kurtz, David L.   II. Title.
HF5415.B53   1989   658.8   87-38143
ISBN 0-03-022814-X

Printed in the United States of America
 90-039-98765432
Copyright © 1989, 1986, 1983, 1980, 1977, 1974 by The Dryden Press, a division
of Holt, Rinehart and Winston, Inc.

Address orders:
The Dryden Press
Orlando, Florida 32887

Address editorial correspondence:
908 N. Elm St.
Hinsdale, IL 60521

The Dryden Press
Holt, Rinehart and Winston
Saunders College Publication

Cover Illustration: "Marché aux Puces" by Michel Delacroix, 1977. Courtesy of
Lublin Graphics, Inc., 95 East Putnam Avenue, Greenwich, CT 06830.

To our families,
Pat, Barry, and Christopher
Diane, Jennifer, Kelli, Fred, and Tom

About the Authors

Louis E. Boone (Ph.D.) holds the Ernest G. Cleverdon Chair of Business and Management at the University of South Alabama. He formerly chaired the Division of Management and Marketing at the University of Tulsa and has taught marketing in Australia, Greece, and the United Kingdom.

Dr. Boone has been active in applying computer technology to marketing education. His research on marketing information systems has been published in the *Proceedings of the American Marketing Association, Business Horizons,* and the *Journal of Business Strategy.* His marketing simulations include *Marketing Strategy* (Charles E. Merrill Publishing Company, 1971 and 1975) and *The Sales Management Game* (McGraw-Hill, 1989). His research has also been published in such journals as the *Journal of Marketing, Journal of Retailing, Journal of Business of the University of Chicago, Business, Health Marketing Quarterly, Journal of Business Research,* and the *Journal of Marketing Education.* He has served as president of the Southwestern Marketing Association and vice-president of the Southern Marketing Association.

David L. Kurtz (Ph.D.) heads the Department of Marketing and Transportation at the University of Arkansas where he holds the R. A. and Vivian Young Chair of Business Administration. Dr. Kurtz has also taught at Seattle University, Eastern Michigan University, Davis & Elkins College, and Chisholm Institute of Technology in Melbourne, Australia.

Dr. Kurtz has authored or coauthored 24 books and more than 60 articles, monographs, cases, book reviews, and computer simulations. His text *Foundations of Marketing* (Louis E. Boone and Dale M. Beckman, coauthors) is used as the introductory marketing text by over 50 percent of all Canadian colleges and universities. Dr. Kurtz has served as president of the Western Marketing Educators Association and vice-president of the Academy of Marketing Science. He currently serves on the editorial review boards of three marketing journals and has been the president of a small corporation.

The Dryden Press Series in Marketing

Preface

During the past 15 years, more than three-quarters of a million students have begun their study of marketing with *Contemporary Marketing*. The book's long-lived popularity stems from its role as the innovation leader among marketing textbooks. With each successive edition it has introduced a number of "firsts" to bring marketing alive for students. It was the first, for example, to use learning aids such as opening vignettes and boxed items to show an actual individual or firm applying the concepts discussed in the chapter. In the fifth edition, *Contemporary Marketing* introduced computer applications following each chapter.

The sixth edition continues in this tradition of innovation. We believe it once again establishes a benchmark that will have a lasting effect on how the introduction to marketing course is taught.

Integrating Print and Video Technology

Technological advances are having a profound effect on college and university teaching. In recent years, publishers have been barraged with increased requests for integrated video materials that are closely aligned with marketing concepts discussed in the textbook. *Contemporary Marketing* is the first text to truly answer those requests. Each of the 20 chapters in *Contemporary Marketing* is accompanied by an Emmy Award-winning 29-minute video. Writers, directors, and other technical specialists responsible for the creation of each video first studied the text chapter and then chose a case example of a company that has successfully applied the concepts and principles comprising that chapter. Included in the 20 videos are giant corporations and tiny start-up businesses, nonprofit organizations, international marketers, minority enterprises, and service firms. A complete listing by chapter of the *Contemporary Marketing* videos is given below.

1. The United States Army
2. Mitsubishi Motor Sales of America
3. Pizza Hop
4. The Disney Channel
5. Kawasaki Motors Corp.
6. Skyfox Corp.
7. Irvine Co.
8. Carushka
9. Robert Mondavi
10. Yamaha Motorcycles
11. Looking Good Calendar Co.
12. Famous Amos

13. Northern Produce Co./Mushrooms, Inc.

14. West Ridge Mountaineering

15. Arrowhead Drinking Water Co.

16. Apple Computer, Inc.

17. Chiat/Day

18. Lipton & Lawry's

19. Fluor Corp.

20. Azure Seas

A video case complete with student homework assignments is included at the end of each chapter. In addition, a separate manual, *Video Case Teaching Notes,* provides detailed outlines for each video, teaching objectives, and specific page references to text concepts shown in the video. All 20 videos are available at no cost to professors who use *Contemporary Marketing* in their classes. With them, we feel we have succeeded in integrating videos with the text.

Computer Applications

Contemporary Marketing accomplishes the dual objectives of increasing the student's level of analytical thinking in the basic marketing course and integrating the use of microcomputers in the marketing curriculum. At the end of each chapter, a special *Computer Applications* section describes the use of a technique or marketing concept that can be adapted to the microcomputer. Each section contains at least five marketing problems that focus specifically on marketing concepts discussed in the chapter. Techniques used in solving marketing problems include such basic models as breakeven analysis, return on investment, inventory turnover, the EOQ model, Engel's laws, the exchange process, markups and markdowns, and sales forecasting. Over 100 computer problems are included in the text; additional problems are contained in the *Study Guide.*

These problems can be solved with the use of the *Boone & Kurtz Marketing Disk,* a software supplement available free to adopters for use with the IBM® PC and Apple® II systems. The following 16 programs, each presented in a user-friendly, menu-driven format for use in solving marketing problems, are included:

1. Exchange Process

2. Decision Tree Analysis

3. Sales Forecasting

4. Sales Analysis

5. Evaluation of Alternatives

6. Competitive Bidding

7. Engel's Laws

8. Return on Investment (ROI)

9. Breakeven Analysis

10. Inventory Turnover

11. Markups

12. Markdowns

13. Economic Order Quantity (EOQ)

14. Promotional Budget Allocations

15. Advertising Evaluations

16. Sales Force Size Determination

At the request of several reviewers, the problems have been structured to require the student to draw conclusions based upon the data being analyzed. In addition, spreadsheet problems such as modified breakeven analysis, competitive bidding, and sales force size determination allow the student to manipulate data and observe the changes in profits, prices, and breakeven points.

Since full descriptions of each technique and sample problems with solutions are included in the text, the instructor can use these computer problems in a variety of formats. If students have ready access to microcomputers, problem assignments can be used as daily homework. If computers are not easily accessible, the problems can be solved by using a calculator. When microcomputer access is difficult, instructors can integrate computer usage in their classes by making one or two assignments during the term and/or by spacing computer assignments for different groups of students throughout the course to relieve demand for computer access in the microcomputer lab. Each of these alternatives will succeed in providing homework assignments involving quantitative problems for every chapter in the textbook.

Strategic Orientation

Contemporary Marketing is written with a strong marketing planning/strategy orientation. As a number of reviewers have pointed out, planning occurs at the beginning of the marketing effort, not at the end. Consequently, coverage of marketing planning and forecasting begins in Chapter 3. The chapter has been revised extensively to provide a strong, logical treatment of both the *why* and *how* of marketing planning. In addition, a new appendix titled *Developing a Marketing Plan* has been added. The appendix includes a discussion of the how of marketing planning and is in response to dozens of requests for specific examples of an actual marketing plan. It is a practically oriented discussion of how to write a marketing plan.

The shift to a more strategic orientation is not limited to a single chapter. Chapter 7, for example, provides detailed coverage of major segmentation bases in both consumer and industrial markets. The treatment of retailing and wholesaling has been thoroughly reworked to replace descriptive materials with more strategy-oriented information. All of the chapters in Part 7 have been rewritten to emphasize a more analytic, decision-oriented approach to promotional strategy.

Integrating Nonprofit and For-Profit Marketing

Many authors of marketing texts treat the subject of marketing in nonprofit organizations as an "add-on" subject by inserting a separate chapter at the end of the book. *Contemporary Marketing* integrates the broadened view of marketing throughout the text. The expanded concept of marketing incorporating nonprofit organizations, places, persons, and causes as well as tangible goods begins in Chapter 1 and continues through Chapter 20.

New Chapter on Services

Contemporary Marketing also extends its coverage to the vital yet often neglected area of service strategy. Chapter 20 is a new chapter devoted to thoroughly treating this important component of marketing. In addition, unique aspects of the marketing of services are discussed at appropriate locations throughout the text. For instance, Chapter 12 contains a section entitled "Marketing Channels for Services."

Focus on Competitiveness and Marketing Ethics

Unlike the frequently interruptive boxed illustrations in many marketing texts, *Contemporary Marketing* integrates examples directly in the text materials to emphasize concepts by showing their application by actual firms. Numerous examples of real-life organizations are found on every page. The generous use of examples has been a trademark of the text since its inception.

Two topics, however, are so important to today's marketing students that they require special emphasis: marketing competitiveness and marketing ethics. Special theme boxes emphasizing these two subjects are included in each chapter.

The Competitive Edge contains a case example emphasizing chapter concepts by introducing an organization whose marketers have achieved competitive success either in the United States or in international markets. In each case, their distinctive competence has been the result of correctly applying marketing concepts described in the chapter. The examples used include the following:

- □ Nordstrom, Inc.
- □ Kleenex Tissues
- □ Domino's Pizza
- □ Cincinnati Microwave
- □ TABASCO Brand Pepper Sauce
- □ Arbor Cinema Four
- □ Boeing
- □ Wal-Mart Stores

The second theme box, *Focus on Ethics,* examines a number of wide-ranging ethical issues facing marketers and their organizations. The following examples illustrate the variety of issues treated in the text:

- □ Can Marketing Ethics Be Taught?
- □ "Your Free Prize is Waiting for You to Claim . . ."
- □ Extending the Product Life Cycle of Cigarettes
- □ New Drugs for AIDS Victims
- □ Buy American?
- □ The Unethical Sales Presentation

Emphasis on Buyer Behavior and Marketing Mix Elements

Contemporary Marketing is designed to meet instructor demands for a thorough treatment of the core topics of market segmentation, buyer behavior, and the elements of the marketing mix. Part 3 devotes three chapters to the first two topics. Coverage of consumer behavior in Chapter 5 has been thoroughly revised and improved. Chapter 6 has been expanded to focus on *organizational* buying behavior by including concise, comprehensive treatments of buyer behavior in the producer, trade industries, institutional, and government markets. Chapter 7 analyzes the concept of market segmentation and describes segmentation techniques used in both consumer and industrial markets.

At least two chapters focus on each of the elements of the marketing mix. Unlike some recent texts, *Contemporary Marketing* does not neglect the vital roles of marketing institutions and physical distribution. Separate chapters are devoted to the subjects of retailing, wholesaling, and the management of physical distribution.

A Completely New Full-Color Art Program

Perhaps the most visible indicator of the improved sixth edition of *Contemporary Marketing* is the new full-color design. Every figure and table is new and has been designed by a team of artists based upon the authors' instructions. The result is a state-of-the-art book using color photographs, advertisements, and illustrations to emphasize text concepts.

Instructional Resource Package

The sixth edition of *Contemporary Marketing* is a comprehensive teaching/ learning package unparalleled in its completeness. The textbook is undoubtedly the most critical element in the package, but it is only one part. Because of extensive research and careful coordination, the complete package is uniquely suited to the needs of marketing professors. Since both authors of *Contemporary Marketing* teach introductory marketing, we are well aware of the challenges facing the instructor. The *Instructional Resource Package* is designed to assist the basic marketing professor, who so often has large classes and a heavy teaching load.

The *Instructional Resource Package* consists of the following supplementary teaching aids:

Instructor's Resource Manual

These two bound volumes of instructional materials contain the following sections for each chapter:

- □ Changes from the Previous Edition
- □ Slide/Lecture Description
- □ Annotated Learning Goals
- □ Key Terms
- □ Lecture Outline
- □ Lecture Illustration File
- □ Answers to Review Questions
- □ Answers to Discussion Questions
- □ Answers to Video Case Questions

- ☐ Solutions to Computer Applications
- ☐ Supplemental Case
- ☐ Teaching Notes for Supplemental Case
- ☐ Experiential Exercises
- ☐ Guest Speaker Suggestions
- ☐ Film/Videocassette Guide
- ☐ Study Guide Solutions

A total of 100 suggested term paper topics are also included in the *Instructor's Resource Manual.*

Test Bank

The completely revised 3,000-question *Test Bank* is available in both a printed and a computerized format. The *Test Bank* had been designed to aid the classroom learning experience with a wide range of testing alternatives. Each chapter includes multiple choice, true/false, and essay questions, as well as two minicases. The minicases, which are followed by multiple-choice questions, present a problem situation that requires a more thorough analysis and synthesis of information than the typical multiple-choice question. Each question is keyed to specific text page numbers and level of difficulty. Questions that are similar to *Study Guide* questions are indicated as such. The *Test Bank* was prepared by Professors Abraham Axelrud, Jonas Falik, and Ben Wieder of Queensborough Community College.

Study Guide

The *Study Guide* is a learning supplement designed to further students' understanding and to provide them with additional practice in applying concepts presented in the text. Each chapter includes a brief summary of the chapter, experiential exercises, a self-quiz, cases, short-answer questions, and computer problems. Also included are crossword puzzles at the end of each part, a marketing plan exercise, and three term projects. The *Study Guide* was prepared by Professor Thomas S. O'Connor of the University of New Orleans.

Marketing Simulation Game

Microsim, a marketing simulation game written by Professor Steven Schnaars of Baruch College, is available for marketing instructors. The game asks students to assume the role of a marketing manager for a microwave oven company and manipulate fundamental marketing variables to maximize profits. It is designed for use with either IBM PC or Apple II microcomputers.

The Boone & Kurtz Marketing Disk

The *Boone & Kurtz Marketing Disk* contains complete programs for the computer applications problems in the textbook and *Study Guide.* It is available free to adopters for use with Apple II or IBM PC microcomputers.

Contemporary Marketing Videos and Video Case Teaching Notes

The 20 *Contemporary Marketing Videos* are available at no cost for professors who use the text in their classes. The videos are available only in one-half inch VHS format. In addition, a separate manual, *Video Case Teaching Notes,* is provided with the videos.

Full-Color Overhead Transparencies

This innovative component includes a set of 150 original full-color transparency acetates, which are also available as 35mm slides. Without duplicating the presentation of material in the text, each transparency is a striking graphic illustration of a concept discussed in *Contemporary Marketing.* Approximately 45% of the transparencies are advertisements illustrating marketing concepts. The set includes teaching notes for each transparency.

Slide/Lecture Series

The series consists of three 50-minute lecture modules, each illustrated by approximately 50 full-color slides and accompanied by a written commentary for instructors. The three modules cover the following marketing subjects:

- Marketing planning and segmentation
- International marketing
- Marketing for small business

The lectures present fundamental marketing concepts, applications, and examples keyed to material in *Contemporary Marketing,* but with new materials, examples, and illustrations not contained in the text.

Acknowledgments

Every successful textbook is the product of many people's work. Textbooks are, after all, merely a reflection of contemporary thought in a discipline. In this respect, marketing is blessed with a strong cadre of academicians and practitioners who are constantly seeking to improve and advance the discipline.

The authors gratefully acknowledge the following academic colleagues who reviewed all or part of the manuscripts for earlier editions:

Keith Absher	Jeffrey T. Doutt	Paul E. Green
Dub Ashton	Sid Dudley	Blaine Greenfield
Wayne Bascom	Phillip E. Egdorf	Matthew Gross
Richard D. Becherer	John W. Ernest	John H. Hallaq
Richard F. Beltramini	Gary T. Ford	Cary Hawthorn
Howard B. Cox	Ralph M. Gaedeke	Sanford B. Helman
Michael R. Czinkota	Gerry P. Gallo	Nathan Himelstein
Kathy Daruty	James Gould	Robert D. Hisrich
Gordon Di Paolo	Donald Granbois	Ray S. House

Michael D. Hutt	Lou Mansfield	Bert Rosenbloom
Don L. James	Robert D. Miller	Carol Rowey
David Johnson	J. Dale Molander	Ronald S. Rubin
Eugene M. Johnson	John F. Monoky	Bruce Seaton
James C. Johnson	James R. Moore	Howard Seigelman
Harold H. Kassarjian	Carl McDaniel	Jack Seitz
Bernard Katz	Colin Neuhaus	Steven L. Shapiro
James H. Kennedy	Robert T. Newcomb	A. Edward Spitz
Stephen K. Keiser	Dennis D. Pappas	William Staples
Charles Keuthan	Constantine Petrides	Robert E. Stevens
Donald L. Knight	Barbara Piasta	Vern Terpstra
Philip Kotler	Dennis Pitta	John E. Timmerman
Francis J. Leary, Jr.	Barbara Pletcher	Howard A. Thompson
Paul I. Londrigan	Arthur E. Prell	Dennis H. Tootelian
Lynn J. Loudenback	Gary Edward Reiman	Fred Trawick
David L. Loudon	Arnold M. Rieger	Dinoo T. Vanier
Dorothy Maass	C. Richard Roberts	Fred Weinthal
James C. Makens	Patrick J. Robinson	Robert J. Williams
James McCormick	William C. Rodgers	Julian Yudelson
James McHugh	William H. Ronald	Robert J. Zimmer

Our work in preparing the sixth edition was enhanced greatly by the following reviewers who made numerous suggestions. In preparing the sixth edition, we sought out the advice of marketing specialists who reviewed text components that matched their specialized research and teaching areas. The new edition is greatly improved as a result of the dozens of suggestions offered by the following individuals:

Robert Bielski, Dean Junior College
Robert Collins, University of Nevada — Las Vegas
G. P. Gallo, Long Island University
William Green, Loyola Marymount University
Hoyt Hayes, Northeast Missouri State University
Nathan Himelstein, Essex County College
Paul Londrigan, C. S. Mott Community College
Robert O'Keefe, DePaul University
Jacqueline Z. Nicholson, Eckerd College
Sukgoo Pak, University of Tennessee — Martin
Bill Quain, University of Nevada — Las Vegas
Rafael Santos, Imperial Valley College
David Steenstra, Davenport College
G. Knude Swenson, Salisbury State University
Toni Valdez, Mt. San Antonio College
Gayle D. Wasson, Johnson County Community College
Cecilia Wittmayer, Dakota State College

We are especially indebted to Thomas S. O'Connor for preparing the *Study Guide.* Our special thanks go to Steven Schnaars of Baruch College for preparing the marketing simulation game *Microsim* and to Abraham Axelrud, Jonas Falik, and Ben Wieder for their preparation of the *Test Bank,* and to Jacqueline Z. Nicholson, who checked every question in the *Test Bank.* We are also appreciative of the suggestions made by colleagues Tom Becker, Don Gibson,

James Grant, John D. Milewicz, and Lynn B. Robinson of the University of South Alabama and Rex Toh of Seattle University. We can never fully express our appreciation to our research associate, Nancy Moudry, for her many contributions. We would also like to thank our capable secretaries and research associates, Deborah Evers, Michael Fitzgerald, Rubi Gardner, Colleen Keleher, Jeanne Lowe, and Gary Prish for their invaluable assistance.

Finally, we gratefully acknowledge the many contributions of the professionals at The Dryden Press. We would particularly like to thank our publisher Bill Schoof and our editor Rob Zwettler for their insights and suggestions for the new edition. Our developmental editor Jan Richardson was a continuing source of good advice. Karen Steib, Barb Bahnsen, Jan Doty, Kathy Harsch, Rose Hepburn, Mary Jarvis, Doris Milligan, Jane Perkins, and Alan Wendt proved on numerous occasions their ability to eliminate seemingly insurmountable obstacles. And our marketing manager Butch Gemin was a constant source of creative suggestions for improving the new edition. The revision was truly a team effort, and we are in their debt.

Louis E. Boone   **David L. Kurtz**
Mobile, Alabama   Fayetteville, Arkansas
October 1988

Brief Contents

Contents

Chapter 2
Marketing: Its Environment and Role in Society   **40**

Part 3
Buyer Behavior and Market Segmentation   159

Chapter 5
Consumer Behavior   160

Chapter 7
Market Segmentation   232

Part 4
Product and Service Strategy   267

Chapter 8
Product Strategy   268

Chapter 9
Product Mix Decisions and New-Product Planning   294

Part 5
Pricing Strategy

Chapter 10
Price Determination

Chapter 11
Managing the Pricing Function   374

Part 7
Promotional Strategy

Chapter 16
Introduction to Promotion

Chapter 17
Advertising, Sales Promotion, and Public Relations   568

The Contemporary Marketing Environment

1

Photo source: Courtesy of Mazola Corn Oil, Best Foods Division of CPC International. Photography: Kelly-Mooney Photography.

1

Marketing in Profit and Nonprofit Settings

Chapter Objectives

1. To explain the types of utility and the role marketing plays in their creation.

2. To relate the definition of marketing to the concept of the exchange process.

3. To contrast marketing activities during the three eras in the history of marketing.

4. To explain the concept of marketing myopia.

5. To identify and briefly explain the types of nonprofit marketing.

6. To identify the variables involved in marketing decision making and the environmental factors that affect these decisions.

7. To explain the universal functions of marketing.

8. To list three reasons for studying marketing.

T he inspiration that made Avi Fattal a marketing success—and a millionaire—came shortly after he arrived in Southern California. The Israeli immigrant, then 25, scorched his palms and thighs getting into his car in his new American attire of shorts and shirt one summer day in 1981. Recognizing the similarities of Southern California's climate to Israel's, Fattal instantly knew that the solution to this problem was a widely used Israeli product: folding cardboard screens that rest inside a car's front windshield and block the sun from the car's interior. This simple, accordian-style piece of cardboard seemed to be the answer for the millions of drivers who must park their cars in the sun for several hours a day.

Fattal teamed with Avi Ruimi, his friend and fellow Israeli immigrant, to establish Auto-Shade in Van Nuys, California, and market the product. First they negotiated a licensing agreement with the owners of the copyright for the shades. Then they created their own cardboard design in the shape of sunglasses, using such colors as blue, red, yellow, or brown on a white background.

Fattal, who had begun his marketing career as a teenager selling home-cooked food to Israeli soldiers on the move, knew that he and his friend had a marketing success in the new product if he could generate sufficient consumer awareness and make the product available through-

out the United States during the summer months. After all, New Jersey seems just as hot as Los Angeles in August. The two entrepreneurs reached agreements with a number of independent representatives in different geographical areas to market the Auto-Shade auto sunglasses to retail outlets ranging from gas stations and convenience stores to hotels and motels, resort gift shops, and department stores in their assigned territories. By 1985, the cardboard sun protectors were selling at a rate of 150,000 per week at prices ranging from $6 at corner drugstores to $3.95 or less at discount stores. By 1988, Fattal and Ruimi had tapped a new market—corporations such as Goodyear, AT&T, and Bank

of America that used the shades as portable billboards, printing company logos on them and offering them as customer gifts. Corporate orders accounted for approximately one-fifth of the 10 million Auto-Shades sold in 1988. At an average profit of $1 per unit sold, the young marketers had made their millions within a few years of their arrival in America. Not only had they spotted a consumer need and filled it; they also expected to continue to fill it. Fattal does not view Auto-Shades as a fad. "They are good for only one summer. Since I am selling something that works, people will buy again next year."[1]

Photo source: David Dempster, Photosynthesis.

Chapter Overview

All organizations perform two basic functions: They produce a good, a service, or an idea, and they market it. This is true of all firms — from giant manufacturers such as RJR Nabisco and United Airlines to Fattal and Ruimi's Auto-Sales or a neighborhood video rental store. It is true of both profit-seeking firms and nonprofit organizations. Production and marketing are the essence of economic life in any society.

Through the production and marketing of goods, services, and ideas, organizations satisfy a commitment to society, to their customers, and to their own-

Table 1.1

Four Types of Utility

Type	Description	Examples	Organizational Function Responsible for Its Creation
Form	Converting raw materials and components into finished products and services	Fantastic Sam's hair stylists Ford Motor Company	Production[a]
Time	Availability of products and services when consumer wants them	Domino's Pizza's 30-minute home delivery service One-hour photo processing	Marketing
Place	Availability of products and services at convenient locations	Vending machines in office buildings 8,000 McDonald's fast-food outlets	Marketing
Ownership (possession)	Ability to transfer title to product or service from marketer to buyer	Retail outlets (in exchange for currency or credit card payment)	Marketing

[a]Marketing provides inputs related to consumer preferences, but the actual creation of form utility is the responsibility of the production function.

utility
Want-satisfying power of a product or service.

ers. They create what economists call **utility** — the want-satisfying power of a product or service. The four basic kinds of utility — form, time, place, and ownership — are shown in Table 1.1

Form utility is created when the firm converts raw materials and component inputs into finished products and services. Glass, steel, fabrics, rubber, and other components are combined to form a new Ford Taurus or Acura Integra. Cotton, thread, and buttons are converted into Benetton shirts. Sheet music, musical instruments, musicians, a conductor, and the facilities of Orchestra Hall are used to create a performance by the Chicago Symphony Orchestra. Although marketing inputs may be important in specifying consumer and audience preference, the actual creation of form utility is the responsibility of the organization's production function.

Time, place, and ownership utilities are created by marketing. *Time* and *place utility* are created when products and services are available to consumers when and where they want to purchase them, respectively. *Ownership utility* is created when title to the product or service may be transferred at the time of purchase.

This chapter sets the stage for the entire text by examining the meaning of marketing and its importance for all organizations. It describes the development of marketing in our society and its contributions and introduces the marketing variables used in a marketing strategy.

What Is Marketing?

To survive, all organizations must create utility. The designing and marketing of want-satisfying products, services, and ideas is the foundation for the creation of utility. However, the role of marketing in an organization's success has only recently been recognized. Management author Peter F. Drucker emphasizes the importance of marketing in his book *The Practice of Management:*

If we want to know what a business is, we have to start with its purpose. And its purpose must lie outside the business itself. In fact, it must lie in society since a business enterprise is an organ of society. There is one valid definition of business purpose: to create a customer.[2]

How does an organization "create" a customer? Professors Guiltinan and Paul explain it this way:

Essentially, "creating" a customer means identifying needs in the marketplace, finding out which needs the organization can profitably serve, and developing an offering to convert potential buyers into customers. Marketing managers are responsible for most of the activities necessary to create the customers the organization wants. These activities include:

□   *Identifying customer needs*

□   *Designing products and services that meet those needs*

□   *Communicating information about those products and services to prospective buyers*

□   *Making the products or services available at times and places that meet customers' needs*

□   *Pricing the products to reflect costs, competition, and customers' ability to buy*

□   *Providing for the necessary service and follow-up to ensure customer satisfaction after the purchase.*[3]

Marketing: A Definition

Ask five persons to define marketing, and five definitions are likely to follow. Due to their continuous exposure to advertising and personal selling, most respondents are likely to link marketing and selling. Over a quarter-century ago, the American Marketing Association, the international professional association in the marketing discipline, tried to standardize marketing terminology by defining marketing as "the performance of business activities that direct the flow of goods and services from producer to consumer or user."

But this definition proved too narrow. It also implied that marketing begins at the end of a producer's loading dock by emphasizing the flow of products and services that already have been produced. It failed to recognize marketing's crucial role in analyzing consumer needs and securing information designed to ensure that the products or services created by the firm's production facilities would match buyer expectations. The old definition ignored the thousands of nonprofit organizations that engage in marketing activities. A broader and more descriptive view was needed, one that would describe the firm or enterprise as an organized behavioral system seeking to generate output of value to consumers.

In 1985, the American Marketing Association replaced its antiquated definition with a broader one: **Marketing** is the process of planning and executing

marketing
Process of planning and executing the conception, pricing, promotion, and distribution of ideas, goods, and services to create exchanges that will satisfy individual and organizational objectives.

Figure 1.1
Applying Marketing Concepts in Profit and Nonprofit Organizations

Sources: Courtesy of United Airlines, Inc. and Mothers Against Drunk Driving, Southeastern Wisconsin Chapter. The advertising agency that produced the poster for MADD is Frankenberry, Laughlin & Constable, Milwaukee.

the conception, pricing, promotion, and distribution of ideas, goods, and services to create exchanges that will satisfy individual and organizational objectives.[4]

The expanded concept of marketing activities permeates all organizational functions. It assumes that the marketing effort will proceed in accordance with ethical practices and that it will be effective from the standpoint of both society and the organization. It also identifies the marketing variables of product, price, promotion, and distribution that are used to provide consumer satisfaction. In addition, it assumes that the consumer segments to be satisfied through the organization's production and marketing activities have been selected and analyzed prior to production. In other words, the customer, client, or public determines the marketing program. Finally, it recognizes that marketing concepts and techniques are applicable to nonprofit organizations as well as to profit-oriented businesses, as shown in the advertisements in Figure 1.1. United Airlines, a for-profit service firm, targets a select group of consumers by providing airline service to Colorado from the other 49 states — the only airline to do so. The MADD poster illustrates how marketing concepts apply to nonprofit organizations. The Southeastern Wisconsin Chapter of Mothers Against Drunk Driving ran this poster during the holiday season to dramatize the consequences of violating the state's tough drunk-driving law.

The Origins of Marketing

The essence of marketing is the **exchange process,** by which two or more parties give something of value to each other to satisfy felt needs. In many cases, the item is a tangible good, such as a newspaper, a compact disk, or a pair of shoes. In others, intangible services, such as a car wash, a haircut, or a concert performance, are exchanged for money. In still others, funds or time donations may be offered to political candidates, a Red Cross office, or a church or synagogue.

exchange process
Process by which two or more parties give something of value to each other to satisfy perceived needs.

The marketing function is both simple and direct in subsistence-level economies. For example, assume that a primitive society consists solely of Person A and Person B. Assume also that the elements of their standard of living are food, clothing, and shelter. The two live in adjoining caves on a mountainside. They weave their own clothes and tend their own fields independently. They are able to subsist even though their standard of living is minimal.

Person A is an excellent weaver but a poor farmer, whereas Person B is an excellent farmer but a poor weaver. In this situation, it would be wise for each to specialize in the work that he or she does best. The net result would be a greater total production of both clothing and food. In other words, specialization and division of labor would lead to a production surplus. But neither Person A nor Person B would be any better off until each had traded the product of his or her individual labor, thereby creating the exchange process.

Exchange is the origin of marketing activity. In fact, marketing has been described as the process of creating and resolving exchange relationships. When there is a need to exchange goods, the natural result is a marketing effort on the part of the people involved. As Wroe Alderson, a leading marketing theorist, points out, "It seems altogether reasonable to describe the development of exchange as a great invention which helped to start primitive man on the road to civilization."[5]

While the cave dweller example is simplistic, it reveals the essence of the marketing function. A complex, industrial society has a more complicated exchange process, but the basic concept is the same: Production is not meaningful until a system of marketing has been established. Perhaps publisher Red Motley's adage sums it up best: "Nothing happens until somebody sells something."

Three Eras in the History of Marketing

Although marketing has always been a part of business, its importance has varied greatly. As Table 1.2 shows, three historical eras can be identified: (1) the production era, (2) the sales era, and (3) the marketing era.

The Production Era

Until about 1925, most firms were production oriented. Manufacturers stressed production of quality products and then looked for people to purchase them. Pillsbury Company is an excellent example of a production-oriented company.

Table 1.2

Three Eras in the History of Marketing

Era	Approximate Time Period	Prevailing Attitude
Production era	Prior to 1920s	"A good product will sell itself."
Sales era	1920s to 1950s	"Creative advertising and selling will overcome consumer resistance and convince them to buy."
Marketing era	Last half of twentieth century	"The consumer is king! Find a need and fill it."

Here is how the company's chief executive officer, the late Robert J. Keith, described Pillsbury during its early years:

We are professional flour millers. Blessed with a supply of the finest North American wheat, plenty of water power, and excellent milling machinery, we produce flour of the highest quality. Our basic function is to mill high-quality flour, and, of course (and almost incidentally), we must hire salesmen to sell it, just as we hire accountants to keep our books.[6]

The prevailing attitude of this era was that a good product (defined in terms of physical quality) would sell itself. This **production orientation** dominated business philosophy for decades — indeed, business success was often defined in terms of production victories.

Although marketing had emerged as a functional activity within the business organization prior to the twentieth century, management's orientation remained with production for quite some time. In fact, what might be called industry's production era did not reach its peak until the early part of this century. The apostle of this approach to business operations was Frederick W. Taylor, whose *Principles of Scientific Management* was widely read and accepted. Taylor's approach reflected his engineering background by emphasizing efficiency in the production process. Later writers, such as Frank and Lillian Gilbreth, the originators of motion analysis, expanded on Taylor's basic concepts.

Henry Ford's mass production line exemplifies this orientation. Ford's slogan "They [customers] can have any color they want, as long as it's black" reflected a then prevalent attitude toward marketing. Production shortages and intense consumer demand were the rules of the day. It is easy to understand how production activities took precedence.

The "Better Mousetrap" Fallacy   The essence of the production era resounds in a statement made over 100 years ago by the philosopher Ralph Waldo Emerson:

If a man writes a better book, preaches a better sermon, or makes a better mousetrap than his neighbor, though he builds his house in the woods, the world will make a beaten path to his door.

But Chester M. Woolworth knows better. Woolworth, who is president of the nation's largest mousetrap producer, once designed a new mousetrap based on thorough research on the type of trap that would be most "appealing" to mice. The new model had a modern, brown plastic design, was completely

production orientation
Business philosophy stressing efficiency in producing a quality product; attitude toward marketing is "a good product will sell itself."

sanitary, and was priced only a few cents more than the commonplace wood mousetrap. Also, it never missed!

But the better mousetrap failed as a new-product venture. While Woolworth's designers had created a quality product, they had forgotten the customer and the environment in which the purchase decision is made. The postmortem analysis of this marketing disaster went something like this. Men bought the majority of the newly designed plastic mousetraps. In most instances, it was also the responsibility of the male member of the household to set the trap before the family retired for the night. But the problem occurred the next morning when he failed to check the trap before leaving for work. Women were most likely to check the trap — during the morning in the case of wives not employed outside the home and in the afternoon after work in the case of working women. With the conventional wood trap, they would simply sweep both trap and mouse into a dustpan, minimizing the effort and time involved in this undesirable task. However, the new trap looked too expensive to throw away, even though it cost only a few cents more. Consequently, the wife was faced with first ejecting the mouse and then cleaning the instrument. In a short time, the new, improved mousetrap was replaced with the traditional wood version.

The moral of the mousetrap story is obvious: A quality product is not successful until it is effectively marketed. Mr. Woolworth expressed it most eloquently when he said, "Fortunately, Mr. Emerson made his living as a philosopher, not a company president."[7]

The Sales Era

Between 1925 and the early 1950s, production techniques became more sophisticated and output grew. Thus, manufacturers began to increase the emphasis on an effective sales force for finding customers for their output. In this era, firms attempted to match their output to customers. Companies with a **sales orientation** assume that customers will resist purchasing products and services not deemed essential and that the task of personal selling and advertising is to convince them to buy.

National Biscuit Company (now Nabisco Brands, Inc.) used advertisements like the one in Figure 1.2 to promote its new Ritz cracker introduced in 1934. The product posted a first-year sales record, and the company not only maintained but actually increased sales in the troubled economy of the Depression years. Marketing efforts during this era were also aimed at wholesalers and retailers in an attempt to motivate them to stock greater quantities of manufacturers' output.

Although marketing departments began to emerge during the sales era, they tended to remain in a subordinate position to production, finance, and engineering. Many chief marketing executives held the title of sales manager. Here is how Pillsbury described itself during the sales era:

We are a flour-milling company, manufacturing a number of products for the consumer market. We must have a first-rate sales organization which can dispose of all the products we can make at a favorable price. We must back up this sales force with consumer advertising and market intelligence. We want our sales representatives and our dealers to have all the tools they need for moving the output of our plants to the consumer.[8]

sales orientation
Business philosophy assuming that consumers will resist purchasing nonessential products and services; attitude toward marketing is that creative advertising and personal selling are required in order to overcome consumer resistance and convince them to buy.

Figure 1.2
A Sales Orientation
Advertisement

Source: Courtesy of Nabisco Brands, Incorporated.

But selling is only one component of marketing. As Theodore Levitt has pointed out, "Marketing is as different from selling as chemistry is from alchemy, astronomy from astrology, chess from checkers."[9]

The Marketing Era

As personal incomes and consumer demand for goods and services dropped rapidly during the Great Depression of the 1930s, marketing was thrust into a more important role. Organizational survival dictated that managers pay closer attention to the markets for their products. This trend was halted by the outbreak of World War II, when rationing and shortages of consumer goods became commonplace. The war years, however, were an atypical pause in an emerging trend that resumed almost immediately after the hostilities ceased. The marketing concept was about to emerge.

Emergence of the Marketing Concept

seller's market
Marketplace characterized by a shortage of goods and/or services.

buyer's market
Marketplace characterized by an abundance of goods and/or services.

consumer orientation
Business philosophy incorporating the marketing concept of first determining unmet consumer needs and then designing a system for satisfying them.

What was the setting for this crucial change in management philosophy? Perhaps it can best be explained by the shift from a **seller's market** — one with a shortage of goods and services — to a **buyer's market** — one with an abundance of goods and services. When World War II ended, factories stopped manufacturing tanks and Jeeps and started turning out consumer goods again — an activity that had, for all practical purposes, stopped in early 1942.

The advent of a strong buyer's market created the need for a **consumer orientation** on the part of U.S. business. Products had to be marketed, not just produced and sold. This realization has been identified as the emergence of the marketing concept. The recognition of this concept and its dominant role in business dates from 1952, when General Electric's *Annual Report* heralded a new management philosophy:

[The concept] introduces the marketing man at the beginning rather than at the end of the production cycle and integrates marketing into each phase of the

business. Thus, marketing, through its studies and research, will establish for the engineer, the design and manufacturing man, what the customer wants in a given product, what price he is willing to pay, and where and when it will be wanted. Marketing will have authority in product planning, production scheduling, and inventory control, as well as in sales, distribution, and servicing of the product.[10]

Marketing would no longer be regarded as a supplemental activity performed after the production process has been completed. The marketer would, for instance, now play the lead role in product planning. Marketing and selling would no longer be synonymous.

The **marketing concept** is a companywide consumer orientation with the objective of achieving long-run success. The key words are *companywide consumer orientation.* All facets of the organization must be involved with first assessing and then satisfying customer wants and needs. The effort is not something to be left only to the marketers. Accountants working in the credit office and engineers employed in product design also play important roles. The words *with the objective of achieving long-run success* differentiate the concept from policies of short-run profit maximization. Since the firm's continuity is an assumed component of the marketing concept, companywide consumer orientation will lead to greater long-run profits than will managerial philosophies geared toward reaching short-run goals.

marketing concept
Companywide consumer orientation with the objective of achieving long-run success.

The marketing concept is a contemporary philosophy for dynamic organizational growth. But not all firms have been as quick as General Electric to embrace it. Until the mid-1980s, McCormick & Company, the 98-year-old spice maker, held on to the production-oriented motto of its founder, "Make the Best — Someone Will Buy It." But McCormick realized that in the early 1980s fewer people were beating a path to grocery store shelves to buy its line of 104 gourmet and 107 regular spices. Spice use in general dropped 20 percent between 1980 and 1984, and McCormick's market share in the grocery store spices category declined from 40 to 35 percent. Why? McCormick wasn't paying attention to its customers. It was producing, rather than marketing, its spices. McCormick marketers believed that all they needed was a variety of spices and enough shelf space and consumers would buy.

In 1985, McCormick conducted research on its market — people who cook meals at home — and learned that an increasing number of working women were buying convenience foods and those who were still preparing meals from scratch didn't feel comfortable improvising with spices unless they followed fancy recipes. To give customers what they wanted — convenience and reassurance — and to ensure its long-term growth, McCormick launched a $200 million consumer marketing and product development program. It introduced more convenience-type spices and started a promotional campaign to give consumers simple how-to tips on using spices. The new, consumer-oriented program was expected to boost spice sales by at least 10 percent a year.[11]

Converting Needs to Wants

Every consumer must acquire goods and services on a continuing basis to fill certain needs. The fundamental needs for food, clothing, a home, and transportation must be satisfied through purchase or, in some instances, temporary

THE COMPETITIVE EDGE

Kleenex Tissues

Competitiveness. The word appears to have been added to every marketer's vocabulary over the past few years as organizations seek out special areas of strength to insulate their markets from the never-ending onslaught of both domestic and foreign competition. Some marketers emphasize increased customer satisfaction through postsale service support, such as Chrysler's longer-term warranty. In other instances, companies enhance the value of their product offerings through specific product changes, such as Glad Lock bags' color-coded seal that ensures complete closure or Clorox's splash-reducing bleach bottle. But paper products manufacturer Kimberly-Clark offers so much added value in its Kleenex tissues that it dominates the marketplace.

It wasn't always this way. The firm spent several years after World War I trying to discover a consumer market application for its Cellucotton wood-cellulose tissue. The product, which proved superior to surgical cotton in absorbency, had been developed for use as a surgical dressing during the war. An even more absorbent version of Cellucotton was used as a gas mask filter, and it was this material that Kimberly-Clark began marketing as Kleenex Kerchiefs, a cold-cream remover that could serve as a disposable substitute for

facial towels. Thus was launched one of the most successful brands of the twentieth century.

Then letters from customers started arriving at the firm's corporate headquarters, asking various versions of the same question: Why doesn't the Kleenex tissue advertising or the Kleenex tissue package mention its most practical use as an inexpensive handkerchief? Kimberly-Clark marketers liked the suggestion, and the product's marketing strategy was modified to emphasize these perceived benefits.

A series of memorable advertisements was devised using the theme "Don't put a cold in your pocket." The message that disposable Kleenex tissues prevented reexposure to stored-up germs in contrast to linen handkerchiefs produced immediate and positive responses on the part of the buying public. The new campaign, combined with the 1929 introduction of the Pop-Up-Tissue box, which allowed the pulling of one tissue to raise the next one into the ready position, caused Kleenex tissue sales to double in a single year. A few years later, sales almost doubled again when Kimberly-Clark marketers decided to expand into the new radio advertising medium by sponsoring a hit radio show, "The Story of Mary Marlin."

And so the disposable-tissue industry was born. Today the linen handkerchief is nearly extinct, and

disposable tissues ring up half a billion dollars in sales every year. Kimberly-Clark has extended the underlying product to a whole generation of cellulose-based disposables, such as napkins, towels, and diapers. The firm employs 37,000 people and generates almost $5 billion in sales worldwide each year — all because its marketers were willing to listen to its customers and position its products to match buyer needs and uses.

Sources: The Kleenex tissue story is described in more detail in "Kleenex," *Modern Packaging* (April 1950), pp. 136–140. See also Molly Wade McGrath, *Top Sellers USA* (New York: Morrow, 1983), pp. 124–125. *Photo source:* Courtesy of Kimberly-Clark Corporation.

use in the form of rented property or hired or leased transportation. By focusing on the *benefits* resulting from these products and services, effective marketing converts needs to wants. A need for clothing may be translated into a desire (or want) for designer clothes. The need for transportation may become a desire for a new Suzuki Samurai. The need for liquid refreshment may be satisfied with a product as basic as water or as expensive as Perrier. As the Hush Puppies advertisement shown in Figure 1.3 illustrates, marketing focuses on basic needs (such as shoes) and converts them into wants for specific products and brands (ventilated Hush Puppies).

Figure 1.3
Marketing: Converting
Needs to Wants

Ventilated Hush Puppies.

Will people ever stop panning over these shoes? Cool mesh casuals, in colors and tropical prints.

Source: Courtesy of Wolverine World Wide, Inc.

Avoiding Marketing Myopia

The emergence of the marketing concept has not been devoid of setbacks. One troublesome situation has been what Theodore Levitt calls *marketing myopia*.[12] According to Levitt, **marketing myopia** is management's failure to recognize the scope of its business. Future growth is endangered when management is product oriented rather than customer oriented. Levitt cites many service industries — dry cleaning, electric utilities, movies, and railroads — as examples of marketing myopia.

Organizational goals must be broadly defined and oriented toward consumer needs. Trans World Airlines, for example, has redefined its business as travel rather than just air transportation. The firm now offers complete travel services, such as hotel accommodations, credit, and ground transportation, in addition to air travel. Esprit de Corps, the San Francisco-based clothing designer and manufacturer, describes itself as a "life-style" company rather than a clothing firm and offers, in addition to clothing collections, accessories, shoes, kids' wear, eyewear, and bed and bath accessories.

Revlon founder and president Charles Revson understood that a broader focus on benefits rather than on products is required in order to avoid marketing

marketing myopia
Term coined by Theodore Levitt in his argument that executives in many industries fail to recognize the broad scope of their businesses. According to Levitt, future growth is endangered because these executives lack a marketing orientation.

Table 1.3
Avoiding Marketing Myopia by Focusing on Benefits Provided by the Organization

Company	Myopic Description of Firm's Business	Marketing-Oriented Description of Firm's Business
Walt Disney Enterprises	"We are in the animated-film business."	"We are in the entertainment business."
Burlington Northern Inc.	"We are in the railroad business."	"We are in the transportation business."
Exxon	"We are in the petroleum business."	"We are in the energy business."
Nynex	"We are a telephone company."	"We are a communications company."

myopia. As Revson described it, "In the factory we make perfume; in the store we sell hope." Table 1.3 illustrates how firms in a number of other industries have overcome myopic thinking with a marketing-oriented description of their businesses that focuses on consumer need satisfaction.

Broadening the Marketing Concept to Nonprofit Marketing

In the early 1960s, several writers suggested that marketing should be concerned with issues beyond the traditional profit-oriented domain. Marketing was beginning to be perceived as having a wider application than was formerly believed. A major breakthrough came in 1969 with the publication of Kotler and Levy's classic article arguing that the marketing concept should be broadened to include the nonprofit sector of society.[13] Marketing, they proposed, is a generic activity for all organizations. Thus, the **broadening concept** extended the marketing concept to nontraditional exchange processes.

broadening concept
Expanded view of marketing as a generic function to be performed by both profit-seeking and non-profit organizations.

The broadening concept was not accepted by all marketers. Some argued that it was an unwarranted extension of the marketing concept.[14] Others said the concept might be responsible for undesirable social changes and disorder.[15] But despite such dissent, the broadening concept has been widely adopted by nonprofit organizations. The U.S. armed forces use advertising to recruit volunteers; United Way conducts market research to help American charities attract donors; and the San Diego Zoo employs a goodwill ambassador who promotes and publicizes the zoo's reputation worldwide.

In recent years, financial pressures resulting from increased competition and cutbacks in government funding have prompted more nonprofit groups to adopt the marketing concept. When Beverly Sills took over as general director of the New York City Opera in 1979, ticket sales were down and the company seemed headed for financial ruin. Sills is credited with bringing the company into the twentieth century by using high-profile advertising and marketing surveys. Her other marketing strategies included cutting subscription prices by 20 percent, programming special operatic festivals, and combining the separate fall and spring seasons into one long July-through-November season. Sills traveled some 250,000 miles a year and used her personal selling talents and celebrity status to raise money for the ailing company. Today ticket sales are at record levels and the Opera's budget has jumped from $10 million to $24 million.[16]

Marketing in Nonprofit Organizations

Although a latecomer to the management of nonprofit organizations, marketing has become an important part of the operational environment of many successful nonprofit groups. A substantial part of the U.S. economy is made up of nonprofit organizations — those whose primary objective is something other than returning a profit to its owners. The more than 900,000 nonprofit organizations operating in the United States employ 10 percent of the American work force and generate an estimated $300 billion in revenues each year.[17] The nonprofit sector includes religious and human service organizations, museums, private libraries, secondary schools, many hospitals, colleges and universities, symphony orchestras, fraternal organizations, and thousands of other groups such as government agencies, political parties, and labor unions.

Nonprofit organizations operate in both public and private sectors. Federal, state, and local government units and agencies whose revenues are derived from tax collection have service objectives that are not keyed to profitability targets. The Department of Defense, for example, provides protection; a state department of natural resources regulates conservation and environmental programs; and the local animal control officer enforces ordinances that protect people and animals.

The private sector has an even more diverse array of nonprofit organizations. Art institutes, the University of Southern California's football team, labor unions, hospitals, private schools, the March of Dimes, the Rotary Club, and the local country club are all examples of private-sector, nonprofit organizations. Some, like USC's football team, may return a surplus to the university that can be used to cover other activities, but the organization's primary goal is to win football games. The diversity of nonprofit groups suggests the presence of numerous organizational objectives other than profitability. In addition to organizational goals, nonprofit groups differ from profit-seeking firms in other ways.

Types of Nonprofit Marketing

Nonprofit organizations have a special set of characteristics that influence their marketing activities. Like profit-seeking firms, nonprofits may market a tangible good or an intangible service. The U.S. Postal Service, for example, offers stamps (a tangible good) and mail delivery (an intangible service). As Table 1.4 reveals, four categories of nonprofit marketing can be identified: person marketing, place marketing, idea marketing, and organization marketing.

Person Marketing   **Person marketing** refers to efforts designed to cultivate the attention, interest, and preferences of a target market toward a person.[18] Campaigns for political candidates and promotions for celebrities are examples of person marketing. In political marketing, candidates target two markets: They attempt to gain the recognition and preference of voters and the financial support of donors. Increasing numbers of campaign managers are using computerized marketing research to identify voters and donors and then design adver-

person marketing
Marketing efforts designed to cultivate the attention, interest, and preference of a target market toward a person (typically a political candidate or celebrity).

Table 1.4
Types of Nonprofit Marketing

Type	Brief Description	Examples
Person marketing	Marketing efforts designed to cultivate the attention, interest, and preference of a target market toward a person	Celebrities (such as David Letterman, David Bowie, Gore Vidal) Political candidates ("Mercer for Governor; Carson for President")
Place marketing	Marketing efforts designed to attract visitors to a particular area, improve consumer images of a city, state, or nation, and/or attract new businesses	"Virginia is for lovers." "Arizona is good for business."
Idea marketing	Identification and marketing of a cause or social issue to selected target markets	"Buy American!" "Buckle up, America." "No Nukes!"
Organization marketing	Marketing efforts of mutual-benefit organizations, service organizations, and government organizations that seek to influence others to accept their goals, receive their services, or contribute to them in some way	"Reach for the union label." "Give to the college of your choice." "Army: Be All That You Can Be." "Support your local police."

tising to reach those markets.[19] Other promotional efforts include personal handshakes, political rallies, fund-raising dinners, and publicity. In an attempt to secure the 1988 Democratic presidential nomination, former Arizona governor Bruce Babbitt tried to gain national recognition by pedaling his 15-speed bicycle across the state of Iowa, white-water rafting down the Colorado River with a reporter and several environmentalists, and climbing Mount Washington in New Hampshire.[20]

place marketing
Marketing efforts to attract people and organizations to a particular geographical area.

Place Marketing **Place marketing** refers to attempts to attract customers to a particular area. Cities, states, and countries publicize their tourist attractions to lure vacation travelers. The State of California is attempting to entice tourists to visit the Golden State by sponsoring a series of advertisements, each devoted to a different region of the state. The ad shown in Figure 1.4, "The Middle Kingdom," features the Hearst Castle among the numerous attractions along the central coast of California.

To stimulate economic growth, many communities launch marketing campaigns aimed at attracting new businesses. Memphis, Tennessee, for example, faced the challenge of revitalizing its sluggish economy. After pinpointing its strengths — one of the most centrally located cities in the country, a well-developed highway system, six national railroad lines, and an excellent airport — Memphis decided to market itself as a distribution center. It spent $6 million on a marketing campaign to attract new businesses by describing how companies could use Memphis as a base from which to send their products throughout the country. The investment paid off. Seven years ago, Memphis was the eighteenth largest distribution center in the United States; today it ranks tenth and is still growing. International Paper and Litton Industries are just two of the many firms that recently have located part of their operations in Memphis.[21]

Figure 1.4
Place Marketing: The California Central Coast

Source: Courtesy of The California Department of Commerce.

Idea Marketing **Idea marketing** refers to the identification and marketing of a cause or social issue to selected consumer market segments. Idea marketing covers a wide range of issues, including physical fitness, gay rights, family planning, prison reform, overeating, pollution control, birth defects, child abuse, gun control, and drunk driving. A cause marketed recently by the American Cancer Society is the need for sun protection. An ACS advertising campaign targets two high-risk groups — leisure tanners and outdoor workers — with the message "Cover up or face the consequences." The ad directed at leisure tanners shows a skeleton with a pair of sunglasses lying on a chaise lounge and carries the heading "Skin Cancer Can Ruin a Beautiful Tan." The ad aimed at outdoor workers shows a brawny construction worker without a shirt. The headline warns: "Staying Cool on the Job Could Cost You Your Life." Both messages attempt to educate the public about avoidance of skin cancer, a disease that kills more than 7,000 Americans a year.[22]

idea marketing
Identification and marketing of a cause to chosen consumer segments.

Figure 1.5
An Example of
Organization Marketing

Source: Courtesy of Portland Art Museum.

organization marketing
Marketing by mutual-benefit organizations, service organizations, and government organizations that seek to influence others to accept their goals, receive their services, or contribute to them in some way.

Organization Marketing **Organization marketing** involves attempts to influence others to accept the goals of, receive the services of, or contribute in some way to an organization. For example, through advertisements like the one in Figure 1.5, the Portland Art Museum invites the public to visit the museum and experience such art as the Renoir masterpiece firsthand. Organization marketing includes mutual benefit organizations (churches, labor unions, and political parties), service organizations (colleges and universities, hospitals, and museums), and government organizations (military services, police and fire departments, and the U.S. Postal Service). An example of organization marketing is Wisconsin Calling, a phonathon program set up by the University of Wisconsin Foundation that targets UW–Madison alumni. Through this fund-raising program, student callers contact alumni across the country to solicit their financial support, update alumni records, and answer questions about the university. Another example is a marketing campaign used by the Trinitarians, an 800-year-old order of Catholic priests, to attract young men into the priesthood. The order discovered that the majority of its candidates were older men, changing in mid-career, and that younger men were not as interested in entering the priesthood as in past years. The new marketing effort is evident in a series of ads with catchy headlines — "Good help is still hard to find" and "The man who answers this ad should be committed" — in the college editions of *Time* and *Newsweek* to attract young men to a career in the Trinitarian order.[23]

Characteristics of Nonprofit Marketing

An important distinction between nonprofits and for-profit companies is that non-profit organizations often market to multiple publics, which complicates the decision regarding the correct market to target. Political candidates, for example, target both voters and campaign contributors. One writer describes it this way:

Nonprofit organizations normally have at least two major publics to work with from a marketing point of view: their clients and their funders. The former pose the problem of resource allocation *and the latter, the problem of* resource attraction. *Besides these two publics, many other publics surround the nonprofit organization and call for marketing programs. Thus, a college can direct marketing programs toward prospective students, current students, parents of students, alumni, faculty, staff, local business firms, and local government agencies. It turns out that business organizations also deal with a multitude of publics, but their tendency is to think about marketing only in connection with one of these publics, namely their customers.*[24]

A second distinguishing characteristic of nonprofit marketing is that a customer or service user may wield less control over the destiny of a nonprofit organization than would be true for a profit-seeking firm. A government employee may be far more concerned with the opinion of a member of the legislature's appropriations committee than with that of a service user. Further, non-profit organizations often possess some degree of monopoly power in a given geographical area. An individual might object to the United Fund's inclusion of a crisis center among its beneficiary agencies. But a contributor who responds to the United Fund appeal recognizes that a portion of total contributions will go to the agency in question.

Another potential problem involves the resource contributor, such as a legislator or financial backer, who interferes with the marketing program. It is easy to imagine a political candidate harassed by financial supporters who want to replace an unpopular campaign manager (the primary marketing position in a political campaign).

Perhaps the most commonly noted feature of the nonprofit organization is its lack of a *bottom line* — a term in business jargon referring to the overall profitability measure of performance. Profit-seeking firms can measure profitability in terms of sales and revenues. While nonprofit organizations may attempt to maximize their return from a specific service, less exact goals, such as service-level standards, are the usual substitute for an overall evaluation. The net result is that it is often difficult to set marketing objectives that are aligned specifically with overall organizational goals.

A final characteristic is the lack of a clear organizational structure. Nonprofit organizations often refer to constituencies that they serve, but these often are considerably less exact than, for example, the stockholders of a profit-oriented corporation. Nonprofit organizations often have multiple organizational structures. A hospital might have an administrative structure, a professional organization consisting of medical personnel, and a volunteer organization that domi-

The goals of the military's aerial demonstration teams, such as the U.S. Army Parachute Team (The Golden Knights), are to boost recruitment and retention, and to cultivate the relationship between civilian communities and the military. These objectives cannot be measured in terms of profit or market share; rather, they are evaluated by feedback from communities and recruiting and retention results.

Photo source: Courtesy of U.S. Army.

nates the board of trustees. These people may sometimes work at cross-purposes and disagree with the organization's marketing strategy.

While some of the above factors may also characterize profit-seeking firms, they are particularly prevalent in nonprofit organizations. However, both for-profit and nonprofit organizations focus on the consumer in the same manner, as marketing goals are aimed at satisfying the needs and wants of consumers.

Selecting a Target Market

Since the focal point of marketing activities is the consumer, market-driven organizations begin their overall strategies with detailed descriptions of their **target market:** the group of consumers toward whom the firm decides to direct its marketing efforts. For firms such as Wal-Mart and Church's Fried Chicken, the target market consists of consumers purchasing for themselves or their families. Other companies, such as General Dynamics Corporation, market most of their products to government purchasers. Still other firms provide goods and services to retail and wholesale buyers. In every instance, however, marketers should

target market
Group of people toward whom a firm markets its goods, services, or ideas with a strategy designed to satisfy their specific needs and preferences.

be as specific as possible in delineating their target markets. Consider the following examples:

☐ Stouffer's Lean Cuisine frozen-food line is targeted at weight-conscious 25- to 45-year-olds willing to pay premium prices for high-quality, microwavable convenience foods with relatively few calories.

☐ Giorgio of Beverly Hills targets affluent women who purchase cosmetics in department stores rather than at supermarkets or discount stores.

☐ The Saab target market consists of well-educated, 30- to 40-year-old professionals and managers with household incomes of $50,000 to $100,000.

Although the identification and satisfaction of a target market are subjects relevant to every chapter in the text, three chapters in Part Three focus specifically on this subject. Consumer behavior is the subject of Chapter 5. Chapter 6 is devoted to the analysis of organizational buying behavior. Methods of segmenting markets are analyzed in Chapter 7.

The Marketing Environment

Marketing decisions are not made in a vacuum. They must take into account the dynamic nature of five dimensions in the marketing environment: competitive, political/legal, economic, technological, and social/cultural. Consider, for example, how the marketing of contraceptives has been affected by economic, legal/political, and social changes. State laws prohibiting condom advertising, sales to minors, and in-store displays greatly limited marketing strategies until these laws were declared unconstitutional in 1977 by the U.S. Supreme Court. Heightened concern over the AIDS epidemic prompted a growing number of magazines, newspapers, and local television stations to accept condom advertising. As sales increased, new firms entered the market. As Figure 1.6 illustrates, Mentor Corporation decided to appeal to women as its target market. Today women account for an estimated 40 to 50 percent of all condom purchases, as compared with only 15 percent in 1975.[25]

Dimensions of the marketing environment are discussed in more depth in Chapter 2. The marketing environment is important because it provides a framework for all marketing activity. It influences the development of marketing plans and forecasts, which are described in Chapter 3, and the process of marketing research, the subject of Chapter 4. Marketers consider the environmental dimensions when they study consumer and organizational buying behavior, the topics of Chapters 5 and 6, respectively, and when they develop segmentation strategies, covered in Chapter 7.

The Marketing Mix Variables

After marketers select a target market, they direct company activities toward profitably satisfying that segment. Although thousands of variables are involved, marketing decision making can be divided into four strategies: product, pricing,

Figure 1.6
Marketing Contraceptives
to Women

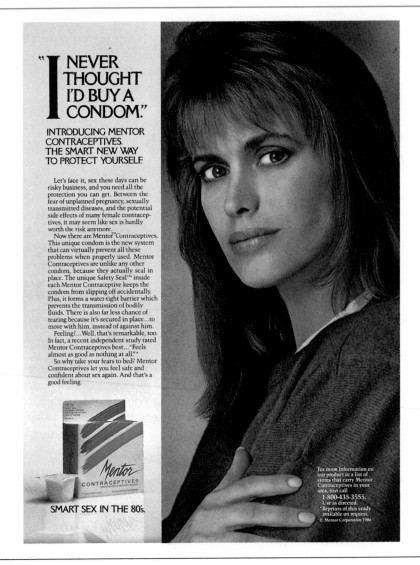

Source: Courtesy of Mentor Corporation.

marketing mix
Blending the four strategy elements of marketing decision making — product, pricing, distribution, and promotion — to satisfy chosen consumer segments.

distribution, and promotion. The total package forms the **marketing mix** — the blending of the four strategy elements to fit the needs and preferences of a specific target market. Each strategy is a variable in the mix. While the fourfold classification is useful in study and analysis, the *combination* of the variables determines the degree of marketing success.

The focus of the marketing mix variables on chosen consumer or organizational target markets is illustrated in Figure 1.7. In addition, decisions about product, price, distribution, and promotion are affected by the environmental factors in the outer circle of the figure. Unlike the controllable marketing mix elements, the environmental variables frequently are beyond the control of marketers. However, they may play a major role in the success of a marketing program and must be taken into consideration by marketers even if they cannot

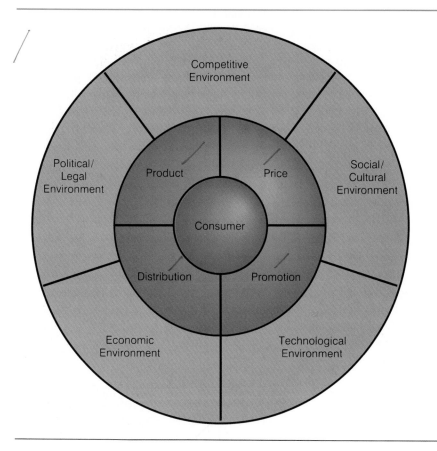

Figure 1.7
Elements of the Marketing Mix as They Operate within an Environmental Framework

be controlled. It should also be stressed that the consumer is not a marketing mix component, since marketers have little or no control over the future behavior of present and potential consumers.

Product Strategy

In marketing, the word *product* means more than a good, service, or idea. Product is a concept that considers the satisfaction of all consumer needs in relation to the good, service, or idea. For example, General Foods developed an easy-to-open, easy-to-reseal plastic bag similar to Ziploc bags for its Post cereals. Liners in cereal boxes often frustrate consumers: They are difficult to open, rip easily, and are impossible to reseal. General Foods' new plastic bag is a part of its product strategy aimed at satisfying a consumer need in relation to the product.[26]

Product strategy not only involves deciding what products or services the firm should offer to a group of consumers; it also includes making decisions about package design, brand names, trademarks, warranties, product life cycles, positioning, and new-product development. American Cyanamid marketers made such decisions recently when they launched the latest in a seemingly unending series of "better mousetraps." Following the success of the firm's

product strategy
Element of marketing decision making comprising activities involved in developing the right product or service for the firm's customers.

roach control tray system, the Combat Mouse Killer Bait System was introduced. The new system was positioned as a product that permits the buyer to
avoid the unpleasant task of cleaning the trap or killing a trapped mouse. The
clear-plastic trap has two bait troughs so that two mice can dine at the same
time. It is designed so that the poisonous food consumed by the mice will not
take effect until the mouse has returned to its hole. The product is also tamper-
resistant, so that pets and children cannot access the trap or its poisonous
contents. For the firm's marketers, the product is a logical addition to the existing line of pest-control products, is handled by the same types of retail outlets,
and is comparably priced.[27]

Two chapters in Part Four focus on product strategy. Chapter 8 introduces
the elements of product strategy. Chapter 9 discusses product mix decisions
and new-product planning.

Pricing Strategy

pricing strategy
Element of marketing decision
making that deals with the methods of setting profitable and justifiable exchange values for goods
and services.

Pricing strategy, one of the most difficult areas of marketing decision making,
deals with the methods of setting profitable and justifiable prices. It is closely
regulated and subject to considerable public scrutiny.

Consider, for example, the pricing strategy of the Department of the Interi-
or's Park Service, which recently began charging entrance fees at 71 of the 337
national parks and double or triple fees at 62 parks that already had fees. Most
Park Service officials say the fees — ranging from $1 to $5 a week for each
person or vehicle — are reasonable and point to Disneyland's daily admission
fee of $20 for adults and $15 for children. The new fee revenue is being used
to improve recreational services — adding visitor attractions, repairing buildings, and hiring more staff to conduct trail walks and run visitor centers. Although park users benefit from these improved services, the pricing strategy
spurred a heated congressional debate and public protest. The U.S. Senate
exempted a planned $1 fee at the Statue of Liberty after Senator Bill Bradley
quoted her inscription: "Give me your tired, your poor, your huddled masses
yearning to breathe free." The New Jersey Democrat added, "She does not
say — 'And give me a dollar.' " In spite of the controversy, the Park Service
plans to continue implementing the new pricing system.[28]

Pricing strategy is the subject of Part Five. Chapter 10 analyzes the elements involved in determining prices. Chapter 11 covers the management aspect of pricing.

Distribution Strategy

distribution strategy
Element of marketing decision
making comprising activities and
marketing institutions involved in
getting the right product or service to the firm's customers.

Marketers develop **distribution strategies** to ensure that their products are
available in the proper quantities at the right time and place. Distribution decisions involve modes of transportation, warehousing, inventory control, order
processing, and selection of marketing channels. Marketing channels, made up
of institutions such as retailers and wholesalers, are the steps a product follows
from producer to final consumer.

White Castle System, a chain of 220 fast-food restaurants, added a marketing channel to its distribution system when it decided to sell a frozen version
of its bite-size hamburgers in supermarkets. The strategy was so successful —
sales jumped from 5 million to 26 million burgers in one year — that White

Figure 1.8   Advertising As Part of Promotional Strategy

Source: Courtesy of Mead Johnson Pablum.

Castle is considering supermarket distribution of its other offerings, including fish sticks, onion rings, and breakfast sandwiches. Part of the success of the supermarket distribution relates to the product itself. White Castle hamburgers are small, weighing only 1.8 ounces, and inexpensive, about 35 cents each. In supermarkets, they are sold in packages of six and are positioned as a snack food.[29]

Distribution strategy is covered in Part Six. Topics include channel strategy (Chapter 12), wholesaling (Chapter 13), retailing (Chapter 14), and physical distribution (Chapter 15).

Promotional Strategy

Promotion is the communication link between sellers and buyers. Organizations use many different means of sending their messages about goods, services, and ideas. The message may be communicated directly by salespeople or indirectly through advertisements and sales promotions. As the advertisement shown in Figure 1.8 illustrates, Mead Johnson uses a playful advertising approach to communicate to parents the importance of healthy food in infants' early diets. In developing a **promotional strategy,** marketers blend together the various elements of promotion that will communicate most effectively with their target market.

Promotional strategies serve different purposes and vary in size and scope. Procter & Gamble, for example, sent free six-ounce samples of its Liquid Cascade to millions of households to introduce customers to a new liquid dish-

promotional strategy
Element of marketing decision making that involves appropriate blending of personal selling, advertising, and sales promotion for use in communicating with and seeking to persuade potential customers.

washer detergent — and move the product from the "unknown" category to the "known."[30] Chrisman, Miller, Woodford — a 38-member design and construction firm — sends 3,000 copies of a quarterly newsletter to clients and prospects as a source of information about the company. Like other firms that use client newsletters as a promotional tool, Chrisman's newsletter is a soft-sell, long-range marketing approach.[31] On a grander scale, the 1988 Winter Olympic Games provided a worldwide opportunity for 3M Company to introduce a new product and to reaffirm its market leader position for another product. As an official sponsor of the games, 3M provided jogging outfits made of its new Thintech fabric to 11,000 runners who took part in the 88-day run to carry the Olympic torch throughout Canada. At Argentina's Cape of Good Hope, 3M sponsored adventurer Ned Gillette, who rowed 550 miles to Antarctica and wore cold-weather gear made of 3M's Thinsulate brand thermal insulation. From Canada to the southern tip of South America, 3M ran retail promotions with the theme "3M Is Warming Up the 1988 Winter Olympic Games." At the local level, a 3M Olympic van traveled to major cities in the United States and Canada to promote the company's products and provide information about the games.[32]

Promotional strategy is covered in Part Seven. The concept of promotion is introduced in Chapter 16. Chapter 17 deals with advertising, sales promotion, and public relations. Personal selling and sales management are the topics of Chapter 18.

Marketing Costs and Marketing Functions

Creation of time, place, and ownership utilities costs money. Numerous attempts have been made to determine marketing costs in relation to overall product and service costs, and most estimates have ranged between 40 and 60 percent. On the average, one-half of the costs involved in a product such as a Godfather's Pizza, an ounce of *Anaïs Anaïs* perfume, a pair of GUESS jeans, or even a Honda Elite scooter can be traced directly to marketing. These costs are not associated with fabrics, raw materials and other ingredients, baking, sewing, or any of the other production functions necessary for creating form utility. What, then, does the consumer receive in return for this 50 percent marketing cost? What functions are performed by marketing?

As Table 1.5 reveals, marketing is responsible for the performance of eight universal functions: buying, selling, transporting, storing, standardization and grading, financing, risk taking, and securing marketing information. Some functions are performed by manufacturers, others by retailers, and still others by marketing intermediaries called wholesalers.

Buying and selling, the first two functions shown in Table 1.5, represent *exchange functions. Buying* is important to marketing on several levels. Marketers must determine how and why consumers buy certain products and services. To be successful, they must seek to understand consumer behavior. In addition, retailers and other intermediaries must seek out products that will appeal to their customers. Since they are generating time, place, and ownership utilities through these purchases, they must make decisions concerning likely consumer preferences that will be expressed through purchases several months after the time orders are placed. *Selling* is the second half of the exchange process. It involves advertising, personal selling, and sales promotion in an attempt to match the firm's products and services to consumer needs.

Table 1.5
Eight Essential Marketing Functions

Marketing Function	Description
A. Exchange Functions	
1. Buying	Ensuring that product offerings are available in sufficient quantities to meet customer demands
2. Selling	Use of advertising, personal selling, and sales promotion to match product and service offerings to customer needs
B. Physical Distribution Functions	
3. Transporting	Moving the product from its point of production to a location convenient for the purchaser
4. Storing	Warehousing of products until needed for sale
C. Facilitating Functions	
5. Standardization and grading	Ensuring that product offerings meet established quality and quantity control standards of size, weight, and other product variables
6. Financing	Providing credit for channel members or consumers
7. Risk taking	Uncertainty about consumer purchases resulting from creation and marketing of products and services that consumers *may* purchase in the future
8. Market information	Collection of information about consumers, competitors, and channel members for use in making marketing decisions

Transporting and storing are *physical distribution functions. Transporting* involves the physical movement of the product from the seller to the purchaser. *Storing* involves the warehousing of goods until they are needed for sale. These functions frequently involve manufacturers, wholesalers, and retailers.

The final four marketing functions — standardization and grading, financing, risk taking, and securing market information — are often called *facilitating functions* because they assist the marketer in performing the exchange and physical distribution functions. Quality and quantity control *standards* and *grades,* frequently set by federal or state governments, reduce the need for purchasers to inspect each item. Specific tire sizes, for example, permit buyers to request a needed size and to know that they will receive a uniform size.

Financing is another marketing function because funds often are required for financing inventories prior to their sales. In many instances, manufacturers may provide financing for their wholesale and retail customers. In other cases, some types of wholesalers perform similar functions for their retail customers. Finally, retailers frequently permit their customers to make credit purchases.

The seventh function, *risk taking,* is part of most ventures. Manufacturers create products and services based on their belief (and research studies) that a consumer need for them exists. Wholesalers and retailers acquire inventory based on similar expectations of future consumer demand. These uncertainties about future consumer behavior must be assumed by entrepreneurial risk takers when they market products and services.

The final marketing function involves *securing market information.* Marketers gather information about their markets to obtain decision-oriented input about their customers — who they are, what they buy, where they buy, and how they buy. By collecting and analyzing market information, marketers also seek to understand why consumers purchase some product offerings and reject others.

FOCUS ON ETHICS

Can Marketing Ethics Be Taught?

General Dynamics Corporation overcharges the government on defense contracts. E. F. Hutton bilks banks out of millions with a check-kiting scheme. Wall Street witnesses an epidemic of insider trading, capped with the astonishing $100 million fine and jail sentence for Ivan Boesky. As scandals rock the business world, many observers wonder why such seemingly low ethical standards abound and whether anything can be done about it. At a time when only 2 percent of the public thinks that business executives have "excellent" ethical standards and 46 percent classifies them as "pretty good," one oft-heard suggestion is increased emphasis on ethics in colleges and business schools. Whether this would be effective is hotly debated.

Donald P. Jacobs, dean of the Kellogg Graduate School of Management at Northwestern University, represents one view. "You learn ethics at home," he argues bluntly. Those who support this widely held view contend that if you didn't learn morality and ethics at home, it's too late for university ethics courses to have much impact on you.

A contrary view seems to be gaining increasing acceptance, however. Its supporters emphasize that many of the ethical decisions in a business or marketing environment differ dramatically from the types of personal ethical decisions that people are ac-

customed to making. Professor Thomas W. Dunfee of the Wharton School, University of Pennsylvania, notes that among students — even business school students — a high level of ignorance exists regarding business ethics questions. "You'd be surprised how many students don't know what a conflict of interest is. They can't define a bribe. They say, 'If I give money to a maitre d', isn't that a bribe?' "

Ethical issues are present in every aspect of marketing. For example, in the area of product strategy, should manufacturers completely retool an assembly line to fix a minor but potentially dangerous product defect? Should larger-than-necessary packages be used to gain shelf space at the expense of the competition's? In distribution strategy, what is the proper degree of control over a distribution channel such as a franchise? Does a company have an ethical duty to continue serving a low-income area that is only marginally profitable but has no alternative source of supply?

Promotional strategy is especially prone to ethical abuses. Misleading advertising, sexism in advertising, and unethical sales techniques are three of the biggest problems. For example, Anheuser-Busch, Inc., brewer of Budweiser, Busch, and Michelob, has on two occasions paid fines totaling $2.75 million to the Bureau

of Alcohol, Tobacco, and Firearms for basing its decision regarding advertising on major league baseball broadcasts on whether teams sold Anheuser-Busch beers at their stadiums.

Historically, pricing abuses, such as price fixing and price discrimination, have been widespread at various times. Other ethical questions include: Should customers pay more in one location rather than another if distribution or other costs are higher in that location? Do marketers have an obligation to warn customers of impending price, discount, or other policy changes?

There are some who believe that answers to these and other ethical questions can and should be dealt with in the classroom. A prominent advocate is John Shad, former head of the Securities and Exchange Commission, who recently gave the Harvard Business School $30 million to establish a program designed to teach students that "ethics pays."

Sources: Michael O'Neal, "Anheuser-Busch: The Scandal May Be Small Beer After All," *Business Week* (May 11, 1987), pp. 72–73; Sallie Gaines, "Teaching Ethics: Uproar Makes B-Schools Bristle," *Chicago Tribune* (May 17, 1987), sec. 7, pp. 1, 8, 10; *Business Week*/Harris Poll, *Business Week* (July 20, 1987), p. 71; John A. Byrne with Alex Beam, "Harvard's $30 Million Windfall for Ethics 101," *Business Week* (April 13, 1987), p. 40; and Beth Brophy, "Ethics 101: Can the Good Guys Win?" *U.S. News & World Report* (April 13, 1987).

The Study of Marketing

Marketing is a pervasive element in contemporary life. In one form or another, it is close to every person. Three of its most important concerns for students are as follows:

1. Marketing costs may be the largest item in the personal budget. As pointed out earlier, marketing costs account for approximately 50 percent of the total costs for the average product. Based on costs alone, marketing undeniably is a key item in any consumer's budget.

Cost alone, however, does not indicate the value of marketing. If someone says that marketing costs are too high, that person should be asked, "Relative to what?" The standard of living in the United States is in large part a function of the country's efficient marketing system. When considered in this perspective, the system's costs seem reasonable. For example, marketing expands sales, thereby spreading fixed production costs over more units of output and reducing total output costs. Reduced production costs offset many marketing costs.

2. There is a good chance that many students will become marketers. Marketing-related occupations account for 25 to 33 percent of the nation's jobs. History has shown that the demand for effective marketers is not affected by cyclical economic fluctuations.

3. Marketing provides an opportunity to contribute to society as well as to an individual company. Marketing decisions affect everyone's welfare. Further, opportunities to advance to decision-making positions come sooner in marketing than in most occupations. (Societal aspects of marketing are covered in detail in later chapters.)

Why study marketing? The answer is simple: Marketing influences numerous facets of daily life as well as future careers and economic well-being. The study of marketing is important because it is relevant to students of today and tomorrow. It is little wonder that marketing is now one of the most popular fields of academic study.

Each succeeding chapter in *Contemporary Marketing* includes detailed analysis and evaluation of at least one ethical issue. Different types of ethical dilemmas that may be confronted in marketing will also be examined.

Summary of Chapter Objectives

1. Explain the types of utility and the role marketing plays in their creation. Utility is the want-satisfying power of a product or service. There are four basic kinds of utility: form, time, place, and ownership. Form utility refers to the conversion of raw materials and component parts into finished products and services. Although marketing provides information about consumer wants and needs, the actual creation of form utility is the responsibility of the production function. In contrast, marketing creates time, place, and ownership utilities. These are created when goods and services are available when and where people want to buy them, and when facilities exist for the transfer of title.

2. Relate the definition of marketing to the concept of the exchange process. The American Marketing Association has defined marketing as the process of planning and executing the conception, pricing, promotion, and distribution of ideas, goods, and services to create exchanges that satisfy individual and organizational objectives. The exchange process, by which two or more parties give something of value to each other to satisfy felt needs, is a critical aspect of this definition.

3. Contrast marketing activities during the three eras in the history of marketing. Firms were production oriented during the production era; the prevailing attitude was that quality products would sell themselves. Marketing was a secondary activity. In the sales era, the emphasis was on convincing people to buy. Marketing was, in essence, defined as selling. The marketing era saw the emergence of the marketing concept, a companywide consumer orientation with the objective of achieving long-run success.

4. Explain the concept of marketing myopia. Both production- and sales-oriented firms frequently do not achieve long-run success because they suffer from marketing myopia. They define the scope of their business around the product rather than customers' needs. The term *marketing myopia* was coined by Harvard marketing professor Theodore Levitt to describe a form of nearsightedness on the marketer's part, a failure to recognize the scope of the business. Future growth of myopic organizations is endangered because management is product rather than customer oriented.

5. Identify and briefly explain the types of nonprofit marketing. There are four types of nonprofit marketing. Person marketing focuses on an individual, such as a celebrity or political candidate. Place marketing attempts to attract people and/or businesses to a particular geographical area — city, state, or country. Idea marketing involves identifying and marketing a cause or idea to chosen consumer segments. Organization marketing refers to marketing efforts to influence others to accept the organization's goals or services or contribute to it in some way. Organization marketing is undertaken by (1) mutual-benefit organizations, such as churches, labor unions, and political parties; (2) service organizations, such as colleges, universities, hospitals, and museums; and (3) government organizations, such as the military services and police and fire departments.

6. Identify the variables involved in marketing decision making and the environmental factors that affect these decisions. The two major variables in a marketing strategy are (1) analysis, evaluation, and selection of a target market and (2) the development of a marketing mix designed to satisfy the chosen target market. Marketing begins with an assessment of consumer wants and needs, the collection of information about potential consumer segments to be satisfied, and the ultimate choice of a consumer segment that will serve as the firm's target market. Once the target market has been selected, the marketing manager directs activities toward its satisfaction. The four strategy elements in marketing decision making are product strategy, pricing strategy, distribution strategy, and promotional strategy. The combination of these four elements is called the *marketing mix.* The five components of the marketing environment are the competitive environment, the political/legal environment, the economic environment, the technological environment, and the social/cultural environment.

7. Explain the universal functions of marketing. Marketing is responsible for the performance of eight universal functions as it creates time, place, and ownership utilities. Some of these functions are performed by manufacturers, others by retailers, and still others by marketing intermediaries such as wholesalers. The eight functions may be divided into three broad categories: (1) exchange functions (buying and selling); (2) physical distribution functions (transporting and storing); and (3) facilitating functions (standardization and grading, financing, risk taking, and securing marketing information).

8. List three reasons for studying marketing. Three basic reasons for studying marketing are: (1) Marketing costs may be the largest item in the personal budget; (2) there is a good chance that individual students will become marketers; and (3) marketing provides an opportunity to contribute to society as well as to an individual organization.

Key Terms

utility	person marketing
marketing	place marketing
exchange process	idea marketing
production orientation	organization marketing
sales orientation	target market
seller's market	marketing mix
buyer's market	product strategy
consumer orientation	pricing strategy
marketing concept	distribution strategy
marketing myopia	promotional strategy
broadening concept	

Review Questions

1. Identify the types of utility created by marketing. What types are being created in the following examples?
   a. One-hour cleaners
   b. National Video movie rental outlet
   c. Honda auto assembly plant in Marysville, Ohio
   d. Annual boat and sports equipment show in a local convention center
   e. Regional shopping mall

2. Relate the definition of marketing to the concept of the exchange process.

3. Discuss the production and sales eras. How does the marketing era differ from the previous eras?

4. Explain the concept of marketing myopia. Why is it likely to occur? What steps can be taken to reduce the likelihood of its occurrence?

5. What is person marketing? Contrast it with marketing of a consumer product such as magazines.

6. Why is idea marketing more difficult than place or organization marketing?

7. What did the General Electric annual report mean when it stated that GE was introducing the marketer at the beginning rather than the end of the production cycle?

8. Identify the major variables of the marketing mix. Briefly contrast the mix variables in nonprofit marketing with those involved in for-profit marketing.

9. What are the components of the marketing environment? Why are these factors not included as part of the marketing mix? Is the target market a component of the marketing mix?

10. Categorize the following marketing functions as an exchange function, a physical distribution function, or a facilitating function. Choose a local retail store, and give an example of how it performs each of the eight functions.
    a. Buying
    b. Financing
    c. Securing marketing information
    d. Standardization and grading
    e. Selling
    f. Risk taking
    g. Storing
    h. Transporting

Discussion Questions

1. What type of nonprofit marketing does each of the following represent?
   - **a.** United Auto Workers
   - **b.** "Alaska: Land of Surprises"
   - **c.** New York Public Library
   - **d.** Save the Whales Foundation
   - **e.** University of Montana
   - **f.** U.S. Girl Scouts
   - **g.** Easter Seals

2. How would you explain marketing and its importance in the economy to someone not familiar with the subject?

3. Identify the product and the consumer market for each of the following organizations:
   - **a.** Local cable television firm
   - **b.** Minnesota Twins baseball club
   - **c.** Planned Parenthood
   - **d.** Jolt Cola

4. Give two examples each of firms that you feel reflect the philosophies of the following eras. Defend your answers.
   - **a.** Production era
   - **b.** Sales era
   - **c.** Marketing era

5. Choose a company in your area, and briefly describe its target market. How are each of the marketing mix variables employed by this firm? Which of these variables appear to be emphasized in its marketing strategy?

VIDEO CASE 1

The United States Army

Nineteen seventy-three was a memorable year in the history of organization marketing. That was the year Congress suspended the draft, leaving the U.S. Army with the problem of how to fill its ranks. Army personnel planners realized that future procurement of officers and enlisted personnel would be difficult since many enlistments had previously been draft-motivated.

For years the Army had been *production-oriented;* it had a product and made little effort to enhance its appeal to potential consumers. If young men and women chose the Army as a career, Army planners were satisfied. If not, they simply drafted enough people to satisfy personnel needs. The all-volunteer concept required that the Army approach the problem from a new viewpoint.

The move to an all-volunteer Army was complicated by the negative images of Army careers created during the 1960s and early 1970s by widespread opposition to American involvement in Vietnam. In the late 1980s, the images of young American draftees risking their lives while slogging through the rice paddies of Vietnam were kept alive for a new generation of prospective enlistees through a series of motion pictures and network television programs.

An additional problem involved the reduced number of eligible Americans from whom the Army could attract enlistees. The Army identifies its target market as men and women between the ages of 18 and 35. However, many of the recruiting efforts focus on 18-year-olds as prime targets to replenish the 130,000 persons needed each year to maintain the Army's current personnel level of about 770,000. The pool of 18-year-olds is dwindling, though, and by 1992 there will be only 3 million, down 25 percent from 1978.

The shrinking market has been made even smaller by the addition of more stringent qualifications for Army recruits. In 1973, when the draft was eliminated, only half of all new recruits were high school graduates. Such an educational level was clearly unacceptable in an increasingly high-tech army, where thousands of dollars were invested to equip each enlistee and thousands more spent on specialized training. Congress decided to step in and specify minimum educational requirements: at least 65 percent of all Army recruits must be high-school graduates.

Skeptics questioned the Army's ability to attract recruits in the absence of a military draft. Marketers at the Department of Defense knew that the risk of failure was high if they did not offer potential recruits a competitive product. Consequently, they took steps to make the product more appealing. Today's successful applicant receives an attractive benefit package, an accelerated promotion schedule, enviable job security, practical training, career advancement, and travel and management opportunities not often available to new entrants into the job market. Prospective recruits receive written guarantees for jobs before enlistment. Recruits with sufficiently high scores on the Armed Services Vocational and Aptitude Battery (ASVAB) can select specific jobs in such fields as aviation, military intelligence, engineering, military police, signal corps, transportation, finance, ordnance, field artillery, air defense artillery, infantry, airborne, armor, quartermaster, medical, Special Forces, and Army Rangers. The delayed enlistment program enables high school students to wait as long as a year before reporting for active duty. In addition to increasingly competitive pay, post exchange and commissary privileges, attractive medical and dental care, and 30 days paid vacation every year, the new GI Bill provides over $10,000 in educational benefits after completion of service time to those persons who contribute $1200 to the program during their tour of duty.

Since the product had changed, it was essential that the nature of the changes be communicated to the Army's target market. Long-standing legal constraints prohibiting the Armed Forces from using paid advertising had recently been lifted and the Army turned first to the N.W. Ayer advertising agency and then to Young & Rubicam in 1987 to create product awareness. For the past decade, the slogan "Be all that you can be" combined with the more recent "Get an edge on life" has communicated the joint themes of technology and personal challenge to millions of prospective recruits. One hundred million dollars is spent each year on advertising designed to inform and persuade young men and women of the merits of a career in the U.S. Army. Typical ads, such as those showing paratroopers bailing out of planes and a young paratrooper writing home to his father, are designed to illustrate that the Army experience teaches qualities such as teamwork and maturity.

The key ingredient in the Army's marketing strategy is the recruiter. Local recruiters devote most of their efforts toward high school seniors and recent high school graduates. They participate in career days on campus, write letters, and make telephone calls to prospects. They make presentations to student groups and to civic organizations and seek out referrals.

Special events are also used to expand contacts with potential recruits. These include military displays such as helicopters and tanks at state fairs, air shows, or similar events; cinema vans on high school and college campuses during registration or career days; and demonstration jumps by the Golden Knights, the Army's All American Parachute Team. Such events, aimed at achieving the dual missions of recruitment and public relations, frequently have long-term impact. Captain Richard Drake, Golden Knights team spokesperson, agrees, "We get a lot of 10-year-old boys. We get some people who say, 'I saw the Golden Knights when I was in grade school, and that influenced me to join the Army.' "

High school and university ROTC programs are important sources of future officers. Approximately 70 percent of the 100,000 Army officers currently on active duty are recruited from college ROTC programs; the remainder come from officer candidate schools (OCS) or the military academies.

In addition to attracting qualified applicants, the Army is also interested in retaining personnel beyond their first enlistment. It is much more cost-effective to convince trained personnel to reenlist than to attract and train new recruits. Substantial bonuses as high as $20,000 for some difficult-to-fill specialty fields are offered. Approximately 43 percent of all Army personnel do reenlist after their initial enlistment, while 85 percent reenlist after their second enlistment.

Army marketers have also lessened the impact of a declining 18-year-old market by focusing on a previously neglected segment: women. When the all-volunteer military was introduced in 1973, women accounted for only 1.9 percent of the U.S. Armed Forces. Today, they make up more than 10 percent of the total. Although combat-risk posts remain off limits, the career choices for women have been greatly increased. Today's female soldiers are permitted to fly U-2 and SR-71 spy planes, and serve as guards at U.S. embassies and in Army forward support battalions in addition to the more traditional assignments.

Thus far, the application of marketing concepts to Army recruiting is working. Personnel needs are being met and applicant qualifications continue to increase. The Congressional mandate of a 65 percent high school graduate quota is hardly remembered; 95 percent of today's Army recruits have at least a high school education.

Sources: Dale quotation from Susan Katz, "Military's Airborne Drawing Cards," *Insight* (February 1, 1988), p. 21. See also "Redefining a Woman's Place," *Time* (February 15, 1988), p. 27; and Janet Meyers, "New Army Spots Go For Heart," *Advertising Age* (November 30, 1987), p. 2.

Questions

1. Relate the marketing of Army careers to the concept of the consumer and the elements of the marketing mix. Describe the target market and compare the product the military is marketing with other products. Discuss how each of the other marketing mix elements is employed in the Army's marketing strategy.

2. Relate the material in this case to each of the environmental factors affecting marketing decisions.

3. Suggest methods by which Army marketing efforts can include such people as parents and friends who influence the decisions of potential recruits.

4. Referrals are a vital component in recruitment efforts. Identify persons who are likely to serve as centers of influence for potential enlistees and propose a systematic approach to maximize the number of referrals.

5. Nonprofit marketing is often more difficult to evaluate than marketing in profit-seeking firms due to the absence of the overall profitability measure of performance. How should the effectiveness of Army marketing be measured?

COMPUTER APPLICATIONS

In this chapter, the origin of marketing activity was traced to the exchange process. Two of the eight fundamental marketing functions — buying and selling — are performed when suppliers exchange surplus products or services for other items or money.

Figure 1 illustrates the most primitive form of exchange, in which producers contact one another directly to exchange surplus output. In this example of what might be termed *decentralized exchange,* the small barter economy consists of eight families living within a few miles of one another on a small island. At one time, each family was completely self-sufficient. Over time, however, each began to realize that it could increase its standard of living by specializing in the production of a limited number of products and then exchanging its surplus production for products produced by the other families. Although the families were uncomfortable at first with the prospect of being dependent on others for products necessary for their own comfort and enjoyment, they gradually accepted this new approach to production and trade due to its ability to provide them with more goods and services than they could produce under the previous system of total self-sufficiency.

Although specialization produced benefits for the eight families, the decentralized exchange proved time consuming, since each family had to make direct contact with each of the other seven families to complete the process. Another source of complaint would occur when one family representative seeking to make an exchange with another family discovered that the second family had traveled to the residence of still another family to make an exchange, leaving no one at home.

Figure 1 illustrates the inefficiency of decentralized exchange by showing all of the connecting lines necessary for completing the transactions among the eight families — a total of 28.

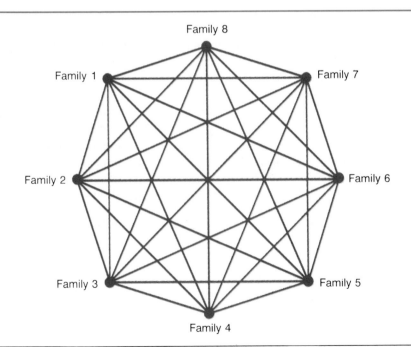

Family 8
Family 1
Family 7
Family 2
Family 6
Family 3
Family 5
Family 4

Figure 1
Decentralized Exchange
among Eight Families

Figure 2
Centralized Exchange among
Eight Families

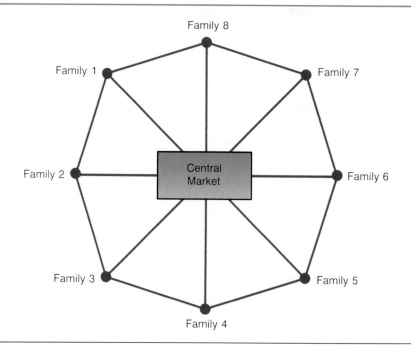

Instead of resorting to drawing and then counting all the lines connecting the families, we can use the following formula to determine the number of transactions required to carry out decentralized exchange:

$$T = \frac{n(n-1)}{2},$$

where T is the number of transactions and n the number of producer families. In this case,

$$T = \frac{8(8-1)}{2} = \frac{8(7)}{2} = \frac{56}{2} = 28.$$

But what happens if the decentralized exchange economy is converted to a *centralized exchange system* through the introduction of some form of marketing intermediary such as a central market? The results are shown in Figure 2. The exchange process becomes much more efficient when a central market is created, because each family can contact the manager of the market directly to exchange surplus production for other needed products. The need to make direct contact with other families in order to facilitate exchange no longer exists. Instead of the 28 transactions required for decentralized exchange, only 8 transactions are needed when a marketing intermediary is introduced. The result is increased efficiency, since the marketing intermediary reduces the amount of work that must be done.

How much more efficient is centralized exchange than the former system of decentralized exchange? The following calculation provides the answer to this question:

$$\text{Percentage of Increased Efficiency} = \frac{\text{Number of Transactions with Decentralized Exchange}}{\text{Number of Transactions with Centralized Exchange}}$$

$$= \frac{28}{8}$$

$$= 350\%.$$

Directions: Use menu item 1 titled "Exchange Process" to solve each of the following problems.

Problem 1   Five small manufacturers were operating in close proximity to one another. Each manufacturer made purchases from and, in turn, sold products to the other four manufacturers. A marketing intermediary offered to serve as a linkage among the firms to reduce the time and costs involved in the old system of decentralized exchange. However, one of the manufacturers argued that the small number of firms was insufficient to justify a marketing intermediary. How much will efficiency increase if the intermediary is used?

Problem 2   A group of nine families located in an isolated region near Nome, Alaska, have been engaged in decentralized exchange of surplus products for several years. They are considering opening a central market that would operate every Saturday in a conveniently located meeting place.
a. How many transactions are involved under the present decentralized exchange system?
b. How many transactions would be involved if the families decided to establish the central market?
c. What effect would the central market have on efficiency?

Problem 3   A small community of 75 farmers residing in a rural area of Wisconsin were considering the development of a central farmer's market for their exclusive use in trading with one another. How many transactions are currently necessary to conduct decentralized exchange among the 75 farmers? How many transactions will be necessary if the farmer's market is constructed and utilized by each farmer? What effect will the farmer's market have on efficiency?

Problem 4   Nine years ago, 30 families emigrated to a small Pacific island located 800 miles east of Tasmania. Since they are completely dependent on trading surplus goods with one another, they have been actively engaged in a decentralized exchange system since 1980. Due to the problems involved in their current informal system of trade, they are considering a proposal to establish a central market.
a. How many transactions are involved under the present system?
b. How many transactions will be involved if the central market is established?
c. Specify the impact of the central market in terms of increases in efficiency.

Problem 5   Ten families currently reside on the small Caribbean island of Anta. Another eight families live on Benzille, another island three miles away. At the present time, the 10 families on Anta are engaged in decentralized exchange but do not trade with the residents of Benzille. Decentralized exchange is also in effect on Benzille. During recent trade discussions between a Benzille representative and an Anta resident, two proposals for increasing efficiency were presented:

1. Establish two central markets, one located on Anta and the other on Benzille. Although a centralized exchange system would replace the previous system on both islands, no inter-island trade would be involved.

2. Establish one large, central market on the currently uninhabited island of Centar, located midway between Anta and Benzille. Residents of both Anta and Benzille would utilize this market, and their original decentralized exchange systems would be eliminated.

Compare the current decentralized exchange systems on Anta and Benzille with the first proposal. How much will efficiency increase on Anta if the first proposal is implemented? On Benzille? How many transactions will be involved if the second proposal is implemented?

2

Marketing: Its Environment and Role in Society

Chapter Objectives

1. To identify the five components of the marketing environment.

2. To explain the types of competition marketers face and the steps in developing a competitive strategy.

3. To describe how government and other groups regulate marketing activities and how marketers can influence the political/legal environment.

4. To outline the economic factors that affect marketing decisions and consumer buying power.

5. To explain the impact of the technological environment on a firm's marketing activities.

6. To explain how the social/cultural environment influences marketing.

7. To describe the role of marketing in society.

8. To identify the three major social issues in marketing.

U ntil as recently as the early 1980s, research and development reigned at DuPont Company. Marketing was relegated to handling the sales arrangements for cellophane, nylon, Teflon, Dacron, and the other breakthrough products that seemed to be emerging regularly from DuPont's research labs. DuPont clearly was the industry leader, and R&D efforts appeared capable of maintaining this position for the firm forever. Then, based on work beginning in the early 1960s, a small group of chemists at the firm's experimental station in Wilmington, Delaware, unveiled their latest miracle product: an amazingly strong fiber called *Kevlar*.

But the production-oriented corporate giant fell victim to its antiquated marketing philosophy. "Kevlar was the answer," says Wayne B. Smith, a marketing manager for the fiber, "but we didn't know for what."

To DuPont executives, experienced in the production and marketing of tire materials such as nylon, the logical product application for the new, resilient material was in passenger-car tires. Compared with steel, its main tire-ingredient competitor, Kevlar could more easily be woven into rubber and was lighter, stronger, and more heat resistant. Early DuPont tire tests using Kevlar as a major component were highly successful and, by 1980, more than half of all the Kevlar being produced was going into tires. That year, DuPont began construction of a $500 million Kevlar manufacturing facility capable of producing huge quantities of the product for what appeared to be a giant market. Later that same year, tire manufacturers chose steel. Steel was less expensive than Kevlar, and tire marketers felt that consumers would prefer the phrase "steel-belted radials."

DuPont marketers now had a problem with their "better mousetrap." By this time, the firm had in-

vested more in Kevlar than in any other product in the company's history. Special product groups were assigned to find markets for this five-times-stronger-than-steel fiber. Several possible markets were suggested based on Kevlar's amazing strength. After all, a Kevlar cable could anchor an oil rig in the North Sea, and Kevlar vests, with a mere three-eighths inch of multiple plies of woven fabric, could stop a .357 Magnum bullet. Demonstrations of prototype bulletresistant vests to police departments were so effective that many police officers — and even their spouses — bought them with their own money when the departments lacked the funds.

A variety of snafus in the marketing environment slowed growth in Kevlar sales during the late 1970s and early 1980s. First, initial production was delayed because a solvent used in the manufacture of an ingredient was a suspected carcinogen. Then lower petroleum prices prompted major reductions in offshore oil and gas drilling, which in turn greatly reduced the size of the market for oil rig anchor lines made with Kevlar. The U.S. Army spent seven years testing Kevlar as a pos-

sible replacement for nylon in flak jackets.

By 1985, DuPont's efforts to find markets for its miracle fiber were beginning to pay off. In 1987, annual sales had approached the $300 million mark, and dozens of markets were being served. Today the product can be found in army helmets and flak jackets, bulletresistant vests, tennis rackets, golf clubs, trawling nets, skis, and racing sails. Kevlar gloves are available for gardeners, fishing enthusiasts, autoworkers, and motorcyclists. Lightweight Kevlar components in airplanes provide added strength with less weight; each pound of Kevlar can save an estimated $300 in fuel costs over an airplane's life.

DuPont's sobering experiences with Kevlar may have produced an unexpected benefit: They forced the firm to overhaul its marketing philosophy. As one writer put it, "Instead of inventing products and then hunting for markets for them, it would figure out first what customers needed and then how to make it."[1]

Photo source: Courtesy of E. I. DuPont de Nemours and Company.

Chapter Overview

Like DuPont, every type of organization is affected by outside forces. Most will never face the life-and-death issue of cyanide-laced capsules that confronted Johnson & Johnson in the early 1980s and again in 1986. But all firms must identify, analyze, and monitor external forces and assess their potential impact on their products and/or services. Although external forces frequently are outside the marketing manager's control, they must be considered together with the controllable variables of the marketing mix in developing marketing plans and strategies.

This chapter begins by describing five forces in marketing's external environment: competitive, political/legal, economic, technological, and social/cultural. These forces, as shown in Figure 2.1, are important because they provide the frame of reference within which marketing decisions are made. The response of marketers to society in general through socially responsible and ethical behavior is also discussed in this chapter.

The Marketing Environment: Not Always Uncontrollable

Although some marketing writers argue that the marketing environment is completely beyond the control of marketing management, this is not always the case.[2] In some instances, marketers can influence the environment in which the firm operates.

environmental management
Attainment of organizational objectives by predicting and influencing the competitive, political/legal, economic, technological, and social/cultural environments.

Environmental management is the attainment of organizational objectives by predicting and influencing the competitive, political/legal, economic, technological, and social/cultural environments.[3] This influence can result from a number of activities by the firm's management. Political power in the form of lobbying among legislative groups and contributions by political action committees (PACs) may result in modifications of regulations, laws, or tariff restrictions. The competitive environment can be affected by new-product developments, joint ventures, and mergers. For example, a firm may strengthen its competitive position through a joint venture or merger with another company whose products complement its own. By acquiring Seven Seas salad dressings and Chiffon margarine from Quaker Oats, Kraft, Inc., boosted its market share of pourable dressings from 33 to 40 percent and raised its share of total margarine sales from 18 to 20 percent. Kraft also realized marketing cost benefits from the acquisition, because it could use its existing sales force and distributors for the new lines.[4]

Successful research and development efforts may result in changes in the technological environment. A research breakthrough may lead to reduced production costs or a technologically superior new product. While the marketing environment may exist outside the confines of the firm and its marketing mix components, effective marketers continually seek to predict its impact on marketing decisions and to modify it whenever possible.

In addition to its effect on current marketing decisions, the marketing environment, due to its dynamic nature, necessitates that management at every level continually reevaluate marketing decisions in response to changing conditions. Even modest environmental shifts can alter the results of marketing decisions.

Figure 2.1
Forces in Marketing's External Environment

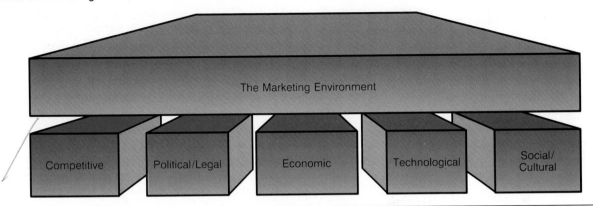

The Competitive Environment

The interactive process that occurs in the marketplace as competing organizations seek to satisfy markets is known as the **competitive environment.** Marketing decisions by an individual firm influence consumer responses in the marketplace. They also affect the marketing strategies of competitors. As a consequence, marketers must continually monitor competitors' marketing activities — their products, channels, prices, and promotional efforts.

In a few instances, organizations enjoy a monopoly position in the marketplace. Utilities, such as natural gas, electricity, water, and cable television service, accept considerable regulation from local authorities of such marketing-related factors as rates, service levels, and geographic coverage in exchange for exclusive rights to serve a particular group of consumers. However, such instances are rare. In addition, traditional monopoly industries, such as telephone service, have been deregulated in recent years. Today American Telephone & Telegraph and the newly formed spin-off companies resulting from its breakup must compete with MCI, U.S. Sprint, and other firms in the sale of telephone receivers, long-distance telephone service, and installation and maintenance of telephone systems in larger commercial and industrial firms. The ability to adapt to change, as AT&T did, is crucial in the competitive environment.

competitive environment
Interactive process that occurs in the marketplace among marketers of directly competitive products, marketers of products that can be substituted for one another, and among marketers competing for the consumer's purchasing power.

Types of Competition

Marketers actually face three types of competition. The most direct form of competition occurs among marketers of similar products. Kinder-Care, Inc. competes with La Petite Academy and other day-care chains. Golden Valley's Act II brand of microwave popcorn faces competition from Beatrice Companies' Orville Redenbacher brand. American Red Cross competes with United Way for charitable contributions.

While the Cycle dog food advertisement shown in Figure 2.2 implies that the nutritional qualities of its products are so superior that nature is its foremost

Figure 2.2
Direct Competition in the Dog
Food Industry

This Is Our Competition.

Source: Courtesy of The Quaker Oats Company.

competition, this is not the case in the supermarket, where dog food shoppers
vote with their purchases. In these instances, Cycle competes directly with Alpo,
Purina Puppy Chow, and dozens of other dog food brands.

A second type of competition involves products that can be substituted for
one another. In the transportation industry, Amtrak competes with auto rental
services, airlines, and bus services. In the plumbing industry, cast-iron pipes
compete with pipes made of synthetic materials such as polyvinyl chloride
(PVC), and steel is losing ground to plastic in automobile manufacturing. Some
car makers prefer plastic because it is lightweight, rustproof, and easier to modify than steel when making design changes, which allows them to quickly adapt
to market changes.[5] In instances in which a change such as a price increase
or an improvement in a product's strength occurs, demand for substitute products is directly affected.

The final type of competition occurs among all organizations that compete
for the consumer's purchases. Traditional economic analysis views competition
as a battle among companies in the same industry or among substitutable products and services. Marketers, however, accept the argument that all firms compete for a limited amount of discretionary buying power. *Competition* in this
sense means that a Mercury Sable competes with a ClubMed vacation and a
Bruce Springsteen record competes with a Steve Martin movie for the consumer's entertainment dollar.

Because the competitive environment often determines the success or failure of a product, marketers must continually assess competitors' marketing
strategies. New product offerings with technological advances, price reductions,
special promotions, or other competitive variations must be monitored, and the
firm's marketing mix may require adjustments with which to counter these

changes. Among the first purchasers of any new product are the product's competitors. Careful analysis of its elements — physical components, performance attributes, packaging, retail price, service requirements, and estimated production and marketing costs — allows marketers to forecast its likely competitive impact. Adjustments to one or more marketing mix components may be needed in order to compete with a new market entry.

Developing a Competitive Strategy

All marketers must develop an effective strategy for dealing with the competitive environment. Some compete in a broad range of markets in many areas of the world. Others specialize in particular market segments, such as those determined by geographical, age, or income factors. Determining a competitive strategy involves answering three questions:

1. Should we compete?

2. If so, in what markets should we compete?

3. How should we compete?

The answer to the first question — should we compete? — must be based on the firm's resources, objectives, and expected profit potential. A firm may decide not to pursue or continue operating a potentially successful venture because it doesn't mesh with its resources, objectives, or profit expectations. Gulf & Western's strategy, for example, is to focus on the three core businesses — financial services, publishing, and entertainment — that offer the strongest growth opportunities. Since 1980, it has sold 50 businesses that were not operating profitably, did not show a satisfactory return on investment, or were not a good fit with its core businesses.[6]

Answering the second question — in what markets should we compete? — requires acknowledging that the marketer has limited resources (sales personnel, advertising budgets, product development capability, and the like) and that these resources must be allocated to the areas of greatest opportunity. Too many marketers have taken a "shotgun" approach to market selection and thus have done an ineffective job in many markets rather than a good one in a selected few. International Multifoods Corporation tried to emulate two of its larger competitors, Pillsbury and General Mills, by diversifying from grain milling into branded consumer products and the restaurant field. IMC acquired many small, regional brands and hoped to build them into major, national ones. But the plan didn't work. The regional brands never generated enough sales volume to justify the huge marketing expenditures required for competing with top consumer goods brands. A strategy review resulted in IMC's selling its line of consumer food products and restaurants. The company decided to concentrate instead on its resource strengths — flour milling, bakery mixes, and animal feed — markets in which the 97-year-old company continues to be a top competitor.[7]

Answering the third question — how should we compete? — requires the marketer to make tactical decisions involved in setting up a comprehensive marketing strategy. Product, pricing, distribution, and promotional decisions, of course, are the major elements of this strategy. The success of Huggies disposable diapers illustrates the importance of a carefully developed and well-executed competitive strategy. Kimberly-Clark, a major newsprint supplier, de-

THE COMPETITIVE EDGE

Campbell Soup

The microwave soup container shown in the accompanying photo hardly seems to reflect the traditional image of Campbell Soup Company. Generations of shoppers have become accustomed to the "Campbell Soup aisle" in supermarkets with its thousands of red-and-white soup labels. But changes are in the works for the company that has traditionally prided itself on its low prices and agonizing deliberateness in new-product development. For Campbell, maintaining competitiveness means willingness to modify previously successful marketing programs to appeal more strongly to the consumer of the late 1980s.

For years, the 10-cent can of condensed soup was Campbell's specialty, winning the company an 80 percent share of the domestic soup market. But Gordon McGovern, who took over as Campbell president in 1980, realized that Campbell's low prices, while a source of pride, were not necessarily a source of added revenues. McGovern set Campbell on a new, market-sensitive, consumer-driven course — one that he hoped would relieve the company of its stodgy reputation and result in 15 percent annual sales gains.

To achieve the goals, Campbell has diversified its product lines. The company introduced 334 new products from 1980 to 1985, more than any other firm in the food industry — an enormous change for a company that previously frowned on new-product development. This was all part of McGovern's guiding principle: that the American marketplace is no longer a homogeneous mass; it has splintered into many different con-

sumer groups that must be individually targeted if Campbell is to maintain its market dominance.

McGovern recently told *Business Week,* "When I grew up, you were at the dinner table at six sharp, your hands washed, and that was that. Today, my son is catching a snack five times a day as he breezes in and out of the house." What McGovern is saying is that family patterns have changed. And so have demographics. Gone are the days of the working father, homemaker mother, and two children. Over 50 percent of all households consist of only one or two persons. In other words, as a Campbell executive has said, there are "niches and more niches."

Campbell's new products are designed to fill those niches. Some of them have been very successful. Campbell's Le Menu frozen dinners, which were designed to compete with Stouffer's for the upscale, single-person market, have been generating $200 million in annual sales during recent years. Consisting of such items as chicken cordon bleu, al dente vegetables, and wine sauces, the dinners have produced a 20 percent growth in Campbell's frozen-menu unit — exactly the effect McGovern wanted.

Other products have failed, which is to be expected. Campbell's Pepperidge Farm division came out with a line of Star War cookies that worked against Pepperidge Farm's premium image. Juice Works, a line of natural juice blends for children, also has had to be completely revamped. In fact, since the initial flurry of McGovern's reign, Campbell has somewhat turned down the tap on new products. McGovern now says

he wants a more thorough review of new-product ventures and a slower pace for national introductions. It's not a return to the production-oriented past, he cautions; rather, he sees it as a natural phase of Campbell's continuing evolution. And new products will continue to come off the line: Refrigerated salads, soups in microwavable containers, Pepperidge Farm ice cream, and granola bread are all on the testing block. Campbell Soup is no longer just the little red-and-white can.

Sources: McGovern quotation from "Campbell's Soup's Recipe for Growth: Offering Something for Every Plate," *Business Week* (December 24, 1984), p. 66. See also Kevin McManus, "Campbell Cooks at U.S. Soup Kitchen," *Advertising Age* (January 30, 1986), p. 20; "Creative Juices Make Gravy for Campbell Soup," *Marketing News* (December 6, 1985), p. 5; and Francine Schwadel, "Revised Recipe: Burned by Mistakes, Campbell Soup Is in Throes of Change," *The Wall Street Journal* (August 14, 1985), p. 1. *Photo source:* Courtesy of Campbell Soup Company.

termined that its future growth depended on diversifying into new businesses and decided to compete in consumer products that were linked to its core business. The disposable-diaper market, dominated by Procter & Gamble's Pampers, embodied the firm's major strengths — expertise in paper and abundant paper resources — and offered Kimberly-Clark enormous growth and profit potential. Huggies' linings and fillings, for example, are made at the company's pulp mills and paper plants. To carry out its strategy, Kimberly-Clark pumped millions of dollars into product research and development and extensive advertising and sales promotion. As a result, Huggies captured one-third of the disposable-diaper market and accounts for 26 percent of total company sales.[8]

The Political/Legal Environment

Before you play the game, learn the rules! It would be absurd to start playing a new game without first understanding the rules. Yet some businesspeople exhibit a remarkable lack of knowledge about marketing's **political/legal environment** — the laws and interpretations of laws that require firms to operate under competitive conditions and to protect consumer rights. Ignorance of or noncompliance with laws, ordinances, and regulations could result in fines, embarrassing negative publicity, and possibly expensive civil damage suits.

political/legal environment
Component of the marketing environment consisting of laws and interpretations of laws that require firms to operate under competitive conditions and to protect consumer rights.

Considerable diligence is required for developing an understanding of the legal framework for marketing decisions. Numerous laws and regulations, often vague and legislated by a multitude of different authorities, characterize the political/legal environment. Our existing legal framework was constructed on a piecemeal basis, often in response to concerns over current issues.

Regulations affecting marketing have been enacted at the federal, state, and local levels, as well as by independent regulatory agencies. They touch on all aspects of marketing decision making — designing, labeling, packaging, distribution, advertising, and promotion of products and services. To cope with the vastness, complexity, and changing nature of the political/legal environment, many large firms maintain in-house legal departments and small firms seek professional advice from attorneys. All marketers, however, should be aware of the major regulations that affect their activities.

Government Regulation

Government regulation in the United States can be divided into four phases. The first phase was the antimonopoly period of the late nineteenth and early twentieth centuries. During this era, major laws such as the Sherman Antitrust Act, Clayton Act, and Federal Trade Commission Act were passed to maintain a competitive environment by reducing the trend toward increasing concentration of industry power in the hands of a small number of competitors. The second phase, aimed at protecting competitors, emerged during the Depression era of the 1930s, when independent merchants felt the need for legal protection against competition from larger chain stores. Federal legislation enacted during this period included the Robinson-Patman Act and the Miller-Tydings Resale Price Maintenance Act. The third phase focused on consumer protection. Although consumer protection is an underlying objective of most laws — the Sherman Act, FTC Act, and Federal Food and Drug Act are good examples — many of the major pro-consumer laws have been enacted during the past 30

Table 2.1
Major Federal Laws Affecting Marketing

Date	Law	Description
A. Laws Maintaining a Competitive Environment		
1890	Sherman Antitrust Act	Prohibits restraint of trade and monopolization; delineates maintenance of a competitive marketing system as national policy
1914	Clayton Act	Strengthens Sherman Act by restricting such practices as price discrimination, exclusive dealing, tying contracts, and interlocking boards of directors where the effect "may be to substantially lessen competition or tend to create a monopoly"
1914	Federal Trade Commission Act	Prohibits unfair methods of competition; established Federal Trade Commission, an administrative agency that investigates business practices and enforces the FTC Act
1938	Wheeler-Lea Act	Amend the FTC Act to further outlaw unfair or deceptive practices in businesses; gives FTC jurisdiction over false and misleading advertising
1950	Celler-Kefauver Antimerger Act	Amends the Clayton Act to include major asset purchases that will decrease competition in an industry
1975	Consumer Goods Pricing Act	Prohibits pricing maintenance agreements among manufacturers and resellers in interstate commerce
1980	FTC Improvement Act	Gives the Senate and House of Representatives joint veto power over FTC trade regulation rules; limits FTC power to regulate unfairness issues
B. Laws Regulating Competition		
1936	Robinson-Patman Act	Prohibits price discrimination in sales to wholesalers, retailers, or other producers; prohibits selling at unreasonably low prices to eliminate competition
1937	Miller-Tydings Resale Price Maintenance Act	Exempts interstate fair trade contracts from compliance with antitrust requirements
C. Laws Protecting Consumers		
1906	Federal Food and Drug Act	Prohibits adulteration and misbranding of foods and drugs involved in interstate commerce; strengthened by the Food, Drug, and Cosmetic Act (1938) and the Kefauver-Harris Drug Amendment (1962)
1939	Wool Products Labeling Act	Requires identification of the type and percentage of wool used in products
1951	Fur Products Labeling Act	Requires identification of the animal from which a fur product was derived
1953	Flammable Fabrics Act	Prohibits interstate sale of flammable fabrics
1958	National Traffic and Safety Act	Provides for the creation of safety standards for automobiles and tires
1958	Automobile Information Disclosure Act	Prohibits automobile dealers from inflating factory prices of new cars

years. The most recent phase, industry deregulation, began in the late 1970s and has continued to the present. This phase, related to the antimonopoly period of the late nineteenth and early twentieth centuries, has sought to increase competition in such industries as transportation and financial services by discontinuing many industry regulations and permitting firms to expand their service offerings to new markets.

Table 2.1 lists and briefly describes the major federal laws affecting marketing. Legislation affecting specific marketing practices, such as product warranties and franchise agreements, is discussed in later chapters.

Table 2.1

Major Federal Laws Affecting Marketing — *continued*

Date	Law	Description
C. Laws Protecting Consumers		
1966	Child Protection Act	Outlaws sale of hazardous toys; 1969 amendment adds products posing electrical, mechanical, or thermal hazards
1967	Fair Packaging and Labeling Act	Requires disclosure of product identification, name and address of manufacturer or distributor, and information on the quality of contents
1967	Federal Cigarette Labeling and Advertising Act	Requires written health warnings on cigarette packages
1968	Consumer Credit Protection Act	Truth-in-lending law requiring disclosure of annual interest rates on loans and credit purchases
1970	Fair Credit Reporting Act	Gives individuals access to their credit records and allows them to change incorrect information
1970	National Environmental Policy Act	Established the Environmental Protection Agency to deal with various types of pollution and organizations that create pollution
1971	Public Health Cigarette Smoking Act	Prohibits tobacco advertising on radio and television
1972	Consumer Product Safety Act	Created the Consumer Product Safety Commission, which has authority to specify safety standards for most consumer products
1975, 1977	Equal Credit Opportunity Act	Bans discrimination-in-lending practices based on sex and marital status (1975) and race, national origin, religion, age, or receipt of payments from public assistance programs (1977)
1978	Fair Debt Collection Practices Act	Prohibits harassing, deceptive, or unfair collection practices by debt collection agencies; exempts in-house collectors such as banks, retailers, and attorneys
D. Laws Deregulating Specific Industries		
1978	Airline Deregulation Act	Granted considerable freedom to commercial airlines in setting fares and choosing new routes
1980	Motor Carrier Act and Staggers Rail Act	Significantly deregulated trucking and railroad industries by permitting them to negotiate rates and services
1980	Depository Institutions and Monetary Control Act ("Banking Act of 1980")	Significantly deregulated financial service industry by permitting all depository institutions to offer checking accounts, expanding the services and lending powers of savings and loan associations, and removing interest rate ceilings on customer deposits

Marketers must also be aware of state and local laws that influence marketing activities. In 1987, for example, Florida passed a law affecting national firms and telemarketers within the state. The law, resulting from repeated consumer complaints, allows people who do not want to receive unsolicited phone calls to request an additional line under their listing in the directory stating, "no sales solicitation calls." Telemarketers within the state must obtain all 71 phone directories and remove from their calling lists the names and numbers of "do-not-call" consumers. Civil penalties for not complying with the law could result in fines of up to $10,000 per violation.[9]

Government Regulatory Agencies

Federal, state, and local governments have established regulatory agencies to enforce laws. At the federal level, the Federal Trade Commission (FTC) has the broadest powers to influence marketing activities. It has the authority to enforce laws regulating unfair business practices and can take action to stop false and deceptive advertising. The scope of other agencies is narrower. The Federal Communications Commission, for example, regulates communication by wire, radio, and television. The Interstate Commerce Commission continues to monitor many of the rates of interstate rail, bus, truck, and water carriers. Other federal regulatory agencies include the Food and Drug Administration, the Consumer Products Safety Commission, the Federal Power Commission, and the Environmental Protection Agency.

The FTC uses several procedures to enforce laws. It may issue a consent order whereby a business accused of violating a law agrees to voluntary compliance without admitting guilt. If a business refuses to comply with an FTC request, the agency can issue a cease-and-desist order, which is a final order to stop an illegal practice. Firms often challenge the cease-and-desist order in court. The FTC can require advertisers to provide additional information about products in their advertisements and can require firms using deceptive advertising to correct earlier claims with new promotional messages. In some cases, the FTC requires that firms give refunds to consumers misled by deceptive advertising. In one such case against Weider Health & Fitness Inc., the FTC ordered the company to reimburse $400,000 to thousands of customers who had bought its muscle-building pills.[10]

Other Regulatory Forces

Marketing activities are also affected by public and private consumer interest groups and self-regulatory organizations. Consumer interest groups have mushroomed in the past 20 years. Today hundreds of these organizations operate at the national, state, and local levels. Groups such as the National Coalition Against Misuse of Pesticides seek to protect the environment. Others attempt to advance the rights of minorities, elderly Americans, and other special-interest groups. The power of these groups has also grown. The Center for Science in the Public Interest recently challenged the advertising claims for McDonald's Chicken McNuggets by filing a complaint with the FTC and the attorney general of New York. The assault on unsafe automobiles by Ralph Nader's Public Citizen group resulted in the passage of the National Traffic and Motor Vehicle Safety Act.

Self-regulatory groups are industry's attempts to set guidelines for responsible business conduct. The Council of Better Business Bureaus is a national organization devoted to consumer service and business self-regulation. The Council's National Advertising Division (NAD) is designed to promote truth and accuracy in advertising. It reviews and resolves advertising complaints from consumers and business on a voluntary basis. If NAD fails to resolve a complaint, an appeal can be made to the National Advertising Review Board, which is composed of advertisers, ad agency representatives, and public members. In addition, many individual trade associations set business guidelines and codes of conduct and encourage members' voluntary compliance.

Figure 2.3
Use of Marketing Techniques to Influence the Political/Legal Environment

Is it time
to teach an old law
new tricks?

Just because a law is old doesn't mean it's necessarily good or bad. But when over the years an industry changes dramatically, it seems reasonable that the laws governing it should also change. For example, America's financial services are governed by a law enacted before computer technology, globalized capital markets, and a wide variety of instruments became part of our financial system.

That law, the Glass-Steagall Act, was passed in the crisis atmosphere of the Great Depression in response to stock market abuses. This 54-year-old law keeps commercial banks from breaking into the Wall Street cartel that dominates stock and bond underwriting and has created a division of services that's outdated and harmful.

By creating a monopoly on certain lines of corporate business, Glass-Steagall has kept the cost of raising capital artificially high. And, ironically, it has prevented U.S. commercial banks from conducting business at home they can successfully pursue overseas—underwriting bonds in London but not in New York, for instance.

Chemical Bank supports appropriate regulation. But we believe that regulations must be removed if they perpetuate unfair competition, hinder our domestic banking system, or raise prices for our corporate clients. If we fail to repeal these archaic regulations, we'll continue to use yesterday's laws to govern today's markets. And that seems to us like the tail wagging the dog. **CHEMICALBANK** The bottom line is excellence.

Source: ©1987 Chemical Bank.

Controlling the Legal/Political Environment

In most cases, marketers comply with laws and regulations. Operating within the legal framework is both socially responsible and ethical. Besides, noncompliance can scar a firm's reputation and hurt profits. In 1987, Velsicol Chemical Company agreed to the Environmental Protection Agency's demand to stop selling its two leading termite control chemicals until it could prove that the potentially cancer-causing products could be used safely. Velsicol's attorney said the company agreed to the pact because "it was getting killed in the marketplace" as a result of negative publicity about the chemicals' hazards.[11]

Marketers can, however, attempt to control forces in the legal/political environment. Individual firms and trade associations can influence public opinion and legislative action through advertising, political action committees, and political lobbying. The advertisement shown in Figure 2.3 illustrates the continuing efforts of Chemical Bank, the nation's fourth largest commercial bank holding company, to repeal federal legislation limiting its ability to expand the types of financial services it offers.

Media groups, including publishers and broadcasters, and individual firms mounted a massive campaign that resulted in the repeal of a 1987 Florida law that placed a 5 percent sales tax on national advertising. CBS and NBC networks assisted such marketers as Johnson & Johnson, Kimberly-Clark, and Rust-Oleum by replacing their commercials on the networks' affiliated stations in Florida with announcements opposing the tax. NBC, the National Association of Broadcasters, and the Television Bureau of Advertisers protested by canceling conventions they had previously scheduled in Florida. Clorox marketers withdrew all of their locally contracted television ads. *National Geographic* magazine offered advertisers a special 49-state edition — minus Florida. The pressure worked, and the law was repealed a few months following its passage.[12]

To influence the outcome of proposed legislation or change existing laws, many industries use political lobbying and political action committees. Dairy farmers, for example, have banded together to form a powerful cooperative lobbying effort and pooled their resources to support political candidates who appear to represent the interests of the dairy industry. Through such efforts, the industry attempts to influence legislation. For example, in 1987 dairy industry efforts succeeded in securing passage of the Truth in Frozen Pizza Labeling Act, requiring pizza makers to label their products to show that they contain imitation cheese. Imitation cheese is used on about 75 percent of all frozen pizzas, a practice the dairy industry claims robs it of a huge market. Current U.S. Department of Agriculture regulations permit pizza makers to replace 90 percent of pizza toppings with imitation products.[13]

The Economic Environment

The health of the economy influences how much consumers spend and what they buy. It also works the other way: Consumer buying plays an important role in the economy's health — indeed, consumer outlays perennially make up some two-thirds of overall economic activity.[14] Since all marketing activity is directed toward satisfying consumer wants and needs, marketers must understand how economic conditions influence consumer buying power.

Marketing's **economic environment** consists of those factors that influence consumer buying power and marketing strategies. They include stage of the business cycle, inflation, unemployment, resource availability, and income.

economic environment
Factors that influence consumer buying power and marketing strategies, including stage of the business cycle, inflation, unemployment, resource availability, and income.

Business Cycles

Historically the economy has tended to follow a cyclical pattern consisting of four stages: prosperity, recession, depression, and recovery. No depressions have occurred since the 1930s, and many economists argue that society is capable of preventing future depressions through intelligent use of various economic policies. Thus, a recession would be followed by a period of recovery. Consumer buying differs in each stage, and marketers must adjust their strategies accordingly.

In times of prosperity, consumer spending is brisk. Marketers respond by expanding product lines, increasing promotional efforts, expanding distribution, and raising prices. During periods of prosperity, consumers often are willing to

Figure 2.4
A Premium Version of a
Well-Known Brand

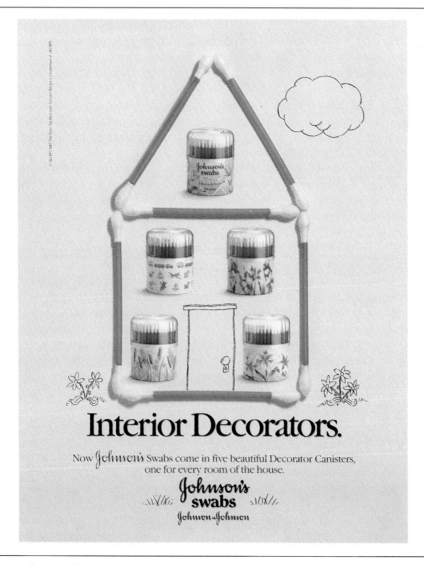

Source: Courtesy of Johnson & Johnson Baby Products Company.

pay more for premium versions of well-known brands. The advertisement shown in Figure 2.4 illustrates how Johnson & Johnson marketers enhanced the value of Swabs by offering shoppers the option of purchasing the products in decorative containers designed for different rooms in the home. Colgate-Palmolive and Procter & Gamble both recently took advantage of a strong economy by raising prices on laundry detergent and toothpaste to widen their profit margins. Clorox marketers introduced a "fresh-scent" version of their bleach that cost 10 cents more than its regular bleach. Sales for the line extension grew more rapidly than the overall bleach market.

Consumer buying power declines during a recession. The most recent recession in the United States was from July 1981 to November 1982. During recessions, consumers frequently shift their buying patterns to basic, functional products that carry low price tags. They spend more at hardware stores and do-it-yourself centers and less on nonessential products such as convenience foods. Sales of low-priced, black-and-white-label generic grocery products, which were introduced in the United States in 1977, initially boomed during the 1981–1982 recession, peaking at $2.8 billion in 1982. By 1987, sales had plummeted to $1.8 billion. In better times, shoppers are less concerned about generics' low price.[15] During recessions, marketers should consider lowering prices, reducing the size of their product lines, and increasing promotional outlays to stimulate demand.

Consumer spending is lowest during a depression. The United States has not suffered a depression since the late 1930s. Although a possibility always exists, the likelihood of another severe depression is slim. Through effective management of monetary and fiscal policies, the federal government attempts to control extreme fluctuations in the business cycle.

In the recovery stage, the economy emerges from a recession to prosperity and consumer purchasing power increases. But while consumers' *ability* to buy increases, their *willingness* to buy is often characterized by caution. Remembering the tougher times of recession, they may be more likely to save than spend or buy on credit. As the recovery strengthens, consumers become more indulgent, buying convenience-type products and higher-priced goods and services such as housecleaning and lawn care. Recovery is a difficult stage for marketers. It requires them to assess how quickly consumers make the psychological transition from recession to prosperity. Hartmarx Corporation misjudged the transition and had to readjust its marketing strategy. Hartmarx operates a chain of 330 higher-priced clothing stores. In 1982, the firm acquired Kuppenheimer Men's Clothiers, a discount chain, to diversify into the under-$200 suit market and started expanding the number of Kuppenheimer stores. But demand for the cheaper suits lessened as consumers, emerging from the recession, began to buy higher-quality clothes. Hartmarx had to alter its strategy by repositioning the no-frills stores to meet this changing consumer demand.[16]

Business cycles, like other aspects of the economy, are complex and seem to be beyond the control of marketers. The key to success is developing flexible plans that can be adjusted to satisfy consumer demands during the various business cycle stages.

Inflation

A major constraint on consumer spending is inflation, which can occur during any stage of the business cycle. *Inflation* is a rising price level that results in reduced consumer buying power. A person's money is devalued in terms of what it can buy. The impact of inflation would be less restrictive if income kept pace with rising prices, but often it does not. The rate of inflation in the United States soared to double digits in the late 1970s and early 1980s, reaching 13.6 percent in 1980. Although the inflation rate dropped below 2 percent in 1987, economists expect it to climb gradually to a 5 percent annual level. If consumer prices continue to rise at an annual rate of 5 percent until the year 2000, it will halve the dollar's current purchasing power by the end of the century.[17] Inflation increases marketers' costs, such as for purchasing materials for production, and may result in declining sales.

Unemployment

Unemployment is defined as the situation in which people who do not have jobs are actively looking for work. Unemployment rises during recessions and declines in the recovery and prosperity stages of the business cycle. Like inflation, unemployment affects marketing by modifying consumer behavior. Unless unemployment insurance, personal savings, and union supplementary unemployment benefits are sufficient to offset lost earnings, the unemployed have less income to spend. Even if people are completely compensated for lost earnings, buying behavior is likely to be affected. Instead of buying, they may choose to build their savings. Consumers, especially during periods of high inflation, become more price conscious in general. This can lead to three possible outcomes, all important to marketers. Consumers can (1) elect to buy now, in the belief that prices will be higher later (automobile dealers often use this argument in their commercial messages); (2) decide to alter their purchasing patterns; or (3) postpone certain purchases.

Resource Availability

Resources are not unlimited. This realization was magnified by the Arab oil embargo during the early 1970s, when much of the industrialized world scrambled for ways to cope with the shortage of petroleum. The energy crisis affected many industries and the marketing of many products. The toy industry, for example, depends on plastic, a petroleum derivative. Some plastics increased substantially in price, and the resulting higher costs were passed on to consumers in the form of toy price increases.

The petroleum shortage had a significant impact on the automobile industry. Consumers decided to trade in their big, gas-guzzling cars for smaller, more efficient models. Consumer demand for smaller cars forced car makers to restructure their production lines, prices, and promotional strategies.

As shortages appeared in many critical industrial areas, marketers faced a relatively strange dilemma: How should limited supplies be allocated to customers whose demands exceed the quantities available for distribution? Many marketers were not prepared to cope with such a situation. The energy crisis and other shortages have forced marketers to devise a fuller range of strategy alternatives.

Shortages — temporary or permanent — can be caused by several factors. A brisk demand may exceed manufacturing capacity or outpace the response time required to gear up a production line. Shortages may also be caused by a lack of raw materials, component parts, energy, or labor. Regardless of the cause, shortages require marketers to reorient their thinking. One approach is **demarketing,** the process of reducing consumer demand for a product to a level that the firm can reasonably supply. Oil companies, for example, publicize tips on how to cut gasoline consumption, and utility companies encourage homeowners to install more insulation to reduce heating costs. Many cities dis-

demarketing
Process of reducing consumer demand for a product or service to a level that the firm can supply.

courage central business district traffic by raising parking fees and violation penalties and promoting mass transit and car pooling.

Shortages present marketers with a unique set of marketing problems. In some instances, they force marketers to be allocators of limited supplies. This is in sharp contrast to marketing's traditional objective of expanding sales volume. Shortages require marketers to decide whether to spread a limited supply over all customers so that none are totally satisfied or to limit purchases by some customers so that others may be completely satisfied. During World War II, consumer demand for Wrigley gum increased while ingredient supplies diminished. Wrigley supplied large quantities of gum to the U.S. armed forces overseas. Since the company could not meet everyone's needs, it took its Spearmint, Doublemint, and Juicy Fruit brands off the civilian market and directed its entire output overseas. It marketed a special wartime brand, Orbit, for civilians but told the public that it wasn't quite good enough to carry the Wrigley label. Top-grade materials eventually became so scarce that Wrigley halted production and marketing of its established brands. But to keep the Wrigley name in consumers' minds, the company ran an advertising campaign showing an empty Wrigley's wrapper with the slogan "Remember This Wrapper." Wrigley's adaptive strategy worked. After being off the market for two years, the brands quickly regained and then exceeded their prewar popularity.[18]

Companies today have also devised ways to deal with shortages. Reynolds Metal Company addresses the dwindling supply of aluminum through its recycling programs, including cash-paying vending machines. Such "reverse" vending machines allow recyclers to insert empty cans and receive money, stamps, and/or discount coupons for merchandise or services.

Income

Income is another important factor in marketing's economic environment, because it influences consumer buying power. Studying income statistics and trends helps marketers estimate market potential and develop plans for targeting specific market segments. Household incomes have grown in recent years and, coupled with a low rate of inflation, resulted in added purchasing power for millions of American households. For marketers, a rise in income represents the potential for increasing overall sales. However, marketers are most interested in *discretionary income,* the amount of money people have to spend after they have paid for necessities such as food, clothing, and housing.

Discretionary income varies greatly by age group and household type. Bureau of the Census statistics show that older couples, for example, have a significant amount of buying power compared to other groups with higher incomes. Contributing to the elderly's buying power are smaller household size, the increased likelihood that children's education outlays will be completed, and the fact that most older people no longer make mortgage payments. Based on this information, many firms are aiming products and services at this once neglected market. Levi Strauss, for example, is producing slacks designed specifically for older customers, and Kraft is emphasizing the benefits that its cheese provides for people over 50, as shown in the advertisement in Figure 2.5. More than half of America's 100 largest companies are targeting advertising at the older market.[19]

Figure 2.5
Marketing Appeals to the
Over-50 Market

Source: ©1985 Kraft, Inc. Reprinted with permission.

The Technological Environment

The **technological environment** represents the application to marketing of knowledge based on discoveries in science, inventions, and innovations. New technology results in new products and services for consumers, improved existing products, and often lower prices through the development of more cost-efficient production and distribution methods. Technology can quickly make products obsolete — calculators, for example, wiped out the market for slide rules — but can just as quickly open up new marketing opportunities. Technology has spawned new industries: Computers, lasers, and xerography all resulted in the development of major industries in the past 30 years. Recent technological advances in superconductivity — the conducting of electricity with virtually no power loss — is expected to result in an annual $20 billion worldwide industry by the year 2000.[20] Scientists and researchers around the globe are working to convert superconductor technology into commercial applications. Superconductors have the potential to eliminate urban air pollution by making electrical cars practical, improve medical imaging systems that will give doctors sharper pictures, save the utilities billions of dollars, and enable computers to perform much more rapidly.[21]

technological environment
Applications to marketing of knowledge based on discoveries in science, inventions, and innovations.

Adapting Technology

Marketers must closely monitor the technological environment for a number of reasons. Adapting technology may be the means by which a firm remains competitive. Remington Arms Company has turned to computers and robots in order to survive in the competitive specialty firearms business, which today is dominated by foreign firms. Remington invested $25 million in computer-driven robotics to compete in this market. Specialty firearms require short production runs when, for example, as few as 200 pieces are to be produced. With Remington's old, less flexible machinery, such short runs were not economical because of the expense of retooling heavy machinery. Now workers need only install new software into their computers to turn out new gun designs in small numbers. The computers and robots have shortened the time Remington needs to bring its products to market, an advantage that previously gave foreign competitors the edge in marketing specialty firearms.[22]

Applying new technology also gives marketers the opportunity to improve customer service. Breakthroughs in electronic communications have brought consumers the convenience of in-home shopping and 24-hour banking at automated teller machines. Security Pacific Corporation plans to bring a new generation of banking technology to its California customers in the 1990s. Its "Branch of the Future" will deliver financial services through terminals that talk, use graphic and live-action video images to dispense user-friendly information, and help guide customers through the steps needed for completing their transactions.[23] The advertisement shown in Figure 2.6 illustrates how firms like NEC America, Inc. have combined such products as advanced personal computers, digital telephones, and high-speed facsimile terminals to provide state-of-the-art solutions for the management and transmission of information for their clients.

Many firms use computer-based electronic systems to give customers information. Larry Robbins, owner of two Philadelphia bookstores, installed computers to help customers select books. The system asks customers which authors, movies, or TV shows they like, correlates that information with a database of more than 100,000 titles, and then prints out a list of recommended books. Fizzazz, a New York retailer, shows music videos of its clothing on a gigantic projection screen that covers the back of its store. A touchscreen computer allows customers to preview items in detail before they start to shop.[24]

New technology can help marketers make decisions that will result in increased productivity and operating efficiency. Computer-aided design, super workstations, and computer-aided manufacturing speed up the process of bringing new products to market. Designing products by computer also allows firms to thoroughly test products for potential problems, thus eliminating costly errors before the products go into manufacturing. Computerized mapping systems give marketers instant geographical and customer information simultaneously. General Motors creates color-coded maps to help determine optimal dealership locations; 3M uses computer-generated maps to analyze its sales territories; and Federal Express uses digitized maps to dispatch its vans.[25] Computer maps also help marketers in targeting markets, planning advertising, analyzing competitors, and distributing products.[26] Advances in communications technology have created computer networks that allow marketers to share information with dealers, salespeople, and coworkers in such areas as finance and research and development. Laptop computers and cellular phone technology

Figure 2.6
Combining Computer and Communications Technology to Manage Information Flows

Source: Courtesy of NEC America, Inc.

have increased sales force productivity, because salespeople do less paperwork and spend more time with clients and prospects.

Sources of New Technology

The United States spends more on research and development than any other country. In 1986, the federal government, industry, universities and colleges, and other nonprofit institutions spent $118 billion on research and development projects. That amounts to 2.8 percent of the U.S. gross national product.[27] Almost half of all R&D funding is provided by the federal government, which is also a major source of technological innovation. The geographic information system used in computer mapping systems stems from the first photographs taken by the government's Landsat spy satellites in the 1960s. The government's research in national defense and space programs has resulted in new technologies that the government encourages industry to apply in the private sector. Industry also plays a major role in the development of new technology.

General Motors, IBM, Ford, AT&T, General Electric, DuPont, and Eastman Kodak each spent over $1 billion for research and development in 1986.[28]

The Social/Cultural Environment

social/cultural environment Component of the marketing environment consisting of the relationship between the marketer and society and its culture.

Americans are on a health and fitness kick — eating more turkey and less red meat, drinking more wine coolers and less hard liquor, buying more low-salt and low-cholesterol substitutes, smoking less, and exercising more. As a nation, we are becoming older and more affluent. Our birthrate is falling, and our population of racial minorities is rising. We value time at home with family and friends, watching videos and eating microwave popcorn. And we love products and services that offer quality and convenience. These are the types of events that shape marketers' **social/cultural environment** — the relationship between marketing and society and its culture.

Marketers must be sensitive to society's changing values and shifts in demographics such as population growth and age distribution. These changing variables affect the way consumers react to different products and marketing practices. What may be out of bounds today may be totally acceptable in tomorrow's marketplace. Subjects that were once taboo — condoms and feminine hygiene products — are now commonly advertised. A change in national attitudes toward sex has altered the way some firms advertise their products. The ad for Calvin Klein Sport clothing shown in Figure 2.7 might have stirred public protest in the 1970s, but it contributed to the line's successful launch in an already crowded industry. Although society in general has become more accepting of such promotions, consumers tend to respond to a sexual approach only when the advertising is geared toward certain products, such as fragrances, fashion clothing, suntan lotions, and lingerie.[29]

Cultural diversity is another important element within society. The United States is a mixed society composed of various submarkets, each of which displays unique cultural characteristics and differs by age, place of residence, and buying behavior. The growing Hispanic population, for example, is highly concentrated with respect to national origin and geography. Most Hispanics in the United States are of Mexican origin and live in the Southwest, while many Americans of Puerto Rican descent live in the New York metropolitan area. In buying behavior, Hispanics tend to be very brand conscious and brand loyal.[30] Recognition of the size, growth rate, and buying power of this market and development of products and services aimed at satisfying Hispanics' needs and wants can open up new marketing opportunities for many firms, large and small. The importance of culture in marketing is explored in more depth in Chapter 5; demographic considerations are discussed in detail in Chapter 7.

Importance in International Marketing Decisions

The social/cultural context for marketing decision making often is more pronounced in the international sphere than in the domestic arena. Competition in the global marketplace has increased considerably in recent years as more and more firms have begun marketing their products and services abroad. Learning about cultural and societal differences among countries is paramount to a firm's success abroad. As stated in the advertisement in Figure 2.8, AIG attributes its

Figure 2.7
Use of Sensuous Advertising to Market Clothing

Source: Courtesy of Calvin Klein.

success in the competitive worldwide insurance business to "becoming part of the social, cultural, and moral fabric of the countries in which we do business." Marketing strategies that work in the United States often cannot be directly applied in other countries. In many cases, marketers must redesign packages and modify products and advertising messages to suit the tastes and preferences of different cultures. The following examples illustrate this point:

☐ S. C. Johnson and Sons, Inc., had trouble marketing its Lemon Pledge furniture polish to people over 40 in Japan. Johnson learned that this group didn't buy the polish because it smelled similar to a latrine

Figure 2.8
Importance of Societal/Cultural Dimension in International Marketing

Sometimes the best way to stand out is to blend in.

It's a very important lesson we learned early in our 65-year history.

Leadership in the worldwide insurance industry isn't won by imposing our corporate culture on local operations. It's won by becoming part of the social, cultural and moral fabric of the countries in which we do business.

That idea is one reason for our current success in providing a broad range of commercial and personal insurance to businesses and individuals around the world. To learn more, contact AIG, Dept. A, 70 Pine St., N.Y., N.Y. 10270.

Thinking more like our customers than other insurance companies is how we won our stripes.

Insurance Companies That Don't Think Like Insurance Companies. **AIG**

Source: Courtesy of American International Group, Inc., New York. Advertising agency: Bozell, Jacobs, Kenyon & Eckhardt, New York.

disinfectant that was widely used in Japan during the 1940s. When Johnson subdued the lemon scent, sales of Lemon Pledge rose sharply.

☐ In Thailand, feet are regarded as despicable. Athlete's foot remedies with packages showing feet would be poorly received by Thai consumers.

☐ A company that had set up a corn processing plant in Italy found that its marketing effort failed because Italians think of corn as pig food.

The social/cultural environment for marketing decisions at home and abroad is expanding in scope and importance. Today no marketer can initiate a strategy without taking into account the society's norms, values, culture, and demographics. Marketers must be aware of how these variables affect their decisions. The constant influx of societal issues requires that marketing managers place more emphasis on addressing these questions instead of concerning themselves with the standard marketing tools. Some firms have created a new position — manager of public policy research — to study the changing societal environment's future impact on the company.

Marketing's Role in Society

Another dimension that goes beyond the five environments described in the previous section is the role that marketing plays in society itself and the consequent effects and responsibilities of marketing activities.

Marketing's relationship to society in general and to various public issues is subject to constant scrutiny by the public. In fact, it may reasonably be argued that marketing typically mirrors changes in the entire business environment. Because marketing is the final interface between the business enterprise and the society in which it operates, marketers often carry much of the responsibility for dealing with various social issues affecting their firms.

Marketing operates in an environment external to the firm. It reacts to its environment and, in turn, is acted upon by it. Relationships with customers, employees, the government, vendors, and society as a whole form the basis of the societal issues that confront contemporary marketing. While they are often a product of the exchange process, these relationships are coincidental to the primary sales and distribution functions of marketing. Marketing's relationship to its external environment has a significant effect on the relative degree of success that the firm achieves. Marketing must continually find new ways to deal with the social issues facing our competitive system.

The competitive marketing system is a product of our drive for materialism. However, it is important to note that materialism developed from society itself. Most of the U.S. culture, with its acceptance of the work ethic, traditionally has viewed the acquisition of wealth favorably. The motto of this philosophy seems to be "more equals better." A better life has been defined in terms of more physical possessions, although that definition may be changing.

Evaluating the Quality of Life

One theme runs through the arguments of marketing's critics: materialism (as exemplified by the competitive marketing system) is concerned only with the quantities of life and ignores the quality aspect. Traditionally, a firm was considered socially responsible in the community if it provided employment for its residents, thereby contributing to its economic base. Employment, wages, bank deposits, and profits — the traditional measures of societal contributions — are quantity indicators. But what about air, water, and cultural pollution? The boredom and isolation of mass assembly lines? The depletion of natural resources? The charges of neglect in these areas go largely unanswered simply because we have not developed reliable indices with which to measure a firm's contribution to the quality of life.

Criticisms of the Competitive Marketing System

An indictment of the competitive marketing system would contain at least the following complaints:

1. Marketing costs are too high.
2. The marketing system is inefficient.

3. Marketers (the business system) are guilty of collusion and price fixing.

4. Product quality and service are poor.

5. Consumers receive incomplete and/or false and misleading information.

6. The marketing system has produced health and safety hazards.

7. Unwanted and unnecessary products are promoted to those who least need them.

Almost anyone could cite specific examples in which these charges have been proven. Because each of us has a somewhat different set of values, it should be recognized that we all evaluate the performance of the marketing system we experience within our own frames of reference.

Bearing this in mind and taking the system as a whole, we can evaluate the success or failure of the competitive marketing system in serving consumers' needs. Most of us will likely arrive at the uncomfortable and somewhat unsatisfying conclusion that the system usually works quite adequately, although there are some aspects of it that we would like to see changed.

Current Issues in Marketing

Marketing faces many diverse social issues. The current issues in marketing can be divided into three major subjects: consumerism, marketing ethics, and social responsibility. While the overlap and classification problems are obvious, the framework provides a foundation for systematically studying these issues.

Consumerism

Unacceptable business practices and changing societal values have led to the consumerism movement. Today everyone — marketers, industry, government, and the public — is acutely aware of the impact of consumerism on the nation's economy and general well-being. **Consumerism** has been defined as a social force within the environment designed to aid and protect the consumer by exerting legal, moral, and economic pressures on business.[31] It is a societal demand that organizations apply the marketing concept.

But not all consumer demands are met. A competitive marketing system is based on the individual behavior of competing firms. Our economic system requires that reasonable profit objectives be achieved. Business cannot meet all consumer demands if it is to generate the profits necessary for remaining viable. This selection process is one of the most difficult dilemmas facing society today. Given these constraints, what should the consumer have the right to expect from the competitive marketing system?

The most frequently quoted statement of **consumer rights** was made by President John F. Kennedy in 1962. While it was not a definitive statement, it is a good rule of thumb with which to explain basic consumer rights:

1. *The right to choose freely.* Consumers should be able to choose from among a range of products and services.

2. *The right to be informed.* Consumers should be provided with enough education and product/service information to enable them to be responsible buyers.

consumerism
Social force within the environment designed to aid and protect the consumer by exerting legal, moral, and economic pressures on business and government.

consumer rights
As stated by President Kennedy in 1962, the consumer's right to choose freely, to be informed, to be heard, and to be safe.

3. *The right to be heard.* Consumers should be able to express their legitimate displeasure to appropriate parties — that is, sellers, consumer assistance groups, and city or state consumer affairs offices.

4. *The right to be safe.* Consumers should be assured that the products and services they purchase are not injurious with normal use. Products and services should be designed in such a way that the average consumer can use them safely.

These rights have formed the conceptual framework of much of the consumer legislation passed in the last 30 years. However, the question of how best to guarantee these rights remains unanswered.

Marketing Ethics

Environmental considerations have led to increased attention to **marketing ethics** — the marketer's standards of conduct and moral values. Ethics concern matters of right and wrong: the decision of the individual and the firm to do what is morally right. A discussion of marketing ethics highlights the types of problems individuals face in their roles as marketers. Such problems must be considered before we can suggest possible improvements in the marketing system.

marketing ethics
Marketers' standards of conduct and moral values.

People develop standards of ethical behavior based on their own systems of values. Their individual ethics help them deal with the various ethical questions in their personal lives. However, when they are put into a work situation, a serious conflict may materialize. Individual ethics may differ from the employer's organizational ethics. An individual may believe that industry participation in developing a recycling program for industrial waste is highly desirable, but his or her firm may take the position that such a venture would be unprofitable. In contrast, unethical behavior of employees may conflict with a firm's high standards of ethical conduct. Anheuser-Busch made it clear to all employees that questionable marketing practices would not be tolerated following a 1987 scandal involving allegations that three of its key marketing executives had taken kickbacks of more than $150,000 from a supplier.[32]

How can these conflicts be resolved? The development of and adherence to a professional ethic may provide a third basis of authority. This ethic should be based on a concept of professionalism that transcends both organizational and individual ethics. A professional peer association can exercise collective sanctions over a marketer's individual behavior. For example, in 1987 the American Marketing Association, the major international association of marketers, revised its code of ethics to include a provision for expelling members who violate its tenets. The revised code is shown in Figure 2.9.

Marketers face a variety of ethical problems. While promotional matters tend to receive the greatest attention, ethical issues also relate to marketing research, product management, channel strategy, and pricing.

Ethical Problems in Marketing Research   Marketing research has been castigated because of its alleged invasion of personal privacy. Citizens of today's urban, mechanized society seek individual identity to a greater degree than ever before. Personal privacy is important to most consumers and therefore has become a public issue. In response to the Florida "do-not-call" law

Figure 2.9
American Marketing Association Code of Ethics

Members of the American Marketing Association (AMA) are committed to ethical professional conduct. They have joined together in subscribing to this Code of Ethics embracing the following topics:

Responsibilities of the Marketer

Marketers must accept responsibility for the consequences of their activities and make every effort to ensure that their decisions, recommendations, and actions function to identify, serve, and satisfy all relevant publics: customers, organizations, and society.
    Marketers' professional conduct must be guided by:
1. The basic rule of professional ethics: not knowingly to do harm;
2. The adherence to all applicable laws and regulations;
3. The accurate representation of their education, training, and experience; and
4. The active support, practice, and promotion of this Code of Ethics.

Honesty and Fairness

Marketers shall uphold and advance the integrity, honor, and dignity of the marketing profession by:
1. Being honest in serving consumers, clients, employees, suppliers, distributors, and the public;
2. Not knowingly participating in conflict of interest without prior notice to all parties involved; and
3. Establishing equitable fee schedules including the payment or receipt of usual, customary, and/or legal compensation for marketing exchanges.

Rights and Duties of Parties in the Marketing Exchange Process

Participants in the marketing exchange process should be able to expect that:
1. Products and services offered are safe and fit for their intended uses;
2. Communications about offered products and services are not deceptive;
3. All parties intend to discharge their obligations, financial and otherwise, in good faith; and
4. Appropriate internal methods exist for equitable adjustment and/or redress of grievances concerning purchases.
It is understood that the above would include, *but it is not limited to,* the following responsibilities of the marketers:
In the area of product development and management,
☐ Disclosure of all substantial risks associated with product or service usage;
☐ Identification of any product component substitution that might materially change the product or impact on the buyer's purchase decision;
☐ Identification of extra-cost added features;
In the area of promotions,
☐ Avoidance of false and misleading advertising;
☐ Rejection of high-pressure manipulations or misleading sales tactics;
☐ Avoidance of sales promotions that use deception or manipulation.
In the area of distribution,
☐ Not manipulating the availability of a product for purpose of exploitation;
☐ Not using coercion in the marketing channel;
☐ Not exerting undue influence over the reseller's choice to handle a product.
In the area of pricing,
☐ Not engaging in price fixing;
☐ Not practicing predatory pricing;
☐ Disclosing the full price associated with any purchase.
In the area of marketing research,
☐ Prohibiting selling or fundraising under the guise of conducting research;
☐ Maintaining research integrity by avoiding misrepresentation and omission of pertinent research data;
☐ Treating outside clients and suppliers fairly.

Organizational Relationships

Marketers should be aware of how their behavior may influence or impact on the behavior of others in organizational relationships. They should not demand, encourage, or apply coercion to obtain unethical behavior in their relationships with others, such as employees, suppliers, or customers. Marketers should:
1. Apply confidentiality and anonymity in professional relationships with regard to privileged information;
2. Meet their obligations and responsibilities in contracts and mutual agreements in a timely manner;
3. Avoid taking the work of others, in whole, or in part, and represent this work as their own or directly benefit from it without compensation or consent of the originator or owner;
4. Avoid manipulation to take advantage of situations to maximize personal welfare in a way that unfairly deprives or damages their organization or others.
Any AMA member found to be in violation of any provision of this Code of Ethics may have his or her Association membership suspended or revoked.

Source: Reprinted with permission from "AMA Adopts New Code of Ethics," *Marketing News* (September 11, 1987), pp. 1, 10, published by the American Marketing Association.

described earlier and other, similar regulatory bills at the state and federal levels, the American Telemarketing Association is developing an ethics code for its members.[33]

Ethical Problems in Product Strategy   Product quality, planned obsolescence, brand similarity, and packaging questions are significant concerns of consumers, managers, and governments. Competitive pressures have forced some marketers into packaging practices that may be considered misleading, deceptive, and/or unethical. Larger than necessary packages are used to gain shelf space and consumer exposure in the supermarket. Odd-size packages make price comparisons difficult. Bottles with concave bottoms give the impression that they contain more liquid than they actually do. The real question seems to be whether these practices can be justified in the name of competition. Growing regulatory mandates appear to be narrowing the range of discretion in this area.

Ethical Problems in Distribution Strategy   A firm's channel strategy is required to deal with two kinds of ethical questions:

1. What is the appropriate degree of control over the channel?

2. Should a company distribute its products in marginally profitable outlets that have no alternative source of supply?

The question of control typically arises in relationships between manufacturers and franchised dealers. Should an automobile dealership, a gas station, or a fast-food outlet be required to purchase parts, materials, and supplementary services from the parent organization? What is the proper degree of control in the channel of distribution? The second question concerns marketers' responsibility to serve unsatisfied market segments even if the profit potential is slight. Should marketers serve retail stores in low-income areas, users of limited amounts of the firm's product, or a declining rural market? These problems are difficult to resolve, because they often involve individuals rather than broad segments of the general public. An important first step is to ensure that channel policies are enforced on a consistent basis.

Ethical Problems in Promotional Strategy   Promotion is the component of the marketing mix that gives rise to the majority of ethical questions. Personal selling has always been the target of ethically based criticism. Early traders, pack peddlers, greeters, drummers, and today's used-car salespeople, for example, have all been accused of marketing malpractice ranging from exaggerating product merits to outright deceit. Gifts and bribes are common ethical abuses.

Advertising, however, is even more maligned than salespeople. It is impersonal and hence easier to criticize. In fact, a study by the American Association of Advertising Agencies showed that advertising ranked second (along with clothing and fashion) in a list of "things in life that we enjoy complaining about but we may not really be serious about our complaints."[34]

While this study may suggest that much of the criticism of advertising is overstated, there is ample evidence and legitimate concern regarding advertising. Charges of overselling, uses of fear-based advertising messages (of social rejection, of growing old), sexism, and the like are common.

FOCUS ON ETHICS

Testing or Fraud? Chrysler and the Odometer Scandal

In 1987, a federal grand jury in St. Louis handed down a 16-count indictment against Chrysler Corporation and two of its executives for disconnecting the odometers on new cars prior to dealer delivery. According to the indictment, at least 80,000 new cars and trucks had been tampered with from July 1985 to December 1986, some having been driven for up to 400 miles by managers at Chrysler plants across the country. Some of the cars damaged during testing were repaired and then sold as new, without informing the buyers of the damage or repairs. Moreover, the practice apparently had been Chrysler policy since 1949, meaning that millions of cars were probably involved during that time.

The discovery that Chrysler was disconnecting odometers came after several Chrysler executives were issued traffic tickets for speeding. The executives confessed that they did not know they were speeding because both the speedometers and the odometers had been disconnected. A Justice Department investigation led to Chrysler's indictment on charges of consumer fraud.

Chrysler's management admitted that odometers had been disconnected but claimed that there was nothing illegal or improper about it, that it was done "as a service to the customer" to identify potential quality

or safety defects. Company spokesperson Baron Bates said that cars were randomly selected for the testing program and driven an average of only 40 miles before shipping. He denied that cars were given to executives for extended periods of time, as claimed in the indictment.

However, the practice of disconnecting odometers runs counter to the policies of the Motor Vehicle Manufacturers Association, an industry trade group. GM has a policy against disconnecting odometers after cars leave the assembly line. Ford does not disconnect or roll back odometers either. At Ford, every vehicle involved in a quality test drive program is labeled with a windshield sticker that states the precise number of miles the car was driven.

Chrysler is hardly the only firm that has run afoul of the dilemma of pretesting products. For example, Maytag Corporation tests all its washing machines before shipping, although only about 15 a day are given a full, 24-hour test. These are reinspected and sent out as new if they pass. But are they new or used? Even consumer advocates disagree. "Any use is use," says Texas official Stephen Gardner. "All we're really talking about is telling people the truth." But others will accept some degree of testing. The main questions are how much test-

ing is reasonable and what sort of notification consumers are entitled to receive.

As a result of the indictment and subsequent embarrassment, Chrysler officials decided to plead *no contest* to criminal charges and agreed to pay at least $16 million, including $500 to any owner whose odometer had been disconnected. They also ended the practice of disconnecting odometers during testing and placed a strict 65-mile limit on the test. In addition, all cars so tested must have notifications placed in the glove compartment. As part of the legal settlement, Chrysler officials agreed to extend the warranty on all cars involved in the testing program and promised to replace all cars that were damaged but were sold as new. To publicize its commitment to the new policy, the company placed ads featuring Chrysler CEO Lee Iacocca promising, "Testing cars is a good idea. Disconnecting odometers is a lousy idea. That's a mistake we won't make again at Chrysler. Period."

Sources: Jacob M. Schlesinger, "Chrysler Finds A Way to Settle Odometer Issue," *The Wall Street Journal* (December 10, 1987), p. 5; John Bussey, "Lee Iacocca Calls Odometer Policy 'Dumb,' " *The Wall Street Journal* (July 2, 1987), p. 2; and "Dear Chrysler: Outsiders' Advice on Handling the Odometer Charge," *The Wall Street Journal* (June 26, 1987), p. 21.

The portrayal of women in advertising is of particular concern to marketers. Too often, it is argued, advertising demeans women by portraying them as frivolous or stereotyping them as housewives. Advertisers, pressured by women's rights groups, are trying to show women in varied situations, especially in nontraditional work roles such as bus driver, bank officer, and heavy-equipment operator.

Another ethical issue concerns advertising to children. Some critics fear that television advertising exerts an undue influence on children. They believe children are easily influenced by toy, cereal, and snack-food commercials. Correspondingly, there is the assumption that children in turn exert substantial pressure on their parents to acquire these items. In recognition of this concern, the Canadian Association of Broadcasters has formulated a comprehensive broadcast code restricting advertising to children. No similar code exists in the United States.

Ethical Problems in Pricing   Pricing is probably the most regulated aspect of a firm's marketing strategy. As a result, most unethical price behavior is also illegal. When asked in a survey to identify unethical practices they wanted eliminated, fewer executives specified such issues as price collusion, price discrimination, and unfair pricing than had a similar group 15 years earlier. This suggests that tighter government regulations exist in these areas now than in the past.[35]

There are, however, some gray areas in the matter of pricing ethics. For example, should some customers pay more for merchandise if distribution costs are higher in their areas? Do marketers have an obligation to warn customers of impending price, discount, or return policy changes? All these queries must be dealt with in developing a professional ethic for marketing.

Social Responsibility

Another major issue affecting marketing is the question of social responsibility. In a general sense, **social responsibility** is the marketer's acceptance of the obligation to consider profit, consumer satisfaction, and societal well-being of equal value in evaluating the firm's performance. It is the recognition that marketers must be concerned with the more qualitative dimensions of consumer and societal benefits as well as the quantitative measures of sales, revenue, and profits by which marketing performance is traditionally measured.

social responsibility
Marketing philosophies, policies, procedures, and actions that have the enhancement of society's welfare as a primary objective.

As Professors Engel and Blackwell point out, social responsibility is a more easily measured concept than marketing ethics:

Actions alone determine social responsibility, and a firm can be socially responsible even when doing so under coercion. For example, the government may enact rules that force firms to be socially responsible in matters of the environment, deception, and so forth. Also, consumers, through their power to repeat or withhold purchasing, may force marketers to provide honest and relevant information, fair prices, and so forth. To be ethically responsible, on the other hand, it is not sufficient to act correctly; ethical intent is also necessary.[36]

The locus for socially responsible decisions in organizations has always been an important issue. Who should be specifically accountable for the social considerations involved in marketing decisions? The direct sales manager? The marketing vice-president? The firm's president? The board of directors? Probably the most valid assessment is to say that *all marketers,* regardless of their stations in the organization, are accountable for the societal aspects of their decisions.

Marketing's Responsibilities   The concept of business responsibility traditionally has concerned the relationships between the manager and customers, employees, and stockholders. Management had the responsibility of providing a quality product at a reasonable price for customers, adequate wages and a

The support of community activities that benefit society is linked to the marketing program of Westinghouse Beverage Group, a soft-drink bottler and distributor. Dressed in native costumes, the children in this photo are being entertained at a child care center established by the Mexican American Opportunity Foundation, a group that Westinghouse has supported for more than a decade.

Photo source: Courtesy of Westinghouse Electric Corporation.

decent working environment for employees, and an acceptable profit level for stockholders. Only occasionally did the concept involve relations with the government and rarely with the general public.

Today the responsibility concept has been extended to the entire societal framework. A decision to continue operation of a profitable but air-polluting plant may be responsible in the traditional sense: Customers receive an uninterrupted supply of the plant's products, employees do not face layoffs, and stockholders receive a reasonable return on their investment in the company. But from the standpoint of contemporary business ethics, this is not a socially responsible decision.

Similarly, a firm that markets foods with low nutritional value may satisfy the traditional concept of responsibility, but such behavior is questionable in the contemporary perspective. This is not to say that all firms should distribute only foods of high nutritional value; it means merely that the previous framework for evaluation is no longer considered comprehensive in terms of either scope or time.

Contemporary marketing decisions must include consideration of the external societal environment. These decisions must also account for eventual, long-term effects. Socially responsible decisions must consider future as well as existing generations.

Marketing and Ecology   Ecology is an important aspect of marketing. The concept of ecology — the relationship between organisms and their environments — appears to be in a constant state of evolution. There are several aspects of ecology with which marketers must deal: planned obsolescence, pollution, recycling waste materials, and preservation of resources.

The original ecological problem facing marketing was *planned obsolescence* — a situation in which a manufacturer produces items of limited durability. In some instances, products are made obsolete by technological im-

Photo source: Courtesy of Reynolds Metals Company.

The Reynolds Metals Company recycling program pays consumers cash for used aluminum cans collected through a network of 1,500 manned sites and 100 convenient "reverse" vending machines. Since 1968, Reynolds has paid recyclers almost $900 million and has recycled more than 3.2 billion pounds of aluminum. This represents an energy saving of more than 21 billion kilowatt-hours of electricity and the conservation of 6.4 million tons of bauxite ore, from which primary aluminum is made.

provements. In others, physical obsolescence is intentional in that products are designed so as to wear out within a short time period. In still others, such as the fashion industry, rapid changes in design produce obsolescence. Planned obsolescence has always represented a significant ethical question for the marketer. On one side is the need for maintaining sales and employment; on the other is the need for providing better quality and durability. A practical question is whether the consumer really wants or can afford increased durability. Many consumers prefer to change styles often and accept less durable items. Increased durability has an implicit cost. It may mean that fewer people can afford the product.

Pollution is a broad term that can be applied to a number of circumstances. It usually means "making unclean." The concern about polluting such natural resources as water and air has reached critical proportions in some areas. The marketing system annually generates billions of tons of packaging materials, such as glass, metal, paper, and plastics, that add to the nation's growing piles of trash and waste. Some environmental groups and waste reduction advocates say that manufacturers should develop new products and design packages that will create less waste.[37] Ecoplastics, a Toronto firm, has developed a plastic resin that disintegrates in the sun, degrading into water and carbon dioxide and leaving no toxic chemicals to leach out in the soil. The plastic resin is being used by manufacturers of plastic bags and containers in Italy, where cities such as Bologna, Florence, and Venice have banned certain plastic packaging and similar national legislation is pending.[38]

Recycling — the processing of used materials for reuse — is another important aspect of ecology. The underlying rationale of recycling is that reprocessed materials can benefit society by saving natural resources and energy as well as by alleviating a major factor in environmental pollution. Tire manufacturers have built artificial fish reefs out of used tires. The 3M Company has printed outlines for splints on its corrugated shipping cartons destined for hospitals; the cartons can then be used by emergency and rescue teams for temporary splints. The beverage industry is using more aluminum cans because of the relative ease of recycling aluminum.

The biggest problem in recycling is getting the used materials from the consumer back to the manufacturer, which will handle the technological aspects of recovery. These "backward" channels are limited, and those that do exist are primitive and frequently lack adequate financial incentives. Marketing can play an important role by designing appropriate channel structures.

Controlling the Marketing System

When the marketing-economic system does not perform as well as we would like, we attempt to change it. We hope to make it serve us better by producing and distributing goods and services in a fairer way. Most people believe that the system is working sufficiently well to require no changes and that relatively minor adjustments can achieve a fair distribution.

Four ways in which we control or influence the direction of the marketing system and try to rid it of imperfections are by (1) helping the competitive market system to operate in a self-correcting manner; (2) educating the consumer; (3) increasing regulation; and (4) encouraging political action. The competitive market system operates to allocate resources and to provide most of the products we purchase to satisfy felt needs. While we may hear many complaints about the system, most of the goods and services we purchase or use flow through it with little difficulty. Competition works if the conditions of many buyers and sellers and other technical requirements of the free-market economic model allow it. We have attempted — sometimes with limited success — to restore competition where monopolies have reduced it.

Combined with the free-market system, consumer education can lead to wise choices. As products become more complex, diverse, and plentiful, the consumer's ability to make wise decisions must also expand. Educational programs and efforts by parents, schools, business, government, and consumer organizations all contribute to a better system. A responsible marketing philosophy should also encourage consumers to voice their opinions. Such comments can result in significant improvements in the seller's products and services.

The marketing concept must include social responsibility as a primary function of the marketing organization. Social and profit goals are compatible, but they require the aggressive implementation of an expanded marketing concept. Explicit criteria for responsible decision making must be adopted in all companies. This is truly marketing's greatest challenge.

Summary of Chapter Objectives

1. Identify the five components of the marketing environment. The five components of the marketing environment are (1) the competitive environment — the interactive process that occurs in the marketplace as competing organizations seek to satisfy markets; (2) the political/legal environment — the laws and interpretations of laws that require firms to operate under competitive conditions and to protect consumer rights; (3) the economic environment — environmental factors resulting from business fluctuations and resultant variations in inflation rates and employment levels; (4) the technological environment — applications to marketing of knowledge based on discoveries in science, inventions, and innovations; and (5) the social/cultural environment — the component of the marketing environment consisting of the relationship between the marketer and society and its culture.

2. Explain the types of competition marketers face and the steps in developing a competitive strategy. The three basic types of competition marketers face are (1) direct competition among marketers of similar products; (2) competition among products or services that can be substituted for one another; and (3) competition among all organizations that compete for the consumer's purchasing power.

The development of a competitive strategy is derived from answers to the following three questions: (1) Should we compete? This question is answered on the basis of the firm's available resources and objectives as well as its expected profit potential; (2) If so, in what markets should we compete? This question acknowledges that the marketer has limited resources that must be allocated to the areas of greatest opportunity; and (3) How should we compete? This question requires the marketer to make the technical decisions involved in setting up a comprehensive marketing strategy.

3. Describe how government and other groups regulate marketing activities and how marketers can influence political/legal environments. Marketing activities are affected by federal, state, and local laws that require firms to operate under competitive conditions and to protect consumer rights. Government regulatory agencies such as the Federal Trade Commission enforce these laws and develop enforcement procedures for unfair marketing practices. Public and private consumer interest groups and industry self-regulatory groups also influence marketing activities. Marketers may seek to influence public opinion and legislative actions through advertising, political action committees, and political lobbying.

4. Outline the economic factors that affect marketing decisions and consumer buying power. The primary economic factors operating in the marketing environment are the stage in the business cycle, inflation and unemployment rates, resource availability, and income. All of these factors are vitally important to marketers because of their effects on consumers' willingness to buy and consumers' conceptions regarding changes in the marketing mix variables.

5. Explain the impact of the technological environment on a firm's marketing activities. The technological environment consists of applications to marketing of knowledge based on discoveries in science, inventions, and innovations. This knowledge can provide both marketing opportunities and threats to current products and services. The technological environment affects marketing in several ways: (1) It results in new products for consumers and improves existing ones; (2) it is a frequent source of price reductions through new production methods or materials; (3) it can make existing products obsolete virtually overnight; and (4) technological innovations can have significant impacts on consumers' life-styles, competitors' products, industrial users' demands, and government regulatory actions.

6. Explain how the social/cultural environment influences marketing. The social/cultural environment relates to the attitudes of members of society toward products and services as well as pricing, promotion, and distribution strategies. Society demands that business be concerned with the quality of life, which has broadened the social impact of marketing. More specifically, the social/cultural environment has the following influences: (1) It influences the general readiness of society to accept a new marketing idea; (2) the public's trust and confidence in business as a whole influence legislation regulating business and marketing; and (3) although it affects domestic marketing, it is an even more critical factor in international marketing.

7. Describe the role of marketing in society. Marketing operates in an environment external to the firm. These environmental relationships exist with customers, employees, the government, vendors, and society as a whole. They form the basis of the societal issues that confront contemporary marketing. Marketing's relationship to its external environment has a significant effect on the relative degree of success the firm achieves. Marketers must continually find new ways to deal with the social issues facing our competitive system.

8. Identify the three major social issues in marketing. Current issues in marketing include consumerism, marketing ethics, and social responsibility. Consumerism is the social force within the environment designed to aid and protect the consumer by exerting legal, moral, and economic pressures on business. Consumer rights include: (1) the right to choose freely; (2) the right to be informed; (3) the right to be heard; and (4) the right to be safe. Marketing ethics are the marketer's standards of conduct and moral values. Social responsibility is the marketer's acceptance of the obligation to consider profit, consumer satisfaction, and societal well-being of equal value in evaluating the performance of the firm.

Key Terms

environmental management
competitive environment
political/legal environment
economic environment
demarketing
technological environment

social/cultural environment
consumerism
consumer rights
marketing ethics
social responsibility

Review Questions

1. Briefly describe each of the five components of the marketing environment. Give an example of each.

2. Explain the types of competition marketers face. What are the steps involved in developing a competitive strategy?

3. Government regulation in the United States has evolved in four general phases. Identify each phase and give an example of laws enacted during it.

4. Give an example of a federal law affecting
   a. Product strategy
   b. Pricing strategy
   c. Distribution strategy
   d. Promotional strategy

5. Explain the methods the Federal Trade Commission uses to protect consumers.

6. What are the major economic factors affecting marketing decisions?

7. Identify the ways in which the technological environment and the social/cultural environment affect marketing activities.

8. Evaluate consumerism's indictment of the competitive marketing system.

9. Describe the ethical problems related to
   a. Marketing research
   b. Product management
   c. Distribution strategy
   d. Promotional strategy
   e. Pricing

10. Identify and briefly explain the major avenues open for the resolution of contemporary issues facing the marketing system.

Discussion Questions

1. Give an example of how each of the environmental variables discussed in this chapter might affect the following firms:
   a. Eastern Airlines
   b. Local aerobics center
   c. Local cable TV franchise
   d. Tupperware products
   e. Sears catalog department
   f. Godfather's Pizza

2. Classify the following laws as (1) assisting in maintaining a competitive environment, (2) assisting in regulating competitors, (3) regulating specific marketing activities, or (4) deregulating industries. Justify your classifications and identify the marketing mix variable(s) most affected by each law.
   a. Miller-Tydings Act
   b. Staggers Rail Act
   c. Fair Packaging and Labeling Act
   d. Clayton Act
   e. Robinson-Patman Act

3. Cite two examples of instances in which the technological environment has produced positive benefits for marketers. Give two instances of the harmful impact of the technological environment on a firm's marketing operations.

4. Should the United States ban advertising aimed at children? Explain.

5. Discuss the problems involved in setting up "backward" channels of distribution for recycling used packages.

VIDEO CASE 2

Mitsubishi Motor Sales of America

What seemed to be an astute marketing decision back in 1970 proved to be one that strategists at Japan's Mitsubishi Heavy Industries would later regret. Mitsubishi is Japan's largest company, a giant conglomerate whose product lines range from shipbuilding to rocketry. Its subsidiary, Mitsubishi Motors Corporation (MMC), is the oldest and third largest Japanese automaker, but its market share is far less than those of market leaders Toyota and Nissan.

In 1970, MMC marketers discovered a low-cost, low-risk way to enter the huge U.S. market, a market they had previously ignored to the benefit of Honda, Nissan, and Toyota. Chrysler Corporation executives, seeking to add small cars to their product line, agreed to purchase a 35 percent share in MMC in return for an exclusive franchise to distribute Mitsubishi models in the U.S. under the Chrysler nameplate. As MMC spokesperson Tohei Takeuchi explains, the arrangement appeared to make sense in 1970, but proved less satisfactory after a few years: "It would have cost MMC a lot of money to expand in the U.S. . . . . Instead, we decided to use Chrysler's distribution network. But suddenly the American consumer liked Japanese cars. The market changed, and we no longer needed help from an existing channel."

Even though one million Mitsubishi cars and small trucks were sold in America between 1971 and 1981, they carried such nameplates as Dodge Colt, Challenger, and Plymouth Sapporo. American car buyers were not being educated about the strengths of Mitsubishi models. In addition, MMC marketers were dissatisfied with Chrysler's marketing efforts and felt that the U.S. firm was emphasizing its own small cars over the Mitsubishi-built Colts and Sapporos because selling its own product was more profitable. They were all too aware of the fact that MMC's market share in Europe, where they controlled their own distribution, was double their U.S. market share.

The opportunity to end Chrysler's exclusive U.S. marketing rights came in 1980. The U.S. firm, in the midst of a financial crisis, was struggling to avoid bankruptcy when Japan's major banks refused to continue their previous practice of financing Mitsubishi shipments to Chrysler. Mitsubishi executives agreed to provide their own financing for Chrysler, but only if the U.S. firm would allow MMC to sell a minimum of 30,000 Mitsubishi cars in the United States through its own dealer network. Chrysler executives had no viable alternative and agreed to the proposal in April, 1981. A new subsidiary, Mitsubishi Motor Sales of America (MMSA) based in Fountain Valley, California, was created to direct the firm's marketing efforts on the U.S. mainland.

Nineteen eighty-two was one of the worst times in automobile history to launch a new product line. The U.S. economy was in the midst of a severe recession further complicated by inflation. The high interest rates and economic uncertainty caused American consumers to postpone major purchases, and the auto industry was in a major sales slump. In addition, the growing share of the American auto market held by imports was prompting increasingly frequent demands for import quotas as a means of reducing the number of foreign cars sold in the U.S.

Japan's Ministry of International Trade & Industry responded by voluntarily limiting auto shipments to the U.S. to 1.68 million units annually. Each Japanese auto company's quota was based on average sales since 1976. Toyota's share of the total amounted to approximately 518,000 cars a year, and Nissan's share was set at about 453,000 cars. While Mitsubishi was granted a quota of 112,500 cars annually, 82,500 of this total had to be shipped to Chrysler. MMSA faced the unenviable task of establishing a widespread distribution network with an annual nationwide sales ceiling of only 30,000 cars. While some auto industry representatives felt that the Voluntary Restraint Agreement would be lifted within a few years, no one knew for certain.

MMSA executives needed a marketing strategy that would produce sales and profit success in an environment filled with uncertainty. In addition to a low quota of cars and the need to create a strong dealership network, they also had to deal with such factors as well-known Japanese and U.S. competitors, low name recognition, and cultural differences that existed in this new market.

Richard Recchia, MMSA's executive vice president, recognized that the first task facing his firm in the highly competitive import market was to convince American consumers that Mitsubishi automobiles were special and unique. He decided to base his marketing strategy on the parent firm's demonstrated strengths.

We didn't want our products to be perceived as just another Japanese car. So the product line we selected and the price lines within those product lines that we established were aimed at placing our products a step above other Japanese car lines in the same segment so people would perceive Mitsubishi as having more features, more technology, more innovation at a better price than the competition.

Three models were selected: the two-door sport hatchback Cordia and the four-door Tredia sedan — both offered at approximately $10,000 — plus the sporty Starion turbo coupe designed to compete with the Mazda RX7 and Nissan's best-selling ZX sports car. In addition, MMSA decided to market a line of small trucks, a product category not included under the Voluntary Restraint Agreement.

Crucial to MMSA's U.S. success was its dealer network. Recchia and his fellow marketers wanted to distribute the Mitsubishi models through a quality network of a few exclusive dealerships. By limiting the number of dealerships, MMSA could assure each dealer sufficient inventory to be successful in the market. Moreover, the presence of high-volume, exclusive Mitsubishi dealers in carefully selected markets would serve as tangible evidence to auto buyers that the new cars represented substantial competition for Toyota, Honda, and other companies that consumers associate with Japanese imports.

The dealerships were strategically placed in geographic areas where concentrations of Japanese car registrations were highest. Special computer programs were developed to create density maps that would pinpoint these locations for prospective dealerships. The first two years of U.S. operation saw Mitsubishi dealerships in only 22 metropolitan markets, but those markets accounted for 43 percent of total car sales in the entire nation.

MMSA marketers worked closely with these dealers to ensure marketplace success. Advertising expenditures were double the per-unit average of other Japanese automakers. Some dealers began to report consumer requests for a fuel-efficient subcompact model; others asked for a more luxurious sedan to compete with the Cressida, Maxima, and Audi. MMSA responded by introducing the subcompact Mirage and the Galant sedan in 1985, enabling Mitsubishi dealers to offer car buyers a complete product line for the first time.

The name recognition issue was addressed in the firm's promotional efforts. Advertising was designed to position Mitsubishi as a premium-class Japanese car, the BMW of Japan. Company marketers realized that many consumers mispronounced *Mitsubishi,* and the promotional theme "takes you where you want to *be*" was created to indicate the correct pronunciation.

During the late 1980s, Mitsubishi benefitted from changing American transportation preferences. In 1960, U.S. consumers bought one truck for every ten cars. In 1987, they bought one truck for every two cars. Compact trucks, such as Mitsubishi's Mighty Max and Montero, are not governed by the Voluntary Restraint Agreement, and they actually outsold the firm's car models in 1987.

To provide its dealers with additional models, Mitsubishi began importing the Hyundai Precis in 1987. Although the Precis (rhymes with "thesis") carries the Mitsubishi nameplate, its South Korean origin exempts it from the restraint quotas, thus permitting MMSA dealers to boost sales and profits without reducing imports of their own higher-priced and more profitable Japanese cars.

In the years since the creation of MMSA, Chrysler Corporation has continued to import and market Mitsubishi car and light truck models under its own nameplate. In fact, of the Big Three U.S. automakers, Chrysler is the most dependent on Japanese imports. About 11 percent of its cars and 40 percent of its light trucks are built by Mitsubishi.

Cooperative relations between Chrysler and Mistubishi continued during the late 1980s as the two firms formed a joint venture to build a giant production facility in Bloomington–Normal, Illinois. The new plant can produce up to 240,000 cars a year, and both firms share the output. Its benefits are enormous for Mitsubishi, since domestic production provides a means of avoiding the sales ceilings imposed by the Voluntary Restraint Agreement. Moreover, it allows MMSA to reduce the headaches resulting from the huge exchange rate fluctuations between the Japanese yen and the U.S. dollar. American sales of MMSA products are expected to approach 250,000 units in 1990, eight times the 1982 totals.

Sources: Takeuchi quotation from Lawrence Minard, "Just What Detroit Needs," *Forbes* (November 21, 1983), pp. 208, 210. See also "Mitsubishi Motors Corp.," *Advertising Age* (November 23, 1987), p. S-35; Andrew Tanzer, "Gentlemen, Start Your Engines," *Forbes* (April 8, 1985), p. 38; and Doug Carroll, "Buyers Keep on Trucking," *USA Today* (February 8, 1988), p. 10E.

Questions

1. Relate the material in this case to each of the elements of the marketing environment.

2. Give specific examples of environmental factors that were truly uncontrollable. How did MMSA marketing responses to these factors differ from those made in response to environmental variables that could be influenced by the firm?

3. What are the major differences between the MMSA marketing approach and the more typical approaches used by other marketers of imported automobiles? What modifications in the MMSA marketing approach do you expect to occur over the next five years?

4. Isuzu Motors is another relatively recent entry in the U.S. auto market with an initial U.S. quota of 16,800 cars. Use the Mitsubishi experience to recommend a course of action for Isuzu.

COMPUTER APPLICATIONS

It is often possible to minimize the adverse effects of environmental factors on operations by predicting their occurrence and taking actions designed to maximize possible benefits resulting from their occurrence. In some cases, the marketer may be able to engage in environmental management and actually influence occurrences in the competitive, political/legal, economic, technological, and social/cultural environments.

A useful method for making decisions in an uncertain marketing environment is *decision tree analysis.* This is a quantitative technique used in identifying alternative courses of action, assigning probability estimates for the profits or sales associated with each alternative, and indicating the course of action with the highest potential profit or sales. The marketer must be able to estimate the likelihood of occurrence in each alternative. In addition, he or she must assign financial payoffs (sales, profits, or losses) for the various alternatives. The following example illustrates how decision tree analysis works.

The vice-president of marketing of a major bicycle manufacturer estimates a 60 percent likelihood that the federal government's Consumer Product Safety Commission will require added safety features on bicycles beginning in 1990. If the new safety features are included in the basic designs now, they will add $10 to the cost of each bicycle produced. On the other hand, if they are not included and if the new safety requirements are enacted in 1990, the cost of adding them to the finished product will be $15 per bicycle. In addition, the inclusion of these features would involve additional time and would delay the shipment of finished bicycles from the manufacturer to its dealers. This would reduce 1990 sales from current estimates of 800,000 units to 600,000 units. Per-unit profits with no changes in product design are estimated at $20. If the new features are built into product design at this time, estimated per-unit profits are $10 as compared with $5 if they must be added to the finished product as a result of new government regulations.

The problem can be illustrated as a type of decision tree lying on its side. Each branch represents a different possible course of acton. The expected profits from a decision to add the new safety features now are $8 million. This determination is made by first multiplying expected total profits ($10 per unit times the 800,000 units) by the .6 probability that the new regulations will be enacted.

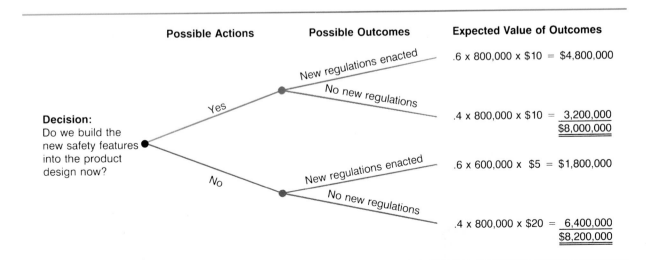

Possible Actions	Possible Outcomes	Expected Value of Outcomes
	New regulations enacted	.6 x 800,000 x $10 = $4,800,000
Yes	No new regulations	.4 x 800,000 x $10 = 3,200,000 / $8,000,000
Decision: Do we build the new safety features into the product design now?		
No	New regulations enacted	.6 x 600,000 x $5 = $1,800,000
	No new regulations	.4 x 800,000 x $20 = 6,400,000 / $8,200,000

Next, the expected total profits ($10 per unit times the 800,000 units) are multiplied by the .4 probability that no new safety regulations will be enacted. Finally, the expected values of the two possible outcomes are combined for a total of $8 million.

The decision to defer installation of additional safety features produces a slightly larger net expected value of profits. Unless the firm's marketers are greatly concerned that the shipment delays would generate ill will among their retail dealers and customers should the proposed regulations be enacted, they should choose the second option.

Directions: Use menu item 2 titled "Decision Tree Analysis" to solve each of the following problems.

Problem 1   Sid Norris, director of marketing for Orlando-based FloridaFruit, recognizes more than most people the difficulty involved in producing time, place, and ownership utilities during winters, when the citrus industry often is devastated by unpredictable, killing freezes. Smudge pots and water spraying — the current methods of reducing the impact of low temperatures — are of little use when the temperatures dip below the 25°F mark. After carefully analyzing the test results of a newly developed citrus grove heating system, Norris is viewing his firm's technological environment in a most positive way. Not only did the new system appear to work; it could be leased on a year-to-year basis, thereby avoiding huge equipment outlays. Norris estimates the likelihood of a severe freeze at 20 percent for the upcoming season. He expects total revenues from next year's crop to reach $700,000 and earnings to amount to 9 percent of sales — as long as no severe freeze occurs. Norris estimates that if one occurs, sales will fall to $200,000 and profits to zero. Norris's calculations show that if FloridaFruit decides to lease the new system, the added leasing costs will trim profits to 5 percent of sales. However, should a freeze occur once the system is in place at FloridaFruit citrus groves, the increased price resulting from the reduced overall industry output would increase the firm's revenues from $700,000 to $850,000. Recommend a course of action for FloridaFruit.

Problem 2   Nancy Akers, vice-president of marketing at Philadelphia Industries, is confident that next year's sales will reach $36 million. However, she is worried about the impact of increased costs on her firm's profits during the coming year. Akers estimates a 70 percent likelihood of a major price increase in one of the petroleum-based raw materials used in the production of her firm's products. Akers feels that she would be unable to raise prices to cover these cost increases. Her major competitors recently have switched to a new, blended process that uses a small amount of petroleum in combination with synthetic materials. Akers projects next year's earnings at 10 percent of sales. If she converts to the new process, earnings are expected to be reduced to 7 percent of sales as a result of the changeover expenses. On the other hand, Akers feels that if she does not make the change and the price increase occurs, her earnings will be reduced to 2 percent of sales as a result of the price-cost squeeze. Recommend a course of action for Philadelphia Industries.

Problem 3   Virginia Beach WaterMania manager Norm Olsen is pleased with next year's $800,000 revenue forecast and projected earnings of 12 percent of sales. However, he is concerned about reports of a new waterslide park opening. In fact, he estimates a 50 percent likelihood that the new competitor will be open for business in time for next year's season. Olsen estimates that if the new park opens at the location under consideration and Virginia Beach WaterMania makes no competitive moves at this time, total revenues will plummet to $300,000 and earnings to only 2 percent of sales. If the competing park fails to materialize and Olsen reduces admission prices by 25 percent to match those charged in other cities by the potential competitor, overall sales revenues will increase to $900,000 and earnings will be 8 percent of sales. If Olsen lowers prices and the new park opens, WaterMania's competitive prices will be sufficient to generate $600,000 in revenues and earn profits of 6 percent of sales. Olsen prefers to postpone his decision until he is certain of his potential competitor's plans, but the need for a new, huge sign and the preparation of tickets, coupons, and advertising materials require him to make the decision now. Recommend a course of action for Olsen.

Problem 4   Maria Fergamo, manager of the Fashion Perfect chain of fashion clothing stores headquartered in San Francisco, realizes that the success of her operations depends on the ability to monitor and predict changes in consumer tastes. Sales projections for next year total $4.2 million, with expected profits of 5 percent of sales. Several of Fergamo's managers, who make up the merchandise buying committee, have recommended a substantial purchase of a new, radical line of clothing that is enjoying huge sales in Europe. Although Fergamo is always concerned about significant inventory investments in unproven lines, she is aware of the consequences of missing major changes in shopper tastes. Fergamo makes the following notes as she listens to the presentation about the new line:

My guess is that the chances of a major consumer taste switch to the new line are 60 percent. If we don't get in on the bandwagon now, our sales next year could fall to $3 million, and at that level Fashion Perfect will earn only 2 percent on sales. On the other hand, if we place the orders and our inventory matches a change in buyer tastes, we could generate as much as $6 million in sales. If this happens, our profits should rise to 7 percent of sales. Even if we place the orders and no radical changes in consumer tastes occur, I think we could still push sales up to $5 million next year. Unfortunately, if tastes don't change as much as those in Europe, the extra inventory and sale merchandise that would result will depress earnings to 2 percent.

a. Recommend a course of action for Fergamo.

b. Would your recommendation change if Fergamo decreased the likelihood of consumer taste changes to 30 percent?

Problem 5   The political/legal environment has been on Cindy Johnson's mind lately. Johnson is vice-president of marketing at Illini Industries, a furniture manufacturer. Although the firm's sales projections are a healthy $14 million for next year and profits are estimated at 8 percent of sales, Johnson is concerned about rumors that the federal government will ban the use of the filler material Illini Industries uses in its furniture cushions. Although substitute filler materials are available (and, in fact, are used by many of the firm's major competitors), they are more expensive. Johnson estimates that a switch to the alternative filler material would reduce profits to 4 percent of sales. On the other hand, if she decides not to switch now and the ban is enacted, the time involved in converting to the new materials next year is likely to represent a loss of $8 million in projected sales and a corresponding profit decline to 2 percent of sales. Johnson feels there is a 30 percent chance that the ban will be enacted.

a. Recommend a course of action for Illini Industries.

b. Would your recommendation change if Johnson reduced her estimate of the likelihood of the ban's enactment to 20 percent?

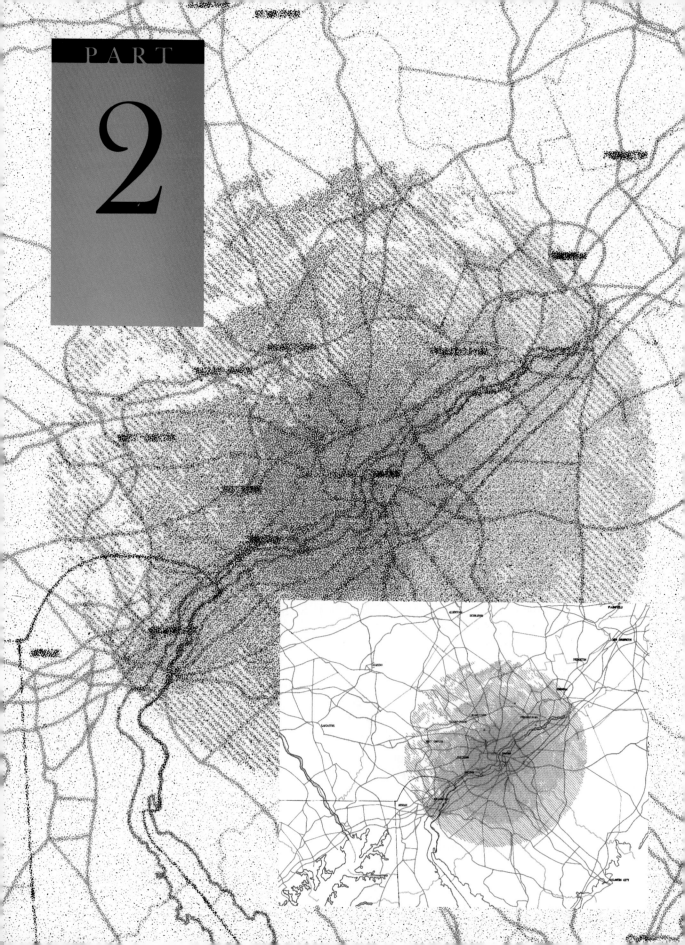

PART

2

Marketing Planning and Information

3

Marketing Planning and Forecasting

Chapter Objectives

1. To distinguish between strategic planning and tactical planning.

2. To explain how marketing plans differ at various levels of the organization.

3. To identify the steps in the marketing planning process.

4. To compare the three basic strategies for matching markets with product/service offerings.

5. To explain how the strategic business unit concept, the market share/market growth matrix, and spreadsheet analysis can be used in marketing planning.

6. To identify the major types of forecasting methods.

7. To explain the steps in the forecasting process.

T he blimp flying over the 1988 Summer Olympics in Seoul did not belong to Goodyear. And it certainly didn't have the name *Fuji* emblazoned on it. After Eastman Kodak's embarrassing loss of the 1984 Los Angeles Olympics sponsorship to Fuji and the specter of the green Fuji blimp floating over American soil, the firm's marketers were determined to secure the rights to use the five-ring emblem at the next Olympic Games. The use of the Kodak blimp was a tangible symbol of Eastman Kodak's determination to regain the dominant market position it once held throughout the world.

Foreign operations have always been a major component of total sales and earnings for the Rochester, New York–headquartered firm that gave birth to modern photography. In fact, almost 40 percent of Eastman Kodak's annual earnings are generated from sales outside the United States.

Although Kodak was the dominant name in film and cameras in Japan during the 1920s and 1930s, its market disappeared with the onset of World War II, and it was not until 1963 that Kodak reestablished its Japanese subsidiary. This delay permitted Fuji Photo Film Company to step in to fill the vacuum left by Kodak. To Kodak's chagrin, Fuji has proven a formidable competitor, both in its home market and abroad.

Over the past few years, Kodak marketers unveiled a complex marketing plan designed to recover the market they surrendered to Fuji and to counter Fuji's expansion into such rapidly growing markets as Taiwan, India, and China. Included in the firm's moves were a variety of joint ventures and aggressive marketing that included new high-tech products, heavy advertising in Japan, displays at major Japanese trade shows, and, of course, the Kodak blimp that cruises the Japanese skies. Kodak marketers are aiming their marketing programs at some very specific goals. Although Kodak holds more than 90 percent of the professional slide film market in Japan, its share of the Japanese consumer film market is only about 10 to 15 percent. And Kodak wants more. A recent version of Kodak's customary New Year's greeting cards in Japan made the firm's intentions clear: The card showed the Kodak blimp with the sacred Japanese mountain, Mt. Fuji, in the background.[1]

Chapter Overview

☐ "Should we grant a license for our new liquid-crystal watch display to a Swiss firm or simply export our models to Europe?"

☐ "Will changing the performance time and date affect concert attendance?"

☐ "Should we utilize company sales personnel or independent agents in the new territory?"

☐ "Should discounts be offered to cash customers? What impact would such a policy have on our credit customers?"

The above questions are examples of the thousands of major and minor decisions that the marketing manager regularly faces. Continual changes in the marketplace resulting from changing consumer expectations, technological improvements, competitive actions, economic trends, and political/legal changes, as well as product innovations and pressures from distribution channel members, are likely to have a substantial impact on the operations of any organization. Although these changes are often beyond the marketing manager's control, effective planning can help the manager anticipate many changes and focus on possible actions. Effective planning is often a major factor in distinguishing between success and failure.

This and the next chapter provide a foundation for all subsequent chapters by demonstrating the necessity for effective planning and reliable information in providing a structure within which a firm can take advantage of its unique strengths. Both the choice of specific target markets and the most appropriate marketing mix to use in satisfying those markets result from marketing planning. This chapter examines marketing planning. Chapter 4 discusses marketing research and the ways in which decision-oriented information is used to plan and implement marketing strategies.

What Is Marketing Planning?

planning
Process of anticipating the future and determining the courses of action necessary for achieving organizational objectives.

Planning is the process of anticipating the future and determining the courses of action for achieving organizational objectives. As the definition indicates, planning is a continuous process that includes specifying objectives and the actions required for attaining them. The planning process creates a blueprint that not only specifies the means for achieving organizational objectives but provides checkpoints at which actual performance can be compared with expectations to determine whether current activities are moving the organization toward its objectives.

marketing planning
Process of anticipating the future and determining the courses of action necessary for achieving marketing objectives.

Marketing planning—the implementation of planning activities as they relate to the achievement of marketing objectives—is the basis for all marketing strategies. Product lines, pricing decisions, selection of appropriate distribution channels, and decisions relating to promotional campaigns all depend on plans formulated within the marketing organization.

Strategic Planning versus Tactical Planning

strategic planning
Process of determining an organization's primary objectives, allocating funds, and then proceeding with a course of action designed to achieve those objectives.

Planning is often classified on the basis of scope or breadth. Some plans are quite broad and long range, focusing on certain organizational objectives that will have a major impact on the organization for a time period of five or more years. Such plans typically are called *strategic plans*. **Strategic planning** is the process of determining the organization's primary objectives and the adoption of courses of action and allocation of resources necessary for achieving them.[2] The word *strategy* is derived from a Greek term meaning "the general's art." Strategic planning has a critical impact on the organization's destiny because it provides long-term direction for decision makers.

Part of what Coca-Cola Company's marketers call their "strategy for the 1980s" is a strategic plan to boost international per capita consumption of their soft drinks, which is well below the U.S. level. Americans drink an average of 806 soft drinks per year, while consumers in international markets drink 118

Photo source: Photo used with permission of The Coca-Cola Company.

The Coca-Cola Company's strategic plan of increasing international per capita consumption of its soft drinks is being implemented in Thailand by installing open coolers, which increase the availability of company products.

soft drinks per year. Initial plans were aimed at increasing international per capita consumption of Coca-Cola soft drinks by 40 percent between 1985 and 1990 by increasing their availability, affordability, and acceptability. To execute this long-term strategy, the company developed a set of tactical plans.[3]

Tactical planning focuses on the implementation of those activities specified in the strategic plan. Tactical plans typically are more short-term than strategic plans, focusing more on current and near-term activities that must be completed to implement overall strategies. Resource deployment is a common decision area for tactical planning. Coca-Cola Company's tactical plans are important for executing its strategies for future international growth. To implement the acceptability strategy, the company's tactical plan is to position soft drinks as appropriate in a wide variety of settings and occasions. For example, in Korea, Brazil, and other global markets, advertising promotes Coca-Cola as a complement to meals. To carry out the affordability strategy, the company is developing larger package sizes, which will offer greater value and convenience

tactical planning
Implementation of activities specified in the strategic plan that are necessary in the achievement of the firm's objectives.

Table 3.1

Planning by Different Management Levels

Managerial Level	Type of Planning Emphasized at This Level	Examples
Top Management Board of directors President Division vice-presidents	Strategic planning	Objectives of organization; fundamental strategies; total budget
Middle Management General sales manager Marketing research director Head of advertising department	Tactical planning	Quarterly and semiannual plans; subdivision of budgets; policies and procedures for each department
Supervisory Management District sales manager Supervisors	Operational planning	Daily and weekly plans; unit budgets; departmental rules and procedures

to consumers. Strengthening its distribution system and introducing new products such as Diet Coke and Cherry Coke are key elements in the long-term strategy of increasing availability. One tactical plan is to install vending and fountain equipment—which is less prevalent outside the United States—in outlets abroad. Another is aimed at developing a stronger bottling system. In Egypt, for example, an independent bottler has been licensed to market soft drinks in packages and flavors not offered by the government-owned bottler.

Planning at Different Organizational Levels

Planning is a major responsibility for every manager. Although managers at all levels devote some of their workdays to planning, the relative proportion of time spent in planning activities and the types of planning vary at different organizational levels.

Top management—the board of directors, president, and functional vice-presidents, such as the chief marketing officer—spend greater proportions of their time engaged in planning than do middle- and supervisory-level managers. In fact, one company president recommends that 30 to 50 percent of a chief executive's time be spent on strategic planning.[4]

Also, top management is more likely to devote more of its planning activities to long-range strategic planning than are middle-level managers (such as the director of the advertising department, regional sales managers, or the physical distribution manager), who tend to focus on operational planning—creating and implementing narrower tactical plans for their departments. Supervisory personnel are more likely to engage in developing specific programs for meeting the goals in their responsibility areas. Table 3.1 indicates the types of planning involved at various organizational levels.

Steps in the Marketing Planning Process

The marketing planning process involves both the development of objectives and specifications for how they will be accomplished. The five basic steps in the process—determination of organizational objectives, assessment of organizational resources, evaluation of environmental risks and opportunities, formulation of marketing objectives and a marketing strategy, and implementation of a marketing strategy through operating plans—are shown in Figure 3.1.

Determination of Organizational Objectives

The basic objectives, or goals, of the organization are the starting point for marketing planning. They serve as guideposts from which marketing objectives and plans are established. As Figure 3.1 shows, these objectives provide direction for all phases of the organization and serve as standards in evaluating performance.

Goals vary among organizations. The goal of the American Egg Board, a nonprofit trade association, is "to improve the demand for eggs, egg products, spent fowl, and the products of spent fowl." Corporate objectives often emphasize profitability, market share, and shareholder value. Coca-Cola Company defines its goal this way: "To increase shareholder value is the objective driving this enterprise." MCI's objective is "to be one of the world's truly great industrial enterprises, a company that delivers meaningful benefits to shareowners, customers, employees, and neighbors."

Soundly conceived objectives should be specific ("a 12 percent increase in profits over last year;" "attain a 20% share of the market by 1991;" "15% increase in sales over last year.") In addition, they should be time-specific, with specifications for time periods within which they will be accomplished.

Assessing Organizational Resources and Evaluating Risks and Opportunities

The second and third steps of the marketing planning process actually occur at about the same time in a back-and-forth assessment of strengths, risks, and available opportunities. Planning strategies are influenced by a number of factors both within and outside the organization. As Figure 3.1 illustrates, marketing opportunities are affected by organizational resources and environmental factors. Both are important considerations in the planning process.

Organizational resources include capabilities in production, marketing, finance, technology, and employees. By evaluating these resources, organizations can pinpoint their strengths and weaknesses. Strengths help organizations set objectives, develop plans for meeting objectives, and take advantage of marketing opportunities. For example, Coca-Cola Company identifies its strengths as having the world's best-known trademark, financial soundness, an exceptional distribution system, marketing and advertising efficiency, new-product innovations, and a dedicated team of managers and employees. The firm's strategy involves capitalizing on these resource strengths in addressing international marketing opportunities. Resource weaknesses, on the other hand,

Figure 3.1
The Marketing Planning Process

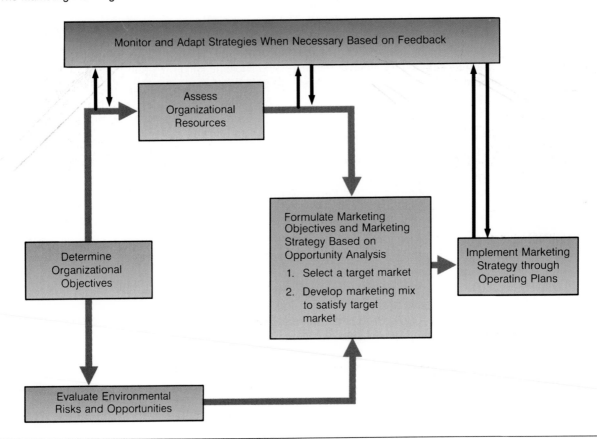

may inhibit an organization from taking advantage of marketing opportunities. General Mills recently decided to end its marketing efforts in the toy and fashion clothing fields and concentrate on food marketing and restaurants—two areas in which it has demonstrated superiority. Although the divested divisions included such well-known names as Parker Brothers and Kenner Products in the toy industry and Izod, Ship 'n Shore, Monet, and Foot Joy among its fashion companies, General Mills' management concluded that these areas did not offer immediate prospects of distinctive competence for the firm and that its marketing strengths could best be exploited in the restaurant and food marketing fields.[5]

The environmental dimensions discussed in Chapter 2—competitive, political/legal, economic, technological, and social/cultural—also influence marketing opportunities. Consider, for example, how a new technology opened up marketing opportunities for a traditionally undermarketed product—carpeting. Americans spend $15 billion a year on carpeting, but until recently the textile-fiber industry spent only $5 million for consumer advertising. And the ads, the

Figure 3.2
Marketing Opportunities Created by Technological Improvements in Carpeting

Source: Courtesy of DuPont Carpet Fibers, E.I. DuPont De Nemours and Company, Inc.

industry admits, were boring. As the DuPoint Stainmaster advertisement shown in Figure 3.2 demonstrates, a new, stain-resistant carpet technology changed all that.

The development of this added benefit convinced carpeting marketers to invest additional marketing funds and creativity in communicating the superiority of this product improvement. In an effort to build brand-name recognition through entertaining and memorable promotions, industry giant DuPont has spent more than $50 million advertising the new carpet's resistance to such stains as motor oil, soft drinks, and ketchup. Another objective of these efforts is to shorten the carpet replacement cycle, which has increased from seven to eleven years for the average homeowner. Stainmaster carpet sales reached $400 million in 1987, making it DuPont's most successful product introduction ever, surpassing even nylon.[6]

The marketing environment may also pose threats to marketing opportunities. In 1987, Genentech marketers were ready to launch TPA, a genetically engineered drug that dissolves blood clots and held the promise of stopping 30 percent of the current 550,000 deaths from heart attacks in the United States each year. TPA was to be biotechnology's first blockbuster drug—potentially a $1 billion-a-year product. But the U.S. Food and Drug Administration stunned company officials by delaying Genentech's request to market TPA in the United States for six months. Because of the regulatory delay, Genentech lost some of its competitive edge, as other biotech firms were already in advanced testing stages for their own versions of TPA.[7]

The Strategic Window   Environmental factors and organizational resources have different impacts on the organization at different times. Derek Abell has suggested the term **strategic window** to define the limited periods during which the key requirements of a market and the particular competencies of a firm best

strategic window
Limited periods during which the "fit" between the key requirements of a market and the particular competencies of a firm is optimal.

Figure 3.3
The Kawasaki ATV:
Taking Advantage of a
Strategic Window

Source: Courtesy of Kawasaki Motors Corporation.

fit together.[8] The reappearance of Halley's Comet in our part of the solar system a few years ago provided a strategic window for Bausch & Lomb. The firm's management, realizing that the comet's approach would stimulate interest in astronomy, expanded the company's telescope distribution system to include department stores, discount houses, and catalog merchandisers. The combination of heightened consumer interest and widespread product availability produced record sales for Bausch & Lomb's astronomical telescopes.

A strategic-window perspective offers a way of relating potential opportunities to company capabilities. Such a view is integrative, requiring a thorough analysis of (1) current and projected *external* environments, (2) current and projected *internal* company capabilities, and (3) how, whether, and when it will be feasible to reconcile the two by implementing one or more marketing strategies. Although Kawasaki was not the first company to introduce all-terrain vehicles (ATVs) to the U.S. market, it did have production and marketing capabilities in the field, and its management recognized a strategic window created by buyer demands and limitations of the Honda ATVs, whose reliance on a solid rear axle limited its turning flexibility. Later Kawasaki offerings, such as shown in Figure 3.3, addressed this issue with four-wheel versions complete with a differential and a reverse gear. These features placed Kawasaki marketers in an enviable position with respect to certain industrial and agricultural users who needed the additional turning capability offered by the Kawasaki concept.

The Marketing Strategy

The net result of opportunity analysis is the formulation of marketing objectives designed to achieve overall organizational objectives and develop a marketing plan. Marketing planning efforts must be directed toward establishing marketing strategies that are resource efficient, flexible, and adaptable. **Marketing strategy** is the overall company program for selecting a particular target market and then satisfying consumers in that segment through careful use of the elements of the marketing mix. The components of the marketing mix—product, pricing, distribution, and promotion—represent subsets of the overall marketing strategy.

marketing strategy
Overall company program for selecting a particular target market and then satisfying target consumers through a blending of the marketing mix elements.

Alternative Marketing Strategies

Much of the strategic planning effort is dedicated to the development of marketing strategies that will best match product offerings to the needs of particular target markets. An appropriate match is vital to the firm's market success. Three basic strategies for achieving consumer satisfaction are available: undifferentiated marketing, differentiated marketing, and concentrated marketing.

Undifferentiated Marketing

Firms that produce only one product or one product line and market it to all customers with a single marketing mix are said to practice **undifferentiated marketing**.[9] This strategy is sometimes called *mass marketing*. Undifferentiated marketing was much more common in the past than it is today. Ignoring the luxury market, Henry Ford built the Model T and sold it for one price to everyone. He agreed to paint the car any color that consumers wanted "as long as it is black." Ford's only concession to more specific customer needs was to add a truck body for those Model T purchasers who needed more hauling capacity.

undifferentiated marketing
Marketing strategy employed by organizations that produce only one product or service and market it to all customers using a single marketing mix.

Although marketing managers using an undifferentiated marketing strategy recognize the existence of numerous segments in the total market, they generally ignore minor differences and focus on the broad market. To reach the general market, they use mass advertising, mass distribution, and broad themes. WD-40 Company, for example, markets its only product—WD-40—as a broad-spectrum maintenance product to all end users, including homeowners, garage mechanics, office workers, and plant supervisors. The product's versatility as a lubricant, penetrant, rust preventative, water displacer, and cleaner allows the firm to use a broad approach for all users, even though they may have specific applications for which they buy WD-40. WD-40 Company uses mass distribution for its product through some 68 trade channels, including hardware, automotive, sporting goods, farm, drug, grocery, and mass merchandising stores.[10]

One advantage of undifferentiated marketing is production efficiency. For WD-40 Company, efficiency is gained by using one formula to make WD-40 concentrate. Similarly, undifferentiated marketing both simplified Ford's production operations and minimized inventories, since neither Ford nor its affiliated automobile dealers had to contend with optional equipment and numerous color combinations.

Figure 3.4
Converting an Undifferentiated
Marketing Strategy to
Differentiated Marketing

Source: Courtesy of The Arrow Company, New York; reprinted by permission.

However, there are dangers inherent in the strategy of undifferentiated marketing. A firm that attempts to satisfy everyone in the market faces the threat of competitors offering specialized products to smaller segments of the total market and better satisfying each segment. Indeed, firms that implement a strategy of differentiated marketing or concentrated marketing may enter the market and capture enough small segments to make the strategy of undifferentiated marketing unworkable for the competition.

Even though The Arrow Company has an enviable, 75-year-old reputation for its quality dress shirts, the firm's marketers recognized the need to offer additional clothing of similar quality to appeal to more diverse segments of the shirt market. In recent years, Arrow's product offerings have been expanded to include both dress shirts and casual wear. As Figure 3.4 illustrates, the new product line enables the firm's marketers to counter the specialized offerings of competitors practicing concentrated marketing or differentiated marketing.

A firm that uses undifferentiated marketing may also encounter problems in foreign markets. The rugged Marlboro Man marketing campaign, so well received in the United States, never scored in Hong Kong. In fact, cigarette sales suffered because Hong Kong smokers perceived the Marlboro Man as a bum. Ads showed him with dirty fingernails, alone, and doing manual labor. A new campaign changed the Marlboro Man's image: He had clean fingernails, became a ranch owner, and owned a personal helicopter. The ad change resulted in Marlboro's emergence as the brand leader in Hong Kong, outselling the next two brands combined.[11]

But for some products, tastes and preferences may vary little among countries. Playtex, for example, successfully used a mass marketing global approach in advertising its new WOW (WithOut Wire) bra. The product universally appeals to underwire-bra users because of the superior comfort of its plastic undershaper. Playtex launched WOW worldwide with identical advertising, which was translated into seven languages and shown in eleven countries. The strategy was cost efficient: The global campaign cost about $250,000 to produce, about half the cost of creating individualized commercials for each country.[12]

Differentiated Marketing

Firms that produce numerous products with different marketing mixes designed to satisfy smaller segments are said to practice **differentiated marketing.** This strategy is still aimed at satisfying a large part of the total market, but instead of marketing one product with a single marketing program, the organization markets a number of products designed to appeal to individual parts of the total market. As Figure 3.5 indicates, Reebok offers various walking shoes to satisfy the needs of different types of walkers. Reebok's strategy is to segment the walking market, recognizing that there is not just one type of walker, and therefore not one shoe to satisfy all walkers' needs; i.e., the Fitness Walker for casual walking, the Power Trainer for workouts, professional racing flats for speed walking, and the Rugged Walker for hiking. The company's slogan is "We have the shoe for wherever you walk." Reebok's objective is to fulfill every type of walker's footwear needs. It accomplishes this by providing a separate marketing mix approach for each product.

Most firms practice differentiated marketing. Kraft markets a variety of cheeses to appeal to different consumer tastes—Philadelphia Brand cream cheese, Kraft American Singles, Cracker Barrel cheddar, Casino natural cheese, and Velveeta and Cheez Whiz process cheese spreads. The Marriott hotel chain offers different types of lodging to satisfy varying traveler needs— large, full-service luxury hotels and resorts; small, full-service hotels; all-suite hotels; and Courtyard hotels.

By providing increased satisfaction for each of numerous target markets, the company with a differentiated marketing strategy can produce more sales than would be possible with undifferentiated marketing. In general, however, the costs of a differentiated marketing strategy are greater than those of an undifferentiated one. Production costs usually rise because additional products mean shorter production runs and increased setup time. Inventory costs rise because of added space needs for the products and increases in the necessary record-

differentiated marketing
Marketing strategy employed by organizations that produce numerous products or services and use different marketing mixes designed to satisfy numerous market segments.

Figure 3.5
A Differentiated Marketing Strategy

Source: Reprinted by permission of Reebok International Ltd.

keeping. Promotional costs also increase because unique promotional mixes are required for each market segment.

Although the costs of doing business typically are greater under a differentiated marketing strategy, consumers are usually better served because products offered are specifically designed to meet the needs of smaller segments. Also, a firm that wants to employ a single marketing strategy for an entire market may be forced to choose a strategy of differentiated marketing instead. If competitors appeal to each target market within the total market, the firm must also use this approach in order to remain competitive.

Concentrated Marketing

concentrated marketing
Marketing strategy that directs all of a firm's marketing resources toward serving a small segment of the total market.

Rather than attempting to market its product offerings to the entire market, a firm may choose to focus its efforts on profitably satisfying a smaller target market. This strategy of **concentrated marketing** is particularly appealing to new, small firms that lack the financial resources of their competitors. Two recent start-ups in the soft-drink business concentrate their efforts on a unique

Figure 3.6
Concentrated Marketing by
SCA Wolff System

Source: Courtesy of SCA Wolff System.

market for their products. Jolt Cola is targeted at consumers who want "all the sugar and twice the caffeine" of other colas, while Soho Natural Soda is aimed at consumers who want an all-natural soda with no artificial flavoring or coloring.

Concentration on a segment of the total market often allows some firms to maintain profitable operations. Fisher-Price has developed an enviable image in the toy industry because of its reputation as a manufacturer and marketer of high-quality children's toys. Other firms recognize a marketing opportunity by focusing on a particular market segment. SCA Wolff System marketers concentrated on satisfying consumers seeking a suntan, but either unwilling to devote the sunbathing hours required to tan outdoors or concerned about the ultraviolet rays in natural sunlight. The SCA Wolff System of suntanning centers found a ready market in the United States. As the advertisement shown in Figure 3.6 illustrates, the firm has not abandoned its concentrated marketing strategy but is broadening its appeal by offering tanning beds for direct sale to consumers.

Concentrated marketing, however, also poses dangers. Since the firm's growth is tied to a particular segment, changes in the size of that segment or in customer buying patterns may result in severe financial problems. Sales may also drop if new competitors appeal to the same market segment.

A decade ago, soaring gasoline prices and product shortages produced predictions that 40 percent of all American passenger cars would be operating on low-maintenance, high-fuel-economy diesel engines by 1990. Foreign car-makers ranging from Mercedes-Benz to Toyota were offering diesel autos to U.S. buyers, and General Motors Corporation was beginning to market diesel-fueled GM cars. Sales prospects were sufficient to convince Walter Genthe to invest $500,000 in a Flora, Illinois, factory to produce and market glow plugs, pocket-sized devices that provide the initial heat needed for starting diesel car engines. But just as quickly as it began, the diesel car market collapsed. By 1989, Mercedes-Benz was the only carmaker offering diesel automobiles in the U.S. market, and Genthe had learned a painful lesson on the risks of a concentrated marketing strategy.[13]

Selecting a Strategy

Although most organizations adopt the strategy of differentiated marketing, there is no single best strategy. Any of the three alternatives may prove most effective in a particular situation. Firms may also decide to change marketing strategies. Minnetonka, which pioneered the market, sold its Softsoap brand together with its other mass market products because the market was saturated with larger competitors such as Procter & Gamble and Lever Brothers. Today, Minnetonka is concentrating on marketing prestige fragrances, such as Obsession by Calvin Klein, and cosmetics that are distributed only through department and specialty stores.[14]

The basic determinants of a market-matching strategy are (1) company resources, (2) degree of product homogeneity, (3) stage in the product life cycle, and (4) competitors' strategies.

A concentrated marketing strategy may be best for a firm with limited resources. Small firms, for example, may be forced to select small target markets because of limitations in financing, size of their sales force, and promotional budgets. On the other hand, an undifferentiated marketing strategy should be used for products perceived by consumers as relatively homogeneous. Marketers of grain sell their products on the basis of standardized grades rather than individual brand names. Some petroleum companies use a strategy of undifferentiated marketing in distributing their gasoline in the mass market.

The firm's strategy also may change as the product progresses through the various stages of its life cycle. During the early stages, an undifferentiated marketing strategy might be useful as the firm attempts to develop initial demand for the product. In the later stages, however, competitive pressures may result in modified products and marketing strategies aimed at smaller segments of the total market.

The strategies used by competitors also affect the choice of a market-matching strategy. A firm may find it difficult to use an undifferentiated strategy if its competitors are actively cultivating smaller segments. In such instances, competition usually forces each firm to adopt a differentiated strategy.

Implementing and Monitoring Marketing Plans

The fifth step of the marketing planning process consists of implementing the marketing strategy that has been agreed upon by management. The overall strategic marketing plan serves as the basis for a series of operating plans

FOCUS ON ETHICS

McDonald's and Nutritional Advertising

Fast-food restaurants have a problem in creating a "healthy" image of their meals when they are so frequently referred to as "junk food." According to marketing researchers, this image has caused consumers to limit their consumption of fast food. McDonald's marketers decided to do something about it. They came up with a two-pronged marketing strategy to counter the idea that McDonald's is a purveyor of junk food.

The first part consisted of new-product introductions and product modifications. While other restaurant chains had introduced salad bars years earlier, McDonald's was a latecomer to the salad game, and its approach was unique. Instead of the typical self-serve salad bars, McDonald's outlets began offering prepackaged, individual salads with names like "Chef's Salad," "Garden Salad," and "Chicken Salad Oriental." In addition, they reduced the sodium content of their products and began using vegetable shortening rather than beef fat for cooking fish and chicken.

The second part of the strategy was launched in 1987 and proved quite controversial. The company had its advertising agency, Leo Burnett U.S.A., design a $20 million promotional campaign to "make consumers feel better" about McDonald's food by touting its nutritional value, according to Burnett vice-president Michael Allen. Ads began appearing in a number of general consumer publications, as well as in several consumer health magazines and medical journals, emphasizing that only a pinch of salt goes into McDonald's french fries and low-fat milk is used in its milkshakes. Other ads repeated the Department of Health and Human Service's seven guidelines for healthy eating, claiming that McDonald's fit right in. Still another ad introduced the new salad offerings. McDonald's goal was to get out front on the nutrition issue.

It did just that—but not the way it expected. The campaign drew fire from consumer advocates, health officials, and the attorneys general of Texas, California, and New York. "The McDonald's ads are hypocrisy," claimed Michael Jacobson, executive director of the Center for Science in the Public Interest. Jacobson believes that the ads "have the potential to deceive millions." He argues that they show only the good side of McDonald's food and omit negative information. For instance, one of the ads emphasizing that there is "less than a pinch" of salt in McDonald's french fries leaves out the fact that a milkshake has three times as much sodium as a regular order of fries. Moreover, the nutritional booklets available at McDonald's restaurants show that a Quarter Pounder with Cheese has 1,220 milligrams of sodium. Thus, a typical meal containing all three items would have 1,629 milligrams of sodium, over half of the Food and Nutrition Board's recommended daily intake of 1,100 to 3,300 milligrams. Another ad that kindled Jacobson's fire touts McDonald's calcium-enriched buns but says nothing about the burgers themselves. "Unfortunately, there's 10 quivering teaspoons of fat in there," he says. "That's the image they want you to forget."

Considerations such as these prompted the move by the three states' attorneys general to threaten McDonald's with legal action if it did not "cease and desist" from making nutritional claims. A McDonald's spokesperson defended the ads as "factual and straightforward," but the legal ramifications have not yet been resolved. It is clear, however, that McDonald's marketers would have encountered less resistance had they stuck to the theme that moderate amounts of their food would fit in with a healthy diet rather than making selective claims about the positive nutritional value of specific items.

Sources: Scott Hume, "Big Mac Attacked," *Advertising Age* (May 4, 1987), p. 110; Barbara Lippert, "Nutrition Debate Gets a Dose of McThoughtfulness," *Adweek's Marketing Week* (January 16, 1987), p. 19; Robert Johnson, "Fast-Food Chains Draw Criticism for Marketing Fare as Nutritional," *The Wall Street Journal* (April 6, 1987), p. 21; Annetta Miller, "A Sizzling Food Fight," *Newsweek* (April 20, 1987), p. 56; and Scott Hume, "McDonald's Heavy in Print for Nutrition," *Advertising Age* (January 19, 1987), pp. 1, 90.

necessary to move the organization toward accomplishment of its objectives. Although marketing planning is discussed throughout the text in connection with the analysis and selection of a target market and the development of a marketing mix designed to satisfy the chosen market, detailed and intensive analysis of operating plans in specific areas of the organization are treated in more advanced marketing classes.

At every step of the marketing planning process, marketing managers use feedback to monitor and adapt strategies when actual performance fails to match expectations. Methods of securing feedback are discussed in Chapter 4.

Tools Used in Marketing Planning

As more organizations have discovered the benefits resulting from effective marketing planning, a number of planning tools have been developed to assist in conducting this important function. These include the strategic business unit concept, the market share/market growth matrix, and spreadsheet analysis. In addition, the marketing audit is frequently used in evaluating marketing planning and marketing performance.

Strategic Business Units

Although smaller firms may offer only a few products and services to their customers, larger organizations frequently produce and market thousands of offerings to widely diverse markets. For example, W. R. Grace & Company's diversified enterprises include specialty chemicals, restaurants, retailing, agricultural chemicals, and natural resources. Corning Glass Works has a portfolio of business that includes consumer products, electronics and telecommunications, health and science, and specialty materials. Top management at major firms needs some type of method for determining the best way to evaluate these diverse businesses and to make decisions concerning promising product lines that warrant additional resources and those that should be weeded from the firm's product portfolio. Management at General Electric approached the problem this way:

> *The GE system grew out of the company's problems in the late 1960s, when setbacks in several areas such as computers, jet engines, and international business proved costly overall. Revenues had steadily grown, but the growth was profitless.*
>
> *To get profits growing along with revenues, GE decided it needed a new, companywide approach. . . . Surveying the organization, management identified 43 units of various sizes, which it dubbed strategic business units. Each SBU . . . (had) a unique business mission within the company . . . (with) identifiable customers . . . and all its major business functions—manufacturing, engineering, finance, and marketing—within the control of the SBU manager.*
>
> *SBUs superseded divisional organization. For example, three separate divisions—portable home products, food preparation products, and personal appliances—were merged into the Housewares Business Division.*[15]

strategic business unit (SBU) Related product groupings of businesses within a multiproduct firm with specific managers, resources, objectives, and competitors; structured for optimal planning purposes.

Strategic business units (SBUs) are divisions composed of key businesses within multiproduct companies with specific managers, resources, objectives, and competitors. SBUs may encompass a division, a product line, or a single product. They can be evaluated as separate entities because they have distinct missions, their own managers, identifiable customer segments, specific competitors, and the ability to be planned independently of other units of the firm.

Figure 3.7
Market Share/Market Growth Matrix

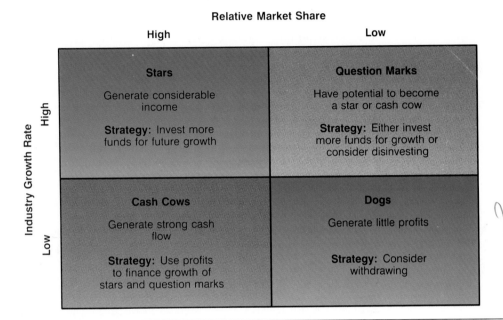

The consequence of this organizational arrangement is that each SBU can be evaluated according to its profit and growth potential. Previously organized by functions, such as marketing and manufacturing, Kodak has reorganized into 24 business units, each with its own profit-and-loss responsibility. During the mid-1980s, Kodak marketers examined each of their products in terms of sales and profitability. After discovering that 80 to 90 percent of them generated only 10 to 20 percent of company revenues, they discontinued 10,000 products, reducing the total number of Kodak products to 55,000.[16]

Since the 1970s, the SBU concept has been adopted by such major firms as Union Carbide, Boise-Cascade, and International Paper. Today 20 percent of the largest U.S. manufacturing corporations use the SBU approach.[17]

The Market Share/Market Growth Matrix

To evaluate the organization's strategic business units, some type of portfolio performance framework is needed. The most widely used framework was developed in the early 1970s by the Boston Consulting Group. The **market share/market growth matrix** is a four-quadrant matrix that plots market share—the percentage of a market a firm controls—and market growth potential. The market share, plotted on the horizontal axis, indicates the SBU's market share relative to competitors in the industry. The market growth rate, plotted on the vertical axis, indicates the annual growth rate of that market. All of a firm's various businesses can be plotted in one of the four quadrants. As Figure 3.7 shows,

market share/market growth matrix
Matrix developed by the Boston Consulting Group that enables a firm to classify its products and services in terms of the industry growth rate and its market share relative to competitive products. The four segments are stars, cash cows, question marks, and dogs.

the quadrants are labeled *cash cows, stars, dogs,* and *question marks,* and each requires a unique marketing strategy.

Stars represent high market share and high market growth. These products or businesses are high-growth market leaders. Although they generate considerable income, even more funds are needed to finance the additional investments in advertising and new equipment required for further growth.

Cash cows represent high market share and low market growth. Marketers want to maintain this status for as long as possible, because these businesses are producing a strong cash flow. Instead of heavily investing in promotions and production, firms use the funds to finance the growth of other SBUs with high growth potential.

Question marks represent low market share and high market growth. These situations require marketers to make the basic decision of "go" or "no go." Due to the high-growth nature of the market, question marks typically require more cash than they are able to generate. Unless marketers can implement plans to convert these question marks to stars, the firm should pull out of these markets and pursue markets with greater potential.

Dogs represent low market share and low market growth. Although dogs may generate some funds for the firm, their future prospects are poor, and marketers attempt to withdraw from these businesses or product lines as quickly as possible.

Evaluating the Matrix Approach to Planning   The market share/market growth matrix emphasizes the importance of creating market offerings that will position the firm to its best advantage. It also indicates that successful SBUs undergo a series of changes as they move through their life cycle. The successful product or business typically begins as a question mark, then becomes a star, and eventually drops into the cash-cow category, generating surplus funds with which to finance new stars. Ultimately it becomes a dog at the end of its life cycle and is eliminated from the firm's product offerings.

Critics of the matrix approach often point to the tendencies of some marketers to apply it in a largely mechanistic manner. In an attempt to develop a product line of stars, marketers may ignore the possible methods of converting products and services labeled as dogs. As former ITT chairperson Harold Geneen put it, "As for the 'dogs,' to my mind it is management's responsibility to figure out why they are 'dogs' and what can be done to turn them into greyhounds."[18] Moreover, the firm with no stars may be forced to seek means of expanding market and sales opportunities of an existing product regardless of its label. Each organization must balance the advantages of the matrix approach against its potential shortcomings.

Spreadsheet Analysis

Spreadsheets are special computer software used in answering "what-if" questions. Electronic spreadsheets are the computerized equivalent of an accountant's hand-prepared worksheet. The electronic spreadsheet, like its manual counterpart, is a rigid grid of columns and rows that enables the manager to organize information in a standardized, easily understandable format. The most popular spreadsheets include *Lotus 1-2-3, Excel, VisiCalc, Multiplan,* and *Appleworks.*

Figure 3.8
Example of Spreadsheet Analysis

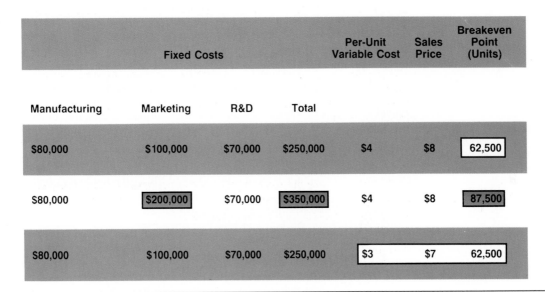

	Fixed Costs			Per-Unit Variable Cost	Sales Price	Breakeven Point (Units)
Manufacturing	Marketing	R&D	Total			
$80,000	$100,000	$70,000	$250,000	$4	$8	62,500
$80,000	$200,000	$70,000	$350,000	$4	$8	87,500
$80,000	$100,000	$70,000	$250,000	$3	$7	62,500

Spreadsheet analysis may be used to anticipate marketing performance given a specified set of circumstances. For example, a spreadsheet might be used to determine the outcomes of different prices for a new product, as shown in Figure 3.8.

In this example, the item will be marketed at $8 per unit and can be produced for $4 in variable costs. The total fixed costs of $250,000 include $80,000 for manufacturing-overhead outlays such as salaries, general office expenses, rent, utilities, and interest charges; $100,000 for marketing expenditures; and $70,000 for research and development for the product. The spreadsheet calculation, using the basic breakdown model, reveals that sales of 62,500 units are necessary in order to break even.

But what if the firm's marketing director convinces other members of the group to increase marketing expenditures to $200,000? As the second part of Figure 3.8 shows, the $100,000 marketing expenditure in the cell (the name of each point at which the rows and columns intersect) is changed to $200,000 and the newly calculated breakeven point is 87,500 units. As soon as a figure in one or more cells changes, all figures are recalculated automatically; this eliminates the need to relocate and revise figures by hand.

The final part of Figure 3.8 demonstrates the impact of a reduction in variable costs (by switching to the lower-cost materials) to $3 coupled with a $1 reduction in the product's selling price. The new breakeven point is 62,500 units.

Figure 3.8 demonstrates the ease with which a manager can use a microcomputer spreadsheet program to determine the potential results of alternative decisions. More complex spreadsheets may have as many as 50 or more columns, but they will make the new calculations as quickly as the manager changes the variables.

spreadsheet analysis
Marketing planning tool that uses a decision-oriented computer program designed to answer "what-if" questions by analyzing different groups of data provided by the manager.

Marketing Audits

William S. Woodside, former president of American Can Company, has been quoted as saying, "The roughest thing to get rid of is the Persian Messenger Syndrome, where the bearer of bad tidings is beheaded by the king. You should lean over backward to reward the guy who is first with the bad news. Most companies have all kinds of abilities to handle problems, if they only learn about them soon enough."[19]

If the marketing organization is to avoid the Persian Messenger Syndrome, it must institute periodic reviews of marketing plans and be willing to accept the objective results of the evaluations. For most organizations, this means using a **marketing audit**—a thorough, objective evaluation of an organization's marketing philosophy, goals, policies, tactics, practices, and results.[20]

marketing audit
Thorough, objective evaluation of an organization's marketing philosophy, goals, policies, tactics, practices, and results.

A comprehensive marketing audit can provide a valuable—and sometimes disquieting—perspective on the progress of the firm's marketing plans. An excellent example of the need to assess performance is the pharmaceutical firm that was delighted with an 83 percent awareness rating for an advertising campaign but shocked on learning that this amounted to only a 28 percent intent-to-buy figure.[21]

A periodic review of marketing plans is invaluable both in identifying the tasks that the organization does well and in revealing its failures. Periodic review, criticism, and self-analysis are crucial to the vitality of any organization. They are particularly critical to a function as diverse and dynamic as marketing. Marketing audits are especially valuable in pointing out areas in which managerial perceptions differ sharply from reality.

Methods of conducting audits are almost as diverse as the firms that use them. Some audits follow informal procedures; others involve elaborate checklists, questionnaires, profiles, tests, and related research instruments.

The marketing audit goes beyond the normal control system. The control process for marketing essentially asks: Are we doing things right? The marketing audit extends this question to: Are we doing the right thing?

Marketing audits are applicable to all organizations—large or small, profitable or profitless, nonprofit or profit oriented. Audits are particularly valuable when performed for the first time or when conducted after having been discontinued for several years. While not all firms use marketing audits, an increasing number of organizations are recognizing their important role in evaluating strategies that will maintain competitiveness and profitability.

Sales Forecasting

sales forecast
Estimate of company sales for a specified future period.

A basic building block of marketing planning is the **sales forecast**—an estimate of the firm's sales or income for a specified future period. In addition to its use in marketing planning, the sales forecast plays a major role in new-product decisions, production scheduling, financial planning, inventory planning and procurement, product distribution, and determining personnel needs. An inaccurate forecast will result in incorrect decisions in each of these areas. The sales forecast is also an important tool for marketing control, because it produces standards against which to measure actual performance. Without such standards, no comparisons can be made. If no criterion of success exists, there can be no definition of failure.

Table 3.2
Benefits and Limitations of Various Forecasting Techniques

Technique	Benefits	Limitations
Qualitative Methods		
Jury of executive opinion	Opinions come from executives in many different departments; quick; inexpensive	Managers may lack sufficient knowledge and experience to make meaningful predictions
Delphi technique	Group of experts can accurately predict long-term events such as technological breakthroughs	Time consuming; expensive
Sales force composite	Salespeople have expert customer, product, and competitor knowledge; quick; inexpensive	Inaccurate forecasts may result from low estimates of salespeople concerned about their influence on quotas
Survey of buyer intentions	Useful in predicting short- and intermediate-term sales for firms that have only a few customers	Intention to buy may not result in actual purchase; time consuming; expensive
Quantitative Methods		
Market tests	Provides realistic information on actual purchases rather than on intent to buy	Alerts competition to new-product plans; time consuming; expensive
Trend analysis	Quick; inexpensive; effective when customer demand and environmental factors are stable	Assumes the future is continuation of past; does not consider environmental changes
Exponential smoothing	Same benefits as trend analysis but emphasizes more recent data	Same limitations as trend analysis but not as severe due to emphasis on recent data

Sales forecasts can be classified as short run, intermediate, or long run. Short-run forecasts usually include a period of up to one year, intermediate forecasts cover one to five years, and long-run forecasts extend beyond five years. The time frame of a forecast depends on many factors, including organizational resources, environmental factors, and the ways in which the forecast will be used.

Although forecasters use dozens of techniques to divine the future—ranging from computer simulations to the study of trends by futurists—their methods fall into two broad categories. *Qualitative forecasting* techniques are more subjective, because they are based on opinions rather than exact historical data. *Quantitative forecasting* methods, by contrast, employ statistical computations such as trend extensions based on past data, computer simulations, and econometrics to produce numerical forecasts. As Table 3.2 shows, each method has benefits and limitations. Consequently, most organizations use a combination of techniques in their attempts to predict future events.

Qualitative Forecasting Techniques

A recent survey of forecasting techniques by 134 firms revealed that marketers rely most on qualitative measures such as estimates by a *jury* of executives or composite forecasts based on sales force estimates as techniques for divining future sales.[22] Other frequently used qualitative sales forecasting methods include the Delphi technique and surveys of buyer intentions.

jury of executive opinion
Qualitative sales forecasting method that combines and averages the future business and sales expectations of executives from functional areas such as finance, production, marketing, and purchasing.

Delphi technique
Qualitative sales forecasting method that involves several rounds of anonymous forecasts and ends when a consensus of the participants is reached.

sales force composite
Qualitative sales forecasting method in which sales estimates are based on the combined estimates of the firm's sales force.

survey of buyer intentions
Qualitative sales forecasting method in which sample groups of present and potential customers are surveyed concerning their purchase intentions.

Jury of Executive Opinion   The **jury of executive opinion** combines and averages the outlooks of top company executives from such areas as finance, production, marketing, and purchasing. It is particularly effective when top managers are experienced and knowledgeable about situations that influence sales, open-minded about the future, and aware of the bases for their judgments. This method is quick and inexpensive and can be effectively used to forecast sales and develop new products. It works best for short-run forecasting.

Delphi Technique   While similar to the jury of executive opinion in that it involves soliciting the opinions of several people, the **Delphi technique** seeks opinions of experts outside the firm, such as university researchers and scientists, rather than relying completely on company executives. It is most appropriately used to predict long-run issues, such as technological breakthroughs, that could affect future company sales and the market potential for new products. The Delphi technique works as follows. A firm first selects a panel of experts and then sends each a questionnaire relating to a future event. Each expert returns his or her answer to the company. The answers are then combined and averaged, and, based on these results, another questionnaire is sent to the experts. The process continues until a consensus of opinion has been reached. Although firms have successfully used Delphi to predict future technological breakthroughs, the method is both expensive and time consuming.

Sales Force Composite   The **sales force composite** is based on the belief that organizational members closest to the marketplace—those with specialized product, customer, and competitor knowledge—are likely to have better insight concerning short-term future sales than any other group. It is typically a *bottom-up approach:* Salespersons' estimates are first combined at the district level, then the regional level, and finally the national level to obtain an aggregate forecast of sales. Few firms rely solely on the sales force composite, however. Since salespeople recognize the role of the sales forecast in determining sales quotas for their territories, they are likely to make conservative estimates. Moreover, their narrow perspectives on their limited geographical territories may prevent them from knowing about trends developing in other territories, forthcoming technological innovations, or the impact of major changes in company marketing strategies on sales. Consequently, the sales force composite is often combined with other forecasting techniques in developing the final forecast.

Survey of Buyer Intentions   The **survey of buyer intentions** uses mail-in questionnaires, telephone polls, or personal interviews to determine the intentions of a representative group of present and potential customers. This method is more appropriate for firms with a limited number of customers and often impractical for those with millions of customers. Also, buyer surveys are limited to situations in which customers are willing to reveal their buying intentions. Moreover, customer intentions do not necessarily translate into actual purchases. These surveys may help predict short-run or intermediate sales, but they are also time consuming and expensive.

Quantitative Forecasting Techniques

Quantitative techniques use a more scientific approach to forecasting sales. They attempt to eliminate the guesswork of the qualitative methods. Quantitative techniques include such methods as market tests, trend analysis, and exponential smoothing.

Market Tests   **Market tests** are frequently used in assessing consumer response to new product offerings. The procedure typically involves establishing a small number of test markets with which to gauge consumer response to a new product under actual marketplace conditions. Market tests also permit the evaluation of different prices, alternate promotional strategies, and other marketing mix variations through comparisons among different test markets. Based on consumer response in test markets, a firm can predict sales for larger market areas.

market test
Quantitative forecasting technique in which a new product, price, promotional campaign, or other marketing variable is introduced in a relatively small test market location in order to assess consumer reactions under realistic market conditions.

Many Walt Disney marketers have long felt that a chain of Disney-owned retail stores featuring the firm's merchandise would be a natural area of expansion. After all, sales of Disney merchandise at the company's theme parks generate over $350 million in a typical year. But other executives were worried about the dangers of cannibalization, pointing out that licensees of Disney characters sell more than $1 billion in merchandise throughout the world. The Disney Store concept was tested by focusing on two likely locations. The Glendale Galleria, a regional shopping mall outside Los Angeles, was the first location to test the effectiveness of a regional mall location. The second location, which offered a festival atmosphere with high tourist foot traffic, was first tested at San Francisco's Pier 39 tourist attraction. Stores were designed to loosely resemble movie sets and store employees called *cast members* received several days of training at the parent firm's Disney University. Disney videos play on overhead monitors located throughout the stores. The results of the test were so successful that twelve Disney Stores had been opened by 1989.[23]

The primary advantage of market tests is the realism it provides for the marketer. On the other hand, it is an expensive and time-consuming approach and may communicate marketing plans to competitors before a product has been introduced to the total market. Test marketing is discussed in more detail in Chapter 9.

Trend Analysis   **Trend analysis** involves forecasting future sales by analyzing the historical relationship between sales and time. It is based on the assumption that factors that collectively determined past sales will continue to exert similar influence in the future. When historical data are available, trend analysis can be performed quickly and inexpensively. For example, if sales were X last year and have been increasing at Y percent for the past several years, the sales forecast for next year would be calculated as follows:

trend analysis
Quantitative sales forecasting method in which estimates of future sales are determined through statistical analyses of historical sales patterns.

$$\text{Sales Forecast} = X + XY.$$

In actual numbers, if last year's sales totaled 520,000 units and the average sales growth rate has been 5 percent, the sales forecast would be:

$$\text{Sales Forecast} = 520,000 + (520,000 \times .05) = 546,000.$$

The danger of trend analysis lies in its underlying assumption that the future is a continuation of the past. Any variations in the determinants influencing sales will result in an incorrect forecast. In addition, historical data may not be readily available in some instances, most notably in the case of new products.

THE COMPETITIVE EDGE

Domino's Pizza

From the very beginning, Thomas Monaghan realized that he would never achieve competitive superiority by simply establishing one more chain of pizza outlets. Giants such as Pizza Hut, Godfather's, Pizza Inn, and others already had established their names and fast-food outlets throughout the United States. So how did Domino's Pizza grow from one small Ypsilanti, Michigan, pizzeria in 1960 to second place behind Pizza Hut by 1989?

Monaghan may not have realized it at the time, but a decision he made in 1965 to strip his menu of everything but pizza and specialize in take-out and delivery created a strategic window that positioned Domino's in the center of the most lucrative niche in the fast-food industry. Sales doubled that year, and Monaghan began an expansion program. New outlets were opened—including the firm's first franchise—and a commissary for supplying pizza ingredients to Domino's outlets was started.

Monaghan also began to play the fast-delivery angle for all it was worth. To do this, he kept the menu simple: two sizes of pizza, a range of only 10 toppings, and cola. And he promised delivery of a piping-hot pizza in less than 30 minutes or $3 off the price. Monaghan has since called that 30-minute promise "the greatest thing we've ever done." Providing time and place utilities for pizza lovers had begun to pay off.

Delivering pizza fast has been Domino's ultimate goal, from which all its planning (and its success) has stemmed. Now Monaghan has added a new goal: to sell more pizza than anybody else. He plans to

have 10,000 stores throughout the world and $10 billion in sales by 1990. Consequently, Monaghan has started Domino's on an expansion program that dwarfs everything he's ever done. Domino's is adding nearly three stores a day, and the company is geared toward doing so with a minimum of problems. There is, for instance, a valuable training program and each potential franchisee is required to begin by working in a store for one year.

One question that remains to be answered is whether the Domino's success formula will "travel well" outside the United States. Monaghan is counting on foreign locations for a substantial proportion of the new outlets, and he feels that his provision of time and place utilities will be equally successful abroad. While early reports show success in Canada and Australia, it remains to be seen whether European, Japanese, and other potential consumers will place

similar values on the Domino's formula of 30-minute delivery and fast-food consumption at home.

Another planning challenge at Domino's these days is the inevitable possibility of major-league competition in its market niche. Pizza Hut, with well over 4,000 outlets, is testing a delivery service. Pizza Inn offers delivery service in addition to in-restaurant pizza dining. But none of that bothers Monaghan, who recently said, "It's the quality of individual stores that makes Domino's a success. As long as I keep my eye on that ball, we're not going to have any problems."

Sources: Domino's growth is described in Tom Monaghan, *Pizza Tiger* (New York: Random House, 1986). See also "The Convenience Industry: Making Life a Little Simpler," *Business Week* (April 27, 1987), pp. 86–94; Richard Behar, "Domino Theories," *Forbes* (February 12, 1984), p. 124; and Raymond Serafin, "Domino's Pizza Delivers on the Basics," *Advertising Age* (July 8, 1985), p. 4. *Photo source:* Courtesy of Domino's Pizza, Inc.

During periods of steady growth and stable demand, the trend extension method of forecasting produces satisfactory results, but it implicitly assumes that the factors contributing to a certain output level in the past will operate in the same manner in the future. When conditions change, the trend extension method often produces incorrect results. For this reason, forecasters have increasingly been using more sophisticated techniques and more complex mathematical models.

Exponential Smoothing   A more sophisticated approach to trend analysis, the **exponential smoothing** technique, assigns a weight factor to each year of sales data. Greater weight is given to the most recent years. For example, an exponential smoothing forecast based on five years of sales data might be weighted as follows:

Year	Weight
1984	.8
1985	.9
1986	1.0
1987	1.1
1988	1.2

Since those factors contributing to the most recent sales data are most likely to continue to interact similarly for the next time period, these data are assigned a greater weighting than those of earlier years.

Steps in Sales Forecasting

Although sales forecasting methods vary, the most typical one begins with an environmental forecast of general economic conditions that marketers use to forecast industry sales and develop a forecast of company and product sales. This approach is referred to as the *top-down method.*

Environmental Forecasting   These broad-based forecasts focus on factors external to the firm that affect its markets. In **environmental forecasting,** projections are likely to be based on factors such as consumer spending/saving patterns, balance-of-trade surpluses and deficits, government expenditures, and business investments. These projections can then be combined to develop an overall economic forecast. The most common measure of economic output is the nation's *gross national product (GNP),* the market value of all final products produced in a country in a given year. Trend analysis is the most frequently used method of forecasting increases in the GNP. Since many federal agencies and other organizations develop regular GNP forecasts, a firm may choose to use their estimates. These forecasts are regularly reported in such publications as *The Wall Street Journal* and *Business Week.*

Developing the Industry Sales Forecast   The general economic forecast is used with other, relevant environmental factors in developing an industry sales forecast. Since industry sales often are related to the GNP or some other measure of the national economy, a forecast may begin by measuring the degree of this relationship and then applying the trend extension method to forecast industry sales. Most industries have trade associations and publications

exponential smoothing
Quantitative forecasting technique that assigns weights to historical sales data, giving greater weight to the most recent data.

environmental forecasting
Broad-based economic forecasting that focuses on the impact of external factors on the firm's markets.

that provide short-, intermediate-, and long-term forecasts. These forecasts are valuable because they combine an economic outlook with trends and environmental factors that influence specific industries.

Forecasting Company and Product Sales   After the industry forecast has been completed, company and product forecasts are developed. These begin with a detailed analysis of previous years' performances. The firm's past and present market shares are reviewed, and product managers, as well as regional and district sales managers, are consulted about expected sales. Since an accelerated promotional budget or the introduction of new products may stimulate additional sales, the marketing plan for the coming year is also considered.

Product and company forecasts must evaluate such factors as sales of each product; future sales trends; sales by customer, territory, salesperson, and order size; and financial resources. After a preliminary sales forecast has been developed, it is reviewed by the sales force and by district, regional, and national sales managers.

Grass-Roots Forecasting   An alternative approach to top-down forecasting is *grass-roots,* or *bottom-up, forecasting.* This forecasting method begins with sales estimates provided by each salesperson for his or her sales territory. These estimates are combined and refined at the divisional, regional, and national levels by sales and marketing managers; they are then submitted to the national sales manager, where they become the aggregate sales estimate for the forthcoming time period. Proponents of the bottom-up approach to forecasting stress employee morale and motivational benefits that result when each member of the sales force participates in developing the forecast that will be used as the primary basis for establishing sales quotas. In addition, the approach ensures inputs from each individual territory, and personal inputs from each salesperson who is in direct and continuing contact with the firm's customers.

One shortcoming of the grass-roots approach is the lack of perspective the individual salesperson has of the organization as a whole. Major trends, such as forthcoming market entries of competitive products, new products about to be introduced by the company, price changes, new promotional campaigns, packaging changes, and other variables likely to affect the marketplace, may not be reflected in the sales estimates for individual territories. In addition, since salespeople realize the relationship between the sales forecast and their sales quotas, they may be tempted to make relatively low forecasts that will be easy to exceed. Consequently, firms using the bottom-up approach depend heavily upon the compromises and final estimates that result from discussions at the divisional, regional, and national levels.

Since both the top-down and grass-roots approaches to sales forecasting possess strengths and weaknesses, it is not surprising that many marketers employ a combination of both approaches to obtain the most realistic forecast possible.

New-Product Sales Forecasting   Forecasting sales for new products is an especially hazardous undertaking because no historical data are available. Companies typically employ consumer panels to obtain reactions to the products and probable purchase behavior. Test market data may also be utilized.

Since few products are totally new, forecasters carefully analyze the sales of competing products that the new entry may displace. A new type of fishing reel, for example, will compete in an established market with other kinds of reels. This *substitute method* provides the forecaster with an estimate of market size and potential demand.

Summary of Chapter Objectives

1. Distinguish between strategic planning and tactical planning. Planning, the process of anticipating the future and determining the courses of action needed for achieving organizational objectives, is the basis for all strategy decisions. Strategic planning is the broad, all-encompassing planning that involves determining the organization's primary objectives and adopting courses of action and allocation of resources necessary for achieving them. Tactical planning focuses on the implementation of activities specified in the strategic plan. Tactical plans typically are more short term than strategic plans, focusing on current and near-term activities that must be executed in order to implement overall strategies. Resource allocation is a common decision area in tactical planning.

2. Explain how marketing plans differ at various levels of the organization. Although all organization managers devote at least some time to planning, the relative proportion of time spent in planning activities and the types of planning vary at different organizational levels. Top management— the board of directors, president, and functional vice-presidents (such as the chief marketing officer) spend more time engaged in planning than do middle- and supervisory-level managers. Top managers are more likely to devote the bulk of their planning activities to long-range strategic planning. Middle-level managers (such as the director of the advertising department, regional sales managers, or the physical distribution manager) tend to focus on narrower, tactical plans for their departments. Supervisory managers are more likely to engage in developing specific programs designed to meet the goals for their responsibility areas.

3. Identify the steps in the marketing planning process. There are five basic steps in the marketing planning process: determination of organizational objectives; assessment of organizational resources; evaluation of environmental risks and opportunities; formulation of marketing objectives and a marketing strategy; and the implementation of a marketing strategy through operating plans.

4. Compare the three basic strategies for matching markets with product/ service offerings. Three alternative strategies exist for matching the firm's offerings to specific target markets. Undifferentiated marketing refers to the strategy of firms that produce only one product or service and market it to all customers with a single marketing mix. Differentiated marketing is used by firms that produce numerous products or services with different marketing mixes designed to satisfy smaller segments. Concentrated marketing means directing all of the firm's marketing resources toward satisfying a small segment of the total market. The choice of which marketing strategy to use involves consideration of company resources, degree of product homogeneity, stage in the product life cycle, and competitors' strategies.

5. Explain how the strategic business unit concept, the market share/ market growth matrix, and spreadsheet analysis can be used in marketing planning. A number of very large, multiproduct firms use the strategic business unit (SBU) concept to aid in marketing planning. SBUs are divisions composed of key businesses within the firm with specific managers, resources, objectives, and competitors. Grouping company operating divisions into SBUs helps the firm focus on customer needs. Distinct strategies can be set up for each SBU based on the needs of its customer segments and its profit or growth potential. The market share/market growth matrix is a four-quadrant matrix that plots market share against market growth potential in the industry. Different marketing strategies may be appropriate for each segment of the matrix. The four segments are stars, cash cows, question marks, and dogs.

6. Identify the major types of forecasting methods. *Sales forecasting* is an important component of both planning and controlling marketing programs. Two basic categories of forecasting techniques exist: quantitative forecasting, which utilizes statistical techniques such as trend analysis based on past data, exponential smoothing, and market tests to produce numerical forecasts of future events, and qualitative forecasting, which uses subjective techniques such as surveys of buyer intentions, sales force composites, jury of executive opinions, and the Delphi technique. Qualitative measures are the more commonly used of the two forecasting approaches.

7. Explain the steps in the forecasting process. Although sales forecasting varies among individual firms, it is possible to divide the approaches into three general categories. With top-down forecasting, the firm begins with an environmental forecast of general economic conditions, which the marketer uses to forecast industry sales and develop a forecast of company and individual product sales. In bottom-up (or grass-roots) forecasting, the firm begins with sales estimates from individual salespersons. These estimates are combined and refined at the divisional, regional, and national levels by sales and marketing managers and then submitted to the national sales manager, at which point they become the aggregate sales estimate for the forthcoming time period. The combination approach is used by many firms to combine the strengths of top-down and bottom-up forecasting to obtain the most realistic forecast possible.

Forecasting sales for new products or services can be especially difficult, since no historical data are available. Marketers of new products or services may have to base their forecasts on market tests or surveys of buyer intentions, which may not provide an accurate picture of actual purchase behavior. A substitute method in which forecasters carefully analyze the sales of competing products that may be displaced by the new entry is also frequently used.

Key Terms

planning
marketing planning
strategic planning
tactical planning
strategic window
marketing strategy
undifferentiated marketing
differentiated marketing
concentrated marketing
strategic business unit (SBU)
market share/market growth matrix

spreadsheet analysis
marketing audit
sales forecast
jury of executive opinion
Delphi technique
sales force composite
survey of buyer intentions
market test
trend analysis
exponential smoothing
environmental forecasting

Review Questions

1. How does strategic planning differ from tactical planning? Which type is more important at each level of management?

2. What are the basic steps in the marketing planning process? Give an example of a decision that might be made at each step.

3. Explain the concept of the strategic window. Provide one example for a for-profit business and one for a nonprofit business.

4. Identify the two major components of a firm's marketing strategy. Why is it important that they be considered in a specific order?

5. Outline the basic features of undifferentiated marketing. Contrast differentiated marketing with concentrated marketing.

6. Differentiate among stars, cash cows, question marks, and dogs in the market share/market growth matrix. Give two examples of products in each of the four quadrants of the matrix, and suggest marketing strategies for each product.

7. What are the potential dangers of rigid application of product portfolio models such as the market share/market growth matrix?

8. Explain how spreadsheet analysis can assist the marketing manager in planning and implementing marketing strategies.

9. Compare the major types of forecasting methods. Explain the steps involved in the forecasting process.

10. Discuss the advantages and shortcomings of basing sales forecasts exclusively on estimates developed by the firm's sales force.

Discussion Questions

1. Choose from among undifferentiated marketing, differentiated marketing, and concentrated marketing in selecting the most appropriate strategy for each of the following situations. Defend your answer.
   a. A product is entering the decline phase of its life cycle.
   b. Management considers it essential to minimize production and inventory carrying costs.
   c. A small, new company is trying to gain a foothold in an established industry.
   d. A firm's major competitors are employing a differentiated marketing strategy.
   e. A firm lacks the financial resources of its major competitors.
   f. A firm is entering a large market made up of several homogeneous products, such as grain.
   g. The market is made up of a series of homogeneous market segments, each having its own particular needs and wants.

2. Suggest methods for forecasting sales for newly introduced products.

3. Discuss the relationship between marketing planning and the marketing audit. How are marketing objectives related to organizational objectives?

4. Why is differentiated marketing the most costly marketing strategy? Under what conditions should it be used?

5. Which forecasting technique(s) do you feel is most appropriate for each of the following? Defend your answer.
   a. Selsun Blue dandruff shampoo
   b. Museum of Modern Art
   c. Office supplies retailer
   d. Maids on Wheels franchise
   e. *Rolling Stone* magazine subscriptions

VIDEO CASE 3

Pizza Hop

Never before in history have so many college and university students chosen to major in business administration and, more particularly, marketing. This year, more than one in every four entering freshmen will decide to study business. A sizable number of these students will choose not to work for existing businesses or nonprofit organizations; instead, they will decide to become entrepreneurs by forming their own businesses.

The risks are considerable. Of the hundreds of thousands of new businesses started each year, 30 percent fail within the first year, and half within two years. The desire to increase the odds of success has prompted a growing number of academic institutions to establish specialized programs in entrepreneurial studies. One such program is located at the University of Southern California, and it was there that Robert A. Schwartz decided to enroll.

Schwartz was not a potential entrepreneur: he already owned a small business and had made enough mistakes to realize that the USC courses should help him turn his shaky venture into a viable one. His first pizzeria had been opened in nearby Van Nuys and he immediately violated the first principle of real estate: "location, location, location." Schwartz had based his budget on a monthly sales forecast of $20,000, but it took him the first six months to reach $10,000 a month in sales.

The USC entrepreneurial studies program is interdisciplinary in nature and is headed by marketing professor Richard H. Buskirk. Among the areas of emphasis in the program is the need for a business plan. As Professor Buskirk puts it, "I read very well, but I don't hear so good." The business plan helps all types of organizations, from start-up businesses to well-established firms, focus their entire operations. It adds realism to entrepreneurial dreams by forcing the would-be business leader to match a good concept to a market. Buskirk and his colleagues teach that a good plan defines the potential market and forces the entrepreneur to seriously consider whether a need exists for the product or service. It also covers channels of distribution, sets a price, and focuses on five-year costs and a financing method, with several alternate financing sources. For start-up firms, a thorough business plan is essential to secure financing. As Charles Kosmont of the venture capital financing firm Princeton/Montrose Partners puts it, "[the business plan] forces entrepreneurs to think through the marketing plan, make financial projections, see how much cash they'll need, whether the market is out there."

Schwartz listened, and put the advice to use. After graduating from the program, he opened Pizza Hop, a new pizzeria within a mile of two universities attended by 35,000 students. He defined his target market as younger adults between the ages of 18 and 35, but he placed particular emphasis on the college and high school market. He also set up a plan based on his forecasts for sales revenues and expenses.

Part of his marketing plan included personal contacts with members of fraternities and sororities on the nearby campuses to build customer awareness of Pizza Hop. Each sales presentation was augmented with two or three free Pizza Hop pizzas to permit his potential market to sample his product offerings. To stimulate patronage from his target market, Schwartz offered a 10 percent discount if customers came in as a group of four or more.

Delivery service was available to provide Pizza Hop customers with maximum convenience. For the restaurant itself, Schwartz decided on a decor from the 1950s, because it was an era that he felt appealed to everyone. In fact, he later changed the name of his pizzerias to the Flashback Cafe.

Schwartz decided to forego the discount route and price his high-quality pizzas at the top end of the market. "I wanted to price my pizza in the most competitive way, but still be at the top 10 percent . . . I went to other pizzerias in town, took their menus, and took my prices from them, staying at the top of the line."

Schwartz soon discovered the importance of flexibility, of being able to quickly adapt a business plan when environmental factors warrant a change. His annual sales forecast was based on a specified dollar amount of advertising, but failure to obtain a bank loan he expected meant that he had to reduce his advertising outlays, directly impacting sales.

Still, Pizza Hop has been successful. The company has expanded from one store with $60,000 in sales in 1984 to five stores with combined sales of $800,000 in 1987. The company's growth allowed Schwartz and his two new partners to concentrate more on management. Back in 1984 Schwartz had lamented that "it takes 14 to 18 hours a day to keep this place going." Now, instead of doing everything from cleaning and cooking to accounting and advertising—and even delivering pizzas—he has time to devote to the continuing planning and forecasting.

What will the future hold for Pizza Hop? Steve Aminian, one of Schwartz' partners, feels the key to marketplace success is franchising. "We're short-handed and need to sell one of the stores. We plan to make that store our first franchise, and we'll use one of our other stores as a training restaurant, where we'll train all our employees."

By expanding, Pizza Hop is exposing itself to the pizzeria chain wars. The major players in the $8 billion market will spend more than $168 million a year in advertising, with Pizza Hut leading the way at $80 million. But the Pizza Hop entrepreneurs feel they can compete based on their new business plan that includes stressing customer service and maintenance of the previous advertising focus, heavy direct-mail advertising, and door hangers, as well as newspaper ads. While Schwartz won't be delivering free pizza to university sororities and fraternities, students in groups will continue to receive price discounts.

Sources: Pizza industry sales and advertising data from Scott Hume, "Pizza Chains Pile on Ads," *Advertising Age* (January 18, 1988), pp. 6, 93. Quotations from telephone interviews (February 23, 1988).

Questions

1. Relate the Pizza Hop decisions to the steps in the marketing planning process shown in Figure 3.1. Identify two examples in the case that reflect tactical planning. Give an example of strategic planning by Pizza Hop marketers.

2. Recommend an approach to sales forecasting for Pizza Hop marketers.

3. Would the start-up business plan for a firm in an industry such as snack foods have the same essential elements as the business plan for a restaurant such as Pizza Hop?

4. In what ways would you expect the Pizza Hop business plan to change when it begins to open franchised outlets?

5. The success of entirely new products such as Rubik's Cube, Pictionary board game, and the Pet Rock is highly unpredictable. Can a business that depends on a novelty or fad survive if its management has developed a good plan?

COMPUTER APPLICATIONS

The sales forecast is a basic building block for marketing planning. A relatively simple quantitative forecasting technique that is frequently utilized for short-term forecasting during periods of steady growth is called *trend analysis*. This technique involves the extrapolation (or extension) of historical data into a specified future time period. This is accomplished by fitting a trend equation to past data on sales, market share, or earnings and using the equation to estimate a future time period. The equation for trend analysis is

$$Y_c = a + bx$$

where

Y_c = predicted amount of sales, market share, or earnings for the specified time period

a = estimated amount of sales, market share, or earnings at the time period when $x = 0$

b = slope of the trend line, that is, average change in sales, market share, or earnings for each specified time period

x = time period (such as one year) used when forecasts are made

To use the trend analysis equation, the marketer must obtain estimates of a and b. These estimates are calculated from historical data using a technique called *least squares*. The following two equations are used for calculating a and b:

$$a = \frac{\Sigma Y}{n}$$

$$b = \frac{\Sigma xY}{\Sigma x^2}$$

The mathematical symbol Σ means "the sum of." The variable n refers to the total number of time periods.

Consider the following example. A small mail-order firm specializing in novelty items is seeking to forecast sales for next year. The firm's president feels that trend extension is an appropriate forecasting technique because of the relatively stable growth in company sales and the forecast's short-term nature. To calculate the needed data for the trend analysis equation, she has created the following table, beginning with a listing of annual sales for each year since the firm's establishment nine years ago:

n Time Period	Y Sales (Thousands of Dollars)	x	xY	x^2
1	100	−4	−400	16
2	112	−3	−336	9
3	130	−2	−260	4
4	160	−1	−160	1
5	205	0	0	0
6	210	1	210	1
7	240	2	480	4
8	280	3	840	9
9	325	4	1300	16
	$1,762		1,674	60

Since the firm has been operating for an odd number of years, the mid-year of Year 5 is coded 0. The years prior to Year 5 are coded -1, -2, and so on. The years following Year 5 are coded with positive 1, 2, and so on. If the data involve an even number of observations, the two mid-years are coded -1 and $+1$. The prior years are then coded in increments of -2 (-3, -5, -7, and so on); all years following the mid-years are coded in increments of $+2$ ($+3$, $+5$, $+7$, and so on). The analysis is completed by calculating ΣxY, Σx^2, and n. The first two values are determined by totaling the two columns labeled xY and x^2. Since the number of time periods included in this example is 9, the value of n is 9. The calculated values for a and b are:

$$a = \frac{1{,}762}{9} = 195.8$$

$$b = \frac{1{,}674}{60} = 27.9$$

Therefore, the trend line for this example is

$$Y_c = a + bx$$
$$= 195.8 + 27.9x$$

To forecast next year's sales for the mail-order firm, it is necessary to count from the Year 5 center value. Since the value for Year 9 is 4, the value for next year (Year 10) would be 5. The forecast is then made by substituting the value of 5 for x in the formula:

$$\text{Annual Sales Forecast for Next Year} = 195.8 + 27.9(5)$$
$$= 335.3$$
$$= \$335{,}300.$$

Directions: Use menu item 3 titled "Sales Forecasting" to solve each of the following problems.

Problem 1   Total annual sales for each of the last seven years for a videocassette rental chain based in Evansville, Indiana, are shown below. Forecast sales for next year using the trend extension method.

Year 1	$ 1,000,000
Year 2	3,000,000
Year 3	6,000,000
Year 4	10,000,000
Year 5	11,000,000
Year 6	13,000,000
Year 7	14,000,000

Problem 2   Career Path, a newly designed board game, was introduced eight months ago. Its sales have continued to grow each month even though it carries a healthy price tag of $32. Moreover, there appears to be no seasonal variation in sales. Monthly unit sales of the product are as follows:

August	14,000
September	16,000
October	23,000
November	24,000
December	28,000
January	29,000
February	33,000
March	36,000

How many unit sales of Career Path would you estimate for April? For May?

Problem 3   During the first year of operation for Garden State University, enrollment totaled 1,200 students. The following year's enrollment grew to 2,100, and by the third year 2,800 students attended the university. Fourth-year enrollments totaled 4,200 students and the growth continued. A total of 4,400 students attended GSU in Year 5, 4,500 in Year 6, 4,800 in Year 7, 5,400 in Year 8, and 6,000 in Year 9. Use the trend extension method to estimate Garden State University enrollments for each of the next two years.

Problem 4   The establishment of a "Birthday Surprise from Home" operation at Ohio State University has proven a market success for its founder, junior marketing major Nancy Wilkes. A direct-mail brochure was prepared and mailed to the parents of each on-campus OSU student offering to personally deliver a birthday cake, complete with a song and a personal message from the parents, on the student's birthday for $20. During the first seven months of operation, Nancy's part-time business has generated the following revenue:

September	$6,400
October	6,800
November	7,000
December	5,600
January	7,200
February	7,200
March	7,400

Forecast revenue for April using the trend extension method.

Problem 5   Ed Smithson set up "Quick Change Artist" (an automobile lubrication service) eight years ago. Since then his sales have grown rapidly. Annual sales revenues have been:

Year 1	$ 46,000
Year 2	78,000
Year 3	120,000
Year 4	132,000
Year 5	156,000
Year 6	190,000
Year 7	230,000
Year 8	278,000

Forecast "Quick Change Artist" revenues for each of the next two years.

APPENDIX

Developing a Marketing Plan

The natural outgrowth of the marketing planning process is a *marketing plan*—a detailed description of resources and actions necessary for achieving stated marketing objectives. Once this plan is formulated and implemented, it may be evaluated periodically to determine its success in moving the organization toward its stated objectives.[24]

Although the format, length, and focus of marketing plans may vary, they typically focus on identifying answers to the following three questions:

☐   Where are we now?

☐   Where do we want to go?

☐   How can we get there?

The following outline illustrates how marketing plans provide answers to each of these questions. The format may be used in a manufacturing, wholesale, retail, or service setting.

Components of the Marketing Plan

I. **Situation Analysis:** Where are we now?
   A. *Historical Background*
      ☐ Nature of the firm, sales and profit history, and current situation.
   B. *Consumer Analysis*
      ☐ Who are the customers this firm is attempting to serve?
      ☐ What segments exist?
      ☐ How many consumers are there?
      ☐ How much do they buy, and why?
   C. *Competitive Analysis*
      ☐ Given the nature of the markets—size, characteristics, competitive activities, and strategies—what marketing opportunities exist for this firm?

II. **Marketing Objectives:** Where do we want to go?
   A. *Sales Objectives*
      ☐ What level of sales volume can we achieve during the next year? During the next five years?
   B. *Profit Objectives*
      ☐ Given the firm's sales level and cost structure, what level of profits should it achieve?
   C. *Consumer Objectives*
      ☐ How will we serve our target market customers?
      ☐ What do we want present and potential customers to think about our firm?

III. **Strategy:** How can we get there?
   A. *Product/Service Strategy*
      ☐ What goods and services should we offer to meet consumers' needs?
      ☐ What is their exact nature?

B. *Pricing Strategy*
  ▫ What level of prices should be used?
  ▫ What specific prices and price concessions are appropriate?
C. *Distribution Strategy*
  ▫ What channel(s) will be used in distributing our product/service offerings?
  ▫ What physical distribution facilities are needed?
  ▫ Where should they be located?
  ▫ What should be their major characteristics?
D. *Promotional Strategy*
  ▫ What mix of personal selling, advertising, and sales promotional activities is needed?
  ▫ How much should be spent using what themes and what media?
E. *Financial Strategy*
  ▫ What will be the financial impact of this plan on a one-year pro forma (projected) income statement?
  ▫ How does projected income compare with revenue expected if we do not implement the plan?

Sample Marketing Plan

The following excerpts from a marketing plan prepared for a large motel, the Driftwood Inn, illustrate the value of such a plan in directing the organization's pursuit of its objectives.

Driftwood Inn Objectives

I. Short Term: 1990
  A. *Sales Objectives*
    To experience an increase in food sales of 100 percent through increased awareness of the Driftwood Inn restaurant and changing consumer attitudes toward motel restaurants—especially the Driftwood Inn restaurant.

Basic Marketing Strategy Statement

I. Lodging
  A. Increase occupancy during seasonal and weekend "slack" periods through development and promotion of special "holiday packages."
  B. Attract participants and spectators to special events through direct mailing of promotional literature where names and addresses are available.

II. Food
  A. Develop an identity and image for the restaurant that are separate and distinct from the Driftwood Inn motel by (1) choosing a new name for the dining facilities, (2) developing a new menu, and (3) making minor changes in decor to create a distinctive dining atmosphere.
  B. Create awareness of the changes in the restaurant among local residents as well as motel guests by developing a complete

promotional campaign and improving in-house promotions (such as lobby signs and promotional "tents" in rooms).

C. Attract civic-group luncheons and rehearsal dinners through price dealing and personal selling.

III. Beverage

A. Develop an atmosphere in the lounge that will complement and extend the restaurant image.

B. Improve awareness of the lounge among local residents through an advertising campaign.

Situation Analysis

I. General Market: Lodging, Food, and Beverage

Table 1 shows the total sales for lodging and eating places between 1986 and 1989 in Baytown and the Driftwood Inn's share of this market. The figures indicate that while total city sales increased 20 percent, the Driftwood Inn's sales increased only 15 percent.

Year	Baytown	Driftwood Inn	Market Share
1986	$12,088,017	$620,740	5.14%
1987	11,537,122	690,552	5.98
1988	12,471,294	711,921	5.70
1989	14,555,443	715,043	4.91

Table 1
Driftwood Inn's Share of Baytown Area Market for Lodging and Food by Year (1986–1989)

II. Lodging

A breakdown of lodging sales for Baytown and Driftwood Inn is shown in Table 2. The last column indicates the Inn's market share. Although the Inn's lodging sales have increased substantially during the 1986–1989 period, its market share has fallen. This is due to an increase in total area lodging sales and increased competition. It is worthwhile to note that the Inn's market share fell to 13 percent between 1988 and 1989. The Inn's sales fell slightly more than 2 percent in those two years, while area lodging sales rose more than 17 percent.

Year	Baytown	Driftwood Inn	Market Share
1986	$2,677,086	$401,556	14.99%
1987	2,604,772	467,829	17.96
1988	3,024,437	489,128	16.15
1989	3,547,427	476,604	13.44

Table 2
Driftwood Inn's Share of the Baytown Lodging Market by Year (1986–1989)

III. Food Sales

Table 3 presents a comparison of Washington County, Baytown, and Driftwood Inn food sales. The last two columns represent the restaurant's respective market shares. During the 1986–1989 period, county sales increased almost 38 percent; city sales 17 percent; and the Inn's food sales only 9 percent. New competitors are one possible explanation for these losses of market share.

Table 3
Driftwood Inn's Share of the Washington County and Baytown Food Market by Year (1986–1989)

Year	Washington County	Baytown	Driftwood Inn	Market Share for Washington County	Market Share for Baytown
1986	$10,172,610	$ 9,410,931	$219,184	2.1%	2.3%
1987	11,273,462	8,932,350	222,723	1.9	2.4
1988	12,215,053	9,446,857	222,793	1.8	2.3
1989	13,994,611	11,008,016	238,439	1.7	2.1

IV. Beverage

No sales data for beverages (liquor) are available for a trend comparison on a state, county, or city level.

Consumer Analysis

I. Lodging

Generally, the lodging market can be broadly divided into the segments shown in the market grid in Table 4.

Table 4
Driftwood Inn Lodging Market

	Individuals or Couples	Groups
Business	Salespeople Management personnel Special events On-premises business	Conventions Seminars, workshops Union negotiations National guard
Nonbusiness	Vacationers Military Moving through, in, or out	Tour groups Party groups Sports groups Reunions

These distinct groups of potential customers represent the market that the Driftwood Inn must attract. The basic consumer characteristics most appropriate for analyzing the lodging market are the nature of the person's stay (business or nonbusiness) and the number of persons staying (individuals and couples or groups). Individuals on business might include salespeople on regular routes, management personnel on special supervisory trips, or people who wish to do business on a temporary basis from their rooms. Groups whose stay might be of a business nature include persons attending conventions, company seminars, and the like (see Table 5).

	Individuals or Couples	Groups
Guests	Vacationers Salespeople Family visits Relocation	Tour groups Conventions Sports groups Military
Nonguests	"Nights out" Special occasions Regular buffets Transients	Tour groups Business meetings Rehearsal dinners Receptions Civic groups

Table 5
Driftwood Inn Food-Service
Market

Food sales may be derived from the public or private dining facilities. An analysis showed that although total food sales increased somewhat in recent years, the growth in food sales revenues was not sufficient to maintain the Inn's market share. Revenues from private dining are derived from three basic sources: wedding rehearsal dinners, wedding receptions, and civic-group luncheons. The potential revenues from these three sources are estimated at over $50,000 annually. The Driftwood Inn appears to have captured a large share of this market, but management recognizes that there are a limited number of competitors for the private dining market. It is believed that little marketing effort has been directed toward local civic organizations, which are important potential customers.

Assignment

Use the format described in this appendix to develop a marketing plan for one of the following:

a. Local retailer

b. Local service provider

c. Local shopping center

d. Nonprofit organization

e. College or university

4

Marketing Research and Information Systems

Chapter Objectives

1. To describe the development and current status of the marketing research function.

2. To list the steps in the marketing research process.

3. To differentiate the types and sources of primary and secondary data.

4. To identify the methods of collecting survey data.

5. To explain the various sampling techniques.

6. To describe a marketing information system and distinguish it from marketing research.

When New Zealand and California kiwifruit was introduced in the United States, the industry turned to Safeway Scanner Marketing Research Services (SMRS), a division of Safeway Stores, for help in planning its advertising and merchandising. SMRS operates an optical scanner checkout network in Safeway stores. SMRS has developed its own techniques for answering questions such as:

□ What effect does in-store sampling have on sales, and for how long?

□ What happens to unit sales when the price is changed?

□ What is the most effective in-store display for a product?

□ How do multi-item displays perform in comparison to single-item displays?

□ Are there any sales benefits from using shelf-dividers or sloped shelving?

After a series of in-store tests, SMRS told the kiwifruit producers to use an additional produce department display and cut the price. It also advised them to implement an advertising program. The net result of these actions was that weekly kiwifruit sales went from 25 to 450 in the average store.

In another instance, SMRS was able to help a snack-food manufacturer with a product identity crisis. The manufacturer's marketing strategy called for the items to be sold

as a health product. However, in-store tests showed that consumers thought it should be located in the snack-food section.[1]

Both of the above situations illustrate the types of problems that marketing research is used to solve.

Photo source: Courtesy of California Kiwifruit Commission.

Chapter Overview

All marketing management decisions depend on the type, quantity, and quality of the information on which they are based. A variety of sources for decision-oriented marketing data needs exist. Some are well-planned investigations designed to elicit specific information. Other valuable information may be obtained from sales force reports, accounting data, and published reports. Still other information may be obtained from controlled experiments and computer simulations.

marketing research
Information function that links the
marketer and the marketplace.

A major source of information for marketing planning takes the form of marketing research. The American Marketing Association defines **marketing research** as follows:

Marketing research is the function which links the consumer, customer, and public to the marketer through information—information used to identify and define marketing opportunities and problems; generate, refine, and evaluate marketing actions; monitor marketing performance; and improve understanding of marketing as a process.

Marketing research specifies the information required to address these issues; designs the method for collecting information; manages and implements the data collection process; analyzes the results; and communicates the findings and their implications.[2]

The critical task of the marketing manager is decision making. Managers must make effective decisions that will enable their firms to solve problems as they arise and must anticipate and prevent future problems. Often, however, managers are forced to make decisions lacking sufficient information. Marketing research aids the decision maker by presenting pertinent facts, analyzing them, and suggesting possible action.

This chapter deals with the marketing research function. Marketing research is closely linked with the other elements of the marketing planning process. All marketing research should be done within the framework of the organization's strategic plan. Research projects should be directed toward the resolution of marketing decisions that conform to an overall corporate plan. The marketing research director for The Singer Company once estimated that research costs 50 to 60 percent more for firms that lack a strategic marketing plan because too much useless information is collected.[3]

Much of the material on marketing planning and forecasting in Chapter 3 and on market segmentation in Chapter 7 is based on information collected as a result of marketing research. Clearly the marketing research function is the primary source of the information needed for making effective marketing decisions.

A Perspective of the Marketing Research Function

Before looking at how marketing research is actually done, it is important to get an overall perspective of the field. What activities are considered part of the marketing research function? How did the field develop? Who is involved in marketing research?

Marketing Research Activities

All marketing decision areas are candidates for marketing research investigations. Marketing research efforts most often focus on determining market potential, market share, and market characteristics. Marketers conduct research to analyze sales and competitors' products, to gauge the performance of existing products and acceptance of new products and package designs, and to develop promotional campaigns. Marketing research resulted in an advertising campaign for Timberland shoes that stresses reliability and durability rather than glamour (see Figure 4.1). In recent years, the shoes have become a fashion

Figure 4.1
Advertising Resulting from Marketing Research

Source: Courtesy of The Timberland Company.

item. But marketing research indicated that consumers bought the shoes because they were durable and improved with age. Based on these findings, the ads for Timberland shoes emphasize how long consumers can expect to wear them rather than promoting them as fashion accessories.[4]

Development of the Marketing Research Function

Marketing research is a relatively new field. More than a hundred years have passed since N. W. Ayer conducted the first organized research project in 1879. A second important milestone in the development of marketing research occurred in 1911 when Charles C. Parlin organized and became manager of the nation's first commercial research department at Curtis Publishing Company.

Parlin actually got his start as a marketing researcher by counting soup cans in Philadelphia's garbage! Parlin was employed as a sales representative for advertising space in the *Saturday Evening Post*. He had failed to sell advertising space to Campbell Soup Company because the firm believed that the magazine reached primarily working-class readers who made their own soup rather than spending 10 cents for a can of prepared soup. Campbell was targeting its product at higher-income people who could afford to pay for convenience. So Parlin began counting the soup cans in the garbage of different neighborhoods. To Campbell's surprise, Parlin's research revealed that more canned soup was sold to the working class than to the wealthy, who had servants to make soup for them. Campbell's soup quickly became a *Saturday Evening Post* client.[5]

Much of the early research represented little more than written testimonials received from purchasers of firms' products. Research became more sophisticated during the 1930s as the development of statistical techniques led to refinements in sampling procedures and greater accuracy in research findings. However, mistakes still occurred. The *Literary Digest* conducted a major national study of U.S. households selected at random from lists of telephone numbers and auto registration records and reported that Alf Landon, not Franklin D. Roosevelt, would be elected president in 1936. The fiasco resulted from the magazine's failure to realize that many voters (most of whom apparently were Democrats) had neither telephones nor automobiles in the midst of the Great Depression.

In recent years, advances in computer technology have changed the complexion of marketing research. Computers not only have accelerated the pace and broadened the base of collecting data; they also have enabled marketers to make informed decisions about problems and opportunities. Computer simulations, for example, allow marketers to evaluate decision alternatives by posing a number of "what-if" questions. Marketing researchers at many consumer goods firms simulate product introductions on computers to help them decide whether to risk a real-world product launch or even subject a product to test marketing. Kraft used a computer simulation before test marketing its Makin' Cajun line of dinner kits and ingredients, and Sara Lee used a simulation before launching its line of frozen Hearty Fruit Muffins.[6]

While high-tech marketing research is common in many medium-size and large firms, smaller companies also find innovative—albeit less sophisticated—ways to research their markets. For example, one car dealer who provides free taxi service to customers dropping off their cars for repair uses a unique marketing research approach: Twice a year the dealer throws a big dinner for the cabdrivers and pumps them for information about customers' comments on the repair service.[7]

Participants in the Marketing Research Function

According to the American Marketing Association, 87 percent of the nation's leading manufacturing firms have a formal marketing research department. Most of these firms market consumer products; however, an increasing number of other firms, such as banks, savings institutions, and insurance companies, and nonprofit organizations are forming marketing research departments. Many smaller firms depend on independent marketing research firms to conduct their research studies. Even large firms typically rely on outside agencies to provide interviews, and they often contract out some research studies to independent agencies as well. The decision of whether to conduct a study through an outside organization or internally is usually based on cost. Another major consideration is the reliability and accuracy of the information collected by an outside organization.

Research is likely to be contracted to outside groups when the following requirements are met:

1. Problem areas can be defined in terms of specific research projects.
2. There is a need for specialized know-how or equipment.
3. Intellectual detachment is needed.[8]

A marketing research firm often is able to provide technical assistance and expertise not available within the firm. Also, the use of outside groups helps ensure that the particular researcher is not conducting the study only to validate the wisdom of a favorite personal theory or a preferred package design. A survey of marketing research by the American Marketing Association revealed that almost one-half of the total marketing research budgets of the responding firms is spent on outside research.

More than 1,000 independent marketing research companies are currently operating in the United States. These range in size from single owners/managers to giant firms such as A. C. Nielsen, IMS International, SAMI/Burke, and Arbitron Ratings Co., each of which generates more than $100 million annually in research revenues. In 1986, total worldwide revenues of 46 leading U.S. marketing research firms were $1.9 billion.[9]

Marketing research companies can be classified as either syndicated services, full-service suppliers, or limited-service suppliers depending on their primary thrust.[10] (However, a full-service organization might be willing to take on a limited-function activity under certain circumstances.)

Syndicated Services   An organization that provides a standardized set of data on a regular basis to all customers is called a *syndicated service.* Mediamark Research, for example, operates a syndicated product research service based on personal interviews with 20,000 adults each year regarding their exposure to advertising media. Clients include advertisers, advertising agencies, magazines, newspapers, broadcasters, and cable networks.

One of the most unique syndicated services is the Brown Bag Institute, a firm that offers quarterly data on the buying habits of people who take their lunches to school or work. Some 80 million people brown-bag it at least part of the time. Approximately 10.7 billion brown-bag meals worth $15 billion are consumed annually. The service, based on 1,000 quarterly telephone interviews, is used by such firms as Aladdin Industries (lunch boxes and thermos bottles), Beatrice Foods, and Oscar Mayer (luncheon meats).

Full-Service Research Suppliers   An organization that contracts with a client to conduct a complete marketing research project is called a *full-service research supplier.* J. D. Power & Associates is a full-service firm that specializes in the domestic and international automotive markets. Full-service suppliers become the client's marketing research arm, performing all the steps in the marketing research process (discussed in the next section).

Limited-Service Research Suppliers   A marketing research firm that specializes in a limited number of activities, such as providing field interviews or data processing services, is called a *limited-service research supplier.* Working almost exclusively for clients in the movie industry, National Research Group specializes in appraising entertainment facilities with audiences of from 100 to

THE COMPETITIVE EDGE

Rubbermaid

"Research is always incomplete." While Rubbermaid probably doesn't know that the obscure eighteenth-century figure Mark Pattison said this, it might as well be the company credo, for Rubbermaid researches like a cloned mad scientist. Rubbermaid never test markets in order to keep new-product ideas safe from competitors. Yet it still achieves a fantastic 90 percent success rate for new products.

Rubbermaid doesn't come by this success through the release of one or two "can't-miss" products a year. Instead, it churns out a spate of products—over 100 a year—to meet its corporate goal of having 30 percent of sales come from products introduced within five years. What would seem worse for sales is Rubbermaid's product mix—humdrum household items such as dish racks and garbage containers.

Rubbermaid's tripling of sales and quadrupling of earnings over the last seven years is remarkable, especially considering that it operates in a mature market and faces intense competition from almost 150 other companies, most of which price below Rubbermaid. The company's continued growth prompted one investment observer to remark, "Rubbermaid is the best argument I've ever seen in my life that American business can be competitive."

How does Rubbermaid achieve its phenomenal success rate? Says current chairman Stanley Gault, "Our formula for success is very open: We watch the market, and we work at it 24 hours a day."

Watching the market includes keeping in touch with customers to

find out which product features they like and which they would like to see added. This kind of consumer research gave Rubbermaid the impetus to release a compact, one-piece dish drainer to meet the needs of apartment dwellers, a growing market segment.

Rubbermaid also conducts numerous focus group interviews. For example, it maintains consumer focus groups on color preferences in six cities throughout the year. For projectability, it then verifies their choices with a larger sample by going to shopping malls to conduct random quizzes.

Rubbermaid doesn't test market, but it does directly monitor consumer response. After it purchased Little Tikes, a small toy company, it infused the existing product line with new toys. But before these were released, Little Tikes researchers observed children in a test lab while they played with the toys and then asked for suggestions. And before its

recent release of a highly successful line of molded patio furniture, Rubbermaid sat on the idea for almost seven years, studying its manufacture, market, and distribution.

Rubbermaid researches obsessively. Company managers often arrive at work by 7 a.m., and 11-hour workdays are common. They spend a lot of their time studying the data generated by user panels, brand awareness studies, and consumer diaries detailing product usage. They also pay close attention to consumer letters, particularly because Rubbermaid is so well known that it often gets complaints from people who have purchased a competitor's product but assume it's Rubbermaid. Rubbermaid never misses the opportunity to do a direct-mail plug for its own product.

Source: Alex Taylor III, "Why the Bounce at Rubbermaid?" *Fortune* (April 13, 1987), pp. 77–78. *Photo Source:* © Andy Freeberg for Rubbermaid Incorporated. Reprinted with permission.

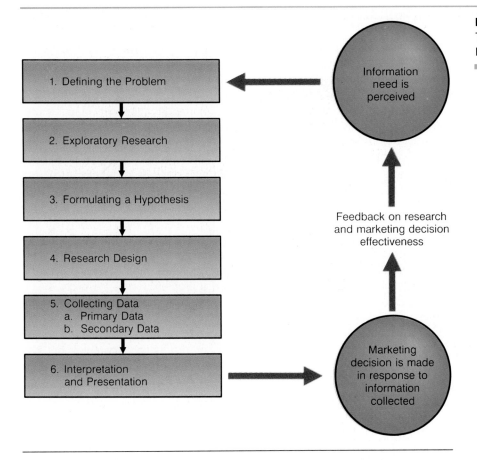

Figure 4.2
The Marketing
Research Process

400 moviegoers, preparing studies for developing advertising strategies, and tracking for awareness and interest. Syndicated services can also be considered limited-service research suppliers.

The Marketing Research Process

How is marketing research actually conducted? The starting point, of course, is the need for information with which to make a marketing decision. For example, a firm that makes frozen pizza would perceive an information need when the product's market share dropped from 25 to 18 percent in six months. Information is needed before the firm can decide what to do to reverse that decline. An information need can relate to a specific marketing decision or an ongoing set of decisions. When an information need is perceived, the marketing research process can be used to produce the needed marketing knowledge.

The marketing research process can be divided into six specific steps: (1) defining the problem; (2) exploratory research; (3) formulating a hypothesis; (4) research design; (5) collecting data; and (6) interpretation and presentation. Figure 4.2 diagrams the marketing research process from the information need to the research-based decision.

Problem Definition

Someone once remarked that well-defined problems are half solved. Problems are barriers that prevent the attainment of organizational goals. A clearly defined problem permits the researcher to focus the research process on securing the data necessary for solving the problem.

Sometimes it is easy to pinpoint problems. A computer manufacturer wanted to learn why owners of businesses with sales ranging from $2 million to $5 million were not buying its products. The firm believed this group represented ideal potential customers. But after interviewing a group of small-business owners, the firm quickly realized it had misjudged its target market. These people were not technologically sophisticated as the company had assumed. They were not buying the computers because they did not understand how they worked and were afraid of them.[11]

In most cases, however, defining a problem is far more difficult. Researchers must not confuse symptoms with the problem itself. A symptom merely alerts marketers that a problem exists. Symptoms are often obvious; for example, a falling market share is a symptom of a problem facing the pizza maker mentioned earlier. To define its problem, the firm must look for underlying causes of market share loss. A logical starting point would be the firm's marketing mix elements and target market. Suppose that the pizza maker has made no recent changes in its product, pricing, or distribution strategies but has adopted a new promotional strategy. A close look at the promotional strategy may reveal the source of the problem. Or perhaps the problem stems from the external environment in the form of new competitors entering the market with superior products and lower prices. The possible causes of problems are further explored in the next step of the marketing research process—exploratory research.

Exploratory Research

exploratory research
Process of discussing a marketing problem with informed sources within the firm as well as outside sources such as wholesalers, retailers, and customers and examining secondary sources of information.

Searching for the cause of a problem allows the researcher to learn about the problem area and to focus on specific areas for study in seeking solutions. This search, often called **exploratory research,** consists of discussing the problem with informed sources within the firm and with wholesalers, retailers, customers, and others outside the firm and examining secondary sources of information. Marketing researchers often refer to internal data collection as the *situation analysis* and to exploratory interviews with informed persons outside the firm as the *informal investigation.* Exploratory research also involves evaluating company records, such as sales and profit analyses, and the sales and profits of competitors' products.

Using Internal Data

An organization's sales records contain valuable sources of information. Analysis of these records should provide a basis for obtaining an overall view of company efficiency and a clue to the problem under investigation.

The basis for analyzing internal data is traditional accounting data provided by the accounting department and usually summarized on the firm's financial statements. Table 4.1 shows a simplified income statement.

Sales		$ 57,830,000
Cost of goods sold		− 32,910,000
Gross margin		$ 24,920,000
Expenses:		
Selling expenses	$7,530,000	
Other expenses	3,010,000	− 10,540,000
Profit before taxes		$ 14,380,000
Income taxes		− 7,190,000
Profit after taxes		$ 7,190,000

Table 4.1
Income Statement for Venture Company for the Year Ended December 31, 198X

District	Average Salary	Average Expenses	Average Sales Costs	Average Sales	Cost/ Sales Ratio
1	$33,600	$10,400	$44,000	$654,000	6.7%
2	31,900	12,800	44,700	534,000	8.4
3	37,200	13,100	50,300	790,000	6.4
4	35,200	12,300	48,000	380,000	12.6
5	34,200	11,700	35,900	580,000	7.9

Table 4.2
Sales and Expense Analysis of Selected Districts

Basic financial statements often are too broad to be useful in marketing analysis. Where nondetailed accounts are used, their main contribution is that of assisting the analyst in raising more specific questions. The income statement in Table 4.1 shows that the company earned a profit for the period involved and that selling expenses represented approximately 13 percent of sales:

$$\text{Cost/Sales Ratio} = \frac{\$7,530,000}{\$57,830,000} = 13\%.$$

Comparison of the 13 percent selling expense to sales ratio with previous years may hint at possible problems, but it will not specifically reveal the cause of the variation. To discover the cause, a more detailed breakdown is necessary.

Sales Analysis   Table 4.2 shows a typical breakdown of sales by territory. This kind of breakdown becomes part of an overall sales analysis. The purpose of the **sales analysis**—the in-depth evaluation of a firm's sales—is to obtain meaningful information from the accounting data.

Easily prepared from company invoices stored on computer tapes, the sales analysis can be quite revealing for the marketing executive. As Table 4.2 shows, the sales force in District 4 has a much higher cost/sales ratio than the sales forces in other districts.

In order to evaluate the performance of the salespersons in the five selected districts, the marketing executive must have a standard of comparison. District 4, for example, may be a large territory with relatively few industrial centers. Consequently, the costs involved in obtaining sales will be higher than for other districts.

The standard by which actual and expected sales are compared typically results from a detailed sales forecast by territory, product, customer, and sales-

sales analysis
In-depth evaluation of a firm's sales.

Table 4.3

Sales Breakdown of Selected Sales Representatives in District 4

Salesperson	Quota	Actual	Performance to Quota
Holtzman	$ 336,000	$ 382,000	114%
Thompson	428,000	453,000	106
Shapiro	318,000	325,000	102
Chandler	446,000	360,000	81
Total	$1,528,000	$1,520,000	

sales quota
Level of expected sales against which actual results are compared.

iceberg principle
Theory suggesting that collected data in summary form often obscure important evaluative information.

marketing cost analysis
Evaluation of such items as selling costs, billing, and advertising to determine the profitability of particular customers, territories, or product lines.

person. Once the **sales quota**—the level of expected sales by which actual results are compared—has been established, it is a simple process to compare the actual results with the expected performance.

Table 4.3 compares actual sales with the quota established for salespersons in District 4. Although Shapiro had the smallest amount of sales for the period, her performance was better than expected. However, the district sales manager should investigate Chandler's performance, since it represented only 81 percent of quota.

The performance of the salespersons in District 4 provides a good illustration of the **iceberg principle,** which suggests that important evaluative information is often hidden by aggregate data. The tip of the iceberg represents only one-tenth of its total size; the remaining nine-tenths lies hidden beneath the surface of the water. Summaries of data are useful, but the marketing researcher must be careful that they do not actually conceal more than they reveal. Had the sales breakdown by salesperson for the district not been available, Chandler's poor sales might have been partially concealed by the good sales performances of the others.

Other possible breakdowns for sales analysis include customer type, product, method of sale (mail, telephone, or personal contact), type of order (cash or credit), and size of order. Sales analysis is one of the least expensive and most important sources of marketing information.

Marketing Cost Analysis   A second source of internal information is **marketing cost analysis**—the evaluation of such items as selling costs, warehousing, advertising, and delivery expenses in order to determine the profitability of particular customers, territories, or product lines.

Marketing cost analysis requires a new way of classifying accounting data. *Functional accounts* must be established to replace the traditional natural accounts used in financial statements. These traditional accounts, such as salary, must be reallocated to the purpose for which the expenditure was made. A portion of the original salary account, for example, will be allocated to selling, inventory control, storage, advertising, and other marketing costs. In the same manner, an account such as supply expenses will be allocated to the functions that utilize supplies.

The costs allocated to the functional accounts will equal those in the natural accounts. But instead of showing only total profitability, they can show the profitability of, say, particular territories, products, customers, salespersons, and order sizes. The most common reallocations are to products, customers, and territories or districts. The marketing decision maker can then evaluate the

Table 4.4
Allocation of Marketing Costs

Marketing Costs	By Customer		By District		
	Large	Small	A	B	C
Advertising	$140,000	$ 300,000	$200,000	$100,000	$140,000
Selling	520,000	620,000	380,000	380,000	380,000
Physical distribution	330,000	260,000	280,000	140,000	170,000
Credit	4,000	26,000	16,000	6,000	8,000
Total	$994,000	$1,206,000	$876,000	$626,000	$698,000

Table 4.5
Income Statement for Districts A, B, and C

	District			
	A	B	C	Total
Sales	$2,600,000	$2,000,000	$1,910,000	$6,510,000
Cost of sales	1,750,000	1,350,000	1,200,000	4,300,000
Gross margin	850,000	650,000	710,000	2,210,000
Marketing expenses	876,000	626,000	698,000	2,100,000
Contribution of each territory	$ (26,000)	$ 24,000	$ 12,000	$ 10,000

profitability of particular customers and districts on the basis of the sales produced and the costs incurred in generating them. Table 4.4 shows how such cost reallocations can be made.

Table 4.5 indicates that District B is the most profitable region and District A the least. Attention can now be given to plans for increasing sales or reducing expenses in this problem district to make market coverage of the area a profitable undertaking.

Formulating Hypotheses

After the problem has been defined and an exploratory investigation conducted, the marketer should be able to formulate a hypothesis—a tentative explanation for some specific event. A **hypothesis** is a statement about the relationship among variables and carries clear implications for testing this relationship.

A marketer of industrial products might formulate the following hypothesis: *Failure to provide 72-hour delivery service will reduce our sales by 20 percent.* Such a statement may prove correct or incorrect. Its formulation, however, provides a basis for investigation and an eventual determination of its accuracy. Also, it allows the researcher to move to the next step: development of the research design.

Fast-food sales generally slump during the first quarter of a year. To stimulate demand and maintain their average price per order, most fast-food restau-

hypothesis
Tentative explanation about some specific event; statement about the relationship among variables, including clear implications for testing it.

Figure 4.3
Use of Two Different
Advertisements to
Test a Hypothesis

Source: Courtesy of Wendy's International, Inc.

rants discount their small-size, lower-priced hamburgers. Wendy's International hypothesized that it could increase sales by offering a "quality" sale, encouraging customers to trade up to buy a bacon cheeseburger. Based on this assumption, Wendy's designed and test marketed two television ads, as shown in Figure 4.3, to determine which one would result in higher sales. The ads targeted heavy fast-food users, mainly male adults aged 18 to 35. While both ads offered consumers the same dollar value, response to the ad on the right, "Only $1.49," was nearly double that of the "Free Bacon" offer.[12]

Research Design

research design
Series of advanced decisions that, when taken together, comprise a master plan or a model for conducting marketing research.

The research design represents a comprehensive plan for testing the hypothesis formulated about the problem. **Research design** refers to a series of decisions that taken together comprise a master plan or model for the conduct of the investigation. Heublein, a marketer of alcoholic beverages, is concerned about the environmental factors that might affect its markets. Therefore, it has set up an environmental monitoring system that scans published data to pick up environmental trends and the like.[13]

Sometimes published data are not enough. In that case, the research design must call for a direct test of a hypothesis. Published data, for example, indicate that people drink diet sodas because they want to control their weight. Ads for Diet Rite, a Royal Crown Cola product, previously focused on low-calorie content, taste, and lower price. But Diet Rite marketers decided they needed ads with an emotional appeal to help distinguish their product from competing Diet Pepsi and Diet Coke. The company interviewed dozens of women dieters and learned that they had poor self-images and felt that dieting was difficult and made them feel more vulnerable. Based on these interviews, Diet Rite decided against commercials showing slim, attractive women in bathing suits, because women with poor self-images do not relate to such models. Instead, the company developed a humorous campaign—one commercial featuring a slightly out-of-shape Tony Danza—that allows viewers to empathize with other dieters who also appear vulnerable.[14]

Data Collection

A major part of research design is determining what data are needed for testing the hypothesis. Data are classified as primary or secondary. **Primary data** refers to data that are collected for the first time during a marketing research study. The Diet Rite interviews with women dieters is an example of primary research. **Secondary data** are previously published matter. They serve as an extremely important source of information for marketing researchers such as those at Heublein.

primary data
Information or statistics collected for the first time during a marketing research study.

secondary data
Previously published data.

Collecting Secondary Data

Secondary data are not only important to the marketing researcher, they are also very abundant. The overwhelming quantity of secondary data available at little or no cost challenges the researcher to select only pertinent secondary data.

Secondary data consist of two types: internal and external. *Internal data* include sales records, product performances, sales force activities, and marketing costs. *External data* are obtained from a variety of sources. Governments—local, state, and federal—provide a wide variety of secondary data, as do private sources.

Use of Databases   Both external and internal data can be obtained from computerized databases. A **database** refers to any collection of data that are retrievable through a computer. A considerable amount of published information is available in this form. Some firms create their own databases that include sales and marketing cost records.

database
Collection of data that are retrievable through a computer.

The three basic types of on-line databases are:

1. Reference databases, which refer to information on a specific topic. Many libraries are equipped with such facilities.

2. Full databases, which produce the complete article being sought.

3. Source databases, which provide detailed information listings. A listing of export trade opportunities is an example.[15]

The growth in popularity of databases has led to an expansion of such services. Widely used commercial on-line database services include Compu-Serve, Data Resources Inc., Dow Jones News/Retrieval, and The Source.

Government Data   The federal government is the nation's most important source of marketing data. The most frequently used government statistics are census data. Although the U.S. government spent more than $1 billion conducting the last Census of Population, census information is available for use at no charge at local libraries, or it can be purchased on computer tapes for

Elaine Winder, an assistant communications specialist for Campbell Company, uses Knight-Ridder's Vu/Text, the world's largest newspaper database, to conduct marketing research on food trends. The database is automatically updated each day and displays articles in full text from 25 newspapers, including the Chicago Tribune, Boston Globe, Miami Herald, *and* Washington Post.

Photo source: Courtesy of Knight-Ridder, Inc.

instantaneous access at a nominal charge. In addition to the Census of Population, the Bureau of the Census conducts a Census of Housing (which is combined with the Census of Population), a Census of Business, a Census of Manufacturers, a Census of Agriculture, a Census of Minerals, and a Census of Governments.

The Census of Population is so detailed that it breaks down population characteristics into very small geographical areas. The 1980 census, for example, broke down population traits by city blocks in large cities. The 1990 census will extend this data breakdown nationwide to include nonmetropolitan areas designated as block-numbering areas (BNAs). The BNAs and census tracts are important for marketing analysis because they show a population with similar traits, unlike that defined by political boundaries such as county lines.[16] Marketers such as local retailers and shopping center developers can easily gather specific information about customers in the immediate neighborhood without spending the time or money to conduct a comprehensive survey.

Of even greater value to marketing researchers is a computerized mapping database that the government plans to complete by 1990. Called *TIGER*—for Topologically Integrated Geographic Encoding & Referencing—the system will combine features such as railroads, highways, and rivers with census data such as household income. Marketers will be able to buy digital tapes of the data from the bureau.[17]

The federal government produces so much information that marketing researchers often purchase summaries such as the *Monthly Catalog of the United States Government Publications,* the *Statistical Abstract of the United States,* the *Survey of Current Business,* and the *County and City Data Book.* Published annually, the *Statistical Abstract* contains a wealth of current data.

Figure 4.4
Delaware Population and Retail Sales Data

DELAWARE

DEL. S&MM ESTIMATES	POPULATION—12/31/86								RETAIL SALES BY STORE GROUP 1986						
METRO AREA County City	Total Population (Thousands)	% Of U.S.	Median Age of Pop.	18–24 Years	25–34 Years	35–49 Years	50 & Over	House-holds (Thousands)	Total Retail Sales ($000)	Food ($000)	Eating & Drinking Places ($000)	General Mdse. ($000)	Furniture/ Furnish./ Appliance ($000)	Auto-motive ($000)	Drug ($000)
WILMINGTON	548.3	.2254	32.2	11.8	17.2	20.1	25.0	195.8	3,660,870	673,915	293,593	505,451	196,627	898,908	114,886
New Castle	413.1	.1698	32.0	12.6	17.3	20.1	24.8	148.3	3,099,561	564,542	247,547	476,213	176,733	753,401	97,751
• Wilmington	70.4	.0289	33.5	10.0	16.5	16.1	31.4	27.6	557,644	50,282	53,822	18,715	28,226	179,478	31,730
Cecil, Md.	67.1	.0276	31.7	9.7	17.1	20.8	23.6	22.8	319,283	57,096	26,025	16,237	7,470	81,565	7,639
Salem, N. J.	68.1	.0280	33.4	9.4	16.1	19.5	28.0	24.7	242,026	52,277	20,021	13,001	12,424	63,942	9,496
SUBURBAN TOTAL	477.9	.1965	32.0	12.1	17.3	20.6	24.2	168.2	3,103,226	623,633	239,771	486,736	168,401	719,430	83,156
OTHER COUNTIES															
Kent	106.3	.0437	30.0	13.1	17.6	20.3	20.8	36.5	687,529	120,742	48,193	103,469	20,921	175,476	18,865
Sussex	110.7	.0455	34.7	9.6	15.7	18.7	30.8	40.8	716,905	145,999	82,484	53,388	40,345	107,732	27,154
TOTAL METRO COUNTIES	413.1	.1698	32.0	12.6	17.3	20.1	24.8	148.3	3,099,561	564,542	247,547	476,213	176,733	753,401	97,751
TOTAL STATE	630.1	.2590	32.1	12.1	17.1	19.9	25.2	225.6	4,503,995	831,283	378,224	633,070	237,999	1,036,609	143,770

Source: Reprinted with permission from *Survey of Buying Power* (July 27, 1987), p. C-36.

The *Survey of Current Business,* updated monthly, focuses on a variety of industrial data. The *County and City Data Book,* typically published every three years, provides a variety of data for each county and each city of over 25,000 residents.

State and city governments serve as other important sources of information on employment, production, and sales activities. In addition, university bureaus of business and economic research often collect and disseminate such information.

Private Data   Many private organizations provide information for the marketing executive. Trade associations are excellent sources of data on activities in a particular industry. Advertising agencies continually collect information on the audiences reached by various media. A wide range of valuable data are found in the annual "Survey of Buying Power" published by *Sales and Marketing Management* magazine. Figure 4.4 illustrates the detailed information the magazine publishes for every county and urban area in the United States.

Several national firms also offer information to businesses on a subscription basis. Information Resources, Inc., one of the largest marketing research firms, offers a national scanning service that tracks consumer purchases of every UPC-coded product sold in supermarkets. Called InfoScan, the system collects sales data from 2,400 supermarkets on a weekly basis and consumer purchasing data from 80,000 households on a daily basis. The system provides marketers with information on promotional conditions that affect consumer purchases by correlating consumer sales with newspaper ads, prices, in-store displays, and coupon redemptions. The integrated store sales and household purchase data give marketers information on their brands' buyers, store loyalty, and general shopping behavior. In addition, InfoScan has developed a PC workstation and special software that allow marketing researchers to analyze InfoScan data in ways that fit their unique information needs.

Strengths and Weaknesses of Secondary Data

The use of secondary data offers two important advantages: (1) Assembly of secondary data is almost always less expensive than collection of primary data, and (2) less time is involved in locating and using secondary data. Completing a research study requiring primary data typically takes about three to four months. Although the time involved in a marketing research study varies considerably depending on such factors as the research subject and the study's scope, an additional time and cost investment is required when primary data are needed.

The researcher, however, must be aware of several potential limitations of secondary data. First, published information can quickly become obsolete. A marketing researcher analyzing the population of the Orlando, Florida, metropolitan market in early 1989 may discover that most of the 1980 census data are obsolete due to the subsequent influx of residents to the area. Second, published data that were collected for a different purpose may not be completely relevant to the marketer's specific needs.

Collecting Primary Data

The marketing researcher has three alternatives in the collection of primary data: observation, survey, or controlled experiment. No single method is best in all circumstances, and any of them may prove the most efficient in a particular situation.

Observation Method Observational studies are conducted by actually viewing the overt actions of the subject. They may take the form of a traffic count at a potential site for a fast-food franchise, the use of supermarket scanners to record sales of certain products, or a check of license plates at a shopping center to determine where shoppers live.

One recent use of the observation method is visiting people's homes to see how they use or consume a product. Breyer's Ice Cream's advertising agency visited six families to observe how they ate ice cream. The researchers concluded that the consumption of ice cream is an inner-directed and sensual activity. This information provided insights for the agency's creative people to use in designing advertisements for Breyer's.[18]

The new technology of "people meters" has changed the way marketing researchers observe television audience viewership. People meters are electronic, remote-control devices that record the viewing habits of each household member. Each person in the household has his or her own button to push to signal television watching. This information is sent overnight, via telephone wire, to the researcher's central computer, providing advertisers with timely and detailed data on audience viewing habits. The viewer information is used to measure a program's success and to set advertising rates. People meters have replaced the ratings system used since the 1950s, in which household meters measured whether a set was on and the channel to which it was tuned and viewers kept diaries of programs watched by each household member.

Survey Method Some information cannot be obtained through observation. The researcher must ask questions to get information on attitudes, motives, and opinions. The most widely used approach to collecting primary data is the sur-

Griffin Williams, a representative of Nielsen Media Research, explains to a family how the Nielsen People Meter works in viewers' homes. This syndicated statistical information service is offered on a subscription basis to advertisers, advertising agencies, and television networks and stations. People Meter data help subscribers buy, sell, plan, and price television time and monitor commericals.

Photo source: © Jeff Jacobson 1987/Archive Pictures and The Dun & Bradstreet Corporation. Used with permission.

vey method, which includes telephone interviews, mail surveys, and personal interviews.

Telephone Interviews. This survey method is inexpensive and quick for obtaining small quantities of relatively impersonal information. Since many firms have leased WATS services (telephone company services that allow businesses to make unlimited long-distance calls for a fixed rate per state or region), the cost of telephone interviewing has decreased. Telephone interviews account for an estimated 55 to 60 percent of all primary marketing research.

Telephone interviews are, however, limited to simple, clearly worded questions. They cannot show respondents a picture of the item under discussion. Also, it is extremely difficult to obtain information on respondents' personal characteristics, and the survey may be prejudiced by the omission of households without phones or with unlisted numbers.

The use of unlisted numbers is commonplace today. It is particularly prevalent among such groups as single women, physicians, and others who do not wish to be disturbed at home. As a result, a number of telephone interviewers have resorted to using digits selected at random and matched to telephone prefixes in the geographical area to be sampled. This technique is designed to correct the difficulty of sampling households with unlisted numbers. However, some states have restricted random dialing, and others have proposed similar restraints. The technological ultimate in telephone interviewing is probably computerized dialing linked with a digitally synthesized voice doing the interviewing.

Mail Surveys. This approach allows the marketing researcher to conduct national studies at a reasonable cost. Whereas the cost of personal interviews with a national sample may be prohibitive, the researcher can contact each potential respondent for the price of a postage stamp. Costs can be misleading, however. For example, returned questionnaires may average only 40 to 50 percent depending on the questionnaire's length and respondents' interest. Some mail surveys even include money to gain the reader's attention, which further increases costs. Unless additional information is obtained from nonrespondents, the results of mail interviews are likely to be biased, since there may be important differences in the characteristics of respondents and nonrespondents. For this reason, follow-up questionnaires are sometimes mailed to respondents or telephone interviews are used to gather additional information.

In April 1990, the U.S. Bureau of the Census will conduct the largest mail survey in history when it mails census questionnaires to 100 million households. The bureau began testing several census questionnaires in 1986 to decide which questions to ask and how to ask them. A major complaint about the 1980 census data was that the figures for whites, blacks, and Hispanics did not add up because Hispanics' answers to race questions varied considerably. To solve this problem, the bureau has redesigned the wording of questions about race and ethnic origin.[19]

Personal Interviews.   This survey method typically is the best means of obtaining detailed information, since the interviewer has the opportunity to establish rapport with each respondent and explain confusing or vague questions. Although mail questionnaires are carefully worded and often pretested to eliminate potential misunderstandings, problems can occur anyway. A university athletic coach described some responses to questionnaires sent to prospective recruits. When asked what he ran the mile in, one respondent wrote, "T-shirt and shorts." In response to a question asking for date of graduation, one athlete replied, "Emmy Lou Watson." And when a questionnaire asked for race, one student replied, "1,500 meters."[20]

Personal interviews are slow and the most expensive method of collecting data. However, their flexibility and the detailed information they can provide often offset these limitations. Recently marketing research firms have rented locations in shopping centers, where they have greater access to potential buyers of the products in which they are interested. Interviews conducted in shopping centers are typically referred to as *mall intercepts.* Downtown retail districts and airports are other on-site locations for marketing research.

Some marketing researchers use computers rather than people to do the interviewing. Although equipment and techniques vary, computer interviews typically use a video-display screen to pose questions, which the interviewee answers by typing responses on a computer keyboard. Interviewing by computer has several advantages over personal interviews. They allow for faster gathering and analysis of data, because the responses are transcribed automatically on a computer disk; the answers given in personal interviews, on the other hand, must be coded for computer tabulation and analysis. Another advantage is that people seem to give more truthful answers to computers than to interviewers, especially when the questions involve disclosing sensitive information. Disadvantages of computer interviews are that they cannot explain misunderstood questions and, unless the interviewee is a good typist, cannot elicit detailed responses.[21]

Focus group interviews are widely used as a means of gathering research information. In a **focus group interview,** eight to twelve individuals are brought together in one location to discuss a subject of interest. Although the moderator typically explains the purpose of the meeting and suggests an opening discus-

focus group interview
Information-gathering procedure in marketing research that typically brings eight to twelve individuals together in one location to discuss a given subject.

Figure 4.5
Advertisement Resulting from
a Focus Group Interview

Source: Courtesy of 3M Commercial Office Supply Division.

sion topic, he or she is interested in stimulating interaction among group members in order to develop discussion of numerous points. Focus group sessions, which are often one or two hours long, are usually taped, allowing the moderator to devote full attention to the discussion, and frequently observed through a one-way mirror. The "yellow-line" advertising approach used by 3M Company to promote its Post-it notes resulted from consumer ideas presented in focus group interviews (see Figure 4.5).[22]

Once used mainly by consumer goods companies, focus groups are now an important research tool for a variety of other organizations. Newspapers and magazines use focus groups to help plan new features and improve graphic design; lawyers use them to test arguments before a trial; and nonprofit organizations use them to develop fund drives and determine how to allocate funds. Benefits of focus group interviews include their immediacy and flexibility. A major limitation is that focus groups are by nature too small to ensure statistical reliability.[23]

Experimental Method   The final and least used method of collecting marketing information is that of controlled experiments. An **experiment** is a scientific investigation in which a researcher controls or manipulates a test group or

experiment
Scientific investigation in which a researcher controls or manipulates a test group(s) and compares these results with those of a group(s) that did not receive the controls or manipulations.

groups and compares the results with that of a control group that did not receive the controls or manipulations. Although such experiments can be conducted in the field or in a laboratory setting, most have been performed in the field. To date, the most common use of this method by marketers has been in test marketing, a topic discussed in Chapter 9.

As Chapter 3 pointed out, marketers often attempt to reduce their risks by *test marketing,* that is, introducing the product or marketing strategy into an area and then observing its degree of success. Marketers usually pick test areas that will reflect what they envision as the market for their product. Seattle was used as a test market for Pepsi Free, because Pepsi outsells Coca-Cola there, and Seattle and Milwaukee share the lead for the highest per capita consumption of diet soft drinks.[24]

The major problem with controlled experiments is controlling all variables in a real-life situation. The laboratory scientist can rigidly control temperature and humidity. But how can the marketing manager determine the effect of, say, reducing the retail price through refundable coupons when the competition simultaneously issues such coupons? Experimentation will become more common as firms develop sophisticated competitive models for computer analysis. Simulation of market activities promises to be one of the great new developments in marketing.

Sampling Techniques

Sampling is one of the most important aspects of marketing research, because it involves the selection of respondents on which conclusions will be based. Figure 4.6 illustrates the importance of sampling in reaching a target market. The total group that the researcher wants to study is called the **population** (or **universe**). For a political campaign, the population would be all eligible voters. For a new cosmetic line, it might be all women in a certain age bracket.

Information is rarely gathered from the total population during a survey. If all sources are contacted, the results are known as a **census.** Unless the total population is small, the costs will be so great that only the federal government will be able to afford them (and it uses this method only once every ten years). Instead, researchers select a representative group called a *sample.* Samples can be classified as either probability samples or nonprobability samples.

A **probability sample** is a sample in which every member of the population has a known chance of being selected. Examples of probability samples include a simple random sample, a stratified sample, and a cluster sample.

The basic type of probability sample is the **simple random sample** in which every item in the relevant universe has an equal opportunity of being selected. Vietnam-era veterans will recall the draft lottery as an example: Each day of the year, and those males born on that day, had the same chance of being selected, thus establishing a conscription list. A **stratified sample** is a probability sample constructed so that randomly selected subsamples of different groups will be represented in the total sample. It differs from quota sampling (discussed in the following section) in that the subsamples are drawn randomly. Stratified samples are an efficient sample methodology in such uses as opinion

population (universe)
Total group that the researcher wants to study.

census
Collection of data from all possible sources in a population or universe.

probability sample
Sample in which every member of the population has a known chance of being selected.

simple random sample
Basic type of probability sample in which every item in the relevant universe has an equal opportunity to be selected.

stratified sample
Probability sample that is constructed so that randomly selected subsamples of different groups are represented in the total sample.

Figure 4.6
Sampling: Crucial in
Marketing Research

Source: Courtesy of Survey Sampling, Inc.

polls, in which various groups hold divergent viewpoints. In a **cluster sample,** areas or clusters are selected and then all or a sample within each become respondents. This type of probability sample is very cost efficient and may be the best option where the population cannot be listed or enumerated. A good example is a market researcher who identifies various U.S. cities and then randomly selects supermarkets within those cities to study.

In contrast, a **nonprobability sample** is arbitrary and does not permit use of standard statistical tests. Examples of nonprobability samples are the convenience sample and the quota sample.

A **convenience sample** is a nonprobability sample based on the selection of readily available respondents. Broadcasting's "on-the-street" interviews are a good example. Marketing researchers sometimes use convenience samples in exploratory research, but not in definitive studies. A **quota sample** is a nonprobability sample that is divided so that different segments or groups are represented in the total sample. An example would be a survey of auto import owners that included 10 Hyundai owners, 10 Honda owners, 10 Volvo owners, and so on.

cluster sample
Probability sample in which geographical areas or clusters are selected and all of or a sample within them become respondents.

nonprobability sample
Arbitrary sample in which most standard statistical tests cannot be applied to the collected data.

convenience sample
Nonprobability sample based on the selection of readily available respondents.

quota sample
Nonprobability sample that is divided so that different segments or groups are represented in the total sample.

FOCUS ON ETHICS

Research or Hype?

A new way to improve a radio or television station's ratings during "sweeps" week, when they are measured and recorded, has generated nationwide controversy and led to at least one lawsuit. It raises the issue of what constitutes unethical marketing research.

In Minneapolis, Atlanta, and Los Angeles, television stations conducted marketing research on viewers during sweeps week, presumably to boost their ratings as measured by A. C. Nielsen Company. Nielsen ratings are important because they largely determine how much a station or network can charge for advertising time on its programs.

Television stations in Minneapolis and Atlanta sent out thousands of questionnaires asking recipients to watch during sweeps week and report how they liked various shows and personalities. In Los Angeles, a station ran stories on the families whose viewing habits were monitored by Nielsen. In the Minneapolis survey, KARE-TV urged recipients of its April 1987 questionnaire to "watch Channel 11 as often as possible for the next seven days" and "watch at 10 p.m. especially" during its nightly news. As a result, ratings for the program jumped 30 percent from the previous period. This

prompted KARE's rival, top-rated WCCO-TV, to cry foul.

WCCO filed a lawsuit (as yet unsettled) against KARE and the marketing research firm it employed, Atkinson Research, charging that the real purpose of the survey was to boost KARE's ratings. According to James Rupp, president and chief executive officer of WCCO's parent, Midwest Communications, Inc., KARE's 30 percent growth spurt was "in defiance of all logic and normal growth patterns." But Ronald F. Atkinson of Atkinson Research defended the survey. On ABC's "Nightline" program, he said that "in the context of broadcasting, the best way to measure realities is to actually ask people to watch the product and then feed back ideas to us." WCCO officials also claimed that the large sample size ("many thousands") of KARE's questionnaire mailing was added proof that the station had attempted to influence the ratings. Rupp noted that the national Nielsen sampling for networks is less than 2,000. "That's not research," Rupp said of KARE's survey, "that's morally wrong."

At the heart of the matter is whether it is ethical to conduct marketing research projects such as KARE's during ratings periods.

Some broadcasting executives argue that you can get the same questionnaire results outside of sweeps as you would during them, so timing them to coincide with the ratings period is just a way to manipulate the ratings. Yet promotions during sweeps are nothing new in the business, and their goal certainly is to boost ratings. But timing marketing research for sweeps week is new and takes advantage of most people's willingness to participate.

The ratings firms are not blind to the problem. In the Los Angeles case, Nielsen canceled the ratings for the sweeps period in which the Nielsen families programs were aired. In Minneapolis, ratings published by Nielsen and Arbitron both indicated that KARE's figures might have been inflated by the survey. And in an editorial about the Minneapolis and Los Angeles cases, one industry journal, *Television/Radio Age,* encouraged the ratings companies to stop publishing listings for stations that try to inflate their ratings.

Source: Gregg Cebrzynski, "TV Station Sues over Alleged 'Phony' Survey," *Marketing News* (August 28, 1987), pp. 1, 42.

Interpretation and Presentation

A number of marketing research books contain information on how to cope with the many problems involved in surveying the public. Among these problems are designing questionnaires; selecting, training, and controlling field interviewers; editing, coding, tabulating, and interpreting data; presenting results; and following up on the survey.

It is imperative that marketing researchers and research users cooperate at every stage in the research design. Too many studies go unused because marketing management believes the results are too restricted due to lengthy discussions of research limitations or unfamiliar terminology.

Marketing researchers must remember that these reports are directed toward management, not other research specialists. As a result, marketing research reports must spell out their conclusions in a clear, concise, and actionable fashion. Technical details of the research can be outlined in an appendix, if at all. This approach will increase the likelihood of management's utilizing the research findings.

Marketing Information Systems

Many marketing managers discover that their information problems result from an overabundance rather than a paucity of marketing data. Their sophisticated computer facilities may provide them with daily printouts about sales in 30 market areas, about 100 different products, and about 6,400 customers. Managers sometimes solve the problem of too much information of the wrong kind and in the wrong form by sliding the printouts to the edge of the desk, where they quietly slip into the wastebasket. Data and information are not synonymous terms. **Data** refers to statistics, opinions, facts, or predictions categorized on some basis for storage and retrieval. **Information** is data relevant to the marketing manager in making decisions.

data
Statistics, opinions, facts, or predictions categorized on some basis for storage and retrieval.

information
Data relevant to the marketing manager in making decisions.

marketing information system (MIS)
Planned, computer-based system designed to provide managers with a continuous flow of information relevant to their specific decision areas.

Obtaining relevant information appears simple enough. One can establish a systematic approach to information management by installing a **marketing information system (MIS),** which is a planned, computer-based system designed to provide managers with a continual flow of information relevant to their specific decision areas. The marketing information system is a subset of the firm's overall management information system (also often called an *MIS*) that deals specifically with marketing information.

A properly constructed MIS can serve as the company's nerve center, providing instantaneous information suitable for each management level. It can monitor the marketplace continuously, allowing management to adjust actions as conditions change.

The role of marketing information in a firm's marketing system can be illustrated with the analogy of how an automatic heating system works. Once the objective of a particular temperature setting (say, 68°F) has been established, information about the actual temperature is collected and compared with the objective and a decision based on this comparison is made. If the temperature drops below the established figure, the decision is to activate the furnace until the temperature reaches the established level. If the temperature is too high, the decision is to turn off the furnace.

Deviation from the firm's goals of profitability, improved return on investment, or greater market share may necessitate changes in price structures, promotional expenditures, package design, or other marketing elements. The firm's MIS should be capable of revealing such deviations and suggesting changes that will result in attaining the established goals. Creating an effective MIS, however, is more easily said than done. Several firms' attempts have succeeded only in further complicating their data retrieval systems.

Figure 4.7
Information Components of the Firm's Marketing Information System

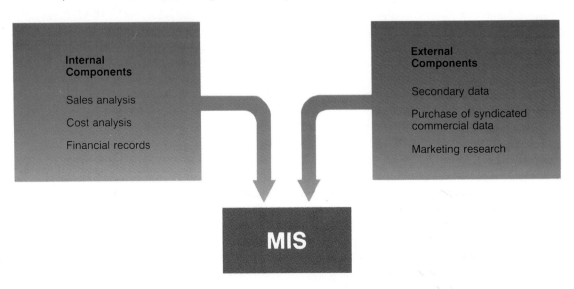

Marketing Research and the Marketing Information System

Many marketing executives think their organizations are too small to use a marketing information system. Others contend that their marketing research departments provide adequate research data for decision making. Such contentions often result from a misconception of the services and functions performed by the marketing research department. Marketing research has already been described as typically focusing on a specific problem or project; its investigations have a definite beginning, middle, and end. Marketing information systems, on the other hand, are much wider in scope, involving the continuous collection and analysis of marketing information. Figure 4.7 indicates the various information inputs—including marketing research studies—that serve as components of a firm's MIS.

By focusing daily on the marketplace, the MIS provides a continuous systematic and comprehensive study of areas that indicate deviations from established goals. The up-to-the-minute information allows problems to be corrected before they adversely affect operations.

Current Status of Marketing Information Systems

Marketing information systems have come a long way from the days when they were responsible primarily for clerical activities (and usually at an increased cost over the old method). Today managers have available special computer programs, remote-access consoles, better data banks, direct communication with computers, and assignment of authority to computers for review and referral.

Marketing managers in many industries use the sophisticated computer technology of *decision support systems (DSSs)*. The DSS is an interactive, single-source storage and retrieval system that incorporates company and com-

Nature of Information Provided

1. Can I compare operating costs across company organizations to permit valid conclusions about relative product costs, margins, and sales volumes?
2. Are my subordinates satisfied with their information resources?
3. Do my competitors have better marketing information systems than I do?

Business, Marketing, and MIS Planning

4. Is there an approved long-range MIS plan?
5. Does my MIS support my business and marketing planning effectively?
6. Are MIS planning, operations, and so forth reviewed at a high organizational level?
7. Am I involved in MIS planning as a marketing manager?
8. Am I kept up to date on the latest MIS technology and applications?

Organization of MIS

9. Do I know how MIS is organized?
10. Do I have the authority and responsibility to get the marketing information I need from MIS?
11. Does MIS keep me informed about cost, time, and performance alternatives?

Costs

12. Do I know how much I am spending on using MIS?
13. Do I have any idea as to whether these costs are excessive, too low, or about right?
14. Do I know how resources are allocated within MIS?
15. Do I agree with the current allocation of expenditures within MIS?

Table 4.6
Questions That Help
Evaluate an MIS

Source: Reprinted by permission of the *Harvard Business Review*. An exhibit from "Managing International Information Systems" by Martin D. J. Buss (September/October 1982). Copyright 1982 by the President and Fellows of Harvard College; all rights reserved.

mercial data. For example, retailers, banks and other financial institutions, and health care firms use Onsite/PC, a geographically based decision support system that integrates retail potential estimates, life-style information, and industry-specific data with clients' internal information. Decision support systems help marketing managers identify new opportunities, study causal relationships, and evaluate alternative plans for pricing, promoting, and distributing products and services.[25]

Developing an MIS

Constructing a marketing information system requires the full support of top management. Management not only must be truly enthusiastic about the system's potential; it also must believe that it is top management's place to oversee its development. Too often the technical staff is left to build the system without that important management contribution. The next step involves a review and appraisal of the entire marketing organization and the policies that direct it. The marketing managers' responsibilities must be clearly defined. If the system is to measure their performances against company plans, each manager's area of accountability must be specified.

Once the organization is readied for development of the MIS, the system's level of sophistication must be determined. Before this can be done, the company's needs and costs of meeting them must be carefully considered. The ability of managers to develop and effectively use a sophisticated system must also be addressed. Managers must be able to state their specific information needs. The questions outlined in Table 4.6 are useful in assessing an MIS.

Summary of Chapter Objectives

1. Describe the development and current status of the marketing research function. Marketing research started when Charles C. Parlin, an advertising space sales representative for the *Saturday Evening Post,* counted empty soup cans in Philadelphia's trash in an effort to convince Campbell Soup Company to advertise in the magazine. Today the most common marketing research activities are determining market potential, market share, and market characteristics and conducting sales analyses and competitive-product studies. Most large companies now have internal market research departments. However, outside suppliers still remain vital to the research function. Some of these outside suppliers perform the complete research task, while others specialize in limited areas or provide other data services.

In 1987, the American Marketing Association redefined marketing research as follows:

Marketing research is the function which links the consumer, customer, and public to the marketer through information—information used to identify and define marketing opportunities and problems; generate, refine, and evaluate marketing actions; monitor marketing performance; and improve understanding of marketing as a process.

Marketing research determines the information needed for these purposes, specifies and implements the data collection process, and interprets and communicates the results.

2. List the steps in the marketing research process. The marketing research process can be divided into six specific steps: (1) defining the problem; (2) exploratory research; (3) formulating hypotheses; (4) research design; (5) collecting data; and (6) interpretation and presentation. A clearly defined problem allows the researcher to obtain the relevant decision-oriented information. Exploratory research refers to information gained both outside and inside the firm. Hypotheses—tentative explanations of some specific event—allow the researcher to set out a specific research design, which is the series of decisions that taken together comprise a master plan or model for the conduct of the investigation. The data collection phase of the marketing research process can involve either or both primary data (original data) and secondary data (previously published data). After the data are collected, researchers must interpret and present them in a way that will be meaningful to management.

3. Differentiate the types and sources of primary and secondary data. Primary data can be collected by the firm's own market researchers or by independent marketing research companies. Three alternative methods of primary data collection can be used: observation, survey, or experimental. Secondary data can be classified as either internal or external. Internal sources include sales records, product evaluations, sales force reports, and records of marketing costs. External sources include the government and private sources such as business magazines and consulting services. Both external and internal data can also be obtained from computerized databases.

4. Identify the methods of collecting survey data. Survey data can be collected through telephone interviews, mail surveys, or personal interviews. Telephone interviews provide over half of all primary marketing research. It is a fast and inexpensive way to get small amounts of information but not detailed or personal information. Mail surveys allow market researchers to conduct national studies at a reasonable cost; their disadvantage is potentially inadequate response. Personal interviews are costly but allow researchers to get detailed information from respondents.

5. Explain the various sampling techniques. Samples can be categorized as either probability samples or nonprobability samples. A probability sample is a sample in which every member of the population has an equal chance of being selected. Probability samples include simple random samples, in which every item in the relevant universe has an equal opportunity to be selected; stratified samples, which are constructed such that randomly selected subsamples of different groups are represented in the total sample; and cluster samples, in which areas are selected and then all or a sample within each become respondents.

A nonprobability sample is arbitrary and does not allow application of standard statistical tests. Nonprobability samples include convenience samples, in which readily available respondents are picked, and quota samples, which are divided so that different segments or groups are represented in the total sample.

6. Describe a marketing information system and distinguish it from marketing research. A marketing information system *(MIS)* is a planned, computer-based system designed to provide managers with a continuous flow of information relevant to their specific decision areas. While marketing research concentrates on a specific problem or project, a marketing information system is wider in scope, involving the ongoing collection and analysis of marketing information.

Key Terms

marketing research	population (universe)
exploratory research	census
sales analysis	probability sample
sales quota	simple random sample
iceberg principle	stratified sample
marketing cost analysis	cluster sample
hypothesis	nonprobability sample
research design	convenience sample
primary data	quota sample
secondary data	data
database	information
focus group interview	marketing information system (MIS)
experiment	

Review Questions

1. Outline the development and current status of the marketing research function.

2. List and explain the various steps in the marketing research process.

3. Distinguish between primary and secondary data.

4. What are the advantages and limitations of using secondary data?

5. Compare and contrast sales analysis and market cost analysis.

6. Collect from secondary sources the following information:
   a. Retail sales in Springfield, Ohio, for last year
   b. Number of persons over 65 in Bend, Oregon
   c. Earnings per share for Ford last year
   d. Coal production in West Virginia in a recent year
   e. Consumer price index for last August
   f. Number of households earning more than $40,000 in Miami, Florida

7. Distinguish among surveys, experiments, and observational methods of data collection.

8. Explain the differences between probability and nonprobability samples, and identify the various types of each.

9. Identify and give an example of each of the three methods of gathering survey data. Under what circumstances should each be used?

10. Distinguish between marketing research and marketing information systems.

Discussion Questions

1. The Council for Economic Action is a nonprofit group that attempts to help inner-city residents establish their own businesses. The model that the group uses has been successfuly implemented in cities ranging from Atlanta to Milwaukee to Stockton, California. The council begins by surveying undersupplied and oversupplied industries in each new city. The future entrepreneurs then take two classes, one dealing with basic business concepts and the other with the creation of a business plan.[26]
   a. What role, if any, should marketing research play in getting a new enterprise started?
   b. Would the Council for Economic Action's program be helpful in your community? Why or why not?

2. It seems that political predictions often miss their mark. Consider the prediction errors made by the *Literary Digest* in the Alf Landon–Franklin D. Roosevelt presidential campaign of 1936, the Truman–Dewey presidential race in 1948, and Reagan's victory over Carter in 1980. What implications do these results have for marketing researchers?

3. You have been asked to determine the effect on Gillette of Schick's revolutionary new blade that is guaranteed to give 100 nick-free shaves. Outline your approach to the study.

4. Many people fear the development of national data banks. What are the responsibilities of marketing researchers with regard to this issue? Discuss.

5. Describe what you see as the future scenario for marketing information systems. Will the MIS ever replace some of the duties now performed by marketing managers? Why or why not?

VIDEO CASE 4

The Disney Channel

When the Bass brothers effectively took control of Walt Disney Company, they installed a new management team. The new executives started to rebuild the $2.5 billion entertainment conglomerate. One of their objectives was to achieve a better revenue balance among the firm's four division: theme parks, film, community development, and consumer products. In a recent year, these divisions contributed to annual sales revenues as follows: theme parks, 61.7 percent; film, 20.7 percent; community development, 12.3 percent; and consumer products, 5.3 percent.

Management specifically wanted to increase the revenue contribution of the film division. The Disney organization abandoned its reliance on G-rated movies and began developing adult-oriented entertainment under the Touchstone Pictures logo. The company also pushed its syndicated offerings of "Wonderful World of Disney." Other television programming included "The Golden Girls," "The Disney Sunday Movie," and "Today's Business."

The Disney Channel was still another part of the firm's efforts to increase the film division's revenue. The Disney Channel is a television channel offered by various cable systems. It was set up in 1983 and by 1986 had moved to a full 24-hour schedule. The Disney Channel is now offered by 4,300 cable systems and has 3.18 million subscribers.

Disney management knew that cable was expected to be the chief growth segment of the television market in the years ahead. The unanswered questions were how to best participate in this market growth and how to maximize revenues. Disney Channel management also knew that it faced a highly competitive environment. Its primary audience (families) was finite. As a result, Disney executives decided to attempt to broaden the channel's appeal to additional market segments. Several efforts were made to appeal to adults without children. Adult programming was increased, and prime time programming began following a structured weekly grid approach in an effort to boost viewer loyalty. The Disney Channel even used a proof-of-purchase promotional tie-in to three different food products.

These efforts indicated that the market for the Disney Channel could indeed be expanded. For instance, the number of subscribers over 40 jumped from 27 percent of all households to 35 percent in a single year. Similarly, the number of subscribers without children went from 25 percent to 33 percent.

Disney executives were also concerned about how to price the channel. The Cable Communications Policy Act frees cable systems from rate regulation by state and local governments. However, the newfound pricing freedom could not be easily translated into substantial price increases. Industry executives knew that cable subscriptions were quite price-sensitive. In fact, only about 57 percent of all households capable of connecting to a cable system actually do so. In one experiment in price sensitivity, Tele-Communications, a large cable company, tested a price cut for The Disney Channel from $10.95 to $7.95 per month. The firm reported a significant increase in the number of Disney subscribers.

Anne Hotchkiss, director of marketing research for The Disney Channel, was involved in many of the channel's developmental decisions. She knew that marketing research had played an important role in the decision to enter the cable market. In fact, marketing research on issues like programming are important throughout the entire cable industry. For example, one survey of cable system operations found that about 67 percent of the most profitable cable companies used marketing research, while only 46 percent of the less profitable ones did.

The Disney Channel used the services of the ASI marketing research organization. In fact, Anne Hotchkiss had just made an appointment with ASI personnel to discuss The Disney Channel's continuing research needs. Specifically, she wanted information on: (1) how to increase market penetration; (2) the various market segments and whether or not programming changes could capture new segments; and (3) the price thresholds for The Disney Channel.

Sources: Ronald Grover, Mark N. Vamos, and Todd Mason, "Disney's Magic," *Business Week* (March 9, 1987), pp. 62–65, 68–69; Myron Magnet, "Putting Magic Back Into the Magic Kingdom," *Fortune* (January 5, 1987), p. 65; "Marketing, Management Practices Separate Cable Winners, Losers," *Marketing News* (April 10, 1987), pp. 4, 35; "Ad Agencies Urged to Concentrate on Strategic Values of Cable TV," *Marketing News* (September 25, 1987), p. 5; Fannie Weinstein, "Disney, Nashville Nets Find Eager Product Tie-Ins," *Advertising Age* (December 7, 1987), p. S-6; Allan Dodds Frank, "Leisure and Recreation," *Forbes* (January 12, 1987), pp. 158–159; "Walt Disney Co.," *Advertising Age* (September 24, 1987), p. 86; David Ansen and Peter McAlevey, "The Mouse That Roared," *Newsweek* (March 3, 1986), pp. 62–65; Laura Landro, "Cable TV's New Freedom Promises Higher Prices — but Fewer Services," *The Wall Street Journal* (December 12, 1986), p. 31; and Pamela Ellis-Simons, "Hi Ho, Hi Ho," *Marketing & Media Decisions* (September, 1986), pp. 52–54, 56–57, 60, 62, 64.

Questions

1. Chapter 4 describes the marketing research process. What steps in that process are evident in this case?

2. What type of information does The Disney Channel require for developing its future marketing strategy?

3. How should The Disney Channel gather the information needed for making a decision?

COMPUTER APPLICATIONS

Sales analysis is defined in this chapter as the in-depth evaluation of a firm's sales. This information is obtained from the organization's sales reports, customer purchase orders, invoices, and other accounting data. The sales analysis concept is explained in detail on pages 133–134. The following problems deal with sales analysis.

Directions: Use menu item 4 titled "Sales Analysis" to solve each of the following problems.

Problem 1   The sales force of Associated Industries of Victoria, Texas, is divided into four sales zones. Average sales for representatives in the various zones are as follows: A—$440,000; B—$407,500; C—$436,000; D—$448,000. The average sales compensation in the four zones is: A—$36,000; B—$39,000; C—$41,000; D—$42,000. Average selling costs are relatively low, with zone D being the most expensive at $6,340. Other average selling cost figures are: A—$5,940; B—$6,380; C—$6,700. Determine the cost/sales ratios for each of Associated's four sales zones.

Problem 2   A Detroit-based corporation organizes its sales force into three sales regions: A, B, and C. The average salaries in these regions are $40,000, $45,000, and $50,000, respectively. Region A sales personnel average $700,000 in sales; Region B, $640,000; and Region C, $945,000. Selling expenses average $12,000 in all regions. Calculate the cost/sales ratios for the three regions.

Problem 3   Jackie Frost, a marketing consultant, has been hired to analyze the sales of a Pittsburgh firm. Management is particularly concerned with Division 4's average selling expenses of $26,400.

The Pittsburg Firm Operates Five Divisions with the Following Average Sales Salaries:		Average Selling Expenses for Personnel in the Divisions Are:		Average Sales Per Representative in these Divisions Are:	
Division 1	$39,300	Division 1	$ 7,670	Division 1	$396,000
Division 2	42,840	Division 2	7,850	Division 2	480,000
Division 3	38,750	Division 3	10,025	Division 3	501,000
Division 4	39,050	Division 4	26,450	Division 4	604,000
Division 5	40,175	Division 5	13,000	Division 5	528,000

What should Frost tell management about the firm's cost/sales ratios?

Problem 4   The Mid-Atlantic Division of a Hartford, Connecticut, company has a seven-person sales force to cover New York, Pennsylvania, and New Jersey. For 1988, the following quotas were assigned according to the territory's sales potential:

Territory 1	$365,000
Territory 2	386,000
Territory 3	476,000
Territory 4	429,000
Territory 5	400,000
Territory 6	411,000
Territory 7	436,000

At the close of business on December 31, 1988, the following annual sales volumes were reported:

Territory 1	$392,000
Territory 2	387,000
Territory 3	442,000
Territory 4	408,000
Territory 5	450,000
Territory 6	416,000
Territory 7	429,000

a. Calculate the performance-to-quota ratios for each of the seven territories.
b. What is the overall performance-to-quota ratio for the Mid-Atlantic Division?

Problem 5   The Chicago Division of a Kirksville, Missouri, firm employs five sales representatives. All were assigned annual sales quotas of $450,000. The division manager, Duane Washington, is now preparing an analysis of how his people did in 1988. The actual sales results were as follows:

Snow	$415,000
Harris	468,000
Beck	389,000
Davis	414,000
Clark	453,000

a. Calculate the performance-to-quota ratio for each of the sales representatives in the Chicago Division.
b. What is the overall performance-to-quota ratio for the Chicago Division?

Buyer Behavior and Market Segmentation

159

5

Consumer Behavior

Chapter Objectives

1. To explain the classification of behavioral influences in consumer decisions.

2. To identify the interpersonal determinants of consumer behavior.

3. To identify the personal determinants of consumer behavior.

4. To outline the steps in the consumer decision process.

5. To differentiate among routinized response behavior, limited problem solving, and extended problem solving.

C hocolate sounds like a marketer's dream product—it tastes terrific, it's compact, and it's fun. It even inspires people; for example, a publisher started a magazine, *Chocolatier,* devoted to the glories of eating chocolate in a wide array of forms. But chocolate sales were flat throughout the 1970s, a troublesome trend for chocolate confectioners.

Selling sweets for the sweet had always been good business, especially since birthdays, anniversaries, Valentine's Day, and the like come every year. So when chocolate sales went flat, manufacturers looked for reasons why. What they found was a fitness-obsessed society that perceived chocolate as junk food.

But consumer attitudes have changed. Today nine in ten Americans eat chocolate regularly, and one in ten eats it every day. People have turned to chocolate to satisfy a host of needs—as a booster on a bad day, as an acceptable and desirable snack, and as a reward for good behavior. Even the physically fit no longer feel guilty about eating a chocolate or two as a treat. Some people buy an expensive box of exotic chocolates as a substitute for luxuries beyond their means. Joan Steuer, president of Chocolate Marketing Inc., observes, "People are buying for themselves, not just as gifts. They can't necessarily take a trip to Tahiti, but they can buy a box of high-quality chocolates and learn to savor it."

Contributing to consumers' attitude changes toward chocolate was a campaign launched by the Chocolate Manufacturers Association. It publicized research findings showing that chocolate does not cause acne, tooth decay, or allergies. Then it began to promote chocolate as a satisfying and permissible product to eat—even between meals.

For chocolate manufacturers, the change in attitudes opened up new marketing opportunities. Inspired by

Treasured Works Of An Old Master.

chocolate's improved image, they responded with new products, positioning strategies, and advertising themes. Ads for Mars' Snickers, America's favorite candy bar, tout it as something to quell midday hunger pangs. Nestlé promotes its new line of Henri Nestlé specialty chocolates as an "affordable luxury." Hershey

Foods has extended its traditional candy bar line by adding upscale products—the GOLDEN ALMOND chocolate bar, GOLDEN III, with butterchips and coconut, and GOLDEN ALMOND SOLITAIRES, chocolate covered almonds. Godiva targets a different market niche with its new line of chocolates, Barringer's, which sell for $14 a pound compared to its gold-boxed, European-style morsels that go for $21 a pound.

Such efforts to satisfy Americans' willingness to indulge their sweet teeth are bound to continue, especially since the attitude change has resulted in an increased per capita consumption from 8.5 pounds in 1980 to 12 pounds per person in 1985.[1]

Photo source: The "Treasured Works of An Old Master" advertisement is reprinted by permission of the copyright owner, Hershey Foods Corporation, Hershey, Pennsylvania, U.S.A. HERSHEY'S, GOLDEN ALMOND, and GOLDEN III are registered trademarks of Hershey Foods Corporation.

Chapter Overview

consumer behavior
All the acts of individuals in obtaining, using, and disposing of economic goods and services, including the decision processes that precede and determine these acts.

Consumer behavior consists of the acts of individuals in obtaining, using, and disposing of economic goods and services, including the decision processes that precede and determine these acts.[2] This definition includes both the ultimate consumer and the industrial products purchaser. A major difference in the purchasing behavior of industrial consumers and that of ultimate consumers is that the former is subject to additional influences from within the organization.

This chapter assesses interpersonal and personal influences on consumer behavior. Chapter 6 deals with industrial and organizational buyer behavior.

Classifying Behavioral Influences: Personal and Interpersonal

Since the study of consumer behavior involves attempts to understand human behavior in purchase/nonpurchase situations, it is not surprising that consumer researchers borrow extensively from areas such as psychology and sociology. The work of Kurt Lewin, for example, provides an excellent classification of influences on buying behavior. Lewin's work is also used in motivation theory, which is part of the management discipline, because it is a general model of behavior. Lewin's proposition is:

$$B = f(P, E),$$

where behavior *(B)* is a function *(f)* of the interactions of personal influences *(P)* and the pressures exerted on them by outside environmental forces *(E)*.[3]

This statement is usually rewritten for consumer behavior as follows:

$$B = f(I, P),$$

where consumer behavior *(B)* is a function *(f)* of the interaction of interpersonal determinants *(I)*, such as reference groups and culture, and personal determinants *(P)*, such as attitudes, learning, and perception. Understanding consumer behavior requires an understanding of both the individual's psychological makeup and the influences of others. The relationship between the interaction of personal and interpersonal determinants and the consumer decision process is shown in Figure 5.1.

The Consumer Decision Process

Consumer behavior may be viewed as a decision process. As Figure 5.1 shows, the act of purchasing is merely one point in the process. To understand consumer behavior, the events that precede and follow the purchase must be

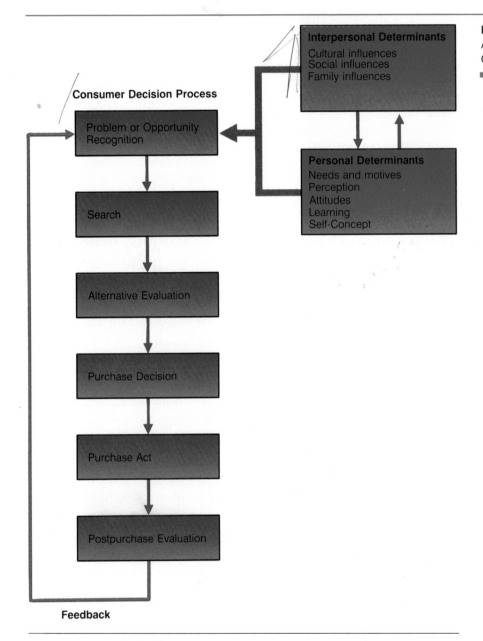

Source: James F. Engel, Roger D. Blackwell, and Paul W. Miniard, *Consumer Behavior,* 5th ed. (Hinsdale, Ill.: Dryden Press, 1986), pp. 29–35.

examined. The steps in the consumer decision process are problem recognition, search, evaluation of alternatives, purchase decision, purchase act, and postpurchase evaluation. Consumers use the decision process in solving problems and taking advantage of opportunities. Such decisions permit consumers to correct differences between their actual and desired states. Feedback from each decision serves as additional experience on which to rely in subsequent decisions.

To illustrate this process, consider the college student whose all-in-one stereo system—an eighth-grade graduation gift—goes on the blink. Life without music is unimaginable, so the student feels a need to buy a new system. First she talks to friends who have recently bought sound systems. She buys a copy of the *Audio/Video Buyer's Guide,* which explains how to choose and buy equipment. Then she visits a specialty store, where she gets advice from a salesperson. She also checks out the selection offered at a discount store and a large audio chain store. After evaluating all the alternatives, she decides to buy an affordable, three-component stereo and makes her purchase at a discount store. She brings the stereo home, hooks it up, and sits back to evaluate the wisdom of her purchase.

This process is common to consumer purchase decisions. Before examining the steps in the decision process in more detail, let us look at the interpersonal and personal influences on consumer behavior.

Interpersonal Determinants of Consumer Behavior

People are social animals. They often buy products and services that will enable them to project a favorable image to others. These influences may result from three categories of interpersonal determinants of consumer behavior: cultural influences, social influences, and family influences.

Cultural Influences

Culture is the broadest environmental determinant of consumer behavior. Marketers often have difficulty overcoming cultural barriers such as language. Errors in translating advertising messages result from failure to understand another culture's colloquialisms and words and phrases with double meanings. Perdue Farms' slogan "It takes a tough man to make a tender chicken" translated into Spanish as "It takes a sexually excited man to make a chick affectionate." A food company advertised a huge burrito as a *burrada,* which in Spanish means "a big mistake."[4]

culture
Complex of values, ideas, attitudes, and other meaningful symbols that help people communicate, interpret, and evaluate as members of society.

Culture can be defined as "the complex of values, ideas, attitudes, and other meaningful symbols that serve humans to communicate, interpret, and evaluate as members of society."[5] It is the completely learned and handed-down way of life that gives each society its unique flavor or values.

Core Values in U.S. Culture

While cultural values change over time, there are always some basic core values that are slow to change. For example, the work ethic and the accumulation of wealth have always played a big part in the development of American society. Other American core values include efficiency, practicality, individualism, freedom, youthfulness, activity, and humanitarianism. Each of these values influences consumer behavior. Americans' value of activity—the notion that keeping busy is healthy and natural—stimulates consumers' interest in products that save time and enhance leisure-time activities. The value of youthfulness stimulates consumers to accept products and services that provide the illusion of maintaining or fostering youth.[6]

Many people thought the generation that grew up in the 1960s had permanently altered American core values. This generation was the product of the baby boom that followed World War II and the Korean conflict. It was raised with the conservative values of the 1950s. Free time was spent watching television shows such as "Ozzie and Harriet" and "Father Knows Best." As it matured, this generation seemed to rebel against most of the values held by their parents and previous generations. This was the generation that challenged traditional cultural values with long hair, antiwar protests, and marijuana. Despite the turmoil of the 1960s, however, most American core values survived.

What are the flower children of the 1960s doing now? They have passed on to early middle age, long since crossing that once dreaded barrier, age 30. They have adopted many of the values their parents held, including worrying about the younger generation. Most baby boomers are now too concerned with mortgages and receding hairlines to protest anything besides high taxes. Even Rolling Stone Mick Jagger once observed: "I can't go on pretending to be 18 much longer."[7]

The current generation of career-oriented college students are sometimes criticized for their lack of social and political activism. Critics suggest that college students have adopted the values of the Eisenhower era. It is significant to note that the shifting contemporary values of this four-decade period clearly illustrate the permanency of American core values.

One American value that survived the social turmoil of recent decades is the family. Although the typical family structure and members' roles have changed, a recent report on the family concluded that Americans value their families as much as ever. The report noted that virtually all Americans believe that when families are happy and healthy, the world is a better place in which to live, and that almost nine out of ten Americans regard their families as one of the most important parts of their lives.[8] Speaking to Americans' value of family and love of cars, ads in Chevrolet's "The Heartbeat of America" campaign, such as the one in Figure 5.2, attempt to influence car buyer behavior.

Cultural Influences: An International Perspective

Cultural differences are particularly important for international marketers. This topic is more fully explored in Chapter 20. For now it is important to note that cultural differences result in different attitudes, mores, and folkways, all of which affect marketing strategy. Consider the case of the candy company that introduced a new chocolate bar with peanuts in Japan. The candy bar failed because Japanese folklore suggests that eating chocolate with peanuts leads to nosebleeds.[9]

Marketing strategies that have proven successful in one country often cannot be applied directly in international markets because of cultural differences. Consider the strategy of an American manufacturer that tried to sell jars of baby food in an African country. The jar labels gave product information and showed a picture of a smiling baby. But most of the potential customers were illiterate. Unable to read the print on the label, they assumed that what was on the outside of the jar was what was inside it—babies.[10]

U.S.-based international marketers face competition from firms in Germany, France, the Soviet Union, Japan, and several other countries, as well as from firms in the host nation. Therefore, they must become familiar with all aspects of the local population, including its cultural heritage. This can be accomplished by treating each country as an additional market segment that must be thoroughly analyzed before developing a marketing mix.

Figure 5.2
Appealing to Family Values

Source: Courtesy of Chevrolet Motor Division.

Subcultures

subculture
Subgroup of a culture with its
own distinct mode of behavior.

Cultures are not homogeneous entities with universal values. Within each culture are numerous **subcultures**—subgroups with their own distinct modes of behavior. Any culture as heterogeneous as that of the United States is composed of significant subcultures based on such factors as race, nationality, age, rural versus urban location, religion, and geographical distribution.

Inhabitants of the southwestern United States display a life-style emphasizing casual dress, outdoor entertaining, and water recreation. Mormons refrain from buying tobacco and liquor. Orthodox Jews purchase kosher and other traditional foods. Understanding these and other differences among subcultures results in successful marketing of products and services. Insensitivity to cultural nuances has the opposite outcome. For example, the state of Maryland had to pull an ad campaign including television commercials, brochures, and posters that featured photos of Al Capone, a gangster who was imprisoned for federal tax evasion. The advertising was intended to publicize the state's tax amnesty program and used Capone to show tax evaders what happens to those who get caught. But leaders of the Italian-American community protested that the campaign was an ethnic slur and that it perpetuated the false stereotype of Italian-Americans as mobsters.[11]

The three largest ethnic subcultures in the United States are blacks, Hispanics, and Asians. Together they account for over 46 million, or a little over 20 percent of the total U.S. population. It is estimated that by the year 2080, 50.1 percent of all Americans will be blacks, Hispanics, and Asians.[12]

Black Consumption Patterns   Blacks represent the largest racial/ethnic subculture in the United States—some 29 million strong. They account for about 12 percent of the U.S. population and more than $200 billion in purchasing power. There are several striking differences between the black and white populations. According to the U.S. Department of Commerce, about 36 percent of blacks are below the poverty level compared to 12 percent of whites. Also, the black population is very young. The median age for blacks in 1990 is expected to be 6.2 years younger than for whites.

While marketers recognize that no group of 29 million can be considered a homogeneous market segment for all products, a number of marketing studies have compared consumption patterns of blacks and whites. One study revealed that the spending patterns of blacks and whites are quite similar in broad categories such as housing, transportation, and food. These categories claim two-thirds of yearly household expenditures for both groups. Blacks, however, spend less on tobacco, alcohol, entertainment, and personal care than do whites.[13] But within these broad categories, there are important differences in the consumer preferences of blacks and whites. A recent Conference Board study reported the following:[14]

□   Although blacks and whites spend the same proportion of their incomes on transportation, blacks spend far less than whites on the purchase of trucks and vans and far more on mass transit and taxis.

□   Blacks represent only 11 percent of all households, but they account for more than one-third of the money spent on rented televisions.

□   Though on average blacks have less money than whites, they account for 10 percent of most expenditures in the television, radio, and sound equipment category.

□   Blacks spend far less than whites for most kinds of reading materials, but they account for 17 percent of expenditures on encyclopedias and other reference books.

□   Blacks spend far less than whites on legal fees, safe deposit boxes, and accounting services.

The most distinguishing feature of black consumers is their brand loyalty. Blacks have been slow to shift to generic and private brands. In fact, it is estimated that blacks may account for 30 to 40 percent of the sales of many national brands. The Wellington Group, a New Jersey–based marketing research and business development company, found the following to be among the brand favorites of blacks: Listerine, Tide, Pine-Sol, Clorox, S.O.S., Reynolds

Wrap, Minute Maid, Maxwell House, Gold Medal, Crisco, Skippy, Kraft mayonnaise, Vaseline Intensive Care, Campbell's baked beans, and Scott towels.[15]

Marketers, whether in majority- or minority-owned firms, must choose their strategies carefully when attempting to reach the growing black consumer market. Several national firms, including McDonald's, Wendy's, and Procter & Gamble, use black-owned advertising agencies to create advertising messages targeted at the black community.

Hispanic Consumption Patterns   Accounting for 7 percent of the U.S. population, Hispanics are the nation's second largest and fastest-growing subculture. The Bureau of the Census predicts that by 2010 Hispanics will account for 14 percent of the population, becoming a larger minority than blacks. Hispanics already constitute a majority of the population in Miami, San Antonio, and El Paso.[16] Hispanics' purchasing power is also increasing—from $53 billion in 1980 to an estimated $172 billion in 1990.[17]

Hispanics are a more heterogeneous subculture than blacks due to their variety of national origin. Mexico is the birthplace of 58 percent of the U.S. Hispanic population. Other places of origin are Puerto Rico, 14 percent; Cuba, 6 percent; and Central and South American countries, the remainder. Hispanics are geographically concentrated, with those of Mexican origin living primarily in the Southwest, Puerto Ricans in the metropolitan New York area, and Cubans in Florida.

A recent study revealed the following buying traits of U.S. Hispanics:[18]

□   Hispanics prefer buying American-made products, and products and services offered by firms that cater to Hispanic needs. More than 40 percent consider a firm's interest in or recognition of Hispanics when they shop.

□   Hispanics are quality and brand conscious. They prefer to buy brand-name products. Almost one-half of Hispanic consumers do not buy unfamiliar brands, even if they cost less. They buy products on a cost-value basis and are willing to pay a premium price for premium quality.

□   Hispanics are very brand loyal. About 45 percent always buy their usual brands, and only 20 percent frequently switch brands. Brand loyalty stems from Hispanics' desire to do the best for their families. Of particular importance to marketers is the youthfulness of the Hispanic market—the median age of Hispanics is only 23.6 years, compared with 32 years for the U.S. population as a whole. This gives marketers the opportunity to capture Hispanics' loyalty at an early age.

Another cultural characteristic of Hispanics is that they spend relatively more of their free time with their extended families than do other population segments. Shopping and moviegoing, for example, are family outings. The focus on family has been used in the marketing efforts of a grocery store in a Los Angeles suburb, which has provided weekend fiestas for Hispanic customers, complete with mariachi bands and prizes for the children.[19]

Marketers are responding to the growing Hispanic market by targeting their advertising to Hispanics, establishing bilingual sales forces, and sponsoring special events in Spanish-speaking communities. Local firms welcome Hispanics by displaying *"Aqui se habla español"* ("Spanish is spoken here") signs in their shop windows. Two Spanish-language television networks and their

Sensitive to Hispanics' focus on family, Mars Market in El Monte, California, caters to this growing market segment by sponsoring special events such as drawings, giveaways, and entertainment, including performances by this mariachi band.

Photo source: Courtesy of Mars Market.

more than 400 affiliated stations reach over 80 percent of the Hispanic population.

Asian Consumption Patterns   Although a smaller market segment than blacks and Hispanics, the U.S. Asian population is expected to grow from 4 million in 1980 to an estimated 10 million by the end of the century. Like Hispanics, Asian-Americans maintain their native languages and are family oriented. Asians, however, are even more culturally diverse and speak more languages than Hispanics. The Asian population is concentrated on the West Coast, in cities such as San Francisco.[20]

Several characteristics of the Asian subculture make it an appealing market. Asian-Americans are two or three times more likely to hold college degrees than the average American adult; they more typically hold positions as managers, executives, and professionals; and the average family income among Japanese, Chinese, and Filipinos is higher than that of whites.[21]

Marketers selling to Asian-Americans must consider several cultural differences. For example, part of the Chinese business culture is bargaining over price, a practice to which most American salespeople are not accustomed. A car dealer in San Francisco gives his salespeople "Asian Sensitivity Training" to help them learn the subtleties of negotiating with Chinese customers. Another part of the training program focuses on dealing with families. Like Hispanics, the Chinese prefer shopping in large family groups. The actual buying decision in the Chinese family is often made by a family elder, such as a grandfather, even though the buyer is a middle-aged family member. The training teaches salespeople to direct their sales pitches at the decision maker rather than the buyer.[22]

Social Influences

The second interpersonal determinant of consumer behavior is the social influences that affect purchase behavior. Children's earliest group experience is their membership in the family. From this group they seek total satisfaction of their physiological and social needs. As they grow older, they join other groups—neighborhood play groups, school groups, Girl Scouts, Little League, and friendship groups, among others—from which they acquire both status and roles. Yamaha's motorcycle ad in Figure 5.3 illustrates the impact of family and friends on buying decisions.

status
Relative position of any individual in a group.

roles
Behavior that members of a group expect of individuals who hold a specific position within it.

Status is the relative position of any individual member in a group; **roles** are what the other members of the group expect of individuals who hold specific positions within it. Some groups (such as Boy Scouts) are formal, and others (such as friendship groups) are informal. Both types of groups supply each member with both status and roles; in doing so, they influence that person's activities.

The Asch Phenomenon

Although most persons view themselves as individuals, groups are often highly influential in purchase decisions. In situations in which individuals feel that a particular group is important, they tend to adhere in varying degrees to the general expectations of that group.

Asch phenomenon
Occurrence first documented by psychologist S. E. Asch that illustrates the effect of a reference group on individual decision making.

The surprising impact that groups and group norms can exhibit on individuals' behavior has been called the **Asch phenomenon,** which was first documented in the following study conducted by psychologist S. E. Asch:

Eight subjects are brought into a room and asked to determine which of a set of three unequal lines is closest to the length of a fourth line shown some distance from the other three. The subjects are to announce their judgments publicly. Seven of the subjects are working for the experimenter and they announce incorrect matches. The order of announcement is arranged such that the naive subject responds last. In a control situation, 37 naive subjects performed the task 18 times each without any information about others' choices. Two of the 37 subjects made a total of 3 mistakes. However, when another group of 50 naive subjects responded after hearing the unanimous but incorrect judgment of the other group members, 37 made a total of 194 errors, all of which were in agreement with the mistake made by the group.[23]

This widely replicated study illustrates the impact of groups on individual decision making. Marketing applications range from the choice of automobile model and residential location to the decision to purchase at lease one item at a home party sponsored by a direct seller.

Figure 5.3
Social Influences that Affect
Consumer Behavior

Show this ad to your friends.

We built the TW200 with only one thing in mind.

Pure, unadulterated fun.

That's why we gave it a knobby rear tire that's not just fat, it's obese. And that's why we gave it fun stuff like Monocross rear suspension, five-speed gearbox and a high-torque, 196cc engine.

All of which makes the TW200 the most righteous, on-road, off-road, off-the-wall example of very un-basic transportation you can buy. But, as the next page shows, your parents will like it anyway.

YAMAHA
We make the difference.

12 month limited warranty. Warranty terms are limited. See your Yamaha dealer for details. Dress properly for your ride with a helmet, eye protection, long sleeved shirt, long trousers, gloves and boots. Yamaha and the Motorcycle Safety Foundation encourage you to ride safely and respect the environment.

Show this ad to your parents.

We built the TW200 with only one thing in mind.

Pure, unadulterated practicality.

That's why we gave it a built-in luggage rack, to carry your lunch box safely. And that's why we gave it electric starting and a low seat, to carry you easily to your meeting of the Concerned Young People Against Rock Lyrics.

All of which makes the TW200 the most practical, functional, plain-old-common-sense example of basic transportation you can buy.

But you'll like it anyway.

YAMAHA
We make the difference.

For further information regarding the MSF rider course please call 1-800-447-4700. Do not drink and drive. It is illegal and dangerous. Rear view mirror(s) standard equipment. Models sold in California equipped with evaporative emission control device. Specifications subject to change without notice.

Source: Courtesy of Yamaha.

Reference Groups

Groups whose value structures and standards influence a person's behavior are called **reference groups.** Consumers usually try to keep their purchase behavior in line with what they perceive to be the values of their reference groups. The extent of reference-group influence varies widely. In order for the influence to be great, two factors must be present:

reference group
Group with which an individual identifies to the point where it dictates a standard of behavior.

1. The item must be one that can be seen and identified by others.

2. The item must be conspicuous; it must stand out, be unusual, and be a brand or product that not everyone owns.

Reference-group influence would be significant in the decision to buy a Rolex watch, for example, but would have little or no impact on the decision to purchase a loaf of bread.

The status of the individual within the reference group produces three subcategories: a *membership group,* in which the person actually belongs to, say, a country club; an *aspirational group,* in which a person desires to associate with a group; and a *dissociative group,* with which the individual does not want to be identified by others. Although a reference group can be a membership group, it is not essential that the individual be a member for the group to serve as a point of reference. This concept helps explain the use of athletes in advertisements: Although few fans possess the skills of John McEnroe, all can identify with the tennis star by owning a pair of Nike shoes.

Social Classes

Although people prefer to think of the United States as the land of equality, a well-structured class system does exist. Research conducted a number of years ago by W. Lloyd Warner identified a six-class system within the social structures of both small and large cities: upper-upper; lower-upper; upper-middle; lower-middle; working-class; and lower-class.

Class rankings are determined by occupation, source (not amount) of income, education, family background, and dwelling area. Income is not a primary determinant; a pipe fitter paid at union scale earns more than many college professors, but his or her purchase behavior may be quite different. Thus, the adage "A rich man is a poor man with money" is incorrect from a marketing viewpoint.

Richard Coleman illustrates the behavior of three families, all earning approximately the same income but in decidedly different social classes. The upper-middle-class family—headed by a young lawyer or college professor—is likely to spend its money on a home in a prestigious neighborhood, expensive furniture from high-quality stores, and social club membership. At the same time, the lower-middle-class family—headed by a grocery store owner or a sales representative—probably purchases a good home in a less expensive neighborhood, buys furniture from less expensive stores, and has a savings account at the local bank. The lower-class family—headed by a truck driver or welder—likely spends less money on a home but buys one of the first new cars sold each year and owns one of the largest color television sets in town. It stocks its kitchen with appliances—symbols of security.[24]

The role of social class in determining consumer behavior continues to be a source of debate in the field of marketing. Some have argued against using social class as a market segmentation variable. Others disagree as to whether income or social class is the better base for targeting markets. The findings tend to be mixed. One study revealed that social class was the superior segmentation variable for food and non-soft-drink/non-alcoholic-beverage markets. Social class also influenced shopping behavior and evening television watching. Income was the superior segmentation variable for major appliances, soft drinks, mixes, and alcoholic beverages. For other categories, such as clothing, a combination of the two variables was found to be the best approach.[25]

Opinion Leaders

Every group usually contains a few members who can be considered **opinion leaders,** or trendsetters. These individuals are likely to purchase new products before others do and to serve as information sources for other group members.[26]

Generalized opinion leaders are rare; instead, individuals tend to be opinion leaders for specific products and services. Their distinguishing characteristics are considerable knowledge and interest in a particular product or service. Their interest in the product motivates them to seek out information from mass media, manufacturers, and other supply sources and, in turn, transmit this information to their non-leader associates through interpersonal communications. Opinion leaders are found within all segments of the population.

Direct, Two-Step, and Multistep Communication Flows   Information about products, retail outlets, and ideas flow through a number of channels. In some cases, the flows are from radio, television, and other mass media to opinion leaders and then from opinion leaders to the population masses. Elihu Katz and Paul Lazarsfeld refer to this channel as the *two-step process of communication*.[27] In other instances, the information flow is *direct*. Continuing access to communications channels allows much information to be transmitted directly to individuals who represent the organization's target market with no intermediaries. Another channel for information flows is a *multistep flow*. In this case, the flows are from mass media to opinion leaders and then on to other opinion leaders before being disseminated to the general public. Figure 5.4 illustrates the three types of communication flow.

Applying the Opinion Leadership Concept   Opinion leaders play a crucial role in interpersonal communication. The fact that they distribute information and advice to others indicates their potential importance for marketing strategy. Opinion leaders can be particularly useful in launching new products. For example, reaching opinion leaders was an important part of GM's distribution strategy when it introduced its Cadillac Allante, a model designed to compete with top European sports cars. GM found that younger car buyers had abandoned its nameplate in favor of BMWs and Mercedes. The Allante was intended to recapture the younger, affluent car buyer. GM introduced the Allante to one market at a time, beginning with New York, Los Angeles, San Diego, and seven other top metropolitan areas. In choosing cities, GM compared its strongest markets with the largest markets for BMWs, Porsches, Jaguars, and Mercedes. Peter Levin, Cadillac's director of merchandising, said, "We found pockets of strength where we could reach opinion leaders with the car, and we went into them first."[28]

Family Influences

One's family is also an interpersonal determinant of consumer behavior. The influence of household members is often significant in the purchase decision process. Because of the close, continuing interactions among family members,

opinion leader
Individual in a group who serves as an information source for other group members.

Figure 5.4
Alternative Channels for
Communication Flows

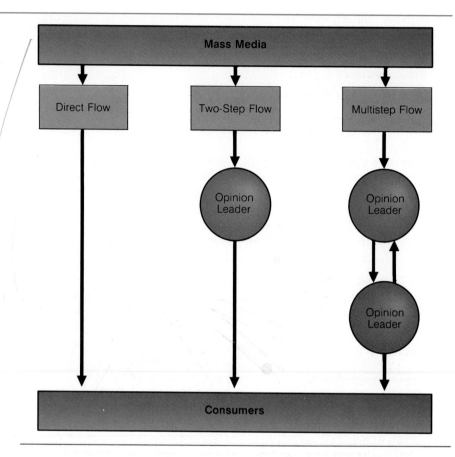

the family often represents the strongest source of group influence on the individual. Most people are members of at least two families during their lifetimes—the family into which they are born and the one they eventually form as they marry and have children.

The establishment of a new household results in new marketing opportunities. A new household means a new house or apartment and accompanying furniture. The need for refrigerators, vacuum cleaners, and paintings for living rooms depends not on the number of persons comprising the household but the number of households.

Fifty-eight percent of all U.S. households now include a married couple, and that percentage is projected to drop to 53 percent by 2000. The tremendous growth of single and other nonfamily households has caused the average household size to fall to 2.7 persons.[29]

Another market is established for parents whose children have moved away from home. These people may find themselves with a four-bedroom residence and a half-acre of lawn to maintain. Lacking maintenance assistance from their children and no longer needing the large house, they become customers for townhouses, condominiums, and high-rise apartments in larger cities. Some become residents of St. Petersburg, Sun City, or other centers for retired persons. Others become target markets for medical insurance, travel, and hearing aids. Designing houses specifically for senior citizens is one effort in reaching that market.

THE COMPETITIVE EDGE

Converse

Apparel makers seem to have a new theme: Get them while they're young—even if they're boys. Levi's, Nike, Lee, Wrangler, Reebok, and Converse are all big-name apparel makers that have discovered the marketing fountain of youth, devising ad campaigns to pitch their products to people from age 2 to 20.

Apparel makers used to give the youth market credit for its ability to whine loud enough to get toys and Zippo Bango Adventure-in-a-Box cereal. As for clothes, kids didn't care. But with single-parent families and working mothers on the rise, kids suddenly had to buy things for themselves, and they started to pay attention to what they purchased. Recent marketing studies show that 85 percent of children influence the brand of clothes bought for them—17 percent more than for cereal and 24 percent more than for toys.

Converse took its venerable line of Chuck Taylor All Star hightops and turned it into a fashion staple for the youth market. Studies indicate that kids want to express themselves as individuals; they don't want to look like every other kid and certainly not like their parents. Converse gave them complete freedom of choice by creating enough colors for its All Stars to rival a box of Crayolas. Converse came up with 18 colors, including pink, raspberry, and turquoise, and then went beyond artistic license

to create wildly colored spin-offs with unique designs and even glow-in-the-dark All Stars. In its quest to satisfy all tastes, Converse even came out with All Star Neehis, a shoe that can cover the calf or be rolled down to the ankle to reveal a completely different color or design on the inside.

Converse then created ads and promotions to hit the whole youth market. The All Star appears in everything from the "Twinkle, Twinkle Little Star" in-store poster, featuring a tot in hightops, to sassy spots on MTV featuring teens and clever print ads with in-between ages in the other major youth medium, magazines, including *Rolling Stone* and those in the Scholastic National Network.

This is perfect market segmenting, and it's paid off big. For instance, Converse hoped to sell 175,000 pairs of Neehis. Instead, it was swamped with orders for 600,000 pairs of two-tone Taylors. To further underscore the effect of the ad campaigns, Converse Chuck Taylor All Stars had the best year in their 75-year history, selling close to 16 million pairs.

"Our dealers say boys down to age two are telling their parents what they want on their feet," says Lou Nagy, director for advertising for Converse. Thanks to Converse marketing efforts, even the littlest shoe

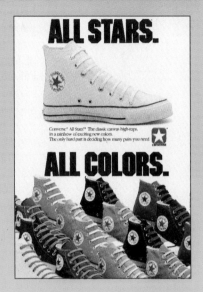

buyer will point out a vibrant pair of All Stars.

Converse also remembers who funds the sales by placing somewhat more staid ads in *People, Redbook, Working Mother,* and other adult-oriented magazines. After all, Chuck Taylor All Stars is a name that parents remember from their own youth.

Source: Jon Berry, "Tiny Trend-setters: Fashion Fits into Boys' Lives," *Adweek* (July 27, 1987), p. 32. *Photo source*: Courtesy of Converse, Incorporated.

Household Roles

Historically, the wife made the majority of family purchases and the husband worked at a paying job most of the day. Although the preferences of children or husband may have influenced her decisions, the wife usually was responsible for food buying and most clothing purchases.

Two forces have changed the female's role as sole purchasing agent for most household items. First, a shorter workweek provides each wage-earning household member with more time for shopping. Second, there are a large number of women in the work force. In 1950, only one-fourth of married women were employed outside the home; now over 50 percent have paid jobs. Studies of family decision making have shown that working wives tend to exert more influence in decision making than nonworking wives. Households with two wage earners also exhibit a large number of joint decisions and an increase in night and weekend shopping.

These changing roles of household members have led many marketers to adjust their marketing programs. For example, *The Wall Street Journal* noted: "In the world of TV commercials, dads now instruct their kids about Crest toothpaste, cook Aunt Jemima waffles for breakfast, cruise supermarket aisles for Kraft cheese, and change diapers with Johnson & Johnson baby powder. Teenagers cook Uncle Ben's rice for dinner, and the whole family pitches in to prepare Minute Rice."[30]

Although an infinite variety of roles can be played in household decision making, four role categories are most often used: (1) autonomic, in which an equal number of decisions is made by each partner; (2) husband dominant; (3) wife dominant; and (4) syncratic, in which most decisions are jointly made by both partners.[31] Figure 5.5 shows the roles household members play in the purchase of a number of products.

Teenagers: The Family's New Purchasing Agent

The role of children in purchasing decisions evolves as they grow older. Children's early influence generally is centered around toys to be recommended to Santa Claus and choice of cereal brands. Younger children are also important to marketers of fast-food restaurants.

As children grow older, they increasingly influence their clothing purchases. One recent study revealed that 29 million teenagers spend an average of $80 a month on clothing and other personal items and $100 a month of their families' money on household items. Total spending power of teenagers in a recent year was $65 billion. Teenagers today are buying more expensive items such as computers, bicycles, portable radio/cassette players, and wristwatches. Instead of spending their money going to the movies, 48 percent of teenagers now rent videotapes to watch at home.[32]

The growing number of married and divorced mothers who work outside the home has had a decided impact on household purchasing patterns. Recent research shows that both teenage boys and girls play an important role in their families' grocery purchases. A study of 1,000 teenagers conducted by Teenage Research Unlimited shows that the majority of teenage girls do some family grocery shopping. Although teenage boys shop less frequently than girls, both make product and brand decisions. Because many teenagers prepare their own meals, they buy food that is easy to prepare and requires little or no cleanup. In general, teenagers enjoy eating snack foods throughout the day. Their number-one fast-food preference is pizza.[33]

Little advertising has been targeted at these important buyers. Research suggests that television, radio, and magazines, not traditional newspaper shop-

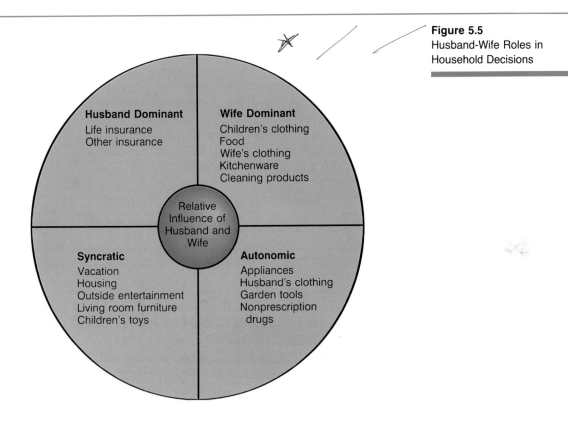

Figure 5.5
Husband-Wife Roles in
Household Decisions

Source: Examples reported in Harry L. Davis and Benny P. Rigaux, "Perception of Marital Roles in Decision Processes," *Journal of Consumer Research* (July 1974), p. 57.

ping sections, may be the best ways to reach this audience. About two-thirds of teenagers learn about new products from television. These young shoppers are not only a sizable part of the current market for many products; they are also the future market. Brand loyalties built now may last for decades. For example, a Yankelovich survey showed that 29 percent of adult women still drink the same coffee they drank as teenagers. The growing role of teenage shoppers is certainly an important new development in the study of consumer behavior.[34]

Personal Determinants of Consumer Behavior

Consumer behavior is a function of both interpersonal and personal influences. The personal determinants of consumer behavior, as shown in Figure 5.1, include the individual's needs and motives, perceptions, attitudes, and self-concept. The interactions of these factors with interpersonal influences cause the individual to act.

Needs and Motives

The starting point in the purchase decision process is the recognition of a felt need. A **need** is simply the lack of something useful. It is an imbalance between the consumer's actual and desired state. The consumer is typically confronted with numerous unsatisfied needs, but a need must be sufficiently aroused before it can serve as a motive to buy something.

Motives are inner states that direct a person toward the goal of satisfying a felt need. The individual is moved to take action to reduce a state of tension and to return to a condition of equilibrium.

need
Lack of something useful; a discrepancy between a desired state and the actual state.

motive
Inner state that directs a person toward the goal of satisfying a felt need.

Hierarchy of Needs

Although psychologists disagree on specific classifications, A. H. Maslow developed a useful theory of the hierarchy of needs, which is based on two important assumptions:

1. People are wanting animals whose needs depend on what they already possess. A satisfied need is not a motivator; only those needs that have not been satisfied can influence behavior.

2. People's needs are arranged in a hierarchy of importance. After one need has been at least partially satisfied, another emerges and demands satisfaction.[35]

Maslow's five-level hierarchy of needs begins with physiological needs and progresses to self-actualization needs. Table 5.1 illustrates products and marketing themes designed to satisfy each need level.

Physiological Needs   Physiological needs are primary needs for food, shelter, and clothing that must be satisfied before the individual can consider higher-order needs. After the physiological needs are at least partially satisfied, other needs enter the picture.

Safety Needs   The second-level safety needs include security, protection from physical harm, and avoidance of the unexpected. Gratification of these needs may take the form of a savings account, life insurance, purchase of radial tires, or membership in a local health club.

Social Belongingness Needs   Satisfaction of physiological and safety needs leads to the third level—the desire to be accepted by members of the family and other individuals and groups—the social needs. The individual may be motivated to join various groups, conform to their standards of dress and behavior, and become interested in obtaining status as a means of fulfilling these needs.

Esteem Needs   The higher-order needs are more prevalent in developed countries, in which a sufficiently high per capita income has allowed most consumers to satisfy the basic needs and thus concentrate on the desire for status, esteem, and self-actualization. These needs, which are near the top of the hierarchy, are more difficult to satisfy. At the esteem level is the need to feel a

Table 5.1
Marketing Strategies Designed for Each Level in Maslow's Needs Hierarchy

Needs	Products	Specific Themes
Self-actualization	Education, hobbies, sports, some vacations, gourmet foods, museums	*U.S. Army:* "Be all you can be." *U.S. Home:* "Make the rest of your life . . . the best of your life." *Outward Bound School:* "Challenges, adventure, growth."
Esteem	Clothing, furniture, liquors, hobbies, stores, cars, and many others	*Schaeffer:* "Your hand should look as contemporary as the rest of you." *St. Pauli Girl:* "People who know the difference in fine things know the difference between imported beer and St. Pauli Girl . . ." *Cricketeer:* "Cricketeer. Because the quality of your clothes should equal the quality of your life." *Cadillac:* " . . . those long hours have paid off. In recognition, financial success, and in the way you reward yourself. Isn't it time you owned a Cadillac?"
Social (Belongingness)	Personal grooming, foods, entertainment, clothing, and many others	*Atari:* "Atari brings the computer age home" (with a picture of a family using an Atari home computer). *Oil of Olay:* "When was the last time you and your husband met for lunch?" *J. C. Penney:* "Wherever teens gather, you'll hear it. It's the language of terrific fit and fashion . . . " *AT&T:* "Reach out and touch someone."
Safety	Smoke detectors, preventive medicines, insurance, social security, retirement investments, seat belts, burglar alarms, tires, safes	*Sleep Safe:* "We've designed a travel alarm that just might wake you in the middle of the night—because a fire is sending smoke into your room. You see, ours is a smoke alarm as well as an alarm clock." *General Electric:* "Taking a trip usually means leaving your troubles behind. But there are times when you just might need help or information on the road. And that's when you need HELP, the portable CB from GE." *Alka-Seltzer:* "Will it be there when you need it?"
Physiological	Limited in the United States. Generic foods, medicines, special drinks and foods for athletes	*Campbell Soup:* "Soup is good food" (with copy that stresses the nutritional benefits of soup). *Raisins:* "Thank goodness I found a snack food kids will sit for. And mothers will stand for." *Kellogg's All-Bran:* "At last, some news about cancer you can live with" (with copy that stresses the role of fiber in the diet).

Source: Reprinted by permission of the publisher from Del I. Hawkins, Roger D. Best, and Kenneth A. Coney, *Consumer Behavior* (Plano, TX: Business Publications, Inc., 1986), pp. 382–383.

sense of accomplishment, achievement, and respect from others. The competitive need to excel—to better the performance of others—is an almost universal human trait.

The esteem need is closely related to social needs. At this level, however, the individual desires not just acceptance but recognition and respect. The person desires to stand out from the crowd in some way.

Self-Actualization Needs   The top rung of the ladder of human needs is self-actualization—the need for fulfillment, realizing one's potential, and fully using one's talents and capabilities. Self-actualization motivates people only after other needs have been satisfied.

Maslow points out that a satisfied need is no longer a motivator. Once the physiological needs are met, the individual moves on to the higher-order needs. Consumers are periodically motivated by the need to relieve thirst or hunger, but their interests are most often directed toward satisfaction of safety, social, and other needs in the hierarchy.

Perceptions

Individual behavior resulting from motivation is affected by how stimuli are perceived. **Perception** is the meaning that the person attributes to incoming stimuli received through the five senses—sight, hearing, touch, taste, and smell. The York® Peppermint Pattie ad in Figure 5.6 demonstrates advertising that appeals to multiple senses.

> **perception**
> Manner in which an individual interprets a stimulus; the often highly subjective meaning that one attributes to an incoming stimulus or message.

Psychologists once assumed that perception is an objective phenomenon—that the individual perceives only what is there to be perceived. Only recently have researchers come to recognize that what people perceive is as much a result of what they *want* to perceive as of what is actually there. This does not mean that dogs may be viewed as pigeons or shopping centers as churches. Saks Fifth Avenue is perceived differently from K mart and Godiva chocolates differently from Fannie May.

The perception of an object or event results from the interaction of two types of factors:

1. *Stimulus factors:* Characteristics of the physical object, such as size, color, weight, or shape

2. *Individual factors:* Characteristics of the individual, including not only sensory processes but experiences with similar items and basic motivations and expectations

Perceptual Screens

People are continually bombarded with many stimuli, but most are ignored. In order to have time to function, people must respond selectively. Determining to which stimuli they do respond is a problem of all marketers. How can marketers gain the consumer's attention so that he or she will read the advertisement, listen to the sales representative, or react to the point-of-purchase display? Increasingly marketers are appealing to consumers' senses of smell and hearing. To gain the attention of shoppers, firms use point-of-purchase displays that emit their products' fragrances or deliver prerecorded advertising messages. For example, when customers pass a Bud Light display, they hear part of the beer's commercial and a brief sales pitch.[36]

> **perceptual screen**
> Perceptual filter through which messages must pass.

Although studies have shown that the average consumer is exposed to more than 500 advertisements daily, most of these ads never break through people's **perceptual screens**—the perceptual filters through which messages

Figure 5.6
Advertisement Appealing
to Multiple Senses

Escape
to a cool mountaintop.

Get the sensation.

Source: Courtesy of Cadbury Schweppes Inc. York® Peppermint Pattie is a registered trademark of Cadbury Schweppes Inc.

must pass. Sometimes breakthroughs are accomplished in the printed media through large ads. Doubling the size of an ad increases its attention value by about 50 percent. Using color in newspaper ads in contrast to the usual black and white is another effective way to break through the reader's perceptual screen. Other contrast methods include using a large amount of white space around a printed area or using white type on a black background.

In general, the marketer seeks to make the message stand out, to make it sufficiently different from other messages that it gains the prospective customer's attention. Realizing that few people ever get close to a Rolls-Royce, the car maker created an ad that gave prospective buyers a chance to smell the essence of owning one. It ran a one-time-only ad in *Architectural Digest* that carried a scented strip with the aroma of the automobile's leather, which the company claims is the finest in the world and has a very distinctive smell. The purpose of the ad was to shift people's perception of the Rolls-Royce as an out-of-reach, snob-appeal product to one more accessible and contemporary.[37]

The psychological concept of closure also achieves the objective of making a message stand out. *Closure* refers to people's tendency to produce a complete picture. Advertisements that allow consumers to do this are successful in breaking through perceptual screens. Salem cigarettes once asked people to complete the advertising theme "You can take Salem out of the country, but . . . ". Kellogg once used outdoor advertising with the last *g* omitted at the billboard's edge.[38] During a Kellogg campaign promoting the use of fruit with cereal, the company emphasized the point by replacing the *l*ls in "Kellogg" with bananas. In a campaign featuring a 25-cent coupon offer, Kellogg emphasized the promotion by replacing the *o* in the brand name with a quarter.

With such selective perception at work, it is easy to see the importance of the marketer's efforts to obtain a "consumer franchise" in the form of brand loyalty. Satisfied customers are less likely to seek information about competing products. Even when it is forced on them, they are less apt than others to allow it to pass through their perceptual filters. They simply tune out information that does not accord with their existing beliefs and expectations.

Subliminal Perception

Is it possible to communicate with persons without their being aware of the communication? In 1956, a New Jersey movie theater tried to boost concession sales by flashing the words "Eat Popcorn" and "Drink Coca-Cola" between frames of Kim Novak's image in the movie *Picnic*. The messages flashed on the screen every 5 seconds at $1/300$ seconds. Researchers reported that these messages, though too short to be recognizable at the conscious level, resulted in a 58 percent increase in popcorn sales and an 18 percent increase in Coca-Cola sales. After these findings were published, advertising agencies and consumer protection groups became intensely interested in **subliminal perception**—the receipt of incoming information at a subconscious level.

subliminal perception
Receipt of information at a subconscious level.

Subliminal advertising is aimed at the subconscious level of awareness to circumvent viewers' perceptual screens. The goal of the original research was to induce consumer purchasing while keeping consumers unaware of the source of their motivation to buy. Further attempts to duplicate the test findings, however, invariably have been unsuccessful.

Although subliminal advertising has been universally condemned as manipulative (and declared illegal in California and Canada), it is exceedingly unlikely that it can induce purchasing except in those instances in which the person is already inclined to buy. The reasons for this are:

1. Strong stimulus factors are required in order to even gain attention.
2. Only a very short message can be transmitted.
3. Individuals vary greatly in their thresholds of consciousness.[39] Messages transmitted at the threshold of consciousness for one person will not be perceived at all by some people and will be all too apparent to others. The subliminally exposed message "Drink Coca-Cola" may go unseen by some viewers, while others may read it as "Drink Pepsi-Cola," "Drink Cocoa," or even "Drive Slowly."

Despite early fears, research has shown that subliminal messages cannot force the receiver to purchase goods that he or she would not consciously want. But some marketers, with the help of social scientists and psychologists, continue to study the impact of their messages on consumers' subconscious levels. One marketing researcher claims that advertisers must be aware of subconscious subtleties that could result in communicating the wrong message. For example, an ad for Grey Flannel cologne that showed only a man's back could be perceived by some as giving the consumer the cold shoulder.[40]

In recent years, subliminal programming has spread to other commercial applications. One growing market is subliminal self-help audiocassette tapes. With these tapes, listeners hear on a conscious level relaxing music or the

FOCUS ON ETHICS

Consumers Want Values with Their Value

One of the fastest-growing trends today in consumer behavior is the increasing importance of ethical concerns in the marketplace. Consumers are now judging companies on a long list of ethical and political issues. This is happening in at least three ways.

First is the rise of "socially responsible" investments, including both money market funds and mutual funds. These funds, such as the $100-million-plus Working Assets money market fund or the $400 million Pioneer Three mutual fund, use ethical screening criteria to select stocks, bonds, or other investments. They usually avoid certain kinds of firms (such as those involved in nuclear power or weapons production, those that invest in South Africa, or those that engage in unfair labor practices) and promote other goals (such as alternative energy sources, housing, or education). The development of these funds was largely an outgrowth of universities and municipalities divesting their stock portfolios of companies doing business in South Africa and their need for professional investment management that would respect this decision.

Second is the growth of "affinity" credit cards, offered by many organizations in conjunction with banks, in which the bank makes small donations to the organization for every dollar charged on the cards. While charitable groups are not the only users of such cards, they do benefit from them. For example, Working Assets has a Visa card, charges on which earn small donations to a variety of charities and social-action groups. Recently over $32,000 was donated through the purchases of 13,000 cardholders.

Third is the expanded use of ethical issues information in making buying decisions. The Council on Economic Priorities publishes *Rating America's Corporate Conscience,* which considers corporate behavior in terms of South Africa, hiring and promotional practices with women and minorities, environmental and nuclear issues, and charitable contributions. While the ratings have been faulted by some business commentators, they do provide ethics-oriented information for consumer use. Prior to this publication, it was difficult to trace products to their producers in the wake of recent corporate reorganizations.

A more basic question is how far individuals will go in the direction of socially conscious buying. When a city or even a university boycotts products because of corporate practices, the impact can be substantial. However, individual shoppers cannot see the impact of their decisions and thus are forced to make what are basically symbolic actions.

How should a marketer respond to this trend? The answer hinges on whether you think consumers respond to perceptions of ethical and unethical corporate behavior. Marketers disagree on this issue. Don Dietrich, unit director of Scott Paper Company's Helping Hand line, says: "You have to offer the consumer something other than the opportunity to help others. The consumer has to get an equivalent value." Disagreeing in part is Tony Wainwright, president of The Bloom Companies: "I wouldn't have to give the consumer anything, but I would have to tell him what I was doing. But I'd sell more products if I added a coupon."

Regardless of how you evaluate this matter, evaluate it you must. As one broker says of the investment angle, "Socially responsible investing is growing at the fastest rate of any undeveloped investment niche." While adding values to products has not yet revolutionized the way America does business, it is definitely a factor in contemporary consumer behavior.

Sources: Kerry Elizabeth Knobelsdorff, "More Shoppers Weigh Ethics," *Christian Science Monitor* (July 10, 1987); "The Case of the Ethical Ketchup," *Fortune* (February 16, 1987), p. 28; Janet Neiman, "Values-Added Marketing," *Adweek* (April 6, 1987), pp. HM 18–20; and Nancy Dunnan, "Socially Conscious Investing," *ABA Journal* (November 1, 1986), p. 107.

sound of ocean waves and on a subconscious level, imperceptible to the ear, thousands of subliminal messages. Consumers buy the tapes to stop smoking, develop creativity, improve athletically, succeed financially, and for many other reasons. Marketing research by a manufacturer of subliminal tapes showed that consumers have accepted the new product because it delivers results with virtually no effort on their part. Although there is no scientific evidence proving that self-help subliminals change human behavior, consumer response has encouraged firms to expand their product lines.[41]

Attitudes

attitudes
One's enduring favorable or unfavorable evaluations, emotional
feelings, or pro or con action
tendencies.

Perception of incoming stimuli is greatly affected by attitudes. In fact, the decision to purchase a product is based on currently held attitudes about the product, store, or salesperson. **Attitudes** are a person's enduring favorable or unfavorable evaluations, emotional feelings, or pro or con action tendencies in
regard to some object or data. They are formed over time through individual
experiences and group contacts and are highly resistant to change.

Because favorable attitudes are likely to be conducive to brand preferences, marketers are interested in determining consumer attitudes toward their
products. Numerous attitude-scaling devices have been developed for this purpose.

Attitude Components

There are three related components of an attitude: cognitive, affective, and behavioral. The *cognitive* component refers to the individual's information and
knowledge about an object or concept. The *affective* component deals with feelings or emotional reactions. The *behavioral* component involves tendencies to
act in a certain manner. For example, in considering the decision to shop at a
warehouse-type food store, the individual would obtain information from advertising, trial visits, and input from family, friends, and associates (cognitive). He
or she would also receive input from others about their acceptance of shopping
at this type of store, as well as information about the type of people who shop
there (affective). The consumer may ultimately decide to make some purchases
of canned goods, cereal, and bakery products there but continue to rely on a
regular supermarket for major food purchases (behavioral).

All three components exist in a relatively stable and balanced relationship
to one another and together form an overall attitude about an object or idea.
Figure 5.7 illustrates the three attitude components.

Changing Consumer Attitudes

Given that a favorable consumer attitude is a prerequisite to marketing success,
how can a firm lead prospective buyers to adopt such an attitude toward its
products? The marketer has two choices: to attempt to change consumer attitudes to make them consonant with the product or to first determine consumer
attitudes and then change the product to match them.

If consumers view the product unfavorably, the firm may choose to redesign
it to make it better conform with their desires. It may make styling changes, vary
ingredients, change package size, or switch retail stores.

The other course of action—changing consumer attitudes—is much more
difficult. Consider the problem the U.S. auto industry has in changing some
Americans' negative attitudes toward domestic cars. U.S. automakers have improved the engineering of their cars, upgraded warranties, and extensively advertised their better-built products. But despite these efforts, they are having a
difficult time persuading Americans to buy their products. Marketing research
shows that Americans are convinced that German and Japanese cars are superior to domestic models. A Department of Commerce survey revealed that 13

Figure 5.7
Attitude Components

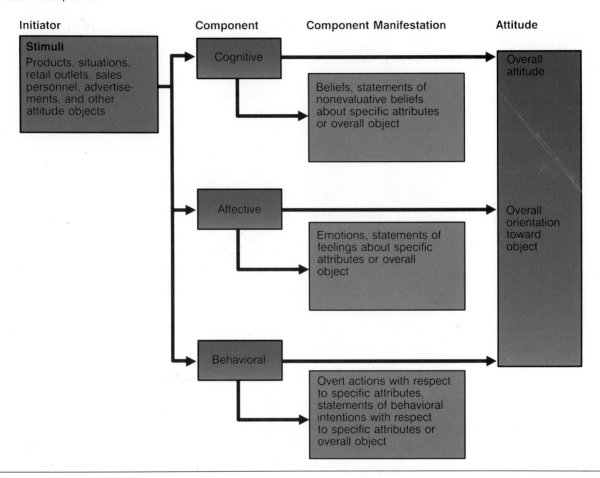

Source: Adapted from M. J. Rosenberg and C. I. Hovland, *Attitude Organization and Change* (New Haven, Conn.: Yale University Press, 1960), p. 3. Reprinted by permission.

percent of consumers would not even consider buying an American car. Most of these potential customers are under 40 and developing lifelong brand loyalties. To them, the "made in Detroit" label means a second-rate product.

Americans' negative attitudes toward U.S. cars have developed over many years and resulted from bad experiences with models such as GM's Vega and Ford's Pinto. According to an auto analyst, one person's bad experience with a car influences the attitudes of ten others. The same concept applies to satisfied owners of foreign models, compounding the U.S. automakers' problem.

Domestic automakers have tried to change Americans' attitudes by pumping billions of dollars into advertising that emphasizes the quality of their products. But one advertising executive claims that the quality approach is ineffective because it runs against what people believe. A Ford executive, however, contends that "persistent corporate advertising is the only way to reach someone who's been turned off by us."

Figure 5.8
Advertisement Designed to Influence the Affective Attitude Component

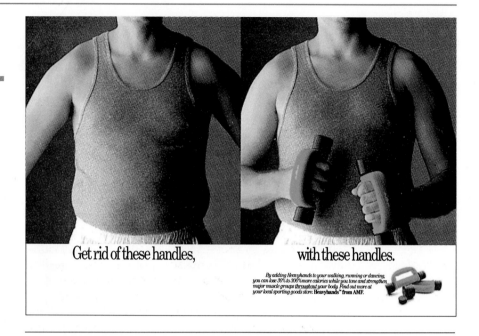

Get rid of these handles,   with these handles.

By adding Heavyhands to your walking, running or dancing, you can lose 30% to 300% more calories while you tone and strengthen major muscle groups throughout your body. Find out more at your local sporting goods store. **Heavyhands™ from AMF.**

Consumer attitudes often change with time. Thirty years ago, Americans equated the "made in Japan" label with poor quality. It took the Japanese 10 to 15 years to change people's attitudes, and it will probably take that long before Americans change their attitudes toward American cars.[42]

Modifying the Attitudinal Components

Attitude change frequently occurs when inconsistencies among the three attitudinal components are introduced. The most common inconsistencies are changes in the cognitive component of an attitude as a result of new information. The Pepsi Challenge was launched in an attempt to convince consumers that they preferred the taste of Pepsi, giving them new information that might lead to increased sales. A Life Savers advertising campaign built around the theme that a Life Saver contains only 10 calories was designed to correct many consumers' misconceptions about the candy's high caloric content.

The affective component may be altered by relating the use of the new product or service to desirable consequences for the user. For example, AMF's ad in Figure 5.8 describes how walkers, dancers, and runners can burn off 30 to 300 percent more calories when they use Heavyhands.

The third alternative in attempting to change attitudes is to focus on the behavioral component by inducing the person to engage in behavior that contradicts currently held attitudes. Attitude-discrepant behavior may occur if the consumer is given a free sample of a product. Trying the product may lead to an attitude change.

Learning

Marketing is as concerned with the process by which consumer decisions change over time as it is with describing those decisions at any given moment. Thus, the study of how learning takes place is important. **Learning** refers to changes in behavior, immediate or expected, as a result of experience.

The learning process includes several components. The first component, **drive,** is any strong stimulus that impels action. Examples of drives are fear, pride, desire for money, thirst, pain avoidance, and rivalry.

A **cue** is any object existing in the environment that determines the nature of the response to a drive. Examples of cues are a newspaper advertisement for a new French restaurant, an in-store display, and an Exxon sign near an interstate highway. For the hungry person, the shopper seeking a particular item, or the motorist needing gasoline, these cues may result in a specific response to satisfy a drive.

A **response** is the individual's reactions to cues and drive. Responses might include such reactions as purchasing a package of Gillette Trac II blades, dining at Burger King, or deciding to enroll at a particular college or university.

Reinforcement is the reduction in drive that results from a proper response. The more rewarding the response, the stronger becomes the bond between the drive and the purchase of the particular product. Should the purchase of Trac II blades result in closer shaves through repeated use, the likelihood of their future purchase is increased.

learning
Changes in behavior, immediate or expected, that occur as a result of experience.

drive
Strong stimulus that impels action.

cue
Any object existing in the environment that determines the nature of the response to a drive.

response
Individual's reaction to cues and drive.

reinforcement
Reduction in drive that results from an appropriate response.

Applying Learning Theory to Marketing Decisions

Learning theory has some important implications for marketing strategists.[43] A desired outcome such as repeat purchase behavior must be developed gradually. *Shaping* is the process of applying a series of rewards and reinforcements to permit more complex behavior to evolve over time. Both promotional strategy and the product itself play a role in the shaping process.

Figure 5.9 shows the application of learning theory and shaping procedures to a typical marketing scenario. Assume that marketers are attempting to motivate consumers to become regular buyers of a certain product. The first step is an initial product trial induced with a free sample package that includes a substantial discount coupon on a subsequent purchase. This example illustrates the use of a cue as a shaping procedure. The purchase response is reinforced by satisfactory product performance and a coupon for the next purchase.

The second step is to entice the consumer to buy the product with little financial risk. The large discount coupon enclosed with the free sample prompts such an action. The package that is purchased has a smaller discount coupon enclosed. Again the reinforcement is satisfactory product performance and the second coupon.

The third step is to motivate the person to buy the item again at a moderate cost. The discount coupon accomplishes this objective, but this time there is no additional coupon in the package. The only reinforcement is satisfactory product performance.

Figure 5.9
Application of Learning Theory and Shaping Procedure to Marketing

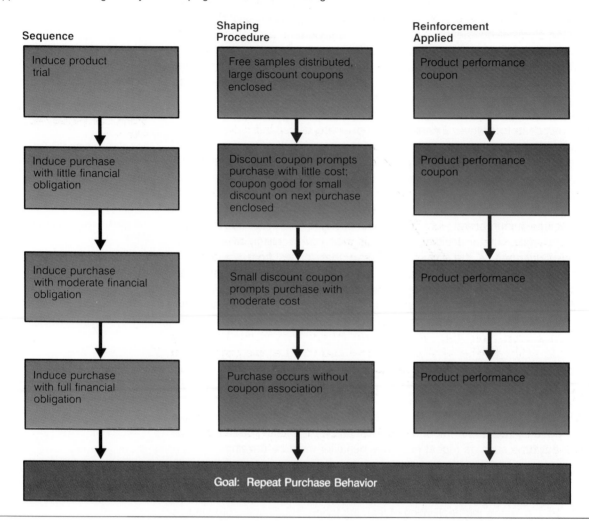

Source: Adapted from Michael L. Rothschild and William C. Gaidis, "Behavioral Learning Theory: Its Relevance to Marketing and Promotions," *Journal of Marketing* (Spring 1981), p. 72.

The final test comes when the consumer is asked to buy the product at its true price without a discount coupon. Satisfaction with product performance is the only continuing reinforcement. Thus, repeat purchase behavior literally will have been shaped by effective application of learning theory within a marketing strategy context.

The introduction of Kellogg's Nutri-Grain brand sugarless whole-grain cereal illustrates the use of learning theory. Coupons worth 40 cents off—about a third of the product's cost—were distributed to elicit trial purchases. Inside boxes of the new cereal were additional cents-off coupons of lesser value.[44]

Self-Concept Theory

The consumer's self-concept plays an important role in consumer behavior. Individuals are physical and mental entities possessing multifaceted pictures of themselves. One young man, for example, may view himself as intellectual, self-assured, talented, and a rising young business executive. People's actions, including their purchase decisions, are related to their mental conceptions of self—their **self-concepts.** The response to direct questions such as "Why do you buy Obsession?" is likely to reflect this desired self-image.

self-concept
Mental conception of one's self, comprised of the real self, self-image, looking-glass self, and ideal self.

The concept of self is the result of the interaction of many of the influences—both personal and interpersonal—affecting buyer behavior. The individual's needs, motives, perceptions, attitudes, and learning lie at the core of his or her conception of self in addition to the environmental factors of family, social, and cultural influences.

The self has four components: real self, self-image, looking-glass self, and ideal self. The *real self* is an objective view of the total person. The *self-image*—the way individuals view themselves—may distort the objective view. The *looking-glass self*—the way individuals think others see them—may also be quite different from self-image, because people often choose to project a different image to others. The *ideal self* serves as a personal set of objectives, since it is the image to which the individual aspires.

In purchasing goods and services, people are likely to choose products that move them closer to their ideal self-image. Those who see themselves as intellectuals are more likely than others to join literary book clubs. The young woman who views herself as a budding tennis star may become engrossed in evaluating the merits of graphite versus steel rackets and view any cheaply made rackets with disdain. The college graduate on the way up the organizational ladder at a bank may hide a love for bowling and take up golf, having determined that golf is the sport for bankers. Many young men see themselves in the romantic scenarios presented in Paco Rabanne's ads, such as the one in Figure 5.10.

The Consumer Decision Process

The model in Figure 5.1 shows that the integration of personal and interpersonal determinants affects the consumer decision process. These influences on the individual create a recognition that a problem or opportunity exists. This recognition triggers the consumer decision process outlined in the following sections.

Problem Recognition

The first stage in the decision process occurs when the consumer becomes aware of a significant discrepancy between the existing state of affairs and a desired state of affairs. Once the problem has been recognized, it must be defined so that the consumer may seek out methods for its solution. As a consequence of problem recognition, the individual is motivated to achieve the desired state.

Figure 5.10
Use of Self-Concept Theory in Paco Rabanne Advertising

Hello?
*How's the Great American
Novel going?*
So far it reads more like the turgid
insights of a lonely Albanian
date-plucker.
Did I hear the word "lonely"?
There's a fog rolling in.
*You're in Pawgansett, dear. It
holds the world record for fog.*
The "t" in my typewriter is
sticking. I have seventeen cans of
lentil soup. And my Paco Rabanne
cologne, which I use to lure shy
maidens out of the woods, is
gone, all gone.
*You're going to have to do better
than that.*
All right, I'm lonely. I miss you.
I miss your cute little broken
nose. I miss the sight of you in
bed in the morning, all pink and
pearly and surly.
*And you want me to catch the
train up.*
Hurry! This thing they call love is
about to burst the bounds of
decency. And, darling...
Yes?
Bring a bottle of Paco Rabanne,
would you? The maidens are
getting restless.
Swine!

Paco Rabanne
A cologne for men
What is remembered is up to you

Source: Courtesy of Paco Rabanne.

Perhaps the most common cause of problem recognition is routine deple-tion of the individual's stock of products. A large number of consumer pur-chases involve the replenishment of items ranging from gasoline to groceries. In other instances, the consumer may possess an inadequate assortment of products. The gardening hobbyist may make regular purchases of different fer-tilizers, seeds, or gardening tools as the garden grows.

A third cause of problem recognition is dissatisfaction with the present brand or product type. This situation is common in the purchase of a new au-tomobile, new furniture, or a new fall wardrobe. In many instances, the con-sumer's boredom with current products and a desire for novelty may be the underlying rationale for the decision process leading to new-product pur-chases.

Another important factor in problem recognition is changed financial status. The infusion of added financial resources from such sources as a salary in-crease, a second job, or an inheritance may permit the consumer to make pur-chases that previously had been postponed.

Search

The second step in the decision process is search—the gathering of information related to the attainment of a desired state of affairs. This stage permits the identification of alternative means of problem solution.

Search may be internal or external. Internal search is a mental review of stored information relevant to the problem situation. This includes both actual experiences and observations and memories of personal communications and exposures to persuasive marketing efforts.

External search is the gathering of information from outside sources by the consumer involved in the search process. Outside information sources may include family members, friends and associates, store displays, sales representatives, brochures, and product-testing publications such as *Consumer Reports.*

In many instances, the consumer solves problems through internal search. The individual merely relies on stored information in making a purchase decision. Achieving favorable results using a certain car polish may sufficiently motivate a consumer to repurchase this brand rather than consider possible alternatives. Since external search involves both time and effort, the consumer will rely on it only when adequate information is unavailable in memory.

Alternative brands for consideration and possible purchase are identified during the search process. The number of brands that a consumer actually considers in making a purchase decision is known as the **evoked set.** In some instances, the consumer is aware of the brands worthy of further consideration; in others, the external search process involves the acquisition of information necessary for permitting the consumer to identify the brands that comprise the evoked set.

evoked set
In consumer decision making, number of brands that a consumer actually considers before making a purchase decision.

Not all brands are included in the evoked set. Sometimes the consumer is unaware of certain brands, others are rejected as too costly, and still others have been tried previously and judged unsatisfactory. Unfavorable word-of-mouth communication or negative reactions to advertising or other marketing efforts may also result in the elimination of some brands from the evoked set. While the number of brands in the evoked set will vary by product category, research indicates that the number is likely to be as few as four or five brands.[45]

Evaluation of Alternatives

The third step in the consumer decision process involves the evaluation of alternatives identified during the search process. Actually, it is difficult to completely separate the second and third steps, since some evaluation takes place simultaneously with the search process as consumers accept, discount, distort, or reject incoming information as they receive it.

Since the outcome of the evaluation stage is the choice of a brand or product in the evoked set (or possibly the search for additional alternatives should all those identified during the search process prove unsatisfactory), the consumer must develop a set of evaluative criteria for use in making the selection. **Evaluative criteria** may be defined as those features the consumer considers in making a choice among alternatives. These criteria can be either objective (government tests of miles per gallon) or subjective (favorable image of Calvin Klein sportswear). Commonly used evaluative criteria include price, brand reputation, perceived quality, packaging, size, performance, durability, and color. Evaluative criteria for detergents include suds level and smell as indicators of

evaluative criteria
In consumer decision making, features considered in a consumer's choice of alternatives.

By providing information, marketers assist consumers in the search and evaluation stages of the decision process. Albertson's, a Boise, Idaho-based chain of retail food and drug stores, helps consumers solve their shopping problems through programs such as "Lean Facts," which provides nutritional information on fresh meat. The program includes in-store displays, brochures, and recipes as well as radio, television, and newspaper advertising.

Photo source: Courtesy of Albertson's, Incorporated.

cleaning power. Most research studies show that consumers utilize six or fewer criteria in the evaluation process.[46]

Purchase Decision and Purchase Act

The end result of the search and alternative evaluation stages of the decision process is the actual purchase decision and the act of making the purchase. In this stage, the consumer has evaluated each alternative in the evoked set, utilizing his or her personal set of evaluative criteria, and narrowed the alternatives down to one.

Another decision facing the consumer is the purchase location. Consumers tend to make store choices by considering such factors as location, price, assortment, personnel, store image, physical design, and services. In addition, store selection is influenced by the product category. Some consumers choose the convenience of in-home shopping via telephone or mail order rather than complete the transaction in a retail store.

Postpurchase Evaluation

cognitive dissonance
Postpurchase anxiety that results when an imbalance exists among an individual's cognitions (knowledge, beliefs, and attitudes).

The purchase act results in either satisfaction to the buyer and removal of the discrepancy between the existing and desired states or dissatisfaction with the purchase. It is also common for consumers to experience some postpurchase anxieties, called **cognitive dissonance.**

Dissonance is a psychologically unpleasant state that occurs when an imbalance exists among a person's *cognitions* (knowledge, beliefs, and attitudes).

For example, consumers may experience dissonance after choosing a particular automobile over several alternative models when some of the rejected models have some desired features not available with the chosen one.

Dissonance is likely to increase (1) as the dollar value of the purchase increases, (2) when the rejected alternatives have desirable features not present in the chosen alternative, and (3) when the decision is a major one. The consumer may attempt to reduce dissonance in a variety of ways. He or she may seek out advertisements or other information supporting the chosen alternative or seek reassurance from acquaintances who are satisfied purchasers of the product. The individual may also avoid information favoring the unchosen alternative. The Toyota purchaser is likely to read Toyota advertisements and avoid Nissan and Subaru ads.

Marketers can assist in reducing cognitive dissonance by providing informational support for the chosen alternative. Automobile dealers recognize "buyer's remorse" and often follow up purchases with a warm letter from the dealership owner offering personal handling of any customer problems and including a description of the product's quality and the availability of convenient, top-quality service.

A final method of dealing with cognitive dissonance is to change options, thereby restoring the cognitive balance. In this instance, the consumer may ultimately decide that one of the rejected alternatives would have been the best choice and vow to purchase it in the future.

Should the purchase prove unsatisfactory, the consumer's purchase strategy must be revised to allow attainment of need satisfaction. Satisfactory or not, feedback on the results of the decision process will serve as experience to be called on in similar buying situations in the future.

Classifying Consumer Problem-Solving Processes

The consumer decision process varies on the basis of the problem-solving effort required. There are three categories of problem-solving behavior: routinized response behavior, limited problem solving, and extended problem solving.[47] The classification of a particular purchase according to this framework clearly influences the consumer decision process.

Routinized Response Behavior   Many purchases are made on the basis of a preferred brand or selection from a limited group of acceptable brands. This type of rapid consumer problem solving is referred to as *routinized response behavior*. The evaluative criteria are set and the available options identified. External search is limited in cases of routinized response behavior, such as the routine purchase of regular brands of beer, cigarettes, or soft drinks.

Limited Problem Solving   Consider the situation in which the consumer has set evaluative criteria but encounters a new, unknown brand. The introduction of a new fragrance line is an example of a *limited problem-solving* situation. The consumer knows the evaluative criteria but has not used them to assess the new brand. A moderate amount of time and external search is involved in such situations. Limited problem solving is affected by the number of evaluative criteria and brands, the extent of external search, and the process by which preferences are determined.

Extended Problem Solving   *Extended problem solving* results from situations in which the brand is difficult to categorize or evaluate. The first step is to compare the item with similar ones. The consumer needs to understand the item before evaluating alternatives. Most extended problem-solving efforts are lengthy and involve considerable external search.

Regardless of the type of problem solving involved, the steps in the basic model of the consumer decision process remain valid. The problem-solving categories described here relate only to the time and effort devoted to each step of the process.

Summary of Chapter Objectives

1. Explain the classification of behavioral influences in consumer decisions. The behavioral influences in consumer decisions are classified as either personal or interpersonal. These categories resulted from the work of Kurt Lewin who developed a general model of behavior.

2. Identify the interpersonal determinants of consumer behavior. There are three interpersonal determinants of consumer behavior: cultural influences, social influences, and family influences. Culture, the broadest of these influences, refers to behavioral values that are created and inherited by a society. The work ethic and the accumulation of wealth were the original determinants of American culture. Cultural norms can change over time. Traditionally the pace of change is slow; however, it may increase in the future.

Cultural influences are particularly significant in international marketing, but they are also crucial factors in domestic marketing. Increased attention is being devoted to the consumption behavior patterns of U.S. subcultures. The three largest American subcultures are blacks, Hispanics, and Asians, which are rapidly growing market segments.

Social influences concern the nonfamily group influences on consumer behavior. The existence of a U.S. class system was demonstrated by W. Lloyd Warner years ago. Opinion leaders, or trendsetters, are another important social influence on consumer behavior. Their reactions to new products are highly influential in the future success of the good or service. Marketers must make special efforts to appeal to these flagships of consumer behavior.

Family influences are the third interpersonal determinant of consumer behavior. Family purchasing patterns vary. In some cases the female is dominant, in others the male. Some purchase decisions are made jointly, while others are made separately, but the number of such decisions is roughly equal for males and females. The traditional role for the female was that of family purchasing agent. This situation is now in flux; for example, more teenagers are doing the household shopping.

3. Identify the personal determinants of consumer behavior. The personal determinants of consumer behavior are needs and motives, perceptions, attitudes, learning, and self-concept. A need is the lack of something useful. Motives are the inner states that direct individuals to satisfy needs. A. H. Maslow proposed a hierarchy of needs that starts with basic physiological needs and proceeds to progressively higher need levels—safety, social, esteem, and self-actualization. Perception is the meaning that a person assigns to stimuli received through the five senses. Because most incoming stimuli are screened or filtered out, the marketer's task is to break through these perceptual screens in order to effectively present the sales message. Attitudes are a person's evaluations and feelings toward an object or idea. There are three components of attitudes: cognitive (what the person knows), affective (what the person feels about something), and behavioral (how the person tends to act). Learning refers to changes in behavior, immediate or expected, as a result of experience. The learning theory concept can be useful in building consumer loyalty for a particular brand. The self-concept refers to an individual's conception of self. Self-concept theory has important implications for marketing strategy, such as in the case of targeting advertising messages.

4. Outline the steps in the consumer decision process. The consumer decision process consists of six steps: problem or opportunity recognition, search, evaluation of alternatives, purchase decision, purchase act, and postpurchase evaluation. The time involved in each stage of the decision process is determined by the nature of individual purchases.

5. Differentiate among routinized response behavior, limited problem solving, and extended problem solving. Routinized response behavior, limited problem solving, and extended problem solving are the three categories of problem-solving behavior. Routinized response behavior refers to purchase situations based on selection of a preferred brand or from a group of acceptable brands. When the alternative criteria are set but a new brand is encountered, limited problem solving takes place. Extended problem solving occurs when a new brand is difficult to evaluate or categorize. Extended problem-solving efforts are lengthy and involve considerable external search.

Key Terms

consumer behavior
culture
subculture
status
roles
Asch phenomenon
reference group
opinion leader
need
motive
perception
perceptual screen

subliminal perception
attitudes
learning
drive
cue
response
reinforcement
self-concept
evoked set
evaluative criteria
cognitive dissonance

Review Questions

1. What are the two primary determinants of behavior according to Kurt Lewin?
2. List the steps in the consumer decision process.
3. Explain the interpersonal determinants of consumer behavior.
4. How does culture affect buying patterns?
5. Relate social class to consumer behavior.
6. Describe family influences on consumer behavior and how they are changing.

7. What are the personal determinants of consumer behavior?

8. Explain the concept of perception. Consider perceptual screens, selective perception, and subliminal perception in your explanation.

9. How do attitudes influence consumer behavior? How can negative attitudes be changed?

10. Differentiate among the four components of the self-concept: ideal self, looking-glass self, self-image, and real self.

Discussion Questions

1. Relate a recent purchase you made to the consumer decision-making process shown in Figure 5.1.

2. For which of the following products is reference-group influence likely to be strong?
   a. Corona beer
   b. Skis
   c. Shaving lather
   d. Eighteen-speed mountain bike
   e. Portable radio
   f. Soft contact lenses

3. Describe the opinion leaders in a group to which you belong. Why are these people the group's opinion leaders?

4. List two products for which the following family members might be most influential:
   a. Mother
   b. Six-year-old child
   c. Father
   d. Teenage son
   e. Teenage daughter
   f. Two-year-old child

5. Poll your friends about subliminal perception. How many believe that marketers can control consumers at a subconscious level? Report the results of this survey to your marketing class.

VIDEO CASE 5

Kawasaki Motors Corp.

Santa Ana, California-based Kawasaki Motors Corp., U.S.A., is a wholly owned subsidiary of Japan's Kawasaki Heavy Industries Ltd. and sells about $375 million worth of motorcycles annually in the United States. Kawasaki offers American consumers two types of motorcycles — sports models and custom models — each of which appeals to a different group of buyers.

Kawasaki asked its advertising agency, Kenyon & Eckhardt, to develop a print advertisement that would appeal to buyers of both sports and custom models without alienating either group. The firm needed an advertisement that would stand out from the 2400 ads that every American consumer is exposed to each week, and that would break through the clutter that characterizes contemporary U.S. advertising.

To accomplish these objectives, Peter Goodwin, the account supervisor for Kawasaki, asked Renee Fraser, a psychologist and the agency's research director, to gather information about motorcycle owners to find out why they buy what they do. The agency's creative people — artists and copywriters — needed this information to create an advertisement that satisfied the needs of motorcycle buyers. The advertisement had to influence the purchase decisions of new buyers and also reassure current owners that they had made the right choice. This latter goal is known as alleviating cognitive dissonance, the post-purchase doubt that accompanies any major purchase.

Fraser understood the importance of her task. She remarked, "To make persuasive advertising we have to really understand what motivates the consumer." Fraser began by checking some databases to learn about the people who buy motorcycles. This secondary research produced considerable demographic statistics such as income, age, and so forth. But Fraser realized that this information was useless because it did not tell her what really motivated people to buy motorcycles.

As a result, Fraser decided to gather some primary data by using focus groups, personal in-depth interviews, and field research. In speaking to motorcycle owners, Fraser learned that the motorcycle buying audience consists of a wide range of people from many social classes — blue collar workers, professionals (doctors, engineers, lawyers), even movie stars. Owners are much more diverse than the stereotypical motorcycle rider.

The motorcycle owners interviewed shared many common traits: cycling gave them a sense of power, a sense of being in control, and a feeling of independence and freedom (which are core values discussed in the interpersonal determinants section of Chapter 5). They liked being outside, feeling the wind on their faces, and enjoyed the thrill and speed of riding, being able to control the risk and dangers involved. Owning and riding a motorcycle was important in their self-concept and in satisfying esteem needs. One of the people that Fraser interviewed expressed the feeling this way: "I sort of feel like a pioneer. . . ." Fraser herself commented: "It was almost as if there was a relationship between them and the bike; it was their thing."

In later meetings with other Kenyon & Eckhardt personnel, Fraser noted that motorcycle riders ". . . want to demonstrate to other people what they really are . . . it's almost like they take off their clothes and they are Superman underneath." The research director continued: "One of the fantasies these men have about themselves on the bike is that they are the lone cowboy . . . they identify very strongly with that image of themselves."

The Kenyon & Eckhardt staff decided that motorcycle riders in general are not so much concerned with vehicle performance as with the way the motorcycle looks and the way it makes them look. The challenge was to come up with a print advertisement that would appeal to this image and break through the advertising clutter discussed earlier.

The agency's art department eventually designed a print advertisement showing a lone rider rounding a bend with the bike leaning to the side and the rider's knee almost touching the ground. The rider's position had been suggested several times by the people Fraser interviewed. The Kawasaki advertisement captures the thrill of riding — the wind, the speed, the danger. It depicts the self-image of cyclists, projecting a positive relationship between the product and the buyer. Both types of cyclists — those who ride sports bikes and those who ride custom models — can see themselves in this ad.

Questions

1. Which categories of the personal and interpersonal determinants of consumer behavior influence a person's decision to purchase a motorcycle?

2. Use this video case to explain the relationship between marketing research and the study of consumer behavior.

3. Discuss how you would respond to the Kawasaki print ad.

COMPUTER APPLICATIONS

Two important concepts discussed in connection with the consumer decision process are evoked set and evaluative criteria. An *evoked set* is defined in this chapter as the number of brands a consumer actually considers in his or her search behavior. *Evaluative criteria* are those features the consumer considers in selecting a specific purchase option. Both concepts are described in detail on pages 191–192.

Consumers develop various methods for making purchase choices from alternative products or brands. For major purchases and cases involving considerable risk, potential buyers may score or rank the brands that comprise their evoked sets on the basis of various evaluative criteria. Then the question becomes how to best make the actual purchase decision. Approaches to this problem include the following:

1. *Overall scoring method.* This approach uses the highest total score to select a brand from the evoked set. All of the evaluative criteria are considered equally important, and the brand with the highest overall score is chosen.

2. *Weighted scoring method.* This approach involves assigning different weights to the various evaluative criteria according to the consumer's perception of their relative importance. Once the variables are assigned their weighted scores, they are totaled and the brand with the highest score is selected.

3. *Minimum-score method.* This approach sets a floor for one or more evaluative criteria below which a brand will not be selected. For example, if the consumer decides that a brand must receive a ranking of 4 or more on "service availability," a brand ranked 3 for this criterion will be rejected even if it receives the highest overall score. The minimum-score method is frequently used in conjunction with either the overall scoring method or the weighted scoring method.

It should be noted that these methods represent quantitative approaches to a typically qualitatively oriented subject. Not all consumers behave in such a fashion. Moreover, those who do may differ significantly in their scoring evaluations. The following problems refer to a specific consumer's perceptions of a purchasing situation in which he or she has already determined the evaluative criteria and the evoked set.

Directions: Use menu item 5 titled "Evaluation of Alternatives" to solve each of the following problems.

Problem 1   Pam Zimmer of Cincinnati is attempting to select a new car based on the following criteria: price, trade-in allowance, styling, riding comfort, and fuel economy. Earlier Zimmer had narrowed her decision to four models: Elegance, Standard, Speedo, and Majestic. She then decided to rate each model on each evaluative criterion, using 3 to represent "excellent," 2 for "good," and 1 for "fair." Her rankings are as follows:

Evoked-Set Alternatives	Evaluative Criteria: Decision Factors				
	(A) Price	(B) Trade-in Allowance	(C) Styling	(D) Riding Comfort	(E) Fuel Economy
1. Elegance	2	2	3	3	2
2. Standard	2	2	2	2	3
3. Speedo	3	3	3	3	1
4. Majestic	3	3	1	1	3

a. Which model would Zimmer select using the overall scoring method?
b. Suppose Zimmer decides that fuel economy, price, and trade-in allowance are each 50 percent more important than the other two evaluative criteria. Which model will she select?
c. Suppose that using the overall scoring method Zimmer also decides she will not accept any model that is rated lower than "good" on fuel economy, price, and trade-in allowance. Which model will she prefer?
d. Would Zimmer's decision in question c change if she decided to use the weighted scoring method?

Problem 2   Like Pam Zimmer in Problem 1, Tom Jenkins is contemplating the purchase of a new car. In fact, he and Zimmer conferred before assigning the ratings for the Elegance, Standard, Speedo, and Majestic. However, Jenkins also considers another auto model, the Olympic, a viable option. His rankings are as follows:

	Evaluative Criteria: Decision Factors				
Evoked-Set Alternatives	**(A)** Price	**(B)** Trade-in Allowance	**(C)** Styling	**(D)** Riding Comfort	**(E)** Fuel Economy
1. Elegance	2	2	3	3	2
2. Standard	2	2	2	2	3
3. Speedo	3	3	3	3	1
4. Majestic	3	3	1	1	3
5. Olympic	3	2	2	2	2

a. Which model would Jenkins select using the overall scoring method?
b. Suppose Jenkins considers riding comfort and fuel economy 100 percent more important than styling and price and trade-in allowance 200 percent more important than styling. Which model will he select?
c. Suppose that using the overall scoring method Jenkins also decides that he will not accept a car that is rated lower than "good" on any variable. Which model will he select?
d. Would Jenkins' decision in question c change if he used the weighted scoring method?

Problem 3   Edna Fram, of Morristown, New Jersey, is considering the purchase of a new refrigerator. Her evoked set consists of five brands: Best Fridge, Chillmaster, Super Fridge, Excellence, and Keep Fresher. Fram's evaluative criteria are price, energy efficiency, appearance, ice-making feature, and reversible doors. She decides to use a seven-point rating scale in making her assessment. Scores range from 1 (unacceptable or feature absent) to 7 (perfect). Fram's scores are as follows:

	Evaluative Criteria: Decision Factors				
Evoked-Set Alternatives	**(A)** Price	**(B)** Energy Efficiency	**(C)** Appearance	**(D)** Ice-Making Feature	**(E)** Reversible Doors
1. Best Fridge	4	5	5	7	1
2. Chillmaster	7	5	7	7	1
3. Super Fridge	2	2	7	7	7
4. Excellence	3	4	2	7	7
5. Keep Fresher	7	7	4	1	7

a. Which model would Fram select using the overall scoring method?
b. Suppose Fram considers price and energy efficiency 100 percent more important than the other criteria. Which model would she select if she assigned this weight to price and energy efficiency?
c. Suppose that using the overall scoring method Fram decides that an ice maker and reversible doors are absolutely essential. What model will she select?
d. Would Fram's decision in question c change if she used a weighted scoring method?

Problem 4   A Sacramento, California, consumer is considering four brands of washing machines: Master Wash, Washer Magic, Washing Wonder, and Super Wash. She has decided to evaluate the brands on the bases of price, quality, warranty, and service availability. She has also decided to give each model a score of 1 (poor) to 5 (best) on each evaluative criterion. Her rankings are as follows:

Evoked-Set Alternatives	Evaluative Criteria: Decision Factors			
	(A) Price	(B) Quality	(C) Warranty	(D) Service Availability
1. Master Wash	4	3	4	4
2. Washer Magic	4	4	4	4
3. Washing Wonder	2	5	5	5
4. Super Wash	5	5	4	2

a. Which model would the consumer select using the overall scoring method?
b. Suppose the consumer considers price 50 percent more important than any of the other evaluative criteria. Which model will she select?
c. Suppose that using the overall scoring method the consumer also decides that she will not accept any model scoring lower than 3 on any variable. Which model will she select?
d. Would your response to question c change if the consumer used the weighted scoring method?

Problem 5   Al Ogden, director of purchasing for Granite Industries of Nassau, New Hampshire, is a very orderly decision maker. When he was asked to purchase a snowblower, Ogden developed a 100-point scoring system to evaluate different models on the bases of price, ease of use, power, warranty, and ease of maintenance. The maximum score is 100. Ogden's evoked set consists of five brands: Snow Tosser, White Energy, Super Blower, The Remover, and Expert Blower. His scores are as follows:

Evoked-Set Alternatives	Evaluative Criteria: Decision Factors				
	(A) Price	(B) Ease of Use	(C) Power	(D) Warranty	(E) Ease of Maintenance
1. Snow Tosser	70	75	65	60	70
2. White Energy	95	45	75	99	100
3. Super Blower	45	85	85	100	100
4. The Remover	75	75	80	45	60
5. Expert Blower	99	50	55	70	60

a. Which model would Ogden select using the overall scoring method?

b. Suppose Ogden considers price and power 100 percent more important than the other criteria. Which model will he select if he assigns this weight to price and power?

c. Suppose that using the overall scoring method Ogden decides he will not accept any snowblower that scores less than 50 on any evaluative criterion. Which brand will he select?

d. Would Ogden's decision in question c change if he used the weighted scoring method?

6

Organizational Buying Behavior

Chapter Objectives

1. To list and define the components of the organizational market.

2. To describe the nature and importance of the industrial market.

3. To identify the major characteristics of industrial markets and industrial market demand.

4. To describe organizational buying behavior.

5. To classify organizational buying situations.

6. To explain the buying center concept.

7. To outline the steps in the organizational buying process.

8. To compare government markets with other organizational markets.

Billions of copies pour out of copy machines each year. But there was a time when the man most responsible for all these machines could not sell his invention anywhere.

Between 1939 and 1944, Chester Carlson's invention was turned down by more than 20 companies. Even the name of his oft-rejected invention was turned down. He called it electrophotography, but the marketers rejected the name as too cumbersome. They changed it to "xerography," for the Greek words "dry" and "writing."

His invention was finally accepted by Haloid, a small photo-paper maker in Rochester, N. Y., which spent $12.5 million and 10 years developing the first automated dry process copier from Carlson's basic work. When the machine took off, Haloid changed its name to — what else? — Xerox.

How important was the development of the modern copier? "It is a milestone," said Eugene Ostroff, curator of photography at the Smithsonian National Museum of American History, where one of the original Xerox 914 copiers is now included in the collection.

"It did truly change the entire complexion of the business of doing business. There is an occasional secretary that almost doesn't know what carbon paper is. Carbon paper was a way of life before these copiers were introduced," said Ostroff.

When Xerox leased its first machine to Standard Pressed Steel in Newton, Pa., in 1960, the copiers then on the market generally produced copies that were wet, and potentially messy, when they came out of the machine. The Xerox machine produced dry copies and was an instant hit.

Charlotte Wresinski, a secretary, is among those who remember when wet process copiers and carbon paper were the office staples. "We had garbage cans full of that," she said. "You wore it home, you wore it on your clothes. It was kind of messy."

Ros Todaro, a vice president of Ko-Rec-Type, a carbon paper manufacturer, remembers those days fondly. In 1960, the year Xerox produced its first machine, Todaro's company sold 10 million boxes of carbon paper. Now it sells about a million boxes a year.

"I would say the use of carbon paper went down at least 60 to 70 percent," said Todaro. "My guess is, chances are the only carbon paper will be pencil carbons, in the form of little pads, receipt things. I foresee that carbon paper will be obsolete."

Wresinski, an executive secretary at Allstate Insurance, was in the typing pool when Allstate got its first dry process copiers 20 years ago.

"We had a copy room for the whole building with two or three machines for 400 people," she said. "You could go stand in line for 25 minutes. It was probably worth it compared to the other methods we had."

Today, copy machines can produce hundreds of exquisite duplicates, in color, on both sides of the paper, in different sizes. Wresinski doesn't even have to leave her desk.

The office copier also has had a side effect that some people don't find pleasing. They are at least partially responsible for the paperwork explosion that seems at times to engulf businesses.

"The ready accessibility of copy machines certainly opens the door wide into the world of proliferation of papers," said Ostroff. "Very often, people are not reluctant to run extra copies over and above what is needed. It is easy, when one has extra copies, to send it to another friend, another business associate, or create another file."

Back in 1950, an avalanche of paper was far from the problem.

"Xerography was too complicated and too expensive, and there was absolutely no demand for it," said David T. Kearns, chairman and chief executive officer of Xerox.

The $12.5 million spent on research and development was more than Haloid-Xerox made between 1950 and 1960, and the first commercial machine cost $2,000 to manufacture. Because wet copiers were selling for about $300, the first Xerox machines were impossible to sell.

So the company leased them. For as little as $95 a month, a company got 2,000 free copies and paid four cents for each additional copy. A meter on each machine kept track. Within a year, 2,300 machines were placed.

"It created an entire new industry," said Kearns. "The 914 made it economically feasible to make a single copy of anything anybody wanted to put on paper."[1]

Photo source: Courtesy of Xerox Corporation.

Chapter Overview

In Chapter 5, we saw how attitudes, perceptions, family and social influences, and other determinants affect consumer buying behavior. Understanding these determinants is important for firms involved in consumer marketing, that is, selling products and services purchased by individuals for personal use. In contrast, many firms sell products and services to other organizations. Federal Signal Corporation makes warning lights and sirens that are purchased by municipal police departments. Manpower provides temporary personnel services for firms that need extra workers. In addition to serving the consumer market, Barnett Bank sells international banking, cash management, and lending services to a variety of large and small corporations. As Figure 6.1 illustrates, Barnett marketers use a humorous advertising approach to warn businesses of the negative impact of company "yes-men" and to describe how Barnett corporate bankers can help businesses overcome such problems.

Some firms concentrate on marketing their products to consumers. Tootsie Roll Industries, for example, sells its candy only to the consumer market. Other firms focus entirely on organizational markets. Methode Electronics manufactures controls, connectors, and printed circuits that it sells to more than 1,000 businesses in the aerospace, automotive, and other industries. These companies use Methode's components in the manufacture of their own products. Still other firms sell to both consumer and organizational markets. Kraft sells cheese and dairy products to consumers and food service institutions such as restaurants. Kraft also sells edible oil, snack seasoning, flavoring, and other ingredients to other food manufacturers.

In this chapter, we will discuss buying behavior in the organizational market. The organizational market can be divided into four major categories: the industrial (producer) market, trade industries (wholesalers and retailers), governments, and institutions.

The Organizational Market

industrial (producer) market
Component of the organizational market consisting of individuals and firms that acquire goods and services to be used, directly or indirectly, to produce other goods and services.

The industrial market is the largest component of the organizational market. The **industrial (producer) market** consists of individuals and firms that acquire goods and services to be used, directly or indirectly, in producing other goods and services. An American Airlines purchase of the new, fuel-efficient Boeing 757 plane, a wheat purchase by General Mills for its cereals, and the purchase of light bulbs and cleaning materials for an Owens-Illinois manufacturing facility all represent industrial purchases by producers. Some products aid in producing another product or service (the new plane); others are physically used up in the production of a product (the wheat); and still others are routinely used in the firm's day-to-day operations (the maintenance items). Producers include manufacturing firms; farmers and other resource industries; construction contractors; and providers of such services as transportation, public utilities, finance, insurance, and real estate.

trade industries
Component of the organizational market composed of retailers or wholesalers that purchase goods for resale to others.

The second component of the organizational market is **trade industries,** which are organizations, such as retailers and wholesalers, that purchase for resale to others. In most instances, such resale products as clothing, appli-

Figure 6.1
Advertising Targeted at an Organizational Market

Source: Courtesy of Barnett Banks, Inc.

ances, sports equipment, and automobile parts are finished goods that are marketed to customers in the selling firm's market area. In other cases, some processing or repackaging may take place. For example, retail meat markets may make bulk purchases of sides of beef and convert them into individual cuts for their customers. Lumber dealers and carpet retailers may purchase in bulk and then provide quantities and sizes to meet customers' specifications. In addition to resale products, trade industries buy cash registers, computers, display equipment, and other products required for operating their businesses. These products (as well as maintenance items and specialized services such as marketing research studies, accounting services, and management consulting) all represent organizational purchases. Detailed discussions of the trade industries are presented in later chapters, wholesaling in Chapter 14, and retailing in Chapter 15.

Governments at the federal, state, and local levels represent the third category of organizational purchaser. This important component of the organizational market purchases a wide variety of products ranging from highways to

Table 6.1
The Organizational Market:
Size and Scope

Category	Number of Organizations	Number of Employees	Employees per Organization
Industrial Producers			
Agriculture, forestry, fisheries	2,747,000	3,179,000	1
Mining	250,000	939,000	4
Construction	1,621,000	6,987,000	4
Manufacturing	619,000	20,879,000	33
Transportation, public utilities	625,000	7,548,000	12
Finance, insurance, real estate	2,140,000	7,005,000	3
Services	5,800,000	33,322,000	6
Total	13,802,000	79,859,000	6
Trade Industries			
Wholesaling firms	511,000	4,341,000	8
Retailing firms	2,830,000	17,955,000	6
Total	3,341,000	22,296,000	7
Governments			
Federal government	1	3,021,000	
State governments	50	3,984,000	
Local governments	82,290	9,685,000	193
Total	82,341	16,690,000	
Overall Totals	17,225,341	118,845,000	

Source: *Statistical Abstract of the United States* (Washington, D.C.: U.S. Government Printing Office, 1987), pp. 280, 388, 540.

F-16 fighter aircraft. The primary motivation of government purchasing is to provide some form of public benefit, such as national defense or public welfare.

Institutions, such as hospitals, universities, and museums and other non-profit groups, comprise the fourth component of the organizational market. The purchasing behavior of the institutional sector is similar to that of the other components.

Size of the Organizational Market

The producer component of the organizational market accounts for about half the value of all the manufactured goods in the United States. The **value added by manufacturing** — the difference between the prices manufacturers charge and the cost of their inputs — totals about $963 billion.

The size and scope of the organizational market are shown in Table 6.1. The producer, trade industry, and government components employ more than 118 million workers in over 17 million organizations. Producers account for approximately 80 percent of the total number of organizations and 67 percent of total employment. However, there are differences among the three components. As expected, the number of employees per unit in the government sector is significantly larger than in the producer and trade industry segments. Also, there are more than four times as many retail establishments as manufacturers. However, the average manufacturing firm employs 33 people, compared with 6 employees in the average retail establishment.[2]

value added by manufacturing
Difference between the price charged for a manufactured good and the cost of the raw materials and other inputs.

Figure 6.2
Geographical Concentration of U.S. Manufacturing Plants

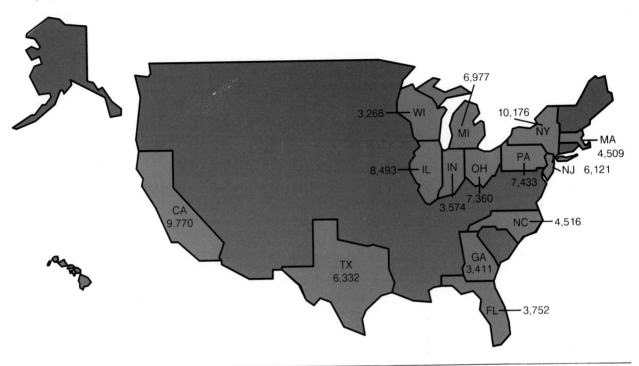

Source: Based on data from "State Summaries of Manufacturing Industries," *Sales and Marketing Management* (April 27, 1987), p. 26.

Characteristics of the Industrial Market

The industrial market can be distinguished from the consumer market on the basis of three distinct characteristics: (1) geographic market concentration, (2) a relatively small number of buyers, and (3) a unique classification system called *SIC codes.*

Geographic Market Concentration

The market for industrial goods in the United States is more geographically concentrated than the consumer market. Figure 6.2 shows the concentration in the northeastern states of Massachusetts, New Jersey, New York, and Pennsylvania; the Sunbelt states of Georgia, Florida, California, North Carolina, and Texas; and the Great Lakes states of Wisconsin, Illinois, Indiana, Michigan, and Ohio. These 14 states account for 73 percent of the $2.2 trillion in annual manufacturing shipments for plants with 20 or more employees.[3]

Limited Number of Buyers

In addition to geographic concentration, the industrial market is made up of a limited number of buyers. Industrial purchasers at four companies represent two-thirds of the entire U.S. automobile tire output. The U.S. aluminum sheet plate and foil industry includes a total of only 55 manufacturing facilities. Even in industries made up of a larger number of producers, a relatively small percentage of the total industry accounts for a large percentage of the entire industrial market. For example, of the 142 firms in the wood office furniture industry, 50 large firms with 100 or more employees account for 89 percent of all industry shipments.

The concentration of the industrial market — in terms both of the number of buyers and of geographic concentration — greatly influences the marketing strategies used in serving it. Some companies have set up a national accounts sales organization that deals solely with buyers at company headquarters. A separate field sales organization is then used to service buyers at regional production facilities. Wholesalers are used less frequently in the industrial field than in the consumer field, and the marketing channel for industrial goods is typically much shorter than for consumer goods. In addition, advertising plays a much smaller role in the industrial market. It is used primarily as an aid to personal selling and to enhance the reputation of the industrial marketer and its products and services.

Standard Industrial Classification (SIC) Codes

Marketers are aided in their efforts to reach the geographically concentrated and limited number of industrial buyers by a wealth of statistical information. The federal government is the largest single source of information. Every five years it conducts a Census of Manufacturers as well as a Census of Retailing and Wholesaling, which provide detailed information on industrial establishments, output, and employment. Specific industry studies are summarized in the annual *U.S. Industrial Outlook,* a government publication providing statistical data and discussing industry trends.

Trade associations and business publications provide additional information on the industrial market. Private firms such as Dun & Bradstreet publish detailed reports on individual firms. These data serve as useful starting points for analyzing industrial markets.

Standard Industrial Classification (SIC)
Numerical system developed by the U.S. government that subdivides the industrial marketplace into detailed market segments.

The federal government's **Standard Industrial Classification (SIC)** system greatly simplifies the process of focusing on an industrial target market. This numerical system subdivides the industrial marketplace into more detailed market segments. The SIC codes are divided into the following broad industry divisions, into which all types of organizations can be classified:

- [ ] 01–09   Agriculture, Forestry, Fishing
- [ ] 10–14   Mining
- [ ] 15–17   Contract Construction
- [ ] 20–39   Manufacturing
- [ ] 40–49   Transportation and Other Public Utilities
- [ ] 50–51   Wholesale Trade
- [ ] 52–59   Retail Trade
- [ ] 60–67   Finance, Insurance, and Real Estate
- [ ] 70–89   Services
- [ ] 91–97   Government — Federal, State, Local, and International
- [ ] 99   Others

Figure 6.3
Standard Industrial Classification System

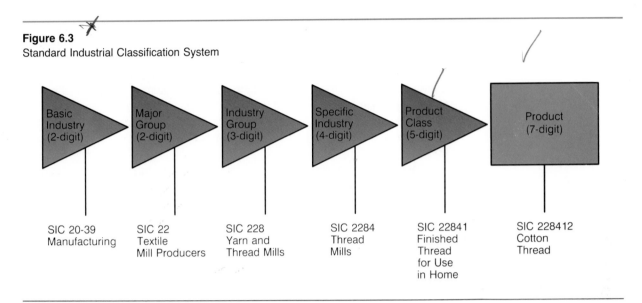

| SIC 20-39 Manufacturing | SIC 22 Textile Mill Producers | SIC 228 Yarn and Thread Mills | SIC 2284 Thread Mills | SIC 22841 Finished Thread for Use in Home | SIC 228412 Cotton Thread |

Each major category within these classifications is assigned its own two-digit number; three- and four-digit numbers subdivide the industry into smaller segments. For example, a major group such as the printing, publishing, and allied industries is assigned SIC 27. A specific three-digit industry group such as books is SIC 273. The next category, specific industries, would use the fourth digit; book printing, for example, is SIC 2732.

In the Census of Manufacturers, the Bureau of the Census also assembles industrial data at two additional levels: five-digit *product classes* and seven-digit *product* or *commodity categories*. Figure 6.3 illustrates the classification system and the detail in which data are available.

Since most published data on industrial markets utilize the SIC system, the SIC codes are invaluable tools in analyzing the industrial marketplace. The detailed information for each market segment provides the marketer with a comprehensive description of the activities of potential customers on both a geographic and specific industry basis.

Characteristics of Industrial Market Demand

Considerable differences exist in the marketing of consumer and industrial products. Consider the case of Tandy Corporation. Tandy prospered in the personal computer market by motivating its successful Radio Shack store managers with profit sharing and stock options. Some store managers had earnings well into six figures.

In 1986, Tandy management decided that it was time to enter the industrial market. The company hired an outbound, or direct, sales force of 1,500 people and set up 386 computer centers from which the field sales force would operate. But Tandy soon ran into problems.

Selling computers to businesses involves installation of more complex systems than Tandy was used to in its consumer markets. Yet the firm refused to pay competitive wages to the computer technicians needed to support the sales force. The sales force, also underpaid, was of little help in technical matters. Sales training was minimal, consisting of eight Saturday sessions after the salespeople had been hired and working in the field. Worse yet, Tandy tried to supervise its new sales force with existing store managers. In effect, the managers were being asked to supervise two entirely different sales operations.

Tandy soon realized its mistakes. The company has since hired experienced field sales managers and cut their administrative burden. Nearly a third of the computer centers have been closed or consolidated. Sales commissions were increased and a month-long training period added.[4]

The Tandy case illustrates that the unique characteristics of industrial settings require that marketing strategies be tailored to the special requirements of this marketplace. But what are the primary characteristics of industrial market demand? Most lists would include derived demand, joint demand, inventory adjustments, and demand variability.

Derived Demand

derived demand
Demand for an industrial product that is linked to demand for a consumer good.

The term **derived demand** refers to the linkage between desires of an industrial marketer to make purchases of such needed items as machinery, components parts and materials, and raw materials and the desires of his or her customers for the firm's output. For example, the demand for automated teller machines, an industrial good, is derived from consumer demand for banking convenience. In recent years, purchases of ATMs by commercial banks have increased because more and more bank customers like the convenience of 24-hour banking by machine.

Industrial marketers may attempt to increase demand for their product by advertising directly to consumers. Carpet can be either an industrial good or a consumer good depending on the purchaser and his or her purchase motivations. For example, carpet purchased by a homeowner for use as replacement for worn or outdated carpet in the home would be a consumer good. The same carpet becomes an industrial good when it is purchased by a builder for installation in a new office building, retail store, or in a newly-built home or apartment that will be offered for sale or lease. The advertisement shown in Figure 6.4 is designed to inform consumers and industrial buyers of the quality and beauty of Masland carpets and to differentiate the brand from competitors. The marketing objective of such efforts is to encourage purchasers of new offices, retail outlets, or homes to specify that the builder or interior designer install Masland carpet rather than another brand.

joint demand
Demand for an industrial good as related to the demand for another industrial good that is necessary for the use of the first item.

Joint Demand

The demand for some industrial products is related to the demand for other industrial goods to be used jointly with the former, a concept known as **joint demand.** For example, coke and iron ore are required for making pig iron. If

Figure 6.4
Increasing Industrial Demand through Consumer Promotions

Source: Courtesy of Masland Carpets.

the coke supply is reduced, there will be an immediate effect on the demand for iron ore.

Inventory Adjustments

Changes in inventory policy can have an impact on industrial demand. Assume that a two-month supply of raw materials is considered the optimal inventory in a particular industry. Now suppose economic conditions or other factors dictate that this level be increased to a 90-day supply. The raw materials supplier will then be bombarded with a tremendous increase in new orders. Thus, inventory adjustments can be a major determinant of industrial demand.

Demand Variability

Derived demand in the industrial market is linked to immense variability in industrial demand. Assume the demand for industrial product A is derived from

THE COMPETITIVE EDGE

Boeing

Boeing is attempting to change the way airplanes are sold. Traditionally, commercial aircraft was sold to airlines by emphasizing such features as fuel economy and labor savings. In other words, the product has been marketed to the intermediary in the channel of distribution (the airline), not the final consumer (the passenger). But stiff competition from Airbus Industrie and McDonnell Douglas is beginning to change the way Boeing markets its airplanes. The firm is now seeking a competitive edge by selling its planes through derived demand—appealing directly to airline passengers.

Boeing's marketing research has indicated that passengers may be willing to pay more for greater comfort. As a result, the Seattle-based manufacturer plans to redesign its interiors to make trips more enjoyable for passengers. Here are some of the changes Boeing anticipates. Cabin pressure will be lowered for the comfort of passengers with inner-ear and sinus problems. Long-distance flights will offer video screens in seat backs. More overhead storage and wider seats and aisles will be installed. Even office compartments will be available in business class.

Boeing's vice-president of marketing for commercial airplanes, Chris Longridge, explains the strategy this way: "In the absence of other incentives, passengers are indifferent to new generation airplanes we've built. And with low fuel prices

forecast to remain low, efficiency alone isn't an incentive for airlines to replace their fleets. A 20-year-old plane can still do the mission today." Longridge continues, "This is a risky strategy, but we're doing it. The success depends on a traveler's willingness to change habits."

Boeing is not the only firm altering its competitive strategy. Airbus is already advertising the comfort features of its airplanes. Its rivalry with

Boeing is likely to redefine how firms compete in this organizational marketplace. It is also clear that Boeing intends to keep the competitive edge that has allowed it to dominate the commercial aircraft market for years.

Source: Gordon Lee, "Fare Wars Falter, Service Wars Erupt in Boeing's 1990 Marketing Scenario," *Puget Sound Business Journal* (November 17, 1986), pp. 1A, 15A. *Photo source:* Courtesy of The Boeing Company.

the demand for consumer product B, an item whose sales volume has been growing at an annual rate of 10 percent. Now suppose that the demand for product B has slowed to a 5 percent annual increase. Management might decide to delay further purchases of product A, using existing inventory until market conditions were clarified. Therefore, even modest shifts in the demand for product B would greatly affect product A's demand. This disproportionate impact that changes in consumer demand have on industrial market demand is called the *accelerator principle.*

Basic Categories of Organizational Products

There are two general categories of organizational products: capital items and expense items. *Capital items* are long-lived business assets that must be depreciated over time. *Depreciation* is the accounting concept of charging a portion of a capital item as a deduction against the company's annual revenue for purposes of determining its net income. Examples of capital items include major installations such as new plants and office buildings as well as equipment.

Expense items, in contrast, are products and services that are used within a short time period. For the most part, they are charged against income in the year of purchase. Examples of expense items include the supplies used in operating the business, ranging from paper clips to machine lubricants. An expense item for firms whose employees work with toxic chemicals would be special gloves, such as those produced by North Hand Protection and shown in Figure 6.5.

Chapter 8 presents a comprehensive classification of industrial products. The initial breakdown of capital and expense items is useful because buying behavior varies significantly depending on how a purchase is treated from an accounting viewpoint. Expense items may be bought routinely and with minimal delay, while capital items involve major fund commitments and thus are subject to considerable review by the purchaser's personnel.

The Make, Buy, or Lease Decision

Organizational buyers considering the acquisition of a new product have three basic options:

1. Make the product themselves.
2. Purchase it from another organization.
3. Lease it from another organization.

If the company has the capability for manufacturing the item itself, it may be desirable to do so. Considerable cost savings may be realized if the purchaser does not have to pay the manufacturing division all of the overhead or profit margin that would otherwise be charged to an outside buyer.

On the other hand, most organizational or industrial products cannot be made internally. Therefore, purchasing them from an outside vendor is the most common choice. This option is discussed in the following section.

Leasing is a third possibility in many industrial marketing situations. It has become more popular as a result of the Tax Reform Act of 1986, which removed several of the advantages of purchasing. Firms are no longer allowed to claim a 10 percent investment tax credit or to depreciate their capital items as advantageously as they did before. As a result, leasing has become more common than it was in previous years.

Figure 6.5
Industrial Gloves:
an Expense Item

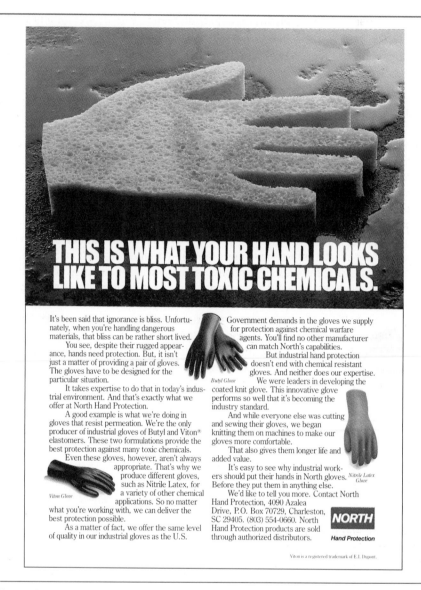

Source: Courtesy of North Hand Protection, Charleston, S.C. 29405.

Organizational Buying Behavior

Organizational buying behavior tends to be more complex than the consumer decision process described in Chapter 5. There are several reasons for this:

1. Many persons may exert influence in organizational purchases, and considerable time may be spent in obtaining the input and approval of various organization members.

2. Organizational buying may be handled by committees, with greater time requirements for majority or unanimous approval.

3. Many organizations attempt to utilize several sources of supply as a type of "insurance" against shortages.

4. Organizational buyers are influenced by both rational (cost, quality, delivery reliability) and emotional (status, fear, recognition) needs.

Most organizations have attempted to systematize their purchases by employing a professional buyer—the purchasing manager or buyers or buying committee in the case of retailers and wholesalers. These technically qualified people are responsible for handling much of the organization's purchases and securing needed products at the best possible price. Unlike the ultimate consumer, who makes periodic purchase decisions, a firm's purchasing department devotes all its time and effort to determining needs, locating and evaluating alternative sources of supply, and making purchase decisions.

Two of the tools purchasers use are value analysis and vendor analysis. **Value analysis** is an examination of each component of a purchase in an attempt to either delete the item or replace it with a more cost-effective substitute. For example, DuPont's Kevlar, a synthetic material, is now used in airplane construction because it weighs less than the product it replaced. The resulting fuel savings are significant for the buyers in this marketplace.

Purchasing managers also use vendor analysis to evaluate potential suppliers. **Vendor analysis** is an ongoing evaluation of a supplier's performance in categories such as price, back orders, delivery time, and attention to special requests. A checksheet set up along these lines helps purchasers determine the most effective supply source for a particular item.

value analysis
Systematic study of the components of a purchase to determine the most cost-effective way to acquire the item.

vendor analysis
Assessment of a supplier's performance in areas such as price, back orders, timely delivery, and attention to special requests.

Complexity of Organizational Purchases

Where major purchases are involved, negotiations may take several weeks or even months and the buying decision may rest with a number of persons in the organization. The choice of a supplier for industrial drill presses, for example, may be made jointly by the purchasing agent and the company's production, engineering, and maintenance departments. Each of these principals may have a different point of view to be taken into account in making a purchase decision. As a result, representatives of the selling firm must be well versed in the technical aspects of the product or service and capable of interacting socially and professionally with managers of the various departments involved in the purchase decision. In the chemicals industry, for instance, it takes an average of seven face-to-face presentations to make a sale.

Illustration of a Typical Organizational Purchase

The manufacturer of a reinforced fiberglass utility lighting pole faced a complicated decision process that involved members of several departments and months of negotiations before a sale could be made. The new pole had several advantages over the traditional steel, wood, or aluminum pole: It was lightweight, had nonelectrical conducting and noncorrosive properties, never needed painting, and met all strength requirements. Its major disadvantage, other than purchaser unfamiliarity, was its high initial purchase price compared

Figure 6.6

Decision to Purchase a New Type of Utility Pole

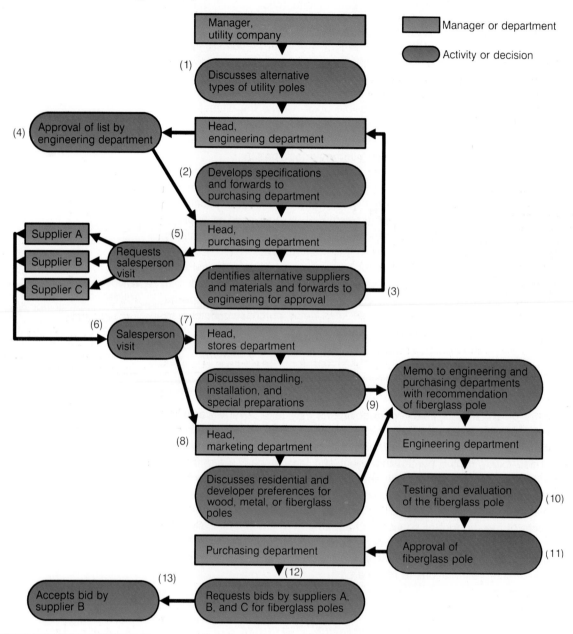

Source: Adapted from Arch G. Woodside, "Marketing Anatomy of Buying Process Can Help Improve Industrial Strategy," *Marketing News* (May 1, 1981), sec. 2, p. 11. Used by permission of the American Marketing Association.

to the metal alternatives. The decision process, which is diagrammed in Figure 6.6, began with the manager of the utility company.[5] Next, the utility's purchasing department manager was contacted; who, in turn, contacted the engineering head. After a list of alternative suppliers and materials had been prepared by purchasing and approved by engineering, the purchasing manager discussed the organization's needs with salespeople representing three suppliers. The salespeople met with the head of the stores department and the marketing department manager. After a series of meetings with the salespeople and numerous discussions among the utility's various department heads, a decision was made to submit the new fiberglass pole to a test conducted by the engineering department. The results of the test were reported to the various department heads. Bids were then requested from suppliers A, B, and C. These bids were reviewed by the department heads, who ultimately decided to select the new fiberglass pole offered by supplier B.

Classifying Organizational Buying Situations

Organizational buying behavior is affected by situational variables. Organizational purchase decisions vary in terms of the degree of effort and involvement by different levels within the organization. There are three generally recognized organizational buying situations: straight rebuy, modified rebuy, and new-task buying.[6]

Straight Rebuy

A **straight rebuy** is a recurring purchase decision in which an item that has performed satisfactorily is purchased again by a customer. This organizational buying situation occurs when a purchaser is pleased with the good or service and the terms of sale are acceptable. The buyer sees little reason to assess other options and therefore follows a routine buying format.

Low-cost products such as paper clips and number 2 pencils for an office are typical examples. If the purchaser is pleased with the products and their prices and terms, future purchases will probably be treated as a straight rebuy from the current vendor. Even expensive items specially designed for a customer's needs are treated as a straight rebuy in some cases. For example, the U.S. Postal Service is committed to buy 99,150 new mail delivery vehicles from Grumman Corporation's Allied Division.

Marketers facing straight-rebuy situations should concentrate on maintaining a good relationship with the buyer by providing adequate service and delivery. Competitors will then find it difficult to present unique sales proposals that would break this chain of repurchases.

Modified Rebuy

A **modified rebuy** is a situation in which purchasers are willing to reevaluate their available options. The appropriate decision makers feel that it may be to their advantage to look at alternative product offerings using established purchasing guidelines. This might occur if a marketer allows a straight-rebuy situation to deteriorate because of poor service or delivery. Perceived quality and cost differences can also create a modified-rebuy situation.

Organizational marketers want to move purchasers into a straight-rebuy position by responding to all of their product and service needs. Competitors, on the other hand, try to move buyers into a modified-rebuy situation by correctly assessing the factors that would make purchasers reconsider their decisions.

straight rebuy
Recurring purchase decision in which an item that has performed satisfactorily is purchased again by a customer.

modified rebuy
Situation in which purchasers are willing to reevaluate available options in a repurchase of the same product or service.

New-Task Buying

new-task buying
First-time or unique purchase situations that require considerable effort on the decision makers' part.

New-task buying refers to first-time or unique purchase situations that require considerable effort on the decision makers' part. After such a need has been identified, evaluative criteria can be established and an extensive search launched. Alternative product/service offerings and vendors are considered. For example, a firm that enters a new field must seek suppliers of component parts that it did not purchase previously. Manufacturing firms moving into automated factory systems face the task of buying new equipment such as robots and computers.

The Buying Center Concept

buying center
Participants in an organizational buying action.

The buying center is a vital concept to the understanding of organizational buying behavior.[7] The **buying center** simply refers to everyone who is involved in some fashion in an organizational buying action. For example, a buying center can include the architect who designs a new research laboratory, the scientist who will use the facility, the purchasing manager who screens contractor proposals, the chief executive officer who makes the final decision, and the vice-president for research who signs the formal contracts for the project.

Buying centers are not part of the firm's formal organizational structure. They are informal groups whose composition varies among purchase situations and firms. Buying centers typically include anywhere from 4 to 20 participants. They tend to evolve as the purchasing process moves through its various stages.

Buying center participants play different roles in the purchasing process. These roles—users, gatekeepers, influencers, deciders, and buyers—have the following characteristics:

- *Users* are the people who will actually use the purchased product or service. Their influence on the purchase decision may range from being inconsequential to extremely important. Users sometimes initiate the purchase action by requesting the product, and they may also help develop product specifications.

- *Gatekeepers* control the information to be reviewed by buying center members. Their information control may be in terms of distributing printed information or advertisements or deciding which salespeople will speak to which individuals in the buying center. For example, a purchasing agent may open the gate to the buying center for some salespeople and close it to others.

- *Influencers* affect the buying decision by supplying information for the evaluation of alternatives or by setting buying specifications. Influencers are typically technical personnel such as engineers, quality control specialists, and research and development staff members. Sometimes a buying organization hires outside consultants, such as engineers and architects, who influence the buying decision.

- *Deciders* actually make the buying decision, although they may not have the formal authority to do so. The identity of the decider is the most difficult role to determine: for example, a firm's buyer may have the formal authority to buy, but the firm's president may actually make the buying decision. A decider could be a design engineer who develops specifications that only one vendor can meet.

Figure 6.7
Model of the Industrial Buying Process

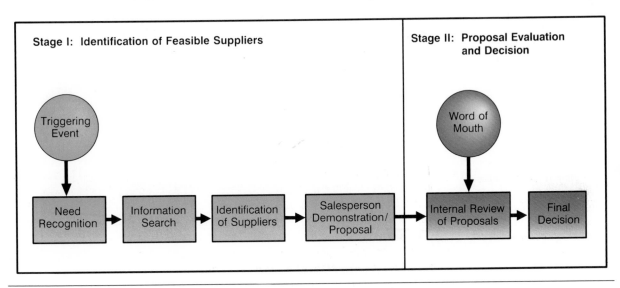

Source: Adapted from Manoj K. Agarwal, Philip C. Burger, and Alladi Venkatesh, "Industrial Consumer Behavior: Toward an Improved Model," in *Developments in Marketing Science,* ed. Venkatakrishna V. Bellur, Thomas R. Baird, Paul T. Hertz, Roger L. Jenkins, Jay D. Lindquist, and Stephen W. Miller (Miami Beach: Academy of Marketing Science, 1981), p. 72.

□   *Buyers* have the formal authority to select a supplier and implement the procedures for securing the product. The buyer's power is often usurped by more influential members of the organization. The buyer's role is assumed often by the purchasing agent, who executes the clerical functions associated with a purchase order.[8]

The critical task for the organizational marketer is to be able to determine the specific role and the relative buying influence of each buying center participant. Sales presentations and information can then be tailored to the precise role that the individual plays at each step of the purchase process. Organizational marketers also have found that while their initial—and, in many cases, most extensive—contacts are all with the purchasing department, the buying center participants having the greatest influence often are not in that department at all.

The Process of Buying Industrial Goods and Services

The exact procedures used in buying industrial goods and services vary according to the buying situation confronted: straight rebuy, modified rebuy, or new-task buying. Most industrial purchases follow the same general process. Research by Agarwal, Burger, and Venkatesh suggested the model presented in Figure 6.7. While this model was formulated for industrial machinery purchases, it has general application to the industrial buying process.[9]

Caterpillar, Inc.'s marketing activities include inviting government and industrial buyers from around the world to product demonstrations held at a facility in Edwards, Illinois, where specially prepared job sites simulate customers' actual working conditions. This gives buyers the chance to see Caterpillar's earth-moving, construction, and materials handling equipment in action and to secure additional information from Caterpillar's technical staff that they need before making a final purchase decision.

Photo source: Courtesy of Caterpillar Incorporated.

Dissecting the Model

The various steps shown in the model of the industrial buying process are divided into two stages. In Stage I, members of the buying center respond to the triggering event by identifying alternative suppliers capable of filling the need and requesting demonstrations and/or proposals. Stage II consists of a detailed analysis of alternative proposals that results in an eventual purchase decision. The specific steps are as follows:

☐ *Need recognition.* A triggering event, such as an equipment failure, stimulates recognition of a need for an industrial purchase.

☐ *Information search.* Buying center members begin to collect information on potential suppliers from sales personnel, advertisements, word of mouth, pamphlets, and other sources. The net result of this stage is to delineate the technical nature of the purchase.

☐ *Identification of suppliers.* Given the specifications established in the previous step, potential suppliers are determined. Budget considerations may be a factor in this step.

☐ *Sales demonstration/proposal.* Vendor sales representatives are invited to provide demonstrations and sales proposals. These proposals typically include technical and economic options as well as prices.

☐ *Word of mouth.* Buying center members may contact current users of the product for their evaluations of its performance. Reliability, costs, and operational abilities are explored. Some vendors are eliminated because of negative information.

☐ *Final decision.* Eventually, a purchase decision is made. In many cases, this extensive buying process leads to a consensus decision, but some buying center members are more important than others in the final decision stage.

Reciprocity

A highly controversial practice in a number of organizational buying situations is **reciprocity**—the extension of purchasing preference to suppliers that are also customers. For example, an office equipment manufacturer may favor a particular supplier of component parts if the supplier has recently made a major purchase of the manufacturer's products. Reciprocal arrangements traditionally have been used in industries with homogeneous products with similar prices, such as the chemical, paint, petroleum, rubber, and steel industries.

Reverse reciprocity—the practice of extending supply privileges to firms that provide needed supplies—is another form of reciprocity. In times of shortages, reverse reciprocity occasionally emerges as firms attempt to obtain raw materials and parts with which to continue operations.

The practice of reciprocity suggests the close links among the various elements of the organizational marketplace. Although some reciprocal agreements still exist, both the Justice Department and the Federal Trade Commission view them as attempts to reduce competition. Federal intervention is common in cases where agreements are used systematically.

reciprocity
Highly controversial practice of extending purchasing preference to suppliers who are also customers.

Government Markets

Government at all levels is a sizable segment of the organizational market. Total spending for goods and services by all three levels of government—federal, state, and local—is in the trillions of dollars. For major defense contractors, such as General Dynamics, government sales are essential. General Dynamics relies on government contracts for 94 percent of its business. Other major defense contractors whose government contracts amount to billions of dollars each year are McDonnell Douglas, Rockwell International, Lockheed, Boeing, and General Electric.[10]

Foreign governments represent another component of the government sector of the organizational market. Thousands of companies have sent delegations to China during the 1980s seeking contracts with the Chinese government. Some have been successful. For example, Management Science America, Inc., the largest independent supplier of mainframe applications software, landed a contract to supply the Chinese government with its software. But other firms have ceased their marketing efforts in China, concluding that their costs were exceeding the amount of business secured.

Selling to Government Markets

By law, most government purchases must be made on the basis of **bids,** or written sales proposals, from vendors. As a result, government buyers develop **specifications**—specific descriptions of needed items—for prospective bidders.

The General Services Administration (GSA), through its Office of Federal Supply and Services, buys many commercial items for use by other agencies. However, a large number of other federal agencies also perform procurement functions. Most states have offices comparable to the GSA.[11]

Prospective government suppliers can learn of opportunities for sales by contacting the various government agencies. Most contracts are advertised by

bids
Written sales proposals from vendors.

specifications
Written description of a product or service needed by a firm. Prospective bidders use this description first to determine whether they can manufacture the product or deliver the service and then to prepare bids.

these agencies, and information on bidding procedures can be obtained directly from them. Directories explaining the procedures involved in selling to the federal government are available from the Government Printing Office, and most states provide similar information.[12]

Problems and Opportunities   The GSA once was unable to find three bidders for some $50,000 in purchases of facial tissues, filing cabinets, garbage cans, and table napkins. Despite its immense size, the government market is often viewed as unprofitable by many suppliers. A survey conducted by *Sales and Marketing Management* reported that industrial marketers have registered a variety of complaints about government purchasing procedures. These include excessive paperwork, bureaucracy, needless regulations, emphasis on low bid prices, decision-making delays, frequent shifts in procurement personnel, and excessive policy changes.[13]

On the other hand, marketers generally credit the government for being a relatively stable market. Once the government purchases an item, the probability of additional sales is good. Other marketers cite such advantages as the instant credibility established by sales to the federal government, timely payment, excise tax and sales tax exemptions, acceptance of new ideas, and reduced competition.

One survey reported that 68 percent of its organizational respondents did not maintain a separate government sales manager or sales force. But many firms report success with specialized government marketing efforts. J. I. Case, Goodyear, Eastman Kodak, and Sony are examples.

Trends in the Government Market

Three trends have influenced the federal government market, and similar developments have affected some state and local governments.[14] The federal developments are as follows:

1. The Office of Management and Budget requires that government agencies use a single set of procurement regulations, the so-called Federal Acquisition Regulation (FAR). The intent is to reduce the red tape and excessive regulation that characterizes the federal government market. By combining government procurement regulations into a single, plain-English document, the FAR has made it easier for private contractors to know exactly what the government wants. By giving government contracting officers greater discretion in carrying out federal procurement policy, the FAR has also made the system more flexible in dealing with the variations among private contractors.

2. In an attempt to reduce spending, the Pentagon, the GSA, and other government buyers are turning to more off-the-shelf goods rather than issuing special-order contracts.

3. *Life-cycle costing*—the cost of using a product over its lifetime rather than just the initial bid price—is now being used. Life-cycle costing essentially takes all the costs associated with purchasing and using a product and divides them by the item's estimated useful life. This approach has resulted in considerable savings. For example, life-cycle-costing procurement of typewriters is estimated to have saved the government $9 million over a three-year period.[15]

J ohn Dorrance created the "Mm! Mm! Good!" taste of Campbell's soup. Campbell's was so popular that when Dorrance died in 1930, he left behind $128 million, then the third largest fortune in American history. Dorrance wouldn't recognize his fortune today—his descendants now hold stock worth $2.2 billion—nor would he recognize his company. But then, a lot of people who have watched Campbell Soup Company for years must blink twice when they see it now.

Heralded as one of the first successful companies in mass marketing, Campbell made and sold products such as chicken noodle and tomato soup that appealed to everyone's tastes. Now the company is at the fore of a dynamic, novel exercise in corporate change. It has divided the country into 22 geographic regions and is developing products, sales efforts, and advertising and promotions targeted at each defined area.

Campbell's move into regional marketing is part of the firm's strategy for long-term growth in an industry facing mature or declining markets. Realizing that few new products will achieve the mass-appeal status of chicken noodle soup, Campbell intends to be flexible by first finding new market niches and then filling them. Geographic segmentation is helping Campbell develop new, region-specific products, such as creole soup, which is sold only in the South, or red-bean soup, which is marketed in Hispanic areas. Campbell also is developing different recipes for the same product and targeting each product variation to specific regions.

Regional marketing also enables Campbell to focus on innovative local advertising and promotion. Sales of Campbell's fresh mushrooms increased five times during a promotion created for the Northern California market. The program included local advertising and joint in-store demonstrations of Campbell's mushrooms and another firm's deep-fried batter. The cumulative effect of such efforts, Campbell believes, will spur corporate growth. Carl V. Stinnett, Campbell's vice-president of sales and marketing, says, "If we have people out there in Bangor, Maine, Fargo, North Dakota, Midland, Texas, and Jackson, Mississippi, doing that, then all of a sudden it will show up in our shipments, and we'll wind up with a higher market share."

Campbell has made several changes in its corporate structure to fit its novel regional approach. It has created the new position of brand sales manager—one for each of the 22 regions—that is responsible for tailoring national marketing plans to the specific region, creating regional

and local ads and promotions, and keeping national headquarters informed of local trends and competitors' activities. Sales representatives, who previously sold only 1 product line, such as canned soups, to as many as 100 stores, now sell Campbell's full line of products to a far smaller number. These changes, executives feel, will help the company to think like it is a local competitor and allow it to react to changing consumer tastes in each region.

Other companies, such as Heinz, General Foods, and Nabisco, are also experimenting with regional marketing strategies. Many industry analysts believe that Campbell's regional approach will be the dominant one in the future of American business. For now, the move has taken the Campbell Kids into new territory—and they're smiling.[1]

Photo source: Courtesy of Campbell Soup Company.

Chapter Overview

Before a marketing mix strategy can be implemented, the marketer must identify, evaluate, and select a target market. The starting point is to understand what is meant by a market.

A market is people and institutions, but they alone do not make a market. A real estate salesperson would be unimpressed by news that 50 percent of a marketing class raised their hands in response to the question "Who wants to buy a condominium in Aspen, Colorado?" More pertinent would be the answer to the question "How many of you have $50,000 for the down payment and can qualify for the mortgage loan?" A **market** requires not only people or institutions and the willingness to buy but also purchasing power and authority to buy.

A successful salesperson quickly learns how to pinpoint which individual in an organization or household has the authority to make particular purchasing decisions. Without this knowledge, he or she may spend too much time convincing the wrong person to buy the product or service.

market
Group of people who possess purchasing power and the authority and willingness to purchase.

Types of Markets

Products are often classified as either consumer goods or industrial goods. **Consumer goods** are products purchased by the ultimate consumer for personal use. **Industrial goods** are products purchased for use either directly or indirectly in the production of other goods or services for resale. A similar dichotomy can be used for services. Most products purchased by individual consumers—books, records, and clothes, for example—are consumer goods. Rubber and raw cotton, however, are generally purchased by manufacturers and are therefore classified as industrial goods. Rubber is used in many products by producers such as Goodyear; textile manufacturers such as Burlington Industries convert raw cotton into cloth.

Sometimes the same product is destined for different uses. Spark plugs purchased for the family car constitute a consumer good, but spark plugs purchased by Chrysler for use on its four-wheel-drive line are an industrial good, since they become part of another good destined for resale. (Some marketers use the term *commercial goods* to refer to industrial products not directly used in producing other goods.) The key to proper classification of goods is determining the purchaser and the reasons for the purchase.

consumer goods
Products purchased by the ultimate consumer for personal use.

industrial goods
Products purchased for use directly or indirectly in the production of other goods for resale.

The Role of Market Segmentation

The world is too large and filled with too many diverse people and firms for any single marketing mix to satisfy everyone. Unless the product or service is an item such as an unbranded, descriptive-label detergent aimed at the mass market, an attempt to satisfy everyone may doom the marketer to failure. Even a seemingly functional product such as toothpaste is aimed at specific market segments. Crest, as the ad in Figure 7.1 shows, focuses on tooth decay prevention; Close-Up hints at enhanced sex appeal; Aim promises both protection and a taste children like; Gleem targets the teeth-whitening segment; and several brands claim to help prevent tartar build-up.

The auto manufacturer who decides to produce and market a single model to satisfy everyone will encounter seemingly endless decisions about such var-

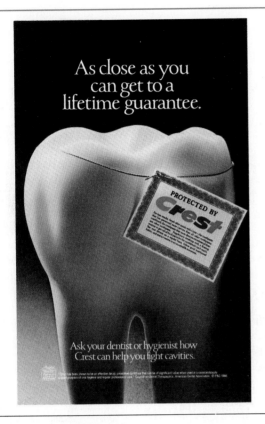

Figure 7.1
Targeting a Specific
Market Segment

Source: Courtesy of The Procter & Gamble Company.

iables as the number of doors, type of transmission, color, styling, and engine size. In its attempt to satisfy everyone, the firm may be forced to compromise in each of these areas and, as a result, may discover that it satisfies no one very well. Firms that appeal to particular segments—the performance-oriented market, the prestige-conscious market, the larger-family market, and so on—may capture most of the total market by satisfying the specific needs of each segment. This process of dividing the total market into several relatively homogeneous groups is called **market segmentation.** Marketing mixes are then adjusted to meet the needs of specified market segments. Market segmentation is used by both profit-oriented and nonprofit organizations.

Criteria for Effective Segmentation

Market segmentation cannot be used in all cases. To be effective, segmentation must meet the following basic requirements:

1. The market segments must be measurable in terms of both purchasing power and size.

2. Marketers must be able to effectively promote to and serve a market segment.

market segmentation
Process of dividing the total market into several relatively homogeneous groups with similar product or service interests based on such factors as demographic or psychographic characteristics, geographic location, or perceived product benefits.

3. Market segments must be sufficiently large to be potentially profitable.

4. The number of segments must match the firm's marketing capabilities.[2]

If one or more of these factors is missing, the marketer should reassess any proposed market segmentation strategy.

Segmenting Consumer Markets

Market segmentation results from the isolation of factors that distinguish a certain group of consumers from the overall market. These characteristics—age, sex, geographic location, income and expenditure patterns, and population size and mobility, among others—are vital factors in the success of the overall marketing strategy. Toy manufacturers such as Ideal, Hasbro, Mattel, and Kenner study not only birthrate trends but shifts in income and expenditure patterns. Colleges and universities are affected by such factors as number of high school graduates, changing attitudes toward the value of college educations, and increasing enrollment of older adults. The four commonly used bases for segmenting consumer markets are geographic segmentation, demographic segmentation, psychographic segmentation, and benefit segmentation. These segmentation bases can be important to marketing strategies provided they are significantly related to differences in buying behavior.

Geographic Segmentation

geographic segmentation
Dividing a population into homogeneous groups on the basis of location.

A logical starting point in market segmentation is the examination of population characteristics. **Geographic segmentation**—the dividing of an overall market into homogeneous groups on the basis of population location—has been used for hundreds of years.

The U.S. population of about 250 million is not distributed evenly; rather, it is concentrated in states with major metropolitan areas. The 25 largest metropolitan areas listed in Table 7.1 account for half of the total U.S. population.

States vary not only in population density but in population migration. Census data indicate three major population shifts over the past two decades: to the Sunbelt states of the Southeast and Southwest; from interior states to seacoast states; and to the West. Between 1970 and 1980, the population of the South increased by 20 percent and that of the West by 24 percent, compared to a modest 4 percent increase in the Midwest and a less than 1 percent gain in the Northeast. These patterns have continued in the 1980s.[3] Foreign immigration accounts for a considerable part of the population growth in the South and West. Since 1975, more than 2.8 million foreign immigrants have settled in the West and 2.3 million in the South. Since 1980, the West has gained twice as many residents from foreign immigration as it has from migration from other regions of the United States.[4] States expected to gain the largest number of residents by the year 2000 are California (5.7 million), Florida (3.7 million), Texas (2.4 million), and Arizona (1.3 million).[5]

Overall the U.S. population growth has been slowing and is expected to continue to decline into the next century. The 13 percent growth rate of the

Rank	Metropolitan Area	Population July 1986	Percentage Change 1980–1986
1	New York	17,967,000	2.4
2	Los Angeles	13,074,800	13.7
3	Chicago	8,116,100	2.3
4	San Francisco	5,877,800	9.5
5	Philadelphia	5,832,600	2.7
6	Detroit	4,600,700	−3.2
7	Boston	4,055,700	2.1
8	Dallas	3,655,300	24.7
9	Houston	3,634,300	17.2
10	Washington, D.C.	3,563,000	9.6
11	Miami	2,912,000	10.1
12	Cleveland	2,765,600	−2.4
13	Atlanta	2,560,000	19.8
14	St. Louis	2,438,000	2.6
15	Pittsburgh	2,316,100	−4.4
16	Minneapolis	2,295,200	7.4
17	Seattle	2,284,500	9.1
18	Baltimore	2,280,000	3.7
19	San Diego	2,201,300	18.2
20	Tampa	1,914,300	18.6
21	Phoenix	1,900,200	25.9
22	Denver	1,847,400	14.1
23	Cincinnati	1,690,000	1.8
24	Milwaukee	1,522,000	−1.2
25	Kansas City	1,517,800	5.9

Table 7.1

The 25 Largest Metropolitan Areas

Source: Census Bureau Press Release, CB87-116, "Dallas/Fort Worth Tops Houston as 8th Largest Metro Area, Census Bureau Reports," July 24, 1987.

1960s fell to 11 percent in the 1970s and 10 percent in the 1980s. The current annual growth rate of less than 1 percent is expected to fall to less than one-half percent by the year 2000. While the growth rate of the white population has steadily decreased since the 1960s, the rate for blacks, Hispanics, and other races has steadily increased. By 1990, the white population is expected to have grown by 8 percent since 1980, compared to 21 percent for blacks and other races.[6]

Population shifts have also occurred within states. Farmers have migrated steadily to urban areas since 1800, and the percentage of farm dwellers has dropped below 3 percent. The United States traditionally has been a mobile society. One of every six Americans moves each year; however, this figure is down from one out of five persons two decades ago. This slowdown is attributed to three factors: a higher percentage of home ownership, increased housing prices, and fluctuating mortgage interest rates. The number of in-county moves accounts for virtually all of this decline. Intercity moves have consistently remained at a higher rate.[7] If this trend continues, it will have a decided impact on marketers' use of geographic segmentation.

The move from urban to suburban areas after World War II, primarily by middle-class families, created a need to redefine the urban marketplace. This trend radically changed cities' traditional patterns of retailing and led to a disintegration of many U.S. cities' downtown shopping areas. It rendered traditional city boundaries almost meaningless for marketing purposes.

In an effort to correct this situation, the government now classifies urban data using three categories:

Consolidated Metropolitan Statistical Area (CMSA)
Major population concentration, including the 25 or so urban giants.

Primary Metropolitan Statistical Area (PMSA)
Major urban area within a CMSA.

Metropolitan Statistical Area (MSA)
Large, free-standing urban area for which detailed marketing-related data are collected by the Bureau of the Census.

- A **Consolidated Metropolitan Statistical Area (CMSA)** includes the 25 or so urban giants such as New York, Los Angeles, and Chicago. It must include two or more Primary Metropolitan Statistical Areas.

- A **Primary Metropolitan Statistical Area (PMSA)** is a major urban area within a CMSA—an urbanized county or counties with social and economic ties to nearby areas. PMSAs are identified within areas of 1-million-plus populations. Long Island's Nassau and Suffolk counties would be part of the New York CMSA, Oxnard-Ventura part of the Los Angeles CMSA, and Aurora-Elgin part of the Chicago CMSA.

- A **Metropolitan Statistical Area (MSA)** is a freestanding urban area with an urban center population of 50,000 and a total MSA population of 100,000 or more. MSAs exhibit social and economic homogeneity. They are usually bordered by nonurbanized counties. Moorhead, Minnesota, Peoria, Illinois, and Sheboygan, Wisconsin, are examples.

Using Geographic Segmentation

There are many instances in which markets for products and services may be segmented on a geographic basis. Dividing the total market into geographic segments is useful when consumer tastes vary among regions. Regional preferences are more pronounced in certain products, such as food, beverages, and automobiles, than in others, such as personal care items. Anheuser-Busch divides the United States into 210 geographic markets to compete effectively with local and regional brewers that cater to local tastes. The company targets each market with special advertising and promotions. It works with its local beer distributors to sponsor community softball teams, bowling matches, and special events such as rodeos.[8]

Some national firms develop products aimed at specific regions. For example, automakers have produced special, limited-edition models for the California market, such as Chrysler's all-white Dodge Lancer Pacifica. Most automakers also position their models differently according to market location. The Chevrolet Blazer ads in Figure 7.2 show advertising approaches used by General Motors that appeal to consumers in different geographic areas. Nationally GM promotes the Blazer as an outdoor vehicle, as shown in the ad on the right. The ad on the left, showing a Blazer parked amid Ferraris and Porsches at a fancy restaurant, targets consumers in California.[9]

Residence location within a geographic area is an important geographic variable. Urban dwellers may have less need for automobiles than their suburban and rural counterparts, and suburban dwellers spend proportionately more on lawn and garden care than do rural or urban residents. Both rural and sub-

Figure 7.2
Advertising Appealing to Consumers in Different Geographic Areas

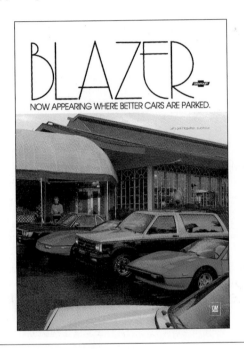

Source: "Backwoods Guide" Courtesy of Chevrolet Motor Division. Agency: Lintas/Campbell-Ewald. "Blazer" Courtesy of Chevrolet Motor Division. Agency: Vic Olesen & Partners.

urban dwellers may spend more of their household incomes on gasoline and automobile needs than urban households.

Climate is another important factor. Snowblowers, snowmobiles, and sleds are important products in the northern sections of the United States. Residents of the Sunbelt states may spend proportionately less of their total incomes on heating and heating equipment and more on air conditioning. Climate also affects patterns of clothing purchases.

Geographic segmentation is useful only when differences in preference and purchase patterns for a product emerge along regional lines. Moreover, geographic subdivisions of the overall market tend to be rather large and often too heterogeneous for effective segmentation without careful consideration of additional factors. In such cases, several segmentation variables may need to be utilized.

Demographic Segmentation

The most common approach to market segmentation is **demographic segmentation**—dividing consumer groups according to demographic variables. These characteristics—sex, age, income, occupation, education, household size, and stage in the family life cycle, among others—typically are used to

demographic segmentation
Dividing a population into homogeneous groups based on characteristics such as age, sex, and income level.

FOCUS ON ETHICS

Coors and Women

"I never shower alone," says Cher, staring at you from the page of the magazine. She is touting a card for women to place in their showers demonstrating how to examine their breasts, and reminding them to do it often, to help detect breast cancer in its early stages.

A typical health tip ad? Not at all. While the card comes from High Priority, a research and information network on breast cancer, the ad itself is paid for by Adolph Coors Company of Golden, Colorado, the number five brewer in the United States.

Using demographic segmentation, Coors has decided that women, who buy $6.5 billion worth of beer annually, are a good bet for increasing that amount—perhaps to as much as $9 billion by 1994. And in an industry where overall market growth has been virtually nonexistent, targeting a segment that looks to buy more is a good idea. In addition to the public service type of ad described above, Coors ran direct appeals to drinking beer, which sounded like its other ads but were specifically directed at women. In all, Coors devoted $500,000 of its 1987 ad budget of $75 million to full-page ads in women's magazines.

But critics have castigated Coors for the ad campaign, comparing it to cigarette manufacturers who have tried to expand sales among women to counteract sales erosion among men. Among them is Victoria Leonard, executive director of the Washington, D.C.–based National Women's Health Network. To her, Coors is going after the women's markets because "men aren't abusing substances at profitable levels any-more." She points out that the National Cancer Institute recently completed a study showing that drinking even one beer a day could increase the risk of breast cancer by 40 percent. The implication is that Coors is promoting a product to people who will be harmed by it.

It may well be a question of consistency. Had Coors simply promoted its product to women, no one might have complained. Lots of products have survived early implications of connection to health problems. The ethical issue arose because Coors had aimed its ads at women, who might incur a greater health risk from the product, while urging them to practice regular breast self-examination.

Source: Marj Charlier, "New Print Ads for Coors Beer Target Women," *The Wall Street Journal* (June 2, 1987), p. 33.

identify market segments and develop appropriate marketing mixes. Demographic variables are used in market segmentation for three reasons:

1. They are easy to identify and measure.
2. They are associated with the sale of many products and services.
3. They are typically referred to in describing the audiences of advertising media so that media buyers and others can easily pinpoint the desired target market.[10]

Vast quantities of data are available for assisting marketers in segmenting potential markets on a demographic basis. The following sections describe demographic variables often used as bases for segmenting markets.

Segmenting by Sex

Sex is a natural variable for segmenting certain markets, because many products—notably magazines, fragrances, and clothing—are sex specific. In recent years, however, more industries have discovered marketing opportunities for sex segmentation.

Research by American Express revealed that women viewed credit cards as a male-specific product. In an effort to expand its cardholder base, American Express focused on women as the most promising target market. It initiated an "Interesting Lives" advertising campaign to attract new female cardholders. The

Figure 7.3
Segmenting Markets by Age

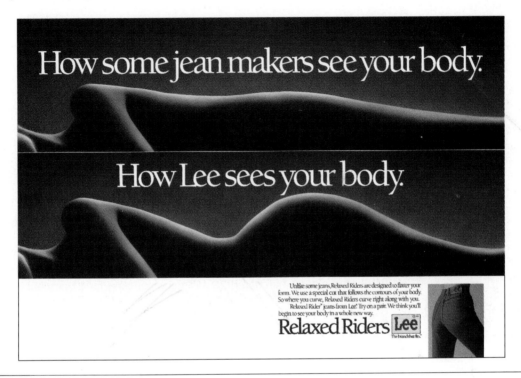

Source: Courtesy of Lee Apparel Company, Incorporated.

strategy worked. Now almost 50 percent of new American Express cardholders are women, compared to 29 percent when the campaign began.[11]

The automobile industry also has recently turned to sex segmentation. Traditionally cars were made for and sold mainly to men. But car buyer research indicates that women buy almost half the number of cars sold and influence more than 80 percent of all sales. As a result, automakers are not only advertising directly to women; they are designing cars with women in mind, forming women's advisory committees to help develop and market cars to women and educating their dealers on how to sell to women. Chevrolet distributes a sales brochure telling dealers that "pretty soon every other guy who walks into your showroom will be a woman."[12]

Segmenting by Age

Many firms identify market segments on the basis of age. Some market products and services only to specific age groups. Gerber focuses on food for infants and toddlers. New Beginnings Adult Care offers medical treatment and recreational services for older people. Firms that market similar products for a wide variety of age groups often develop different marketing approaches for each group. The ad for Lee Relaxed Rider jeans in Figure 7.3 is aimed specifically at women 18 to 35 years old and focuses on the problem women in this age group have finding jeans that fit properly. Lee uses different approaches for its other target markets: children 6 through 13, mothers of children 6 and under, and men.

Age distribution and projected changes in age groups are important to marketers because consumer needs and wants differ among groups. Markets for some products shrink in declining age groups. The young-adult population, aged 18 to 25, decreased steadily during the 1980s, a trend that is not expected to reverse itself until the mid-1990s. For colleges and universities, this decline has resulted in a change from a seller's market to a buyer's market. It has forced most institutions to sell their services in order to compete for a smaller number of students. To attract students, colleges are spending more money on advertising and public relations and offering unique programs. Northeastern University in Boston offers a program that allows all full-time students to work every other quarter for one of 29,000 different employers. Through its Adelphi-On-Wheels program, Adelphi University in New York offers business courses taught on commuter trains. Other institutions are targeting women and students age 25 and older—the fastest-growing groups of college students.

The most notable trend in the U.S. population is referred to as the "graying of America." In 1980, the elderly—those defined by the Bureau of the Census as 65 and older—numbered 26 million, accounting for 11 percent of the population. The number in this age group is expected to rise to 64 million by the year 2030, accounting for one-fifth of the population of 304 million. This growth will reflect the aging of the baby boomers, the 76 million 25- to 44-year-olds who represent the largest and fastest-growing age group in the 1980s.

The aging of the American population has opened many marketing opportunities. For example, book publisher Doubleday & Company has launched a new, large-type book club for older Americans. But marketing experts say that selling to older Americans is difficult because they perceive themselves as being younger than their actual ages. Older Americans respond to products and advertising that appeal to their interests, needs, and wants but turn off to approaches that focus on age and mention terms such as "senior citizen," "golden years," and "retirees." Older people, for example, did not take to Johnson & Johnson's initial advertising campaign for Affinity shampoo because it promoted the product as beneficial for older, brittle hair. Sales increased after the company repositioned Affinity as a product that would enhance the beauty of age and changed the advertising message to suggest that women can be alluring at any age.

Segmenting by Family Life Cycle Stage

family life cycle
Process of family formation and dissolution that includes five major stages: (1) young single, (2) young married without children, (3) other young, (4) middle-age, and (5) older.

The **family life cycle** is the process of family formation and dissolution. Using this concept, the marketing planner combines the family characteristics of age, marital status, and number and ages of children to develop a marketing strategy.

Patrick E. Murphy and William A. Staples have proposed a five-stage family life cycle with several subcategories. The major stages are young singles under 35; young marrieds under 35 without children; other young people under 35,

Photo source: Courtesy of BIC Corporation.

The market for exciting recreational products consists mainly of young single people. BIC Corporation targets this group in marketing its BIC sailboards and BIC SportRack, a car-top carrier system.

including divorced people with and without children and young marrieds with children; middle-agers between 35 and 64; and older people 65 and over.[13]

The behavioral characteristics and buying patterns of persons in each life cycle stage often vary considerably. Young singles have relatively few financial burdens; tend to be early purchasers of new fashion items; are recreation oriented; and make frequent purchases of basic kitchen equipment, cars, and vacations. In contrast, young marrieds with small children tend to be heavy purchasers of baby products, homes, television sets, toys, washers, and dryers. Their liquid assets tend to be relatively low, and they are more likely to watch television than are young singles or young marrieds without children. The empty-nest households in the middle-age and older categories with no dependent children tend to have more disposable income, more time for recreation, self-education, and travel, and more than one member in the labor force than their full-nest counterparts with younger children. Similar differences in behavioral and buying patterns are evident in the other stages of the family life cycle.[14]

Analysis of life cycle stages often gives better results than reliance on single variables such as age. The buying patterns of a 25-year-old bachelor are very different from those of a father of the same age. A family of five headed by parents in their forties is a more likely prospect for the World Book Encyclopedia than a childless, 40-year-old divorced person.

Marketing planners can use published data such as census reports and divide their markets into more homogeneous segments than would be possible if they were analyzing single variables. Such data are available for each classification of the family life cycle.

Segmenting by Household Type

When the first census was taken in 1790, the average household had 5.8 persons. Today the typical household has 2.67 persons and is projected to shrink to 2.48 persons by the year 2000. The U.S. Department of Commerce cites several reasons for the trend toward smaller households: lower fertility rates; young people's tendency to postpone marriage or never marry; the increasing tendency among younger couples to limit the number of children or have no children; the ease and frequency of divorce; and the ability and desire of many young singles and the elderly to live alone.

Almost 22 million people live alone today—about 24 percent of the 89.5 million U.S. households—compared to 10 million in 1970. The single-person household has emerged as an important market segment with a special title: *SSWD,* for *s*ingle, *s*eparated, *w*idowed, and *d*ivorced. SSWDs are customers for single-serve food products, such as Campbell's Soup for One and Green Giant's single-serve casseroles and vegetables. A survey by the Bureau of Labor Statistics reported differences in spending patterns between men and women who live alone. Women spend more than twice as much as men on medical services, prescription drugs, and health insurance. A larger share of women's budgets goes to buying gifts, and women make three times the cash contributions to charities that men do. Men spend more on entertainment, food, and alcohol. Because men eat meals away from home more often, they spend twice as much as women on food outside the home.[15]

Historically about 5 percent of Americans never marry, but that number is likely to increase to 10 percent, according to census bureau estimates. The proportion of never-married men and women in their late twenties and early thirties more than doubled between 1970 and today. Specialized services, such as singles travel agencies and dating services, cater to the never-married. In some cases, the buying habits of singles are similar to those of married couples. For example, an increasing number of singles are buying homes and furnishing them with fine china, silver, and crystal. To attract never-married customers, many major department stores have changed their traditional bridal registries to "gift" registries. Unlike married couples, singles, especially women, are more apt to buy "life organizer" and "rent-a-wife" services that purchase groceries, arrange parties, unpack moving boxes, wait for plumbers, and perform many other everyday tasks for clients.[16]

The majority of U.S. households are married-couple families, which number about 51 million. But the percentage of these households has dropped from 70 percent in 1970 to 57 percent today and is expected to account for only 53 percent of all households by the turn of the century. The number of unmarried individuals living together increased almost fourfold between 1970 and 1986. As a result, the Bureau of the Census has designated another category— *POSLSQ*—for unmarried *p*eople of the *o*pposite *s*ex *l*iving in the *s*ame *qu*arters.

Finally, one of the most highly sought-after market segments in the late 1980s are *DINKs*—*d*ual-*i*ncome couples with *n*o *k*ids. With a high level of spendable income, such couples are big buyers of gourmet foods, luxury items, and travel. DINKs have become one of the most important market segments to emerge in the last five to ten years.

An offshoot of the emergence of DINKs is the "cocooning" trend. The pressure of two careers has made DINKs more conscious of convenience and

Table 7.2
Households Classified by Age and Income

Income	Number of Households (Thousands)						
	Under 25	25–34	35–44	45–54	55–64	65–74	75 and Over
Under $10,000	1,750	2,984	1,992	1,565	2,384	3,562	3,545
$10,000–$19,999	1,826	4,748	2,948	1,995	2,708	3,461	2,137
$20,000–$29,999	1,140	4,764	3,634	2,255	2,311	1,898	879
$30,000–$39,999	460	3,643	3,360	2,134	1,736	977	399
$40,000–$49,999	179	2,058	2,271	1,711	1,299	500	198
$50,000–$59,999	73	1,064	1,542	1,261	872	281	108
$60,000–$74,999	41	695	1,137	1,028	709	205	107
$75,000 and over	33	455	1,115	1,151	834	272	67

Source: Thomas Exter, "Where the Money Is," *American Demographics* (March 1987), p. 29. Reprinted with permission © American Demographics, March 1987.

household comforts. Therefore, DINKs call Domino's frequently and are major purchasers of expensive home entertainment centers and sofas.

Segmenting by Income and Expenditure Patterns

Earlier we defined markets as people with purchasing power. A common method of segmenting the consumer market is on the basis of income. Fashionable specialty shops stocking designer clothing make most of their sales to high-income shoppers. Other retailers aim their appeals at middle-income groups. Still others focus almost exclusively on low-income shoppers.

The number of households in various income groups is shown in Table 7.2. This information is further classified by age of the head of household, illustrating how two segmentation variables can be used jointly.

Household expenditures can be divided into two categories: (1) basic purchases of essential household needs and (2) other purchases made at the discretion of household members after necessities have been purchased. About one-third of U.S. households have discretionary income.

Engel's Laws

How do expenditure patterns vary with increased income? More than 100 years ago, Ernst Engel, a German statistician, published what became known as **Engel's laws**—three general statements based on his studies of the impact of household income changes on consumer spending behavior. According to Engel, as family income increases,

1. A smaller percentage of expenditures goes for food.
2. The percentage spent on housing and household operations and clothing remains constant.
3. The percentage spent on other items (such as recreation and education) increases.

Engel's laws
Three general statements on spending behavior: As a family's income increases, (1) a smaller percentage of income goes for food; (2) the percentage spent on household operations, housing, and clothing remains constant; and (3) the percentage spent on other items increases.

Are Engel's laws still valid? Recent studies supply the answers. A steady decline in the percentage of total income spent on food, beverages, and tobacco occurs from low to high incomes. Although high-income families spend a greater absolute amount on food items, their purchases represent a smaller percentage of their total expenditures than is true of low-income families. The second law is partly correct, since the percentage of expenditures for housing and household operations remains relatively unchanged in all but the very lowest income group. The percentage spent on clothing, however, rises with increased income. Households that earn less than $10,000 annually spend a smaller percentage of their incomes on clothing than those who earn more than $10,000. The third law is also true with the exception of medical and personal care, which appear to decline with increased income.

Engel's laws provide the marketing manager with useful generalizations about the types of consumer demand that evolve with increased income. They can also be helpful for the marketer evaluating a foreign country as a potential target market.

Psychographic Segmentation

Although geographic and demographic segmentation traditionally have been the primary bases for dividing consumer and industrial markets into homogeneous segments for use as target markets, marketers have long recognized the need for fuller, more lifelike portraits of consumers in developing marketing programs. While traditionally used variables such as age, sex, family life cycle, income, and population size and location are important in segmentation, life-styles of potential customers may prove equally significant.

Life-style refers to the consumer's mode of living; it is how an individual lives. Consumers' life-styles are regarded as composites of their individual psychological makeups—their needs, motives, perceptions, and attitudes. A life-style also bears the mark of many other influences, such as reference groups, culture, social class, and family members.

life-style
The way people decide to live their lives, including family, job, social activities, and consumer decisions.

Using Psychographic Segmentation

In recent years, a new technique that promises to elicit more meaningful bases for segmentation has been developed. Although definitions vary among researchers, **psychographic segmentation** generally means the psychological profiles of different consumers developed from asking consumers to agree or disagree with **AIO statements,** which are a collection of several hundred statements dealing with activities, interests, and opinions.

Marketing researchers conduct psychographic studies on hundreds of goods and services ranging from beer to air travel. Hospitals and other health care organizations use psychographic studies to assess consumer behavior and attitudes toward health care in general, to learn the needs of consumers in a particular marketplace, and to determine how consumers perceive individual institutions. Marriott Corporation, Avon, and other businesses have turned to psychographics in an effort not only to learn what seniors need but to under-

psychographic segmentation
Dividing a population into homogeneous groups on the basis of behavioral and life-style profiles developed by analyzing consumer activities, opinions, and interests.

AIO statements
Collection of statements in a psychographic study to reflect respondents' activities, interests, and opinions.

stand what becomes important to them as they grow older. Such studies help marketers target their services and marketing approaches more effectively.

The President's Commission on Americans Outdoors conducted a psychographic study to determine what kinds of parks, beaches, campgrounds, and other outdoor recreation areas will be needed in the coming decades. The research, which included 20 focus groups and a nationwide survey of 2,000 adults, divided Americans into the following five groups based on recreational values and life-styles:

- *Excitement-Seeking Competitives,* who represent 16 percent of the adult population, rate excitement and competition as main reasons for outdoor recreation. They participate in team sports such as basketball and baseball and competitive sports such as golf and tennis. Almost half belong to sports clubs, teams, or groups. The median age of this group is 32, and two-thirds are men.

- *Get-Away Actives,* one-third of the population, use outdoor recreation as a chance to be alone and an opportunity to experience nature. They like backpacking, day hiking, tent camping, fishing, and bird watching. Over half of this group use outdoor recreation as a way to reduce stress. Their median age is 35, and they are divided equally between men and women. Almost half are baby boomers.

- *The Fitness Driven,* about 10 percent of adults, participate in outdoor activities mainly to keep fit. They are the joggers and walkers. This group is the highest on the socioeconomic scale and includes more women (56 percent) than men (44 percent). Almost 40 percent are college graduates, and their median age is 46.

- *Health-Conscious Sociables,* another one-third of adults, like picnicking, sightseeing, attending sports events, and pleasure driving. They participate in outdoor recreation for physical fitness and social companionship. They have no desire for excitement, competition, or solitude. Their median age is 49, and about two-thirds are women.

- The *Unstressed and Unmotivated,* about 8 percent of the population, have no motivation to participate in outdoor recreation. This group is split about evenly between men and women. Their median age is 49.

Based on this study, the commission learned that because of the size of the baby boom generation and their participation in outdoor recreation, the demand for parks, marinas, bicycle paths, nature preserves, and other recreational facilities is likely to increase in future decades.[17]

The marketing implications of psychographic segmentation are considerable. Psychographic profiles produce a much richer description of a potential target market and can assist in promotional decisions in attempting to match the company's image and product offerings with the type of consumer who uses the products.

Psychographic segmentation often serves as a component of an overall marketing strategy in which markets are also segmented on the basis of demographic/geographic variables such as age, income, city size, education, family life cycle stage, and geographic location. These more traditional bases give

Figure 7.4
Segmenting Markets by
Income and Life-Style

Source: Courtesy of Porsche Cars North America, Incorporated.

the marketer accessibility to consumer segments through orthodox communications channels such as newspapers, radio and television, and other promotional outlets. Psychographic studies may then be implemented to develop life-like, three-dimensional profiles of the life-styles of consumers in the firm's target market.

When combined with demographic/geographic characteristics, psychographics is an important tool for understanding the behavior of present and potential target markets. For example, luxury-car makers segment their market by income. A psychographic study of luxury-car buyers, however, identified distinct personality and life-style differences among consumers in this group even though they shared the trait of ability to afford a high-priced car. According to the study, Cadillac owners desire comfort, want to be chauffeured, and are concerned about the impression their cars make on others. They care little about their cars' color or mechanical aspects. Porsche owners, in contrast, demand performance over luxury. They prefer the color red and are knowledgeable about their cars' mechanical operation. Jaguar owners are more austere and have a taste for elegance and darker colors, while Mercedes owners like to feel they are in control of their lives and their vehicles and prefer muted shades of tan, gray, and silver. In short, luxury-car owners view their cars as extensions of themselves.[18] Such descriptive profiles help marketers learn why a buyer might choose a Porsche over a Jaguar. Using this information, marketers can divide the luxury-car market into smaller segments and develop a marketing mix appropriate for each target. The advertisement for Porsche in Figure 7.4 emphasizes the car's performance and appeals to owners' preference for the color red.

Benefit Segmentation

Benefit segmentation focuses on such attributes as product usage rates and benefits derived from a product. These factors may reveal important bases for pinpointing prospective target markets. One analysis of 34 segmentation studies indicated that benefit analysis provided the best predictor of brand use, consumption level, and product type selected in 51 percent of the cases.[19] Many marketers now consider benefit segmentation the most useful approach to classifying markets.

benefit segmentation
Dividing a population into homogeneous groups on the basis of benefits consumers expect to derive from a product or service.

Usage Rates

Marketing managers may divide potential segments into two categories: users and nonusers. Users may be subdivided as heavy, moderate, and light. A poll of California lottery players revealed that 30 percent of the adult population did not buy lottery tickets. Of the nonusers, most were women, 84 percent were white, and the overwhelming majority had more education and higher incomes than the average Californian. The poll also identified heavy users—those who bought 20 tickets in a 45-day period. While the heavy users constituted only 18 percent of the state's adult population, they purchased 71 percent of all lottery tickets. The heavy users were more likely to be minorities and have less income and education than the average Californian.[20]

By identifying heavy users, marketers can develop advertising and promotions targeted at this group in an attempt to build customer loyalty. Several firms have adopted the airlines' frequent-flyer concept of rewarding heavy users. Park 'n Fly's frequent-parker program gives customers up to 7 days' free airport parking for every 35 days of paid parking. Customers who spend $6,000 a year at Neiman-Marcus stores receive a box of chocolates each month for a year. Those who spend $60,000 get a Super Bowl trip.[21]

Sales analysis, discussed in Chapter 4, is a common method of identifying heavy users. Much of this information can be obtained from internal records. Photon Entertainment developed a unique customer database that identified boys under age 17 as the single largest user group of its laser tag combat centers. The company tracks player frequency by issuing permanent identification cards that give a demographic profile of each player. Computers at each of 20 laser tag arenas record player hits, final scores, and other statistics that are fed into computers at company headquarters. Containing about 1 million names, the database can track zip code areas in which members of target groups are concentrated. Marketers use the database to analyze patterns of play and then customize individual mailing lists for target groups in each arena area.[22]

Product Benefits

Market segments may also be identified by the benefits buyers expect to derive from a product or brand. In a pioneering investigation, Daniel Yankelovich revealed that much of the watch industry was operating with little understanding of the benefits watch buyers expect in their purchases. At the time of the study,

TABASCO Brand Pepper Sauce

Like the Tin Man in *The Wizard of Oz,* most of us do not like to see people cry. But the McIlhenny family banks on a product that brings tears to anyone's eyes: TABASCO brand Pepper Sauce. Their sauce, derived from a special strain of *calipsum frutescens* pepper bred in the 1860s by the company founder, Edmund McIlhenny, is the hottest of the commercial pepper sauces and, when used in sufficient quantity, takes food beyond mouth watering to eye watering.

Tabasco sauce sounds like a product with limited appeal, but its market has grown steadily. Since 1868, when McIlhenny wholesaled his first batch of 350 bottles of sauce at $1 a bottle, McIlhenny Company has seen sales of TABASCO grow to $40 million a year. TABASCO dominates the pepper sauce market, its growth stemming largely from the company's efforts to expose everlarger segments of the public to it.

McIlhenny Company is based on Avery Island, off the coast of Louisiana. Thus, it is only fitting that Louisianians are the heaviest users, consuming more Tabasco sauce per person than any other state, although California generates the highest sales volume. But TABASCO sauce is used around the world; the biggest foreign market is Japan, where some 6 million bottles are sold each year.

Still, prior to the 1940s TABASCO sauce was marketed largely by word of mouth and via billboards and poster bills. Then came Walter McIlhenny, the fourth head of the company, who realized that while some people used tremendous amounts of the sauce, most associated it only with cocktails such as Bloody Marys or seafoods such as oysters.

Walter McIlhenny wanted to give the product a wider appeal, so he introduced modern advertising techniques to McIlhenny Company, hiring

TABASCO® SAUCE MAKES A SPLASH WITH OYSTERS. AND CLAMS. AND SWORDFISH. AND SOLE. AND CATFISH. AND REDFISH. AND [...]

Circle 129 on reader service card.

AND SCA[...] AND FLOUNDER. AND CRAB. AND MUSSELS. AND TROUT. AND MAHI MAHI. AND SHRIMP.

advertising agencies to create campaigns for print journalism, and, much later, television. An avid traveler, McIlhenny also searched the world for foods that blended well with TABASCO sauce and then created a series of recipes that used TABASCO.

The recipes were something of a master stroke. As company vice president Paul McIlhenny points out: "Over 50 percent of the U.S. homes have a bottle on the shelf. Our problem is to get them to use it."

New president Edward McIlhenny Simmons (McIlhenny Company has turned down numerous takeover offers for its essentially one-product firm) intends to continue exploring new methods of marketing to increase the number of TABASCO users. Its most recent marketing idea is to put TABASCO sauce in small packets for use at McDonald's restaurants.

Sources: Phyllis C. Richman, "Pepper Sauce with a Pedigree: The Life and Legends on Avery Island," *Washington Post* (June 8, 1983), and John Cade, "Red Hot: The Spice of Life Is a Way of Life on Louisiana's Avery Island," *Philip Morris Magazine* (Fall 1986), pp. 27–30. *Photo source:* Courtesy of McIlhenny Company.

most watch companies were marketing relatively expensive models through jewelry stores and using prestige appeals. However, Yankelovich's research revealed that about one-third of the market purchased the lowest-priced watch and another 46 percent focused on durability and overall product quality. U.S. Time Company decided to focus its product benefits on those two categories and to market its Timex watches in drugstores, variety stores, and discount houses. Within a few years of adopting the new segmentation approach, U.S. Time Company became the largest watch company in the world.[23]

Benefit segmentation has also been successfully employed in a number of other consumer markets. One study, for example, revealed seven market segments based on the perceived benefits of drinking liquor. "Mood modification" was the objective of a consumer group that sought to escape stress, boredom, and so forth; another segment sought "social lubrication," believing the liquor improved social interaction.[24]

Where differences among competing brands are slight, a firm may introduce a brand with a new benefit that appeals to a certain market segment. According to one study, 55 percent of consumers see few differences among laundry detergents, most of which are promoted as making clothes clean and bright and smell fresh and fragrant. In its search for a new benefit, Lever Brothers decided to target consumers concerned about body odor in clothes, a problem that has increased because more Americans are exercising and more clothing is being made of synthetic fibers that hold odors. Based on this benefit, Lever Brothers formulated Surf, a detergent with odor-tackling properties, which quickly became the number two detergent brand in the country.[25]

Segmenting Industrial Markets

While the bulk of market segmentation has concentrated on consumer markets, the concept also applies to the industrial sector. The overall process is similar. For example, many of IBM's competitors have decided to compete against the computer giant by specializing in specific market segments. Qantel services small hotels and football and athletic teams. Control Data concentrates on the engineering and scientific markets. NCR markets many of its computers to banks and retailers.[26]

Segmentation approaches used in the industrial market include geographic segmentation, product segmentation, and segmentation by end-use application.

Geographic Segmentation

Geographic segmentation is useful in industries whose customers are concentrated in specific geographical locations. This approach is used effectively in the automobile industry, concentrated in the Detroit area, and the tire industry, centered in Akron. It might also be used where markets are limited to just a few locations. The oil field equipment market, for example, is largely concentrated in such cities as Houston, Dallas, and Tulsa.

Figure 7.5
How Industrial Goods Meet Specific Buyer Requirements

Source: Courtesy of Hercules Incorporated.

Product Segmentation

product segmentation
Dividing an industrial market into homogeneous groups on the basis of product specifications identified by industrial buyers.

Product segmentation is often used in the industrial marketplace because industrial users tend to have much more precise product specifications than do ultimate consumers. Thus, industrial products often fit narrower market segments than consumer products. Designing an industrial good or service to meet specific buyer requirements is a form of market segmentation. A. Schulman, a plastics compounder, concentrates on market segments demanding materials that meet exact customer specifications. Schulman buys resins from oil and chemical firms and then adds coloring and other additives to produce plastics for specific customer applications ranging from skateboard wheels to lobster pots to flame-retardant compounds for electronics firms.[27] The advertisement in Figure 7.5 describes how Hercules, Inc., developed a tackifying resin for an adhesives formulator that required meeting exact specifications. The adhesive on the banana label had to be resistant to the fruit's natural oils, stick on more than just one type of banana, and withstand frequent temperature changes.

Segmentation by End-Use Application

A third segmentation base is **end-use application segmentation,** or the precise way in which the industrial purchaser will use the product. For example, a manufacturer of printing equipment may serve markets ranging from a local utility to a bicycle manufacturer to the U.S. Department of Defense. Each end use of the equipment may dictate unique specifications for performance, design, and price. Instead of competing in markets dominated by large firms, many small and medium-size companies concentrate on specific market segments. Glassmaker AFG Industries receives more than half of its sales from specialty lines of tempered and colored glass. It makes 70 percent of the glass used in microwave oven doors and 75 percent of that used in shower enclosures and patio table tops.[28] Regardless of how it is done, market segmentation is as vital to industrial marketing as it is to consumer marketing.

end-use application segmentation
Dividing an industrial market into homogeneous groups on the basis of precisely how different industrial purchasers will use the product.

The Market Segmentation Decision Process

To this point, we have discussed the various segmentation bases used by consumer and industrial marketers. In both types of markets, marketing managers follow a systematic five-step decision process, which is outlined in Figure 7.6.[29]

Stage I: Select Market Segmentation Bases

Segmentation begins when a firm seeks bases on which to segment markets. These bases are one or more characteristics of potential buyers that allow the marketer to classify them into market segments for further analysis. Segmentation bases should be selected so that each segment contains customers who respond similarly to specific marketing mix alternatives; customers in different segments respond differently. For example, before Procter & Gamble decides to market Crest to a segment made up of large families, management should be confident that most large families are interested in preventing tooth decay and thus will be receptive to the Crest marketing offer. In some cases, this objective is difficult to achieve. Consider the marketer seeking to reach the consumer segment that is over 50 years of age. Saturday evening television commercials can reach this group, but much of the expenditure may be wasted, since the other major viewer group is composed of teenagers.

Stage II: Develop Relevant Profiles for Each Segment

Once segments have been identified, marketers should seek to understand the customers in each segment. Segmentation bases provide some insight into the nature of customers, but typically not enough to base the kinds of decisions that marketing managers must make. Sufficient description of customers is needed to allow managers to more accurately match customer needs with marketing offers. Characteristics that explain the similarities among customers within each segment as well as account for differences among segments must be identified. Thus, the task at this stage is to develop profiles of the typical customer in each segment. Such profiles might include life-style patterns, attitudes toward product attributes and brands, brand preferences, product use habits, geographic location, and demographic characteristics. The Broadway–Southern California, a

Figure 7.6
The Market Segmentation
Decision Process

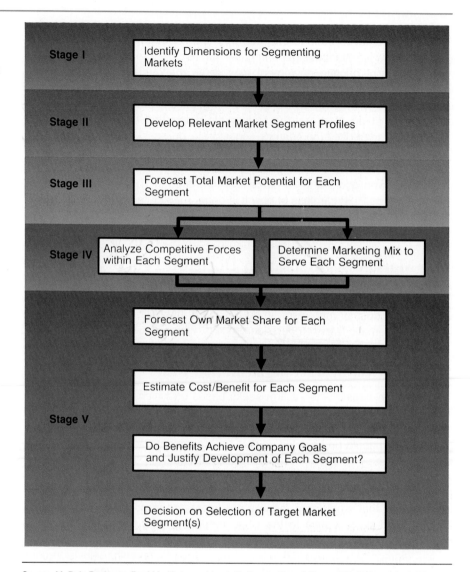

Source: M. Dale Beckman, David L. Kurtz, and Louis E. Boone, *Foundations of Marketing,* 3d ed. (Toronto: Holt, Rinehart and Winston of Canada, 1985), p. 181. The figure was originally prepared by Professor J. D. Forbes of the University of British Columbia and is reprinted by permission of the authors and publisher.

leading Los Angeles–based retailer, profiled its female customers as being between ages 25 to 55; 4 feet 10 inches to 5 feet 3 inches tall; weighing 85 to 120 pounds; career oriented; and having $20,000-plus household incomes. The Broadway used this profile to set up separate petite sections — one of the fastest-growing segments of the women's fashion industry.[30]

Stage III: Forecast Market Potential

In the third stage, market segmentation and market opportunity analysis continue to coincide to produce a forecast of market potential within each segment. Market potential sets the upper limit on the demand that can be expected from a segment and therefore determines maximum sales potential.

In response to competitors' increased emphasis on promoting and advertising their hamburgers, Wendy's launched new products targeted at specific market segments in an effort to expand market share. Wendy's Big Classic hamburger, for example, targets primarily 18- to 24-year-old males. To increase its share of the young-family market, Wendy's upgraded its Kids' Meals and plans to introduce products particularly attractive to children.

Photo source: Courtesy of Wendy's International, Inc.

This step should be a preliminary go or no-go decision point for management, since it must determine whether the total sales potential in each segment is sufficient to justify further analysis. Some segments will be screened out because they represent insufficient potential demand; others will be sufficiently attractive for the analysis to continue.

Consider the toothbrush segment of the dental supplies and mouthwash market. This segment would nearly triple if a marketer could convince the public to replace toothbrushes on a regular basis. Americans should buy 3 to 4 toothbrushes a year with average usage, but the current replacement rate is only 1.3 brushes annually.[31] Obviously a tremendous market potential exists.

Stage IV: Forecast Probable Market Share

Once market potential has been estimated, the proportion of demand that the firm may capture must be determined. This step requires a forecast of probable market share. Market share forecasts depend on both an analysis of competitors' positions in target segments and the specific marketing strategy and tactics designed to serve these segments. These two activities may be performed simultaneously. Moreover, design of marketing strategy and tactics determines the expected level of resources, that is, the costs that will be necessary for tapping the potential demand in each segment.

Colgate once trailed Procter & Gamble in heavy-duty detergents, dishwashing liquids, and soaps—overall, in half of its business. Thus, Colgate diversified its product line. Today 75 percent of the firm's offerings do not face a directly competitive Procter & Gamble product, or, if they do, they compete effectively.[32]

Stage V: Select Specific Market Segments

The information, analysis, and forecasts accumulated through the entire market segmentation decision process allow management to assess the potential for achieving company goals and to justify the development of one or more segments. For example, demand forecasts, when combined with cost projections, are used to determine the profit and return on investment that can be expected from each segment. Analysis of marketing strategy and tactics will determine the degree of consistency with corporate image and reputation goals as well as with unique organizational capabilities that may be realized by serving a segment. These assessments will, in turn, help management select specific segments as the target markets.

At this point in the analysis, the costs and benefits to be weighed are not only monetary; they also include many difficult-to-measure but critical organizational and environmental factors. For example, the firm may not have enough experienced personnel to launch a successful attack on what clearly promises to be certain monetary success. Similarly, a firm with 80 percent of the market may face legal problems with the Federal Trade Commission if it increases its market concentration. The assessment of both financial and nonfinancial factors is a difficult but vital step in the decision process.

There is no simple answer to the market segmentation decision—nor should there be. The marketing concept's prescription for serving the customer's needs and earning a profit while doing so implies that the marketer must evaluate each potential marketing program on its ability to achieve this goal in the marketplace. By performing the detailed analysis outlined in Figure 7.6, the marketing manager can increase the probability of success in profitably serving consumers' needs.

Target Market Decision Analysis

target market decision analysis
Evaluation of potential market segments by dividing the overall market into homogeneous groups. Cross-classifications may be based on variables such as type of market, geographic location, frequency of use, or demographic characteristics.

Target market decision analysis is a useful tool in the market segmentation process. Targets are chosen by segmenting the total market on the basis of a given characteristic. Figure 7.7 illustrates the application of target market decision analysis.

Applying Target Market Decision Analysis

Consider the decisions of a small firm that analyzes the market potential for a proposed line of typewriters. Because of limited financial resources, the company must operate on a regional basis. Grid A in Figure 7.7 illustrates the firm's first two decisions: choosing a geographic area and marketing the typewriters to the ultimate consumer. The typewriter company could also have chosen the industrial market, but a separate marketing strategy would have been required since each market in grid A represents unique characteristics.

The next step involves the decision to market the typewriters to high-income households in the young and middle-age stages of the family life cycle, which in turn requires evaluating the market for typewriters as gifts for school-age children. These decisions are shown in grid B. Data can be gathered on

Figure 7.7
Target Market Decision Analysis for Typewriters

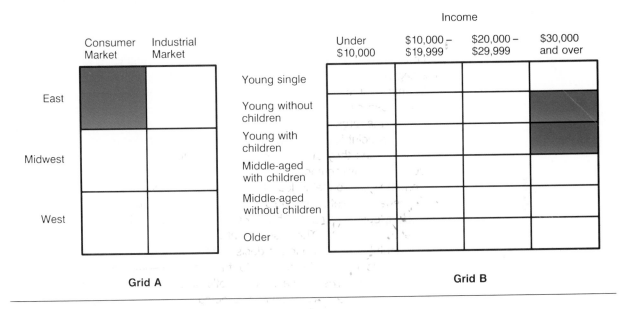

Grid A

Grid B

the size of the target market in the eastern United States and the firm's predicted market share.

The cross-classifications in grid B can be further subdivided to gather
more specific data on the characteristics of the proposed target market. The
potential bases for segmenting markets are virtually limitless, and although
divisions are sometimes made intuitively, they are usually supported with concrete
data.

While this illustration used geographic and demographic segmentation
bases, benefit and psychographic segmentation can also be used in target market decision analysis. Similarly, geographic, product, and end-use application
segmentation bases can be used in targeting industrial market segments.

Summary of Chapter Objectives

1. Explain what is meant by a *market*. A market consists of people and
organizations with the necessary purchasing power and willingness and
authority to buy. Markets may be classified according to product type.
Consumer goods are products purchased by the ultimate consumer for
personal use. Industrial goods are products purchased for use directly or
indirectly in the production of other goods and services.

**2. Outline the role of market segmentation in developing a marketing
strategy.** Market segmentation refers to the process of dividing the total
market into several homogeneous groups. It plays an important role in the
development of marketing strategies, because most products are targeted at

specific market segments. The segmentation process allows marketers to choose their target markets more accurately.

3. Explain each of the four bases for segmenting consumer markets. Consumer markets may be divided on the bases of geographic, demographic, psychographic, or benefit segmentation. Geographic segmentation, one of the oldest forms, is the process of dividing the overall market into homogeneous groups on the basis of population location. The continual shifts in the U.S. population necessitate considerable effort in identifying the various geographic segments. The most commonly used form of segmentation is demographic segmentation, which classifies the overall market into homogeneous groups based on such characteristics as age, sex, and income level. Psychographic segmentation, a relatively new approach, uses behavioral profiles developed from analyses of consumers' activities, opinions, interests, and life-styles to identify market segments. Benefit segmentation, perhaps the most useful approach, segments markets on the basis of the perceived benefits consumers expect to derive from a product or service.

4. Describe the three bases for segmenting industrial markets. There are three bases for industrial market segmentation. Geographic segmentation is commonly used in concentrated industries. Product segmentation focuses on product specifications of industrial buyers. Segmentation by end-use application is based on how industrial purchasers will use the good or service.

5. Identify the steps in the market segmentation process. Market segmentation is the division of large, heterogeneous markets into several relatively homogeneous groups. The segmentation process follows a five-step sequence: determining the bases on which to segment markets; developing consumer and/or industrial user profiles for appropriate market segments; assessing the overall market potential for the relevant market segments; estimating market share and costs/benefits of each market segment given the existing competition and the selected marketing mix; and selecting the segments that will become the firm's target markets.

6. Explain how target market decision analysis can be used in segmenting markets. Target market decision analysis is a useful tool in the market segmentation process. It involves developing a grid outlining the various market segments by their distinguishing characteristics. All bases for segmentation may be employed in target market decision analysis. The approach can be used for both consumer and industrial markets.

Key Terms

market	demographic segmentation
consumer goods	family life cycle
industrial goods	Engel's laws
market segmentation	life-style
geographic segmentation	psychographic segmentation
Consolidated Metropolitan Statistical Area (CMSA)	AIO statements
	benefit segmentation
Primary Metropolitan Statistical Area (PMSA)	product segmentation
	end-use application segmentation
Metropolitan Statistical Area (MSA)	target market decision analysis

Review Questions

1. Explain why each of the four components of a market is needed in order for a market to exist.

2. Bicycles are consumer goods; iron ore is an industrial good. Are trucks consumer goods or industrial goods? Support your answer.

3. Identify and briefly explain the bases for segmenting consumer markets.

4. Identify the major population shifts that have occurred in recent years. How do you account for these shifts?

5. Distinguish among CMSAs, PMSAs, and MSAs.

6. Why is demographic segmentation the most commonly used approach to market segmentation? How can life-styles be used in market segmentation?

7. Explain the use of product usage rates as a segmentation variable.

8. What market segmentation base would you recommend for the following?
   a. Professional basketball team
   b. Subaru X/T sports car
   c. RCA records
   d. Listerine mouthwash

9. Identify and briefly explain the bases for segmenting industrial markets.

10. List the steps in the market segmentation process.

Discussion Questions

1. California is Chrysler's biggest market segment for full-size vans. In contrast, relatively few Aries and Reliants are sold in the state.[33] Relate this situation to the material in this chapter.

2. Minute Maid Squeeze-Fresh, a frozen juice concentrate packaged in a 12-ounce squeeze bottle, is currently being test marketed by Coca-Cola Foods. The concentrate, which makes 60 ounces of orange juice, is aimed at smaller households.[34] What role does market segmentation play for this new Minute Maid product?

3. Match the following bases for market segmentation with the appropriate items. Explain your choices.
   a. Geographic segmentation
   b. Demographic segmentation
   c. Psychographic segmentation
   d. Benefit segmentation
   _____ A government-financed study divided U.S. households into five categories of eating patterns: meat eaters, healthy eaters, conscientious eaters, in-a-dither eaters, and on-the-go eaters.
   _____ Bamberger's decision to emphasize suburban department stores (its only downtown outlet is the original store in Newark, New Jersey).
   _____ "7-Up, clear, crisp with no caffeine."
   _____ Spiegel Inc. targets its catalogs at 25-to-54-year-old working women with household incomes of $35,000.

4. Discuss how each of the four consumer-oriented segmentation bases can be used in target market decision analysis.

5. Discuss how each of the three industrial market segmentation bases might be used in target market decision analysis.

VIDEO CASE 7

Irvine Co.

The original 90,000 acres of the Irvine Ranch were purchased by James Irvine and his partners for 35 cents an acre in the 1860s. Running inland 22 miles from the Pacific Ocean, the ranch is located between Los Angeles and San Diego in what is now called Orange County. The tract includes the city of Irvine and sections of several other wealthy Los Angeles suburbs, such as Newport Beach.

For generations, the property was operated as a farm and ranch. In fact, nearly 60,000 acres of this highly fertile land are still used for agricultural pursuits. Major crops include tomatoes, avocados, asparagus, and Valencia oranges.

The area was virtually uninhabited until the 1950s. Then the Los Angeles megapolis spread into the region, and Orange County quickly became one of the fastest-growing areas in the United States. As a result, the land soon became more valuable for housing development than for agricultural purposes. Thus the Irvine Co. set up a project to develop the property by creating planned communities. The Irvine plan was part of the so-called "New Town" concept that was popular at the time. Like developers of such East Coast New Towns as Columbia, Maryland and Reston, Virginia, Irvine's marketing plan involved setting up planned communities that included shopping, schools, churches, and recreational areas along with housing.

Today some 66,500 acres of the Irvine property — 15 percent of Orange County — remain undeveloped. As it is one of the largest undeveloped plots of land near a major U.S. city, its future worth is immeasurable.

Irvine's marketers planned to utilize a textbook approach to market segmentation. Since people have differing housing needs based upon their life-cycle stage, the firm should have made alternative housing available to cater to these varying needs. However, the traditional approach to building ignored these needs and treated the housing market as a monolith, recognizing different households' requirements with only variations in the number of bedrooms or overall square footage. The Irvine marketing approach involved an initial analysis of the housing market and the development of a product mix designed to appeal to different types of buyers. Families would live near families, adult households near other adult households, and so forth.

Market segmentation — the process of dividing a market into homogeneous target markets — provided the key to Irvine's planned community concept. Irvine's management felt that market segmentation would allow the firm to meet both social and marketing goals by providing a structure for growth while allowing the development to proceed more rapidly. Market segmentation can be done on geographic, demographic, psychographic, or benefit bases. Irvine's management initially selected psychographic segmentation for characterizing its market. As noted in the chapter, psychographic segmentation is based upon an analysis of consumer lifestyles. The company accumulated all sorts of information, from the cars people drove to the wines they consumed. However, no one could relate this data to the types of housing people desired.

Irvine Co. soon turned to other means of segmenting its market. It began interviewing its home buyers, both to promote public relations and to obtain demographic data that would assist in future segmentation efforts. Builders were persuaded to design homes specifically targeted at given market segments. Thus, demographic segmentation enabled Irvine to build the homes people really wanted. In addition to standard one-, two-, and three-bedroom formats to match various household sizes, it offered options such as a triplex plan, which gave first-time buyers affordable but spacious housing, and nonrelated-adults dwellings with individual master bedrooms.

Irvine's market segmentation efforts hit a snag in the late 1970s. Inflation and substantial in-migration created an unprecedented housing boom in Southern California. Consumer demand soon exceeded product availability, forcing housing prices up 25 to 30 percent per year. Some houses were even being sold through lottery drawings. Also, some homes that cost $80,000 in the 1950s had been sold with 25-year land leases rather than as deeded land. When the leases were reopened in the late 1970s, Irvine Co. sought increases as high as 3,333 percent. It later backed away from this position, offering to sell the land or proposing new leases that were higher priced but far less so than was originally proposed.

If the price hikes did not force buyers out of the housing market, mortgage rates did. A restrictive monetary policy designed to combat double-digit inflation produced interest rates of nearly 20 percent. As a result, new houses remained unsold. Irvine's market segmentation strategy was a shambles, as targeted groups could no longer afford the available housing. In fact, Orange County's industrial growth was stymied as well, since people will not take jobs where they cannot afford to buy homes.

The housing boom began to subside in the early to mid-1980s, when home prices and mortgage rates came into closer balance with consumers' ability to purchase housing. Irvine Co. returned to its segmentation strategy. Once again, the challenge was to provide housing that would accommodate diverse needs and encourage families to remain in the community throughout their life cycles.

Property continued to be developed at a planned pace of about 700 acres per year. The company's present marketing approach involves planning new housing in accordance with segmentation strategy, constructing roads and sewers, and obtaining government permits. The actual construction and sales, however, are handled by outside contractors.

Sources: Julie Flynn and Mark Frons, "Owning Irvine, Calif., Isn't What It Used to Be," *Business Week* (March 9, 1987), pp. 80, 82, and Gary Hector, "The Land Coup in Orange County," *Fortune* (November 14, 1983), pp. 91–92, 96, 100, 102.

Questions

1. Discuss the importance of market segmentation for Irvine Co.

2. Why was demographic segmentation more effective than psychographic segmentation for Irvine Co.?

3. What specific aspects of demographic segmentation are evident in this case?

COMPUTER APPLICATIONS

In one of the earliest reported studies of how consumer expenditure patterns change when household income increases, German statistician Ernst Engel proposed three general conclusions:

1. A smaller percentage of the household budget will be allocated to food purchases.
2. The percentage of the household budget spent on housing, household operations, and clothing will remain constant.
3. The percentage spent on other items (such as education and recreation) and the percentage devoted to savings/investments will increase.

These generalizations became known as *Engel's laws.*

Directions: Use menu item 7 titled "Engel's Laws" to solve each of the following problems.

Problem 1   Alice Garcia is a single, 26-year-old marketing research analyst at a major consumer goods company in Boston. Last year Alice saved $3,200 and spent the remainder as follows: food, $6,400; housing and clothing, $12,800; and miscellaneous (including entertainment and vacations), $9,600. But a recent promotion and salary increase has prompted Garcia to reevaluate her personal budget. She has decided to use a payroll deduction program to increase her savings to $4,200, go on a diet and cut her food expenditures to $4,600, increase her housing and clothing outlays slightly to $14,000, and spend the rest of next year's $36,000 salary on miscellaneous items (includng a short winter vacation). Does Garcia's budget conflict with Engel's laws? If so, how?

Problem 2   The Martin family of San Diego uses a budget to monitor and control household expenditures. The family has just prepared this year's budget to reflect the salary increases that both spouses expect at the beginning of the year. The general categories of expenditures and savings and the amounts allocated to each category are shown in the accompanying table. Is the Martins' budget for this year consistent with Engel's laws? With which, if any, of the laws does it conflict?

Budget Category	Last Year's Expenditures	This Year's Budgeted Amount
Food	$18,000	$19,500
Clothing and housing	24,000	29,250
Other	18,000	16,250
Total	$60,000	$65,000

Problem 3   Sam and Carla Benson of Wilmington, North Carolina, recently consulted a financial planner for assistance in developing a household budget and making investments. In the process, the planner made several suggestions about the Bensons' personal expenditures. Noting that the couple's combined income would increase next year by 12 percent, the planner suggested that they purchase the home they had been considering. The planner pointed out that while their monthly housing costs would rise 50 percent above their current rent, most of the increase would be tax deductible as an interest expense. However, Carla was interested in using the additional income to purchase stocks and bonds rather than to serve as a down payment on the house. Last year's expenditures and next year's budget proposals are as follows:

Budget Category	Expenditures	Planner's Proposed Budget for Next Year	Carla's Proposed Budget for Next Year
Food	$ 14,000	$ 15,000	$ 15,000
Beverages	1,000	2,000	2,000
Clothing	20,000	22,000	22,000
Housing	17,000	25,000	17,000
Entertainment	10,000	11,000	11,000
Investments	5,000	5,000	17,000
Other	33,000	32,000	28,000
Total	$100,000	$112,000	$112,000

a. Does the planner's suggestion conflict with Engel's laws?
b. How consistent is Carla's proposed budget with Engel's laws?

Problem 4 Pat and Jan Gardner of Cleveland have never used a formal household budget. But the couple does engage in an annual ritual of sitting in front of their fireplace every New Year's Eve, evaluating the past year and making some general plans for the coming one. The discussion this past December 31 went something like this:

Jan: Well, this year was certainly good to us, with each of us getting a $5,000 raise effective tomorrow.
Pat: Yes, I agree. So maybe it is about time we moved on that condo with the "For Sale" sign that we drive past every day.
Jan: Pat, you read my mind every time! I don't care if it does increase our spending on housing from $15,000 to $19,500 next year. We could make it up somewhere else in our spending plans.
Pat: Well, we still have to eat, but we could stay away from the gourmet section and cut back on our percentage spent on food. My quick tally of the checkbook shows we spent $8,000 on food items this year. We could try to hold our food spending to, say, $9,000 next year.
Jan: And I would be willing to spend our vacation in Florida rather than flying to Europe like we planned. According to my mental calculator, that means we would have $3,500 left from our $32,000 take-home pay next year for miscellaneous— including the vacation. That's $500 less than the $4,000 we allocated for miscellaneous spending this past year out of our combined $27,000 in take-home pay.
Pat: Jan, next New Year's Eve, we've just got to start talking about a savings and investment plan. . . .

Do the Gardners' financial plans conflict with Engel's laws? If so, how?

Problem 5 Virgil Romanos is a relief pitcher with the Minnesota Twins. Romanos, who is 23 and single, has just completed the best year of his baseball career, posting a 9-7 win/loss record with 16 saves. His agent has just negotiated a new contract for next year that will boost Romanos to $350,000 from the $280,000 he earned last year. The agent, an attorney and CPA, has also developed a personal budget for Romanos that reflects his raise and the fact that the young pitcher will marry soon. Since the couple plans to start a family right away, the bride-to-be has decided to give up her teaching position in Bloomington. Determine whether the agent's proposed budget coincides with Engel's laws. (Hint: Taxes and the agent's fees should be included in the "other" category.)

Budget Category	Last Year's Expenditures	This Year's Budgeted Amount
Clothing	$ 29,000	$ 35,000
Food	9,000	11,000
Entertainment	23,000	28,000
Travel	10,000	25,000
Housing	37,000	57,000
Professional fees	28,000	35,000
Taxes	84,000	95,000
Savings and investments	60,000	64,000
Total	$280,000	$350,000

Product and Service Strategy

267

8

Product Strategy

Chapter Objectives

1. To identify the classifications of consumer goods and briefly describe each category.

2. To identify the types of industrial goods.

3. To explain the concept of the product life cycle.

4. To identify the determinants of the rate of adoption of a product.

5. To explain the methods for accelerating the speed of adoption.

T he Post-it Notes saga began in 1970, when Spencer Silver, a 3M scientist, was working on a new, extra-strong adhesive. His new product proved a failure as an adhesive. Since it was considerably less effective than current 3M products, Silver sent his research report and several samples to other 3M scientists for ideas on how to use it.

Several years later, one of these scientists, Art Fry, who had been having trouble every Sunday marking his place in his church hymnal, realized that a weak adhesive was just what he was looking for. Fry needed a temporary place marker, and that was exactly what the new adhesive offered.

The 3M product that evolved from these events, Post-it Notes, is simply a pad of notepaper with an adhesive strip on the back of each sheet. Because the adhesive is so weak, the strips can be attached to objects without damaging them—unlike staples, for instance. In addition, they do not restrict page turning, as do paper clips, and they don't fall off, as do ordinary paper strips. Post-it Notes were an instant success, quickly moving through the introductory stage of the product life cycle after they were introduced in 1980.

Fry's idea would never have been converted into a viable product had it not been for 3M's unique corporate culture. Once he had hit upon the idea of Post-it Notes, Fry was able to use his bootlegging research time on

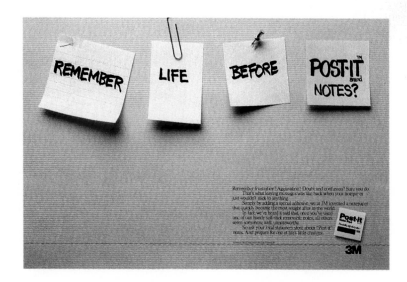

the project. At 3M, "bootlegging" refers to the 15 percent of researchers' work time that they are allowed to spend on anything that interests them. Fry spent a year and a half perfecting Post-it Notes and then convincing the right 3M executives of the idea's commercial possibilities. By late 1975, the product was ready for a market test.

The test proved a failure—but this was the point at which 3M's willingness to exhaust every possibility before abandoning a championed idea paid off. One of 3M's marketing executives suspected that the test failure was due to the testers' inability to get the product into the hands of the right people. A new test was commissioned in Boise, Idaho, this time with the promotional emphasis on free samples. The strategy

worked, and Post-it Notes were an immediate hit.

One of 3M's goals is to generate 25 percent of each year's annual sales from products that didn't even exist five years before. That's a pretty tall order, since the 3M product line consists of some 45,000 different items. 3M wants to be sure that its researchers are constantly feeding new ideas into the introductory stage of the product life cycle. The commitment to new products and, to a certain extent, the free rein given for developing new products from ideas even when the ultimate payoff is uncertain have paid off more than once for 3M. Art Fry's Post-it Notes represent just one of many commercial successes.[1]

Photo source: Courtesy of 3M Commercial Office Supply Division.

Chapter Overview

The first three parts of this book deal with preliminary marketing considerations such as marketing research and consumer behavior aimed at identifying the firm's target market. Now the attention shifts to the firm's marketing mix.

This and the next chapter analyze the decisions and problems involved with the first element of the marketing mix—the products and services the firm offers to its target market. Planning efforts begin with the choice of products to offer the target market. The other variables of the marketing mix—pricing structures,

Figure 8.1

Aloha Airlines Advertising: A Broader Definition of Product

Source: Courtesy of Aloha Airlines.

distribution channels, and promotional plans—must be based on product planning.

A narrow definition of the word *product* focuses on the physical or functional characteristics of a good or service. For example, a videocassette recorder is a rectangular container of metal and plastic with wires that connect it to a television set, accompanied by a series of special tapes for recording and viewing. But the purchaser has a much broader view of the recorder. Some buyers may want to use it to see soap operas they missed because of work; others may be interested in the warranty and service facilities of the manufacturer; still others may want it to rent recently released movies for home viewing.

Marketing decision makers must have this broader conception of product in mind and realize that people buy want satisfaction. For example, most consumers know little about the gasoline they buy. In fact, many view it not as a product but as a premium they must pay for the privilege of driving their cars. Aloha Airlines recognizes that consumers want more than just air transportation; they also want the convenience of on-time standards, as illustrated in Figure 8.1.

Some products have few or no physical attributes. A haircut and blow-dry by a hairstylist produces only well-groomed hair. A tax counselor produces only advice. Therefore, a broader view of products must include services. Consequently, a **product** is a bundle of physical, service, and symbolic attributes designed to enhance consumer want satisfaction.

product
Bundle of physical, service, and symbolic attributes designed to enhance consumer want satisfaction.

Classifying Consumer and Industrial Goods

How a firm markets a product depends largely on the product itself. For example, Chanel stresses subtle promotions in prestige media such as *The New Yorker* and *Vogue* magazines and markets its perfumes through department stores and specialty shops. Hershey markets its candy products through candy wholesalers to thousands of supermarkets, variety stores, discount houses, and vending machine companies. A firm manufacturing and marketing forklifts may use sales representatives to call on industrial buyers to ship its product either directly from the factory or from regional warehouses.

Product strategy differs for consumer goods and industrial goods. As defined earlier, *consumer goods* are products destined for use by the ultimate consumer and *industrial goods* are products used directly or indirectly in producing other goods for resale. These two major categories can be further subdivided.

Types of Consumer Goods

Several classification systems for consumer goods have been suggested. One basic distinction is based on whether or not the buyer perceives a need for the item. Thus, an *unsought good* is one for which the consumer does not yet recognize a need. For example, in early October 1987, weekend travelers who went to see the autumn colors in upstate New York did not realize that they had a need for snow tires until they were caught in an early winter storm that dumped up to 20 inches of snow in some areas. In contrast, most consumers recognize the need for various types of consumer goods. The most commonly used classification divides consumer goods into three groups: convenience goods, shopping goods, and specialty goods.[2]

Convenience Goods

The products that the consumer wants to purchase frequently, immediately, and with a minimum of effort are called **convenience goods.** Milk, bread, butter, eggs, and beer (the staples of most 24-hour convenience food stores) are all convenience goods. So are newspapers, chewing gum, candy, magazines, cigarettes, and most vending machine items.

convenience goods
Products that consumers want to purchase frequently, immediately, and with a minimum of effort.

Convenience goods are usually sold by brand name and are low priced. They fall into three subcategories: staples, impulse items, and emergency items. Many of them — such as bread, milk, and gasoline — are *staple items,* the consumer's supply of which must constantly be replenished. In most cases, the buyer has already decided to purchase a particular brand of gasoline or candy or to buy at a certain store and spends little time deliberating on the purchase decision. Products purchased on the spur of the moment or out of habit when the supply is low are referred to as *impulse goods.* For instance, it is estimated that over half of all supermarket purchases are unplanned.[3] The purchase of emergency items is prompted by unexpected and urgent needs. A repair kit for a broken water pipe, medical supplies, or an ice scraper purchased in the midst of an unexpected winter storm are all examples of the final sub-category of convenience goods.

The consumer rarely visits competing stores or compares price and quality when purchasing convenience goods. The possible gains from such compari-sons are outweighed by the costs of acquiring the additional information. This does not mean, however, that the consumer is destined to remain permanently loyal to one brand of beer, candy, or cigarettes. People continually receive new information from radio and television advertisements, billboards, and word-of-mouth communication. Since the prices of most convenience goods are low, trial purchases of competing brands or products are made with little financial risk and often create new habits.

Since the consumer is unwilling to spend much effort in purchasing conve-nience goods, the manufacturer must strive to make them as convenient as possible. Candy, cigarettes, and newspapers are sold in almost every super-market, service station, and restaurant. Sellers also place vending machines in spots that are convenient for customers, such as office buildings and factories.

Retailers usually carry several competing brands of convenience products and are unlikely to promote any particular one. The promotional burden, there-fore, falls on the manufacturer, who must advertise extensively to develop con-sumer acceptance of the product. The Coca-Cola promotional program consists of radio and television commercials, magazine ads, billboards, and point-of-pur-chase displays in stores. These efforts to motivate the consumer to choose Coke over competing brands are good examples of a manufacturer's promotion designed to stimulate consumer demand.

Shopping Goods

shopping goods
Products purchased only after the consumer has made compar-isons of competing goods in competing stores on such bases as price, quality, style, and color.

In contrast to convenience goods, **shopping goods** are purchased only after the consumer has made comparisons of competing goods in competing stores on such bases as price, quality, style, and color. Shopping goods, which typi-cally are more expensive than convenience goods, include clothing, furniture, appliances, jewelry, and shoes. The purchaser of shopping goods lacks com-plete information prior to the shopping trip and gathers information during it.

A woman intent on adding a new dress to her wardrobe may visit many stores, try on a number of dresses, and spend a weekend making the final choice. She may follow a regular route from store to store in surveying compet-ing offerings and ultimately will select the dress that most appeals to her. New stores carrying assortments of shopping goods must ensure that they are lo-

Figure 8.2
Racing Bikes: Heterogeneous Shopping Goods

Source: Courtesy of Schwinn Bicycle Company.

cated near other shopping-goods stores so that they will be included in shopping expeditions.

Some shopping goods, such as refrigerators and washing machines, are considered *homogeneous;* that is, the consumer views them as essentially the same. Others, such as the Schwinn Tempo bicycle shown in Figure 8.2, are considered *heterogeneous,* or essentially different. Price is an important factor in the purchase of homogeneous shopping goods, while quality and styling are relatively more significant in the purchase of heterogeneous goods.

Important features of shopping goods are physical attributes, price, styling, and place of purchase. The store's name and reputation also have a considerable influence on consumer buying behavior. The brand is often less important, in spite of the large amounts of money manufacturers frequently spend promoting their brands.

Since buyers of shopping goods expend some effort in making their purchases, shopping goods manufacturers utilize fewer retail stores than do convenience goods producers. Retailers and manufacturers work closely together in promoting shopping goods, and retail purchases often are made directly from the manufacturer or its representative rather than the wholesaler. Fashion merchandise buyers for department stores and specialty shops make regular buying trips to regional and national markets in New York, Dallas, Los Angeles, and Seattle. Buyers for furniture retailers often go directly to the factories of furniture manufacturers or attend furniture trade shows.

Specialty Goods

specialty goods
Products with unique characteristics that cause the buyer to prize them and make a special effort to obtain them.

The specialty goods purchaser is well aware of what he or she wants and is willing to make a special effort to obtain it. The nearest Cartier dealer may be 50 miles away, for example, but the watch purchaser willing to spend several thousand dollars will go there to buy this prestigious timepiece. **Specialty goods** possess some unique characteristics that cause the buyer to prize those particular brands. For these products, the buyer has complete information prior to the shopping trip and is unwilling to accept substitutes.

Specialty goods typically are high priced and frequently branded. Since consumers are willing to exert considerable effort to obtain them, fewer retail outlets are required. For instance, Mercury outboard motors and Porsche sports cars may be handled by only 1 or 2 retailers for every 100,000 people.

Applying the Consumer Goods Classification System

The three-way classification system allows the marketing manager to gain additional information for use in developing a marketing strategy. Consumer behavior patterns differ for each type of consumer good. For example, once a new food product has been classified as a convenience good, insights are gained about marketing needs in branding, promotion, pricing, and distribution methods. Table 8.1 summarizes the impact of the consumer goods classification system on the development of an effective marketing mix.

But the classification system also poses problems. The major problem is that it suggests only three categories into which all products must fit. Some products fit neatly into one category, but others fall into the grey areas between categories. For example, how should a new automobile be classified? It is expensive, sold by brand, and handled by a few exclusive dealers in each city. But before classifying it as a specialty good, other characteristics must be considered. Most new-car buyers shop extensively among competing models and auto dealers before deciding on the best deal. A more effective way to utilize the classification system is to consider it as a continuum representing degrees of effort expended by the consumer. At one end of the continuum are convenience goods, at the other end lie specialty goods, and in the middle fall shopping goods.[4] On this continuum, the new-car purchase can be located between the categories of shopping and specialty goods but closer to the specialty goods end.

A second problem with the classification system is that consumers differ in their buying patterns. One person will make an unplanned purchase of a new Honda Prelude, while others will shop extensively before purchasing a car. But one buyer's impulse purchase does not make the Prelude a convenience good. Goods are classified by the purchase patterns of the majority of buyers.

Factor	Convenience Goods	Shopping Goods	Specialty Goods
Consumer factors:			
Planning time involved in purchase	Very little	Considerable	Extensive
Purchase frequency	Frequent	Less frequent	Infrequent
Importance of convenient location	Critical	Important	Unimportant
Comparison of price and quality	Very little	Considerable	Very little
Marketing mix factors:			
Price	Low	Relatively high	High
Advertising	By manufacturer	Both manufacturer and retailer	Both manufacturer and retailer
Channel length	Long	Relatively short	Very short
Number of retail outlets	Many	Few	Very few; often one per market area
Store image	Unimportant	Very important	Important

Table 8.1
Marketing Impact of the Consumer Goods Classification System

Types of Industrial Goods

Industrial goods can be subdivided into five categories: installations, accessory equipment, component parts and materials, raw materials, and industrial supplies. Industrial buyers are professional customers; their job is to make effective purchase decisions. The purchase decision process involved in buying supplies of flour for General Mills, for example, is much the same as that used in buying the same commodity for Pillsbury. Thus, the classification system for industrial goods is based on product uses rather than on consumer buying patterns.

Installations

The specialty goods of the industrial market are called **installations.** Included in this classification are such major capital items as new factories and heavy machinery, computers, Boeing 737s for Continental Airlines, and locomotives for Burlington Northern.

Since installations are relatively long-lived and involve large sums of money, their purchase represents a major decision for an organization. Negotiations often extend over several months and involve the participation of numerous decision makers. In many cases, the selling company must provide technical expertise. When custom-made equipment is involved, representatives of the selling firm work closely with the buyer's engineers and production personnel to design the most feasible product for the buying firm.

Price is almost never the deciding factor in the purchase of installations. The purchasing firm is interested in the product's efficiency and performance over its useful life. It also wants a minimum of breakdowns. "Downtime" is expensive, because employees are nonproductive (but still paid) while the machine is being repaired.

Since most of the factories of firms purchasing installations are geographically concentrated, the selling firm places its promotional emphasis on well-

installations
Major capital items, such as new factories and heavy machinery, that typically are expensive and relatively long-lived.

trained salespeople, many of whom have a technical background. Most installations are marketed directly on a manufacturer-to-user basis. Even though a sale may be a one-time transaction, contracts often call for regular product servicing. In the case of extremely expensive installations, such as computer and electronic equipment, some firms lease the installations rather than sell them outright and assign personnel directly to the lessee for operating or maintaining the equipment.

Accessory Equipment

accessory equipment
Capital items, usually less expensive and shorter-lived than installations, such as typewriters, hand tools, and adding machines.

Fewer decision makers are usually involved in purchasing **accessory equipment**—capital items that typically are less expensive and shorter-lived than installations. Although quality and service are important criteria in purchasing accessory equipment, the firm is likely to be much more price conscious. Accessory equipment includes such products as desk calculators, hand tools, portable drills, small lathes, and word processors. Although these goods are considered capital items and are depreciated over several years, their useful lives generally are much shorter than that of an installation.

industrial distributor
Wholesaling marketing intermediary that operates in the industrial goods market and typically handles small accessory equipment and operating supplies.

Because of the need for continuous representation and the more widespread geographic dispersion of accessory equipment purchasers, a wholesaler—often called an **industrial distributor**—contacts potential customers in each geographic area. Technical assistance usually is not necessary, and the manufacturer of accessory equipment often can effectively utilize wholesalers in marketing its products. Manufacturers also use advertising more than do installation producers.

Component Parts and Materials

component parts and materials
Finished industrial goods that actually become part of the final product.

Whereas installations and accessory equipment are used in producing the final product, **component parts and materials** are the finished industrial goods that actually become part of the final product. Spark plugs complete a new Chevrolet; batteries often are added to Mattel toys; tires are included with a Dodge pickup truck. A digital flight control computer system produced by Allied-Signal is a component part of the F-16 shown in Figure 8.3. Some fabricated materials, such as flour, undergo further processing before the finished product is produced.

Purchasers of component parts and materials need a regular, continuous supply of uniform-quality goods. These goods generally are purchased on contract for a period of one year or more. Direct sale is common, and satisfied customers often become permanent buyers. Wholesalers sometimes are used for fill-in purchases and in handling sales to smaller purchasers.

Raw Materials

raw materials
Industrial goods, such as farm products (wheat, cotton, soybeans) and natural products (coal, lumber, iron ore), used in producing final products.

Farm products—such as cattle, cotton, eggs, milk, pigs, and soybeans—and *natural products*—such as coal, copper, iron ore, and lumber—constitute **raw materials.** They are similar to component parts and materials in that they actually become a part of the final product.

Figure 8.3

Component Parts Become Part of the Final Product

this aircraft is reacting to things
its pilot hasn't seen yet.

**Allied
Signal**
Technologies

technology: Bendix digital flight controls, the first all-digital fly-by-wire flight control computer system in a production aircraft, will be introduced on new F-16C/D.

benefit: automated aircraft reaction in low level terrain-following and other demanding situations. better mission capabilities, greater flexibility, lower life cycle cost. less weight.

future: will be the basis for integrated avionics, flight and engine controls planned for new advanced technology fighters. will be standard on many aircraft in the next decade.

Bendix digital flight controls. one of the Allied-Signal advanced technologies—focused on aerospace, electronics, automotive products, and engineered materials. for facts, call 1-800-243-8160.

Source: © 1986 Allied-Signal Incorporated. Photo: Gregory Heisler.

Since most raw materials are graded, the purchaser is assured of standardized products of uniform quality. As with component parts and materials, direct sale of raw materials is common, and sales typically are made on a contractual basis. Wholesalers are increasingly involved in the purchase of raw materials from foreign suppliers.

Price is seldom a deciding factor in the purchase of raw materials, since it is often quoted at a central market and is virtually identical among competing sellers. Purchasers buy raw materials from the firms they consider most able to deliver in the required quantity and quality.

Supplies

If installations represent the "specialty goods" of the industrial market, operating supplies are the "convenience goods." **Supplies** are regular expense items that are necessary in the firm's daily operation but are not part of the final product.

supplies
Regular expense items necessary in the firm's daily operation but not part of the final product.

MRO items
Supplies for an industrial firm, categorized as maintenance items, repair items, or operating supplies.

Supplies are sometimes called **MRO items,** because they can be divided into three categories: (1) *maintenance items,* such as brooms, floor-cleaning compounds, and light bulbs; (2) *repair items,* such as nuts and bolts used in repairing equipment; and (3) *operating supplies,* such as heating fuel, lubricating oil, and office stationery.

The regular purchase of operating supplies is a routine aspect of the purchasing agent's job. Wholesalers are often used in the sale of supplies due to the items' low unit prices, small sales, and large numbers of potential buyers. Since supplies are relatively standardized, price competition is frequently heavy. However, the purchasing agent spends little time making purchase decisions. He or she frequently places telephone or mail orders or makes regular purchases from the sales representative of the local office supply wholesaler.

The Product Life Cycle

Products, like individuals, pass through a series of stages. Whereas humans progress from infancy to childhood to adulthood to retirement to death, successful products progress through four basic stages: introduction, growth, maturity, and decline. This progression, known as the **product life cycle,** is depicted in Figure 8.4, along with products in the recording industry that currently fit into each stage.

product life cycle
Four stages through which a successful product passes—introduction, growth, maturity, and decline.

Introductory Stage

The firm's objective in the early stages of the product life cycle is to stimulate demand for the new market entry. Since the product is unknown to the public, promotional campaigns stress information about its features. They also may be directed toward marketing intermediaries in the channel to induce them to carry the product. In this phase, the public becomes acquainted with the product's merits and begins to accept it.

As Figure 8.4 indicates, losses are common during the introductory stage due to heavy promotion and extensive research and development expenditures. But the groundwork is being laid for future profits. Firms expect to recover their costs and begin earning profits when the new product moves into the second phase of its life cycle — the growth stage.

Growth Stage

Sales volumes rise rapidly during the growth stage as new customers make initial purchases and early buyers repurchase the product. Word-of-mouth and mass advertising induce hesitant buyers to make trial purchases. Gourmet coffee is a product in the growth stage, with industry sales accounting for 7 percent of the $6.5 billion in total domestic coffee sales, up from 2 percent in 1981. To promote its Private Collection label of whole coffee beans and premium ground coffee, Maxwell House spent $20 million on advertising in magazines such as *Bon Appetit* and direct-mail campaigns.[5] Another product category in the growth stage is fitness and exercise equipment, with industry sales expected to increase from $1.2 billion in 1986 to $2.1 billion in 1991.[6]

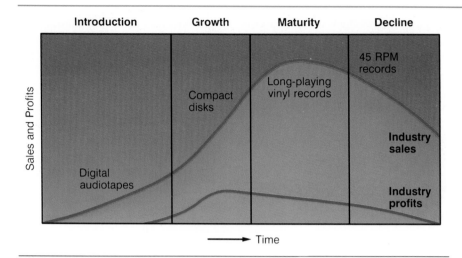

Figure 8.4
Stages in the Product
Life Cycle

As the firm begins to realize substantial profits from its investment during the growth stage, the product attracts competitors. Success breeds imitation, and other firms inevitably rush into the market with competitive products. In fact, the majority of firms in a particular market enter during the growth stage.

Maturity Stage

Industry sales continue to grow during the early part of the maturity stage, but eventually they reach a plateau as the backlog of potential customers dwindles. By this time, a large number of competitors have entered the market, and the firm's profits decline as competition intensifies.

In the maturity stage, differences among competing products diminish as competitors discover the product and promotional characteristics most desired by the market. Heavy promotional outlays emphasize subtle differences among competing products, and brand competition intensifies.

For the first time in the product life cycle, available products exceed industry demand. Companies attempting to increase their sales and market share must do so at the expense of competitors. As competition intensifies, competitors tend to cut prices in an attempt to attract new buyers. Although a price reduction may be the easiest method of inducing additional purchases, it is also one of the simplest moves for competitors to duplicate. Reduced prices result in decreased revenues for all firms in the industry unless the price cuts produce enough increased purchases to offset the loss in revenue on each item sold.[7]

Decline Stage

In the final stage of the product's life, innovations or shifting consumer preferences bring about an absolute decline in industry sales. The safety razor and electric shaver replaced the straight razor years ago. More recently, universal life insurance policies have replaced many whole life insurance policies because of a shift in consumer preferences. As Figure 8.5 indicates, the decline stage of an old product doubles as the growth stage for a new market entry.

Figure 8.5
Overlap of Life Cycles for
Products A and B

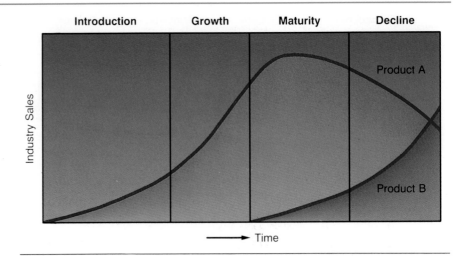

Industry profits decline and in some cases actually become negative as sales fall and firms cut prices in a bid for the dwindling market. Manufacturers gradually begin to leave the industry in search of more profitable products.

The traditional product life cycle needs to be distinguished from fad cycles. Fashions and fads have a profound influence on marketing strategy. *Fashions* are currently popular products that tend to follow recurring life cycles. Women's apparel and accessories provide the best examples. After being out of fashion for over a decade, the miniskirt was reintroduced in the early 1980s and again in the late 1980s.

In contrast, *fads* are fashions with abbreviated life cycles. Most fads, such as Pet Rocks and variations of the yellow "Baby on Board" car window stickers, experience short-lived popularity and then quickly fade. However, there are some fads that maintain a residual market among certain market segments.

✳ Using the Product Life Cycle Concept in Marketing Strategy

The product life cycle, with all its variants, is a useful tool in marketing strategy decision making. For instance, the knowledge that profits assume a predictable pattern through the stages and that promotional emphasis must shift from product information in the early stages to brand promotion in the later ones should allow the marketing decision maker to expand sales and profits in each stage of the product life cycle through appropriate marketing efforts.

A firm's marketing efforts should emphasize stimulating demand at the introductory stage. The focus should shift to cultivating selective demand in the growth period. Market segmentation should be used extensively in the maturity period. During the decline stage, the emphasis should return to increasing primary demand. Table 8.2 suggests appropriate pricing, distribution, product development, and service and warranty strategies for each life cycle stage.

Table 8.2

Organizational and Environmental Conditions with Appropriate
Marketing Efforts for Various Product Life Cycle Stages

Stage	Organizational Conditions	Environmental Conditions	Marketing Efforts
Introduction	High costs	Few or no competitors	Stimulate primary demand
	Inefficient production levels	Limited product awareness and knowledge	Establish high price
	Cash demands	Limited demand	Offer limited product variety
			Increase distribution
Growth	Smoothing production	Expanding markets	Cultivate selective demand
	Lowering costs	Expanded distribution	Improve product
	Operation efficiencies	Competition strengthens	Strengthen distribution
	Product improvements	Prices soften slightly	Increase price flexibility
Maturity:			
Early maturity	Efficient scale of operation	Slowing growth	Emphasize market segmentation
	Product modification work	Strong, heightened competition	Improve service and warranty
	Decreasing profits	Expanded market	Reduce prices
Late maturity	Low profits	Faltering demand	Intensify market segmentation
	Standardized production	Fierce competition	Make pricing competitive
		Established distribution patterns	Retain distribution
Decline		Permanently declining demand	Increase primary demand
		Fewer competitors	Profit opportunity pricing
		Limited product offerings	Prune and strengthen distribution
		Price stabilization	

Source: Adapted from Burton H. Marcus and Edward M. Tauber, *Marketing Analysis and Decision Making* (Boston: Little, Brown, 1979), pp. 115–16. Copyright © 1979 by Burton H. Marcus and Edward M. Tauber. Reprinted by permission of Little, Brown and Company.

Extending the Product Life Cycle

A frequently used marketing strategy involves taking steps to extend the product life cycle as long as possible. Marketing managers can accomplish this if they take action early in the maturity stage. Product life cycles can be extended indefinitely through actions designed to increase the frequency of use by current customers, add new users, find new uses for the product, and/or change package sizes, labels, or product quality.[8]

Increasing Frequency of Use During the maturity stage, the industry sales curve for a product or service reaches a maximum point as the firm exhausts the supply of customers who previously have not been purchasers. However, if current purchasers increase their purchase frequency, total industry sales will rise even though no new customers enter the market.

FOCUS ON ETHICS

Extending the Product Life Cycle of Cigarettes

Whenever you have a product on the downside of the product life cycle, you must consider changing your marketing strategy and eventually deleting the product if profit margins begin to decline significantly. If most of your sales volume is in that particular product, however, it is essential to try to extend the product's life as long as possible. But what if your product is, according to most medical evidence, both a health hazard and addictive? This is the situation facing the cigarette industry.

At the individual level, surveys have shown that most workers in the cigarette industry do not think it has been proven that cigarettes are harmful to health. On the other hand, cigarette companies sometimes have found it difficult to attract employees for top positions precisely because many people believe smoking is dangerous. "At least 50% to 75% of the people I contact for Philip Morris have objections now," says one New York–based recruiter. And despite tobacco companies' continuing high profitability, top positions often go unfilled for quite some time. According to Dennis Cott of the Maxwell Group, a marketing executive recruiter, "R. J. Reynolds Tobacco has had a couple of assistant brand manager positions open for at least six months now." It should be noted that tobacco is also disfavored because it is a mature industry and be-

cause there is less for a marketer to learn in a situation in which TV and radio advertising are banned.

Despite increasing sales volume, more and more laws banning smoking in public places, active campaigning by the Surgeon General, and the prospect of a national prohibition of tobacco advertising, the industry is forging ahead with new ways to extend the product's life. One important route is to expand sales abroad. Of the 5 trillion cigarettes sold overseas, U.S. producers sell about 20 percent. However, two top American producers, Philip Morris and R. J. Reynolds, have been able to increase their sales volume by 5 to 6 percent annually. The only problem is that profit margins abroad are much narrower; thus, despite selling more cigarettes overseas than in the United States, Philip Morris has made nearly 10 times as much money ($3.3 billion versus $340 million) in the United States as it has abroad.

Another competitive tactic is to target specific domestic market segments. Cigarette companies sponsor numerous social events in black and Latino communities and make contributions to the NAACP and the League of United Latin American Citizens. In addition, they advertise heavily in minority publications, since minority group members are still increasing their per capita cigarette

consumption. Tobacco companies also continue to go after the youth market, using new packaging ideas to try to attract younger smokers.

A third approach to extending the product's life is to attempt to come up with safer cigarettes. Capri cigarettes are about 30 percent thinner and are being touted as a "more courteous and conscientious smoke." More important is a search for a cigarette that will be totally safe. This could create a big spurt in usage as the introduction of the filter tip did in the 1950s.

The final move by the tobacco companies is unarguably benign. Several of them are diversifying into other products. In 1985, Philip Morris acquired General Foods (taking down notices for stop-smoking clinics in the bargain), and Reynolds merged with Nabisco.

Sources: Ronald Alsop, "Cigarette Packs Look Flashier to Attract Younger Smoker," *The Wall Street Journal* (April 30, 1987), p. 29; Joan O'C. Hamilton and Emily T. Smith, " 'No Smoking' Sweeps America," *Business Week* (July 27, 1987), pp. 40–46; Scott Ticer, "Big Tobacco's Fortunes Are Withering in the Heat," *Business Week* (July 27, 1987), pp. 47–52; Linda Williams, "Tobacco Companies Target Blacks with Ads, Donations and Festivals," *The Wall Street Journal* (October 6, 1987), p. 35; Daniel Seligman, "Don't Bet Against Cigarette Makers," *Fortune* (August 17, 1987), pp. 70–77; Christine Donahue, "If There's Smoke, They're Hirin,' " *Adweek's Marketing Week* (June 20, 1987), pp. 1, 6; and Trish Hall, "Popular Employer," *The Wall Street Journal* (July 25, 1986), pp. 1, 12.

In the mid-1960s, the fourth quarter of the year accounted for 95 percent of U.S. turkey sales. But the industry has successfully changed turkey's holiday-only image. Today the fourth quarter accounts for only 40 percent of all sales, and U.S. consumption of turkey is up significantly.[9] Figure 8.6 shows a Louis Rich advertisement aimed at making turkey an "anytime" meal.

Increasing Number of Users   A second strategy for extending the product life cycle is to increase the overall market size by attracting new customers who previously have not used the product.

Source: Courtesy of Oscar Mayer Foods Corporation. Louis Rich is a registered trademark of Oscar Mayer Foods Corporation.

Figure 8.6
Increasing the Frequency of Turkey Consumption

Lorimar's $15 million movie, *American Anthem,* featuring U.S. Olympic gymnast Mitch Gaylord, was a box office failure within weeks of its opening. Rather than give up on the movie, Lorimar added two music video sequences and re-released it as a video rental.[10]

Finding New Uses   Still another strategy for extending a product's life cycle is to identify new uses for the item. Kraft, Inc., extended the life cycle of two of its mature products — Cheez Whiz process cheese spread, on the market for 34 years, and Philadelphia Brand cream cheese, a 106-year-old product. Kraft developed advertising to reposition Cheez Whiz as a microwavable sauce and added new labels that highlight the product's microwavability and include recipes. As a result, Cheez Whiz sales increased 40 percent in one year. Kraft also used advertising to reposition its cream cheese as an alternative to margarine and butter, a move that increased sales by 21 percent in just three years.[11]

THE COMPETITIVE EDGE

Barnum's Animal Crackers

Barnum's animal crackers defy the product life cycle theory. Nabisco's brand started strong: All 189,000 5-cent boxes sold out in the first month following their introduction in December 1902. Today the price is 59 cents a box, but sales still roll in, with 50 million boxes sold annually, or more than 1 billion cookies, bringing the total number of animal crackers purchased to 35 billion (enough cookies to circle the earth 38 times). Barnum's Animals have become so much a part of Americana that Nabisco spends almost nothing to promote or advertise them.

The success of Barnum's animal crackers has become self-perpetuating, thanks mostly to Nabisco's original marketing strategy. Other companies were marketing animal crackers in 1902, but Nabisco guaranteed the initial success of its crackers when it looked to capture the imagination—and the market—of America's children.

For the product release, Nabisco sought and received generally less desirable shelf space on the lower shelves of stores—at a child's eye level. Children walking through a store would come face to face with pictures of the famed Barnum circus animals inside the brightly colored P. T. Barnum wagons. Nabisco released its animal crackers in December in the hope that they would be used as Christmas presents and

Christmas tree surprises—hence the cotton string attached to the box.

The clever package design and perfect shelf position kept sales of Barnum's animal crackers from fading after the initial Christmas season. Today, though the words "The circus is in town!" no longer seem to rate an exclamation point, Barnum's animal crackers still generate plenty of excitement. The package is the same as ever: blue Barnum circus wagons topped with a cutout circus figure and a cotton string (now a convenient handle); boxes now also come in red and yellow. The menagerie inside the box has changed a bit, but most of the 17 are only shaped differently from their ancestors. The recipe is unaltered, and stores still stock them on lower

shelves. Even the number of cookies inside—22 to 23—is the same.

American children are not the only lovers of Barnum's animal crackers, either. Children in 17 countries and territories also have the fun of opening the "wagon" to see the animals inside and let animals become playmates before they are eaten.

Nabisco just proved that a good product indeed sells itself when it is given the right package and has all the attributes that satisfy customer wants.

Sources: 42 Million a Day: The Story of Nabisco Brands, 1986, p. 22, and Nabisco Brands, Inc., press releases commemorating the 85th anniversary of Barnum's Animals animal crackers.

Changing Package Size, Labels, or Product Quality   Many firms implement significant physical changes in their products in an attempt to extend the product life cycle. Reducing package sizes to appeal to one-person households has proven a successful strategy for firms ranging from Swanson to Campbell Soup. Raisinets and Goobers were sold only in movie theaters for over 50 years. But when Nestlé acquired these brands, it reformulated and repackaged them for distribution in supermarkets and convenience stores.[12]

The Consumer Adoption Process

Consumers also make decisions about a new product offering. In the **adoption process,** potential consumers go through a series of stages from learning of the new product to trying it and deciding to purchase it regularly or to reject it. These stages in the consumer adoption process can be classified as:

1. *Awareness.* Individuals first learn of the new product but lack information about it.

2. *Interest.* They begin to seek information about it.

3. *Evaluation.* They consider whether or not the product is beneficial.

4. *Trial.* They make trial purchases to determine its usefulness.

5. *Adoption/Rejection.* If the trial purchase is satisfactory, they decide to use the product regularly.[13]

The marketing manager needs to understand the adoption process so that he or she can move potential consumers to the adoption stage. Once the manager is aware of a large number of consumers at the interest stage, steps can be taken to stimulate sales by moving consumers through the evaluation and trial stages. For example, Ralston Purina used a cash premium promotion to encourage consumers to try its new Almond Delight cereal. For six weeks, the company inserted U.S. and foreign paper currency in 4.3 million boxes of the product. Customers could win $1, $5, $50, or $500 bills as well as currencies such as Bolivian pesos, Irish punts, and Indonesian sens.[14]

adoption process
Series of stages in the consumer decision process regarding a new product, including awareness, interest, evaluation, trial, and rejection or adoption.

Adopter Categories

Some people purchase a new product almost as soon as it is placed on the market. Others wait for additional information and rely on the experiences of **consumer innovators**—first purchasers—before making trial purchases. Consumer innovators are likely to be present in each product area. Some families were the first in the community to buy videocassette recorders. Some doctors are the first to prescribe new drugs. Some farmers plant new hybrid seeds much earlier than their neighbors.

A number of investigations analyzing the adoption of new products have resulted in the identification of five categories of purchasers based on relative time of adoption. These categories, shown in Figure 8.7, are innovators, early adopters, early majority, late majority, and laggards.

The **diffusion process** is the acceptance of new products and services by the members of a community or social system. Figure 8.7 shows this process as following a normal distribution. A few people adopt at first; then the number of adopters increases rapidly as the value of the innovation becomes apparent. The adoption rate finally diminishes as fewer potential consumers remain in the nonadopter category.

Since the categories are based on a normal distribution, standard deviations are used to partition them. Innovators are the first 2.5 percent to adopt the new product; laggards are the last 16 percent to do so. Excluded from Figure 8.7 are nonadopters—those who never adopt the innovation.

consumer innovator
First purchaser of a new product or service.

diffusion process
Acceptance of new products and services by the members of a community or social system.

Figure 8.7
Categories of Adopters Based
on Relative Time of Adoption

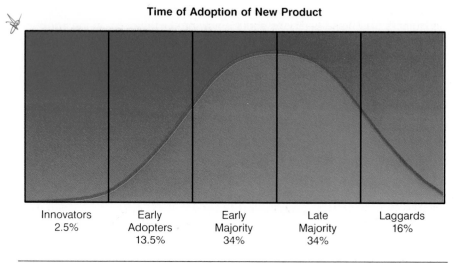

Time of Adoption of New Product

Innovators	Early	Early	Late	Laggards
2.5%	Adopters	Majority	Majority	16%
	13.5%	34%	34%	

Identifying First Adopters

Locating first buyers of new products is a challenge for the marketing manager. If first buyers can be reached early in the product's development or introduction, they can serve as a test market, evaluating the products and making suggestions for modifications. Since early purchasers are often opinion leaders from whom others seek advice, their attitudes toward new products are quickly communicated to others. Acceptance or rejection of the innovation by these purchasers can help forecast its expected success.

Unfortunately, first adopters of one new product are not necessarily first adopters of other products or services. A large number of research studies, however, have established some general characteristics of most first adopters. First adopters tend to be younger, have higher social status, be better educated, and enjoy higher incomes than others. They are more mobile than later adopters and change both their jobs and home addresses more often. They are also more likely to rely on impersonal information sources than are later adopters, who depend more on promotional information from the company and word-of-mouth communication.

Rate of Adoption Determinants

Frisbees progressed from the product introduction stage to the market maturity stage in a period of six months. But it took the U.S. Department of Agriculture 13 years to convince corn farmers to use hybrid seed corn—an innovation capable of doubling crop yields. The adoption rate is influenced by five characteristics of the innovation:

1. *Relative advantage*—the degree to which the innovation appears superior to previous ideas. The greater the relative advantage—manifested in terms of lower price, physical improvements, or ease of use—the faster the adoption rate.

2. *Compatibility*—the degree to which the innovation is consistent with the values and experiences of potential adopters. Consider, for example, the failure of Avert, Kimberly-Clark's germ-killing facial tissue that cost about four times more per tissue than regular tissues. Avert was designed to prevent the spread of colds when used by a sick person, but it did not protect consumers who bought the tissues to avoid catching colds from others. The product failed in the marketplace because consumers were not willing to pay the high price for something used to protect others from getting their colds.[15]

3. *Complexity*—the relative difficulty of understanding the innovation. In most cases, the more difficult a new product is to understand or use, the longer it will take to gain general acceptance.

4. *Divisibility*—the degree to which the innovation can be used on a limited basis. First adopters face two types of risk—financial loss and ridicule from others—if the new product proves unsatisfactory. The option of sampling the innovation on a limited basis reduces these risks and generally accelerates the rate of adoption.

5. *Communicability*—the degree to which the results of using the product are observable or communicable to others. If the innovation's superiority can be displayed in a tangible form, the adoption rate will increase.[16]

These five characteristics can be implemented to some extent by the marketing manager to accelerate the rate of adoption. Product complexity must be overcome with informative promotional messages. Products should be designed to emphasize their relative advantages and, whenever possible, be divisible to permit sample purchases. If divisibility is physically impossible, in-home demonstrations or trial home placements can be used. Positive attempts must also be made to ensure the innovation's compatibility with adopters' value systems.

These actions are based on extensive research studies of innovators in agriculture, medicine, and consumer goods. They should pay off in increased sales by accelerating the adoption rate in each adopter category.

Summary of Chapter Objectives

1. Identify the classifications of consumer goods and briefly describe each category. The three categories of consumer goods are convenience goods, shopping goods, and specialty goods. Convenience goods are products that the consumer wants to purchase frequently, immediately, and with a minimum of effort. Shopping goods are products that are purchased after extensive shopping on such bases as price, quality, style, and color. Specialty goods are those with unique features that will cause the buyer to seek them out.

2. Identify the types of industrial goods. Industrial goods are classified on the basis of product uses. The five categories in the industrial goods classification are installations, accessory equipment, component parts and materials, raw materials, and supplies.

3. Explain the concept of the product life cycle. Most successful products pass through the four stages of the product life cycle—introduction, growth, maturity, and decline—before their death. The product life cycle concept affects other components of the marketing mix; pricing, distribution, and promotion strategies as well as product strategy must be adjusted in different life cycle stages. Marketers should also attempt to extend life cycles of successful products for as long as possible. This objective can be accomplished by: (1) increasing the frequency of use; (2) increasing the number of users; (3) finding new uses; and (4) changing package size, label, or product quality.

4. Identify the determinants of the rate of adoption of a product.
Consumers go through a series of stages in adopting new products: initial product awareness, interest, evaluation, trial purchase, and adoption or rejection. Although first adopters vary among product classes, several common characteristics have been isolated. First adopters are often younger, better educated, and more mobile; they typically have higher incomes and higher social status than later adopters.

The rate of adoption for new products and services depends on five characteristics: (1) relative advantage—the degree of superiority of the innovation over the previous product or service; (2) compatibility—the degree to which the new product or idea is consistent with the value systems of potential purchasers; (3) complexity of the new product or service; (4) divisibility—the degree to which small-scale trial purchases are possible; and (5) communicability—the degree to which the innovation's superiority can be conveyed to other potential buyers.

5. Explain the methods for accelerating the speed of adoption. Product complexity must be overcome by informative promotional messages. Products should be designed to emphasize their relative advantages and, whenever possible, be divisible to allow for sample purchases. If divisibility is physically impossible, in-home demonstrations or trial home placements can be used. Positive attempts must also be made to ensure the innovation's compatibility with adopters' value systems. These actions should pay off in increased sales by accelerating the rate of adoption in each adopter category.

Key Terms

product	raw materials
convenience goods	supplies
shopping goods	MRO items
specialty goods	product life cycle
installations	adoption process
accessory equipment	consumer innovator
industrial distributor	diffusion process
component parts and materials	

Review Questions

1. Explain the broader definition of *product* used in the chapter.

2. What is meant by an unsought good?

3. Why does the basis used for categorizing industrial goods differ from that used for classifying consumer goods?

4. Compare a typical marketing mix for convenience goods with one for specialty goods.

5. Outline the typical marketing mix for a shopping good.

6. Discuss the marketing mix for the various types of industrial goods.

7. Illustrate and explain the product life cycle concept.

8. Suggest several means by which a product's life cycle can be extended.

9. Identify and briefly explain the stages in the consumer adoption process.

10. Describe the determinants of the rate of new-product adoption.

Discussion Questions

1. For each stage of the product life cycle, select a specific product (other than those mentioned in the text) that fits into it. Explain how marketing strategies vary by life cycle stage for each product.

2. Trace the life cycle of a recent fad. What marketing strategy implications can you derive from your study?

3. Home burglar alarm systems using microwaves are a fast-growing product in the home-security market. Such systems operate by filling rooms with microwave beams, which set off alarms when an intruder intercepts one of them. What suggestions can you make for accelerating the rate of adoption for this product?

4. Classify the following consumer goods:
   a. Sofa
   b. Reebok running shoes
   c. Felt-tip pen
   d. Swimsuit
   e. BMW 325i
   f. Binaca breath freshener
   g. *Discovery* magazine
   h. Original oil painting

5. Classify the following products into the appropriate industrial goods category. Briefly explain your choice for each product.
   a. Word processor
   b. Land
   c. Light bulb
   d. Cotton
   e. Paper towel
   f. Nylon
   g. Airplane
   h. Tire

VIDEO CASE 8

Carushka

The bodywear industry has grown by leaps and bounds over the past decade. It began with dancewear, which later was picked up by millions of aerobics class participants. The next step — from aerobics classes to fitness centers — was a logical extension of the product's sales curve. Today bodywear, alternatively called *dancewear* or *exercise wear,* has become acceptable street dress.

   Ric Wanetik, a Marshall Field's vice-president, has assessed the reason for this evolution: "I happen to believe people buying this merchandise aren't necessarily doing it to run out and exercise in; they're buying it because it's fashion-smart." Designer Rebecca Moses echoes this view: "People like the way they look in workout clothes, so they incorporated elements of these designs into their everyday wardrobes." Perhaps one of the clearest indications of the growth of the bodywear industry is that even L. L. Bean has produced a fitness-fashion catalog.

But despite its rapid growth, designer bodywear is a highly volatile market. Designs, labels, and even manufacturers are continually emerging and disappearing as consumer tastes shift. In fact, the entire life cycle of designer bodywear is only about three months.

Firms that seek to compete in this marketplace must have a coherent product strategy, One designer, Carushka, has based her overall product and competitive strategy on innovation: "I am willing to take the step where no one else is. I am a pioneer." Carushka got the idea for her first leotard, a striped model, while watching a Gene Kelly movie. She was the first designer to do stripes, the first to do cottons, and the first to do prints. It is no wonder that the motto of Carushka's company became "Expect the unexpected." As Carushka put it, "I will take the risks and do the unusual."

When she began her business, Carushka would load her station wagon with her merchandise and deliver it personally to her first 100 accounts. The leotards were packaged in plastic bags with invoices attached since Carushka operated on a cash-only basis at the time.

Then her line became popular with specialty boutiques that sold it to the consumer innovators in this marketplace. Since her firm was too small to advertise to such a large market, Carushka developed an alternative marketing strategy: She began sending her designs free to celebrities. The resulting media coverage brought her the broader audience she was seeking. Word-of-mouth promotion then took over, and Carushka became an overnight success. Later she tripled her sales by selling her line through department stores.

The innovative designer applied some unorthodox theories to her company and her lines. A believer in inner personality, numerology, and astrology, Carushka used astrology to pick people for the various functions within the company and numerology to number her garments, avoiding numbers she considered unlucky. But these tactics did not help Carushka when she tried to market a line of men's bodywear. She had teamed up with actor/dancer John Travolta, and the initial response to the line was quite positive, with $1 million of product shipped in the first four months. However, the men's bodywear segment of the industry did not hold up in the long run.

Despite this failure, Carushka remained true to her strategic emphasis on innovation. She refused to test market her new lines, explaining, "This is my look. You either buy it or you don't." But Carushka also admitted that "you have to be crazy to be an entrepreneur."

Entrepreneurial enterprises like Carushka's face two types of risk. First, there is the constant danger that consumers will reject the product offering, as in the case of the Travolta line. Second, in a fashion-oriented industry such as bodywear even the most innovative ideas can be quickly copied. For instance, Carushka estimates that competitors copied most of her designs within six weeks to a full season after their introduction. As a result, the pace of innovation becomes a key factor in the long-term success of a firm like Carushka's.

Carushka also believes that the bodywear market will go back to basics. In fact, this is exactly what happened to her own business. The designer was forced to take off for a few years due to health reasons. When she reopened in January 1987, she again concentrated on her original customer base — specialty boutiques. She remarked, "They are more fun than selling to department stores." Carushka no longer uses sales reps; she now sells via consumer and retail mail-orders and through wholesalers. However, in the spring of 1988, Carushka was giving serious consideration to opening her own retail store in Sherman Oaks, California.

It is obvious that Carushka still believes in the importance of innovation in the bodywear industry. Her company's slogan remains "Expect the unexpected."

Sources: Allison Kyle Leopold, "Workout Clothes: From the Gym. . . to the Street," . . . *The New York Times Magazine* (September 28, 1986), pp. 67–68, 110; "Carushka Is Still Shipping, Says Company Won't Close," *Women's Wear Daily* (June 14, 1985), p. 10; and Jim Seale, "Exercise Wear," *Stores* (June 1987), pp. 13–19.

Questions

1. How would you classify Carushka with respect to product life cycle stage?

2. Relate this case to the chapter's discussion of fashions and fads.

3. How did Carushka's product strategy facilitate the consumer adoption process?

4. What part of the consumer goods classification would best match Carushka's product lines?

5. Assess Carushka's decision to return to her original marketing strategy of selling through specialty boutiques.

COMPUTER APPLICATIONS

The creation of new product and service offerings for industrial purchasers, organizational buyers, or ultimate consumers is an expensive and risky undertaking. Since marketers usually face a number of alternatives from which to choose a product or service to offer their selected target markets, they need a method for evaluating the most appropriate use of the firm's limited financial and human resources. A commonly used technique for this purpose is *return on investment (ROI)*. This quantitative tool is particularly useful in evaluating proposals for alternative courses of action. ROI equals the rate of profit (net profit divided by sales) multiplied by the firm's turnover rate (sales divided by the required investment):

$$\text{ROI} = \frac{\text{Net Profit}}{\text{Sales}} \times \frac{\text{Sales}}{\text{Investment}}$$

Consider a proposed new product for which the firm's marketers estimate a required investment of $200,000. The company expects to achieve $500,000 in sales, with a projected net profit of $40,000. The proposed product's ROI is calculated as follows:

$$\text{ROI} = \frac{\$40,000}{\$500,000} \times \frac{\$500,000}{\$200,000}$$

$$= .08 \times 2.5$$

$$= 20\%.$$

Whether or not the 20 percent return on investment is acceptable depends on similar ROI calculations for alternative uses of company funds. In addition, the marketing decision makers are likely to carefully consider such variables as the fit of the proposed product or service with existing product lines and with long-range marketing plans.

In comparing ROIs of different proposals, it is important to recognize several factors that can affect ROI calculations. In situations in which different depreciation schedules are being used, profits—and therefore ROI—will vary. External conditions can also affect ROI. Favorable economic conditions may be associated with high rates of return, while lower rates may be more common during economic downturns. A third factor affecting ROI is the time period over which product development expenditures are made. The ROI of a product that requires considerable developmental work may be adversely affected.[17]

Directions: Use menu item 8 titled "Return on Investment" to solve each of the following problems.

Problem 1   The management of Light Manufacturing of Youngstown, Ohio, is considering the development of a new type of industrial shears. The estimated cost of developing the new product is $5 million. The firm expects to sell $20 million of the shears for a profit of $2 million. What is the product's ROI?

Problem 2   Southern Michigan Industries of Jackson, Michigan, has marketed an industrial drill for years. Current annual sales are $5 million, but last year Southern Michigan earned only $150,000 on the drill because of the rapidly rising cost of component parts. A recent proposal from the production department suggests that shifting to less expensive components would increase profits to

$300,000 while maintaining sales at $5 million. However, this would require several plant layout changes costing $1.25 million. What is the ROI of the proposed switch to less expensive parts?

Problem 3   San Francisco–based Bay Dental Clinics markets franchises to young dentists just starting their practices. The company projects that a franchisee will earn $45,000 in the first year of operation based on $180,000 in professional fees. Total first-year expenses of $135,000 include franchise fees, equipment, personnel, rent, utilities, and other setup costs. In addition, the $135,000 includes interest charges on a special financial arrangement Bay Dental Clinics has developed for new dentists with limited current funds but high future revenue expectations. What is the typical first year's ROI for a dentist who establishes a Bay Dental Clinic?

Problem 4   Northwoods Industries of Mankato, Minnesota, has developed a new type of ski. Special placement tests at ski instruction schools throughout the United States proved highly successful. In fact, ski instructors preferred the new skis over their current skis by a three-to-one margin. Northwoods' top management estimates that the firm would be able to generate $10 million in revenue from the sale of the skis at wholesale prices. However, development expenses for the prototype skis are estimated at $4 million. Management believes that the new line would add $750,000 to the firm's annual profits. Calculate the ROI for the proposed new line of skis.

Problem 5   A Lopez Island, Washington, inventor has developed a new fad item about which she refuses to divulge any details until she completes a licensing proposal for a major novelty manufacturer in New York. One part of the proposal is a return-on-investment calculation. The inventor estimates that the manufacturer would have to spend a total of $15 million in production and promotional outlays to successfully launch the fad item. Annual sales are estimated to be $60 million. After subtracting such expenses as shipping, retail price discounts necessary for motivating retailers to carry the item in inventory, and licensing fees, the firm should earn profits of $5 million. What ROI should the inventor include in her proposal to the novelty manufacturer?

9

Product Mix Decisions and New-Product Planning

Chapter Objectives

1. To identify the major product mix decisions that marketers must make.

2. To explain why most firms develop a line of related products rather than a single product.

3. To identify alternative new-product development strategies and the determinants of each strategy's success.

4. To explain the various organizational structures for new-product development.

5. To list the stages in the new-product development process.

6. To explain the roles of brands, brand names, and trademarks in a marketing strategy.

7. To describe the major functions of the package.

8. To explain the nature of customer service and list its major components.

9. To outline the functions of the Consumer Product Safety Commission and the concept of product liability.

N ew products frequently create corporate growth. But creating a new product that can enhance a balance sheet is no easy undertaking, considering that 95 percent of the more than 2,000 new food and beverage products introduced each year are flops. So when PepsiCo moved to fill the gap in its soft-drink product line—a lemon-lime soda to compete with 7-Up and Sprite—it knew it faced a struggle. PepsiCo already had a lemon-lime product, Teem, but it had never managed to gain the popularity of its competitors, partly because it was a me-too takeoff on the leading brands—exactly what PepsiCo wanted to avoid.

With this in mind, PepsiCo told its research and development team to create a lemon-lime drink that was better tasting yet different. What they formulated was so much better and different that it became an entire new product category—juice-added soft drinks.

Consumers recognize PepsiCo's new product as Slice, the drink with 10 percent fruit juice. But in initial consumer taste tests, PepsiCo pushed the product's flavor, only to find that consumers were not impressed by another lemon-lime soda. Marketing researchers then decided to tell the taste testers about the product's point of difference and discovered that they were impressed by the added value—the fruit juice.

PepsiCo shifted its focus to the fruit aspect of the drink and assigned a two-person team to create the new product's image. The team consisted of the vice-president of new-product development and the brand manager for the as yet unnamed product. Working with package designers, marketing personnel, and PepsiCo's advertising agency, they came up with "Slice," a name easily associated with a piece of fruit. On the package they dotted the *i* with a vibrantly colored fruit. For ads they created the slogan "We Got the

Juice," with television commercials featuring enormous slices of fruit bursting through a clear liquid.

PepsiCo has an extensive network of small, regional bottling companies, and it used one to distribute its new creation to a limited test market. Slice, in both regular and diet versions, was an instant success in this initial test, and PepsiCo rushed the product into nationwide production to prevent competitors from beating it to market. Slice also was an instant success nationally and became one of the most successful new products of the 1980s, reaching $1 billion in sales in two years. (Most companies are happy to have a new product hit $100 million in sales.)

PepsiCo juiced up on Slice's success by whirling other fruit-added drinks into production. The first line extension was Mandarin Orange Slice, which was test marketed some six months after the original. Cherry Cola Slice and Apple Slice soon followed. However, Slice brands were selling so well that PepsiCo didn't even test market Cherry Cola and Apple Slice, which some analysts say may have led to cannibalization of sales.

Despite Slice's "can't-miss" results, the product almost didn't happen. PepsiCo's chemists were unable to mix the blend of ingredients needed to keep the product from souring, clouding, changing color, or suffering any of a variety of other technical ailments. But just when it appeared that PepsiCo's efforts with Slice would be fruitless, the lab produced a perfect batch. Then it took more months of work to figure out a way to mass produce the recipe and test the product in prototype bottling plants. After 18 months of product development, one of the most successful new products in years blossomed.

Competitors only wish they'd developed it first as they scramble to get their juice-added products on grocery shelves.[1]

Photo source: © Andrew Moore.

Chapter Overview

Chapter 8 considered several basic product concepts. This chapter expands the discussion of product strategy by examining the product mix and new-product planning. A starting point is the concept of product mix.

product mix
Assortment of product lines and individual offerings available from a marketer.

product line
Various related goods offered by a firm.

A **product mix** is the assortment of product lines and individual offerings available from a marketer. Its two primary components are **product line,** a series of related products, and individual offerings that make up the product line. PepsiCo's product mix, shown in Figure 9.1, consists of three basic product lines—soft drinks, snacks, and restaurants—and individual items within the lines such as Pepsi-Cola, Slice, Ruffles potato chips, and Pizza Hut restaurants.

Product mixes typically are measured in terms of width, length, and depth of assortment. Selected items from the PepsiCo product mix illustrate these concepts. *Width* of assortment refers to the number of product lines the firm offers. Soft drinks, snacks, and restaurants would be considered the width of PepsiCo's product mix. *Length* refers to the number of products in the mix. For Pepsi it is 16, with 6 brands of soft drinks, 7 snack lines, and 3 restaurant lines. (In reality, PepsiCo markets many more brands, but only the major ones are listed in Figure 9.1.) *Depth* refers to variations of each product in the mix. PepsiCo deepened its Doritos brand by adding two new flavorings—Nacho Cheese and Cool Ranch.

The Existing Product Mix

An established firm initiates product planning by first assessing its current product mix. What product lines does it now offer? How deep are the offerings within each product line? The marketer looks for gaps in the assortment that can be filled with new products or modified versions of existing ones.

Cannibalization

cannibalizing
Refers to a product that takes sales from another offering in a product line.

A firm wants to avoid a costly new-product introduction that will adversely affect sales of one of its existing products. A product that takes sales from another offering in a product line is said to be **cannibalizing** the line.

Such was the case when General Foods introduced its Maxim instant coffee. The company hoped that the popularity of the Maxwell House name would help Maxim. It did, but it also took millions of sales dollars from the established offering.[2] Combe, Inc. avoided the danger of cannibalizing sales of its Grecian Formula 16 hair coloring for men when it developed a second hair-coloring product. On the market since 1961, Grecian Formula gradually tints gray hair

Figure 9.1
The PepsiCo Product Mix

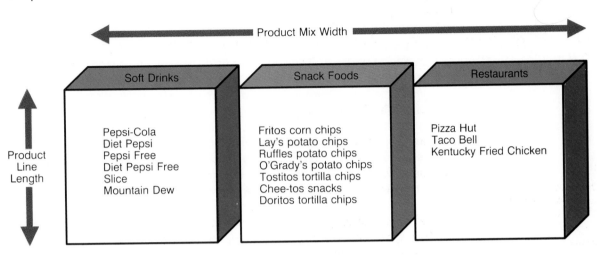

over a three-to-four-week period. The new product, Just for Men, is a shampoo-in hair coloring that transforms gray hair into brown in a matter of minutes. Combe research indicated that many contemporary men want an immediate hair color change. The new product targets that group, while Grecian Formula appeals to those who want a more subtle color transformation. In cities in which Just for Men was test marketed, no cannibalization occurred—in fact, Grecian Formula's sales rose 14 percent in those cities.[3]

While the introduction of a new product may take some sales from existing related products, marketing research should ensure that the new offering will guarantee sufficient additional sales to warrant the investment involved in its development and market introduction.

Line Extension

An important rationale for assessing the current product mix is to determine whether line extension is feasible. A **line extension** refers to the development of individual offerings that appeal to different market segments but are closely related to the existing product line. If cannibalization can be minimized, line extension provides a relatively inexpensive way to increase sales revenues with minimal risk. Since Sony introduced its Walkman portable stereo in 1979, the company has extended the product line by adding about 100 models, ranging from a $32 playback-only model to a $450 Walkman that records as well as plays and has the sound quality of a tape deck. For walkers and runners, Sony offers an ultralight radio-only model that attaches to a sweatband. A solar-powered, waterproof Walkman is designed for use at the beach. The deluxe Boodo Khan model has oversize headphones that produce a concert hall sound.[4]

After assessing the existing product mix and considering appropriate line extensions, marketing decision makers must turn their attention to product line planning and the development of new products.

line extension
New product that is closely related to other products in the firm's existing product line.

The Importance of Product Lines

Firms that market only one product are rare today. Most offer their customers a product line, that is, a series of related products. Reynolds Metals Company, for example, began operations in 1919 by producing lead and tinfoil packaging for the tobacco industry. In 1926, it added aluminum foil to its line of metal-packaging products. Since then, Reynolds has become a producer of aluminum and has developed hundreds of aluminum products for both industrial and consumer markets. These include aluminum cans, Reynolds Wrap household aluminum foil, aluminum siding and other building products, solar hot water heating systems, electrical wire and cable, can and packaging machinery systems, and parts for the automotive, railroad, aircraft, and aerospace industries. To expand its line of consumer products, Reynolds introduced a plastic household wrap in the early 1980s.[5] Several factors explain why firms such as Reynolds develop a complete line rather than concentrate on a single product.

Desire to Grow

A company limits its growth potential when it concentrates on a single product. Firms are introducing new products at an ever increasing rate to boost market growth and company profits. Rubbermaid launches about 100 new products each year and attempts to generate 30 percent of its sales from products no more than five years old. New products and line extensions have enabled Rubbermaid to double sales and triple earnings in the past six years. Sales of its garbage containers accelerated 20 percent when Rubbermaid deepened the product line by adding a slate-blue model.[6]

Firms often introduce new products to offset seasonal variations in the sales of their current products. Most toy purchases, for example, are made during the Christmas season. To boost year-round toy sales, Fisher-Price has added spring/summer toys such as the Bubble Mower lawn mower. The company also recognizes growth potential in nontoy areas and recently has introduced a line of juvenile furnishings, including high chairs, car seats, and portable cribs and playpens.

Optimal Use of Company Resources

By spreading the costs of its operations over a series of products, a firm may be able to reduce the average production and marketing costs of all of its products. Texize Chemicals Company started with a single household cleaner and learned the painful lessons on marketing costs of a firm that has only one major product. Management rapidly added the products K2r and Fantastik to the line. The company's sales representatives now call on marketing intermediaries with a series of products at little more than the cost of doing so with a single product. In addition, Texize's advertising produces benefits for all products in the line.

Similarly, production facilities can be used economically in producing related products. Chrysler, for example, gains maximum production efficiency by producing different car models based on one design. Since 1980, all new Chrysler models, including compacts, sports cars, minivans, and full-size cars, have been variations of the K car design.[7] Finally, the expertise of all of the firm's personnel can be utilized more economically for a line of products than for a single product.

Increasing Company Importance in the Market

The company with a line of products often is more important to both consumers and marketing intermediaries than is the firm with only one product. A shopper who purchases a tent often buys related items, such as tent heaters, sleeping bags and air mattresses, camping stoves, and special cookware. Recognizing this tendency, Coleman Company now includes in its product line dozens of items associated with camping. The firm would be little known if its only product were lanterns. Similarly, new cameras from Eastman Kodak help the firm sell more film—a product that carries a 60 percent profit margin.[8]

Industrial buyers often expect a firm that manufactures a product to also offer related products. Firms that buy computers, for example, expect computer manufacturers to sell software and computer services. Based on this consumer demand, computer giants such as IBM, Tandem, and NCR are increasingly selling software and services. Large computer firms predict that by the 1990s about 50 percent of their revenues will come from the sale of software and services. In the early 1980s, these related products accounted for only about 25 percent of their revenues.[9]

Exploiting the Product Life Cycle

As its output enters the maturity and decline stages of the product life cycle, the firm must add new products if it is to prosper. The regular addition of new products to the firm's mix helps ensure that it will not become a victim of product obsolescence. Schlage Lock Company was in a mature business; every front door in the United States has an average of 1.57 locks. But because only 8 percent of American homes have an alarm system, Schlage decided to develop home security system products for a market that is growing some 25 percent each year.[10]

New-Product Planning

The product development effort requires considerable advance planning. New products are the lifeblood of any business firm, and a steady flow of new entries must be available if the firm is to survive. Some new products may involve major technological breakthroughs. For example, Procter & Gamble developed a male-baldness cure and a margarine containing olestra, which cuts blood cholesterol. Other new products are simple product line extensions; in other words, a new product is simply a product new to either the company or the customer. A recent survey revealed that only about 10 percent of new-product introductions were truly new products.

New-product development is time consuming, risky, and expensive. Approximately two-thirds of all new products fail once they are on store shelves.[11] Dozens of new-product ideas are required to produce even one successful

Figure 9.2
Alternative Product
Development Strategies

	Old Product	New Product
Old Market	Product Improvement	Product Development
New Market	Market Development	Product Diversification

product. As ideas are evaluated and tested, most are discarded in the firm's pursuit of products that will enjoy sufficient marketplace success to justify the required investments.

Product Development Strategies

The firm's strategy for new-product development varies according to the existing product mix and the extent to which current marketing offerings match overall marketing objectives. The current market position of the firm's products and services also affects product development strategy. Figure 9.2 identifies four alternative development strategies: product improvement, market development, product development, and product diversification.[12]

A *product improvement strategy* refers to a modification of the product offering. Packaged-goods marketers often use this strategy to boost market share for mature products in mature markets. Procter & Gamble introduced no-scent versions of its Charmin bathroom tissue, Bounce fabric softener, and Tide laundry detergent. After Colgate added a lemon-lime scent to its Palmolive dishwashing detergent, the product's market share increased by three percentage points.[13] Product positioning often plays a major role in such a strategy. **Product positioning** refers to the consumer's perception of a product's attributes, use, quality, and advantages and disadvantages relative to competing brands. Marketing research methodology allows marketers to analyze consumer preferences and construct product positioning maps that plot a product in relation to competitive offerings.

A *market development strategy* concentrates on finding new markets for existing products. Market segmentation, discussed in Chapter 7, is a useful tool in such an effort. The Arm & Hammer division of Church & Dwight developed new markets for its baking soda by promoting it as a refrigerator cleanser, bathwater treatment, sink drain deodorizer, plaque remover, and leavening agent.

Product development strategy, as defined here, refers to the introduction of new products into identifiable or established markets. Sometimes the new product is the firm's first entry in a particular marketplace. In other cases, firms

product positioning
Consumer's perception of a product's attributes, use, quality, and advantages and disadvantages.

choose to introduce new products into markets in which they already have established positions in an attempt to increase overall market share. These new offerings are called *flanker brands.* Miller Genuine Draft is Miller Brewing Company's flanker to its premium Miller High Life beer. The company introduced the new brand to boost market share of its higher-priced beer.[14]

Product diversification strategy refers to the development of new products for new markets. In some cases, the new target markets complement existing markets; in others, they do not. Firms often diversify through acquisition. Maytag Company, maker of washers, dryers, and dishwashers, broadened its line of major appliances by acquiring Magic Chef, Inc., which manufactures gas ranges and refrigerators.[15]

New-product planning is a complex area. The critical nature of product planning decisions requires an effective organizational structure.

Organizational Structure for New-Product Development

An effective organizational structure is required in order to stimulate and coordinate new-product development. Most firms assign new-product development to one or more of the following entities: new-product committees, new-product departments, product managers, and venture teams.

New-Product Committees

The most common organizational arrangement for new-product development is the new-product development committee. It is typically composed of representatives of top management in such areas as marketing, finance, manufacturing, engineering, research, and accounting. Committee members are less concerned with the conception and development of new-product ideas than with reviewing and approving new-product plans. Publishing houses, for instance, often have editorial review committees that must approve new project ideas before editors can work with authors in developing new books.

Since the members of new-product committees are key executives in the functional areas, their support for any new-product plan is likely to result in approval for further development. However, new-product committees tend to be slow in making decisions and conservative in their views, and sometimes they compromise so that members can get back to their regular company responsibilities.

New-Product Departments

Many companies establish separate, formally organized new-product departments. The departmental structure overcomes the limitations of the new-product committee system and makes new-product development a permanent, full-time activity. The department is responsible for all phases of the product's development within the firm, including screening decisions, developing product specifications, and coordinating product testing. The head of the department has sub-

Coca-Cola Foods made optimal
use of its resources when it
entered a new product area by
introducing Minute Maid Fruit
Juice frozen snacks. The product
uses Minute Maid's established
juice technology and frozen-
products distribution system and
benefits from the popular brand
name.

Photo source: Courtesy of The Coca-Cola Company.

stantial authority and typically reports to the president or the top marketing officer.

Colgate-Palmolive recently set up a new-product group separate from its Colgate Venture Company (a concept discussed in a later section). Colgate's new-product group was responsible for introducing liquid Palmolive automatic dishwashing detergent and, later, a lemon-scented version.[16]

Product Managers

product manager
Individual in a manufacturing firm assigned a product or product line and given complete responsibility for determining objectives and establishing marketing strategies.

Product managers, also called *brand managers,* are individuals assigned one product or product line and given responsibility for determining its objectives and marketing strategies. Procter & Gamble assigned its first product manager in 1927 when it made one person responsible for Camay soap. The product manager concept was adopted by such marketers as General Foods, Pillsbury, Bristol-Myers, Gillette, and Quaker Oats.

Product managers set prices, develop advertising and sales promotion programs, and work with sales representatives in the field. Although product managers have no line authority over the field sales force, the objective of increasing brand sales is the same, and managers attempt to help salespeople accomplish their task. In multiproduct companies, product managers are key people in the marketing department. They provide individual attention for each product and can utilize the firm's sales force, marketing research department, and advertising department.

In addition to having primary responsibility for marketing a particular product or product line, the product manager is often responsible for new-product development, creation of new-product ideas, and recommendations for improving existing products. These suggestions become the basis for proposals submitted to top management.

The product manager system has one of the same disadvantages as the new-product committee: New-product development may get secondary treatment because of the manager's time commitments for existing products. Although a number of extremely successful new products have resulted from ideas submitted by product managers, it cannot be assumed that the skills required for marketing an existing product line are the same as those needed for successfully developing new products.[17]

In recent years, advocates of the brand management system have modified the approach to deal with changes in marketing's environment. The system was developed to sell leading brands to mass market consumers with similar tastes. But the increasing fragmentation of the mass market into smaller segments has forced firms to rethink the brand management approach. Several firms, including Procter & Gamble, have turned to a team approach, whereby brand managers are assigned to a team to work along with research, manufacturing, and sales managers.

Venture Teams

The **venture team** concept is an organizational strategy for developing new product areas by combining the management resources of technological innovations, capital, management, and marketing expertise. Like new-product committees, venture teams are composed of specialists from different areas of the organization: engineering representatives for product design and prototype development; marketing staff members for development of product concept tests, test marketing, sales forecasts, pricing, and promotion; and financial accounting representatives for detailed cost analyses and decisions concerning the concept's probable return on investment.

Unlike committees, venture teams do not disband after every meeting. Team members are assigned a project as a major responsibility, and teams possess the authority necessary for both planning and implementing a course of action. To stimulate product innovation, the venture team typically is linked directly with top management, but it functions as an entity separate from the organization. Some sources also differentiate venture teams from task forces. A new-product *task force* is an interdisciplinary group on temporary assignment that works through functional departments. Its basic task is to coordinate and integrate the work of the functional departments on a specific project. In contrast, venture teams work independently and are not tied to functional departments.

The venture team must meet such criteria as prospective return on investment, uniqueness of product, existence of a well-defined need, compatibility of the product with existing technology, and strength of patent protection. Although

venture team
Organizational strategy for identifying and developing new-product areas by combining the management resources of technological innovation, capital, management, and marketing expertise.

Polaroid

When the instant camera market faded drastically, falling by almost 6 million camera sales a year from its 1978 high of 9.6 million, Polaroid made a snap decision. It told marketing to develop the next Polaroid instant camera—an unprecedented move. Polaroid's revenues quickly jumped 30 percent and profits skyrocketed 250 percent. The reason? Spectra, which Polaroid released in April 1986, marking the first big hit in the instant camera market since 1972.

Polaroid's production of Spectra provides a textbook example of how to market a product. Polaroid gave marketing the lead role in developing the new camera in response to consumer research showing that consumers thought instant cameras were bulky, the film was too expensive, and, worst of all, instant cameras were not truly convenient.

Marketing went to work with zeal. First, it conducted what was for Polaroid an unprecedented marketing research campaign to discover what consumers wanted from an instant camera. From the information it gathered through extensive market studies and consumer interviews, marketing developed the camera's specifications, among them a smaller camera, sonar auto-focus, sharper images, and a film chemistry giving brighter, more lifelike colors. Then the marketing team went to the engineers.

At this point, Spectra became the brainchild of a venture team of marketers and engineers, another first for Polaroid. The team had its problems, but the engineers caught the marketing fever and developed nothing less than a success. "They delivered 10 out of 10," said Joseph McLaughlin, group vice-president of worldwide marketing for Polaroid. "Everything we asked for, they gave us."

Marketing also changed the way Polaroid targeted its product. Tradi-

tionally, Polaroid's engineers would produce a new camera and then the company would run ads trumpeting its new features. Spectra had a specific target, namely the upscale consumer market — people who usually purchased 35mm cameras and accessories. Spectra was priced at $150, more than twice as much as any Polaroid instant camera has ever cost. The targeting went far beyond the price tag, though. The marketers wanted Spectra to look like an upscale product, and they hired a design firm to make sure it did. The result was a sleek, slender, binocular-like camera in a dark metallic grey—the look of a luxury European automobile.

Targeting the upscale market may have given Polaroid its biggest boost. As it happened, Spectra made optimal use of the company's resources by increasing Polaroid's market presence, for while Polaroid concentrated some 95 percent of its ad budget on Spectra, sales of other Polaroid instants jumped along with Spectra sales.

Sources: Stephen MacDonald, "Looking Good: More Firms Place Higher Priority on Product Design," *The Wall Street Journal* (January 22, 1987), p. 33; "Spectra's Instant Success Gives Polaroid a Shot in the Arm," *Business Week* (November 3, 1986), pp. 32–34; and Brian Dumaine, "How Polaroid Flashed Back," *Fortune* (February 16, 1987), pp. 72–76. McLaughlin quotes are from "Spectra Unites Polaroid's 'Family,'" *Advertising Age* (October 6, 1986).

the venture team is considered temporary, its actual life span is flexible, often extending over a number of years. When the commercial potential of a new product has been demonstrated, the product may be assigned to an existing division, become a division within the company, or serve as the nucleus of a new company. Procter & Gamble has established a separate division to manage the potentially major business created by olestra, a synthetic fat substitute mentioned earlier. P&G plans to develop a complete line of products that contain olestra.

Stages in the New-Product Development Process

Once the firm has organized for new-product development, it can establish procedures for evaluating new-product ideas. The new-product development process involves six stages: (1) idea generation, (2) screening, (3) business analysis, (4) development, (5) testing, and (6) commercialization. At each stage, management faces the decision of whether to abandon the project, continue to the next stage, or seek additional information before proceeding further.

Idea Generation

New-product development begins with ideas that emanate from many sources: the sales force, customers who write letters asking "Why don't you . . . ," marketing employees, research and development specialists, competitive products, retailers, and inventors outside the company. Consumer hotlines are a source of many new-product ideas. New products from Whirlpool and General Electric have come from suggestions or complaints received through consumer hotlines. Complaints about noisy dishwashers resulted in Whirlpool's new Quiet Wash dishwasher. General Electric developed new, easier to use VCRs and less complicated VCR manuals in response to consumer complaints. General Electric's 250 hotline employees are trained to communicate to marketing, advertising, and product development departments the most frequent consumer complaints.[18] Other firms, such as Black & Decker, set up dealer advisory panels as a source of new ideas. One panel member's suggestion resulted in Black & Decker's new, heavy-duty reciprocating power saw.[19] It is important for the firm to develop a system for stimulating new ideas and rewarding their creators.

Screening

The critical screening stage involves separating ideas with potential from those incapable of meeting company objectives. Some organizations use checklists to determine whether product ideas should be eliminated or subjected to further consideration. These checklists typically include such factors as product uniqueness, availability of raw materials, and the proposed product's compatibility with current product offerings, existing facilities, and present capabilities. In other instances, the screening stage consists of open discussions of new-product ideas among representatives of different functional areas in the organization. Toymaker Hasbro Inc. screens new-product ideas by looking for three traits in a toy: lasting play value, ability to be shared, and ability to stimulate the imagination.[20]

Figure 9.3
Basic Criteria for Screening
New-Product Ideas

Checklist for Screening Ideas

Yes   No

☐ ☐   Will the proposed new product be in a field of activity in which the corporation is currently engaged?

☐ ☐   If the idea involves a companion product to others already being manufactured, can it be made from materials with which the corporation is familiar?

☐ ☐   Is the proposed new product capable of being produced on the type and kind of equipment the corporation normally operates?

☐ ☐   Can the proposed new product be handled readily by the corporation's existing sales force through the established distribution pattern?

☐ ☐   Is the potential market for the product at least $_____?

☐ ☐   Is the market expected to grow at a faster rate than the nation's gross national product over the next five years?

☐ ☐   Will the expected return on investment, after taxes, reach a minimum level of ____ percent?

Source: Adapted with permission of Macmillan Publishing Company from *Product Planning and Management* by William S. Sachs and George Benson, p. 231. Copyright 1981 by Penwell Books, Inc.

Screening is an important stage in the developmental process because any product ideas that proceed further will cost the firm time and money. Figure 9.3 presents some basic criteria for the screening process.

Business Analysis

Product ideas that survive the initial screening are subjected to a thorough business analysis. The analysis involves an assessment of the new product's potential market, growth rate, and likely competitive strengths. Decisions must be made about the compatibility of the proposed product with such company resources as financial support for necessary promotion production capabilities, and distribution facilities.

Concept testing, or the consideration of the product idea prior to its actual development, is an important aspect of the business analysis stage. **Concept testing** is a marketing research project that attempts to measure consumer attitudes and perceptions relevant to the new-product idea. Focus groups and in-store polling can be effective methods for assessing a new-product concept.

concept testing
Measuring consumer attitudes and perceptions of a product idea prior to its actual development.

Development

Product ideas with profit potential are converted into a physical product. The conversion process is the joint responsibility of the development engineering department, which turns the original concept into a product, and the marketing department, which provides feedback on consumer reactions to product designs, packages, colors, and other physical features. Numerous changes may be necessary before the original mock-up is converted into the final product. Some firms use computer-aided design to reduce the number of prototypes developers must build, thus hastening the development stage. 3M, for example, cut six months off the three years it usually needs to develop a microfilm reader

During development, COMPAQ personal computers undergo a series of rigid tests. Here a COMPAQ engineer "zaps" a computer with static electricity to ensure that the product will withstand a similar charge in an office. In other tests, computers are frozen and baked in a climatic chamber to test their ability to function under extreme temperature conditions.

Photo source: Courtesy of Compaq Computer Corporation.

because the model designed on the computer was good enough to go straight into production.[21]

The series of tests, revisions, and refinements should ultimately result in the introduction of a product with great likelihood of success. Some firms obtain the reactions of their own employees to proposed new-product offerings. Employees at Levi Strauss test new styles by wearing them and reporting on the various features. Thom McAn asks its workers to report regularly on shoe wear and fit over an eight-week testing period.

Part of the $3.1 billion that Ford invested in developing the new Taurus involved careful scrutinization of competitive models. The objective was to see what Ford could learn from competitors. Ford selected cars it considered the best in the class of mid-size, four-door models and then took the cars apart piece by piece to see how they were made (a process known in the auto industry as a *layered stripdown*). During this process, Ford employees identified 400 features they believed they could either improve on or emulate. Of the 400, Ford incorporated 360 features in the Taurus, which in 1987 became the number-one-selling car in the United States.[22]

Testing

To determine consumer reactions to a product under normal conditions, many firms test market their new-product offerings. Up to this point, they have obtained consumer information by submitting free products to consumers, who then give their reactions. Other information may come from shoppers asked to evaluate competitive products. Test marketing is the first stage at which the product or service must perform in a real-life environment.

Figure 9.4

Top Ten Test Market Locations in the United States

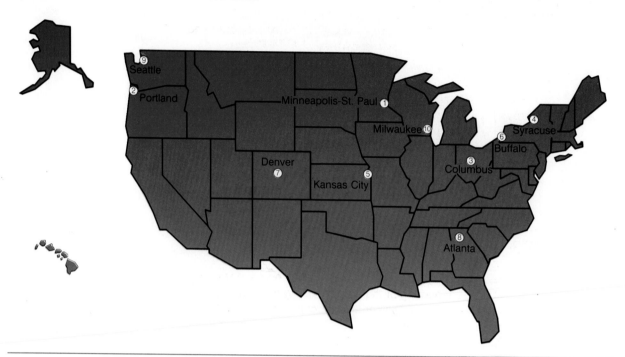

Source: Saatchi & Saatchi DFS Compton, as reported in *The Wall Street Journal* (January 26, 1988), p. 42.

test marketing
Process of selecting a specific city or television coverage area considered reasonably typical of a new total market and introducing the product with a marketing campaign in this area.

Test marketing is the process of selecting a specific city or television-coverage area that is considered reasonably typical of the total market and introducing the product or services with a complete marketing campaign in this area. If the test is carefully designed and controlled, consumers in the test market city will respond to the new offerings without knowing that a test is being conducted. After the test has been underway for a few months and sales and market shares in the test market city have been calculated, management can estimate the product's likely performance in a full-scale introduction.

In selecting test market locations, marketers look for a location with a manageable size. In addition, its residents should represent the overall population in such characteristics as age, education, and income. Finally, the media should be self-contained so that the promotional efforts can be directed to people who represent the target market of the product or services being tested. The ten most popular U.S. markets for testing food and drug products are shown in Figure 9.4.

Some firms omit test marketing and move directly from product development to full-scale production. These companies cite four problems with test marketing:

1. Test marketing is expensive. It can cost $250,000 to $1 million depending on the size of the test market city and the cost of buying media to advertise the product.[23]

2. Competitors who learn about the test market often disrupt the findings by reducing the prices of their products in the test area, distributing cents-off coupons, installing attractive in-store displays, or giving additional discounts to retailers to induce them to display more of their products. In a court settlement, Hartz Mountain once agreed not to engage in advertising designed to disrupt the test of a new pet product by a subsidiary of A. H. Robins.

3. Long-lived durable goods, such as dishwashers, hair dryers, and compact laser disc players, are seldom test marketed due to the major financial investment required for their development, the need to establish a network of dealers to distribute the products, and the parts and servicing required. Whirlpool Corporation recently invested $160 million to redesign and install a new manufacturing line for a new automatic washer and another $120 million to change from porcelain to plastic liners for refrigerators. To develop each silicon chip that performs a single function in an Apple microcomputer costs approximately $100 million and takes at least six months. Producing a prototype for a test market is simply too expensive. Thus, the go/no-go decision for the new, durable product typically is made without the benefit of test market results.

4. Test marketing a new product or service communicates company plans to competitors prior to its introduction. Kellogg Company discovered a new product with sales potential by learning of the test marketing of a new, fruit-filled tart designed to be heated in the toaster and served for breakfast. Kellogg rushed a similar product into full-scale production and became the first national marketer of the product with its Pop Tarts. Other test marketed products beaten by competitors in the national market race include Helene Curtis' Arm in Arm deodorant (preempted by Church & Dwight's Arm & Hammer brand deodorant); General Foods' Maxim (beaten by Nestlé's Taster's Choice); Hills Brothers High Yield Coffee (Procter & Gamble's Folger's Flakes); and Hunt-Wesson's Prima Salsa Tomato sauce (Chesebrough-Pond's Ragu Extra Thick & Zesty).[24]

The decision to skip the test marketing stage should be based on the conclusion that the new product or service has an extremely high likelihood of success. The cost of developing a new detergent, for example, from idea generation to national marketing has been estimated at $25 million! Even if a company experiences losses on a good or service that fails at the test marketing stage, it will save itself from incurring even greater losses and embarrassment in the total market. Otherwise, the product or service may join the ranks of such monumental failures as DuPont's Corfam synthetic leather or Polaroid's ill-fated Polavision instant movie system.

Commercialization

The few product ideas that survive all the steps in the development process are ready for full-scale marketing. Marketing programs must be established, outlays for necessary production facilities made, and the sales force, marketing intermediaries, and potential customers acquainted with the new product.

A systematic approach to new-product development is essential. The traditional method for developing new products, called *phased development,* follows a sequential pattern whereby products are developed in an orderly series of steps. Responsibility for each phase passes from product planners to design-

FOCUS ON ETHICS

Product Deception or Test Market Sabotage?

When PepsiCo wanted to test market a new diet cola, it chose Seattle as one site because 40 percent of all soft-drink sales there are diet drinks compared to about 25 percent nationwide. The new cola, Jake's, differed from most diet drinks in that it used a combination of corn syrup and NutraSweet for a 30-calorie-per-can drink, unlike the 1-calorie drinks that use NutraSweet exclusively. With this combination, PepsiCo hoped to attract drinkers who wanted fewer than the 150 calories in a regular soft drink but disliked the bitter aftertaste of one-calorie drinks. Test marketing is usually an uncontroversial affair, certainly closely monitored by sponsor and competitors, but civilized. With Jake's, however, things worked out very differently.

First, in its test market advertising PepsiCo wasn't entirely upfront about its sponsorship of Jake's, saying that it was made by Jake's Cola Company. Second, PepsiCo advertised Jake's as having "15 calories per serving" without mentioning that there are 2 servings in a 12-ounce can for a total of 30 calories per can. These actions aroused the ire of industry leader The Coca-Cola Company, along with the claim that peo-

ple in taste tests liked Jake's better than Diet Coke, the leading diet soda, with 7.3 percent of the total soft-drink market.

Coke fought back. The company took out full-page newspaper advertisements in Seattle and the two other cities in which Jake's was being test marketed—Indianapolis and Jacksonville—attacking PepsiCo's claim that Jake's was made by Jake's Cola Company and for its allegedly misleading statements about calories. The ads also pointed out that the calories in Jake's "come from nearly two teaspoons of sugar," so Jake's was not a sugar-free drink like Diet Coke and other true diet drinks. Finally, the ads challenged the claim that people in taste tests liked Jake's better than Diet Coke, asserting that in independent taste tests people "liked the taste of Diet Coke better than Jake's, 57 percent to 39 percent."

To what extent Coca-Cola's advertisements affected the test marketing of Jake's is uncertain. Jake's sales in Seattle were reported as quite good, while those in Indianapolis were mixed and those in Jacksonville somewhat sluggish. As a result PepsiCo eventually gave up on Jake's.

But the ethical issues involved are to some extent unique. For example, how far does a firm have the right to go in promoting a product's image? Specifically in this case, can a firm try to divorce itself from the product's public image? A different and more common question concerns the "serving" debate. A PepsiCo distributor's spokesperson said the company was following Food and Drug Administration standards by quoting the calories in a six-ounce serving. Critics, on the other hand, noted that no one sells six ounces of a soft drink. At the same time, Coca-Cola's response may be seen as excessive and questionable in terms of disrupting the test market of a competitor's product. What sort of situation, if any, would justify such a disruption? The answers are far from obvious.

Sources: "Everything's Not Jake, Says Coca-Cola," *Puget Sound Business Journal* (March 2, 1987), pp. 1–2; Robin Updike, "New Low-Calorie Drink Test Marketed in Seattle," *The Seattle Times* (January 15, 1987), p. F1; "Catching Up with Jake," *Beverage Industry* (April 1987), p. 12; and Josh Levine, "Against All Odds, Some Surprise Hits," *Adweek's Marketing Week* (December 21, 1987), p. 32.

ers and engineers, then to manufacturers, and finally to marketers. This method works well for firms that dominate mature markets and develop variations on existing products. It is less effective for firms in industries affected by rapidly changing technology, in which the slow process of phased development is a liability. In the electronics industry, for example, bringing a new product to market nine months late can cost the product half of its potential revenue.

Instead of proceeding sequentially, many firms have adopted the *parallel approach,* which uses teams of design, manufacturing, marketing, sales, and service people who are involved with development from idea generation to commercialization. Venture teams, discussed earlier, are an example of the parallel approach. One of the biggest advantages of this approach is that it reduces the time needed for developing products. Parallel development enabled Compaq

Computer to create the Deskpro 386 personal computer in just 9 months, compared with the 13 months IBM took to develop its original personal computer.[25]

Systematic planning of all phases of new-product development and introduction can be accomplished through the use of such scheduling methods as the Program Evaluation and Review Technique (PERT) and the Critical Path Method (CPM). These techniques, originally developed by the U.S. Navy in connection with construction of the Polaris missile and submarine, map out the sequence in which each step must be taken and show the time allotments for each activity. Detailed PERT and CPM flowcharts coordinate all activities entailed in the development and introduction of new products.

Product Deletion Decisions

Although many firms devote a great deal of time and resources to the development of new products, the prospect of eliminating old ones is painful for many executives. Often sentimental attachments to marginal products with declining sales preclude objective decisions to drop them.

To avoid waste, product lines must be pruned and old, marginal products eventually eliminated. Marketers typically face this decision during the late maturity and early decline stages of the product life cycle. Periodic reviews of weak products should be conducted to eliminate them or justify retaining them.

In some instances, a firm continues to carry an unprofitable product in order to provide a complete line of goods for its customers. For example, while most grocery stores lose money on bulky, low-unit-value items such as salt, they continue to carry them to meet shopper demand.

Shortages of raw materials have prompted some companies to discontinue production and marketing of previously profitable items. Due to such a shortage, Alcoa discontinued its brand of aluminum foil. In other cases, profitable products are dropped because they fail to fit into the firm's existing product line. The introduction of automatic washing machines necessitated the development of low-sudsing detergents. Monsanto produced the world's first detergent of this sort, All, in the 1950s. All was an instant success, and Monsanto was swamped with orders from supermarkets throughout the nation. The Monsanto sales force was primarily involved in marketing industrial chemicals to large-scale buyers, and the company would have needed a completely new sales force to handle the product. Nine months after the introduction of All, Procter & Gamble introduced the world's second low-sudsing detergent, Dash. Because the Procter & Gamble sales force handled hundreds of products, the company could spread the cost of contacting dealers over all its products. In contrast, Monsanto had only All. Rather than attempt to compete, Monsanto sold All in 1958 to Lever Brothers, a Procter & Gamble competitor that had a marketing organization capable of handling the product.

Product Identification

Manufacturers identify their products with brand names, symbols, and distinctive packaging; so do certain large retailers, such as J.C. Penney and Sears. Almost every product that is distinguishable from another contains a means of identification for the buyer. Sunkist Growers stamps its oranges with the name *Sunkist*. The purchasing agent for a construction firm can turn over a sheet of aluminum and find the Alcoa name and symbol. Choosing the means of identifying the firm's output represents a major decision for the marketing manager.

Brands, Brand Names, and Trademarks

A **brand** is a name, term, sign, symbol, design, or some combination used to identify the products of one firm and differentiate them from competitive offerings. The American Marketing Association has defined a **brand name** as the part of the brand consisting of words or letters that comprise a name used to identify and distinguish the firm's offerings from competitors'. It is, therefore, the part of the brand that can be vocalized. A **trademark** is a brand that has been given legal protection exclusive to its owner. Trademark protection includes not only pictorial design but the brand name, a slogan, or a product name abbreviation, such as "Bud" for Budweiser or "The Met" for the New York Metropolitan Opera. The courts ruled in favor of Budweiser when it claimed that an exterminating company using the slogan "This Bugs for You" constituted trademark infringement. Firms can also receive trademark protection for packaging elements and product features such as color, shape, design, and typeface. Pink, for example, is a protectable color for Owens-Corning's fiberglass insulation.[26] To receive protection, firms must register the brand or brand name with the U.S. Patent and Trademark Office. More than 700,000 trademarks are currently registered in the United States.

For the consumer, the process of branding allows repeat purchases of the same product, since the product is identified with the name of its producer. The purchaser thus can associate the satisfaction derived from an ice cream bar, for example, with the brand name Häagen-Dazs. For the marketing manager, the brand serves as the cornerstone of the product's image. Once consumers have been made aware of a particular brand, its appearance becomes additional advertising for the firm. Shell Oil's seashell symbol is instant advertising to motorists who glimpse it while driving.

Well-known brands also allow the firm to escape some of the rigors of price competition. Although any chemist will confirm that all brands of aspirin contain the same amount of the chemical acetylsalicylic acid, Bayer has developed such a strong reputation that it can successfully market its aspirin at a higher price than competitive products. Well-known gasoline brands typically sell at slightly higher prices than independent brands because many purchasers feel that they are buying higher-quality gasoline. Several food companies are applying their established brand names to fresh produce. Campbell, for example, markets tomatoes, lettuce, mushrooms, cucumbers, sprouts, peppers, and other fresh produce under its Campbell Fresh logo. One marketing research study estimated that profit margins for such well-known branded produce are 10 to 60 percent higher than those for similar, unbranded products.[27]

Characteristics of Effective Brand Names

Effective brand names are easy to pronounce, recognize, and remember. Short names, such as Bounce, Agree, Raid, and Swatch, meet these requirements. Multinational marketing firms face a particularly acute problem in selecting

brand
Name, term, sign, symbol, design, or some combination of these used to identify the products of one firm and differentiate them from competitive offerings.

brand name
Part of a brand consisting of words or letters that comprise a name used to identify and distinguish the firm's offerings from competitors'.

trademark
Brand that has been given legally protected status exclusive to its owner.

Campbell Soup Company decided to use the firm's venerable brand name when it moved into the fresh-produce market under the Campbell Fresh logo.

Photo source: Courtesy of Campbell Soup Company.

brand names; an excellent brand name in one country may prove disastrous in another. When International Harvester Corp. executives decided to develop a new image of their firm and its products, they began the search for a new name. Word fragments were fed into the firm's central computer. The resulting list of 300 combinations was narrowed to 15, and the finalists were checked to determine prior use, translatability into foreign languages "without meaning something naughty," and possibility for graphic presentation. The result was Navistar. As one company executive explained, "Navistar means nothing; it's a made-up word that sounds like a real word. But it has positive meanings in 30 different languages."[28]

Every language has *o* and *k* sounds, and *okay* has become an international word. Every language also has a short *a;* thus, Coca-Cola and Texaco are effective brands in any country. An advertising campaign for E-Z washing machines failed in the United Kingdom, however, because the British pronounce *z* as *zed.*

Marketers try to overcome the problem of easily mispronounced brand names by teaching consumers how to pronounce them correctly. Advertisements for the Korean car Hyundai explained that the name rhymes with *Sunday.* When Pizza Hut introduced its Priazzo pie, it printed the phonetic symbols on placemats and in newspaper advertisements.[29]

Brand names should also give buyers the correct connotation of the product's image. The bicycle brand name Allez carries the image of champion French bicyclists. The Tru-Test name used on the True Value Hardware line of paints suggests reliable performance. Accutron suggests the quality of the high-priced, accurate timepiece.

The brand name must also be legally protectable. The Lanham Act of 1946 states that registered trademarks must not contain words in general use, such as *automobile* or *suntan lotion.* These generic words actually describe a particular type of product and cannot be granted exclusively to any company. A. J. Canfield Company, maker of Diet Chocolate Fudge Soda, sued for trademark infringement when competitors later introduced similar beverages with names that included the words *chocolate fudge.* But the court ruled that those words simply describe a specific drink flavor and are not legally protectable.[30]

generic name
Brand name that has become a generally descriptive term for a product.

When a unique product becomes generally known by its original brand name, the brand name may be ruled as a descriptive **generic name.** If this occurs, the original owner loses exclusive claim to it. For example, in 1983 the U.S. Supreme Court ruled that the trademark for Parker Brothers' Monopoly was invalid because it had become a general term for such games. The case involved Parker Brothers, who first produced Monopoly in 1935, and a San Francisco State University economics professor who developed a game called *Anti-Monopoly.* The generic names *nylon, aspirin, escalator, kerosene,* and *zipper* formerly were brand names. Other generic names that were once brand names include *cola, yo-yo, linoleum,* and *shredded wheat.*

There is a difference between brand names that are legally generic and those that are generic in many consumers' eyes. Jell-O is a brand name owned exclusively by General Foods, but to most consumers Jell-O is a descriptive name for gelatin desserts. Legal brand names such as Jell-O are often used by consumers as descriptive names. Many English and Australian consumers use the brand name Hoover as a verb for *vacuuming.* Similarly, Xerox is such a well-known brand name that it is frequently—though incorrectly—used as a verb. To protect its valuable trademark, Xerox Corporation has created advertisements explaining that Xerox is a brand name and registered trademark and should not be used as a verb.

To prevent their brand names from being ruled descriptive and available for general use, most owners take steps to inform the public of their exclusive ownership of the names. Coca-Cola uses the ® symbol for registration immediately after the names *Coca-Cola* and *Coke* and sends letters to newspapers, novelists, and others who use *Coke* with a lowercase *c* informing them that the name is owned by Coca-Cola.[31] These companies face the dilemma of attempting to retain exclusive rights to a brand name when it is generic to a large part of the market. Since any dictionary name may eventually be ruled generic, some companies create new words for their brand names. Names such as *Tylenol, Keds, Rinso,* and *Kodak* have been created by their owners.

Protecting Trademarks Abroad   A problem that many U.S. firms face is the protection of their trademarks in foreign countries. An Indonesian court, for example, ruled that the cartoon character Donald Duck is the property of an Indonesian firm even though Walt Disney Productions claims worldwide rights to it. Many American brand name goods, from handbags to computer software, are counterfeited abroad and marketed in violation of U.S. trademark law. It is estimated that counterfeiting practices cost U.S. firms up to $20 billion a year in lost sales. To remedy the problem, Congress has introduced legislation that would make it easier for American firms to seek court judgments under U.S. trade laws that would punish foreign counterfeiters.[32]

Measuring Brand Loyalty

Brands vary widely in consumer familiarity and acceptance. While a boating enthusiast may insist on a Johnson outboard motor, one study revealed that 40 percent of U.S. homemakers could not identify the brands of furniture in their own homes. Brand loyalty can be measured in three stages: brand recognition, brand preference, and brand insistence.

Brand recognition is a company's first objective for its newly introduced products to make them familiar to the consuming public. Often this is achieved through offers of free samples or discount coupons for purchases. Several new brands of toothpaste have been introduced on college campuses in free sample kits called *Campus Pacs.* Once consumers have used a product, it moves from the unknown to the known category, and the probability of its being repurchased is increased provided the consumer was satisfied with the trial sample.

Brand preference is the second stage of brand loyalty. In this stage, consumers, relying on previous experience with the product, will choose it over its competitors if it is available. A college student who prefers Stroh's beer usually will switch to another brand if it is not available at the tavern where he or she meets friends after an evening class. Companies with products at the brand preference stage are in a favorable position for competing in their industry.

Brand insistence, the ultimate stage in brand loyalty, is the situation in which consumers will accept no alternatives and will search extensively for the product or service. A product at this stage has achieved a monopoly position with that particular group of consumers. Although brand insistence is the goal of many firms, it is seldom achieved. Only the most exclusive specialty goods attain this position with a large segment of the total market.

Importance of Brand Loyalty   A study of 12 patented drugs illustrates the importance of brand loyalty. The sample included such well-known drugs as Librium and Darvon. The research indicated that patent expiration had minimal effect on the drugs' market shares or price levels. This resiliency was credited to the brand loyalty for the pioneer product in the field.[33] Another measure of the importance of brand loyalty is found in the Brand Utility Yardstick used by the J. Walter Thompson advertising agency. These ratings measure the percentage of buyers who remain brand loyal even if a 50 percent cost savings is available from generic products. Beer consumers were very loyal, with 48 percent refusing to switch brands. Sinus-remedy buyers were also brand loyal, with a 44 percent rating. In contrast, only 13 percent of the aluminum foil buyers would not switch to the generic product.[34]

Some brands are so popular that they are carried over to unrelated products because of their marketing advantages. The strategy of using a popular brand name for a new-product entry in an unrelated product category is known as **brand extension.** It should not be confused with *line extension,* which refers to new sizes, styles, or related products. Brand extension, in contrast, refers only to carrying over the brand name.

Examples of brand extension abound in contemporary marketing. The well-known Titleist golf ball brand name has been extended to golf accessories such as bags, gloves, and carts, a line of putters, and a clothing line including slacks, shirts, sweaters, and rainsuits. The Coca-Cola Company markets a line of

brand recognition
Stage of brand acceptance at which the consumer is aware of the existence of a brand but does not prefer it to competing brands.

brand preference
Stage of brand acceptance at which the consumer will select one brand over competitive offerings based on previous experience with it.

brand insistence
Stage of brand acceptance at which the consumer will accept no alternatives and will search extensively for the product or service.

brand extension
Decision to use a popular brand name for a new-product entry in an unrelated product category.

Figure 9.5
Example of a Family Brand Name

Source: Courtesy of KitchenAid Incorporated.

Coca-Cola brand clothing. Similarly, General Foods has extended its Jell-O brand to Jell-O Pudding Pops, Jell-O Fruit and Cream Bars, and Jell-O Gelatin Pops. Although most people associate the Mrs. Paul's brand with fish sticks, it has been extended to frozen fried chicken.

Family Brands and Individual Brands

family brand
Name used for several related products, such as the Johnson & Johnson line of baby care products.

individual brand
Strategy of giving an item in a product line its own brand name rather than identifying it by a single family brand name used for all products in the line.

Brands can be classified as family brands or individual brands. A **family brand** is a single brand name used for several related products. KitchenAid has a complete line of appliances under the KitchenAid name, as displayed in the ad in Figure 9.5. Johnson & Johnson offers a line of baby powder, lotions, disposable diapers, plastic pants, and baby shampoo under one name.

On the other hand, a manufacturer may choose to utilize **individual brands,** items known by their own brand names rather than by the names of the companies producing them or by an umbrella name covering similar items. Lever Brothers, for example, markets Aim, Close-Up, and Pepsodent toothpastes; All and Wisk laundry detergents; Imperial margarine; Caress, Dove,

Lifebuoy, and Lux bath soaps; and Shield deodorant soap. Quaker Oats markets Aunt Jemima breakfast products, Gatorade soft drinks, and Celeste Pizza. Individual brands are more expensive to market because a new promotional campaign must be developed to introduce each new product to its target market. But they are an extremely effective aid in implementing a market segmentation strategy.

When family brands are used, a promotional outlay benefits all the products in the line. For example, a new addition to the Heinz line gains immediate recognition because the family brand is well known. Use of family brands also makes it easier to introduce the product to both the customer and the retailer. Since supermarkets stock an average of 17,000 items, they are reluctant to add new products unless they are convinced of potential demand. A marketer of a new brand of turtle soup would have to promise the supermarket buyer huge advertising outlays for promotion and evidence of consumer buying intent before getting the product into the stores. On the other hand, Campbell Soup Company, with its dominant share of the U.S. soup market, could merely add turtle soup to its existing line and secure store placements more easily than could another company offering only individual brand names.

Family brands should be used only when the products are of similar quality, or the firm will risk harming its product image. Using the Mercedes-Benz name on a new, less expensive auto might severely tarnish the image of the other models in the Mercedes-Benz product line.

Individual brand names should be used for dissimilar products. Quaker Oats' dog food line is marketed under the Ken-L Ration brand name and its cat food line under the Puss 'n Boots brand name. Large marketers of grocery products, such as Procter & Gamble, General Foods, and Lever Brothers, employ individual brands to appeal to unique market segments. These brands also enable the firm to stimulate competition within the organization and to increase total company sales. Consumers who do not want Tide can choose Cheer, Dash, or Oxydol—all Procter & Gamble products—rather than a competitor's brand.

Manufacturers' Brands and Private Brands

Most of the brands mentioned in this chapter have been brands offered by manufacturers, commonly termed **manufacturers' (national) brands.** But many large wholesalers and retailers also place their own brands on the products they market. The brands offered by wholesalers and retailers are usually called **private brands.** Sears, the nation's largest retailer, sells its own brands—Kenmore, Craftsman, DieHard, and Harmony House. DieHard is the leading brand of battery today. Sears heavily promotes its private brands through national advertisements such as that in Figure 9.6. Safeway shelves are filled with such company brands as Bel Air, Canterbury, Cragmont, Party Pride, Manor House, and Scotch Buy. In total, these private brands represent 28 percent of total retail sales of all U.S. Safeway stores. Private brands and generic products expand the number of alternatives available to consumers. There are now about 48,000 nationally advertised brands in the United States.[35]

The growth of private brands is largely attributed to the fact that they allow retailers and wholesalers to maintain control over the products' image, quality, and price. Private brands are usually sold at lower prices than the national brands offered by manufacturers.

manufacturer's (national) brand
Brand name owned by a manufacturer or other producer.

private brand
Brand name owned by a wholesaler or retailer.

Figure 9.6
Advertisement Promoting a
Private Brand

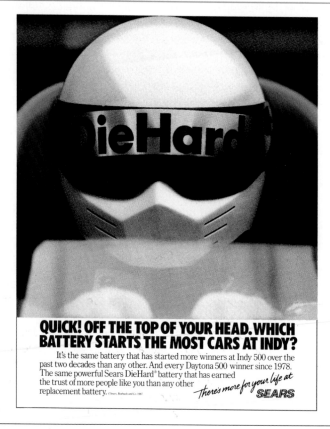

**QUICK! OFF THE TOP OF YOUR HEAD. WHICH
BATTERY STARTS THE MOST CARS AT INDY?**

It's the same battery that has started more winners at Indy 500 over the
past two decades than any other. And every Daytona 500 winner since 1978.
The same powerful Sears DieHard® battery that has earned
the trust of more people like you than any other
replacement battery. © Sears, Roebuck and Co. 1987

There's more for your life at
SEARS

Source: Courtesy of Sears, Roebuck and Company.

Generic Products

generic product
Food or household item characterized by a plain label, little or no advertising, and no brand name.

Food and household staples characterized by plain labels, little or no advertising, and no brand names are called **generic products.** These "no-name" products were first sold in Europe, where their prices were as much as 30 percent below brand name products, and introduced in the United States in 1977. Generic products account for 1.5 percent of total store sales. In 1982, at the height of an economic recession, generics captured 2.4 percent of store sales. Market share has decreased steadily since then as the economy has improved and the inflation rate has dropped. Today the most popular generic items are cigarettes and paper products such as towels and tissues.[36]

Battle of the Brands

Competition between manufacturers' brands and private brands offered by wholesalers and large retailers has been called the "battle of the brands." Although the battle appears to be intensifying, the marketing impact varies widely among industries. For example, private brands account for 52 percent of shoe sales but only 34 percent of gasoline sales.

The growth of private brands has paralleled that of chain stores in the United States, most of which has occurred since the 1930s. Chains that market their own brands become customers of the manufacturer, which places the chains' private brand names on its own products. Such leading manufacturers as Westinghouse, Armstrong Rubber, and Heinz are obtaining ever increasing percentages of their total incomes by selling private-label goods. Private-label sales to Sears and other major customers account for about 45 percent of Whirlpool's sales. Polaroid is now manufacturing private-label instant cameras for Sears. Although some manufacturers refuse to produce private-brand goods, most regard such production as a way to reach another segment of the total market.

Great inroads have been made into the dominance of manufacturers' national brands. Private brands have proven that they can compete with national brands and often have succeeded in effecting price reductions by national brand marketers to make them more competitive.

Packaging

Questions about packaging also must be addressed in a firm's product strategy. When Kimberly-Clark was designing one version of Kleenex, it asked several consumers to keep diaries listing their tissue usage. The study resulted in a new Kleenex package containing 60 tissues—the average number of times the product is used when someone has a cold.[37]

Packaging is a vital component of product strategy. Firms increasingly are using scientific approaches in making packaging decisions. Rather than experimenting with physical models or drawings, more and more package designers are using special graphics computers that create three-dimensional images of packages in thousands of colors, shapes, and typefaces. Another computer system helps firms design effective packaging by simulating what shoppers see when they walk down supermarket aisles. Companies use marketing research to test alternative package designs. Kellogg, for example, tested Nutri-Grain's package as well as the product itself.[38]

The package has several objectives. These can be classified under three general goals:

1. To protect against damage, spoilage, and pilferage
2. To assist in marketing the product
3. To be cost effective

Protection Against Damage, Spoilage, and Pilferage

The original packaging objective was to offer physical protection for the product. The typical product is handled several times between manufacture and consumer purchase, and its package must protect the contents from damage. Furthermore, perishable products must be protected against spoilage in transit, storage, or awaiting consumer selection. Because darkness protects the flavor of beer, Latrobe Brewing Company packages its Rolling Rock bottles in light-tight cardboard containers. Ads for the beer emphasize the important role the package plays in safeguarding flavor (see Figure 9.7).

Product tampering has forced many firms to improve package design. Over-the-counter medicinal products now have tamper-resistant packages, many of which warn consumers not to purchase the product if protective seals are broken. SmithKline Beckman redesigned the packaging for its Contac capsules after some were contaminated with rat poison. Capsules are now sealed

Figure 9.7
Protective Packaging

Source: Courtesy of Latrobe Brewing Company, Latrobe, Pennsylvania. This ad was produced by Gumpertz/Bentley/Fried for Sundor Brands Incorporated (1987).

with gelatin bands to make tampering more difficult and more easily detectable. They are individually sealed in clear plastic blister packs and sold in plastic-wrapped boxes.[39]

Another important safeguard many packages provide for the retailer is prevention of pilferage. At the retail level, customer shoplifting costs retailers about $840 million annually and employee theft another $1.2 billion. Many products are packaged with oversize cardboard backing too large to fit into a shoplifter's pocket or purse.

Assistance in Marketing the Product

Packaging is taking on a more important role as a marketing tool. The proliferation of new products, changes in consumer life-styles and buying habits, and marketers' emphasis on targeting smaller market segments have increased the importance of packaging as an effective way to promote products.

In a grocery store containing as many as 17,000 different items, a product must capture the shopper's attention. Walter Margulies, chairman of Lippincott & Margulies advertising, summarizes the importance of first impressions in the retail store: "Consumers are more intelligent, but they don't read as much. They relate to pictures." Margulies also cites another factor: One out of every six shoppers who needs eyeglasses does not wear them while shopping. Consequently, many marketers offering product lines are adopting similar package designs to create more visual impact in the store. Packaging Stouffer's frozen foods in orange boxes and the adoption of common package designs by product lines such as Weight Watchers foods and Planters nuts represent attempts to dominate larger sections of retail stores.[40]

Packages can also offer the consumer convenience. Pump dispenser cans facilitate the use of products ranging from mustard to insect repellent. Pop-top cans provide added convenience for soft drinks, beer, and other food products. The six-pack carton, first introduced by Coca-Cola in the 1930s, can be carried with minimal effort. Packaging plays a key part in convenience foods such as microwave meals and snacks, juice drinks in small, aseptic packages, and single-serving portions of frozen entrées and vegetables.

A growing number of firms are providing increased consumer utility with packages designed for reuse. Peanut butter jars and jelly jars have long been used as drinking glasses. Bubble bath can be purchased in plastic bottles shaped like animals and suitable for bathtub play. Packaging is a major component in Avon's overall marketing strategy. The firm's decorative reusable bottles have even become collectibles.

Like brand names, packages should evoke the product's image and communicate its value. Colors such as black, gold, and maroon and design elements such as borders and crests help promote a product's premium image.[41] The original white package for Breyer's ice cream was redesigned with a black background to promote an upscale, contemporary image that would appeal to premium ice cream buyers.[42] Similarly, Seagram Beverage Company chose a distinctive black-and-gold label for its Golden Wine Cooler. The product is positioned as a sophisticated drink and is targeted at 25-to-49-year-olds rather than the 21-to-35-year-olds at which other coolers are aimed.[43]

Cost-Effective Packaging

Although packaging must perform a number of functions for the producer, marketer, and consumer, it must do so at a reasonable cost. Packaging currently represents the single largest item in the cost of producing a can of beer. It also accounts for 55 percent of the total cost of the single-serving packets of sugar found in restaurants.[44]

Designing a cost-effective package was a major decision facing All American Gourmet Company when it launched its line of Budget Gourmet frozen dinner entrées. Higher-priced frozen dinners such as Le Menu are packaged in expensive boxes, and the food is presented in domed plastic containers. To keep its product in the budget range without sacrificing the quality of the food, All American had to develop an inexpensive package. It designed a sturdy, polyester-coated cardboard container that can be used in both conventional and microwave ovens. All American estimates that the package is 30 to 40 percent cheaper than traditional frozen dinner packaging, allowing the firm to keep Budget Gourmet dinners priced at $1.69. According to the firm's marketing director, consumers understand that the package, not lack of quality, is the reason they pay less. Consumer acceptance of the product seems to back the claim, as Budget Gourmet captured 13.4 percent of the $2.5 billion frozen entrée market within three years of its launch.[45]

The Metric System

U.S. marketers are increasingly adopting the metric measurement system in their packaging and product development decisions. Most soft drinks now come in metric-size containers as a substitute for pints and quarts. Many canned and packaged foods list metric equivalents to ounces and pounds on their labels. General Motors and Ford now design and manufacture their cars to metric specifications alone. One survey found that 34 percent of all new products were designed in metrics, while 16 percent of the firms studied reported losing some sales because they did not offer a metric product.[46]

U.S. marketers must make the switch to metrics if they are to compete in the world marketplace. The United States and Burma are the only countries in the world that have not either adopted metrics or mandated its future adoption. Such firms as Caterpillar Tractor, John Deere, Navistar, and IBM have been using metrics for years in their foreign trade. The switch to metrics should increase export sales of small U.S. firms that cannot afford to produce two sets of products for different markets.

Labeling

Although in the past the label often was a separate item that was applied to the package, today it is an integral part of most plastic packages. Labels perform both promotional and informational functions. In most instances, a **label** contains the brand name or symbol, the name and address of the manufacturer or distributor, the product composition and size, and recommended uses for the product.

Consumer confusion and dissatisfaction over such incomprehensible descriptions as "giant economy size," "king size," and "family size" led to passage of the Fair Packaging and Labeling Act in 1966. The act requires that a label offer adequate information concerning the package contents and that a package design facilitate value comparisons among competitive products.

Food and Drug Administration regulations require that the nutritional contents be listed on the label of any food product to which a nutrient has been added or for which a nutritional claim has been made. Figure 9.8 shows a label listing nutritional ingredients.

Voluntary packaging and labeling standards have also been developed in a number of industries. As a result, the number of toothpaste sizes was reduced from 57 to 5 and the number of dry detergent sizes from 25 to 6. In other industries, such as drugs, food, fur, and clothing, federal legislation has been enacted to force companies to provide information and prevent misleading branding. Marketing managers in such industries must be fully acquainted with these laws and design packages and labels to comply with them.

Universal Product Code　The Universal Product Code designation is another very important part of a label or package. Figure 9.8 shows the zebra-stripe UPC on the Ragu spaghetti sauce label. In other cases, the code lines are printed right into the package, such as on a can of Tab.

The **Universal Product Code (UPC),** introduced in 1974 as a method for cutting expenses in the supermarket industry, is a code read by optical scan-

label
Descriptive part of a product's package, listing brand name or symbol, name and address of manufacturer or distributor, ingredients, size or quantity of product, and/or recommended uses, directions, or serving suggestions.

Universal Product Code (UPC)
Special code on packages read by optical scanners.

Figure 9.8
Product Label Listing Nutritional Ingredients and Displaying the UPC code

Source: Courtesy of Chesebrough-Pond's Incorporated.

ners that print the item and its price on the cash register receipt. Virtually all packaged grocery items contain the UPC lines. While UPC scanners are costly, they permit considerable labor savings and improved inventory control. The Universal Product Code is also a major asset for marketing research. For example, some marketing research companies are providing consumer test participants with hand-held wands capable of reading UPC codes, which the participants use to record their purchases at home.[47]

But despite its advantages, UPC faces obstacles. The most serious is some localities' specific requirement of individually priced items, which negates the labor-saving advantage of UPC scanners. Overall, however, the Universal Product Code will likely play an even greater role in product management in the coming decade.

Customer Service

The term **customer service** simply refers to the manner in which marketers deal with their customers. Sometimes these dealings are less effective than they should be. Many people have noted that customer service has declined considerably in recent years. Complaints about rude personnel, schedulers who refuse to specify delivery times, long lines at banks, and shoddy repairs are too frequent for an otherwise consumer-oriented society. As a result, many marketers now believe that customer service may become the primary competitive battlefield.

Like branding and packaging, customer service is a crucial element of overall product strategy. It is as important to service marketers as it is to goods marketers and is a major enhancer of competitiveness. Consider the case of the Stouffer Madison Hotel in Seattle. Thousands of Japanese businesspeople come through Seattle on their way to or from Japan; in fact, the Stouffer Madison handles about 480 Japanese guests each month. Hence, in order to get a competitive edge over other Seattle hotels, the Stouffer Madison began offering

customer service
Manner in which marketers treat their customers.

Figure 9.9
Effective Customer Relations in Action

COMMAND AIRWAYS INC.
DUTCHESS COUNTY AIRPORT
WAPPINGERS FALLS, NEW YORK 12590 (914) 462-6100 TELEX 289371 COMD UR

January 21, 1985

Mr. David Kemp
176 West 87th Street
New York, NY 10024

Dear Mr. Kemp:

Clearly we screwed up. Please accept our apologies.

Attached is a check for $168.00, which represents a full refund.

Again, please accept our apologies.

Sincerely,

Kingsley G. Morse,
President

KGM:nj
Enclosure

Source: Courtesy of Command Airways Inc.

traditional Japanese breakfasts, including dried seaweed, fermented soybeans, fish and raw eggs, rice, pickles, and green tea.[48] The breakfasts give the hotel a major marketing advantage in a highly competitive marketplace.

Components of Customer Service

There are four major components of customer service: customer relations, delivery, repair service, and warranties. Most aspects of customer service can be placed in one of these categories.

Customer Relations Marketers must maintain good interpersonal relationships with their customers. The friendliness of customer contact people such as bank tellers, flight attendants, and retail sales personnel is a major factor in one's perception of customer service. Handling of customer complaints is one aspect of good customer relations. Figure 9.9 shows how one firm effectively dealt with a complaint.

Delivery At Domino's Pizza, delivery is the key to success or failure in the area of customer service. As a result, Domino's management goes to considerable effort to ensure that its drivers meet the 30-minute guaranteed delivery: If a pizza is delivered in over 30 minutes, the customer is given $3 off; if it leaves the store in over 30 minutes, it is free. Phil Bressler, the regional district manager for 18 Baltimore-area Domino's restaurants, takes the delivery guarantee so seriously that he once sent out 330 free pizzas on a snowy evening even though corporate policy allowed him to lift the 30-minute guarantee in the event of bad weather.[49]

Repair Service   Late or poorly done repairs are a source of many customer service complaints. But companies such as Dallas's Sewell Village Cadillac prove that this does not have to be. When a customer buys a Cadillac from Sewell Village, he or she is assigned a personal service adviser for the life of the car. The adviser handles all the aspects of getting the car serviced, even providing 24-hour emergency road service if necessary. In addition, the dealership has a fleet of 150 loaner cars with which to serve its customers.[50]

Warranties   An important feature of many products is the **warranty**—the guarantee to the buyer that the manufacturer or service provider will replace or refund the product's purchase price if it proves defective during a specified time period. Warranties increase consumer purchase confidence and often represent an important means by which to stimulate demand.

A warranty trend has permeated many businesses in recent years, including airlines, hotel chains, car manufacturers, computer firms, banks, and appliance companies. General Electric has made its "Satisfaction Guaranteed" program a major part of its competitive strategy. The program, which promises buyers of major appliances a refund or replacement if they are not satisfied within 90 days after purchase, is heavily promoted through ads such as the one in Figure 9.10.[51]

warranty
Guarantee to the buyer that the manufacturer will replace a product or refund its purchase price if the product proves defective during a specified time period.

Product Safety

If a product is to fulfill its mission of satisfying consumer needs, it must, above all, be safe. Manufacturers must design their products to protect users. Packaging plays an important role in product safety. Aspirin bottle tops have been made childproof (and virtually parentproof) by St. Joseph's and Bayer since 1968. This safety feature is estimated to have reduced by two-thirds the number of children under five years of age who accidentally swallow overdoses of aspirin.

Prominently placed safety warnings on the labels of such potentially hazardous products as cleaning fluids and drain cleaners inform users of the dangers of these products and urge them to store them out of the reach of children. Changes in product design have reduced the hazards involved in the use of such products as lawn mowers, hedge trimmers, and toys.

Consumer Product Safety Commission

Federal and state legislation have long played a major role in promoting product safety. Many of the piecemeal federal laws passed over a 50-year period were unified by the Consumer Product Safety Act of 1972, which created a powerful regulatory agency—the Consumer Product Safety Commission (CPSC). The agency has assumed jurisdiction over every consumer product except food, automobiles, and a few other products already regulated by other agencies. The

Figure 9.10
General Electric's Guarantee Program

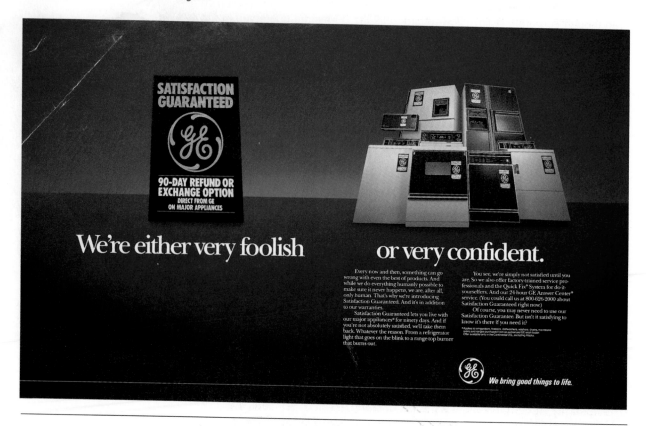

Source: Courtesy of General Electric Company.

CPSC has the authority to ban products without a court hearing, order the recall or redesign of products, and inspect production facilities. It can charge managers of accused companies with criminal offenses.

The Concept of Product Liability

product liability
Concept that manufacturers and marketers are responsible for injuries and damages caused by their products.

Product liability refers to the concept that manufacturers and marketers are responsible for injuries and damages caused by their products. There has been a tremendous increase in product liability suits in recent years. Although many such claims are settled out of court, others are decided by juries, who sometimes have awarded multimillion-dollar settlements.

Not only have marketers stepped up efforts to ensure product safety; product liability insurance has become an essential ingredient in any new or existing product strategy. Premiums for this insurance have risen alarmingly, and in some cases coverage is almost impossible to obtain. A Detroit producer of components for pleasure boats discovered that its liability insurance premiums had increased from $2,500 to $160,000 in a two-year period even though the insurance company had never paid a claim on the firm's behalf.

Efforts are underway in several states to exempt companies from liability for injuries or property loss resulting from misuse of the products or from customer negligence. Such an exemption would have protected the retailer who paid damages to two men hurt by a lawn mower that they had lifted off the ground to trim a hedge.

CPSC activities and the increased number of liability claims have prompted companies to improve their safety standards voluntarily. For many companies, safety has become a vital ingredient of product strategy.

Summary of Chapter Objectives

1. Identify the major product mix decisions that marketers must make.
A product mix is the assortment of product lines and individual offerings available from a marketer. Its two primary components are product line (a series of related products) and individual offerings (single products). Product mixes are assessed in terms of length, width, and depth of assortment. Length refers to the number of products in the mix. Width means the number of product lines the firm offers. Depth refers to variations of each product in the mix.

2. Explain why most firms develop a line of related products rather than a single product. Firms usually produce several related products rather than single products to achieve the objectives of growth, optimal use of company resources, and increased company importance in the market, and to exploit the product life cycle.

3. Identify alternative new-product development strategies and the determinants of each strategy's success. Many new-product ideas are required in order to produce one commercially successful product. The success of a new product depends on a host of factors and can result from four alternative product development strategies. A product improvement strategy refers to the modification of existing products to better match consumer needs. The finding of new markets for established products is called a market development strategy. The introduction of new products into established or identifiable markets is referred to as a product development strategy. The creation of new products for new markets is called a product diversification strategy.

4. Explain the various organizational structures for new-product development. New-product organizational responsibility in most large firms is assigned to new-product committees, new-product departments, product managers, or venture teams. New-product committees are review committees for new-product ideas. New-product departments are organizational units charged with the actual development of new products. Individuals given the responsibility for determining marketing strategies for a product, brand, or product line are called product managers. Venture teams are temporary groups set up to develop a specific product or product line.

5. List the stages in the new-product development process. New-product ideas evolve through six stages on the way to their market introduction: idea generation, screening, business analysis, product development, testing, and commercialization.

6. Explain the roles of brands, brand names, and trademarks in a marketing strategy. A brand is a name, term, sign, symbol, design, or some combination used to identify the products of one firm and differentiate them from competitive offerings. A brand name is the name part of a brand. A trademark is a brand that has been given legal protection that is granted exclusively to its owner. A trademark includes both the brand's pictorial design and the brand name.

7. Describe the major functions of the package. Modern packaging is designed to protect against damage, spoilage, and pilferage; to assist in marketing the product; and to be cost effective.

8. Explain the nature of customer service and list its major components. Customer service refers to the manner in which marketers deal with their customers. It has become a major factor in the competitive environment of the late 1980s. The major components of customer service are customer relations, delivery, repair service, and warranties.

9. Outline the functions of the Consumer Product Safety Commission and the concept of product liability. Product safety has become an increasingly important component of the total product concept. It has evolved through voluntary attempts by product designers to reduce hazards, through various pieces of legislation, and through the establishment of the Consumer Product Safety Commission. The CPSC was established by the Consumer Product Safety Act of 1972. It has jurisdiction over every consumer product except food, automobiles, and a few other products already regulated by other agencies. It can ban products without a court hearing, order the recall or redesign of products, inspect production facilities, and charge violators of its rules with criminal offenses. The concept of product liability refers to the producer's or marketer's legal responsibility for injuries or damages caused by a defective product. It is becoming an increasingly important factor in contemporary marketing.

Key Terms

product mix	brand preference
product line	brand insistence
cannibalizing	brand extension
line extension	family brand
product positioning	individual brand
product manager	manufacturer's (national) brand
venture team	private brand
concept testing	generic product
test marketing	label
brand	Universal Product Code (UPC)
brand name	customer service
trademark	warranty
generic name	product liability
brand recognition	

Review Questions

1. What is meant by a *product mix?* How is the concept used in making effective marketing decisions?

2. Why do most business firms market a line of related products rather than a single product?

3. Outline the alternative organizational structures for new-product development.

4. Identify the steps in the new-product development process.

5. What is the chief purpose of test marketing? What potential problems does it involve?

6. List the characteristics of an effective brand name. Illustrate each characteristic with an appropriate brand name.

7. Identify and briefly explain each of the three stages of brand loyalty.

8. What are the objectives of modern packaging?

9. Why is customer service becoming an increasingly important aspect of product strategy?

10. Explain the chief functions of the Consumer Product Safety Commission. What steps can it take to protect consumers from defective and hazardous products?

Discussion Questions

1. The Coca-Cola Company's line of colas includes Coke, Coca-Cola Classic, Diet Coke, Caffeine Free Diet Coke, Caffeine Free Coke, Cherry Coke, and Diet Cherry Coke. Relate Coca-Cola's lineup of colas to the concept of product mix. What generalizations can you make about the company's product strategies? Discuss.

2. General Foods gave up Lean Strips, a textured vegetable-protein strip designed as a bacon substitute, after eight years of test marketing. Lean Strips sold well when bacon prices were high but poorly when they dropped. General Foods hoped to offer a protein-analog product line that included Crispy Strips, a snack and salad-dressing item. Consumers liked the taste of Crispy Strips, but it was too expensive for repeat purchases, and the product was abandoned before Lean Strips' demise. General Foods said that it would concentrate on new-product categories rather than on individual items such as Lean Strips. What can be learned from General Foods' experience with Lean Strips?

3. Selchow & Righter Co. followed the initial success of its Trivial Pursuit game with the Baby Boomer, Silver Screen, All-Star Sports, Genus II, RPM, and Young Players editions. It also developed special editions for dozens of foreign countries. What type of product development strategy did it employ for Trivial Pursuit?

4. Every year, MarketSource Corp. distributes 1.2 million free Campus Pacs to students at 400 colleges and universities. In addition, 100,000 Pacs are delivered through the top 50 schools with large black and Hispanic enrollments. Describe how a marketer could utilize such distributions in the new-product development and introduction process.

5. The new package for General Mills' Count Chocula cereal had been approved by the responsible company officials and the firm's advertising agency. The new package designs featured Dracula wearing a pendant that resembled the Star of David. Jewish consumers were quick to complain, and General Mills hastily deleted the pendant from its package design.[52] What packaging lessons can be learned from this experience?

VIDEO CASE 9

Robert Mondavi

For decades, most Americans thought of wine as either an exotic elixir or something similar to grape juice in a jug. But in the last 20 years, American drinking habits have changed to the point where more than $7 billion worth of wine is sold in the United States each year. While the market has not achieved the 6 to 8 percent annual growth rate that was predicted for the 1980s, its current size is an impressive tribute to the influence of marketing.

To broaden the beverage's appeal, wine marketers had to alter deeply embedded attitudes. The efforts of a few benefitted the industry as a whole. Indeed, until the late 1970s, most wineries portrayed wine as an upscale "tuxedo" drink, one that was not for everyone. The shift in marketing strategies started in 1967, when the Robert Mondavi Winery introduced Fume Blanc.

Fume Blanc, a white wine, was a risky proposition since white wines accounted for less than one fourth of total U.S. wine sales when it was introduced. It is also made from Sauvignon grapes, and Sauvignon wines have traditionally sold poorly in the U.S. market. Robert Mondavi, the firm's founder, decided to go ahead with Fume Blanc because he sensed that Americans were ready for a dry white wine. Still, the name posed a problem.

"I didn't want to call it Sauvignon Blanc, because I know the American people didn't seem to care for the name," said Mondavi. "I had to have something with more appeal."

Marketing provided the breakthrough that Mondavi sought. He thought of Blanc Fume, a long-established French Sauvignon wine. Mondavi simply reversed the name, and Fume Blanc went on to become the second best-selling white wine in California. "The only mistake I made was in not copyrighting the name," said Mondavi, who has since seen a number of wineries introduce their own Fume Blancs.

White wine sales in general have surged, rising from a 25 percent market share in 1970 to a majority market share today. Mondavi wines have shared in this success; the Mondavi winery, opened in 1966, is now one of America's 20 largest wineries.

Mondavi's marketing prowess is considered the best in the wine industry; a high compliment since Ernest Gallo, of the dominant E & J Gallo Winery, is regarded as a marketing genius. But the Mondavi Winery does not advertise. Instead, Mondavi has made a commitment to educate consumers about wine, a complete departure from the former practice of putting wine on the shelf and letting the consumers educate themselves, if they choose.

Robert Mondavi cannot compete head-to-head with Gallo, and it does not attempt to. "We can't be all things to all people," says Michael Mondavi, Robert's son and company president. "The goal is to select a specific niche, then be the best in that niche."

Mondavi's niche is the upper 5 percent of the wine drinking market, which represents the opinion leaders for the rest of the market. No expense is spared to ensure that the wines are of superior quality. Unlike many wineries, Mondavi does not specify a production cost figure for each barrel. This gives Robert's other son and winemaster Tim Mondavi room to make the best wine that he can. The firm also limits its product line and maintains strict control of the product quality. Mondavi Winery uses advanced lab techniques and daily tests of each batch of wine to ensure proper levels of acidity, sugar, and fermentation.

The winery employs some 55 people nationwide to conduct seminars and wine-tasting events, and to meet with wine distributors. But the big push comes at the winery itself. Robert Mondavi designed it for entertaining, and he makes sure the entertainment includes extensive discourses on wine. Every year some 300,000 people visit the vineyards, taking a required tour of the winery. The winery courtyard hosts six jazz concerts a year, starring jazz greats such as Ella Fitzgerald. The Mondavis host a cooking seminar, monthly art shows, and winemaking demonstrations.

Most wineries advertise extensively, spending millions on radio, television, and print ads, although ads for alcohol are increasingly controversial. Others focus on product improvements, challenging Mondavi for innovative supremacy.

For instance, the Benmarl Winery started its Society of Winemakers in 1971. Its wines are given a birth certificate, and the labels are personalized for its members. The concept has worked so well that other wineries have copied it, and some have taken it a step farther, selling the production of particular vines to customers. As another example, St. Julian's, a Michigan winery, operates a chain of stores along an interstate highway, just one of many regional wineries to play to regional ties.

The label of a wine is emphasized by marketers, who discovered that wine drinkers frequently choose wines because of a particularly attractive label. Many wineries invest significant amounts of money in label design.

Even the smallest wineries now issue newsletters, informing wine aficionados and other people included on their mailing lists of their product offerings and the prices of each product and vintage year. Traditionally, wineries were not aggressive marketers, but when Coca-Cola acquired Wine Spectrum in the late 1970s, it brought "cola wars" marketing with it, and consumers responded to the new advertisements. Other wineries took notice, and the big companies, such as Almaden, Inglenook (Heublein), and Paul Masson (Seagrams) are now aggressive marketers.

Mondavi remains a marketing leader; it was the first winery to sell futures on its wine production. Mondavi also introduced a joint venture with the famed French winery Rothschild — Opus One, which debuted at more than $50 a bottle, but sold out rapidly.

Sources: "Now, Chateau Cash Flow," *Time* (June 1, 1987), p. 55; *Fortune* (January 21, 1985), p. 84; *Advertising Age* (January 16, 1984), Special Report on Wine Marketing, M31–M43; Ruth Stroud, "Flat Sales Force Winery Changes," *Advertising Age* (March 12, 1984), p. 3; Eunice Fried, "Sauvignon Blanc," *Black Enterprise* (August 1984), p. 78.

Questions

1. Relate the introduction of Robert Mondavi Fume Blanc wine to the alternative development strategies shown in Figure 9.2. Which type of strategy was used by the winery?

2. What role has the introduction of new products played in the growth of the Robert Mondavi Winery?

3. Do you agree with the marketing strategy employed by Robert Mondavi? What changes might you make?

4. Robert Mondavi limits the kinds of wine it produces to high quality varieties. What are the advantages and disadvantages of this practice?

COMPUTER APPLICATIONS

In Chapter 5, three approaches to making choices from among alternatives were described. The *overall scoring method* involves scoring or ranking each of the evaluative criteria (or decision factors) used in choosing among alternatives and then selecting the alternative with the highest total score. The *weighted scoring method* involves assigning different weights to the various decision factors according to the decision maker's perception of their relative importance; the weighted scores are then totaled and the alternative with the highest score selected. Finally, the *minimum-score method* establishes a minimum score for one or more decision factors; any alternative with a score below this specified minimum is rejected regardless of its overall score. The minimum-score method can be used in conjunction with either of the other two approaches.

These approaches are described in detail on page 198. While they are used in making consumer purchase decisions, as discussed in Chapter 5, they can also be used to quantify the alternatives in product strategy decisions ranging from selection of package design to choice of brand name.

Directions: Use menu item 5 titled "Evaluation of Alternatives" to solve each of the following problems.

Problem 1   Omaha Industries is trying to pick one of three line extensions for its line of batteries. The alternatives are named Sparky, Big Lite, and Light Forever. Management is evaluating these options on the basis of compatibility with the existing line, production lead time, and potential profitability. The product development group at Omaha Industries has rated each alternative on a system of 3 (excellent), 2 (good), and 1 (fair). The ratings are as follows:

Evoked-Set Alternatives	Evaluative Criteria: Decision Factors		
	(A) Compatibility	(B) Production Lead Time	(C) Profitability
1. Sparky	1	2	3
2. Big Lite	1	3	2
3. Light Forever	2	3	2

a. Which line extension should Omaha Industries select using the overall scoring method?
b. Suppose management considers potential profitability 200 percent more important than any other evaluative factor. Which line extension will it select?
c. Suppose that using the overall scoring method management will not accept any line extension rated less than "good" on any factor. Which line extension will it select?

Problem 2   Toledo Enterprises is considering one of three package designs for its electronic components. It has identified three major factors to consider in this decision: safety, promotional appeal, and ease of storage. Toledo's management has scored each package design on a scale of 1 (poor) to 5 (excellent) for each decision factor. The scores are as follows:

Evoked-Set Alternatives	Evaluative Criteria: Decision Factors		
	(A) Safety	(B) Promotional Appeal	(C) Ease of Storage
Package design 1	4	2	2
Package design 2	2	5	2
Package design 3	5	1	4

a. Which package design would the company select using the overall scoring method?

b. Suppose management considers safety 100 percent more important than any other decision factor. Which package design will it select?

c. Suppose that using the overall scoring method management also decides not to accept any package design that scored less than 2 on any factor. Which package design will it select?

d. Would your response to question c change if management used the weighted scoring method?

Problem 3   Regina Taylor, marketing vice-president at an Elmira, New York, toy company, must select a brand name for use on a new toy line targeted at preschool children. All five finalists, coded A, B, C, D, and E to maintain their secrecy, have been cleared by the firm's legal department. Taylor's marketing research department has concluded that the marketing impact of the brand names will vary among the parties involved in the toy-buying decision: parents, grandparents, and the children themselves. Each brand name has been evaluated for each group on a five-point scale ranging from excellent (5) to unacceptable (1). The rankings are as follows:

Evoked-Set Alternatives	Evaluative Criteria: Decision Factors		
	(A) Impact with Grandparents	(B) Impact with Parents	(C) Impact with Children
1. Brand A	4	4	3
2. Brand B	4	2	5
3. Brand C	2	5	2
4. Brand D	3	3	4
5. Brand E	5	5	2

a. Which brand name would be selected using the overall scoring method?

b. Suppose Taylor considers the brand name's marketing impact with children to be 200 percent more important than its impact with parents and grandparents. Which brand name should she select?

c. Suppose that using the overall scoring method Taylor decides that she will not accept a brand name rated less than 3 by any of the parties who might be involved in a purchase decision. Which brand name should she select?

d. Would Taylor's decision in question c change if she used the weighted scoring method?

Problem 4   Miguel Fernandez, director of marketing at San Antonio Industries, wants to add a line extension to his firm's offering of toothbrushes. Various toothbrush configurations are under consideration; these are labeled option 1, 2, 3,

4, and 5. Five factors will be used to evaluate each option: profitability, production lead time, compatibility with the existing product line, adaptability to the standard San Antonio Industries in-store display, and retailer's margin. Fernandez has rated each possible line extension by each variable. His scoring system ranges from 1 (poor) to 5 (excellent). The specific scores are as follows:

Evoked-Set Alternatives	Evaluative Criteria: Decision Factors				
	(A) Profitability	(B) Production Lead Time	(C) Compatibility	(D) Adaptability	(E) Retail Margin
Option 1	2	4	3	2	2
Option 2	5	5	5	2	3
Option 3	3	3	3	3	3
Option 4	3	3	4	3	3
Option 5	5	2	2	5	5

a. Which line extension option should Fernandez select using the overall scoring method?

b. Suppose Fernandez decides to assign a weight of 400 percent more to retail margin than to production lead time due to the importance of retailers' acceptance of the new toothbrush line. In addition, he decides to weight adaptability as 300 percent more important than production lead time, profitability as 200 percent more important than production lead time, and compatibility with the existing product line as 100 percent more important than production lead time. Which line extension option should he select?

c. Suppose that using the overall scoring method Fernandez decides to reject any option rated less than 3 on any factor. Which line extension option will he select?

d. Would your response to question c change if Fernandez decided to use the weighted scoring method in making his selection?

Problem 5   Ray Langston, marketing director of a St. Louis garden tool manufacturer, is in the process of choosing one of five new retail display racks. Langston is considering four major factors: promotional appeal, maximum display inventory, cost, and convenient size. He has scored each display design on a scale ranging from 1 (poor) to 5 (excellent) for each decision factor. Langston's ratings are as follows:

Evoked-Set Alternatives	Evaluative Criteria: Decision Factors			
	(A) Promotional Appeal	(B) Maximum Inventory	(C) Cost	(D) Convenient Size
Display rack 1	5	3	3	4
Display rack 2	4	4	1	5
Display rack 3	3	5	5	2
Display rack 4	3	3	5	3
Display rack 5	5	5	1	5

a. Which display will Langston select if he uses the overall scoring method?

b. Suppose Langston considers convenient size as the least important of the four decision factors. Promotional appeal and maximum inventory are considered as 100 percent more important than convenient size and cost 400 percent more important than convenient size. Which display rack should Langston select if he applies these weights to the various decision factors?

c. Suppose that using the overall scoring method Langston also decides that he will not accept any display rack with less than a 3 rating on any decision factor. Which display should he select?

d. Would your response to question c change if Langston decided to use the weighted scoring method in making his decision?

Pricing Strategy

10 Price Determination

Chapter Objectives

1. To outline the legal constraints on pricing.

2. To identify the major categories of pricing objectives.

3. To explain the concept of elasticity and the determinants of the degree of price elasticity for a product or service.

4. To list the practical problems involved in applying price theory concepts to actual pricing decisions.

5. To explain the major cost-plus approaches to price setting.

6. To list the major advantages and shortcomings of using breakeven analysis in pricing decisions.

7. To explain the superiority of modified breakeven analysis over the basic breakeven model.

I t's a question heard throughout the world. In France, the words are *Combien est-ce?* In Germany, it is stated *Wieviel kostet es?* Italians phrase it *Quanto costa?* Russians ask, *Skol'ko eto stoit?* In every instance, though, the question is the same: How much does it cost?

This question weighed heavily on John Whitney Payson's mind as he waited for the day when Sotheby's would auction Vincent Van Gogh's masterpiece *Irises.* Certainly there was no clue to the painting's worth from the sales that occurred during Van Gogh's lifetime. The tormented artist lived almost exclusively on funds provided by his devoted brother Theo and, in fact, sold only one painting in his life—*The Red Vineyard,* for about $80. Less than a year after Van Gogh painted *Irises* in the garden of the mental asylum in Saint-Rémy, he took his own life.

Payson did have concrete information on the original purchase price. His mother—lumber, banking, and real estate heiress Joan Whitney Payson—acquired the work in 1947 for $84,000. Her son grew up with the painting. "I remember it well in my mother's apartment. It was in the living room on a wall facing Fifth Avenue over an unused fireplace. It

was practically alive with the light hitting it. I used to go into the living room and sit and look at it and see what was going on inside of it. It has movement; you can feel the irises moving in the wind. It mesmerized me."

Payson inherited the painting when his mother died in 1975 and decided to have it appraised for insurance purposes. The appraised value was less than $1 million. He had planned to eventually donate the work to Westbrook College in his hometown of Portland, Maine, but changes in the tax laws forced him to modify his plan. He would sell the work and donate 20 percent of the proceeds to Westbrook.

Sotheby's officials were delighted at Payson's decision to consign the painting to them for auction. Just eight months earlier, the firm's chief competitor, Christie's, had auctioned Van Gogh's *Sunflowers* for an unprecedented $39.9 million. The combination of collectors' interest in Van Gogh's tragic life and the artist's unique style of bright colors and thick, curvy brushstrokes had pushed the prices of his works to previously unheard-of levels.

The payoff for the auction house would be considerable, and it was directly related to the price of the work. Sotheby's charges the buyer a 10

percent premium, and the seller pays a 10 percent commission.

The combination of Van Gogh's reputation, media coverage of the event, and Sotheby's marketing efforts produced a standing-room-only crowd at the auction company's New York showroom. When the gavel came down and the auctioneer cried "Sold!" the price of *Irises* had been set: An anonymous telephone bidder had agreed to buy the 1889 masterpiece for $53.9 million.[1]

Photo source: Courtesy of Kee-Byrd Productions, Incorporated. Art Director: Shelly Tannenbaum. Concept: Norman I. Newman.

Chapter Overview

In Chapters 8 and 9, we examined the first element of a firm's marketing mix: the determination of the goods and services to be offered to the target market. The second variable — price — is the subject of both this and the following chapter. Marketers' decisions in setting the price for a product or service are influenced by dozens of factors, including marketing objectives, consumer demand, costs, competition, profit requirements of marketing intermediaries, and government regulations.

Although each marketing mix variable is examined in considerable detail in separate sections of the text, all are clearly interrelated. The decision by Japan's Seiko Time Corporation to have its product compete directly with Rolex, Piaget, Audemars-Piguet, and other watches in the higher-price market involved every marketing mix variable: product, pricing, distribution, and promotion. As the advertisement in Figure 10.1 suggests, for $75 one buys a watch and for

Figure 10.1

Combining Product, Price, Distribution, and Promotion to Create a High-Quality Image

Source: Courtesy of Seiko Time Corporation.

$2,000 one buys a "timepiece." While the standard Seiko products are priced at less than $500, the new Jean Lassale brand offerings range in price from $900 to $35,000. Seiko marketers decided to acquire the "borrowed European authority" of the Swiss names by purchasing them from their Swiss manufacturer.[2] Print advertising in such upscale magazines as *The New Yorker, Architectural Digest,* and *Connoisseur* was designed to enhance the image of Jean Lassale. A beautiful, high-quality solid-gold product marketed in exclusive retail outlets completed the marketing mix.

The starting point for examining pricing strategy is to understand the meaning of the term *price.* As the story of the auction of *Irises* illustrates, **price** is the exchange value of a good or service, and the value of an item is what it can be exchanged for in the marketplace. In earlier times, the price of an acre of land might have been 20 bushels of wheat, 3 head of cattle, or 1 boat. When the barter process was abandoned in favor of a monetary system, *price* came to mean the amount of funds required to purchase an item. As one writer has pointed out, contemporary society uses a number of names to refer to price:

Price is all around us. You pay rent *for your apartment,* tuition *for your education, and a* fee *to your physician or dentist.*

price
Exchange value of a good or service.

The airline, railway, taxi, and bus companies charge you a fare; *the local utilities call their price a* rate; *and the local bank charges* interest *for the money you borrow.*

The price for driving your car on Florida's Sunshine Parkway is a toll, *and the company that insures your car charges you a* premium.

The guest lecturer charges an honorarium *to tell you about a government official who took a* bribe *to help a shady character steal* dues *collected by a trade association.*

Clubs or societies to which you belong may make a special assessment *to pay unusual expenses. Your regular lawyer may ask for a* retainer *to cover her services.*

The "price" of an executive is a salary; *the price of a salesperson may be a* commission; *and the price of a worker is a* wage.

Finally, although economists would disagree, many of us feel that income taxes *are the price we pay for the privilege of making money!*[3]

Determination of profitable and justifiable prices results from considering such factors as pricing objectives and alternative approaches to setting prices. These topics are the subject of this chapter. Chapter 11 focuses on management of the pricing function and discusses pricing strategies, price-quality relationships, and pricing in both the industrial and public sectors.

Legal Constraints in Pricing

Pricing decisions are subject to a variety of legal constraints at both the federal and state levels. Pricing is also regulated by the general constraints of U.S. antitrust legislation (outlined in Chapter 2). Some of the most important pricing legislation is discussed in the following sections.

Robinson-Patman Act

The **Robinson-Patman Act** (1936) typifies Depression-era legislation. Known in some circles as the *Anti-A&P Act,* it was inspired by price competition from the developing grocery store chains—in fact, the original draft was prepared by the United States Wholesale Grocers Association. The country was in the midst of the Depression, and legislative interest was primarily in saving jobs. The developing chain stores were seen as a threat to traditional retailing and employment, and this act was a government effort designed to counteract it.

Robinson-Patman Act
Federal legislation prohibiting price discrimination that is not based on a cost differential; also prohibits selling at an unreasonably low price to eliminate competition.

The Robinson-Patman Act, which technically was an amendment to the Clayton Act, prohibits price discrimination in sales to wholesalers, retailers, and other producers that is not based on cost differentials. It also disallows selling at an unreasonably low price in order to eliminate competition. The Clayton Act had applied only to price discrimination by geographic area, which injured local sellers. The rationale for the Robinson-Patman legislation was that the chain stores might be able to secure supplier volume discounts that were unavailable to small, independent stores.

The major defenses against charges of price discrimination are that price differentials are used to meet competitors' prices and that they are justified by cost differences. When a firm asserts that price differentials are used in good faith to meet competition, the logical question is "What constitutes good-faith pricing behavior?" The answer depends on the particular situation.

When cost differentials are claimed as a defense, the price differences must not exceed the cost differences resulting from selling to various classes of buyers. A major problem with this defense is that of justifying the differences; indeed, many authorities consider this one of the most confusing areas in the Robinson-Patman Act.

The varying interpretations of the act certainly qualify it as one of the vaguest marketing laws.[4] For the most part, charges brought under the act are handled on an individual basis. Therefore, marketers must continually evaluate their pricing actions to avoid potential Robinson-Patman violations.

Unfair-Trade Laws

unfair-trade laws
State laws requiring sellers to maintain minimum prices for comparable merchandise.

Unfair-trade laws are state laws requiring sellers to maintain minimum prices for comparable merchandise. Enacted in the 1930s, these laws were intended to protect small specialty shops, such as dairy stores, from the loss-leader pricing used by chain stores for some products. Such stores might sell a certain product below cost to attract customers. Typically a state law would set retail price floors at cost plus some modest markup. Although most of these laws remain on the books, they have become less important in recent years. However, one area in which they are still enforced is in the production and marketing of milk.[5]

Fair-Trade Laws

fair-trade laws
Statutes enacted in most states that permitted manufacturers to stipulate a minimum retail price for a product.

Fair trade is a concept that has affected pricing decisions for decades. **Fair-trade laws** permit manufacturers to stipulate minimum retail prices for products and to require their retail dealers to sign contracts agreeing to abide by these prices.[6]

The basic argument behind this legislation is that a product's image, which is implied by its price, is a property right of the manufacturer, which should have the authority to protect its asset by requiring retailers to maintain a minimum price. Fair-trade legislation can be traced to lobbying by organizations of independent retailers who feared chain store growth. The economic mania of the Depression years was clearly reflected in these statutes.

In 1931, California became the first state to enact fair-trade legislation. Most other states soon followed suit; only Missouri, the District of Columbia, Vermont, and Texas failed to adopt such laws.

A U.S. Supreme Court decision holding fair-trade contracts illegal in interstate commerce led to the passage of the *Miller-Tydings Resale Price Maintenance Act* (1937), which exempted interstate fair-trade contracts from compliance with antitrust requirements. The states were thus authorized to keep these laws on their books if they so desired.

Over the years, fair-trade laws declined in importance as discount retailers emerged and price competition became a more important marketing strategy. These laws became invalid with the passage of the *Consumer Goods Pricing Act* (1975), which halted all interstate use of resale price maintenance, an objective long sought by consumer groups.

FOCUS ON ETHICS

General Dynamics Corporation Makes Amends

In 1985 the heat was on General Dynamics Corporation, one of the nation's leading defense contractors. The company was being investigated for allegations of deliberate overbilling on military contracts from about 1978 to 1980. Navy Secretary John F. Lehrman demanded management changes and held up processing some of the contracts, telling the news media that the actions that had led to the investigation were "merely manifestations of an approach, an attitude, that has pervaded their doing business with the government. . . . It isn't the problem of one or two individuals doing the wrong things. It is a pervasive record of corporate policy that we want changed."

Later that year, indictments for fraud were handed down against General Dynamics and four of its executives. Following the indictments, the company was suspended from contracting with the executive branch of government but was given a chance to show that it was cleaning up its act. As a result of Secretary Lehrman's earlier demands, General Dynamics had already begun doing just that.

Besides overhauling management procedures to prevent a recurrence of the problem, General Dynamics introduced a corporate ethics program that is widely considered the most comprehensive in the industry. Overseen by a committee of the firm's board of directors, the program has instituted ethics workshops, all at least two hours long, attended by almost every employee. All workers have access to a hotline to the corporate ethics director where they can get advice on ethical matters or report violations. A steering committee ensures that the company complies with its new policies, which are listed in its 20-page code of ethics. Among the provisions are:

Conflict of interest. Being an investor, director, or officer of a supplier of goods and services to General Dynamics is not strictly forbidden, but it must be disclosed in advance and approved by the company.

Marketing. When illegal or unethical activity is seen as a requirement for getting certain business, the employee must stop pursuing that business as soon as the necessity for such activity becomes apparent.

Marketing. Proposals must be realistic in terms of cost, product performance, and delivery schedule.

Cash. All cash transactions must be recorded in the company's book of accounts and handled so as to prevent even a suspicion of illegal or improper conduct.

Gifts. Receiving or soliciting gifts is expressly prohibited. In addition, employees are not allowed to pursue business through the use of gifts, entertainment, or other favors. In countries in which custom dictates exchanging gifts, the company must provide the gift given and take possession of the gift received.

The federal government was persuaded that General Dynamics was striving to put its house in order, and in 1986 it lifted the restrictions against awarding the company contracts. General Dynamics' ethics hotlines handled 3,646 calls in 1986, but only 10 percent of these involved possibly illegal activities or ones that could seriously embarrass the company.

Sources: General Dynamics Standards of Business Ethics and Conduct (St. Louis, Mo.: General Dynamics Corporation, 1985). See also "This Industry Leader Means Business," Sales and Marketing Management (May 1987), p. 44, and "Probe Scuttled," Time (June 1, 1987), p. 51.

The Role of Price in the Marketing Mix

Ancient philosophers recognized the importance of price in the functioning of an economic system. Some of their early written accounts refer to attempts to determine a fair or just price. However, their limited understanding of time, place, and possession utilities thwarted such efforts.

Price continues to serve as a means of regulating economic activity. Employment of any or all of the four factors of production—land, capital, human resources, and entrepreneurship—depends on the prices each factor receives. For an individual firm, prices and the corresponding quantities purchased by its customers represent the revenue to be received. Prices, therefore, influence a firm's profit as well as its employment of the factors of production.

How Marketing Executives Rank the Price Variable

A quarter-century ago, marketing professor Jon G. Udell conducted a survey of marketing executives to determine the relative importance of price as an element of their firms' marketing mixes. When the various factors included in the questionnaire were reorganized into the four major mix variables, price was ranked third behind product and promotion and ahead of distribution.[7]

But times have changed. A recent study of marketing executives revealed that price currently ranks as the single most important marketing mix variable.[8] Product planning and management is a close second, and distribution and promotion rank third and fourth, respectively.

Pricing Objectives

Just as price is a component of the total marketing mix, so are pricing objectives a component of the organization's overall objectives. As Chapter 3 explained, marketing objectives represent the outcomes that executives hope to attain. They are based on the overall objectives of the organization. Pricing objectives are also a critical component of the means-end chain extending from the firm's overall aims. The objectives of the firm and the marketing organization provide the basis for developing pricing objectives, which in turn are used to develop and implement the more specific pricing policies and procedures.

A firm's major overall objective may be to become the dominant factor in the domestic market. Its marketing objective might then be maximum sales penetration in each region and the related pricing objective sales maximization. This means-end chain might lead to the adoption of a low-price policy implemented with the highest price discounts to channel members of any firm in the industry.

While pricing objectives vary from firm to firm, they can be classified into four major groups: (1) profitability objectives, (2) volume objectives, (3) meeting competition objectives, and (4) prestige objectives. Profitability objectives include profit maximization and target return goals. Volume objectives can be categorized as either sales maximization or market share goals.

A recent study of U.S. businesses asked marketers to identify their firms' primary and secondary pricing objectives. Meeting competitors' prices was most often mentioned as a primary or secondary pricing objective. This was followed closely by two profitability-oriented objectives: a specified return on investment and particular total profit levels. These two objectives ranked first and second, respectively, as primary pricing objectives.[9] The findings are shown in Table 10.1.

Profitability Objectives

In classical economic theory, the traditional pricing objective has been to maximize profits. The study of microeconomics is based on certain assumptions, namely that buyers and sellers are rational and that rational behavior constitutes an effort to maximize gains and minimize losses. In terms of actual business practice, this means that profit maximization is assumed to be the basic objective of individual firms.

Table 10.1
Primary and Secondary Pricing Objectives of U.S. Firms

Pricing Objective	Percentage of Respondents Ranking the Item[a]		
	As Primary Objective	As Secondary Objective	As Either Primary or Secondary Objective
Profitability Objectives			
Specified rate of return on investment	61%	17%	78%
Specified total profit level	60	17	77
Increased total profits above previous levels	34	38	72
Specified rate of return on sales	48	23	71
Volume Objectives			
Increased market share	31	42	73
Retaining existing market share	31	36	67
Serving selected market segments	27	39	66
Specified market share	16	41	57
Meeting Competition Objectives			
Meeting competitive price level	38	43	81
Prestige Objectives			
Creation of a readily identifiable image for the firm and/or its products	22	41	63

[a]Totals exceed 100 percent because most firms list multiple pricing objectives.

Source: Louis E. Boone and David L. Kurtz, *Pricing Objectives and Practices in American Industry: A Research Report.* All rights reserved.

Although Americans own more cats than dogs (57.8 million versus 49.4 million), the pet food market is so saturated with competitors that canned cat food category growth is only about 6 percent annually. Cat food marketers have decided to focus on single serving convenience by introducing gourmet brands such as Fancy Feast, Friskies PetCare Division, Carnation Company, shown in Figure 10.2. The image of the silver shaded Chinchilla Persian cat nibbling from a crystal bowl is appropriate, since the upscale brands retail for 12 percent more than regular brands. By 1987, gourmet cat food brands such as Fancy Feast and H. J. Heinz's Amoré accounted for 12 percent of the 2 billion pounds of cat food sold.[10]

Profits are a function of revenue and expenses:

$$\text{Profits} = \text{Revenue} - \text{Expenses}.$$

Revenue is determined by the product's selling price and number of units sold:

$$\text{Total Revenue} = \text{Price} \times \text{Quantity Sold}.$$

Price, therefore, should be increased to the point at which it will cause a disproportionate decrease in the number of units sold. A 10 percent price increase that results in only an 8 percent cut in volume will add to the firm's revenue. However, a 10 percent price hike that results in an 11 percent sales decline will reduce revenue.

Economists refer to this approach as *marginal analysis.* They identify **profit maximization** as the point at which the addition to total revenue is just bal-

profit maximization
In pricing strategy, point at which the additional revenue gained by increasing the price of a product equals the increase in total cost.

Figure 10.2
Use of Gourmet Brands to Achieve Profitability Objectives

Source: © 1987 Friskies PetCare Division, Carnation Company; used by permission.

anced by the increase in total cost. The basic problem is how to achieve this delicate balance between marginal revenue and marginal cost. Relatively few firms actually achieve the objective of profit maximization. A significantly larger number prefer to direct their efforts toward goals that are more reasonably implemented and measured.

Consequently, target return objectives have become common in industry, particularly among the larger firms in which public pressure typically prohibits consideration of the profit maximization objective. Automobile companies are an example of this phenomenon. **Target return objectives** are either short-run or long-run goals usually stated as a percentage of sales or investment. For example, General Electric's stated pricing objective is a 20 percent annual rate of return on investment or a 7 percent rate of return on sales. Alcoa marketers operate with a 20 percent ROI objective. A specified rate of return on investment was the most commonly reported primary pricing objective in Table 10.1. These types of goals also serve as useful guidelines in evaluating corporate activity. As one writer has aptly put it, "For management consciously accepting less than maximum profits, the target rate can provide a measure of the amount of restraint. For firms making very low profits, the target rate can serve as a standard for judging improvement."[11]

Target return objectives offer several benefits for the marketer. As noted above, they serve as a means for evaluating performance. They also are designed to generate a "fair" profit as judged by management, stockholders, and the general public.

target return objectives
Short-run or long-run pricing objectives of achieving a specified return on either sales or investment.

Volume Objectives

Many business executives argue that a more accurate explanation of actual pricing behavior is that firms strive for *sales maximization* within a given profit constraint. In other words, they set a minimum acceptable profit level and then seek to maximize sales (subject to this profit constraint) in the belief that the increased sales are more important than immediate high profits to the long-run competitive picture. The companies continue to expand sales as long as their total profits do not drop below the minimum return acceptable to management.

Another volume-related pricing objective is the *market share objective*— the goal set for the control of a portion of the market for a firm's product or service. The company's specific goal may be either to maintain its share of a particular market or to increase its share, say, from 10 to 20 percent. As Table 10.1 indicates, almost two-thirds of all responding firms list volume objectives as either a primary or secondary pricing objective.

Although *growth* is typically the end result of volume objectives, some firms with relatively high market shares may even prefer to reduce their shares of specific markets at times due to possible government action in the area of monopoly control. Market share is a frequently used indicator in court evaluations of cases involving alleged monopolistic practices.

The PIMS Studies Market share objectives may prove critical to the achievement of other organizational objectives. High sales, for example, often mean more profits. The extensive **Profit Impact of Market Strategies (PIMS) project,** conducted by the Marketing Science Institute, analyzed more than 2,000 firms and revealed that two of the most important factors influencing profitability were product quality and market share.

Profit Impact of Market Strategies (PIMS) project
Major research study that discovered a strong positive relationship between a firm's market share and its return on investment.

The linkage between market share and profitability is clear. PIMS data reveal an average 32 percent return on investment for firms with market share of over 40 percent. In contrast, average ROI decreases to 24 percent for firms whose market share is between 20 and 40 percent. Firms with a minor market share (less than 10 percent) generate average pretax investment returns of 13 percent.[12]

The relationship also applies to individual brands offered by the firm. In comparing the top four brands in a market segment, PIMS research data revealed that the leading brand generates after-tax returns on investment of 18 percent, considerably higher than the second-ranked brand. Weaker brands, on average, fail to earn adequate returns. The ad in Figure 10.3 demonstrates IBM's enviable brand strength in the office typewriter market. Not only does the firm have the industry's best-selling product in the Wheelwriter 3 typewriter, but a second IBM typewriter, the Wheelwriter 6, holds the second-place position in the market.

Quaker Oats marketers offer a portfolio of grocery products well positioned for future profitability. Brands with leading market shares accounted for over 63 percent of total sales during 1986. Included in this category are Quaker brand hot cereals and Granola Bars, Aunt Jemima breakfast products, Gatorade thirst quencher, Van Camp's pork and beans, and Ken-L Ration dog foods.

The underlying explanation of the positive relationship between profitability and market share appears to be the greater operating experience and lower overall costs of high-market-share firms relative to competitors with smaller market shares. Accordingly, the most astute segmentation strategies may be those that focus on obtaining larger shares of smaller markets and avoiding smaller shares of larger ones. The financial returns may be greater for a major competitor in several smaller market segments than for a relatively minor competitor in a larger market.

Figure 10.3
Brand Strength: Closely Related to Return On Investment

Source: Courtesy of International Business Machines Corporation.

Meeting Competition Objectives

The third pricing objective, that of meeting competitors' prices, is much less aggressive than profitability or volume objectives. Competing firms operationalize this objective simply by matching the prices of the established industry price leader. As Table 10.1 indicates, 81 percent, or four out of every five respondent firms, listed this as a primary or secondary objective, making meeting competition the most frequently mentioned pricing objective.

The net result of this objective is to de-emphasize the price element of the marketing mix and focus more strongly on nonprice competition. Although pricing is a highly visible mix component and an effective method of obtaining a differential advantage over competitors, a price reduction is an easily duplicated move. The airline price competition of recent years exemplifies the actions and reactions of competitors for passenger and freight business. Because of the direct impact of such price changes on overall profitability, many firms attempt to promote stable prices by utilizing the objective of simply meeting competition and competing for market share by focusing on product/service strategies, promotional decisions, and distribution—the nonprice elements of the marketing mix.

Prestige Objectives

The final category of pricing objectives, unrelated to either profitability or sales volume, is prestige objectives. Prestige objectives involve establishing relatively high prices to develop and maintain an image of quality and exclusiveness that appeals to status-conscious consumers. Such objectives reflect marketers' recognition of the role of price in creating an overall image for the firm and its products and services.

Prestige pricing is used for such products as Baccarat crystal, Rolls-Royce automobiles, Rolex watches, Tiffany jewelry, and perfumes that sell for $135 or more an ounce. Advertisements for Joy promote the fragrance as the "costliest perfume in the world."

In contrast to low-price strategies used by some cruise shiplines to fill unsold berths, Royal Viking Line marketers emphasize the royal amenities of their Mediterranean cruises. The cruises are targeted at "those who collect the best of everything." Advertisements for the cruises, such as that in Figure 10.4, appeal to people with discriminating tastes—those who appreciate the best in food, wine, and music. Amenities include onboard experts in wine, music, and current events. One cruise features performances of the San Francisco Opera; another includes a visit to the château of a noted wine connoisseur.

Pricing Objectives of Nonprofit Organizations

Pricing typically is a very important element of the marketing mix for nonprofit organizations. Pricing strategy can be used to achieve a variety of organizational goals in nonprofit settings:

1. *Profit maximization.* While nonprofit organizations by definition do not cite profitability as a primary goal, there are numerous instances in which they do try to maximize their returns on single events or series of events. The $1,000-a-plate political fund raiser is a classic example.

2. *Cost recovery.* Some nonprofit organizations attempt to recover only the actual cost of operating the unit. Mass transit, publicly supported colleges, and bridges are common examples. The amount of recovered costs is often dictated by tradition, competition, and/or public opinion.

3. **Providing market incentives.** Other nonprofit groups follow a lower than average pricing policy or offer a free service to encourage increased usage of the product or service. Seattle's bus system offers free service in the downtown area in an attempt to reduce traffic congestion, encourage retail sales, and minimize the effort required to use downtown public services.

4. *Market suppression.* Price is sometimes used to discourage consumption. In other words, high prices are used to accomplish societal objectives and are not directly related to the costs of providing the product or service. Illustrations include tobacco and alcohol taxes, parking fines, tolls, and gasoline excise taxes.[13]

Figure 10.4
Royal Viking Line: Using Price to Achieve Prestige Objectives

Source: © 1987, Royal Viking Line/Lowe-Marshalk Inc., San Francisco.

How Prices Are Determined

The determination of price may be viewed in two ways: the theoretical concepts of supply and demand and the cost-oriented approach that characterizes current business practice. During the first part of this century, most considerations of price determination emphasized the classical concepts of supply and demand. Since World War II, however, the emphasis has shifted to a cost-oriented approach. Hindsight reveals that both concepts have certain flaws.

Another concept of price determination—one based on the impact of custom and tradition—is often overlooked. **Customary prices** are retail prices that consumers expect as a result of tradition and social habit. Candy makers' attempt to hold the line on the traditional 10 cent candy bar led to considerable reduction in product size. Similar practices have prevailed in the marketing of soft drinks as bottlers attempt to balance consumer expectations of customary prices with the realities of rising costs.

Hershey Food Corporation marketers approached the dilemma of increased product costs for snack items by simultaneously increasing the product size and its price. Hershey's milk chocolate bar and Reese's Peanut Butter

customary prices
In pricing strategy, the traditional prices that customers expect to pay for certain products and services.

THE COMPETITIVE EDGE

Arbor Cinema Four

It's show time, folks, so let the magic begin! In Austin, Texas, movietime means cinemagic—at least if you decide to go to Arbor Cinema Four. The Arbor is a special theater, one that recalls fading visions of Chicago's Oriental or New York's Paramount in their heydays, a time when the movie palaces were as much a part of a night at the theater as the films themselves. (In fact, MGM's founder Marcus Loew once said, "We sell tickets to theaters, not movies.")

The Austin Arbor itself attracts people. The architect was directed to design not a lobby but a stage set. Instead of a ceiling, the Arbor offers stars twinkling through the cloud cover on a romantic evening, with the rumble of thunder and lightning off in the distance. Instead of a mundane concession stand, there's a two-story clock tower. The way to the auditorium is marked by lampposts and a prewar British phone booth.

Arbor Cinema's design has won awards, and people come from as far as Houston and Dallas just to see it. The lobby is only the start. Presidio invested serious money inside the auditorium, which opens with French-made seats set a roomy 42 inches apart; builds to the state-of-the-art projection system, which features both 35mm and 70mm projectors; and culminates with the genuine Lucasfilm Limited THX sound system, which gives moviegoers a sense of listening in 3D.

All these extras have made the Arbor Four Cinema a $2.8 million complex, about 25 percent more than it would have cost without them. But it helps make the magic—and sell tickets. Presidio theaters house only 42 percent of the movie seats in the area, but they sell more than 60 percent of the theater tickets.

The Presidio marketers make sure that the bewitching theater is not spoiled by churlish concessionaires or obnoxious ushers. Rigorous training and regular motivation sessions for all four employee levels combine to keep them as customer friendly as possible. Out of a page from Disney, they become part of the theater experience, often dressing up as characters from the movies being featured.

The whole show makes the Arbor the best place in America to watch a movie, according to *Star Wars* producer George Lucas and the people of Austin. Despite its location in the 98th largest market in America, Arbor sales revenues are large enough to rank it as one of the top 10 in the nation.

The unique theater experience is also a major contributor in Presidio's efforts to make the Arbor a profitable operation. These days, theaters are often compared to razor blade manufacturers who (almost) give away their razors so they can generate revenue from sale of blades. Since Presidio has to return approximately 50 percent of the ticket revenues to the film distributor, it must look elsewhere for profits—the concession stand. Popcorn, with a 539 percent markup, is the key ingredient; the other concessions carry markups av-

Figure 11.2
Using a High-Price Marketing Strategy to Enhance a Prestige Image

Source: Courtesy of J. M. Weston.

chicken noodle soup. Pet's marketing strategy for Progresso and other food products is to project a high-quality image that brings top prices and high profit margins.

One benefit of a skimming strategy is that it allows the firm to quickly recover its research and development costs. The assumption is that competition will eventually drive down the price. Such was the case with videocassette recorders, electric toothbrushes, and personal computers. A skimming strategy for many new products, therefore, attempts to maximize the revenue received from the sale of a new product before the entry of competition.

A skimming strategy is also useful in segmenting the overall market on a price basis. In the case of new products that represent significant innovations, relatively high prices convey an image of distinction and appeal to buyers who are less sensitive to price. Ballpoint pens were introduced shortly after World War II at a price of about $20. Today the best-selling ballpoint pens are priced at less than $1. Other examples of products that were introduced using a skimming strategy include television sets, Polaroid cameras, digital watches, and pocket calculators. Subsequent price reductions allowed the marketers of these products to appeal to additional, more price-sensitive market segments.

A third advantage of a skimming strategy is that it permits the marketer to control demand in the introductory stages of the product's life cycle and adjust

FOCUS ON ETHICS

New Drugs for AIDS Victims

A firm usually uses a skimming pricing strategy when it introduces a new product with significant technological advantages over its competitors. Such a pricing approach allows the marketer to quickly recover its research and development, marketing, and other costs and turn a profit on the product more rapidly. But what about a product that could be a life-or-death matter for its users? This was the issue facing Burroughs-Wellcome Company, maker of AZT, the first drug to offer hope for sufferers of the deadly acquired immune deficiency syndrome (AIDS).

The firm's marketers have followed the textbook approach of a skimming strategy, setting a wholesale price that would produce retail prices of between $7,000 and $14,000 a year per patient depending on dosage amounts and pharmacy markups. But few AZT recipients can afford that price tag. Even for middle-class AIDS patients the cost of treatment eventually exceeds insurance maximums. Patients who qualify for Medicaid may live in states in which Medicaid does not pay for prescriptions. An example is Florida, which has the fourth largest number of AIDS cases but limits Medicaid drug payments to $22 a month.

"Only the privileged and rich will be able to handle the cost," according to Lionel Resnick of Mount Sinai Medical Center in Miami. Jerome Groopman of New England Deaconess Hospital in Boston adds, "I think the extraordinarily high price of the drug needs to be justified in very clear terms, because it will clearly limit access to patients who could benefit." The controversy has resulted in hearings by the House of Representatives' Subcommittee on Health and the Environment, chaired by California congressman Harry Waxman, another critic of the pricing strategy.

Burroughs-Wellcome defends its move. Its executives point out that the firm has spent $80 million to test and produce the drug, not even counting research and development costs. Dr. David Barry, vice-president of research, says, "I have no compunction about charging this price. No one flinches at hundreds of dollars a day in hospital costs, but everyone expects a drug that prevents hospitalization to be much less." Company officials estimate that by reducing infections and hospitalization the drug will decrease the cost of caring for AIDS patients, which can range from $70,000 to $140,000 or more before death occurs.

By 1988, 19,000 patients were receiving AZT (3,000 free in clinical tests), drug sales were at $100 million a year, and the sales curve was continuing to climb. Burroughs-Wellcome executives made another pricing move: They reduced the price of AZT by 20 percent, explaining that the production improvements and manufacturing efficiencies made possible by growing sales allowed the price cut.

Despite this price reduction, however, the controversy continues. Some critics say it was not nearly enough; others claim the move was merely a response to political pressure.

Sources: Quotations from Marilyn Chase, "AIDS Drug Comes to a Worried Market," *The Wall Street Journal* (March 23, 1987), p. 6. See also Marilyn Chase, "Wellcome Unit Cuts Price of AIDS Drug 20%, Cites Production Improvements," *The Wall Street Journal* (December 15, 1987), p. 30; "The Killer Cost of AIDS," *American Demographics* (June 1987), p. 13; Sally Squires, "The High Cost of Treating AIDS," *Washington Post* (March 10, 1987), p. H7; "Uproar over AIDS Drugs," *Newsweek* (April 6, 1987), p. 24; and Bernard Weintraub, "Panel Says New AIDS Drug May Cost Too Much," *The New York Times* (March 11, 1987).

its productive capacity to match demand. One danger in low initial prices for a new product is that demand may outstrip the firm's production capacity, resulting in consumer and retailer complaints and possibly permanent damage to the product's image. Excess demand occasionally results in poor-quality products, because the firm strives to satisfy consumer desires but lacks adequate production facilities.

During the late growth and early maturity stages of the product life cycle, the price is typically reduced for two reasons: (1) the pressure of competition and (2) the desire to expand the product's market. Figure 11.3 shows that 10 percent of the market for product X would buy the item at $10 while another 20 percent would be attracted into the market at $8.75. Successive price declines will expand the firm's market as well as meet new competition.

Figure 11.3
Use of Price Reductions to
Expand Total Market

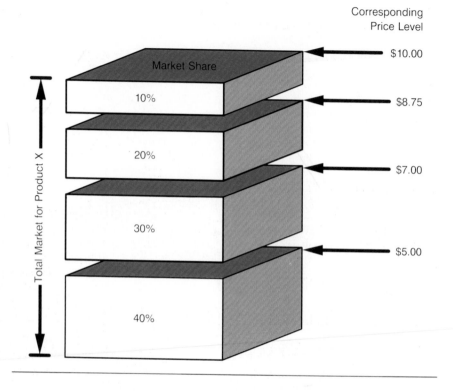

Corresponding
Price Level

Market Share

10%　— $10.00

20%　— $8.75

30%　— $7.00

40%　— $5.00

Total Market for Product X

A skimming strategy has one chief disadvantage: It attracts competition. Potential competitors see that the innovating firms receive large financial returns and thus decide to enter the market. This forces the price even lower than what it might be under a sequential skimming procedure. However, if a firm has patent protection, as Polaroid did, or a proprietary ability to exclude competition, it may use a skimming strategy for a relatively long period. After winning a patent infringement lawsuit that caused rival Eastman Kodak to leave the instant photography business, Polaroid marketers raised prices on two cameras and their twin-pack instant film. A spokesperson stated that the products had been underpriced to compete with Kodak's prices, but "we no longer have to struggle with that kind of predatory pricing."[3]

One-sixth of the respondents in a recent study of pricing practices among large companies reported frequent use of a skimming strategy.[4] Skimming appears to be more common in industrial markets than in consumer markets.

penetration pricing strategy
Pricing strategy involving the use
of a relatively low entry price as
compared with competitive offerings; based on the theory that
this initial low price will help secure market acceptance.

Penetration Pricing Strategy

A **penetration pricing strategy** uses low prices as a major marketing weapon. Products or services are priced noticeably lower than competing offerings. In some instances, penetration pricing is used to introduce new products in indus-

Figure 11.4
Penetration Pricing Used as a Competitive Tool

Traditionally, in the world of business, those who perform best charge most. UPS proudly flies in the face of tradition.

When it comes to package delivery companies, UPS is a leader in the industry. But unlike the competition, our high level of service is not reflected in our prices. Because at UPS we work hard at being efficient. In fact, it's an obsession with us. After all, it enables us to deliver packages for less. And, in turn, charge less.

We deliver Next Day Air to any address coast to coast for up to half what the competition charges.

And if you can afford to wait one more day, you can use UPS 2nd Day Air and save even more.

Our service and low prices also extend to Japan and most of Western Europe.

So if you need a package delivery company you can depend on, call UPS. Especially if being efficient is as much an obsession with you as it is with us. We run the tightest ship in the shipping business. UPS

tries characterized by dozens of competing brands. Once the product has achieved some market recognition as a result of consumer trial purchases stimulated by the lower prices, marketers may increase the price to the level of competitive products. Consumer products such as toothpaste and detergent often use this strategy. In other cases, a penetration pricing strategy may be used throughout several stages of the product life cycle as the firm seeks to maintain a reputation as a low-price competitor. Such a strategy has been used by United Parcel Service since its inception as a competitor of the U.S. Postal Service. As the advertisement in Figure 11.4 illustrates, UPS continues to maintain its reputation as a low-price competitor in the package delivery industry.

A penetration pricing strategy is sometimes called a *market-minus* approach and is based on the premise that a lower-than-market price will attract buyers and move the brand from the "unknown" category to at least the brand recognition stage, or even the brand preference stage. Since in many instances the firm intends to increase the price in the future, large numbers of consumer trial purchases are critical to the success of a penetration strategy. One advantage of this strategy is that it discourages competition, since the prevailing low price does not suggest the attractive financial returns associated with a skimming strategy.

While variable pricing has the advantage of flexibility in selling situations, it may conflict with Robinson-Patman Act provisions. It may also lead to retaliatory pricing by competitors, and it is not well received by those who have paid the higher price.

Product Line Pricing

product line pricing
Practice of marketing different lines of merchandise at a limited number of prices.

Since most firms market several different lines of products or services, an effective pricing strategy must consider the relationship among all of these products or services instead of viewing each in isolation. **Product line pricing** is the practice of marketing merchandise at a limited number of prices. For example, a clothier might have three lines of men's suits—one priced at $225, a second at $350, and the most expensive at $450. These price points are important factors in achieving product line differentiation and in trading up and trading down by the firm's customers.

Product line pricing, which is really a combined product/price strategy, is used extensively in retail marketing. The old five-and-dime variety stores were operated using this approach. It can be an advantage to both retailer and customer. Shoppers can choose the price range they desire and then concentrate on other product variables such as color, style, and material. Retailers can purchase and offer specific lines at a limited number of price categories instead of more general assortments with dozens of different prices.

Product line pricing requires identifying the market segment or segments to which the firm is appealing. Saab-Scania auto marketers use the theme line "The most intelligent cars ever built," because research studies have revealed that more than half of all U.S. purchasers of the unusually designed Swedish auto hold postgraduate degrees. The four Saab models shown in Figure 11.9 range in price from approximately $15,000 to $30,000. (The supersonic Saab fighter plane carries a $20 million price tag.)[13]

One problem with a product line pricing decision is that once it is made retailers and manufacturers may have difficulty adjusting it. Rising costs, therefore, force the seller to either change the price lines, which results in confusion, or reduce costs through production adjustments, which opens the firm to the complaint that "XYZ Company's merchandise certainly isn't what it used to be!"

Promotional Pricing

promotional pricing
Pricing policy in which a lower-than-normal price is used as a temporary ingredient in a firm's marketing strategy.

In **promotional pricing,** a lower-than-normal price is used as a temporary ingredient in a firm's selling strategy. In some cases, promotional prices are recurrent, such as the annual shoe store "buy one pair, get the second pair for one cent" sale. Another example is a new pizza restaurant that has an opening special to attract customers. In other situations, a firm may introduce a promotional model or brand to allow it to compete in another market.

loss leader
Product offered to consumers at less than cost to attract them to retail stores in the hope that they will buy other merchandise at regular prices.

Most promotional pricing occurs at the retail level. One type is **loss leaders**—goods priced below cost to attract customers who, the retailer hopes, will then buy other, regularly priced merchandise. The use of loss leaders can be effective. However, loss-leader pricing is not permitted in states with unfair-trade acts, which were discussed in Chapter 10.

One of the most successful loss-leader pricing pioneers was Cal Mayne. He was one of the first marketers to systematically price specials and evaluate

The Transfer Pricing Dilemma

A pricing problem peculiar to large-scale enterprises is the determination of an internal **transfer price**—the price for sending goods from one company profit center to another. As companies expand, they tend to decentralize management and set up profit centers as a control device in the newly decentralized operation. A **profit center** is any part of the organization to which revenue and controllable costs can be assigned, such as a department.

In large companies, profit centers can secure many of their resource requirements from within the corporate structure. The pricing problem becomes: What rate should profit center A (maintenance department) charge profit center B (sales department) for the cleansing compound used on B's floors? Should the price be the same as it would be if A did the work for an outside party? Should B receive a discount? The answers to these questions depend on the philosophy of the firm involved.

The transfer pricing dilemma is an example of the variations that a firm's pricing policy must address. Consider the case of UDC-Europe, a Universal Data Corporation subsidiary with 10 subsidiaries. Each subsidiary is organized on a geographic basis, and each is treated as a separate profit center. Intercompany transfer prices are set at the annual budget meeting. Special situations, such as unexpected volume, are handled through negotiations by the subsidiary managers. If complex tax problems arise, UDC-Europe's top management may set the transfer price.[19]

transfer price
Cost assessed when a product is moved from one profit center in a firm to another.

profit center
Any part of an organization to which revenue and controllable costs can be assigned.

Pricing in the Public Sector

The pricing of public services has also become an interesting—and sometimes troublesome—aspect of contemporary marketing. Traditionally government services were very low cost or were priced using the full-cost approach: Users paid all costs associated with the services. More recently there has been a move toward incremental or marginal pricing, which considers only those expenses specifically associated with a particular activity. However, it is often difficult to determine the costs that should be assigned to a particular activity or service. Government accounting problems frequently are more complex than those of private enterprises.

Another problem in pricing public services is that taxes act as an *indirect* price of a public service. Someone must decide on the relationship between the direct and indirect prices of such a service. A shift toward indirect tax charges (where an income or earnings tax exists) is pricing based on the *ability-to-pay* principle rather than on the *use* principle.

The pricing of any public service involves a basic policy decision to determine whether the price is an instrument for recovering costs or one for achieving some other social or civic objective. For example, public health services may be priced near zero to encourage their use. On the other hand, parking fines in some cities are high in order to discourage the use of private automobiles in the central business district. Pricing decisions in the public sector are difficult, because political and social considerations often outweigh the economic aspects.

Summary of Chapter Objectives

1. Explain the organizational structures for pricing decisions. Two basic steps in making pricing decisions are (1) to assign someone to administer the pricing structure and (2) to set the overall structure. The person or groups in the firm most commonly chosen to set pricing structures are (1) a pricing committee composed of top executives; (2) the company president; or (3) the chief marketing officer. In a recent study, the chief marketing executive was responsible for administering the price structure in 51 percent of the firms surveyed, while overall marketers administered the pricing structure in over 68 percent.

2. Compare the alternative pricing strategies and explain when each strategy is most appropriate. The alternative pricing strategies are a skimming pricing strategy, a penetration pricing strategy, and a competitive pricing strategy. Skimming pricing is commonly used as a market entry price for distinctive products or services with little or no initial competition. Penetration pricing is used when there is a wide array of competing brands. Competitive pricing is employed when the marketers wish to concentrate their competitive efforts on marketing variables other than price. More than two-thirds of the firms surveyed in a recent study used the competitive pricing approach.

3. Describe how prices are quoted. Methods for quoting prices depend on such factors as cost structures, traditional practices in the particular industry, and policies of individual firms. Prices quoted can involve list prices, market prices, cash discounts, trade discounts, quantity discounts, and allowances such as trade-ins, promotional allowances, and rebates.

Shipping costs often figure heavily in the pricing of goods. A number of alternatives for dealing with these costs exist: FOB plant, in which the price includes no shipping charges; freight absorption, which allows the buyer to deduct transportation expenses from the bill; uniform delivered price, in which the same price, including shipping expenses, is charged to all buyers; and zone pricing, in which a set price exists within each region.

4. Identify the various pricing policy decisions that marketers must make. A pricing policy is a general guideline based on pricing objectives and is intended for use in specific pricing decisions. Pricing policies include psychological pricing, unit pricing, price flexibility, product line pricing, and promotional pricing.

5. Relate price to consumer perceptions of quality. The relationship between price and consumer perceptions of quality has been the subject of considerable research. In the absence of other cues, price is an important indicator of how the consumer perceives the product's quality. A well-known and accepted concept is that of *price limits*—limits within which the perception of product quality varies directly with price. The concept of price limits suggests that extremely low prices may be considered too cheap, thus indicating inferior quality.

6. Contrast negotiated prices and competitive bidding. Negotiated prices and competitive bidding are pricing techniques used primarily in the industrial sector and in government and institutional markets. Sometimes prices are negotiated through competitive bidding, in which several buyers quote prices on the same service or good. Buyer specifications describe the item that the government or industrial firm wishes to acquire. Negotiated contracts are another possibility in many procurement situations. The terms of the contract are set through talks between buyer and seller.

7. Explain the importance of transfer pricing. A phenomenon in large corporations is transfer pricing, in which a company sets prices for transferring goods or services from one company profit center to another. A *profit center* refers to any part of the organization to which revenue and controllable costs can be assigned. In large companies whose profit centers acquire resources from other parts of the firm, the prices charged by one profit center to another have a direct impact on the cost and profitability of the output of both profit centers.

8. Describe pricing in the public sector. The pricing of public services has become an interesting and sometimes troublesome aspect of contemporary marketing. Related decisions include (1) which costs to assign to a particular activity or service; (2) the relationship between the direct and indirect prices, such as taxes on a service; and (3) whether price should be an instrument for recovering costs or for accomplishing other social or civic objectives. Public-sector pricing traditionally used a full-cost approach, but the current tendency is toward incremental pricing.

Key Terms

skimming pricing strategy
penetration pricing strategy
competitive pricing strategy
list price
market price
cash discount
trade discount
quantity discount
trade-in
promotional allowance
rebate
FOB plant
freight absorption
uniform delivered price

zone pricing
basing point system
pricing policy
psychological pricing
odd pricing
unit pricing
price flexibility
product line pricing
promotional pricing
loss leaders
escalator clause
transfer price
profit center

Review Questions

1. What is meant by the term *price structure?* Who in the organization is most likely to be responsible for setting the price structure? Who is most likely to administer the price structure?

2. What are the benefits of using a skimming pricing strategy?

3. Under what circumstances is penetration pricing most likely to be used?

4. Explain why most marketing executives choose meeting competitors' prices as a pricing strategy.

5. Contrast the freight absorption and uniform delivered pricing systems.

6. Prepare a list of arguments for use in justifying a basing point pricing system.

7. List and discuss the reasons for establishing pricing policies.

8. When does a price become a promotional price? What are the pitfalls in promotional pricing?

9. What is the relationship between price and consumer perceptions of quality? Give examples of what you consider acceptable price ranges for a common consumer good or service, such as toothpaste, a haircut, or mouthwash. How would a price outside this range affect the product's quality image?

10. What types of decisions must be made in the pricing of public services? What role could escalator clauses play in this area?

Discussion Questions

1. Skimming pricing, penetration pricing, and competitive pricing are the three alternative pricing strategies. Which of the three appears most appropriate for the following items? Defend your answers.
   a. Software package used for spreadsheet analysis
   b. Compact disk player
   c. Fuel additive that substantially increases automobile mileage
   d. Ultrasensitive burglar, smoke, and fire alarm
   e. New brand of toothpaste

2. Frequent-flyer programs are discount schemes designed by airlines to attract and reward regular customers. What type of discount plan describes these programs? Explain. What are the potential dangers of such programs?

3. How are prices quoted for each of the following?
   a. Delta Airlines ticket to Orlando
   b. Installation of aluminum siding by a local contractor
   c. Jogging suit from a sportswear retailer
   d. New Acura Legend automobile

4. Assume that a product sells for $100 per ton and that Pittsburgh is the basing point city for transportation charges. Per-ton shipping from Pittsburgh to a potential customer in Cincinnati costs $10 per ton. The actual shipping costs of suppliers in three other cities are $8 per ton for supplier A, $11 per ton for supplier B, and $10 per ton for supplier C. Using this information, answer the following questions.
   a. What delivered price would a salesperson for supplier A quote to the customer?
   b. What delivered price would a salesperson for supplier B quote to the customer?
   c. What delivered price would a salesperson for supplier C quote to the customer?
   d. How much would each supplier net (after subtracting actual shipping costs) per ton on the sale?

5. Comment on the following statement: "Unit pricing is not only expensive for retailers but also useless because everyone ignores it."

VIDEO CASE 11

Looking Good Calendar Co.

Pricing a product seems a relatively simple task: add up the production and marketing costs, then pick a price that will guarantee a profit. But costs do not determine prices and control over the price frequently does not rest with the producer — the caprices of the market set the price.

"There is no relation between what it costs to make a product and what it sells for," confirms Dr. Richard Buskirk, marketing professor and director of the University of Southern California's entrepreneurship program. Therefore, it should come as no surprise that pricing is at the same time one of the most important and trickiest parts of developing a marketing mix for a good or service. If the price is too high, the product may remain on store shelves. A too-low price means lost profit opportunities and the possibility of consumer demand too great for supply.

Jim and Nick Colachis, founders of Looking Good Calendar Co., recognized the importance of pricing from the time they founded their company. They paid special attention to the price variable when they developed their initial business plan. Their overriding company objective was to make money, and they thought they had an infallible method to achieve their goal.

"Back then, it was a beginning thing: no one had heard of a male calendar," said Nick. "It was brand new, and while some people said 'Why is it going to sell?' that didn't matter to us, because we knew the co-eds wanted it."

As it turned out the Colachis brothers underestimated consumer demand. They approached the USC bookstore manager about ordering some Looking Good calendars, hoping for an initial order of five or six dozen. The manager examined the calendar carefully and ordered 3,500.

"We left the room in shock," said Nick. "We printed 5,000, so we could sell 1,500 to the fraternities and sororities, the bookstore took 3,500, and we made $12,000 in about a minute. It was a good feeling."

First-year sales for Looking Good amounted to $30,000. By 1988, sales had soared to $2 million a year and Looking Good had expanded into a company with six full-time and two part-time employees. Jim Colachis feels that much of the credit goes to a clever pricing strategy that he and his brother have used from the start. Even though they felt the market would support a considerably higher price, they deliberately priced the calendar low in order to achieve maximum market penetration.

"We've made, in our first few years, very little money, in order to promote that name," said Jim. "Sell the calendar a little bit cheaper, give someone a better deal, because we had to get the name out there, because that's valuable when it comes time to do things like posters. . . ."

To get an idea of what the market might bear in terms of price, the Looking Good partners conducted their own very informal, very unscientific marketing research. They showed the calendar to female students at USC and then asked them what they would pay for it. Nick summarized the results of the research: "Some said $4, and some said $5, and some said $6. . . . When they saw [cover model Mike Flynn's] picture they'd die, they'd say 'I want this now!' "

Jim and Nick chose to price their first calendar at $5.95 because "most of the other calendars in the store were selling for $6.95, so why not be $1 cheaper?" said Nick. By 1988, the firm was offering 14 different calendars, both in color and in black and white, ranging in size from 11 to 13 inches square, and in price from $7.95 to $9.95. Since most calendars are now priced at $8.95, the typical Looking Good calendar continues to be priced one dollar below the average competitor's price.

"We undercut the market in terms of price and value," says David Gothard, Looking Good's vice president. "We use more expensive materials than other calendar companies, higher-quality photography, more expensive paper, metal spiral binding, and special processing."

Today the calendars have worldwide distribution through some 24 independent representatives. Expansion into international markets has just begun and 95 percent of current sales are generated in the United States.

Even though the success of Looking Good is impressive, even more impressive is the fact that the Colachis twins planned for this kind of growth when they started their company. "You have to plan from the beginning that you're going to be national, you're going to be the best, and you're going to put money into making your calendar stay on top," said Nick.

Looking Good's founders and their associates continue to work extended hours in pursuit of their growth and profit objectives. The 1988 acquisition of another calendar company enabled them to double the previous year's sales.

Source: Telephone interviews with Nick Colachis and David Gothard (March 17, 1988).

Questions

1. What pricing strategy is being used by Looking Good for its calendars? Justify the choice of this strategy.

2. Suggest methods by which the Colachis brothers can continue to grow and protect their product concept from competitors.

3. Relate the following pricing concepts to the material in this case:
   a. trade discounts
   b. promotional allowances
   c. psychological pricing
   d. product-line pricing

4. Discuss the price-quality relationship as it relates to Looking Good pricing decisions. What other factors might serve to offset this relationship?

5. Discuss the impact of increased production costs on the ability of Looking Good to continue its current pricing strategy.

COMPUTER APPLICATIONS

Problems 1 through 4 deal with situations involving competitive bidding by firms offering products and services to industrial purchasers or government organizations. The description of the *expected net profit (ENP)* approach to competitive bidding on page 229 should be reviewed before attempting to solve these problems.

Problems 5 and 6 focus on the application of two pricing strategies discussed in the chapter: skimming strategies and penetration pricing. The discussion of breakeven analysis on pages 360–364 should be reviewed before attempting to solve these problems.

Directions: Use menu item 6 titled "Competitive Bidding" to solve Problems 1–4. Use menu item 9 titled "Breakeven Analysis" to solve Problems 5 and 6.

Problem 1   The manager of Rochester, New York–based Empire State Construction hopes to earn an expected net profit (ENP) of $9,000 on a job with an estimated cost of $4,000.
a. What probability of acceptance is being assigned if the manager submits a bid of $20,000?
b. What probability of acceptance is being assigned if the manager submits a bid of $14,000?

Problem 2   Joe Worthington, marketing manager at Washington, D.C.–based Capitol Construction, wants to submit a bid for a job that he estimates will cost $80,000. He has prepared two preliminary proposals: (1) a bid for $120,000 and (2) a bid for $105,000. If Worthington estimates a 40 percent chance of the buyer accepting the first bid and a 60 percent chance of his accepting the second bid, which bid will yield the higher expected net profit?

Problem 3   Jane Dawson is owner/manager of Hawkeye Contractors based in Des Moines, Iowa. She has estimated the probability of acceptance of her firm's bid on a state contract at 70 percent. Since her planned bid is $60,000 and the estimated cost of completing the project is $36,000, Dawson has calculated the expected net profit as $16,800.
a. What would the expected net profit be if the cost estimate turned out to be $2,000 too low?
b. What would the expected net profit be if total costs could be held to only $35,000?

Problem 4   Houston Suppliers' marketing executive, Charlie Robbins, has spent a number of days developing a bidding strategy for two bid invitations his firm recently received from Harris County. The cost of each bid is estimated as $18,000.
a. What bid should Robbins submit in order to ensure an expected net profit of $15,000 if he estimates the expected probability of acceptance of bid 1 at 65 percent?
b. The owner of Houston Suppliers has specified a minimum acceptable expected net profit of $15,000. Robbins estimates the probability of acceptance of bid 2 at 55 percent. What bid should he submit?
c. What bid should Robbins submit if Houston Suppliers' owner requires a minimum acceptable expected net profit of $15,000 and also asks Robbins to lower the probability of bid 2's acceptance to 45 percent?

Problem 5   Midwest Industries of Kansas City is considering the possible introduction of a new service. Focus group research has revealed that consumers expect the service to be priced at approximately $50. Total fixed costs are $620,000, and average variable costs are calculated as $22.

a. What is the breakeven point (in units) for the proposed service?

b. The firm's director of marketing has suggested a target profit return of $100,000 for the service. How many units must be sold in order to both break even and achieve the target return?

c. Another proposal is to use a 12 percent return on sales as a target return instead of a fixed dollar amount. How many units must be sold in order to both break even and achieve the 12 percent return?

d. How would your answers to questions a, b, and c change if the firm's marketing director decided to implement a skimming strategy and price the service at $85?

e. How would your answers to questions a, b, and c change if the firm's marketing director decided to implement a penetration strategy and price the service at $35?

Problem 6   Ole Johansen is marketing vice-president of Seattle-based Puget Sound Manufacturing, a major appliance manufacturer with its own chain of retail outlets. Johansen is evaluating a product development department proposal for a new portable washer. Fixed costs are estimated at $1.2 million, variable costs are expected to be $40 per unit, and typical retail prices on similar products are $125.

a. What is the breakeven point for Puget Sound Manufacturing if Johansen decides to meet competition by choosing the $125 price for the portable washer?

b. Johansen is also considering a skimming strategy for the new washer and a price of $160. This strategy will help improve the image of other Puget Sound appliances and will assist Johansen in adjusting his production level to match consumer demand. However, he feels that the firm will have to spend an additional $500,000 on advertising, store displays, and other promotional materials in order to ensure the new washer's success if he decides to implement the price-skimming strategy. Determine the breakeven point if these expenditures are made and the skimming strategy is used.

c. Johansen's national sales manager feels that a penetration pricing strategy might prove effective in gaining quick consumer acceptance for the new product and in attracting to the firm's retail stores customers who might purchase additional appliances with higher margins. He suggests $100 as a retail price. How many units of the new portable washer will have to be sold in order to break even if the firm chooses the penetration strategy?

d. Suppose that Puget Sound Manufacturing selects the penetration strategy but also establishes a minimum target return of 15 percent of sales. How many units must be sold in order to both break even and achieve the target return?

Distribution Strategy

405

Photo source: Courtesy of Southern Pacific Transportation Company.

12 Channel Strategy

Chapter Objectives

1. To explain the role of distribution channels in marketing strategy.

2. To describe the various types of distribution channels.

3. To explain the concept of power as it relates to the distribution channel.

4. To describe the concept of channel leadership.

5. To discuss conflict and cooperation within the distribution channel.

6. To outline the major channel strategy decisions.

7. To identify and discuss the various types of vertical marketing systems.

C hannel strategy has played a major role in the success of Docktor Pet Centers. The Wilmington, Massachusetts based company has 260+ outlets in 37 states. This expansion has resulted from an aggressive franchising effort. Franchises are a contractual agreement between a franchisor and a dealer who agrees to meet certain operating requirements. The success of this franchise has resulted in some two-thirds of the Docktor Pet Centers being operated by owners who have two or more outlets; in fact, one franchisee owns 22 centers. While the firm believes that "anyone can run a Docktor Pet Center," it does specifically try to attract, as franchisees, experienced retailers and veterinarians among other men and women who have had face-to-face experience with consumers.

Most Docktor Pet Centers are located in regional shopping malls. The company is now expanding into strip centers. The stores do little advertising, but an average of 10,000 potential buyers enter each Docktor Pet Center every week because the presentation and product lines are so in demand by customers. The company's research indicates that different people buy different kinds of pets. Adult females buy cats. Adult

males buy large birds and fish. Children buy small birds and small animals. In contrast, puppies are purchased by people of both sexes and all ages. As a result, store sales personnel called *pet counselors* are trained to help customers find the right products and pets to fulfill their needs. The stores also have "animal love rooms" so that potential buyers can get to know animals before purchasing.

Docktor Pet Centers allows their franchisees considerable flexibility in running their stores. For instance, the company's recommended prod-

uct mix of 50 percent pets and 50 percent dry goods can be varied if the franchisee so desires. One thing is for certain: Docktor Pet Centers' unique franchising concept has been successful for its franchisees. The typical store now does $500,000 annually, up from $350,000 just three years ago and as compared to $160,000 for the average local pet shop. This concept allows individuals to bring their personal strengths into their own businesses.[1]

Photo source: Courtesy of Docktor Pet Centers, Incorporated.

Chapter Overview

Part 6 discusses the activities, decisions, and marketing intermediaries involved in moving products and services to consumers and industrial users. Basic channel strategy is the starting point for our discussion of the distribution function and its role in the marketing mix.

This chapter analyzes such basic issues as the role and types of distribution channels, channel strategy decisions, and conflict and cooperation in the channel of distribution. Chapters 13 and 14 deal, respectively, with wholesaling and retailing—the marketing institutions in the distribution channel. Although not considered part of the distribution channel, physical distribution is a vital facilitating agency that assists regular channel members. It is discussed in Chapter 15.

We begin this chapter with an examination of what marketers call *distribution channels.*

Figure 12.1
NAPA as a Distributor of
Automobile Parts

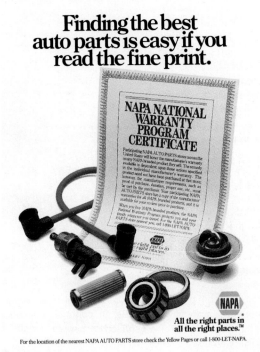

Source: Courtesy of NAPA.

Distribution Channels

Although Dresser Industries' gasoline pumps are made in Salisbury, Maryland, they are sold all over the United States. Boeing aircraft made in the state of Washington are marketed to numerous domestic and foreign airlines. The Nissan truck bought by someone in Dallas, Texas, was most likely made in Smyrna, Tennessee. In each case, methods must be devised for bridging the geographical gap between producer and consumer. Distribution channels are the method used to provide ultimate users with a convenient means of obtaining the products and services they desire.

distribution channel
Entity consisting of marketing institutions and their interrelationships responsible for the physical and title flow of goods and services from producer to consumer or industrial user.

marketing intermediary
Business firm, either wholesale or retail, that operates between the producer of goods and the consumer or industrial user; sometimes called *middleman*.

    Distribution channels represent marketing bridges between producer and consumer or industrial user. They are comprised of the various marketing institutions and the interrelationships responsible for the physical and title flow of goods and services from producer to consumer or industrial user. **Marketing intermediaries,** or middlemen, are the marketing institutions in the distribution channel; that is, business firms that operate between producers and consumers or industrial purchasers. In this book, the terms *jobber* and *distributor* are considered synonymous with wholesaler. For example, NAPA is a wholesaler, or distributor, that sells its NAPA-branded products through independently owned retailers. NAPA supports its retailers with advertising such as that shown in Figure 12.1.

Confusion can result from the practices of some firms that operate both wholesaling and retailing operations. Sporting-goods stores, for example, often maintain wholesaling operations to market lines of goods to high schools and sports teams as well as operate retail stores. For simplicity, this text treats these operations as separate entities.

A second source of confusion is the misleading practice of some retailers claiming to be wholesalers. Such stores may actually sell at wholesale prices and can validly claim to do so. However, stores that sell products purchased by individuals for their own use rather than for resale are by definition *retailers,* not wholesalers.

The Role of Distribution Channels in Marketing Strategy

Distribution channels play a key role in marketing strategy because they provide the means by which goods and services are conveyed from producers to consumers and users. Marketing intermediaries exist at both the wholesale and retail levels. As specialists in the performance of marketing functions—rather than producing or manufacturing functions—they perform these activities more efficiently than producers or consumers. The importance of distribution channels and marketing intermediaries can be explained in terms of the utility they create and the functions they perform.

The Creation of Utility

Distribution channels create three types of utility for consumers. *Time utility* is created when distribution channels make products and services available for sale when the consumer wants to purchase them. *Place utility* is created when goods and services are available at a convenient location. *Ownership* (or *possession) utility* is created when title to the goods passes from the producer or intermediary to the purchaser. Possession utility can also result from transactions in which the title does not pass to the purchaser, such as in the case of a rental car.

Physicians' Pharmaceutical Services (PPS) is a firm that plans to provide time, place, and ownership utilities to patients needing prescriptions. The Rockville, Maryland, firm sells generic drugs to physicians who are now authorized by the Federal Trade Commission to dispense prescription drugs. The drugs are to be sold to doctors by a sales force of licensed pharmacists. Direct sales by physicians now account for only $15 million of the $20 billion prescription drug market, because only 1 percent of all physicians sell their own prescriptions. However, PPS believes that this distribution channel will eventually hold a 14 percent market share, since it is providing patients with prescriptions at the times and places of their choosing. The sale of prescriptions in the doctor's office will also create ownership utility.[2]

Functions Performed by Distribution Channels

The distribution channel performs several functions in the overall marketing system. These include facilitating the exchange process, sorting to alleviate discrepancies in assortment, standardizing transactions, and the search process.[3]

Facilitating the Exchange Process   The evolution of distribution channels began with the exchange process described in Chapter 1. As market economies grew, the exchange process itself became more complicated. Because there were more producers and potential buyers, marketing intermediaries emerged to facilitate transactions by cutting the number of marketplace contacts. For example, if 10 apple orchards in eastern Washington sell to 6 supermarket chains each, there are a total of 60 transactions. However, if the producers set up and market their apples through a cooperative, the number of contacts declines to 16.

Sorting to Alleviate Discrepancies in Assortment   Another essential function of the distribution channel is to adjust discrepancies in assortment via a process known as *sorting*. A producer tends to maximize the quantity of a limited line of products, while the buyer needs a minimum quantity of a wide selection of alternatives. Sorting alleviates such discrepancies by adjusting both the buyer's and the producer's needs.

   Returning to the apple orchard example, an individual orchard's output can be divided into separate homogeneous categories, such as various types and grades of apples. The apples are then combined with similar crops of other orchards—a process known as *accumulation*. These accumulations are broken down into smaller units or divisions, such as boxes of apples. In marketing literature, this is often called *breaking bulk*. Finally, an assortment is built for the next level in the distribution channel. For example, the eastern Washington cooperative might prepare an assortment of four boxes of Golden Delicious and six crates of Red Delicious apples for a Jewel supermarket in a Chicago suburb.

Standardizing Transactions   If each transaction in a complex market economy were subject to negotiation, the exchange process would be chaotic. Distribution channels standardize exchange transactions in terms of the product, such as the grading of apples into types and grades, and of the transfer process itself. Order points, prices, payment terms, delivery schedules, and purchase lots tend to be standardized by distribution channel members. For example, supermarket buyers might have online communications links with the cooperative. Once a certain stock position is reached, more apples are automatically ordered from either current output or controlled-atmosphere storage.

The Search Process   Distribution channels also accommodate the search behavior for both buyers and sellers. Buyers search for specific products and services to fill their needs, while sellers attempt to find out what consumers want. A college student looking for some Golden Delicious apples might go to the fruit section of a Jewel store near Chicago. Similarly, the manager of that department would be able to provide the Washington cooperative with information about sales trends in his or her marketplace.

Types of Distribution Channels

Literally hundreds of marketing channels exist today, and obviously there is no such thing as one best distribution channel. The best channel for Mary Kay Cosmetics is directly from manufacturer to consumer through a sales force of 140,000 beauty consultants. The best channel for frozen french fries may be

THE COMPETITIVE EDGE

FireKing International, Inc.

When Van Carlisle took over Fire-King International, a firm his grand-father had founded, the New Albany, Indiana, company had the lowest market share of any of the nation's six producers of fireproof filing cabi-nets. Thirteen years later, FireKing has a dominant 37 percent market share and sales of $16 million.

How did FireKing become a small-business success? When Car-lisle took over at age 24, he soon re-alized that FireKing's problems were with his wholesalers and retailers, not his customers. FireKing filing cabinets were perceived as being of the highest quality in the industry be-cause they were the heaviest, weigh-ing an average of 750 pounds. While the ultimate consumer liked the Fire-King product, the firm's dealers were concerned about freight costs and other factors.

Carlisle soon realized that he would have to improve FireKing's re-lations with its distribution channel. He began by pointing out an essen-tial difference between FireKing and its competition. Three of FireKing's competitors used a less costly pro-duction process that cut costs but of-ten led to rust, since it allowed wet insulation to dry within the steel framework of the cabinet. Carlisle was quick to point out the threat of a rusting inventory to dealers.

Since weight meant quality to consumers, Carlisle decided against making his product lighter. Instead, he set up a network of contract car-riers and offered dealers a prepaid freight program. Carlisle observed: "Before weight could be a positive, it had to be eliminated as a negative."

Fireproof filing cabinets are given either C or D ratings by Underwriters Laboratories. Both are fire resistant, but a C rating means that the cabinet could survive a 30-foot fall or a roof cave-in, both possible circumstances in a fire. At the time, FireKing made both C- and D-rated cabinets, but most of the competition concentrated on the latter. Carlisle decided a change was in order. He switched FireKing's production to C-rated cab-inets only and priced them at the for-mer D-rated unit level.

When later marketing research in-dicated that consumers wanted 25-inch filing cabinets (regular ones are 31.5 inches deep), Carlisle added a new, smaller line. The new product line was introduced to dealers with travel incentive programs, again aimed at building dealer relations.

FireKing's growth pattern was not without problems. A vendor once sent 15,000 defective locks, which were mistakenly installed in FireKing cabinets. When the error was discov-ered, Carlisle quickly replaced his dealers' inventories and installed new locks on already sold units. He even sent $25 gift certificates to cus-tomers who had bought cabinets with defective locks.

FireKing's 24 percent annual compound growth rate during Car-lisle's tenure illustrates the success of his marketing efforts. Further, he intends to keep his competitive edge in the future.

Source: David E. Gumpert, "Which Cus-tomer Is Always Right?" *INC.* (June 1987), pp. 145–147. *Photo source:* Courtesy of FireKing International Incorporated.

from food processor to agent marketing intermediary to merchant wholesaler to supermarket to consumer. Instead of searching for the best channel for all products, the marketing manager must analyze alternative channels in light of consumer needs to determine the most appropriate channel or channels for the firm's products and services.

However, even once the proper channels have been chosen and established, the need for the marketing manager's channel decisions has not ceased. Channels, like so many marketing variables, change, and today's ideal channel may prove inappropriate in a few years.

Tupperware International's 90,000-strong sales force attends housewares parties for 22 million consumers each year. The firm's home party plan has been a successful distribution strategy for years. But recent changes in this marketplace have forced Tupperware to adapt its strategy to reach working women. These customers are no longer eager to spend their limited free time at an evening Tupperware party. As a result, the firm is now hosting lunchtime parties and product displays in office buildings. Tupperware has also added a toll-free number through which potential customers can locate dealers in their areas. The dealers also reach working women with a 32-page catalog that has been distributed to 30 million people. In short, Tupperware's distribution channel has been modified to reflect changes in consumer buying patterns.[4]

Alternative Distribution Channels

Figure 12.2 depicts the major channels available for marketers of consumer and industrial products and services. In general, industrial products channels tend to be shorter than consumer goods channels due to geographical concentrations of industrial buyers and a relatively limited number of purchasers. In addition, retail sales are characteristic only of consumer goods purchases; therefore, the retailer is not found in industrial channels. Service channels also tend to be short because of the intangibility of services and the need to maintain personal relationships within the channel. Service channels are discussed in greater detail in Chapter 20.

Producer to Consumer or Industrial User   The simplest, most direct distribution channel is not necessarily the most popular, as evidenced by the relatively small percentage of dollar volume of sales that moves along this route. Fewer than 5 percent of all consumer goods move from producer to consumer. In consumer markets, the producer-to-consumer channel is broken down into two segments. **Direct selling** involves direct sales contact between the buyer and seller. Direct-sales companies include Avon, Mary Kay Cosmetics, Tupperware, Amway, and Shaklee. **Direct marketing,** in contrast, refers to direct communication other than personal sales contact between buyer and seller. Catalogs and direct-mail advertisements illustrate this distribution channel. Direct marketing and direct selling are discussed in greater detail in Chapter 14.

Direct channels are much more important in the industrial goods market. Most major installations, accessory equipment, and even component parts and raw materials are marketed through direct contacts between seller and buyer.

direct selling
Direct sales contact between buyer and seller.

direct marketing
Direct communication, other than personal sales contacts, between buyer and seller.

Figure 12.2
Alternative Distribution Channels

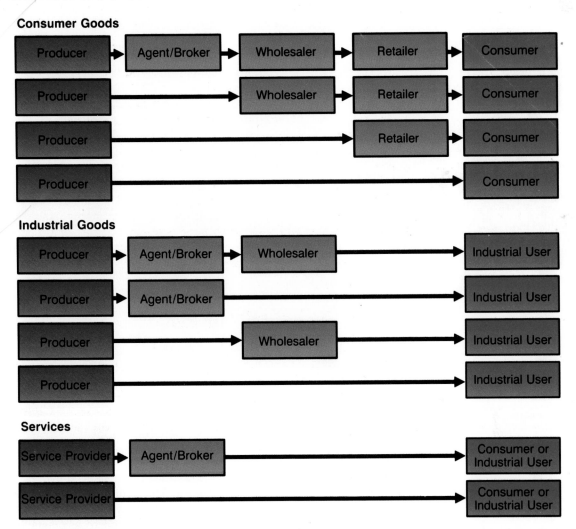

Consumer Goods

Producer → Agent/Broker → Wholesaler → Retailer → Consumer

Producer → Wholesaler → Retailer → Consumer

Producer → Retailer → Consumer

Producer → Consumer

Industrial Goods

Producer → Agent/Broker → Wholesaler → Industrial User

Producer → Agent/Broker → Industrial User

Producer → Wholesaler → Industrial User

Producer → Industrial User

Services

Service Provider → Agent/Broker → Consumer or Industrial User

Service Provider → Consumer or Industrial User

Producer to Wholesaler to Retailer to Consumer   The traditional channel for consumer goods proceeds from producer to wholesaler to retailer to user. It is the method used by small retailers and literally thousands of small producers that make limited lines of products. Small companies with limited financial resources utilize wholesalers as immediate sources of funds and as a means of reaching the hundreds of retailers who will stock their products. Small retailers rely on wholesalers as buying specialists that ensure a balanced inventory of goods produced in various regions of the world.

The wholesaler's sales force is responsible for reaching the market with the producer's output. Many manufacturers also use specialized sales representatives to contact their retailer accounts. These representatives serve as sources of marketing information, but they do not actually sell the product.

Figure 12.3
Use of Industrial Distributors in
Organizational Marketing

Source: Courtesy of Janesville Apparel Division, Lion Apparel, Incorporated.

Producer to Wholesaler to Industrial User   Similar characteristics in the organizational market often lead to the utilization of marketing intermediaries between producer and industrial purchaser. The term *industrial distributor* is commonly utilized in the industrial market to refer to wholesalers that take title to the goods they handle. For example, in an effort to reach customers that are inaccessible through its own sales force, IBM has turned to industrial distributors. IBM industrial distributors sell a variety of products, including supplies and moderately priced display terminals. IBM continues to sell its entire product line, but its sales force can now concentrate on larger computer systems.

Firefighting equipment and gear are also typically sold through industrial distributors. Figure 12.3 shows how one such firm uses distributors and dealers as its channel of distribution.

Producer to Agent to Wholesaler to Retailer to Consumer   When products are produced by a large number of small companies, a unique intermediary—the agent—performs the basic function of bringing buyer and seller together. The agent is, in fact, a wholesaling intermediary that does not take title to the goods. The agent merely represents the producer or the regular wholesaler (that does take title to the goods) in seeking a market for the manufacturer's output or in locating a source of supply for the buyer. Chapter 13 describes two types of wholesaling intermediaries—merchant wholesalers, which take title to the goods they handle, and agent wholesalers, which do not.

Agents are used in such industries as canning and frozen-food packing. In these industries, many producers supply a large number of geographically scattered wholesalers. The agent wholesaling intermediary performs the service of bringing buyers and sellers together.

Producer to Agent to Wholesaler to Industrial User Similar conditions often exist in the industrial market, in which small producers attempt to market their offerings to large wholesalers. The agent wholesaling intermediary, often called a *manufacturer's representative,* serves as an independent sales force in contacting the wholesale buyers.

Producer to Agent to Industrial User Where the unit sale is small, merchant wholesalers must be used in order to economically cover the market. By maintaining regional inventories, they achieve transportation economies through stockpiling goods and making final small shipments over short distances. Where the unit sale is large and transportation accounts for a small percentage of the total product cost, the producer-agent-industrial user channel is usually employed. The agent wholesaling intermediaries in effect become the company's industrial sales force.

Service Provider to Consumer or Industrial User Distribution of services to both consumers and industrial users usually is simpler and more direct than in the case of industrial and consumer goods. This is partly due to the intangibility of services. The marketer of services is often less concerned with storage, transportation, and inventory control and typically uses shorter channels.

Another consideration is the need for continuing personal relationships between producers and users of many services. Consumers will remain clients of the same insurance agent, bank, or travel agent as long as they are reasonably satisfied. Similarly, public accounting firms and attorneys are retained on a relatively permanent basis by industrial buyers.

Service Provider to Agent to Consumer or Industrial User When marketing intermediaries are used by service firms, they are usually agents or brokers. Common examples include insurance agents, securities brokers, travel agents, and entertainment agents. For instance, travel and hotel packages sometimes are created by intermediaries and then marketed at the retail level by travel agents to both vacationers and firms that want to offer employee incentive awards.

Dual Distribution

Dual distribution refers to the use of two or more distribution channels to reach the same target market. This distribution strategy is usually used to either maximize the firm's coverage in the marketplace or make its marketing effort more cost effective. The first objective is illustrated by automobile parts manufacturers who use both a direct sales force and independent jobbers. In contrast, the cost-effectiveness goal is exemplified by a manufacturer that uses its own sales

dual distribution
Network in which a firm uses more than one distribution channel to reach its target market.

force to sell in high-potential areas while relying on manufacturers' representatives (independent, commissioned salespeople) in lower-volume areas.

Fuller Brush is now testing a dual distribution system. The Sara Lee division, which was started in 1906, now has 13,000 door-to-door sales representatives. This distribution channel has long been the way Fuller Brush did business. Then, a few years ago, Fuller Brush began providing a direct-mail catalog for reaching working women and a younger customer base than its traditional market. Fuller Brush took dual distribution one step further when it opened two Dallas retail stores in 1987.[5]

Distribution Channels for Nonprofit Organizations

Distribution channels for nonprofit organizations tend to be short, simple, and direct. Any marketing intermediaries present in the channel usually are agents such as independent ticket agencies or fund-raising specialists. A major distribution decision involves the specific location of the nonprofit organization.

Nonprofit organizations often fail to exercise caution in planning and executing distribution strategies. Urban hospitals located in declining areas sometimes find it difficult to attract suburban patients. In contrast, some public agencies, such as health and social welfare departments, have set up branches in neighborhood shopping centers in order to be more accessible to their clientele.

Reverse Channels

reverse channel
Path goods follow from consumer back to manufacturer.

While the traditional concept of marketing channels involves the movement of products and services from producer to consumer or industrial user, there is continued interest in reverse channels. **Reverse channels** refer to the backward movement of goods from the user to the producer.

Reverse channels will increase in importance as raw materials become more expensive and additional laws are passed. Bottle deposits have long been required in Michigan, Oregon, and several other states. New Jersey recently passed legislation requiring businesses and households to separate their trash to make recycling more feasible. The Garden State also gives tax credits to firms that buy equipment using recycled materials.[6]

For recycling to succeed, the following four basic conditions must be satisfied:

1. A technology for efficiently processing the material being recycled must be available.

2. A market must be available for the end product—the reclaimed material.

3. A substantial and continuous quantity of secondary products (recycled aluminum, reclaimed steel for automobiles, recycled paper) must be available.

4. A marketing system that can profitably bridge the gap between suppliers of secondary products and end users must be developed.

In some instances, the reverse channel consists of traditional marketing intermediaries. In the soft-drink industry, retailers and local bottlers perform these functions. In other cases, manufacturers take the initiative by establishing redemption centers and "cleanup" days, developing systems to rechannel paper products for recycling, and creating specialized organizations to handle waste disposal and recycling.

Other reverse-channel participants may include community groups that organize cleanup days and develop systems and organizations for handling recycling and waste disposal.

Reverse Channels for Product Recalls and Repairs   Reverse channels are also used for product recalls and repairs. Ownership of some products is registered so that proper notification can be sent in the event of recalls. For example, in the case of automobile recalls, owners are advised to have the problem corrected at their dealerships. Similarly, reverse channels have been used for repairs for some products. The warranty for a small appliance might specify that if repairs are needed within the first 90 days of sale, the item should be returned to the dealer and after that period to the factory. Such reverse channels are a vital element of product recall and repair procedures.

A reverse channel was established for Kodak instant cameras in 1986 following a U.S. Supreme Court ruling prohibiting the firm from marketing instant cameras and film. The ruling stemmed from a patent infringement suit initiated by Polaroid. Since owners of the 16.5 million Kodak instant cameras could no longer purchase compatible film, Kodak marketers, within hours of the court ruling, offered camera owners the option of turning in each camera for either a disk camera and film with a retail value of $50, coupons for $50 worth of other Kodak products, or a share of Kodak stock, then selling for about $50. Camera owners were instructed to call a toll-free number, and callers were sent a postage-paid envelope for mailing cameras. Merchandise, coupons, or stock certificates were then mailed to the respondents. Although Eastman Kodak was not legally obligated to make this exchange, the recall was an effective, albeit expensive, method of maintaining the firm's positive image with its customers.[7]

Facilitating Agencies

A **facilitating agency** provides specialized assistance for regular channel members (such as producers, wholesalers, and retailers) in moving products from producer to consumer. Included in the definition of facilitating agencies are insurance companies, marketing research firms, financial institutions, advertising agencies, and transportation and warehousing firms.

> **facilitating agency**
> Institution, such as an insurance company, bank, or transportation company, that provides specialized assistance for channel members in moving products from producer to consumer.

Facilitating agencies perform a number of special services. Insurance companies assume some of the risks involved in transporting the goods, marketing research firms supply information, financial institutions provide the necessary financing, advertising agencies help sell the goods, and transportation and warehousing firms store and physically move the goods. In some instances, the major channel members perform these services. Facilitating agencies are not, however, involved in directing the flow of goods and services through the channel.

Power in the Distribution Channel

Some marketing institutions must exercise leadership in the distribution channel if the channel is to be an effective aspect of marketing strategy. Decisions must be made and conflicts among channel members resolved. Channel leadership is a function of members' power within the distribution channel.

Bases of Power

There are five bases of power within the distribution channel: reward power, coercive power, legitimate power, referent power, and expert power.[8] All of these bases can be used to establish a position of channel leadership.

Reward Power   If channel members can offer some type of reward to another member, they possess *reward power*. Examples are the granting of an exclusive sales territory or franchise.

Coercive Power   The threat of economic punishment is known as *coercive power*. For instance, a manufacturer might threaten an uncooperative retailer with loss of its dealership. Another example is Sears' strength with its suppliers. The giant retailer's market size is a significant base of power in its distribution channel.

Legitimate Power   Distribution channels that are linked contractually are examples of *legitimate power*. For example, a franchisee might be contractually required to perform such activities as maintaining a common type of outlet, contributing to general advertising, and remaining open during specified time periods.

Referent Power   Agreement among channel members as to what is in their mutual best interests is known as *referent power*. For instance, many manufacturers maintain dealer councils to help resolve potential problems in distributing a product or service. Both parties have a mutual interest in maintaining effective channel relationships.

Expert Power   Knowledge is the determinant of *expert power*. For instance, a manufacturer might assist a retailer with store layout or advertising based on its marketing expertise with the product line.

Channel Leadership

channel captain
Dominant and controlling member of a marketing channel.

The dominant and controlling member of a channel is called the **channel captain.** Historically the channel leadership role was performed by the producer or wholesaler, since retailers tend to be both small and localized. However, retailers increasingly are taking on the role of channel captain as large chains assume traditional wholesaling functions and even dictate product design specifications to manufacturers.

Producers as Channel Captains   Since producers and service providers typically create new product and service offerings and enjoy the benefits of large-scale operations, they fill the role of channel captain in many marketing channels. Examples of such manufacturers include Armstrong Cork, General Electric, Magnavox, and Sealy Mattress.

Retailers as Channel Captains   Retailers are often powerful enough to serve as channel captains in many industries. Large chain operations may bypass independent wholesalers and utilize manufacturers as suppliers in producing the retailers' private brands at quality levels specified by the chains. Major

Wetterau Incorporated, the nation's third largest full-service food wholesaler, prints more than 1.5 million advertising circulars each week for its independent retailer customers. As a channel captain, Wetterau provides many other services for its 2,800 grocery retailer customers, including retail accounting, merchandising and business counseling, shelf space and price management, point-of-sale scanning, and in-store microcomputers.

Photo source: Courtesy of Wetterau Incorporated.

retailers, such as Kmart, Sears, J.C. Penney, and Montgomery Ward, serve as leaders in many of the marketing channels with which they are associated.

Wholesalers as Channel Captains   Although their relative influence has declined since 1900, wholesalers continue to serve as vital members of many marketing channels. Large-scale wholesalers, such as the Independent Grocers Alliance (IGA), serve as channel captains as they assist independent retailers in competing with chain outlets.

Brand Hostaging

As noted above, retailers increasingly are assuming the role of channel captain. Part of their power comes from their control of the shelf spots in their stores, for which manufacturers must compete. In the average supermarket, there are 17,000 shelf spots; yet manufacturers create 22,000 to 25,000 new offerings each year.

A common marketing strategy for manufacturers is to develop line extensions in order to claim more of the limited shelf facings. For instance, in a recent year it was estimated that 92 percent of Procter & Gamble's new products were line extensions. In 1987, Lever Brothers took the unusual step of confronting the problem head-on in trade advertising. Lever Brothers was concerned that its market's leading Dove brand was being denied adequate shelf facings because of the flood of multiple line extensions. The trade advertisements pointed out that Dove had a dominant 7 percent market share. However, because it had the same amount of shelf space as a decade ago, it was frequently out of stock.[9]

The battle for shelf space has led to a situation known as **brand hostaging,** in which retailers force a manufacturer to pay trade promotion monies or be denied shelf space for its brand. Trade promotion money is essentially a price discount. Several factors have given retailers this new power:

brand hostaging
Situation in which a retailer demands trade promotion funds from a manufacturer in exchange for shelf space.

1. Retailers are less dependent on manufacturers' brands than they were in the past. Today supermarket chains do their own advertising and develop their own merchandising strategies. Further, only 19 percent of all buyers pick brands before they go shopping compared to 35 percent a decade ago.

2. There are fewer stores today than in the past. For example, there were 223,000 food stores in 1968; today there are only 115,000.

3. Sophisticated scanning systems give retailers a tremendous informational advantage. They allow retailers to continually assess prices, shares, and volume trade-offs for various brands. They know what will happen if they shift shelf space to another brand priced at a certain level.

For manufacturers, the best defense is to build market share even at the expense of short-term profitability. A strong market share is the best argument anyone can give for carrying a specific brand.[10]

Channel Conflict

Channel captains often are called upon to mediate or resolve channel conflicts. Distribution channels must be organized and regarded as systematic, cooperative efforts if operating efficiencies are to be achieved. Yet channel members often perform as separate, independent, and even competitive forces. Too often marketing institutions within the channel believe it extends only one step forward or backward. They think in terms of suppliers and customers rather than of vital links within the total channel.

Types of Conflict

Two types of conflict may occur—horizontal or vertical. Both are hindrances to the normal functioning of distribution channels.

Horizontal Conflict   Horizontal conflict may develop among channel members at the same level, such as two or more wholesalers or two or more retailers, or among marketing intermediaries of the same type, such as two competing discount stores or several retail florists. More often, however, horizontal conflict occurs among different types of marketing intermediaries that handle similar products. The retail druggist competes with variety stores, discount houses, department stores, convenience stores, and mail-order houses, all of which may be supplied by the producer with identically branded products. Consumer desire for convenient, one-stop shopping has led to multiple channels and the use of numerous outlets for many products.

Sometimes horizontal conflict occurs among retailers that carry the same names. Consider the Rod Carew commemorative Coke bottle that was produced in conjunction with the retirement of the baseball hero's uniform number.

FOCUS ON ETHICS

Distribution Problems at Porsche

When problems crop up in the distribution channel, a manufacturer can face hard choices involving ethical norms as well as business judgment. The German sports car producer Porsche was faced with just such a situation in 1984.

In the United States, Porsches were being imported, marketed, and serviced by Volkswagen of America through a network of 330 dealers, some of which also sold Volkswagens and Audis. But former Porsche CEO Peter Schutz was troubled by some negative reports concerning the U.S. distribution system. Certain dealers were experiencing inventory shortages and, rather than losing a sale, would buy cars at a premium from other dealers and pass along the additional costs to customers. Other problems included high inventory costs and getting cars to match customer specifications. Moreover, since Porsches were being distributed by Volkswagen, their image was to some extent being confused with the latter's.

Schutz anticipated that one or more of the Japanese car makers would soon enter the high end of the U.S. sports car market. He wanted to make sure that before that happened Porsche's distribution system was the best it could be. Schutz decided to cut ties with Volkswagen and institute a company-controlled distribution network. It would include 40 Porsche centers located throughout the country, which would supply the existing dealerships as well as sell cars directly to the public. Instead of buying cars from the company, dealerships would order vehicles from the Porsche centers as they made sales. In addition, the centers would perform the tasks of dealer prep and delivery, which traditionally are handled by dealerships. As a result of all these changes, dealers would be hit in the pocket as well, because commissions would decrease from the 16-to-18 percent range stipulated in the Volkswagen of America agreements with the dealers to a flat 8 percent under the new distribution plan.

Predictably, dealers revolted. The new plan meant that dealers would be competing with the centers but would be unable to either carry inventory or get clear information on their market potential. Robert Mc-Elwaine, president of the American International Automobile Dealers Association, said, "These dealers have made huge investments in their dealerships under the premise that they would be able to buy and sell Porsche autos."

In the face of dealer opposition, Schutz decided to back off from the proposed changes in the distribution network. As John Cook, president of Porsche Cars North America, put it: "We need an enthusiastic organization." Porsche did, however, cut its ties with Volkswagen and implemented several changes to improve customer service. For example, it installed computers at each dealership to provide Porsche owners with computerized service records and to help new customers locate specially equipped models.

Sources: Matt DeLorenzo, "Porsche Casts a Pall on Franchise System," *Automotive News* (February 20, 1984), p. 57; "Dealer Groups Assail Changes by Porsche," *Automotive News* (February 20, 1984), p. 54; "Porsche, Volkswagen Sued by Distributor on U.S. Sales," *The Wall Street Journal* (March 7, 1984), p. 4; and Matt DeLorenzo, "Porsche Changes Its Mind," *Automotive News* (March 19, 1984), p. 1.

The commemorative bottles were supposed to raise scholarship monies for Minnesota baseball players and to help pay the college expenses of Carew's daughters. Plans called for the 43,000 commemorative Coke bottles to be sold for $1.49 through Red Owl stores within reach of the Minnesota Twins' radio network. But two months after Rod Carew Day at the Metrodome, Red Owl returned 16,800 bottles to the local Coca-Cola bottler. The special promotion had failed because of conflict among Red Owl stores. The company-owned stores sold the bottles, but many of the 100 franchised units elected not to do so. Jim Almsted, Red Owl's vice-president of marketing, commented: "Everybody comes up with a different agenda. You may hate baseball. Or maybe there were some hard feelings (about Carew). He didn't even finish his career here, and he left on kind of a sour note." Meanwhile, the bottler is attempting to sell the commemorative Coke bottles through sporting goods and convenience stores and to collectors. Dan Cassidy, sales director for the Minnesota Twins, remarked: "We could be selling these for 10 years."[11]

Vertical Conflict Vertical conflict can occur between channel members at different levels, for example, between producers and wholesalers or retailers. Vertical conflict occurs frequently and often is the more severe form of conflict in the channel. Conflict may occur between producers and retailers when retailers develop private brands to compete with the producers' or when producers establish their own retail stores or create mail-order operations that compete with retailers. Conflict between producers and wholesalers may occur when producers attempt to bypass wholesalers and make direct sales to retailers or industrial users. In other instances, wholesalers may promote competitive products.

Vertical conflict is seen in recent advertising by Cadillac dealers. Cadillac has been heavily promoting its two-seat Allante as an alternative to sporty European luxury cars purchased by young, affluent buyers. However, Cadillac dealers have been reluctant to downplay their traditional market, which is primarily 55-and-over males who seek size and comfort in a luxury car. An advertising campaign run by many Cadillac dealer groups (not General Motors) points out that the Cadillac Fleetwood Brougham is America's biggest luxury car.[12]

Achieving Channel Cooperation

The basic antidote to channel conflict is effective cooperation among channel members. Most channels have more harmonious relationships than conflicting ones; if they did not, the channels would have ceased to exist long ago. Cooperation is best achieved by considering all channel members as part of the same organization. Achieving cooperation is the prime responsibility of the dominant member, the channel captain, which must provide the leadership necessary for ensuring the channel's efficient functioning.

Channel conflict is sometimes the product of dual distribution in which a manufacturer uses both its own sales force and a dealer network. IBM uses a dual distribution strategy, but when it introduced its new line of personal computers, "Big Blue" (as IBM is known) took elaborate steps to ensure dealer cooperation. Dealers received inventory more promptly than they had in the past. Most of the initial production run went to the dealers rather than to IBM's own sales force. Dealers also benefited from a liberal return policy and favorable payment terms.[13] As the channel captain, IBM was determined not to let channel conflict interfere with its product launch.

Channel Strategy Decisions

Marketers face several channel strategy decisions. The selection of a specific distribution channel is the most basic of these decisions. The level of distribution intensity must also be determined. Channel decision makers must also address the issue of vertical marketing systems.

Selection of a Distribution Channel

What makes a franchised retail dealer network best for Ford Motor Company? Why do operating supplies often go through both agents and merchant wholesalers before being purchased by industrial firms? Why do some firms employ multiple channels for the same products? The firm must answer many such questions in choosing distribution channels. The choice is based on an analysis of market, product, producer, and competitive factors. All factors are important, and often they are interrelated. But the overriding consideration is where, when, and how consumers choose to buy the product or service. Consumer orientation is as important to channel decisions as it is in other areas of marketing strategy.

Market Factors   A major determinant of channel structure is whether the product is intended for the consumer or industrial market. Industrial purchasers usually prefer to deal directly with the manufacturer (except for supplies or small accessory items), but most consumers make their purchases from retail stores. Often products for both industrial users and consumers are sold through more than one channel.

The needs and geographical location of the firm's market affect channel choice. Direct sales are possible where the firm's potential market is concentrated. A small number of potential buyers also increases the feasibility of direct channels. Consumer goods are purchased by households everywhere. Since these households are numerous and geographically dispersed and because they purchase a small volume at a given time, marketing intermediaries must be employed to market products to them.

A good illustration of how market factors influence distribution is provided by Jostens, which has been able to capture more than 40 percent of the market for high school class rings and yearbooks by using an 800-member, independent, direct-selling sales force. This direct channel, serviced by a highly educated sales force consisting largely of former high school teachers and coaches, has proven extremely successful.

Order size also affects the channel decision. Producers are likely to use shorter, more direct channels in cases where retail customers or industrial buyers place relatively small numbers of large orders. Retailers often utilize buying offices to negotiate directly with manufacturers for large-scale purchases, while wholesalers may be used to contact smaller retailers.

Shifts in consumer buying patterns also influence channel decisions. The desire for credit, the growth of self-service, the increased use of mail-order houses, and the greater willingness to purchase from door-to-door salespeople all affect a firm's choice of marketing channels.

Product Factors   Product factors also play a role in determining optimal distribution channels. Perishable products, such as fresh produce and fashion products with short life cycles, typically move through relatively short channels directly to the retailer or ultimate consumer. Nabisco Brands, Inc. distributes its cookies and crackers from the bakery to retail shelves. Chips Ahoy!, Fig Newtons, Oreos, Ritz crackers, and other Nabisco brands are delivered to retail customers by a fleet of 1,800 company-owned trucks and a 3,000-member sales force. Each year Hines & Smart Corporation ships some 5 million pounds of live lobsters in specially designed styrofoam containers directly to restaurants and hotels throughout North America.

Complex products, such as custom-made installations and computer equipment, typically are sold by the producer to the buyer. In general, the more standardized the product, the longer the channel. Standardized goods usually are marketed by wholesalers. Products that require regular service or specialized

To ensure that customers receive personalized service and the freshest supplies of its premium ice cream, Dreyer's Grand Ice Cream, Inc. uses a direct store delivery system. It is time consuming and expensive, but Dreyer leverages the costs by carrying other manufacturers' selected premium products. Onboard computers used throughout Dreyer's distribution network monitor sales by store and product type, enabling route salespeople to customize deliveries to satisfy individual stores' flavor and product needs.

Photo source: Courtesy of Dreyer's and Edy's Grand Ice Cream.

repairs normally are not distributed through channels employing independent wholesalers. Automobiles are marketed through a franchised network of retail dealers whose employees receive training on how to properly service the cars.

Another generalization about distribution channels is that the lower the product's unit value, the longer the channel. Convenience goods and industrial supplies with typically low unit prices frequently are marketed through relatively long channels. Installations and more expensive industrial and consumer goods employ shorter, more direct channels.

Producer Factors Companies with adequate financial, managerial, and marketing resources are less compelled to utilize intermediaries in marketing their products. A financially strong manufacturer can hire its own sales force, warehouse its own products, and grant credit to retailers or consumers. A weaker firm must rely on marketing intermediaries for these services (although some large retail chains purchase all of the manufacturer's output, thereby bypassing the independent wholesaler). Production-oriented firms may be forced to utilize the marketing expertise of marketing intermediaries to offset their organizations' lack of finances and management.

A firm with a broad product line usually is able to market its products directly to retailers or industrial users, since its sales force can offer a variety of products. Larger total sales permit the selling costs to be spread over a number of products and make direct sales feasible. The single-product firm often discovers that direct selling is an unaffordable luxury.

The manufacturer's need for control over the product also influences channel selection. If aggressive promotion is desired at the retail level, the producer

Table 12.1
Factors Affecting Selection of Distribution Channel

	Characteristics of Short Channels	Characteristics of Long Channels
Market Factors	Industrial user	Consumers
	Geographically concentrated	Geographically diverse
	Technical knowledge and regular servicing required	Technical knowledge and regular servicing not required
	Large orders	Small orders
Product Factors	Perishable	Durable
	Complex	Standardized
	Expensive	Inexpensive
Producer Factors	Manufacturer has adequate resources for performing channel functions	Manufacturer lacks adequate resources for performing channel functions
	Broad product line	Limited product line
	Channel control important	Channel control not important
Competitive Factors	Manufacturer feels that marketing intermediaries are inadequately promoting products	Manufacturer feels that marketing intermediaries are adequately promoting products

chooses the shortest available channel. For new products, the producer may be forced to implement an introductory advertising campaign before independent wholesalers will agree to handle the items.

Competitive Factors   Some firms are forced to develop unique distribution channels because of inadequate promotion of their products by independent marketing intermediaries. Popular alternatives are for the manufacturer to add a direct sales force or set up its own retail distribution network (a concept discussed later in the chapter).

Table 12.1 summarizes the factors affecting the selection of a distribution channel and examines the effect of each on the channel's overall length.

Determining Distribution Intensity

Adequate market coverage for some products could mean one dealer for 50,000 people. Mars, Inc. marketers defined adequate distribution for Snickers, Milky Way, and Mars candy bars as almost every supermarket, convenience store, drugstore, and variety store, plus many vending machines. The degree of distribution intensity can be viewed as a continuum with three general categories: intensive distribution, selective distribution, and exclusive distribution.

Intensive Distribution   Producers of convenience goods practice **intensive distribution** when they provide saturation coverage of the market, enabling the purchaser to buy the product with a minimum of effort. Examples of goods distributed through this market coverage strategy include soft drinks, candy, gum, and cigarettes.

intensive distribution
Policy in which a manufacturer of a convenience good attempts to saturate the market with the product.

Bic pens, lighters, and razors can be purchased in more than 200,000 retail outlets in the United States. As the retail prices of floppy disks have declined, manufacturers have begun to move toward intensive distribution; consumers can buy Elephant or Verbatim floppies at retail computer and office supply stores, the traditional retail outlets for computer software. In addition, these floppy disks can be purchased at mass merchandisers such as Kmart, Sears, and Montgomery Ward.

Mass coverage and low unit prices make the use of wholesalers almost mandatory for such distribution. An important exception is Avon Products, which sells directly to the consumer through a nationwide network of independent neighborhood sales personnel. These representatives purchase cosmetics, toiletries, jewelry, and toys directly from the manufacturer at 50 to 65 percent of the retail price. Their initial assignments include a territory of 100 homes; their territories may expand depending on their sales results.

selective distribution
Policy in which a firm chooses only a limited number of retailers to handle its product line.

Selective Distribution   **Selective distribution** is a market coverage strategy in which a firm chooses only a limited number of retailers in a market area to handle its product line. By limiting the number of retailers, the firm can reduce its total marketing costs while establishing better working relationships within the channel. Cooperative advertising (in which the manufacturer pays a percentage of the retailer's advertising expenditures and the retailer prominently displays the firm's products) can be utilized for mutual benefit, and marginal retailers can be avoided. Where product service is important, the manufacturer usually provides dealer training and assistance. Price cutting is less likely, since fewer dealers are handling the firm's line. For example, Massachusetts-based Epicure Products, Inc. requires its dealers to be technically proficient in marketing and servicing its high-fidelity speakers. Dealers are also required to maintain listening rooms for the convenience of customers.[14]

exclusive distribution
Policy in which a firm grants exclusive rights to a wholesaler or retailer to sell in a particular geographical area.

Exclusive Distribution   When producers grant exclusive rights to a wholesaler or retailer to sell in a specific geographic region, they are practicing **exclusive distribution,** an extreme form of selective distribution. The best example of exclusive distribution is within the automobile industry. For example, a city with a population of 100,000 will have a single Mazda dealer or a single Pontiac agency. Exclusive-distribution agreements also occur in the marketing of some major appliances and fashion apparel.

Some market coverage may be sacrificed through a policy of exclusive distribution, but this loss is often offset by the development and maintenance of an image of quality and prestige for the product and by the reduced marketing costs associated with a small number of accounts. In exclusive distribution, producers and retailers cooperate closely in decisions concerning advertising and promotion, inventory to be carried by the retailers, and prices.

Legal Problems of Exclusive Distribution   The use of exclusive distribution presents a number of potential legal problems in three areas—exclusive-dealing agreements, closed sales territories, and tying agreements. While none of these practices is illegal per se, all may be ruled illegal if they reduce competition or tend to create a monopoly situation.

Exclusive-Dealing Agreements   An **exclusive-dealing agreement** prohibits a marketing intermediary (a wholesaler or, more typically, a retailer) from handling competing products. Producers of high-priced shopping goods, specialty goods, and accessory equipment often require such agreements as assurance by the marketing intermediary of total concentration on the firm's product line. These contracts are considered violations of the Clayton Act if the producer's or dealer's sales volume represents a substantial percentage of total sales in the market or sales area. The courts have ruled that sellers that are initially entering the market can use exclusive-dealing agreements as a means of strengthening their competitive positions. But the same agreements are considered violations of the Clayton Act when used by firms with sizable market shares, since they may bar competitors from the market. In 1985, 12 oil companies—including Amoco, Chevron, Exxon, Mobil, Shell, and Texaco—paid $25 million in damages and agreed not to force the nation's 55,000 independent service station operators to buy gas exclusively from them for 5 years.[15]

exclusive-dealing agreement Arrangement between a manufacturer and a marketing intermediary that prohibits the intermediary from handling competing product lines.

Closed Sales Territories   Producers with **closed sales territories** restrict the geographical territories for each of their distributors. Although the distributors may be granted exclusive territories, they are prohibited from opening new facilities or marketing the manufacturers' products outside their assigned territories. The legality of closed sales territories depends on whether the restrictions decrease competition. If competition is lessened, closed sales territories are considered as being in violation of the Federal Trade Commission Act and of provisions of the Sherman Act and Clayton Act.

closed sales territory Restricted geographical selling region specified by a manufacturer for its distributors.

The legality of closed sales territories is also determined by whether the restrictions are horizontal or vertical. Horizontal territorial restrictions involve agreements by retailers or wholesalers to avoid competition among products from the same producer. Such agreements consistently have been declared illegal. However, the U.S. Supreme Court has ruled that vertical territorial restrictions—those between producers and wholesalers or retailers—may be legal. While the ruling is not entirely clear-cut, such agreements are likely to be legal in cases where the manufacturer occupies a relatively small part of the market. In such instances, the restrictions may actually increase competition among competing brands. The wholesaler or retailer faces no competition from other dealers carrying the manufacturer's brand and therefore can concentrate on effectively competing with other brands.

Tying Agreements   The third legal question of exclusive dealing involves the use of a **tying agreement**—an agreement that requires a dealer that wishes to become the exclusive dealer for a producer's products to also carry other products of that producer. In the apparel industry, for example, such an agreement may require the dealer to carry a line of less popular clothing in addition to the fast-moving items.

tying agreement Arrangement between a marketing intermediary and a manufacturer that requires the intermediary to carry the manufacturer's full product line in exchange for an exclusive dealership.

Tying agreements violate the Sherman Act and Clayton Act when they lessen competition or create monopoly situations by keeping competitors out of major markets. For this reason, International Salt Company was prohibited from selling salt as a tying product with the lease of its patented salt-dispensing machines for snow and ice removal. The Supreme Court ruled that such an agreement unreasonably eliminated competition among sellers of salt.

Figure 12.4
Example of a Corporate
Marketing System

Source: Courtesy of Hart Schaffner & Marx Clothes.

Vertical Marketing Systems

**vertical marketing system
(VMS)**
Preplanned distribution channel
organized to be cost effective
and achieve improved distribution efficiency.

Efforts to reduce channel conflict and make distribution more effective have led
to the development of vertical marketing systems. These channel systems contrast markedly with earlier distribution channels in the United States. A **vertical
marketing system (VMS)** is defined as a planned channel system designed to
improve distribution efficiency and cost effectiveness. These objectives are
achieved through economies of scale and elimination of duplicated services.
There are three types of vertical marketing systems: corporate, administered,
and contractual.

Corporate System

corporate marketing system
VMS in which there is single
ownership of each stage of the
marketing channel.

Where there is single ownership of each stage of the marketing channel, a
corporate marketing system exists. Hartmarx markets its Hart Schaffner &
Marx, Pierre Cardin, Austin Reed, and other brands through its company-owned
network of 259 stores as well as through independent retailers throughout the
United States. Figure 12.4 shows an advertisement promoting the firm's Hart
Schaffner & Marx brand. At one time, Holiday Corp. owned a furniture manu-

facturer and a carpet mill that supplied its Holiday Inn hotels. Just a few years ago, telephone giant Nynex purchased 100 retail product centers from IBM to handle not only telephone equipment but such logical communications products as personal computers and related electronic products. Other well-known corporate systems include Firestone and Sherwin-Williams.

Administered System

In an **administered marketing system,** channel coordination is achieved through the exercise of power by a dominant channel member. Magnavox, for example, obtains aggressive promotional support from its retailers because of its brand's strong reputation. Although the retailers are independently owned and operated, they cooperate with the manufacturer because of the effective working relationships built up over the years.

administered marketing system
VMS in which channel coordination is achieved through the exercise of power by a dominant channel member.

Contractual System

The most significant form of vertical marketing system is the **contractual marketing system,** which accounts for nearly 40 percent of all retail sales. Instead of the common ownership of channel components that characterizes the corporate VMS or the relative power of a component of an administered system, the contractual VMS is characterized by formal agreements among channel members. In practice, there are three types of such agreements: the wholesaler-sponsored voluntary chain, the retail cooperative, and the franchise.

contractual marketing system
VMS characterized by formal agreements among channel members.

Wholesaler-Sponsored Voluntary Chain   The *wholesaler-sponsored voluntary chain* represents an attempt by the independent wholesaler to preserve a market for the firm's products by strengthening the firm's retail customers. To enable the independent retailers to compete with the chains, the wholesaler enters into a formal agreement with them wherein the retailers agree to use a common name, maintain standardized facilities, and purchase the wholesaler's products. Often the wholesaler develops a line of private brands to be stocked by the members of the voluntary chain.

A common store name and similar inventory allow the retailers to achieve cost savings on advertising, since a single newspaper ad promotes all the retailers in the trading area. IGA (Independent Grocers' Alliance) Food Stores, with a membership of approximately 3,300 stores in 48 states and annual sales of $8.5 billion, is a good example of a voluntary chain. McKesson & Robbins Drug Company has established Value-Rite, a large voluntary chain in the retail drug industry that includes some 1,600 stores. Other wholesaler-sponsored chains include Associated Druggists and Sentry Hardware.

Retail Cooperative   A second type of contractual VMS is the *retail cooperative,* a wholesaling operation established by a group of retailers to help them better compete with chains. The retailers purchase ownership shares in the wholesaling operation and agree to buy a minimum percentage of their inventory from it. The members may also choose to use a common store name and develop their own private brands to carry out cooperative advertising. Retail cooperatives such as Associated Grocers have been extremely successful in the grocery industry, accounting for one-fifth of all retail grocery sales.

franchise
Contractual arrangement in which a wholesaler or retail dealer (the franchisee) agrees to meet the operating requirements of a manufacturer or other franchiser.

Franchise   A third type of contractual vertical marketing system is the **franchise**—a contractual arrangement in which a wholesaler or retail dealer (the franchisee) agrees to meet the operating requirements of a manufacturer or other franchiser. Typically the dealers receive a variety of marketing, management, technical, and financial services in exchange for a specified fee. The costs of opening a franchise vary widely. For instance, at this writing it costs $9,750 to open a Coustic-Glo ceiling cleaning franchise, while a McDonald's store can cost $350,000.[16]

Franchising has become a huge industry. There are now 478,452 franchised outlets in the United States. Franchising employs over 7 million Americans, or 6.3 percent of the work force. Further, total franchise sales now exceed the combined gross national products of the United Kingdom.[17]

Although franchising has attracted considerable interest since the late 1960s, the concept actually began 100 years earlier when The Singer Company established franchised sewing machine outlets following the Civil War. Early impetus for the franchising concept came after 1900, in the automobile industry. Increasing automobile travel created demand for nationwide distribution of gasoline, oil, and tires, for which franchising was used. The soft-drink industry provides another example of a franchise, notably a contractual arrangement between a syrup manufacturer and a wholesale bottler.

The franchising format that has created the most excitement in retailing during the past 30 years has been the retailer franchise system sponsored by a service firm. McDonald's is an excellent example of such a franchise operation. The company brings together suppliers and a 9,530-unit chain of hamburger outlets.[18] It provides a proven system of retail operation (the operations manual for each outlet weighs several pounds) and lower prices through its purchasing power for meat, buns, napkins, and other necessary supplies; in return, the franchisee pays a fee for the use of the McDonald's name plus a percentage of gross sales. Other familiar examples of franchises are H&R Block, Pearle Vision Center, Holiday Inn, 7-Eleven, Baskin Robbins, Century 21, Pizza Hut, and Weight Watchers. Today, the fastest growth segment of the franchise industry is in personal and business services.

Franchising does not guarantee business success; in fact, the California Department of Corporations estimates that bad "business opportunities and franchising deals" cost Americans over $500 million annually.[19] Potential franchise investors should be familiar with the Federal Trade Commission's *Disclosure Requirements and Prohibitions Concerning Franchising and Business Opportunities,* which is designed to protect would-be investors by requiring disclosure of factual information concerning franchiser claims, guarantees, franchising experience, occurrence of bankruptcy, and evidence of the moral character of key personnel in the franchise. Also specified are the services to be provided by each party and the specific terms of the franchising agreement, including all costs involved.

Whether corporate, administered, or contractual, vertical marketing systems are already a dominant factor in the consumer goods sector of the U.S. economy. An estimated 64 percent of the available market is currently in the hands of retail components of VMSs.

Summary of Chapter Objectives

1. Explain the role of distribution channels in marketing strategy.
Distribution channels refer to the various marketing institutions and the interrelationships responsible for the physical and title flow of goods and services from producer to consumer or industrial user. Wholesalers and retailers are the marketing intermediaries in the distribution channel. Distribution channels bridge the gap between producer and consumer. By making products and services available when and where the consumer wants to purchase and by arranging for transfer of title, distribution channels create time, place, and ownership utilities.

2. Describe the various types of distribution channels. A host of alternative distribution channels are available for makers of consumer products, industrial products, and services. They range from selling directly to the consumer or industrial user to using a variety of marketing intermediaries. Multiple channels are also becoming increasingly common today. A unique distribution system is the reverse channel used in recycling, product recalls, and some service situations.

3. Explain the concept of power as it relates to the distribution channel.
Channel leadership is primarily a matter of relative power within the channel. Five bases for power are reward power, coercive power, legitimate power, referent power, and expert power.

4. Describe the concept of channel leadership. The marketing intermediary that makes the major decisions concerning the operation of a particular channel is called the channel captain. In some channels, the manufacturer or service provider is the channel captain. In others, powerful retailers, such as nationwide operations, may fill this role. In still others, wholesalers serve as channel captains.

5. Discuss conflict and cooperation within the distribution channel.
Channel conflict is a problem in distribution channels. There are two types of conflict: horizontal—among channel members at the same level—and vertical—among channel members at different levels. Marketers should work toward cooperation among all channel members as the remedy for channel conflict.

6. Outline the major channel strategy decisions. Basic channel strategy decisions involve channel selection, level of distribution intensity, and use of vertical marketing systems. The selection of a distribution channel is based on market, product, producer, and competitive factors. The decision on distribution intensity involves choosing from among intensive distribution, selective distribution, and exclusive distribution. Another channel strategy decision concerns vertical marketing systems.

7. Identify and discuss the various types of vertical marketing systems.
Three major types of vertical marketing systems exist: corporate, administered, and contractual. A corporate VMS refers to a situation in which there is single ownership of each stage of the marketing channel. An administered VMS is one in which a dominant channel member exercises its power to achieve channel coordination. A contractual VMS includes wholesaler-sponsored chains, retail cooperatives, and franchises.

Key Terms

distribution channel
marketing intermediary
direct selling
direct marketing
dual distribution
reverse channel
facilitating agency
channel captain
brand hostaging
intensive distribution

selective distribution
exclusive distribution
exclusive-dealing agreement
closed sales territory
tying agreement
vertical marketing system (VMS)
corporate marketing system
administered marketing system
contractual marketing system
franchise

Review Questions

1. What types of products are most likely to be distributed through direct channels?
2. Explain the concept of power in the distribution channel.
3. Under what circumstances is the retailer likely to assume a channel leadership role?
4. Discuss the trend toward brand hostaging in distribution channels.
5. What are the primary types of channel conflict?
6. In what ways could the use of dual distribution produce channel conflict?
7. Explain and illustrate the major factors affecting distribution channel selection.
8. Why would a manufacturer deliberately choose to limit market coverage through a policy of exclusive distribution?
9. Explain and illustrate each type of vertical marketing system.
10. What advantage does franchising offer the small retailer?

Discussion Questions

1. Outline the distribution channel used by a firm in your area. Why did the company select these particular channels?
2. The University of North Carolina was forced to recall the 3,100 diplomas it granted in 1975 because the ink disappeared on a third of the certificates.[20] How might a product recall of this nature be handled?
3. Find a real-world example of channel conflict. Suggest an approach to resolving this conflict.
4. Which degree of distribution intensity is appropriate for each of the following?
   a. *People* magazine
   b. Liz Claiborne sportswear
   c. Camay soap
   d. Hyundai
   e. Waterford crystal
5. Select a specific industry and discuss the major issues that will confront its channel strategists over the next decade.

VIDEO CASE 12

Famous Amos

Today, most of us recognize Wally "Famous" Amos, the man who gave his name to the original gourmet cookie. The company founded by Amos has achieved virtual nationwide distribution of several flavors of its cookies in stores, and has scattered retail stores world-wide, with franchises in Japan, Australia, and Canada, as well as the United States.

In 1975, Wally Amos was just another talent agent trying to succeed in Hollywood. However, he soon developed another calling. Friends told him that the cookies he made were so good that he should sell them, and eventually Amos took their advice. Some of these friends backed up their advice by investing $25,000 in his venture, the Famous Amos Chocolate Chip Cookie Company, and the world's first gourmet cookie shop opened in 1975. It was an instant success. By 1981, sales had reached $7 million, and grew to $10 million in 1985.

News of Famous Amos spread by word of mouth, and in a classic example of pull-through demand, consumers would walk into stores and ask the owners why they did not stock Famous Amos cookies. The company relied solely on this informal sort of marketing for its first five years, before beginning to develop other types of promotions.

When Amos started his company, he had made no plans for such growth. His first retail "hot bake" shop appeared to be earning a profit and, after all, in his words, "All I wanted to do was make a living." Consumer demand grew and requests began to pour in from other areas, but Amos did not have the funds to expand his cookie shop concept into a chain. He also wanted to avoid the risk of expanding through borrowing funds. Then the idea struck him — just as it had McDonald's Ray Kroc 20 years earlier: franchising. The firm distributed its frozen dough directly to the franchised "hot bake" shops located in suburban shopping centers and downtown walk-in locations.

Amos also used other distribution alternatives to get the cookies into supermarkets, convenience outlets, "mom-and-pop" stores, and gift shops that make up the Famous Amos market, by contracting with an independent wholesale distributor. This distribution channel saved the company the cost of starting its own network, while giving it access to an already established distribution system, without which the young company might have failed. Even though many store owners were unhappy about doing business with products offering such a low markup, consumer demand was so strong that retailer complaints soon fell to a trickle and distribution became more widespread.

The distributor takes both possession and ownership when its trucks pick up cookies twice weekly from the Famous Amos bakery. The distributor's representatives — different ones for each market segment — meet with store buyers, and are usually able to secure shelf space for the cookies, thanks either to word-of-mouth demand or through having the store buyer taste the cookies.

Famous Amos has tailored its cookies to its markets. Frozen dough is shipped directly to the firm's franchised "hot bake" shops. For supermarkets, it offers several different sizes of cookies, and sets up racks for the packages in the fresh baked goods section, rather than on the cookie shelf. For convenience stores, one- and two-ounce bags were created to save space and to encourage impulse sales. It now makes several flavors of cookies (oatmeal-based cookies are the nation's best sellers), and in its retail stores, it has soft cookies available.

Demand was created in part by the cookie's taste. The gourmet cookie shop concept was entirely novel, and to outlast the novelty, Famous Amos cookies had to be good. Today, with widespread competition, Famous Amos is entering its

13 Wholesaling

Chapter Objectives

1. To identify the functions performed by wholesaling intermediaries.

2. To explain how wholesaling intermediaries improve channel efficiency.

3. To distinguish between merchant wholesalers and agents and brokers.

4. To identify the major types of merchant wholesalers and the situations in which each might be used.

5. To describe the major types of agents and brokers.

6. To outline how a wholesaling strategy is developed.

A Skokie, Illinois–based firm, W. W. Grainger, Inc. is an industrial distributor of electric motors, fans, air compressors, paint-spraying equipment, lighting fixtures, and some 15,000 other items. Sales volume is in excess of $1 billion. Grainger's just under 2 percent market share is the largest in the electrical and mechanical products market.

The 60-year-old firm operates 231 sales branches that serve contractors and other small businesses. A high percentage of Grainger's sales volume comes from over the counter business. The firm has nearly 900,000 customers and completes an average of 44,000 transactions daily.

Grainger's expansion strategy called for the opening of six new sales branches each year. Most of those outlets were to be located in medium-size cities. But a marketing research study, conducted with the help of a consultant, changed the firm's strategy. The study concluded that Grainger was missing a lot of sales potential in major metropolitan areas. The firm's management had assumed that these areas were already saturated. However, marketing research revealed that big-city customers would drive only a short distance to buy their supplies. Location was a more important factor in their purchase behavior than were low prices and an extensive product line.

Armed with this information, Grainger's management decided to

add at least 100 new outlets over the next 3 to 4 years. For example, 16 new sales branches were targeted in the New York metropolitan area, 11 in the Chicago area, and 10 in the Los Angeles area.

The distributor also took steps to improve its marketing strategy. A telemarketing program was set up to reach Grainger's smallest customers, those buying less than $300 a year. The firm's 700 sales representatives can now target high-volume buyers.

Grainger also set up a direct ship unit to stock low-volume items that could not be profitably handled through a sales branch. Finally, in an effort to boost impulse buying, the company adopted a sales center display program that features high-volume products in each branch. Grainger's experience indicates the importance of marketing research on the wholesale level of distribution.[1]

Photo source: Courtesy of W. W. Grainger, Incorporated.

Chapter Overview

Chapter 12 introduced the concept of channel strategy and the role of wholesalers and retailers. This chapter expands the discussion by dealing exclusively with wholesaling.

Wholesaling involves the activities of persons or firms that sell to retailers or to other wholesalers or industrial users and only in insignificant amounts to ultimate consumers. The term **wholesaler** applies only to wholesaling intermediaries that take title to the products they handle. **Wholesaling intermediaries**

wholesaler
Wholesaling intermediary that takes title to the goods it handles; also called *jobber* or *distributor*.

wholesaling intermediary
Broad term describing both wholesalers and agents and brokers that perform important wholesaling activities without taking title to the goods.

Figure 13.1
Wholesaling in the Service Sector

Source: Courtesy of Marine Midland Automotive Financial Corporation. Agency: Fallon McElligott; Mike Fazende, Art Director; John Stingley, Copywriter.

is a broader term that describes not only marketing intermediaries that assume title to the goods they handle but agents and brokers that perform important wholesaling activities without taking title to the goods. Under this definition, then, a wholesaler is a merchant intermediary.

Wholesaling activity also exists in the marketing of some services. For example, wholesaling intermediaries operate in the travel industry. They are largely responsible for the GIT (group-inclusive tour) marketing in which "land packages" (hotels and meals) are offered to retail travel agents that combine them with air travel for their customers as a complete, prepaid vacation. Figure 13.1 illustrates another wholesaling activity in the service sector. The Marine Midland advertisement is aimed at retail car dealers that use their financial services in selling to ultimate consumers. The wholesale market illustrates the importance of channel members working together in an integrated fashion, enabling the channel to operate efficiently.

The most recent Census of Wholesale Trade lists nearly 416,000 wholesaling establishments with a total sales volume of nearly $2 trillion. The New York City metropolitan area alone accounts for 11 percent of all wholesale trade, and California is responsible for another 10 percent of total sales at the wholesale level.

Functions of Wholesaling Intermediaries

The route that goods follow on the way to the consumer or industrial user is actually a chain of marketing institutions. Goods that "bypass" the marketing intermediaries in the chain and move directly from manufacturer to consumer constitute only 3 percent of the total in the consumer goods market. Some consumers complain that marketing intermediaries are an unnecessary cost in the distribution system. Many discount retailers claim lower prices as a result of direct purchases from manufacturers. Chain stores often assume wholesaling functions and bypass independent wholesalers.

Are these complaints and claims valid? Are wholesaling intermediaries still appropriate today? Answers to these questions can be found by considering the functions and costs of these marketing intermediaries.

Services Provided by Wholesaling Intermediaries

A marketing institution can continue to exist only as long as it performs a service that fulfills a need. Its demise may be slow, but it is inevitable once other channel members discover they can survive without it. Table 13.1 examines a number of possible services provided by wholesaling intermediaries. It is important to note that numerous types of wholesaling intermediaries exist and that not all of them provide every service listed in Table 13.1 Producer-suppliers and their customers, who rely on wholesaling intermediaries for distribution, select those that will provide the desired combination of services.

The listing of possible services supplied by wholesaling intermediaries clearly indicates the marketing utilities — time, place, and possession or ownership — that these intermediaries provide. The services also reflect the provision of the basic marketing functions of buying, selling, storing, transporting, risk taking, financing, and supplying market information.

Sometimes the wholesaler is the difference between success and failure in the marketplace. British-made MacLaren strollers are popular purchases for American parents. The secret of the product's success seems to lie in the modifications made by its U.S. distributor, Marshall Electronics, Inc. of Chicago. The American wholesaler replaced the standard British components with brighter fabrics and bigger wheels. Marshall also added seat belts to comply with U.S. safety rules.[2]

The critical marketing functions listed above form the basis for evaluating the efficiency of any marketing intermediary. The risk-taking function is present in each service that the wholesaling intermediary provides.

Transportation and Product Storage   Wholesalers transport and store products at locations convenient for customers. Manufacturers ship products from their warehouses to numerous wholesalers, which in turn ship smaller

Table 13.1

Possible Wholesaling Services for Customers and Producer-Suppliers

Service	Service Provided	
	Customers	Producer-Suppliers
Buying Anticipates customer demands and possesses knowledge of alternative sources of supply; acts as purchasing agent for customers.	•	
Selling Provides a sales force to call on customers, thereby providing a low-cost method of servicing smaller retailers and industrial users.		•
Storing Provides a warehousing function at lower cost than most individual producers or retailers could provide. Reduces risk and cost of maintaining inventory for producers and provides customers with prompt delivery service.	•	•
Transporting Customers receive prompt delivery in response to their demands, reducing their inventory investments. Wholesalers also break-bulk by purchasing in economical carload or truckload lots, then reselling in smaller quantities to their customers, thereby reducing overall transportation costs.	•	•
Providing Market Information Serves as important marketing research input for producers through regular contacts with retail and industrial buyers. Provides customers with information about new products, technical information about product lines, reports on competitors' activities, industry trends, and advisory information concerning pricing changes, legal changes, and so forth.	•	•
Financing Aids customers by granting credit that might be unavailable if customers purchased directly from manufacturers. Provides financing assistance to producers by purchasing goods in advance of sale and through prompt payment of bills.	•	•
Risk Taking Assists producers by evaluating credit risks of numerous distant retail customers and small industrial users. Extends credit to customers that qualify. Wholesaler responsible for transporting and stocking goods in inventory assumes risk of spoilage, theft, or obsolescence.	•	•

quantities to retail outlets in locations convenient for purchasers. A large number of wholesalers assume the inventory function (and cost) for manufacturers. They benefit through the convenience afforded by local inventories. The manufacturer benefits through reduced cash needs, since its products are sold directly to the retailer or wholesaler.

Costs can be reduced at the wholesale level by making large-volume purchases from the manufacturer. The wholesaler receives quantity discounts from the manufacturer and incurs lower transportation costs because economical carload or truckload shipments are made to the wholesaler's warehouse. At the warehouse, the wholesaler divides the goods into smaller quantities and ships them to the retailer over a shorter distance (but at a higher rate) than would be the case if the manufacturer filled the retailer's order directly from a central warehouse.

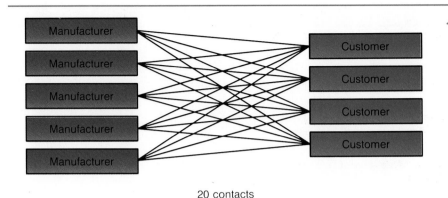

20 contacts

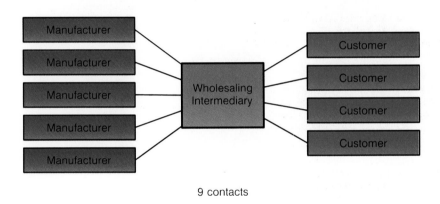

9 contacts

Figure 13.2
Achieving Transaction
Economy with Wholesaling
Intermediaries

The economics of small-scale shipments places a premium on efficient warehousing at the wholesale level. For example, Vonnegut Industrial Products, an Indianapolis-based distributor, purchased an automated storage and retrieval system that could be operated by just one person. The new system handles 9,000 different products, while a manual system in another part of the warehouse requires 6 employees for stocking 15,000 items.[3]

Lowering Costs through Reduced Contacts   As the Computer Applications in Chapter 1 demonstrate, when a marketing intermediary represents numerous producers, the costs involved in buying and selling often decrease. The transaction economies are shown in Figure 13.2. In this illustration, five manufacturers are marketing their outputs to four different retail outlets. A total of 20 transactions result if no intermediary is utilized. By adding a wholesaling intermediary, the number of transactions is reduced to nine.

Source of Information   Because of their central position between manufacturers and retailers or industrial buyers, wholesalers serve as important information links. Wholesalers give their retail customers useful information about

THE COMPETITIVE EDGE

Georgia-Pacific Corporation

The building products industry is responsible for about two-thirds of Georgia-Pacific's revenue and nearly 75 percent of its profits. As a result, the firm is determined to have reliable market information. It does this through more than 150 wholesale building products outlets, which sell to builders and retail home improvement centers, building material retailers, industrial manufacturers, and manufactured housing and commercial markets.

Georgia-Pacific's wholesaling operations feed data into a computerized marketing information system that tracks what is happening in the building products market. This allows the company to identify new product needs and gives it a competitive advantage over other manufacturers in the industry.

Wholesaling clearly is the key to actionable marketing information at Georgia-Pacific. For example, when the firm's distribution center managers began to see opportunities in fencing and lattice panels, they turned to Georgia-Pacific's manufacturing divisions for support in supplying the product. Consequently the company expanded its Cross City, Florida, plant to make cypress fenc-

ing, and added a new line to its Holly Hill, South Carolina, plant to make lattice panels, thus achieving a significant level of vertical integration.

These examples illustrate the importance of obtaining marketing information at the wholesaling level. In Georgia-Pacific's case, it is the key

to maintaining a competitive edge in the manufacturing of building products.

Source: David Henry, "Ear to the Ground," *Forbes* (October 19, 1987), p. 71. *Photo source:* Courtesy of Georgia-Pacific Corporation. © 1987 Georgia-Pacific Corportation. All rights reserved.

new products. In addition, they supply manufacturers with information about market acceptance of their product offerings.

Source of Financing   Wholesalers also serve a financing function. They often provide retailers with goods on credit, allowing the retailers to minimize their cash investments in inventory and pay for most of the goods as they are sold. This allows them to benefit from the principle of leverage, whereby spending a minimum amount on goods in inventory inflates the return on invested funds.

Wholesalers of industrial goods provide similar services for the purchasers of their products. In the steel industry, intermediaries (referred to as *metal service centers*) currently market one-fourth of all steel shipped by U.S. mills. One such center, the Earle M. Jorgensen Company in Los Angeles, stocks 10,500 items for sale to many of the 50,000 major metal users that buy in large quantities directly from the steel mills but turn to service centers for quick delivery of special orders. While an order from the mills may take several weeks to deliver, a service center can usually deliver locally within 24 hours. To attract business from key customers, such as AMF, which makes bicycles locally, Jorgensen carries inventory for them without demanding a contract. The cost and risk of maintaining the stock are assumed by the service center to allow it to provide overnight delivery service for its customers.[4]

Marketing Channel Functions: Who Should Perform Them?

While wholesaling intermediaries often perform a variety of valuable functions for their manufacturer, retailer, and other wholesaler clients, these operations could be performed by other channel members. Manufacturers may choose to bypass independent wholesaling intermediaries by establishing networks of regional warehouses, maintaining large sales forces to provide market coverage, serving as sources of information for their retail customers, and assuming the financing function. In some instances, they may decide to push the responsibility for some of these functions through the channel on to the retailer or the ultimate purchaser. Large retailers that choose to perform their own wholesaling operations face the same choices.

A fundamental marketing principle applies to marketing channel decisions:

Marketing functions must be performed by some member of the channel. They can be shifted, but they cannot be eliminated.

Large retailers that bypass wholesalers and deal directly with manufacturers can assume the functions previously performed by wholesaling intermediaries, or these activities can be performed by the manufacturers. Similarly, manufacturers that deal directly with the ultimate consumer or industrial buyer can assume the functions of storage, delivery, and marketing information previously performed by marketing intermediaries. Intermediaries can be eliminated from the channel, but someone must perform the channel functions.

The potential gain for the manufacturer or retailer is summarized in Table 13.2. The table shows the possible savings if other channel members perform the wholesaling functions as effectively as the independent wholesaling intermediary. Such savings, indicated in the net profit column, could be used to reduce retail prices, increase the profits of the manufacturer or retailer, or both.

The most revealing information in Table 13.2 is the low profit rates earned by most wholesalers. Four types of wholesalers (meats and meat products, tobacco and tobacco products, confectionery, and dairy products) earned less than 1.5 percent net profit as a percentage of net sales, while the group with the highest profits as a percentage of sales (hardware) earned 3.8 percent.

A trend toward consolidation of wholesaling intermediaries partially explains the low profit margins. There are now just 80 pharmaceutical distributors in the United States, down from over 300 a decade ago. The increased competition inherent in this narrowing process is credited with reducing profit margins by 5 percent. The net result has been lower prices for consumers.[5]

Table 13.2 also indicates a negative relationship between annual turnover rate (as measured by total sales divided by average inventory) and net profits as a percentage of net sales. Wholesaling intermediaries such as those in dairy and meat products enjoyed relatively high turnover rates. These rates permitted

Table 13.2
Median Net Profits and
Turnover Rates of Selected
Wholesalers

Kind of Business	Profits as a Percentage of Net Sales[a]	Annual Turnover Rate[b]
Automotive parts and supplies	3.7%	4.2
Beer, wine, and distilled beverages	2.5	14.3
Clothing and furnishings	3.6	7.8
Confectionery	1.4	13.0
Dairy products	1.4	43.1
Drugs, proprietaries, and sundries	1.9	7.6
Electrical appliances, television, radio sets	2.9	7.4
Farm machinery and equipment	1.7	2.8
Furniture and home furnishings	3.7	8.6
Groceries, general line	1.5	6.2
Hardware	3.8	5.9
Meats and meat products	0.9	39.6
Petroleum and petroleum products	1.5	32.0
Tires and tubes	2.2	6.7
Tobacco and tobacco products	0.9	17.5

[a]Return on net sales.

[b]Net sales to inventory.

Source: "The Ratios," *Dun's Business Monthly* (February 1983), pp. 116–117.

the firms to generate sufficient financial returns with lower net profits (on a percentage-of-net-sales basis) than many of the other intermediaries with lower turnover rates. The advertisement in Figure 13.3 for Hercules Chemical Company emphasizes the importance of turnover to wholesalers.

Types of Wholesaling Intermediaries

Various types of wholesaling intermediaries are present in different marketing channels. Some provide a wide range of services or handle a broad line of products, while others specialize in a single service, product, or industry. Figure 13.4 classifies wholesaling intermediaries by two characteristics: *ownership* (whether the wholesaling intermediary is independent, manufacturer owned, or retailer owned) and *title flows* (whether title passes from the manufacturer to the wholesaling intermediary). There are three basic types of ownership: (1) independent wholesaling intermediaries, (2) manufacturer-owned sales offices and branches, and (3) retailer-owned cooperatives and buying offices. The two types of independent wholesaling intermediaries are merchant wholesalers, which take title to goods, and agents and brokers, which do not.

Manufacturer-Owned Facilities

For several reasons, an increasing volume of products is being marketed directly by manufacturers through company-owned facilities. Some products are perishable; others require complex installation or servicing; some need aggressive promotion; still others are high-unit-value goods that the manufacturer can profitably sell to the ultimate purchaser. Among those who have shifted from

Source: Courtesy of Hercules Chemical Company, Inc.

Figure 13.3
Inventory Turnover as an
Essential Element of
Wholesaling Success

using independent wholesaling intermediaries to using company-owned channels are manufacturers of apparel, construction materials, lumber, paint, paper, and piece goods.[6] More than half of all industrial goods are sold directly to users by manufacturers and slightly fewer than one-third are marketed through manufacturer-owned channels.[7]

Sales Branches and Offices The basic distinction between a company's sales branches and sales offices is that a **sales branch** carries inventory and processes orders to customers from available stock. Branches duplicate the storage function of independent wholesalers and serve as offices for sales representatives in the territory. They are prevalent in the marketing of chemicals, commercial machinery and equipment, motor vehicles, and petroleum products. Operating expenses for the 22,121 sales branches in the United States average 9 percent of sales. General Electric has sales branches in every major U.S. city. Its subsidiary, General Electric Supply Corporation, provides regular contacts and overnight delivery to GE retailers and industrial purchasers.

Since warehouses represent a substantial investment in real estate, small manufacturers and even large firms developing new sales territories may choose to use **public warehouses**—independently owned storage facilities. For a rental fee, manufacturers can store their goods in any of the more than

sales branch
Establishment maintained by a manufacturer that serves as a warehouse for a particular sales territory, thereby duplicating the services of independent wholesalers; carries inventory and processes orders to customers from available stock.

public warehouse
Independently owned storage facility that stores and ships products for a rental fee.

Figure 13.4

Major Types of Wholesaling Intermediaries

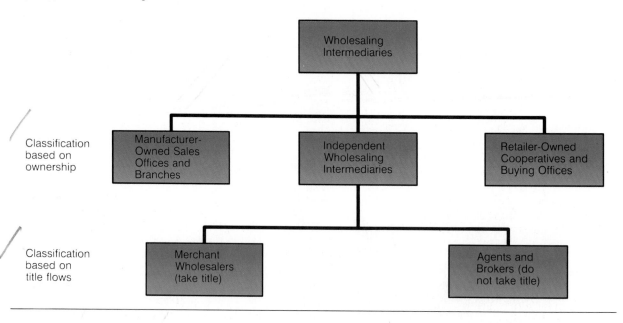

10,000 public warehouses in the United States for shipment by the warehouses to customers in the area. Warehouse owners will package goods into small quantities to fill orders and even handle billing for manufacturers by issuing warehouse receipts for inventory. Manufacturers can use these receipts as collateral for bank loans.

A **sales office,** in contrast, does not carry inventory but serves as a regional office for the firm's sales personnel. Sales offices located close to the firm's customers help reduce selling costs and improve customer service. For example, numerous offices in Southfield, Michigan, serve Detroit's automobile industry. A firm's listing in the local telephone directory often results in new sales for the local representative. Many buyers prefer to telephone the office of a supplier rather than take the time to write to distant suppliers. Since the nation's 16,113 sales offices do not perform a storage function, their operating expenses are relatively low, averaging 4.5 percent of total sales.

Other Outlets for Manufacturers' Products   In addition to using sales forces and regionally distributed sales branches, manufacturers often market their products through trade fairs and merchandise marts.

A **trade fair** (or *trade exhibition*) is a periodic show at which manufacturers in a particular industry display their wares for visiting retail and wholesale buyers. The annual New York City toy fair and the yearly furniture show in High Point, North Carolina, are examples. The cost of making a face-to-face contact with a prospective customer at a trade fair is only 44 percent of the cost of a personal sales call. In addition, such exhibitions are effective means of generating additional sales. One study of attendees at the National Computer Con-

sales office
Manufacturer's establishment that serves as a regional office for salespeople but does not carry inventory.

trade fair
Periodic show at which manufacturers in a particular industry display wares for visiting retail and wholesale buyers.

FOCUS ON ETHICS

Thomas Distributors Protest Unfair Treatment

What responsibilities does a firm have in servicing companies formed solely to distribute its products? That is the question faced by S. B. Thomas, a subsidiary of CPC International Inc., which makes English muffins and other bakery products.

After acquiring another specialty baker, Arnold Foods Company, in December 1986, CPC proceeded to merge its two baking operations. Because Arnold's distribution routes largely overlap with Thomas's, CPC decided to eliminate from its distribution network 24 of the 25 wholesale firms formed solely to distribute Thomas products.

Feeling betrayed, the Thomas distributors are squealing in protest, especially those who, with CPC's encouragement, relocated to Florida several years ago to help build Thomas's distribution network in that state. Steven Dick, for example, moved from Maryland to set up Sunrise Distributors of Central Florida Inc. in Orlando. He says, "I moved 956 miles to Florida, giving up a secure job, all my business contacts, close relationships and family ties. If they had said, 'We can terminate the arrangement with 30 days' notice,' I

don't think anyone in their sane mind would have taken that risk."

A contract specifying a 30-day notice of termination is the norm in the wholesaling industry—a precarious arrangement for distributors. But many Thomas distributors worked with no written contract. Dick relates, "We had a contract, but it was verbal." He and the other distributors felt they could rely on the supplier's good faith. In addition, the distributors claim that Thomas encouraged them to operate in terms of a long-lasting relationship. According to Mark Loesberg of Serv-Mor Distributors Inc. in Fort Lauderdale, "They said, 'You can't look at it for short-term profits. You're building a business.' " So Loesberg and other distributors put their profits back into their companies, as Thomas officials encouraged them to do. Now they feel the rug has been pulled out from under them despite their work for the baker. Loesberg, for example, had increased muffin sales from $800,000 in 1983 to $4.8 million in 1987, while overall Florida sales of Thomas products skyrocketed from $2 million to $10 million in the same period.

Thomas is offering the terminated wholesalers some compensation, but they feel it is woefully inadequate. To Thomas J. Murrin of Tampa, the $96,000 he was offered is less than 20 percent of what he should get based on standard methods of valuing grocery distribution operations. Using a formula of 10 times weekly sales, Murrin contends he should get about $575,000. CPC claims it is not legally required to pay the wholesalers anything at all because it assigned only "temporary" distribution rights. Moreover, as Robert B. Snyder, president of Best Foods Baking Group (the CPC unit formed to manage Thomas and Arnold), points out, the company produced a written contract with a 30-day notice of termination in 1984. Though the Florida distributors refused to sign the contract, Snyder argues, "They knew what our intention was anyway. They chose not to sign it. Whatever vulnerability that left them in, they were aware of it."

Source: Steven P. Galante, "Merger of Two Bakers Teaches Distributors a Costly Lesson," *The Wall Street Journal* (September 14, 1987), p. 23.

ference revealed that, within the eleven months following the event, four out of five attendees had purchased at least one product on display and that the average purchase had been $254,100.[8]

A **merchandise mart** provides space for permanent exhibits at which manufacturers rent showrooms for their product offerings. The largest is the Merchandise Mart in Chicago. This facility is 2 blocks long, 1 block wide, and 24 floors high. The entire Mart Center complex includes 7 million square feet, consisting of the Merchandise Mart, the Apparel Center, and Expocenter/Chicago, hosts 33 industry markets each year, and accounts for more than 1.4 million buying visits by retailers, designers, architects, and industrial purchasers. Industries represented at the Mart Center include residential furnishings, office furnishings, floor coverings, giftware, apparel, and business products. The Mart Center enables exhibitors in these industries to display their latest products in a central location. Over 1 million items are on permanent exhibit.[9]

merchandise mart
Permanent exhibition facility in which manufacturers rent showrooms to display products for visiting retail and wholesale buyers, designers, and architects.

Figure 13.5

Comparison of Wholesale Trade by Sales Volume and Number of Establishments

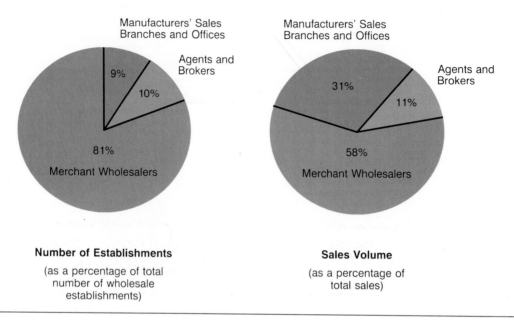

Number of Establishments
(as a percentage of total number of wholesale establishments)

Sales Volume
(as a percentage of total sales)

Source: *1982 Census of Wholesale Trade* (Washington, D.C.: Government Printing Office, 1984), p. 3.

Independent Wholesaling Intermediaries

As Figure 13.5 indicates, independent wholesaling intermediaries account for 91 percent of the wholesale establishments and over two-thirds of the whole-sale sales in the United States. They can be divided into two categories: merchant wholesalers and agents and brokers.

merchant wholesaler
Wholesaling intermediary that takes title to the goods it handles.

Merchant Wholesalers   The **merchant wholesaler** takes title to the goods it handles. Merchant wholesalers account for slightly more than 58 percent of all sales at the wholesale level, with sales of about $1.1 trillion. They can be further classified as full-function or limited-function wholesalers, as indicated in Figure 13.6

Full-Function Merchant Wholesalers   A complete assortment of services for retailers and industrial purchasers is provided by full-function merchant wholesalers. These wholesalers store merchandise in convenient locations, thereby allowing their customers to make purchases on short notice and minimize their inventory requirements. They also usually maintain sales forces that call regularly on retailers, make deliveries, and extend credit to qualified buyers. In the industrial goods market, full-function merchant wholesalers (often called *industrial distributors*) usually market machinery, inexpensive accessory equipment, and supplies.

Full-function merchant wholesalers prevail in industries in which retailers are small and carry large numbers of relatively inexpensive items, none of

Figure 13.6
Classification of Independent Wholesaling Intermediaries

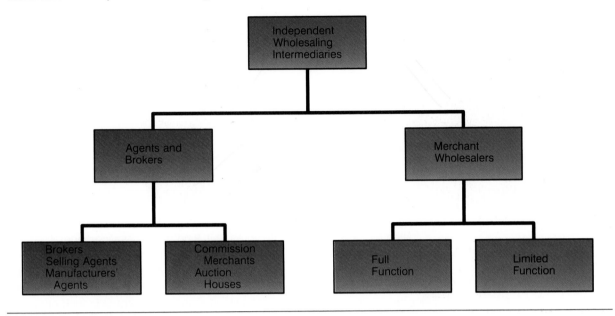

which they stock in depth. The drug, grocery, and hardware industries traditionally have been serviced by full-function merchant wholesalers.

A unique type of service wholesaler emerged after World War II as grocery retailers began to stock high-profit-margin nonfood items. Because food store managers knew little about products such as health and beauty items, housewares, paperback books, records, and toys, rack jobbers provided the necessary expertise. A **rack jobber** supplies the racks, stocks the merchandise, prices the goods, and makes regular visits to refill the shelves. In essence, rack jobbers rent space from retailers on a commission basis. They have expanded into discount, drug, hardware, and variety stores.

Since full-function merchant wholesalers perform a large number of services, their operating expenses average nearly 13 percent, and sometimes as high as 20 percent, of sales. Attempts to reduce the costs of dealing with these wholesalers have led to the development of a number of limited-function intermediaries.

Limited-Function Merchant Wholesalers Four types of limited-function merchant wholesalers are cash-and-carry wholesalers, truck wholesalers, drop shippers, and mail-order wholesalers.

The **cash-and-carry wholesaler** performs most wholesaling functions except for financing and delivery. These wholesalers first appeared on the marketing scene in the grocery industry during the Depression era of the 1930s. In an attempt to reduce costs, retailers began driving to wholesalers' warehouses, paying cash for their purchases, and making their own deliveries. By eliminating the delivery and financing functions, cash-and-carry wholesalers were able to reduce their operating costs to approximately 9 percent of sales.

rack jobber
Full-function merchant wholesaler that markets specialized lines of merchandise to retail stores and provides the services of merchandising and arrangement of goods, pricing, maintenance, and stocking of display racks.

cash-and-carry wholesaler
Limited-function merchant wholesaler that performs most wholesaling functions except financing and delivery.

Table 13.3

Possible Wholesaling Services for Customers and Producer-Suppliers

| | | Limited-Function Wholesalers | | | |
Services	Full-Function Wholesalers	Cash-and-Carry Wholesalers	Truck Wholesalers	Drop Shippers	Mail-Order Wholesalers
Anticipates customer needs	Yes	Yes	Yes	No	Yes
Carries inventory	Yes	Yes	Yes	No	Yes
Delivers	Yes	No	Yes	No	No
Provides market information	Yes	Rarely	Yes	Yes	No
Provides credit	Yes	No	No	Yes	Sometimes
Assumes ownership risk by taking title	Yes	Yes	Yes	Yes	Yes

Although feasible for small stores, this kind of wholesaling generally is unworkable for large-scale grocery stores. Chain store managers are unwilling to perform the delivery function, and today cash-and-carry is typically one department of a regular, full-service wholesaler. However, the cash-and-carry wholesaler has proven successful in the United Kingdom, where 600 such operators produce over $1 billion a year in sales.

truck wholesaler
Limited-function merchant wholesaler that markets perishable food items; also called *truck jobber.*

A **truck wholesaler,** or *truck jobber,* markets perishable food items such as bread, tobacco, potato chips, candy, and dairy products. Truck wholesalers make regular deliveries to retail stores and perform the sales and collection functions. They also aggressively promote their product lines. The high costs of operating delivery trucks and the low dollar volume per sale mean relatively high operating costs of 15 percent.

drop shipper
Limited-function merchant wholesaler that receives orders from customers and forwards them to producers, which ship directly to the customers.

A **drop shipper** receives orders from customers and forwards them to producers, which ship directly to the customers. Although drop shippers take title to the goods, they never physically handle or even see them. Since they perform no storage or handling functions, their operating costs are a relatively low 4 to 5 percent of sales.

Drop shippers operate in industries in which products are bulky and customers make their purchases in carload lots. Transportation and handling costs represent a substantial percentage of the total cost of products such as coal and lumber. Drop shippers do not maintain an inventory of these products, which eliminates the expenses of loading and unloading carload shipments. Their major service is developing a complete assortment of products. Since various types and grades of coal and lumber are produced by different companies, drop shippers can assemble a complete line to fill any customer's order.

mail-order wholesaler
Limited-function merchant wholesaler that utilizes catalogs instead of a sales force to contact customers in an attempt to reduce operating expenses.

The **mail-order wholesaler** is a limited-function merchant wholesaler that relies on catalogs rather than a sales force to contact retail, industrial, and institutional customers. Purchases are then made by mail or telephone by relatively small customers in outlying areas. Mail-order operations are found in the hardware, cosmetics, jewelry, sporting goods, and specialty foods lines as well as in general merchandise.

Table 13.3 compares the various types of merchant wholesalers in terms of services provided. Full-function merchant wholesalers and truck wholesalers are relatively high-cost intermediaries due to the number of services they perform, while cash-and-carry wholesalers, drop shippers, and mail-order whole-salers provide fewer services and have relatively lower operating costs.

Agents and Brokers   A second group of independent wholesaling interme-diaries—**agents and brokers**—may or may not take possession of the goods, but they never take title. They normally perform fewer services than merchant wholesalers and typically are involved in bringing buyers and sellers together. Agent wholesaling intermediaries can be classified into five categories—com-mission merchants, auction houses, brokers, selling agents, and manufacturers' agents.

The **commission merchant,** which predominates in the marketing of agri-cultural products, takes possession when the producer ships goods such as grain, produce, and livestock to a central market for sale. Commission mer-chants act as the producer's agents and receive an agreed-upon fee when the sale is made. Since customers inspect the products and prices fluctuate, com-mission merchants receive considerable latitude in making decisions. The owner of the goods may specify a minimum price, but the commission merchant will sell them on a "best-price" basis. The commission merchant's fee is de-ducted from the price and remitted to the original owner.

Auction houses bring buyers and sellers together in one location and al-low potential buyers to inspect merchandise before purchasing it. Auction house commissions typically are based on a specified percentage of the sales prices of the auctioned items. The auction method of marketing is common in the distribution of products such as tobacco, used cars, artworks, livestock, furs, and fruit.

Brokers bring buyers and sellers together. Brokers operate in industries characterized by a large number of small suppliers and purchasers, for exam-ple, real estate, frozen foods, and used machinery. They represent either the buyer or the seller in a given transaction but not both. Brokers receive fees from clients when the transactions are completed. Since the only service they per-form is negotiating for exchange of title, their operating expense ratio can be as low as 2 percent.

Because brokers operate on a one-time basis for sellers or buyers, they cannot serve as an effective marketing channel for manufacturers seeking reg-ular, continuing service. A manufacturer that seeks to develop a more perma-nent channel utilizing agent wholesaling intermediaries must evaluate the use of the selling agent or manufacturer's agent.

Selling agents often are referred to as *independent marketing depart-ments,* because they can be responsible for the total marketing program of a firm's product line. Typically a **selling agent** has full authority over pricing de-cisions and promotional outlays and often provides financial assistance for the manufacturer. The manufacturer can then concentrate on production and rely on the selling agent's expertise for all marketing activities. Selling agents are common in the coal, lumber, and textile industries. In the coal industry, for ex-ample, A. T. Mossey Company of Richmond, Virginia, and Primary Coal, Inc., of New York are selling agents. For small, poorly financed, production-oriented manufacturers, they may prove the ideal marketing channel.

While manufacturers may utilize only one selling agent, they typically use a number of **manufacturers' agents,** who often refer to themselves as *manufac-turers' reps.* These independent salespeople work for a number of manufactur-ers of related but noncompeting products and receive commissions based on a

agents and brokers
Independent wholesaling inter-mediaries that may or may not take possession of goods but never take title to them.

commission merchant
Agent wholesaling intermediary that takes possession of goods when they are shipped to a cen-tral market for sale, acts as the producer's agent, and collects an agreed-upon fee at the time of sale.

auction house
Establishment that brings buyers and sellers together in one loca-tion for the purpose of permitting buyers to examine merchandise before purchase.

broker
Agent wholesaling intermediary that does not take title to or pos-session of goods and whose pri-mary function is to bring buyers and sellers together.

selling agent
Agent wholesaling intermediary responsible for the total market-ing program of a firm's product line.

manufacturer's agent
Agent wholesaling intermediary who represents a number of manufacturers of related but noncompeting products and re-ceives a commission based on a specified percentage of sales.

Table 13.4

Services Provided by Agents and Brokers

Services	Commission Merchants	Auction Houses	Brokers	Manufacturers' Agents	Selling Agents
Anticipates customer needs	Yes	Some	Some	Yes	Yes
Carries inventory	Yes	Yes	No	No	No
Delivers	Yes	No	No	Some	No
Provides market information	Yes	Yes	Yes	Yes	Yes
Provides credit	Some	No	No	No	Some
Assumes ownership risk by taking title	No	No	No	No	No

specific percentage of sales. Although some commissions are as high as 23 percent of sales, most usually average between 7 and 13 percent.[10] Unlike selling agents, who may be given exclusive world rights to market a manufacturer's product, manufacturers' agents operate in specified territories.

Manufacturers' agents reduce their total selling costs by spreading the cost per sales call over a number of different products. An agent in the plumbing supplies industry, for example, may represent a dozen manufacturers.

Manufacturers develop their marketing channels through the use of manufacturers' agents for several reasons. First, when they are developing new sales territories, the costs of adding salespeople to "pioneer" the territories may be prohibitive. Agents, who are paid on a commission basis, can perform the sales function in these territories at a much lower cost.

Second, firms with unrelated lines may need to employ more than one channel. One line of products may be marketed through the company's sales force and another through independent manufacturers' agents. This is particularly common where the unrelated product line is a recent addition and the firm's sales force has had no experience with it.

Finally, small firms with no existing sales force may turn to manufacturers' agents to gain access to their markets. A newly organized firm producing pencil sharpeners may use office equipment and supplies agents to reach retailers and industrial purchasers.

The importance of selling agents has declined since 1940, because manufacturers desire to better control their marketing programs. In contrast, the volume of sales by manufacturers' agents has more than doubled and now comprises 32 percent of all sales by agent wholesaling intermediaries. The nation's 22,000 agents account for more than $67 billion in sales. Table 13.4 compares the major types of agents and brokers on the basis of the services they perform.

Retailer-Owned Facilities

Retailers also assume numerous wholesaling functions in an attempt to reduce costs or provide special services. Independent retailers occasionally band together to form buying groups to achieve cost savings through quantity purchases. Other groups of retailers establish retailer-owned wholesale facilities as a result of the formation of a cooperative chain. Large-size chain retailers often

Figure 13.7

Operating Expenses of Wholesaling Intermediaries as a Percentage of Sales

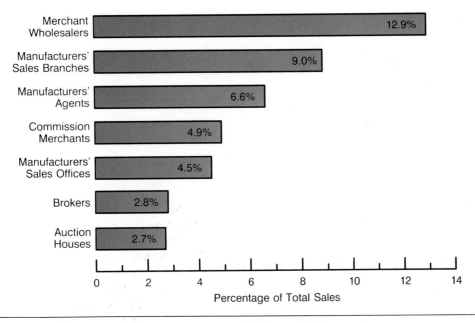

Source: U.S. Department of Commerce, *1982 Census of Wholesale Trade* (Washington, DC: Government Printing Office, 1984), p. 4.

establish centralized buying offices to negotiate large-scale purchases directly with manufacturers for the chain members. For a discussion of these facilities, see Chapter 12.

Costs of Wholesaling Intermediaries

Costs of the various wholesaling intermediaries are calculated as a percentage of total sales. Figure 13.7 lists the cost for each major category. The chief conclusion to be drawn from the chart is that expense variations result from differences in the number of services each intermediary provides. Cost ratios are highest for merchant wholesalers and manufacturers' sales branches because both provide such services as maintenance of inventories, market coverage by a sales force, and transportation. Auction houses perform only one service: bringing buyers and sellers together. As a consequence, they have the lowest expense ratios. Of course, these ratios are averages and will vary among firms within each category depending on the actual services provided.

Independent Wholesaling Intermediaries: A Durable Marketing Institution

Many marketing observers of the 1920s felt that the end had come for independent wholesaling intermediaries as chain stores grew in importance and threatened to bypass them. Over the 10-year period from 1929 to 1939, independent

Figure 13.8
Wholesaling in the United States: A 53-Year Perspective

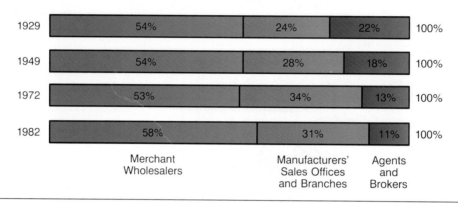

	Merchant Wholesalers	Manufacturers' Sales Offices and Branches	Agents and Brokers
1929	54%	24%	22%	100%
1949	54%	28%	18%	100%
1972	53%	34%	13%	100%
1982	58%	31%	11%	100%

Source: U.S. Department of Commerce, *1982 Census of Wholesale Trade,* and previous census reports.

wholesalers' sales volume indeed dropped, but it has increased since then. Figure 13.8 shows how the relative shares of total wholesale trade have changed since 1929.

While the period from 1929 to the present has seen agents and brokers decline in importance and company-owned channels increase, independent wholesaling intermediaries are far from obsolete—in fact, they are responsible for over two-thirds of all wholesale trade. Their continuing importance is evidence of their ability to adjust to changing conditions and needs. A number of wholesalers involved in marketing consumer goods have chosen to practice vertical integration by establishing retail chains. For example, Wettrau, a leading food products wholesaler, operates over 100 retail stores.

In addition, the services wholesale establishments provide are evolving to match their customers' changing needs. A growing number of wholesalers offer such services as individualized retail pricing, gross margin reports by item, accounting and payroll services, and equipment procurement. In the food industry, links between wholesalers' and suppliers' computers reduce order response time and minimize dollar investments in inventory. It is estimated that by 1990 three out of every four food wholesalers will use online order-entry systems.[11]

The wholesaling field is becoming more professional, boasting computerization, automation, and vertical integration. Wholesalers' willingness to innovate in response to changing market needs explains much of their continuing ability to compete with alternative channels. Their market size proves that they continue to fill a need in many marketing channels.

Wholesaling Strategy

While developing a taxonomy of wholesaling intermediaries is important, it is only one facet of this vital element of the distribution channel. These channel members must develop an effective strategy like other marketers. They do this

Figure 13.9
Trade Advertisement Used
as a Component of a
Wholesaler's Marketing Mix

Source: Courtesy of Andis Company, Racine, Wisconsin.

by determining a target market and then creating an appropriate marketing mix
with which to reach it.

Target Market

A wholesaling intermediary's target market can be defined in terms of product
lines, customer size, customer needs, and promotional strategy employed. The
following types of wholesaling intermediaries illustrate each of these dimensions:

- Product line: Food broker
- Customer size: Cash-and-carry wholesaler
- Customer needs: Rack jobber
- Promotional strategy employed: Mail-order wholesaler

Andis Company uses wholesale intermediaries to sell to its target market—
hair stylists. Figure 13.9 shows a trade advertisement that Andis has used to
support its distribution channel.

Once the target market has been specified, the wholesaling intermediary's
attention shifts to the marketing mix.

Product/Service Strategy

The wholesaling intermediary's product/service strategy is primarily a matter of the width, length, and depth of its assortment. As noted earlier, some wholesaling intermediaries, such as manufacturers' reps, carry no inventory, while others, such as many merchant wholesalers, carry an extensive product line. For the most part, a wholesaling intermediary's product/service strategy is largely a function of the target market it has chosen.

Pricing Strategy

The pricing strategy of these channel members depends on the extent of service they provide for their customers. Merchant wholesalers perform many services; as a result, the prices they charge retail customers are higher than those charged by wholesaling intermediaries that perform only a few functions.

Distribution Strategy

Distribution strategies vary among wholesaling intermediaries. Drop shippers can work through a combination of post office boxes and public warehouses. In contrast, a food broker would be required to have an extensive warehousing and delivery operation.

Promotional Strategy

Personal selling is the primary ingredient of a wholesaling intermediary's promotional strategy. Advertising is limited to trade publications that reach their particular marketplaces.

Summary of Chapter Objectives

1. Identify the functions performed by wholesaling intermediaries.
Wholesaling intermediaries provide time, place, and ownership utilities. They do this by performing the basic marketing functions of buying, selling, storing, transporting, risk taking, financing, and supplying market information.

2. Explain how wholesaling intermediaries improve channel efficiency.
Wholesaling intermediaries improve channel efficiency by cutting the number of buyer-seller transactions required. For example, if 4 manufacturers marketed their output to 4 different retail outlets, a total of 16 transactions would be needed. Using a wholesaling intermediary, however, would reduce the total number of transactions to eight.

3. Distinguish between merchant wholesalers and agents and brokers.
Merchant wholesalers take title to the goods they handle. Agents and brokers may take possession of the goods, but they do not take title.

4. Identify the major types of wholesalers and the situations in which each might be used. The two major categories of merchant wholesalers are full-function merchant wholesalers, such as rack jobbers, and limited-function merchant wholesalers, including cash-and-carry wholesalers, truck wholesalers, drop shippers, and mail-order wholesalers. Full-function wholesalers are common in the drug, grocery, and hardware industries. Limited-function wholesalers are sometimes used in the food, coal, lumber, cosmetics, jewelry, sporting goods, and general-merchandise industries.

5. Describe the major types of agents and brokers. Commission merchants, auction houses, brokers, selling agents, and manufacturers' agents are classified as agent wholesaling intermediaries because they do not take title to the goods they sell.

6. Outline how a wholesaling strategy is developed. Like other marketing strategies, a wholesaling strategy starts with determining the target market, which can be defined in terms of product line, customer size, customer needs, and promotional strategy employed. After the target market is set, a marketing mix is developed. The wholesaling intermediary's product/service strategy is primarily a matter of the width, length, and depth of its inventory assortment. Wholesaling pricing strategy depends on the extent of the services offered. Distribution strategies employed vary among wholesale intermediaries. Finally, promotional strategy basically emphasizes personal selling.

Key Terms

wholesaler
wholesaling intermediary
sales branch
public warehouse
sales office
trade fair
merchandise mart
merchant wholesaler
rack jobber
cash-and-carry wholesaler

truck wholesaler
drop shipper
mail-order wholesaler
agents and brokers
commission merchant
auction house
broker
selling agent
manufacturers' agent

Review Questions

1. Distinguish between a wholesaler and a retailer.
2. In what ways do wholesaling intermediaries assist manufacturers? How do they help retailers?
3. Explain how wholesaling intermediaries can assist retailers in increasing their return on investment.
4. Distinguish between sales offices and sales branches. Under what conditions might each type be used?
5. What role does the public warehouse play in distribution channels?
6. Distinguish merchant wholesalers from agents and brokers.
7. Why are the operating expenses of the merchant wholesaler higher than those of the typical agent or broker?
8. How do commission merchants and brokers differ?
9. Distinguish between a manufacturer's agent and a selling agent.
10. Under what conditions would a manufacturer utilize manufacturers' agents for a distribution channel?

Discussion Questions

1. In outlying areas of Central America, packaged food products are distributed by wholesaling intermediaries on three to five different levels. The first intermediary buys the products in lots of several cases and then breaks bulk by selling to other wholesalers in smaller quantities. They, in turn, resell in smaller quantities to other intermediaries. The products continue to be resold until finally a peddler on a mule travels into the jungles with a couple of cans and several other manufacturers' products for resale to small retailers. Discuss the contributions made by this unique wholesaling system.

2. Match each of the following industries with the most appropriate wholesaling intermediary:

   ___ Hardware   **a.** Drop shipper
   ___ Perishable foods   **b.** Truck wholesaler
   ___ Lumber   **c.** Auction house
   ___ Wheat   **d.** Full-function merchant wholesaler
   ___ Used cars   **e.** Commission merchant

3. Comment on the following statement: "Drop shippers are good candidates for elimination. All they do is process orders; they do not even handle the products they sell."

4. The term *broker* also appears in the real estate and securities fields. Are these brokers identical to the agent wholesaling intermediaries described in this chapter? Discuss.

5. List the following wholesaling intermediaries in ascending order on the basis of operating expense percentages:
   a. Full-function merchant wholesaler
   b. Cash-and-carry wholesaler
   c. Broker
   d. Manufacturer's sales branch
   e. Truck wholesaler

VIDEO CASE 13

Northern Produce Co./Mushrooms, Inc.

It is 4:00 a.m. on a Monday morning when Joey Weiss arrives at the Central Produce Market in Los Angeles. With the eye of an experienced buyer, Joey moves quickly from stall to stall, assessing the quality and quantity of fresh fruits and vegetables displayed by many suppliers. The produce he buys in large volume must fill the orders of hundreds of restaurant, hotel, and grocery-store customers that expect delivery of their daily supply of fresh produce within a few hours.

Joey Weiss is president of Northern Produce Co./Mushrooms, Inc. of Los Angeles. As a full-function merchant wholesaler, Northern takes title to the produce it distributes and provides a broad range of services for customers and suppliers. Joey and his brother Barry are third-generation owners of a family business, set up by their father and grandfather in 1938, as a wholesaler of fresh produce. In the

1950s, the Weiss family expanded their business by distributing cultivated mushrooms. During the late 1970s, they moved into specialty produce, buying and selling fresh herbs and such exotic fare as miniature vegetables, edible flowers, and unusual varieties of wild and cultivated mushrooms. Today the company has 85 employees and rings up annual sales of $20 million.

Northern buys produce to service more than 400 customers, including Vons, Safeway, and other major retail food stores; Irvine Ranch specialty markets; Hilton and Sheraton hotels; Royal Viking cruise ships; and some of Southern California's most fashionable restaurants.

To satisfy diverse customer needs, Joey buys from alternative supply sources. Buying decisions take into account fluctuating market conditions and the seasonal availability of many produce items. Joey buys about half of the firm's inventory during his early morning trips to three produce markets in Los Angeles. He frequently revisits the markets at the end of the day to plan his buying strategy for the following day. Fruits and vegetables in plentiful supply at the end of a day means that he will have more bargaining power the next morning.

Joey buys many specialty and off-season items directly from food brokers, shippers, and growers in other countries. To reduce the air freight costs on some imported produce, Joey has imported seeds from Europe and lined up farmers in the United States to grow such crops as edible flowers, white carrots, haricot vert (a French green bean), and radiccio (a red Italian lettuce).

Each produce shipment arriving at Northern's two warehouses is inspected carefully to ensure that the merchandise is not damaged or spoiled. The quality check reduces the company's risk of taking title to produce it may not be able to sell to customers. Fruits and vegetables passing inspection are moved to refrigerated areas and placed on pallets. Warehouse workers continually rotate inventory, a task that helps alleviate confusion about which produce is brought in to be cooled and which is going out to be delivered to customers. Other warehouse workers sort through bulk packages of produce and repack them so that customers receive produce that is uniform in size, color, and degree of ripeness.

Northern maintains a fleet of 25 refrigerated delivery trucks, each one handpainted with a giant mural of different fruits and vegetables. For many customers, prompt delivery is as important as produce quality and price. A cruise-ship customer says, "We need to be able to ensure that the product is delivered to us when the wholesaler says he will deliver to us. A truck stopped on the freeway is of no use to us because the ship must sail on time."

Northern Produce takes pride in its reputation of being a service-oriented wholesaler. Says Joey, "We tell our customers that if they need two or three deliveries a day, they will have them." The company also sends out several delivery trucks to the same geographic area to ensure that produce is delivered to customers when they want it. Produce is shipped by air to customers in faraway places — for example, the Grand Hyatt Hotel in New York and cruise ships in Europe, Peru, Tahiti, Hawaii, and Japan.

Another service Northern provides for customers is financing. Customers are given up to 30 days to pay for merchandise. If they bought directly from brokers or the market, they would have to pay within a week.

Each week Northern sends customers a newsletter to keep them updated on produce availability and price. This information helps hotels and restaurants plan their menus. It also gives Northern the opportunity to tell customers about specialty produce flown in directly from different countries, such as the purple, yellow, and white bell peppers it imports from Holland.

Keeping customers informed is a top priority of Northern's eight full-time salespeople. Because Northern specializes in exotic produce, much of which may be unfamiliar to many customers, salespeople regularly contact customers, explaining new items in detail so that customers understand their features and uses. In addition to servicing existing accounts, salespeople continually monitor the opening of new hotels, restaurants, and specialty food stores in an effort to bring in new business.

Source: Telephone interviews with Joey and Barry Weiss, February 18 and 19, 1988.

Questions

1. Explain why Northern Produce is classified as a full-function merchant wholesaler.

2. How does Northern Produce attempt to reduce the risks it assumes in taking title to goods?

3. What functions does Northern Produce perform in linking producers with customers?

4. Competition among chic restaurants in Los Angeles is fierce. To remain competitive, chefs constantly look for new ideas to attract their upscale clientele. Do you think Northern Produce could make a difference in the success or failure of a restaurant? Why or why not?

5. Which marketing mix elements do you think contributed most to the growth of Northern Produce? Which elements will be most important to the wholesaler's future growth and expansion?

COMPUTER APPLICATIONS

Inventory turnover, the number of times the dollar value of the firm's average inventory is sold annually, is an important ratio in evaluating the performance of wholesaling intermediaries and their retailer customers. Since trade associations publish average inventory turnover rates for different types of firms, products, and geographical areas, a comparison of the firm's turnover with those of similar organizations provides tangible evidence of the firm's performance. In addition, comparing current turnover rates with those for prior years enables marketers to evaluate changes in performance over time.

Inventory turnover rates are also likely to be reflected in the markups of a wholesaling intermediary. In most instances, wholesaling intermediaries with relatively low turnover rates charge higher average markups than those with higher turnover rates. (Exceptions are instances in which a wholesaler performs few services relative to another wholesaler that might have a similar annual turnover rate but performs a large number of services for its customers.)

To calculate the rate of inventory turnover for a wholesaling intermediary, the firm's average inventory for the year must be known. Average inventory can be determined by adding beginning and ending inventories and dividing by 2. Inventory turnover is then calculated with one of the following formulas depending on whether the firm's inventory is recorded at *retail* (the prices at which the products will be sold to the wholesaler's customers) or *cost* (the prices paid for the products in inventory):

$$\text{Inventory Turnover Rate (at retail)} = \frac{\text{Sales}}{\text{Average Inventory}}$$

$$\text{Inventory Turnover Rate (at cost)} = \frac{\text{Cost of Goods Sold}}{\text{Average Inventory}}$$

The following example illustrates the two methods of determining annual inventory turnover rates. Wholesaler A, with $100,000 in sales and an average inventory of $20,000 at retail, has an annual turnover rate of 5. Wholesaler B, with a cost of goods sold of $120,000 and an average inventory of $30,000 at cost, has an annual turnover rate of 4:

Wholesaler A:

$$\text{Inventory Turnover Rate (at retail)} = \frac{\text{Sales}}{\text{Average Inventory}}$$

$$= \frac{\$100,000}{\$20,000} = 5$$

Wholesaler B:

$$\text{Inventory Turnover Rate (at cost)} = \frac{\text{Cost of Goods Sold}}{\text{Average Inventory}}$$

$$= \frac{\$120,000}{\$30,000} = 4$$

In cases in which average inventory is recorded at cost and only the inventory's selling price is known, the markup percentage must be subtracted from the selling price to calculate the inventory turnover rate on a cost basis. For example, consider the operations of a small wholesaler that carries an average inventory at a cost of $750,000, generates annual sales of $3,850,000, and operates on a 15 percent markup percentage on the selling price. To calculate the firm's inventory turnover rate, the $3,850,000 total sales must be reduced by the 15 percent markup for a total of $3,272,500. The second formula can then be used to determine the firm's turnover rate:

$$\text{Inventory Turnover Rate (at cost)} = \frac{\text{Cost of Goods Sold}}{\text{Average Inventory}}$$

$$= \frac{\$3,272,500}{\$750,000}$$

$$= 4.4$$

Directions: Use menu item 10 titled "Inventory Turnover" to solve each of the following problems.

Problem 1   A Columbia, South Carolina, wholesaling intermediary carries an average inventory recorded at cost of $6 million. Its total cost of goods sold is $42 million. What is the firm's inventory turnover rate?

Problem 2   Tucson Mart is a merchandise mart in Tucson, Arizona. Retailers can order displayed merchandise for shipment directly from the factories of the exhibiting firms. But since many of the manufacturers' factories are located in distant cities, Tucson Mart requires its tenants to carry modest inventories. Total inventories at Tucson Mart average $1,200,000 (at retail). The mart's management estimates that about $9,600,000 in merchandise (at retail) is sold out of these inventories each year. What is the annual inventory turnover rate for the inventories carried at Tucson Mart?

Problem 3   Coleman Brothers, Inc. is a book jobber (wholesaler) in York, Pennsylvania. The firm carries an average inventory at a cost of $1 million. Its annual sales are approximately $7 million. Coleman Brothers operates on a 30 percent markup percentage on selling price. What is the firm's annual turnover rate.

Problem 4   A wholesaler in Flint, Michigan, had a $10 million cost-based inventory on January 1, 1989, but was able to reduce it to $9 million by the end of the year. The firm had a 24 percent markup percentage on selling price. Its 1989 sales volume was $50 million. Calculate the 1989 inventory turnover rate for the Flint wholesaler.

Problem 5   A Wilmington, Delaware, wholesaler began 1989 with an inventory of $4 million at retail. During the year, the wholesaler decided to increase its overall inventory position to better serve its customers. The firm ended 1989 with a $5 million inventory (at retail). Sales in 1989 were $27 million. What was the wholesaler's inventory turnover rate for the year?

14 Retailing

Chapter Objectives

1. To describe the evolution of retailing.

2. To outline the various elements of retailing strategy.

3. To identify and explain each of the five bases for categorizing retailers.

4. To describe the concept of scrambled merchandising.

John Malloy's *The Woman's Dress for Success Book* convinced many businesswomen that the climb up the corporate ladder might be hastened with a wardrobe consisting of more than the traditional navy blue suit and tie. But where could women of accomplishment turn for wardrobes that suited their lifestyles?

Michael Jeffries and Colleen Brady had the answer. In 1984, the two former department store executives opened the first Alcott & Andrews specialty clothing store for career women. "Alcott & Andrews was born out of the idea that there was a new customer—an affluent, successful woman—who needed something she wasn't getting from department stores," says Jeffries. The partners recognized career women as a largely untapped and potentially lucrative market. Alcott & Andrews came on the retailing scene to cater to this specialized segment. Since opening its first two stores in Washington, D.C., it has expanded to urban locations from New York to California and plans to have 36 stores by 1990.

Alcott & Andrews' formula for success is based on its founders' belief that many working women have neither the time nor the inclination to shop. The retailer's strategy is to attract these women by designing store layouts that facilitate quick shopping, providing personalized service, and offering tightly edited collections of career clothes—suits, blouses, blazers, dresses, and accessories. There are no jeans, evening dresses, or lingerie.

Alcott & Andrews' merchandising concept is to help women build wardrobes rather than buy individual garments. Clothing displays are organized according to color schemes so that shoppers can easily mix and match individual items. Salespeople, whom Alcott & Andrews refers to as *wardrobe consultants,* are trained to help the shopper coordinate gar-

WASHINGTON, D.C. · NEW YORK · CHICAGO · ATLANTA · WEST HARTFORD · SOUTH COAST PLAZA · SHORT HILLS

ALCOTT&ANDREWS

124 GEARY STREET AT UNION SQUARE (415) 981-2121   STANFORD SHOPPING CENTER (415) 322-2014
Mon.-Fri. 10 to 8, Sat. 10 to 6, Sun. 12 to 5.   Mon.-Fri. 10 to 9, Sat. 10 to 6, Sun. 12 to 5

ments and think in terms of investing in a wardrobe. The company takes great care in selecting, training, and motivating associates. It has two full-time recruiters who seek out the best possible sales personnel and motivates associates by giving them high sales commissions and offering earnings potential of more than $50,000.

Because store image in fashion retailing is often more important than merchandise, Alcott & Andrews

plays up its executive image to the hilt. Piped-in classical music, leather-topped antique desks, potted palms, and bowls of potpourri create an in-store atmosphere of elegance and refinement. Successful role models such as Barbara Walters and Geraldine Ferraro have given in-store lectures, and the company sends representatives to college campuses to advise female business students on creating appropriate wardrobes. Print and broadcast advertising depicts beautiful, confident women in a variety of attitudes and fashions.

Appealing to a broad-based clientele, Alcott & Andrews offers merchandise of supreme quality at affordable prices. "Our customer uses fashion to express her individuality, and successful women no longer wear uniforms," says Brady. "We find that women at all career levels need elegant, appropriate wardrobes for all the public moments in their lives." Since more people strive than arrive, Alcott & Andrews seems poised for continued success.[1]

Photo source: Courtesy of Alcott & Andrews, Incorporated.

Chapter Overview

The nation's 2 million retail outlets serve as contact points between channel members and the ultimate consumer. In a very real sense, retailers are the distribution channel for most consumers, since the typical shopper has little contact with manufacturers and virtually none with wholesaling intermediaries. Retailers represent the consumer as a purchasing agent to the rest of the distribution channel. The services retailers provide—location, store hours, quality of salespeople, store layout, selection, and return policies, among others—often are more important than the physical product in developing consumers' images of the products and services offered. Both large and small retailers perform the major channel activities: creating time, place, and ownership utilities.

Retailers are both customers and marketers in the channel. They market products and services to ultimate consumers and at the same time are customers of wholesalers and manufacturers. Because of their critical location in the channel, retailers often perform an important feedback role: They obtain information from customers and transmit it to manufacturers and other channel members.

Retailing may be defined as all of the activities involved in the sale of products and services to the ultimate consumer. Although the bulk of all retail sales occurs in retail stores, the definition of retailing also includes several forms of nonstore retailing, which involves such activities as telephone and mail-order sales, vending machine sales, and direct selling.

retailing
All activities involved in the sale of products and services to the ultimate consumer.

Evolution of Retailing

Early retailing can be traced to the establishment of trading posts, such as the Hudson Bay Company, and to pack peddlers who carried their wares to outlying settlements. The first type of retail institution in the United States was the general store, which stocked merchandise to meet the needs of a small community or rural area. Here customers could buy clothing, groceries, feed, seed, farm equipment, drugs, spectacles, and candy. General stores flourished for many years, but the basic needs that had created them also doomed them to a limited existence. Since storekeepers attempted to satisfy customers' needs for all types of goods, they carried a small assortment of each item. As communities grew, new stores opened; these concentrated on specific product lines, such as drugs, dry goods, groceries, and hardware. The general stores could not compete, and their owners either converted them into more limited-line stores or closed them. Most of the few hundred general stores still operating today serve customers in rural areas of the South and West.

Southland Corporation's "MovieQuik" videocassette rental program is one of the many services that attract almost 8 million customers each day to the firm's 7-Eleven convenience stores. In addition to accessible locations and round-the-clock operating hours, 7-Eleven's marketing strategy emphasizes electronic services, such as automatic teller machines, and fresh fast-food items to bring in new customers and increase current customers' business.

The development of retailing illustrates the marketing concept in operation. Innovations in retail institutions have emerged to satisfy changing consumer wants and needs. Supermarkets appeared in the early 1930s in response to consumers' desire for lower prices. The innovation in the 1950s of discount department stores in suburban locations offered consumers convenient parking and appealed to price-sensitive shoppers who were willing to give up many of the services provided by downtown department stores. The emergence of convenience food stores in the 1960s satisfied consumer demand for fast service, convenient location, and expanded hours of operation. The development of off-price retailers in the 1980s reflects consumer demand for brand name merchandise at price levels considerably lower than those of traditional retailers.

The Wheel of Retailing

Marketing professor Malcolm P. McNair attempted to explain the patterns of change in retailing through what has been termed the **wheel of retailing.** According to this hypothesis, new types of retailers gain a competitive foothold by offering their customers lower prices through the reduction or elimination of services. Once established, however, they add more services, and their prices gradually rise. They then become vulnerable to a new, low-price retailer that enters with minimum services—and so the wheel turns.

Most of the major developments in retailing appear to fit the wheel pattern. Early department stores, chain stores, supermarkets, discount stores, hypermarkets, and catalog retailers emphasized limited service and low prices. For most of these retailers, price levels gradually increased as services were added.

There have been some exceptions, however. Suburban shopping centers, convenience food stores, and vending machines were not built around low-price appeals. However, the wheel pattern has been evident sufficiently in the past to enable it to serve as a general indicator of future retailing developments.[2]

wheel of retailing
Hypothesis stating that new types of retailers gain a competitive foothold by offering lower prices through reduction or elimination of services. Once established, they add more services, gradually raise their prices, and then become vulnerable to the emergence of a new, low-price retailer with minimum services.

Figure 14.1
Components of Retailing Strategy

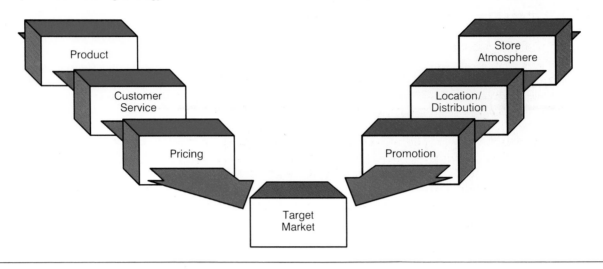

Retailing Strategy

Like manufacturers and wholesalers, retailers develop marketing strategies based on overall organizational goals and strategic plans. They monitor environmental factors and assess organizational strengths and weaknesses to ascertain marketing opportunities and constraints. Retailers' marketing decisions center on the two fundamental steps of (1) analyzing, evaluating, and selecting a target market and (2) developing a marketing mix designed to profitably satisfy the chosen market. Components of retailing strategy, presented in Figure 14.1, include product, customer service, pricing, target market, promotion, location/distribution, and store atmosphere. The combination of these elements projects the **retail image**—the consumer's perception of the store and the shopping experience it provides. Retail image communicates to consumers whether the store is, say, economical, prestigious, conservative, or contemporary. Regardless of the type of image the retailer wishes to project, all components of retailing strategy must work together to appeal to and satisfy the target market.

retail image
Consumers' perception of the store and the shopping experience it provides.

Target Market

Retailers must start by selecting a market to appeal to. In identifying a target market, retailers take into account its size and profit potential and the level of competition. Alcott & Andrews, for example, decided to target career women, a market segment that was growing in terms of both size and purchasing power and offered a low level of competition.

Retailers segment markets according to demographic, geographic, and psychographic bases. Kmart, for example, targets middle-income Americans—families who earn between $15,000 and $60,000 a year. Fiesta Mart, Inc., a

Houston grocery store chain, targets an international clientele—Southeast Asians, Hispanics, Chinese, Koreans, Filipinos, Indians, and immigrants of other nationalities. Capitalizing on the current baby boom, many retailers are opening stores targeted specifically at children. The Gap, Inc. has opened GapKids apparel shops to serve children age 2 to 12, and Waldenbooks, Inc. is targeting the for-kids-only segment through its new chain of Waldenkids bookstores.

One of the most dominant trends in retailing is that of increased market segmentation. Retailers that traditionally sought to serve the mass market have shifted their strategy to target more narrowly defined segments. General merchandisers such as F. W. Woolworth are placing more emphasis on specialty store formats because they provide greater sales per square foot and higher profit margins and returns on investment than do general merchandise stores. Woolworth's shoe business, for example, began with Kinney shoe stores, which sell a full range of casual and dress shoes, boots, and accessories for men, women, and children. In 1974, Kinney opened its first Foot Locker athletic shoe store to cater to Americans' growing interest in physical fitness. In recent years, Kinney has further segmented its shoe business by opening Lady Foot Locker and Kids Foot Locker stores.

After identifying a target market, retailers position themselves among competitors by developing a marketing plan consisting of a blend of the retailing strategy components.

Product Strategy

Product strategy involves making decisions about what type of merchandise the retailer will offer that target customers want to buy. In developing a product mix, the retailer must decide on general product categories, product lines, specific products within lines, and the depth and width of assortment. Pier 1 Imports groups its merchandise into six general product categories: wicker and rattan furniture, gifts and personal care items, decorative home furnishings, housewares, casual clothing, and baskets. By carrying more than 10,000 individual items, Pier 1 offers customers a wide and deep merchandise assortment.[3] Product-mix strategies used by different types of retailers are discussed in later sections of the chapter.

In deciding which products to include in the merchandise assortment, retailers must consider the competitive environment. Sales of many department stores have eroded in recent years due to increased competition from specialty and discount stores. To improve their profitability, many department stores have narrowed their traditionally broad product lines by eliminating high-overhead, low-profit categories such as toys, appliances, sporting goods, and furniture. Department stores are now focusing on expanding their assortment of women's clothing, men's and women's sportswear, jewelry, cosmetics, and linens—product categories that bring higher returns on investment.[4]

Understanding target customers' wants and needs is vital to developing a successful product strategy. By conducting marketing research, retailers can determine what their customers expect and adjust their product offerings accordingly. Vons Companies, a California-based grocery retailer, uses neighborhood and in-store surveys, demographic studies, and computer-generated sales and inventory data to customize the product offerings at each of its 135 neigh-

To sharpen its competitive position, Sears, Roebuck and Co. is developing market-oriented merchandising programs. In this photo, sportswear buyers of Sears' regional buying office in Los Angeles review designs with a California manufacturer. In response to local market demographics, Sears is remerchandising existing mid-size stores. At its Flagstaff, Arizona, store, it has expanded the lawn and garden, enlarged sporting goods and casual apparel departments and added a new line of merchandise — light-truck accessories — to reflect the community's active, outdoor, family-oriented life-styles.

Photo source: Courtesy of Sears, Roebuck and Co.

borhood supermarkets. One demographic study of customers at Vons' Fresno store revealed that current customers are more often Spanish speaking and poorer than those of previous years. As a result, Vons reevaluated 30,000 items sold at the store. It decided to drop 5,000 products, including egg noodles, Dove bars, fancy pet treats, Chinese pea pods, and Pepperidge Farm bread, and add 2,000 new items, such as Mexican cookies, inexpensive ice cream novelties, and broader lines of limeade and punch.[5]

Customer Service Strategy

Retailers provide shoppers with a variety of customer services. Examples are gift wrapping, alterations, return privileges, bridal registries, consultants, interior designers, and merchandise delivery and installation. In developing a customer service strategy, the retailer must determine which services to offer and whether to charge customers for them. Those decisions are influenced by several factors: store size, type, and location; kind of merchandise; level of service offered by competitors; customer expectations; and financial resources.

The basic objective of all customer services is to attract and retain target customers, thus increasing store sales, profits, and market share. Some services, such as restrooms, lounges, complimentary coffee, and drinking fountains, are designed for shoppers' comfort. Quicksilver, a children's clothing store, has set aside a store area for parents that has a rocking chair, bottle warmer, and diaper kits.

Other services offer customers convenience. Carson Pirie Scott & Company's department stores offer customers overnight package delivery via Federal Express, a service that is especially popular during the holiday season. Layaway plans, automatic bill payment, and credit arrangements facilitate payment of merchandise. To make shopping easier, some retailers have installed interactive video systems. Video terminals at Florsheim Shoe Company stores allow customers to order shoes in any size and color of Florsheim's 300 styles. The system places an order directly with the company's warehouse, and shoes are delivered to customers within one week.[6]

A customer service strategy can also be used to build demand for a line of merchandise. In an attempt to upgrade its image from a no-frills discount store to a retailer of fashionable merchandise, Kmart has hired food and entertainment expert Martha Stewart to promote its new kitchen, bed, bath, and home decorating merchandise available in its Kitchen Korners boutiques. As a shoppers' consultant, Stewart makes personal appearances in Kmart stores nationwide. Shoppers also receive Kitchen Kornerstone brochures that offer Stewart's tips on cooking, table decor, and home entertaining.[7]

Recognizing the importance of customer service as a competitive tool, some retailers have established companywide customer service programs. One example is C.A.R.E.—Customers Are Really Everything—operating throughout Dayton Hudson's Target chain of discount clothing stores. To instill a "customers-come-first" attitude, Target honors employees for outstanding customer service and gives them report cards summarizing comments on their service from weekly interviews with customers. Other features of the program focus on customer convenience. Target redesigned service counters and store directories and added automated teller machines and customer assistance phones. To help move customers more quickly through checkout lanes, Target installed scanners and has an employee at the entrance to checkout lanes to answer shopper inquiries and direct customers to the shortest lines.[8]

Pricing Strategy

Prices play a major role in the consumer's perception of the retailer. The $6,055 price of the Brazilian gemstone necklace featured in the H. Stern advertisement in Figure 14.2 clearly positions the retailer as a prestigious store. Prices reflect the retailer's price-setting objectives and policies described in Chapters 10 and 11. Because prices are based on the cost of merchandise, efficient and timely buying is an essential part of the retailer's pricing strategy. For example, to keep prices at discount levels of 30 percent below those of comparable merchandise, IKEA, a retailer of unassembled furniture and other household goods, buys an entire year's supply of goods in advance for the 76 stores it operates throughout the world.[9]

refuse to pay the price or when improved products or fashion changes render current merchandise less salable, the marketer must seriously consider reducing the product's price in the form of a markdown.

markdown
Amount by which the retailer reduces the original selling price of a product.

Markdowns   A **markdown** is the amount by which the retailer reduces the original selling price of a product. The markdown percentage—the discount amount typically advertised for the "sale" item—can be computed as follows:

$$\text{Markdown Percentage} = \frac{\text{Dollar Amount of Markdown}}{\text{"Sale" (New) Price}}.$$

Returning to the above example, suppose no one has been willing to pay $1 for the item. The marketer has decided to reduce the selling price to 79 cents. Advertisements for the special "sale" item might emphasize that the product has been marked down 27 percent:

$$\text{Markdown Percentage} = \frac{\$.21}{\$.79} = 26.6\%.$$

Markdowns are sometimes used for evaluative purposes. For example, store managers or buyers in a large department store may be evaluated partly on the basis of the average markdown percentage on the product lines for which they are responsible.

Location/Distribution Strategy

Real estate professionals often point out that location may be the determining factor in the success or failure of a retail business. Retailers may choose to locate at an isolated site, in a central business district, or in a planned shopping center. The location decision depends on many factors, including the type of merchandise sold, the retailer's financial resources, characteristics of the target market, and site availability. In recent years, fast-food retailers have altered their location strategies because their traditional sites have become saturated by the nation's 113,000 fast-food outlets. New, alternative locations include museums, corporate headquarters, casinos, department stores, motels, and even hospitals. McDonald's operates a restaurant in the Field Museum of Natural History in Chicago; Wendy's has an outlet at the Columbus Zoo in Ohio; and Burger King has opened an outlet at Wang Laboratories, Inc.'s corporate headquarters in Lowell, Massachusetts.[10]

The retailer's location must be appropriate for its target market. In appealing to the upscale customer, The Gap selected a location on Newbury Street in Boston's prestigious Back Bay area. The advertisement in Figure 14.3 emphasizes the location by showing a photograph of the site with the advertising copy simply giving the street address. The site accommodates both The Gap and the retailer's new GapKids store.

planned shopping center
Group of retail stores planned, coordinated, and marketed as a unit to shoppers in a geographic trade area.

Planned Shopping Centers   The pronounced shift of retail trade away from the traditional downtown retailing districts and toward suburban shopping centers has been building since 1950. A **planned shopping center** is a group of retail stores planned, coordinated, and marketed as a unit to shoppers in their

Figure 14.3
Choosing a Location That
Targets Customers

The Gap & GapKids, 201 Newbury St., Boston, MA

the
gap

Source: Barbara Karant/Karant & Associates, Incorporated.

geographical trade areas. These centers followed population shifts to the suburbs and concentrated on avoiding many of the problems associated with shopping in downtown business districts. They provide a convenient location for
shoppers as well as free parking facilities based on the number and types of
stores. Shopping is facilitated with uniform hours of operation and evening and
weekend shopping hours. There are now about 28,500 shopping centers in the
United States.

Types of Shopping Centers   There are three main types of planned shopping
centers. The smallest is the neighborhood shopping center, which most often is
composed of a supermarket and a group of smaller stores such as a drugstore,
a laundry and dry cleaner, a small-appliance store, and perhaps a beauty shop
and barber shop. These centers provide convenient shopping for perhaps 5,000
to 50,000 shoppers who live within a few minutes' commuting time of the centers. They typically contain 5 to 15 stores, and the product mix is usually con-
fined to convenience goods and some shopping goods.

Community shopping centers serve 20,000 to 100,000 persons in a trade
area extending a few miles. These centers are likely to contain from 10 to 30
retail stores and a branch of a local department store or a large variety store
as the primary tenant. In addition to the stores found in a neighborhood center,

the community center is likely to have more stores featuring shopping goods, some professional offices, and a branch bank.

The regional shopping center is a large shopping district of at least 400,000 square feet of shopping space. It is usually built around one or more major department stores and includes as many as 200 smaller stores. In order to be successful, regional centers must be located in areas in which at least 250,000 people reside within 30 minutes' driving time of the centers. Regional centers provide a wide assortment of convenience, shopping, and specialty goods, plus many professional and personal service facilities.

Planned shopping centers generate about $550 billion in annual sales, or slightly more than 40 percent of total U.S. retail sales.[11] The growth of planned shopping centers has slowed in recent years, because the most lucrative locations are occupied and the market is becoming saturated in many areas. As a result, several new shopping center strategies are being pursued. A new regional mall approach combines shopping with entertainment. Scheduled to open in Minneapolis in 1990, the Fashion Mall of America will offer an indoor amusement park complete with a roller coaster, an indoor water park with 20 water slides, and a hotel in addition to 800 stores and 100 restaurants. With 9 million square feet of space, Fashion Mall will be 10 times the size of the currently largest regional shopping center. Similar centers that combine shopping and theme-park entertainment are planned in Cincinnati, Denver, Tampa, and Columbia, South Carolina.[12]

Another trend gaining in popularity is the specialty store shopping center. Unlike community or regional centers, the specialty store centers are not anchored by a department store; they consist only of specialty shops and restaurants and target the upscale consumer. The advertisement in Figure 14.4 promotes the 28 fashion stores in the Galleria, a specialty store shopping center in Edina, Minnesota. Instead of displaying the stores' merchandise, Galleria's advertising presents the season's fashion color palette. Serving the Minneapolis–St. Paul area, the Galleria has a total of 60 shops, including fashion retailers, home furnishings stores, gift shops, and restaurants.

Other Distribution Decisions　Retailers also face a variety of other distribution decisions, many of which ensure that adequate quantities of stock are available when consumers want to buy. Sears recently adopted a plan to streamline its distribution system and cut 5 of its 12 distribution centers. The objectives of the program are to cut distribution costs and speed delivery to stores.[13]

Promotional Strategy

The objective of the retailer's promotional strategy is to position the consumer's perception of the store in line with the other components of the retailing mix. Retailers meet this goal by designing advertisements, staging special events, and developing sales promotions aimed at the target market. Benetton, a sportswear retail chain, targets the college market with a campus promotional program. Benetton advertises in college magazines such as *Campus Voice, Newsweek on Campus,* and *College Woman.* In cities with large campuses, Benetton uses billboard advertising with electronic video displays to carry messages about monthly campus events. The retailer actively participates in on-campus

Figure 14.4
Promoting Fashion Retailers in a Specialty Store Shopping Center

Source: Courtesy of Galleria Merchants Association.

promotions and tie-ins with magazines by sponsoring events such as fashion shows with *Rolling Stone* and *Seventeen.*[14]

Through promotional efforts, retailers communicate information about their stores—their locations, merchandise, store hours, and prices. Retailers selling merchandise that changes frequently due to fashion trends can effectively use advertising to promote current styles.

Retailers also use the promotional component as a persuasive and motivational tool. Owners of a new type of retail store that sells reproductions of classic furniture designed by renowned architects such as Adolf Loos, Frank Lloyd Wright, and Ludwig Mies van der Rohe are relying heavily on promotions to persuade potential customers to purchase their high-priced merchandise. (A wooden chair designed by Charles Rennie Mackintosh may carry a price tag of $1,700, and a lamp designed by Loos may be priced at $1,500.) Targeting the affluent, educated consumer, these new stores offer special courses for customers on the history of design, co-sponsor design exhibitions at museums and galleries, and advertise in the printed programs of local symphonies and theaters and in exclusive design magazines.[15]

Retail salespeople are another important promotional element in helping retailers communicate store image, inform shoppers, and persuade them to buy. As a source of information, salespeople must be knowledgeable about such store policies and procedures as credit, discounts, special sales, delivery, layaways, and returns. As a source of increasing store sales, salespeople must be able to persuade customers that what they are selling is what the customers need. To this end, salespeople should be trained to use selling up and suggestion selling techniques.

selling up
Retail sales technique of convincing a customer to buy a higher priced item than he or she originally intended.

Selling up means convincing the customer to buy a higher-priced item than he or she originally intended. For example an automobile salesperson may convince a customer to buy a more expensive model than the person intended to purchase. It is important that the practice of selling up always be used within the constraints of the customer's real needs. If the salesperson sells the customer something that he or she really does not need, the potential for repeat sales by that seller will be substantially diminished.

suggestion selling
Form of retail selling that attempts to broaden the customer's original purchase with related items, special promotions, and holiday or seasonal merchandise.

Suggestion selling seeks to broaden the customer's original purchase with related items, special promotions, and/or holiday and seasonal merchandise. Here too suggestion selling should be based on the idea of helping the customer recognize true needs rather than selling him or her unwanted merchandise. Suggestion selling is one of the best methods of increasing retail sales and should be practiced by all sales personnel.

Customers' attitudes toward a retailer are greatly influenced by the impression made by sales personnel. Increasing customer complaints about unfriendly, inattentive, and unknowledgeable salespeople have prompted many retailers to pay more attention to training and motivating salespeople. Marshall Field & Company, a Chicago-based department store chain, initiated a program to upgrade the standards of its salespeople. Field implemented a computer scheduling program to place salespeople where they are most needed. Before the system was installed, it took the average salesperson 10 minutes to approach a customer; now the average approach time has been reduced to 2 minutes. Field also developed an incentive plan to motivate employees. Each time a store manager sees an employee being extra helpful to a customer, the clerk receives a silver "Frangloon" coin. When employees accumulate 10 coins, they can trade them in for a box of Field's Frango mint chocolates. Employees earning 100 coins get an extra day of paid vacation.[16] Other retailers are motivating employees by paying them sales commissions.

Store Atmosphere

atmospherics
Combination of physical store characteristics and amenities provided by the retailer that results in developing a retail image and attracting customers.

While store location, merchandise selection, customer service, pricing, and promotional activities all contribute to the store's overall image, a store's personality is also projected by **atmospherics** — the physical characteristics and amenities that attract customers and satisfy their shopping needs. Atmospherics include both the store's exterior and interior.

The store's exterior, which includes architectural design, window displays, signs, and entryways, helps identify the retailer and attract its target market. The Saks Fifth Avenue script logo on storefronts and McDonald's golden arches are exterior elements that readily identify these retailers. Bookstores and fashion retailers often attempt to draw customers inside stores by creating exciting window displays.

FOCUS ON ETHICS

Ethical Issues in Retail Sales

Numerous ethical dilemmas arise in the retail sales environment. How they are resolved will have profound consequences for a store. Job performance can suffer and customers may become angry if a salesperson is unable to handle ethical problems properly. Retail managers must understand how their behavior can contribute to ethical dilemmas, because the store's long-run interests, such as customer satisfaction and goodwill, can conflict with short-term sales goals.

Alan J. Dubinsky and Michael Levy divide the ethical situations salespeople face into three classifications depending on whom they involve:

1. Customer-related situations are those that involve contact with customers, such as failing to assist them or deliberately giving them incorrect change for purchases.

2. Peer-related situations include interactions with fellow nonmanagerial employees and with friends and relatives who do not work at the store. An example would be pressure not to report employee theft.

3. Work-related situations are those related to company practice or the job itself. An example would be giving a new employee an unduly heavy workload for which he or she is not yet fully trained.

Dubinsky and Levy surveyed 122 people working for department and specialty stores in a major metropolitan area to learn which issues were ethically troublesome to them. Two-thirds of the respondents were female. Some 35 percent of those surveyed had worked in retail sales for over a year, and 46 percent had been with the same company for more than a year. The respondents were given a list of 37 situations and were asked whether these constituted ethical problems, if they knew of a company policy relevant to them, and whether a policy for these issues should exist.

Only eight of the situations on the questionnaires were considered ethical issues by half or more of the respondents. Four of them were customer related. These situations and the percentage of respondents who believed they were ethical issues were as follows: charging full price for a sale item, 62 percent; deliberately giving incorrect change, 62 percent; not telling the whole truth about a product, 59 percent; and giving customers markdowns on items that they themselves had damaged, 54 percent. Two were peer related: being pressured not to report employee theft, 63 percent, and pressure from friends or relatives to let them use employee discounts, 55 percent. Two were work related: cheating on employees' time cards, 57 percent, and giving an inexperienced employee an unfair workload, 50 percent.

Interestingly, in only four of these situations did the respondents believe there was a stated company policy on the problem. Dubinsky and Levy concluded that management must ascertain the potential ethical problems in their particular businesses and ensure that there are clearly understood policies covering these situations. They suggest that all policies be in writing to avoid the ambiguity that often surrounds unwritten policies but stress that sales personnel also need latitude in order to perform their jobs effectively.

Source: Alan J. Dubinsky and Michael Levy, "Ethics in Retailing: Perceptions of Retail Salespeople," *Journal of the Academy of Marketing Science* (Winter-Spring 1985), pp. 1–16.

The interior of a store should complement the retailer's image, be responsive to customers' interest, and, most important, induce the shopper to buy. Interior elements include store layout, merchandise presentation, lighting, color, sounds, scents, and cleanliness. With live plants, waterfall, stocked trout pond, and special sound effects, the interior of L. L. Bean's store in Freeport, Maine, creates an outdoor environment that appeals to its clientele and matches the type of merchandise it sells—outdoor sports clothing and accessories. Every detail inside Ralph Lauren's $14 million Madison Avenue store in New York City, from elegant tapestry cushions to singing canaries Paul and Ringo, enhances the store's image of gentility, high style, and "the good life." In keeping with the refined tastes of its clientele, the store plays jazz and Vivaldi music and serves shoppers strawberries and raspberries during the day. After-five customers are served cocktails and canapés and listen to Frank Sinatra recordings.[17]

Tandy Corporation plans to complete a 5-year, $80 million remodeling of its 7,100 Radio Shack stores by 1991. With a gray, black, and red color scheme, the new "Technology Store" design projects a high-tech image and provides more space for the firm's expanding product line. Customer surveys following test marketing of the new design revealed that the stores' new layout appeals especially to women shoppers.

Photo source: Courtesy of Radio Shack Division of Tandy Corporation.

Retailers often use atmospherics to change a store's image. A retailer may decide to change its image to attract a new group of buyers. Many auto parts, hardware, and consumer electronics stores are shedding their traditional for-men-only image by remodeling or redesigning interiors and adding amenities that appeal to the growing number of female buyers. The ServiStar hardware store in Gloucester, Virginia, transformed its dark, untidy store by adding bright lights, chrome gridwork, and wall murals. A Bumper-to-Bumper auto parts store in Fort Worth, Texas, decorated its walls with portraits of women working on their cars. To make women feel more comfortable, hardware stores have added shopping carts and mock-up displays that demonstrate how to operate drills and other tools. Tandy Corporation is remodeling its Radio Shack stores in an attempt to change its hardware outlet image. A major part of the renovation focuses on store layout. Tandy is moving electronic gadgets to the backs of the stores and moved radios, phones, and other assembled-products displays up front.[18]

Other retailers design new store environments to better serve their target markets. The Ups & Downs chain of women's clothing shops realized that sales were slipping because the presentation of merchandise and store atmosphere failed to capture the interest of its active and visually oriented 16-to-20-year-old customers. Store interiors were redesigned to project a vibrant image, with a new lighting scheme, lilac-colored, high-tech mannequins, and large photo wall murals showing models wearing the stores' clothing. To make shopping at Ups & Downs a fun experience, merchandise is now displayed on kinetic carousels that revolve with the touch of a customer's hand. The facelift resulted in an 80 percent sales increase at the first store in the chain sporting the new look.[19]

Shoppers' behavior has fueled the retailing trend of creating environments that entertain and has elevated the importance of atmospherics in retail image making. Recent studies indicate that most people shop for reasons other than purchasing needed items. According to one marketing research survey of 34,000 mall shoppers nationwide, only 25 percent of the respondents said they came to buy a specific item. Other reasons given for shopping were to dispel boredom, alleviate loneliness, relieve depression, escape the routine of daily life, and fulfill fantasies. Challenged to satisfy these broad-based needs and desires, retailers increasingly are turning to atmospherics to lure shoppers. A dramatic example is the atmosphere of Banana Republic stores, whose thatched roofs, ivory-tusk door handles, and packing-crate displays marked for faraway places such as the Congo and Chad offer shoppers the adventure of a jungle safari.[20]

Types of Retailers

The nation's 2 million retailers come in a variety of forms. Since new types of retail operations continue to evolve in response to changing consumer demands, no universal classification has been devised. The following bases can be used in categorizing them: (1) shopping effort expended by customers; (2) services provided to customers; (3) product lines; (4) location of retail transactions; and (5) form of ownership.

Any retailing operation can be classified according to each of the five bases. A 7-Eleven food store may be classified as a convenience store (category 1); self-service (category 2); relatively broad product lines (category 3); store-type retailer (category 4); and a member of a corporate chain (category 5).

Classification by Shopping Effort

In Chapter 8, consumer goods were classified as convenience goods, shopping goods, or specialty goods based on consumer purchase patterns in securing a particular product or service. This three-way classification system can be extended to retailers by considering the reasons consumers shop at particular retail outlets. The result is a classification scheme in which retail stores are categorized as convenience, shopping, or specialty retailers.[21] This determination has a significant influence on the marketing strategies a retailer selects.

Convenience retailers focus on accessible locations, long store hours, rapid checkout service, and adequate parking facilities. Local food stores, gasoline stations, and some barber shops may be included in this category.

Shopping stores typically include furniture stores, appliance retailers, clothing outlets, and sporting goods stores. Consumers will compare prices, assortments, and quality levels of competing outlets before making purchase decisions. Managers of shopping stores attempt to differentiate their outlets through advertising, window displays and in-store layouts, knowledgeable salespeople, and appropriate merchandise assortments.

Specialty retailers provide a combination of product lines, services, or reputation that results in consumers' willingness to expend considerable effort to shop at their stores. Nordstrom, Neiman-Marcus, Lord & Taylor, and Saks Fifth Avenue have developed a sufficient degree of preference among many shoppers to be categorized as specialty retailers.

Classification by Services Provided

Some retailers seek to develop a differential advantage by creating a unique combination of service offerings for the customers in their target market. It is possible to distinguish various retailer types by focusing on the services they offer. According to this type of classification system, the types of retailers are self-service, self-selection, limited-service, and full-service.

Since self-service and self-selection retailers provide few services for their customers, retailer location and price are important considerations. These retailers tend to specialize in staple convenience goods that are purchased frequently and require little product service or advice from retail personnel.

Full-service retail establishments focus on fashion-oriented shopping goods and specialty items and offer a wide variety of services for their clientele. As a result, their prices tend to be higher than those of self-service retailers due to the higher operating costs these services generate.

Classification by Product Lines

Retail strategies can also be based on the product lines carried. Grouping retailers by product line produces three major categories: specialty stores, limited-line retailers, and general merchandise retailers.

Specialty Stores

A specialty store typically handles only part of a single product line. However, this portion is stocked in considerable depth for the store's customers. Specialty stores include fish markets, men's and women's shoe stores, bakeries, furriers, and millinery shops. Although some are run by chains, most are independent, small-scale operations. They are perhaps the greatest stronghold of independent retailers that develop expertise in providing a very narrow line of products for their local markets.

Specialty stores should not be confused with specialty goods. Specialty stores typically carry convenience and shopping goods. The label *specialty* comes from the practice of handling a specific, narrow line of merchandise.

Limited-Line Retailers

limited-line store
Retail establishment that offers a large assortment of one-product lines or just a few related product lines.

A large assortment of one product line or a few related lines of goods are offered in the **limited-line store.** The development of this type of retail operation paralleled the growth of towns to a population size sufficient to support it. These operations include retailers such as appliance, furniture, grocery, hardware, and sporting goods stores. Examples of limited-line stores are IKEA (home furnishings and housewares), Levitz (furniture), Handy Dan and Handy Man (home repair products), and The Gap (clothing). These retailers cater to the needs of people who want to select from a complete line in purchasing a particular product. For example, Toys "R" Us claims it is the world's largest toy store. Figure 14.5 shows one of its Christmas season advertisements.

Figure 14.5
Advertising by a Limited-Line
Retailer

Source: Courtesy of Toys "R" Us.

With profit margins averaging only about 1 percent of sales after taxes, supermarkets compete through careful planning of retail displays in order to sell a large amount of merchandise each week and thereby retain a low investment in inventory. Product location within the store is carefully studied to expose the consumer to as much merchandise as possible and thus increase impulse purchases.

Supermarkets carry nonfood products, such as magazines, records, small kitchen utensils, toiletries, and toys, for two reasons: Consumers have displayed a willingness to buy such items in supermarkets, and supermarket managers like the profit margins on these items, which are higher than those on food products.

These trends are evident in the supermarket industry. First, several chains, such as Safeway, have begun building so-called "superstores" — large-square-footage stores that carry a broad range of food and nonfood items along with specialty sections such as delis. Second, upscale or upgraded supermarkets now operate in many marketplaces. For example, St. Louis–based Dierbergs Markets now offers an in-store cooking school, motorized shopping carts for the handicapped, FTD florists, post offices, banks, fresh seafood, video rentals, pharmacies, and American and French bakeries.[22] Third, supermarkets are adding services. For instance, Inter-Ad, a Rochester, New York, firm, offers a $6,500 electronic map of a supermarket that indicates where some 1,500 products are located. The company also offers a $12,000 machine that prints out recipes and gives video cooking demonstrations.[23]

General Merchandise Retailers

general merchandise retailer
Establishment that carries a wide variety of product lines, all of which are stocked in some depth.

General merchandise retailers may be distinguished from limited-line and specialty retailers by the large number of product lines they carry. The general store described earlier in this chapter is a primitive form of **general merchandise retailer**—a retail establishment that carries a wide variety of product lines, all stocked in some depth. Included in this category are variety stores, department stores, and mass merchandisers such as catalog retailers, discount stores, hypermarkets, and off-price retailers.

variety store
A retail firm that offers an extensive range and assortment of low-price merchandise.

Variety Stores   A retail firm that offers an extensive range and assortment of low-priced merchandise is called a **variety store.** Variety stores are less popular than they once were. Many have evolved into or been replaced by other retailing categories such as discount stores. The nation's 11,000 variety stores now account for only 1 percent of all retail sales.

department store
Large retail firm that handles a variety of merchandise, including clothing, household goods, appliances, and furniture.

Department Stores   The **department store** is actually a series of limited-line and specialty stores under one roof. By definition, it is a large retail firm that handles a variety of merchandise, including men's and boy's wear, women's wear and accessories, household linens and dry goods, home furnishings, and furniture. It serves the consumer as a one-stop shopping center for almost all personal and household items. Department stores account for about 10 percent of all retail sales.

These retailers are organized around departments for the purpose of providing service, promotion, and control. A general merchandising manager is responsible for the store's product planning. Reporting to the general manager are the department managers. These managers typically run the departments almost as independent businesses; they are given considerable latitude in merchandising and layout decisions. The retailing axiom that well-bought goods are already half sold is borne out by the department manager's title of *buyer.*

Department stores are known for offering their customers a wide variety of services, such as charge accounts, delivery, gift wrapping, and liberal return privileges. In addition, some 50 percent of their employees and 40 percent of their floor space are devoted to nonselling activities. As a result, they have relatively high operating costs, averaging from 45 to 60 percent of sales.

Department stores have faced intensified competition over the past 30 years. Their relatively high operating costs have made them vulnerable to retailing innovations such as discount stores, catalog merchandisers, and hypermarkets. In addition, department stores usually were located in downtown business districts and experienced the problems associated with limited parking, traffic congestion and population migration to the suburbs.

However, department stores have been willing to adapt to changing consumer desires. They have added bargain basements and expanded parking facilities in attempts to compete with discount operations and suburban retailers. They have also followed the population movement to the suburbs by open-

THE COMPETITIVE EDGE

Nordstrom, Inc.

The wheel of retailing can spin in the opposite direction—with the right touch. Nordstrom, Inc., a 47-store chain based in Seattle, is an excellent example. Selling pricey products for the upscale market, in direct competition with such department store chains as Macy's of California and The Broadway, Nordstrom has grown 25 percent annually since 1984—an astonishing level for the embattled market segment—and is expected to sustain this pace until the early 1990s. Nordstrom's competitors admire its growth rate, but the store's sales per square feet, an important measure of retail store success, is the envy of the industry: At $310 per square foot in 1986, it is $150 over the industry average, and no other department store company even approaches it.

Nordstrom achieves its sales figures with no tricks. Its formula for success is simple and in keeping with traditional department store strategies: gift wrapping, home delivery, purchase returns, and personal service. But Nordstrom performs these services with a relish generally missing from today's so-called service economy, and customers keep shopping at its stores—a modern example of customer loyalty in a retailing environment whose customers usually are loyal only to the lowest price.

Part of the reason behind Nordstrom's growth to a $2-billion-a-year

company stems from its stores' atmosphere. They sell high-quality apparel, shoes, and accessories in a setting that includes an in-store pianist. But the atmosphere only begins to account for Nordstrom's appeal. What Nordstrom wants is satisfied customers. To get that, it virtually spoils its shoppers. As one Nordstrom's sales clerk says, "Nordstrom tells me to do whatever I need to do to make [the customer] happy. Period."

Making the customer happy includes approaching all customers within two minutes of their arrival in a department and free gift wrapping at the counters at which goods are purchased. Goods are delivered to customers' homes at no extra charge. Return items are accepted with no questions asked.

The foundation of the Nordstrom service ethic is simple: The customer is always right—indeed, the customer can never be wrong.

Nordstrom's reputation for excellent services has retailers east of the Rockies scrambling as Nordstrom prepares to expand. Consumers seem destined to win; venerable department stores in New York and Chicago are hiring more service personnel and looking for ways to improve customer service. They are up against the best, however.

Sources: Joan O'C. Hamilton and Amy Dunkin, "Why Rivals Are Quaking as Nordstrom Heads East," *Business Week* (June 15, 1987), pp. 99–100; "Nordstrom's High Style," *Newsweek* (January 5, 1987), p. 43; and Tom Peters, "The Store Is Where the Action Is," *U.S. News & World Report* (May 12, 1987), p. 58. *Photo source:* © 1987 Robert Holmgren.

ing major branches in outlying shopping centers. They have attempted to revitalize downtown retailing in many cities by modernizing their stores, expanding store hours, attracting the tourist and convention trade, and focusing on the central-city residents.

Mass Merchandisers   Mass merchandising has made major inroads on department stores' sales during the past two decades by emphasizing lower prices for well-known brand name products, high turnover of goods, and reduced ser-

mass merchandiser
Store that stocks a wider line of goods than does a department store but usually does not offer the same depth of assortment.

discount house
Store that charges lower-than-normal prices but may not offer typical retail services such as credit, sales assistance, and home delivery.

vices. The **mass merchandiser** often stocks a wider line of products than department stores but usually does not offer depth of assortment within each line. Discount houses, off-price retailers, hypermarkets, and catalog retailers are all mass merchandisers.

Discount Houses   The birth of the modern **discount house** came at the end of World War II when a New York-based company called Masters discovered that a large number of customers were willing to shop at a store that charged lower-than-usual prices and did not offer such traditional services as credit, salesperson assistance, and delivery. Soon retailers throughout the country were following the Masters formula, either changing over from their traditional operations or opening new stores dedicated to discounting. At first discount stores sold mostly appliances, but they have expanded into furniture, soft goods, drugs, and even food.

Discount operations had existed before World War II, but they sold goods chiefly from manufacturers' catalogs; they kept no stock on display and often had limited potential customers. The more recent discounters operate large stores, advertise heavily, emphasize low prices for well-known brands, and are open to the public. Elimination of many of the "free" services provided by traditional retailers has allowed these operations to keep their markups 10 to 25 percent below their competitors'. Consumers had become accustomed to self-service by shopping at supermarkets, and they responded in great numbers to this retailing innovation. Conventional retailers such as Kresge joined the discounting practice by opening its own Kmart stores. Some of the early discounters have since added services, begun to stock name brands, and boosted their prices; in fact, they now resemble traditional department stores.

The newest wave of true discounters is the *warehouse club*. These stores are no-frills, cash-and-carry outlets. Customers must buy club memberships in order to shop at warehouse clubs. Seattle-based Costco is an example of this type of retailer. In 1987 there were 228 wholesale clubs, and they did $8 billion in annual sales volume.[24]

off-price retailer
Retailer that sells designer labels or well-known brand name clothing at less than typical retail prices.

Off-Price Retailers   The latest version of the discount house is the **off-price retailer.** These retail merchants buy only designer labels or well-known brand name clothing at regular wholesale prices or less and pass the cost savings along to the consumer. Their inventory frequently changes as they take advantage of special price offers from manufacturers desiring to sell excess merchandise. Off-price retailers such as Loehmann's, Marshalls, T. J. Maxx, and Hit or Miss tend to keep their prices below traditional retailers' by purchasing fashion merchandise at lower-than-normal wholesale prices and offering fewer services. Consumer acceptance has been dramatic, making off-price retailing a major retail growth trend.[25]

outlet mall
Shopping center consisting entirely of off-price retailers.

While many off-price retailers are located in downtown areas or freestanding buildings, a growing number are concentrating in **outlet malls** — shopping centers consisting entirely of off-price merchandisers.

hypermarket
Giant mass merchandiser of soft goods and groceries that operates on a low-price, self-service basis.

Hypermarkets   A relatively recent but growing retailing innovation in the United States is the **hypermarket** — a giant, one-stop shopping facility that offers a wide selection of grocery items and general merchandise at discount prices. Safeway's superstores, mentioned earlier, are an example. Store size is the major difference between hypermarkets and supermarkets. Hypermarkets typically have 200,000 or more square feet of selling space compared to about 44,000 for the average new supermarket.

The hypermarket concept originated in France and has spread to Canada and South America as well as the United States. One of the most successful U.S. hypermarkets is Meijers Thrifty Acres in suburban Detroit. The 245,000-square-foot store has 40 checkout counters and sells food, hardware, soft goods, building materials, auto supplies, appliances, and prescription drugs. It also has a restaurant, beauty salon, barbershop, branch bank, and bakery.

Hypermarkets are expected to make major inroads in U.S. retailing in the 1990s. These oversize stores are part of the expansion plans of mass merchandisers such as Wal-Mart Stores and Kmart Corporation. Hypermarkets may be the next stage in the evolution of retailing, providing busy, working consumers with the convenience of shopping for everything from broccoli to bicycles under one roof.

Catalog Retailers: Catalog, Showroom, and Warehouse Catalog retailers mail catalogs to their customers and operate from showrooms that display samples of each product they handle. Orders are filled from backroom warehouses. Price is an important factor for catalog store customers. Low prices are made possible by few services, warehouse storage of most inventory, reduced shoplifting losses, and handling of long-lived products such as luggage, small appliances, gift items, sporting equipment, toys, and jewelry. Some major catalog retailers include Best Products, Service Merchandise, Consumer Distributor, Zales, and Gordon Jewelry Corporation.

Classification by Location of Retail Transactions

Some retailers choose to implement their marketing strategies outside the store environment. Although the overwhelming majority of retail transactions occur in retail stores, nonstore retailing is important for many products. Nonstore retailing includes direct selling, direct-response selling, and automatic merchandising. Such sales account for nearly 10 percent of all retail sales.

Direct Selling

The concept of direct selling was introduced in Chapter 12. Direct selling provides maximum convenience for the consumer and allows the manufacturer to control its marketing channels.

A number of merchandisers use direct selling, including manufacturers of bakery products, dairy products, and newspapers. Amway distributors market a variety of consumer products directly to their customers, who often are friends and acquaintances. Firms emphasizing product demonstrations also tend to use the direct-selling channel. Among them are companies that sell vacuum cleaners (Electrolux Corporation), household items (Fuller Brush Company), encyclopedias (The World Book Encyclopedia), and insurance. Some firms, such as Stanley Home Products, use a variation called *party selling,* in which a customer hosts a party to which neighbors and friends are invited. During the party, an independent salesperson makes a presentation of the products. The salesperson receives a commission based on the amount of products sold. The largest direct-selling retailers are Amway Corporation, Avon Products, Electrolux Corporation, Encyclopedia Britannica, Home Interiors & Gifts, Mary Kay Cosmetics, Princess House, Scott Fetzer (The Kirby Company, World Book), Shaklee Corporation, and Tupperware.

Direct-Response Selling

The customers of direct-response retailers can order merchandise by mail, via telephone, or by visiting the mail-order desk of a retail store. Goods are then shipped to the customer's home or to the local retail store. Many department and specialty stores issue catalogs to create telephone and mail-order sales and to promote in-store purchases of items featured in the catalogs.

Mail-order selling actually began in 1872, when Montgomery Ward issued its first catalog to rural midwestern families. That catalog contained only a few items, mostly clothing and farm supplies. Today mail-order houses offer a wide range of products, from novelty items (Spencer Gifts) to hunting and camping equipment (L. L. Bean) to an eighteenth-century Chinese screen priced at $60,000 (Horchow). Many mail-order catalog organizations also generate retail sales by having consumers buy from retail outlets of their catalog stores.

A recent innovation in mail-order marketing is the use of computer-based catalogs. CompuServe offers such an electronic catalog, which features over 250,000 products. Figure 14.6 shows how the CompuServe system works. Another firm, Comp-U-Card, also offers a computer-based catalog. Comp-U-Card provides its members with an 800 number to call if they want an operator to conduct a computer search of the best buy for a certain product.[26]

While mail-order sales have sky rocketed in recent years, these retailers are not without their problems. Research has found that 43 percent of all U.S. shoppers can be classified as "anti-catalog." As a result, mail-order sellers are trying to direct their catalog distribution to those most likely to buy through this channel. Eddie Bauer, Tiffany & Company, Williams-Sonoma, and 200 other firms now sell their catalogs through bookstores and newsstands. The catalogs are priced at $1 to $3 and usually include a $5 coupon toward a purchase. These retailers have found that asking the customer to buy a catalog is an effective way to reduce waste circulation.[27]

home shopping
Use of cable television to merchandise product via telephone order.

The biggest growth area in direct-response retailing is **home shopping** — the use of cable television networks to sell merchandise through telephone orders. Various forms of home shopping have existed for years, such as the late-night 30-second commercials featuring products such as K-Tel Records and Veg-O-Matic. Similarly, interactive cable television, such as Warner-Amex's QUBE system, was another early effort at making home shopping a significant aspect of direct-response retailing.

Home shopping as we know it in the late 1980s began just a few years ago when Home Shopping Network, Inc., was launched. Numerous competitors quickly followed, and the home shopping boom was on. Today half of all U.S. households with television sets will watch one or more home shopping networks. Sales statistics indicate that over 9 percent of those who watch will buy via this type of direct-response retailing. Some industry experts expect home shopping sales to hit $9 billion by 1990.

Programming ranges from 24-hour-a-day commercials to call-in shows to game show formats. In fact, nearly a quarter of all TV shoppers report that

Figure 14.6
A Computer-Based Catalog

Source: Courtesy of CompuServe Incorporated, an H&R Block Company.

entertainment is the primary reason they watch these shows. Shoppers are given an 800 number to call for products they wish to purchase. Orders are then placed, and the goods are delivered to the buyers' homes. A recent trend is specialization of home shopping channels by merchandise category, thus allowing viewers to tune into only those items that interest them.

Home shoppers tend to be heavy users of this form of retailing. These consumers average six orders a year. In fact, in many ways they are similar to catalog shoppers. As a result, The American Catalogue Shoppers Network was formed. It offers the products featured in 100 catalogs and is specifically targeted at catalog shoppers.[28]

Automatic Merchandising

The world's first vending machines dispensed holy water for a five-drachma coin in Egyptian temples around 215 B.C. However, the period of most rapid growth came after World War II when coffee and soft-drink vending machines were introduced in the nation's offices and factories. Today automatic merchandising machines are a convenient way to purchase a vast array of convenience goods ranging from Pepsi-Cola to Marlboros to Michigan lottery tickets.

Where does the vending machine dollar go? According to the National Automatic Merchandising Association, 44.5 cents of each dollar goes for the product, 54 cents for operating expenses, and 1.5 cents for profit. Typically the owner of the building receives more money from a machine just for allowing it on the premises than does the owner of the machine for installing, stocking, and servicing it.

Classification by Form of Ownership

A final method of categorizing retailers is by ownership. The two major types are corporate chain stores and independent retailers. In addition, independent retailers may join a wholesaler-sponsored voluntary chain, band together to form a retail cooperative, or enter into a franchise arrangement through contractual agreements with a manufacturer, wholesaler, or service organization. Each type has its own unique advantages and strategies.

Chain Stores

chain store
Group of retail stores that are centrally owned and managed and handle essentially the same product lines.

Chain stores are groups of retail stores that are centrally owned and managed and handle the same product lines. One major advantage that chain operations have over independent retailers is economies of scale. Volume purchases through a central buying office allow chains to pay lower prices than independents. Since chains may have thousands of retail stores, they can use layout specialists, sales training, and computerized merchandise ordering, inventory, forecasting and accounting systems to increase efficiency. The large sales volume and wide geographic expanse of many chains enable them to advertise in a variety of media, including television and national magazines.

About 21 percent of all retail stores are part of some chain, and their dollar volume of sales amounts to approximately 52 percent of all retail sales. Chains account for 98 percent of all department store sales, 88 percent of variety store sales, and 76 percent of grocery store sales. Table 14.1 lists the 10 largest retailers in the United States, some of which have expanded their operations worldwide.

For years, Sears, Roebuck has ranked as the nation's largest retailer and currently is the third largest advertiser in the country. Eight out of ten Americans shop at Sears at least once a year, and one out of every two households has a Sears credit card.[29] Appropriately, the firm's headquarters are located in the tallest building in the world — the 110-story Sears Tower in Chicago.

Independent Retailers

Although most retailers are small, independent operators, the larger chains dominate a number of fields. The U.S. retailing structure can be characterized as having a large number of small stores, many medium-size stores, and a small number of large stores. While only 7 percent of all stores have annual sales of $1 million or more, they account for almost two-thirds of all retail sales in the United States. On the other hand, almost half of all stores in the United States have sales of less than $100,000 each year.

Rank	Company	Sales (Thousands of Dollars)
1	Sears, Roebuck (Chicago)	$44,281,500
2	Kmart (Troy, Michigan)	24,246,000
3	Safeway Stores (Oakland)	20,311,480
4	Kroger (Cincinnati)	18,386,408
5	J.C. Penney (New York)	14,740,000
6	American Stores (Salt Lake City)	14,021,484
7	Wal-Mart Stores (Bentonville, Arkansas)	11,909,076
8	Southland (Dallas)	11,081,835
9	Federated Department Stores (Cincinnati)	10,512,425
10	May Department Stores (St. Louis)	10,376,000

Table 14.1
The 10 Largest Retailers

Source: "The 50 Largest Retailing Companies," *Fortune* (June 8, 1987), p. 210.

Independents have attempted to compete with chains in a number of ways. Some have been unable to do so efficiently and are now out of business. Others have joined retail cooperatives, wholesaler-sponsored voluntary chains, or franchise operations. Still others have concentrated on a traditional advantage of independent stores: friendly, personalized service.

Scrambled Merchandising

It is becoming increasingly difficult to classify retailers because in many cases the traditional delineations no longer exist. Anyone who recently has attempted to fill a physician's prescription has been exposed to the concept of **scrambled merchandising**—the retail practice of carrying dissimilar lines in an attempt to generate additional sales volume. The drugstore carries not only prescription and proprietary drugs but garden supplies, gift items, groceries, hardware, housewares, magazines, records, and even small appliances.

Scrambled merchandising was born out of retailers' willingness to add dissimilar merchandise lines to satisfy consumer demand for one-stop shopping. Consider Sears' purchase of Coldwell Banker, a real estate firm, and Dean Witter Reynolds Inc., a stock brokerage firm. Sears already had an insurance company, Allstate, operating within its stores. Other recent examples of scrambled merchandising include the following:

scrambled merchandising
Retailing practice of carrying dissimilar product lines in an attempt to generate additional sales volume.

□ A&P shoppers in Delaware now can get their cholesterol levels checked for $8.

□ Kmarts in selected locations now offer services ranging from banking, real estate, consumer loans, mortgage prequalification, and ATMs to insurance.

□ Black & Decker flashlights, coffee makers, and cordless mixers are now available in 36 supermarket chains.

□ Hardee's franchises have been installed in some 7-Eleven stores.[30]

Scrambled merchandising complicates manufacturers' channel decisions. In most cases, their attempts to maintain or increase market share will require them to develop multiple channels in order to reach the diverse variety of retailers handling their products.

Summary of Chapter Objectives

1. Describe the evolution of retailing. Retail institutions generally have evolved in accordance with the wheel of retailing, which holds that new types of retailers gain a competitive foothold by offering their customers lower prices through reduction or elimination of services. Once established, however, they add more services and increase their prices, thus becoming vulnerable to the next low-price retailer.

2. Outline the various elements of retailing strategy. A retailer must first identify a target market and then develop a product strategy. Then it must establish a customer service strategy. Retail pricing strategy involves such decisions as markups and markdowns. Location/distribution strategy often is the determining factor in a retailer's success or failure. A retailer's promotional strategy, along with store atmosphere, plays an important role in establishing a store's image.

3. Identify and explain each of the five bases for categorizing retailers. Retailers can be categorized on five bases: shopping effort expended by customers, customer services provided, product lines, location of retail transactions, and form of ownership. Retailers, like consumer goods, may be divided into convenience, shopping, and specialty categories based on the effort shoppers are willing to expend in purchasing products. A second method of classification categorizes retailers on a spectrum ranging from self-service to full-service. The third method divides retailers into three categories: limited-line stores, which compete by carrying a large assortment of one or two product lines; specialty stores, which carry a very large assortment of only part of a single product line; and general merchandise retailers, including department stores, variety stores, and mass merchandisers such as discount houses, off-price retailers, hypermarkets, and catalog retailers, all of which handle a wide variety of products. A fourth classification method distinguishes between retail stores and nonstore retailing. While most U.S. retail sales take place in retail stores, such nonstore retailing activities as direct selling, direct-response retailing, and automatic merchandising machines are important in marketing many types of products and services. The fifth method of classification categorizes retailers by form of ownership. The major types include corporate chain stores, independent retailers, and independents that have banded together to form retail cooperatives or join wholesaler-sponsored voluntary chains or franchises.

4. Describe the concept of scrambled merchandising. Scrambled merchandising refers to retailers' practice of carrying dissimilar product lines in an attempt to generate additional sales volume. Scrambled merchandising has made it increasingly difficult to classify retailers.

Key Terms

retailing
wheel of retailing
retail image
markup
markdown
planned shopping center
selling up
suggestion selling
atmospherics
limited-line store
general merchandise retailer

variety store
department store
mass merchandiser
discount house
off-price retailer
outlet mall
hypermarket
home shopping
chain store
scrambled merchandising

Review Questions

1. Explain the major elements of retailing strategy.

2. A Columbus, Ohio, discount store purchases garden hoses for $4 each and sells them for $6 each. What are its markup percentages on selling price and on cost?

3. A Sedona, Arizona, arts and crafts shop purchases decorative wooden carvings for $10 each and sells them for $30 each. What are the shop's markup percentages on selling price and on cost?

4. A carpet store in Manchester, New Hampshire, uses a markup percentage on cost of 66.67 percent. If the store decided to convert to basing markup on retail, what would be the equivalent markup percentage of retail?

5. Identify and describe the different types of shopping centers.

6. Outline the five bases for categorizing retailers.

7. Identify the major types of general merchandise retailers.

8. Explain the concepts of off-price retailing and outlet malls.

9. Differentiate between direct selling and direct-response retailing.

10. Why has the practice of scrambled merchandising become so common in retailing?

Discussion Questions

1. Give several examples of the wheel of retailing in operation. Also identify situations that do not conform to this hypothesis. What generalizations can be drawn from this exercise?

2. Specialty chains such as Fedco, Federated's Main Street Stores, Radio Shack, and C. R. Anthony emphasize target marketing in their promotional efforts. These stores try to concentrate their promotional mailings on people most likely to use their products. They point out that many mailings are wasted—for example, a garden equipment flyer distributed around an apartment complex. Psychographic segmentation is these stores' usual approach to target marketing. [31] Relate this illustration to the text discussion of retailing strategy.

3. Some Kroger supermarkets in Georgia now feature CheckRobot, which customers use to scan their own purchases which in turn are placed on a conveyer belt to a bagging station. Customers then take the receipts to a

cashier for payment. The system is designed to cut labor costs, but tests have shown that customers take longer than clerks to scan purchases.[32] What do you think the future holds for this retailing innovation?

4. Research and then classify each of the following retailers:
   a. Dollar Stores
   b. Lane Bryant
   c. AM-PM Mini Marts
   d. Taco Bell
   e. Levitz Furniture Stores
   f. J. C. Penney

5. Clean & Lean of Vista, California, is a laundromat-fitness center. It features exercise bikes and weight machines along with washers and dryers. The new retailing establishment charges 75 cents per wash and $3.50 for the workout, which is timed to coincide with the wash cycle.[33] Relate Clean & Lean to the material presented in Chapter 14.

VIDEO CASE 14

West Ridge Mountaineering

West Ridge Mountaineering targets its retail offerings to a select group of buyers — risk takers and thrill seekers who enjoy the psychic pleasures of climbing a mountain or skiing down a snowy slope. Unlike general sporting goods stores that carry products for all types of sports enthusiasts, West Ridge is a Los Angeles retailer specializing in mountaineering and skiing equipment, clothing, and accessories.

The original owners of West Ridge were expert climbers and offered their customers only top-of-the-line climbing hardware, tents, backpacks, and other gear. When Ed Brekke bought the business, he added merchandise in various styles and price ranges to appeal to a broader customer base. At one time, for example, West Ridge carried only high-quality sleeping bags ranging in price from $100 to $400. To accommodate customers' requests for less expensive bags, Brekke added bags in the $30 to $50 range. The store maintains its specialty appeal, however, by selling mostly high-quality, brand-name products, many of which customers ask for by name when they come in to shop.

Brekke's retailing strategy is based on a combination of offering customers a wide range of product styles plus a full complement of services, a plan designed to generate greater sales. Services that bring customers into the store include a ski rental shop, and a one-day ski repair and binding adjustment service. Customers who rent skis, boots, and poles often end up buying merchandise, especially such accessories as sunglasses, goggles, lip protectors, socks, and thermal underwear. Skiers who are pleased with the store's repair work are likely candidates to buy new equipment at West Ridge in the future and to become loyal customers.

Other services offered to West Ridge customers include up-to-the-minute reports of snow conditions at many ski areas. Display racks hold an assortment of free brochures and pamphlets that describe products as well as organized hikes, climbs, and instructional programs. For a small fee, backpackers can buy maps of popular hiking areas, which are conveniently arranged in alphabetical order in large filing cabinets. The low-cost maps and free handouts take up valuable floor space that could be used for displaying profitable merchandise such as ski sweaters, but Brekke realizes the contributions of these customer services in generating store traffic. As he points out, "It's more important to us to have a lot of people in the store than one or two big sales. The results are always better if we have a lot of people in the stores, even if the sales are down, as opposed to high sales for the day with only a few people. In the long run, we do much better."

Advertising also builds store traffic. West Ridge ads appear in local newspapers and on cable programs and local commercial television stations. Regular customers frequently receive advertising flyers to remind them about the store and its products and services. To remain competitive, West Ridge advertises heavily during the ski season. In November, at the start of the ski season, ads announce special buys; for example, a ski boot regularly priced at $225 is featured at $99.95. Follow-up ads focus on special ski packages — skis, boots, bindings, and poles. Ads placed directly before and after ski events broadcast on cable television are especially effective in reaching the store's target audience.

Selling mountaineering and skiing equipment requires a knowledgeable sales staff. West Ridge salespeople are expected to learn not only about the products they sell; they are also encouraged to gain experience in skiing and climbing. They do this by attending "demo days," manufacturer-sponsored events that allow them to try out products, and through participation in skiing and climbing excursions. Because West Ridge is open seven days a week, most of these trips take place early in the morning before the store opens. Salespeople can also test products (and practice their climbing techniques) on El Bunde, the red brick wall on the west side of the store.

Brekke wants customers to think of West Ridge as a friendly specialty store whose salespeople are capable of offering expert advice. He trains his employees to project that image. In interviewing prospective employees, Brekke looks for individuals with personalities that exude enthusiasm, energy, candidness, and trustworthiness. During sales training sessions, he teaches employees to avoid hard-sell techniques and to approach customers with a warm greeting, determine their interests and then match products to fit their needs. Above all, he stresses that salespeople must be aware of the importance of the advice they give, which in some cases could save a customer's life. For example, salespeople must understand the concept of layering clothing in selling supplies to mountaineers, who must be prepared to withstand life-endangering sub-zero temperatures.

Brekke pays both part- and full-time salespeople a straight salary, although store managers participate in an incentive program that is directly tied to store sales. They receive their first bonus when sales reach a specified breakeven point and additional financial incentives as sales increase to higher levels. By paying part-time help the minimum wage, Brekke is able to lower his average wage cost. He keeps payroll costs in mind when planning employees' work schedules. Full-time salespeople work days, and part-timers work mornings and evenings. This arrangement ensures that enough salespeople — but not too many — are on hand at all times to assist customers.

Controlling costs was a major concern for Brekke when he chose a site for West Ridge. He considered affordable rent as more important than store location, arguing that specialty store customers will seek out the store wherever it is located.

Brekke also keeps costs in mind when buying merchandise for West Ridge. His buying strategy differs from that of the former owners, who purchased merchandise from manufacturers in large quantities and kept much of it in the back as reserve stock. Brekke learned that buying products in smaller amounts and placing orders more frequently improved the store's cash flow by eliminating thousands of dollars' worth of inventory in back stock. This buying strategy also meshes with Brekke's merchandising philosophy. He believes that all merchandise should be displayed on the sales floor where customers can see it rather than storing it in a back room where they cannot.

Manufacturers often assist retailers in making buying decisions. The manufacturer's representatives who regularly visit West Ridge provide the retailer with valuable information. Brekke says, "If those reps service their accounts, we don't have to buy as much product, because they keep us aware of what's moving, they keep us aware of what's not moving, and they help us fill in where we might have holes in our inventory. That's a service that gives us a real advantage in buying, and we use that."

Questions

1. Classify West Ridge Mountaineering on the following bases:
   a. shopping effort expended by customers
   b. services provided to customers
   c. product lines
   d. location of retail transactions
   e. form of ownership

2. West Ridge owner-manager Ed Brekke wants his customers to perceive his store as a friendly specialty store that offers reliable service. Summarize the elements of the West Ridge retailing strategy and evaluate how well each element combines with the other elements to project this desired image.

3. Location is typically considered to be a key factor in successful retail operations. However, in the case of West Ridge, rental expenses were considered more important. Why? Do you agree with Brekke's decision in this area?

4. Which selling techniques — selling up or suggestion selling — would Ed Brekke be most likely to encourage his salespeople to use? Explain your answer.

COMPUTER APPLICATIONS

A *markup* is the amount added to a product's or service's cost to determine its selling price. The amount of the markup usually depends on (1) the *services* the retailer performs (the more services provided, the larger the markup required) and (2) the *inventory turnover rate* (the higher the turnover rate, the smaller the markup needed).

By contrast, a *markdown* is the amount by which the retailer reduces the product's or service's original selling price. Detailed explanations for calculating markups and markdowns are included on pages 474–476.

Directions: Use menu item 11 titled "markups" to solve Problems 1 through 5. Use menu item 12 titled "markdowns" to solve Problems 6 through 8.

Problem 1   Suppose that the Eastern Michigan University bookstore uses a markup percentage on selling price of 50 percent for its line of EMU T-shirts. What would be the markup percentage on cost for the T-shirts?

Problem 2   A Jackson, Mississippi, shoe store always adds a 40 percent markup (based on selling price) for its shoes. A shipment of shoes just arrived carrying an invoice cost of $54 per pair. What should the retail selling price be for each pair of shoes?

Problem 3   At a recent meeting of the management committee of Litman and Daughter, a Newark, New Jersey, retailer, one of the buyers reported that a new line of dresses carried a markup percentage on cost of 66.67 percent. The firm's president asked the buyer to determine the markup percentage on the line's selling price. How should the buyer respond?

Problem 4   A Louisville, Kentucky, florist sells a special gift arrangement for $30. The florist's costs are $15. What are the florist's markup percentage on selling price and markup percentage on cost?

Problem 5   The Fish Market, a Santa Barbara, California, seafood restaurant, sells a house wine for $7.50 a carafe. The wine actually costs the restaurant $2.50 per carafe. What are the restaurant's markup percentages on selling price and cost?

Problem 6   A Missoula, Montana, retailer pays $156 per dozen for a particular brand of men's shirts. The store attempted to sell these shirts at $30, but sales have been disappointing. In an effort to stimulate additional sales, the store manager decides to mark the shirts down to $25. Determine the store's markdown percentage on the shirts.

Problem 7   A Joliet, Illinois, bookstore has been selling a collection of local recipes for $9.95. The store buys the books from a local gourmet club for $5 each. No returns are allowed. The recipe collection has sold well, and only 19 copies remain. Management recently decided to make space for new inventory by putting the recipe books on the store's discount table at $5.95 each. Determine the bookstore's markdown percentage on the books.

Problem 8   A local economic downturn has adversely affected the sales of a store's line of $150 dresses. The manager decides to mark the dresses down to $120. What markdown percentage should it feature in advertising the sale items?

15

Physical Distribution

Chapter Objectives

1. To explain the role of physical distribution in an effective marketing strategy.

2. To identify and compare the major components of a physical distribution system.

3. To outline the suboptimization problem in physical distribution.

4. To explain the impact of transportation deregulation on physical distribution activities.

5. To compare the major transportation alternatives on the basis of factors such as speed, dependability, cost, frequency of shipments, availability in different locations, and flexibility in handling products.

T he physical distribution component of a total marketing program is frequently viewed as a somewhat mundane but necessary evil. However, it may well be the basis for Baxter Healthcare Corporation's domination of the hospital supply business. The $6.2-billion-a-year company supplies everything from tongue depressors to blood analyzers.

Admittedly the Deerfield, Illinois–based marketer has several strengths, including a crackerjack sales force and an aggressive, high-tech marketing program. But one key to Baxter's marketing success lies in the computer terminals it installed in thousands of hospitals. These computers help Baxter's customers order supplies — and that eliminates a lot of slow, cumbersome, and expensive paperwork. As Baxter marketers hoped, they also seem to have cut down on customers' orders from competitors, since hospitals tend to favor the computers' convenience and efficiency.

Before Baxter installed its analytical systems automated purchasing (ASAP) computer system, hospital supply distribution had been a rather unglamorous business. As one hospital consultant said, "It's a no-technology business — basically, a lot of warehouse shelves and a truck." Add to that the lack of product differentiation (all distributors sell the same things) and the generally low profit margins, and the result is a field that is hard to dominate.

But in 1974, Baxter's predecessor, American Hospital Supply Corp., began installing the industry's first order-taking terminals in the stockrooms of large hospitals. At first, hospital employees planned to use the terminals only in emergencies, since they were still accustomed to regular visits from salespeople. But before long, stock clerks found themselves ordering just about everything through their new terminals, because they were more convenient to use

and usually produced faster, more efficient service.

The ASAP system also cut down on hospitals' inventory carrying costs, since Baxter was able to combine it with its unrivaled distribution network. Inventory control previously had accounted for a good deal of hospitals' procurement costs, but Baxter taught its customers how to "turn" inventory more rapidly. Also, its distribution network put it in a position to deliver products faster than its competitors. In essence, Baxter stored hospitals' inventories for them.

The marketplace experiences of Baxter's and other firms' computer systems have generated some rules about such applications of technology to physical distribution activities. One, the first system to appear usually wins a large share of the busi-

ness (Baxter's net income grew an average of 17 percent annually during the five years following the introduction of its computer system). Two, once a system is entrenched, it is difficult for competitive marketers to challenge it by convincing customers to install duplicate systems. Three, computer systems tend to persuade their users to buy from the systems' suppliers (Baxter's system, for many years, listed only its own products, effectively blocking out the competition). These rules explain the firm's success. While other distributors are playing catch-up, AHS's position at the peak of the medical supply mountain appears secure.[1]

Photo source: Courtesy of Baxter Healthcare Corporation.

Chapter Overview

Chapters 12, 13, and 14 concentrated on distribution channel strategy and the marketing activities of wholesaling and retailing. This chapter focuses specifically on the physical flow of goods. Improving customer service through more efficient physical distribution remains an important aspect of any organization's marketing strategy. As Baxter Healthcare Corp.'s success in the medical supplies industry demonstrates, such efficiency improvement can mean substantial cost savings in addition to better satisfied customers.

Physical distribution involves a broad range of activities aimed at efficient movement of finished products from the end of the production line to the consumer. Although the term *transportation* is sometimes used interchangeably with *physical distribution,* they are not synonymous. As the advertisement in Figure 15.1 demonstrates, the physical movement of people and freight throughout major Asian cities is an important component of Northwest Airlines' marketing operation. But the airline's success, like Baxter Healthcare's, depends on the careful blending of *all* physical distribution activities. These activities include such important decision areas as customer service, inventory control, materials handling, protective packaging, order processing, transportation, warehouse site selection, and warehousing. In this chapter, the term *logistics* is used interchangeably with *physical distribution.*

physical distribution
Broad range of activities concerned with efficient movement of finished products from the end of the production line to the consumer. Includes customer service, transportation, inventory control, packaging and materials handling, order processing, and warehousing.

The Importance of Physical Distribution

In recent years, physical distribution activities have received increasing attention. A major reason is that these functions represent almost half of total marketing costs.

Historically, management's focal point for cost cutting was production. These attempts began with the Industrial Revolution of the 1700s and 1800s, when businesses emphasized efficient production, stressing their ability to decrease production costs and improve the output levels of factories and production workers. But managers now recognize that production efficiency has reached a point at which further cost savings are difficult to achieve. Increasingly managers are turning to physical distribution activities as a possible cost-saving area.

In a recent year, U.S. industry spent about $300 billion on transportation, $180 billion on warehousing, $130 billion on inventory carrying costs, and $40 billion to administer and manage physical distribution. Total physical distribution costs amounted to $650 billion — approximately 21 percent of the nation's gross national product.[2]

A second — and equally important — reason for the increased attention on physical distribution activities is their role in providing customer service. By storing products in convenient locations for shipment to wholesale and retail customers, firms create time utility. Place utility is created primarily by transportation. These major contributions indicate the importance of the physical distribution component of marketing.

Customer satisfaction heavily depends on reliable movement of products to ensure availability. Eastman Kodak committed a major marketing error in the late 1970s when it launched a multimillion-dollar advertising campaign for a new line of cameras before adequate quantities had been delivered to retail outlets.

Figure 15.1
Transportation: One Component of a Physical Distribution System

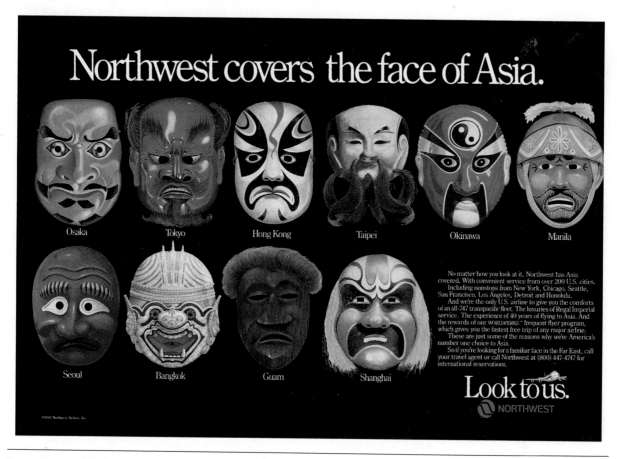

Source: Courtesy of Northwest Airlines, Inc. Saatchi & Saatchi DFS, Inc.

Many would-be purchasers visited the stores, but when they discovered that the new cameras were unavailable, they bought competing brands.

When the firm delivers an intangible service rather than a physical good, information is often a key component of the offering. Fidelity Investor Centers achieved a competitive edge over other discount brokers by increasing its telephone-operator-to-client ratio. On Black Monday in late 1987, when the Dow Jones Industrial Average had tumbled more than 500 points in a single day, several discount brokers reportedly dealt with the influx of telephone calls by leaving their phones off the hook. But Fidelity had recently tripled its staff of operators to about 800. As a result, each of the 580,000 calls logged that day was answered within 48 seconds on average.[3]

Providing desired customer service eventually is reflected in company profitability. For example, in a recent survey Ford Motor Company marketers found that a loyal customer is worth more than $100,000 in repeat purchases during his or her lifetime. Clairol, Inc. marketers report that a satisfied customer will buy a particular hair-coloring product every four weeks for the rest of her life.[4]

By providing consumers with time and place utilities, physical distribution contributes to implementing the marketing concept. Robert Woodruff, former president of Coca-Cola Company, emphasized the role of physical distribution in his firm's success when he stated that its policy is to "put Coke within an arm's length of desire."

The Physical Distribution System

The study of physical distribution is one of the classic examples of the systems approach to business problems. The basic notion of a system is that of a set of interrelated parts. The word is derived from the Greek word *systema,* which refers to an organized relationship among components. The firm's components include such interrelated areas as production, finance, and marketing. Each component must function properly if the system is to be effective and organizational objectives are to be achieved.

A **system** may be defined as an organized group of components linked according to a plan for achieving specific objectives. The physical distribution system contains the following elements:

1. *Customer service:* What level of customer service should be provided?

2. *Transportation:* How will the products be shipped?

3. *Inventory control:* How much inventory should be maintained at each location?

4. *Protective packaging and materials handling:* How can efficient methods be developed for handling products in the factory, warehouse, and transport terminals?

5. *Order processing:* How should the orders be handled?

6. *Warehousing:* Where will the products be located? How many warehouses should be utilized?

The above components are interrelated; decisions made in one area affect the relative efficiency of others. Attempts to reduce transportation costs by using low-cost, relatively slow water transportation may increase inventory costs because the firm may have to maintain large inventory levels to compensate for longer delivery times. The physical distribution manager must balance each component so that no single aspect is stressed to the detriment of the system's overall functioning.

The Problem of Suboptimization

The objective of an organization's physical distribution system may be stated as follows: to establish a specified level of customer service while minimizing the costs involved in physically moving and storing the product from its production point to its ultimate purchase. Marketers must first agree on the necessary level of customer service and then seek to minimize the total costs of moving the product to the consumer or industrial user. All physical distribution elements must be considered as parts of a whole rather than individually when attempting to meet customer service levels at minimum cost. But this does not always happen.

system
Organized group of components linked according to a plan for achieving specific objectives.

Figure 15.2
Cost Trade-offs: Achieving Lower Transport Costs via Slow-Speed Water Transportation

Source: Courtesy of Alabama Development Office.

Suboptimization is a condition in which the manager of each physical distribution function attempts to minimize costs but, due to the impact of one physical distribution task on the others, obtains less than optimal results. One writer explains suboptimization using the analogy of a football team that consists of numerous talented individuals but seldom wins games. Team members hold league records in a variety of skills: pass completions, average yards gained per rush, blocked kicks, and average gains on punt returns. Unfortunately, however, the overall team goal — scoring more points than the opponents — is rarely achieved.[5]

Why does suboptimization frequently occur in physical distribution? The answer lies in the fact that each logistics activity is often judged by its ability to achieve certain management objectives, some of which are at cross-purposes with other goals. For example, water transportation is an extremely low-cost method of shipping heavy, bulky products such as coal and lumber. As the advertisement in Figure 15.2 points out, coal suppliers such as Drummond

suboptimization
Condition in which individual objectives are achieved at the expense of broader organizational objectives.

Company frequently use this transport mode. But it is also the _slowest_ transport mode and may be unsuitable in situations that call for the use of faster but more expensive transportation, such as air freight.

Effective management of the physical distribution function requires some cost trade-offs. Some of the firm's functional areas will experience cost increases and others cost decreases, resulting in minimization of total physical distribution costs. Of course, the reduction of any physical distribution cost should be made with the goal of maintaining the required level of customer service.

Customer Service Standards

customer service standards
Quality of service that a firm's customers will receive.

Customer service standards are the quality of service that the firm's customers will receive. For example, a customer service standard for one firm might be that 60 percent of all orders are shipped within 48 hours after they are received, 90 percent in 72 hours, and all within 96 hours.

Setting the standards for customer service is an important marketing decision. The PIMS studies of the financial performance of some 2,600 businesses over the past 15 years (discussed in Chapter 11) show that financial performance is directly tied to product quality and market share. Among the most powerful tools for influencing buyer perceptions of overall quality is customer service.

To ensure that retail grocers receive products they need when they need them — even if it sometimes means disrupting production to load, ship, and bill an emergency order in a single day — Campbell Soup Company management assigns a salesperson full-time to each of its frozen-food plants. A company spokesperson believes this novel approach strengthens the firm's relationship with its customers: "Most companies have a transportation or warehousing type to handle this function. But we find that keeping a salesman at the plant makes everybody there respond better to customers."[6] In addition, the firm's practice of sending experienced manufacturing people into the field to discover new ways to improve physical distribution service led to changes in the method of loading cases of Swanson frozen dinners in order to cut down on damage.

A vital assignment of the physical distribution specialist is to delineate the costs involved in fulfilling proposed standards. Increased service levels typically cost more, and all members of the marketing department — salespeople and physical distribution specialists — must be aware of the costs of providing the service levels necessary for maintaining both satisfied customers and profitable operations.

In an attempt to increase its share of the market, a major manufacturer of highly perishable food items set a 98 percent service level; that is, 98 percent of all orders were to be shipped the same day they were received. To meet this extremely high level of service, the firm leased warehouse space in 170 cities and kept large stocks in each location. However, the large inventories often meant shipment of dated merchandise. Customers interpreted this practice as evidence of a low-quality product — that is, poor "service."[7]

Table 15.1 indicates possible specific objectives for each factor involved in customer service. It also illustrates the importance of coordinating order pro-

Table 15.1
Customer Service Standards

Service Factor	Objectives
Order-cycle time	To develop a physical distribution system capable of effecting delivery of the product within 8 days from the initiation of a customer order: Transmission of order — 1 day Order processing (order entry, credit verification, picking and packing) — 3 days Delivery — 4 days
Dependability of delivery	To ensure that 95% of all deliveries will be made within the 8-day standard and that under no circumstances will deliveries be made earlier than 6 days nor later than 9 days from the initiation of an order
Inventory levels	To maintain inventories of finished goods at levels that will permit: 97% of all incoming orders for class A items to be filled 85% of all incoming orders for class B items to be filled 70% of all incoming orders for class C items to be filled
Accuracy in order filling	To be capable of filling customer orders with 99% accuracy
Damage in transit	To ensure that damage to merchandise in transit does not exceed 1%
Communication	To maintain a communication system that permits salespersons to transmit orders on a daily basis and that is capable of accurately responding to customer inquiries on order status within 4 hours

Source: From *Strategic Marketing* by David T. Kollat, Roger D. Blackwell, and James F. Robeson, p. 316. Copyright © 1972 by Holt, Rinehart and Winston.

cessing, transportation, inventory control, and the other components of the physical distribution system in achieving these service standards.

Use of Customer Service Standards by Airlines

The next time you are at an American Airlines counter, someone with a stopwatch and clipboard may be hovering nearby. This person is there to see how long it takes you to get your ticket: The company standard is that 85 percent of the passengers should not have to stand in line more than five minutes. When you land, you may find another American Airlines employee checking to see how long it takes to get the luggage off the plane.

American Airlines employees are held to dozens of standards — and are checked constantly. Reservation phones must be answered within 20 seconds; 80 percent of the flights must take off within five minutes of departure time; 79 percent of the flights must arrive within 15 minutes of the published schedule; and 95 percent of the time a gate agent must be available to open the airplane cabin door on arrival. There is even a specification for the proper supply of magazines on board. Monthly performance summaries tell management how the airline is doing and where the problems lie. An outbreak of dirty ashtrays may be traced to a particular cleanup crew; if so, the manager responsible for the crew will hear about it. His or her pay and promotion depend on meeting standards. If the manager fails to meet them three months' running without extenuating circumstances, he or she may soon be looking for a job.[8]

FOCUS ON ETHICS

Customer Service in Deregulated Skies

Customer service standards often are difficult to achieve under rapidly changing market conditions. Beginning with deregulation in the late 1970s, the airline industry has seen some of the most chaotic changes of any U.S. industry. From an early wave of start-ups, of which discount carrier People Express was the largest and most important, to the current, continuing wave of bankruptcies and mergers, conditions have never changed more rapidly. Some consumers of airline services would also argue that customer service has never suffered so much.

In recent years, the Federal Aviation Administration has reported new annual records for late departures (takeoffs at least 15 minutes after scheduled departure time). Airlines' practice of overbooking to compensate for expected "no-shows" combined with increases in the number of air travelers has made "bumping" (denial of seats to ticketed passengers) a part of the transportation vo-

cabulary of the late 1980s. Baggage losses have become so common that a proposed law requiring airlines to give free tickets to passengers whose bags have been lost has already been approved by the House of Representatives. Midair near-collisions increased an ominous 48 percent between 1986 and 1987. In a recent study commissioned by the Air Line Pilots Association, 50 percent of the pilots surveyed reported that plane maintenance has deteriorated. The respondents attributed this to the airlines' cost-cutting efforts and pressures to meet scheduled departure times.

Moreover, the reemergence of oligopoly conditions in the industry (95 percent of the market is now controlled by just 10 airlines) has made fares to and from smaller and medium-size cities with relatively little competitive traffic substantially higher than those in more competitive markets. In some instances, marginal routes were simply abandoned

following deregulation. South Dakota senator Larry Pressler told of having to pay $600 to fly round-trip from Sioux City, South Dakota, to the nation's capital. "I could go to Rome and back on that," he pointed out.

What are the airlines' responsibilities in this environment? Airline executives might well argue that their ultimate responsibility is to their shareholders and thus making a profit is their first priority. Critics are likely to contend that airlines are awarded routes in order for them to provide a public service and that provision of that service is a prerequisite to the right to earn a profit. The debate has already moved to Congress, where the airlines' legal requirements will probably be at least temporarily settled.

Sources: Pressler quotation from Laurie McGinley, "Bad Air Service Prompts Call for Changes," *The Wall Street Journal* (November 9, 1987), p. 29. See also Francis C. Brown III, "Airlines Come to the Aid of Consumers — Sort Of," *The Wall Street Journal* (November 9, 1987), p. 29.

Elements of the Physical Distribution System

The establishment of acceptable levels of customer service provides the physical distribution department with a standard by which to compare actual operations. The physical distribution system should be designed to achieve this standard by minimizing the total costs of the following components: (1) transportation, (2) warehousing, (3) inventory control, (4) order processing, and (5) protective packaging and materials handling. Relative costs for each component are shown in Figure 15.3.

Transportation

Transportation costs are the largest expense item in physical distribution. At Boise Cascade Corporation, for example, transportation costs equal 10 percent of sales, or $340 million. But for many products — particularly perishable goods — transportation is the key to customer service. Most national cookie

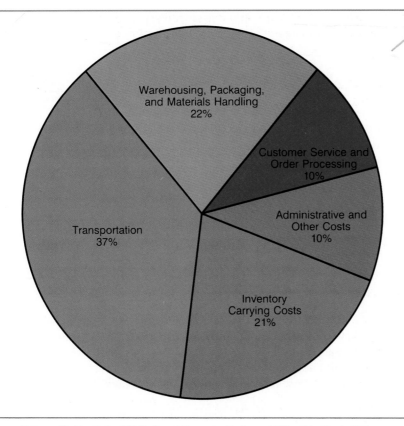

makers, including Duncan Hines, Nabisco, and Keebler, deliver products to stores from inventory that is five to ten days old; nationally marketed breads may be five days out of the oven. But Pepperidge Farm marketers are seeking a competitive advantage by trimming average transport times to fewer than five days for cookies and fewer than three days for bread. Pepperidge Farms CEO Richard Shea summarizes his firm's transportation objective this way: "Our goal is to get the cookies from the ovens to the stores in 72 hours, and we're scaring the life out of that now."[9]

The U.S. transportation system historically has been a regulated industry, much like the telephone and electricity industries. The railroads were first regulated under the Interstate Commerce Act of 1887. This act established the Interstate Commerce Commission (ICC), the first regulatory body in the United States. The ICC regulates some rates and services of railroads, slurry pipelines, motor carriers, and inland water carriers. The Federal Maritime Commission regulates U.S. ocean carriers.

Rate Determination

There are two basic freight rates: class and commodity. The **class rate** is the standard rate for every commodity moving between any two destinations. The class rate is the higher of the two rates. The **commodity rate** is sometimes

class rate
Standard transportation rate established for shipping various commodities.

commodity rate
Special transportation rate granted by carriers to shippers as a reward for either regular use or large-quantity shipments.

called a *special rate,* since it is given by carriers to shippers as a reward for either regular use or large-quantity shipments. It is used extensively by railroads and inland water carriers.

A third type of rate commonly used in the railroad industry today is the *negotiated, or contract, rate.* This type of rate, legalized by the Staggers Rail Act of 1980, allows the shipper and railroad to negotiate a rate for a particular service. The terms of the rate, service, and other variables are then finalized in a contract between the two parties. In the first five years following the passage of the Staggers Rail Act, more than 20,000 such contracts were established and filed with the ICC.

Transportation Deregulation

During the past 12 years, the United States transportation industry has experienced federal deregulation. It began in 1977 with the removal of regulations for cargo air carriers not engaged in passenger transportation. In 1978, the Airline Deregulation Act was passed; this granted airlines considerable freedom in establishing fares and choosing new routes.

In 1980, the Motor Carrier Act and the Staggers Rail Act significantly deregulated the trucking and railroad industries, respectively. These laws enabled transportation carriers to negotiate rates and services, eliminating much of the bureaucracy that traditionally had hampered the establishment of new and innovative rates and services. As the advertisement shown in Figure 15.4 points out, transporters now have added flexibility in designing services and rates to match shippers' unique needs. In this case, the combination of Conrail's rail lines and other highway transportation was necessary for achieving Sunkist's goal of rushing fresh western citrus to eastern supermarkets.

The new transportation environment has increased the importance of physical distribution managers, because their areas of responsibility are even more complex than in a highly regulated situation. It is now possible to simultaneously increase service levels and decrease transportation costs. General Foods recently negotiated a service-oriented contract with the Santa Fe Railroad in which highway trailers would be placed on railcars and transported from Houston to Chicago. In obtaining the contract to ship 6 million pounds of General Foods' products each year, the railroad guaranteed availability of sufficient truck capacity. As a bonus, it will receive an additional $75 per trailer for each month in which 90 percent of its trailers make the trip in 96 hours or less.[10]

Classes of Carriers

Freight carriers are classified as common, contract, and private.

Common carriers, sometimes called the backbone of the transportation industry, are for-hire carriers that serve the general public. Their rates and services are regulated, and they cannot conduct their operations without permission of the appropriate regulatory authority. Common carriers exist for all modes of transport.

Contract carriers are for-hire transporters that do not offer their services to the general public. Instead, they establish specific contracts with certain cus-

Figure 15.4
Custom Transportation Systems Made Possible by Deregulation

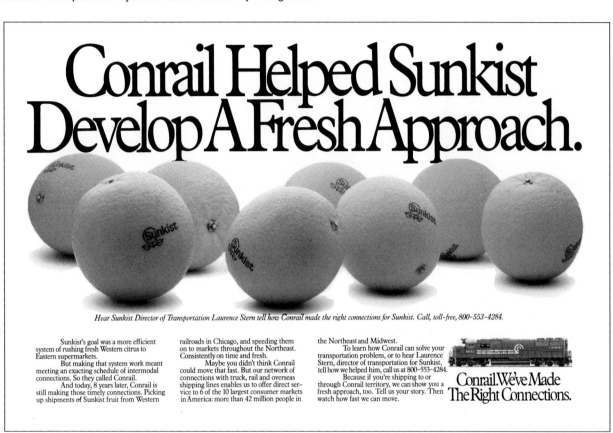

Source: © 1987 Conrail; used by permission.

tomers and operate exclusively for a particular industry (most commonly the motor freight industry). These carriers are subject to much less regulation than are common carriers.

Private carriers are not-for-hire carriers. Their operators transport products only for a particular firm and traditionally have been prohibited from soliciting other transportation business. Since the transportation they provide is solely for their own use, there is no rate or service regulation.

In 1978, the ICC began permitting private carriers to also operate as common or contract carriers. Many private carriers have taken advantage of this new rule to operate their trucks fully loaded at all times. For instance, Nabisco's fleet of private carriers that haul the firm's products to regional warehouses can reduce total transportation costs by transporting other shippers' products on the return trip to the factory. Instead of returning in an empty truck, the Nabisco driver acts as a common carrier or contract carrier and receives a transport fee from the outside shipper.

Figure 15.5

Percentage of Total Intercity Ton-Miles by the Various Transport Modes, 1940–1986

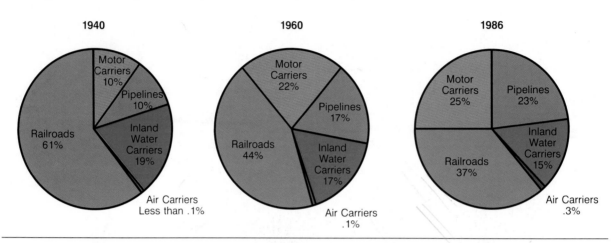

Source: *Transportation in America,* Transportation Policy Associates, Washington, D.C.; and *Yearbook of Railroad Facts* (Washington, D.C.; Association of American Railroads, 1987).

Major Transportation Modes

The physical distribution manager has five major transportation alternatives: railroads, motor carriers, water carriers, pipelines, and air freight. Figure 15.5 indicates the percentage of total ton-miles shipped by each major mode from 1940 to 1986. The term *ton-mile* refers to moving one ton of freight one mile. Thus, a 3-ton shipment moved 8 miles equals 24 ton-miles.

The water carriers' percentage has gradually declined over the years, railroads have experienced a significant decrease, and pipelines and motor carriers have experienced substantial increases. Air carriers are dwarfed by the other transportation alternatives, accounting for fewer than 1 percent of all shipments.

Railroads: The Nation's Leading Transporter The most frequently used method of transportation continues to be railroads, by about a 1.5-to-1 margin over their nearest competitors. They represent the most efficient mode for the movement of bulky commodities over long distances. For instance, two-thirds of domestic coal and almost 70 percent of grain are transported by rail. Chemicals, nonmetallic minerals, and lumber and wood products are other major commodity groups that the railroads carry. Rail carriers such as Burlington Northern, Union Pacific, Santa Fe Southern Pacific, and Norfolk Southern transport three-eighths of all goods shipped in the United States.

In recent years, the railroads have launched a drive to improve their service standards and attract more business and have introduced a number of innovative concepts in pursuit of these objectives. Unit trains, run-through trains, and intermodal (piggyback) operations have played a major role in improving the efficiency and reducing the cost of rail transport.

The unit train, now widely used in coal, grain, and other high-volume movements, runs back and forth between a single loading point (such as a mine) and

Trucks are a vital component in the physical distribution system of Pier 1 Imports, the Fort Worth, Texas-based retailer of decorative home furnishings and accessories. Containerized products shipped from more than 60 countries arrive in U.S. ports where Pier 1 motor carriers then transport them to the company's six distribution centers and from there to 450 U.S. and Canadian retail outlets.

Photo source: Courtesy of Pier 1 Imports.

a single destination (such as a power plant) to deliver one commodity. The run-through train, which bypasses intermediate terminals to speed up schedules, is similar in concept. The difference between them is that the run-through may carry a variety of commodities.

Piggyback operations—in which highway trailers and containers ride on rail flatcars—are the fastest-growing segment of the rail business, combining the long-haul capacity of the train with the door-to-door flexibility of the truck. A highly successful example of this is the Seaboard System's Orange Blossom Special, which hauls more than 1,000 trailerloads of fruit and vegetables each month from Florida to a Delaware terminal for distribution to northeastern markets. The service provides delivery of fresh produce from Florida to New York grocery stores within 48 hours.

In addition to these services, railroads are providing innovative equipment. There are covered hopper cars, which may be loaded with 100 tons of grain in 12 minutes and unloaded in 3. Dual-mode vehicles with two sets of wheels—flanged-steel wheels for use on rails and rubber-tired wheels for use on highways—may be driven away from rail terminals within minutes. Double-stacked containers on flatbed cars enable twice as much freight to be carried for only a slightly greater cost.

Motor Carriers: Flexible and Growing   The trucking industry has shown dramatic growth over the past decades. Its primary advantage over the other transportation modes is its relatively fast, consistent service for both large and small shipments. Motor carriers concentrate on manufactured products, while railroads haul more bulk and raw-material goods. Motor carriers therefore receive greater revenue per ton shipped—more than 23 cents per ton-mile—than do railroads, which earn just over three cents per ton-mile.

Less-than-truckload (LTL) shipments — those weighing less than 10,000 pounds — are consistently transported from coast to coast in fewer than 6 days. A typical example is an 8,000-pound shipment of color televisions from San Diego to Charlotte, North Carolina. The shipment given to Consolidated Freightways on Friday at 4:00 p.m. is joined with others and by Saturday is in Tucumcari, New Mexico. By Sunday, the shipment is in Oklahoma City; on Monday, it arrives in Memphis; and it is delivered to the receiver on Tuesday at 10:30 a.m.[11]

Water Carriers: Slow but Inexpensive   There are two basic types of water carrier — inland or barge lines and oceangoing deepwater ships. Barge lines are efficient transporters of bulky, low-unit-value commodities such as grain, gravel, lumber, sand, and steel. A typical lower Mississippi River barge line may be more than a quarter-mile in length and 200 feet wide.

Oceangoing ships operate in the Great Lakes, transporting goods among U.S. port cities, and in international commerce. Water carrier costs average one cent per ton-mile.

Pipelines: Specialized Transporters   Although the pipeline industry ranks second only to railroads in number of ton-miles transported, many people are barely aware of its existence. More than 213,000 miles of pipelines crisscross the United States. Pipelines serve as extremely efficient transporters of natural gas and oil products, as evidenced by the latter's average revenue per ton-mile of 1.2 cents. Oil pipelines carry two types of commodities — crude (unprocessed) oil and refined products, such as gasoline, jet fuel, and kerosene. In addition, one slurry pipeline currently operates in the United States. In this method of transport, a product such as coal is ground up into a powder, mixed with water, and transported in suspension through the pipeline.

Although pipelines represent a low-maintenance, dependable method of transportation, they have a number of characteristics that limit their use. Their availability in different locations is even more limited than that of water carriers, and their use is restricted to a small number of products. Finally, pipelines represent a relatively slow method of transportation; liquids travel through pipelines at an average speed of only three to four miles per hour.

Air Freight: Fast but Expensive   The use of air carriers as a transportation alternative has been growing significantly. In 1961, U.S. domestic airlines flew about 1 billion ton-miles. By 1985, this figure had jumped to 2.3 billion ton-miles. However, air freight is still a relatively insignificant percentage of the total ton-miles shipped, amounting to three-tenths of 1 percent in 1986.

Because of air freight's relatively high cost, it is used primarily for valuable or highly perishable products. Typical shipments consist of computers, furs, fresh flowers, high-fashion clothing, live lobsters, and watches. Air carriers often offset their higher transportation costs with reduced inventory holding costs and faster customer service.

When General Motors marketers decided to develop a sophisticated luxury sports model to compete directly with the Mercedes 560SL, they turned to the Italian design firm Pininfarina to design the car body. The result was the Cadillac Allanté, which, at almost $60,000, is the most expensive car GM has ever offered. To retain the aura of European sophistication, the Italian firm also handcrafts every Allanté car body. Three times a week, a chartered 747 flies from Turin to Michigan with 56 of the car bodies shown in Figure 15.6 on board.[12]

Figure 15.6
The Cadillac Allanté: Highway Transportation Delivered by Air

Source: Courtesy of General Motors Corporation.

Table 15.2 compares the five transport modes on several bases. Although shippers are likely to consider such items as reliability, speed, and cost in choosing the most appropriate transportation method, these factors will vary in importance for different products. For example, while motor carriers rank highest in availability in different locations, shippers of petroleum products frequently choose the lowest-ranked alternative, pipelines, due to factors such as cost.

Examples of types of products most often handled by the various transport modes include the following:

- *Railroads:* Lumber, iron and steel, coal, automobiles, grain, chemicals
- *Motor carriers:* Clothing, furniture and fixtures, lumber and plastic products, food products, leather and leather products, machinery
- *Water carriers:* fuel, oil, coal, chemicals, minerals, petroleum products
- *Pipelines:* Oil, diesel fuel, jet fuel, kerosene, natural gas, coal (in slurry form)
- *Air carriers:* Flowers, technical instruments and machinery, specialty, high-priced products

Table 15.2
Comparison of Transport Modes

Mode	Speed	Dependability in Meeting Schedules	Frequency of Shipments	Availability in Different Locations	Flexibility in Handling	Cost
Rail	Average	Average	Low	Extensive	High	Medium
Water	Very slow	Average	Very low	Limited	Very high	Very low
Truck	Fast	High	High	Very extensive	Average	High
Pipeline	Slow	High	High	Very limited	Very low	Low
Air	Very fast	High	Average	Average	Low	Very high

Freight Forwarders: Transportation Intermediaries

Freight forwarders are considered transportation intermediaries, because their function is to consolidate shipments to get lower rates for their customers. The transport rates on less-than-truckload (LTL) and less-than-carload (LCL) shipments often are twice as high on a per-unit basis as the rates on truckload (TL) and carload (CL) shipments. Freight forwarders charge less than the higher rates but more than the lower rates. They make their profit by paying the carriers the lower rates. By consolidating shipments, freight forwarders offer their customers two advantages — lower costs on small shipments and faster delivery service than LTL and LCL shippers provide.

Supplemental Carriers

The physical distribution manager can also utilize a number of auxiliary, or supplemental, carriers that specialize in transporting small shipments. These carriers include bus freight services, United Parcel Service, Federal Express, DHL International, and the U.S. Postal Service.

Intermodal Coordination

The various transport modes often combine their services to give shippers the service and cost advantages of each. *Piggyback,* discussed earlier, is the most widely accepted form of coordination. The combination of truck and rail services generally gives shippers faster service and lower rates than either mode does individually, since each method is used where it is most efficient. Shipper acceptance of piggybacking has been tremendous. In 1955, fewer than 200,000 piggyback railcars were shipped; by 1989, more than 2.5 million cars were involved. Piggyback shipments are expected to account for 40 percent of all railcar loadings by 1995. The ICC has exempted piggyback service from government regulation, a move that is expected to increase competition and improve growth prospects for this concept.

Another form of intermodal coordination is *birdyback.* Here motor carriers deliver and pick up a shipment, and air carriers take it over a longer distance. *Fishyback* is a form of intermodal coordination between motor carriers and water carriers.

Figure 15.7
Producing Optimal Customer Service through Multimodal Transportation

Source: Courtesy of CSX Corporation.

/**Multimodal Transportation Companies**   Another form of intermodal co-ordination is performed by multimodal transportation companies. Piggyback generally is done by two separate companies — a railroad and a trucking company. A multimodal firm provides intermodal service in which all the transportation modes are owned and operated by one company. The advantage to the shipper is that the one-carrier service has responsibility from origin to destination. There can be no argument over which carrier caused the shipment to be late or is responsible for a loss or damage.

CSX Corporation is an example of this trend. In 1987 CSX, the nation's third largest railroad, bought Sea-Land, the United States' largest containership operator. Today the firm owns and operates trucks, container ships, barges, and pipelines in addition to the railroad. The firm now offers intermodal transportation services on an international level. As its chief executive officer, Hays T. Watkins, puts it, "We were the first domestic intermodal company. So why not?"[13] The advertisement in Figure 15.7 describes how the diverse freight transportation needs of the firm's customers can be satisfied by the multimodal approach.

Warehousing

storage warehouse
Traditional warehouse in which products are stored prior to shipment.

distribution warehouse
Facility designed to assemble and then redistribute products to facilitate rapid movement of products to purchasers.

Two types of warehouses exist: storage and distribution. A **storage warehouse** stores products for moderate to long time periods in an attempt to balance supply and demand for producers and purchasers. They are most often used by firms whose products' supply or demand are seasonal. A **distribution warehouse** assembles and redistributes products, keeping them on the move as much as possible. Many distribution warehouses or centers physically store goods for fewer than 24 hours before shipping them on to customers.

In an attempt to reduce transportation costs, manufacturers have developed central distribution centers. A manufacturer located in Philadelphia with customers in the Illinois-Wisconsin-Indiana area could send each customer a direct shipment. But if each customer placed small orders, the transportation charges for the individual shipments would be relatively high. A feasible solution is to send a large, consolidated shipment to a *break-bulk center*—a central distribution center that breaks down large shipments into several smaller ones and delivers them to individual customers in the area. For the manager in Philadelphia, the feasible break-bulk center might be located in Chicago.

Conversely, the *make-bulk center* consolidates several small shipments into one large shipment and delivers it to its destination. For example, a giant retailer such as Safeway Stores may operate several satellite production facilities in a given area. Each plant can then send shipments to a storage warehouse in Dallas. This, however, could result in a large number of small, expensive shipments. If a make-bulk center were created in San Francisco and each supplier sent its shipments there, all Dallas-bound deliveries could be consolidated into a single, economical shipment.

The top five distribution center cities in the United States, as measured by the total number of break-bulk distribution centers, are Chicago, Los Angeles–Long Beach, the New York City area, Dallas–Fort Worth, and Atlanta.

Automated Warehouses

Warehouses lend themselves well to automation, with the computer as the heart of the operation. Outstanding examples of automation at work are the six J.C. Penney Catalog Distribution Centers located throughout the country. In Penney's Manchester, Connecticut, center, a facility larger than 35 football fields, a complex system of computers moves over 25,000 pieces of merchandise on and off more than 196,000 shelves every hour. Computers are involved in every phase of the distribution operation, including merchandise receipt, inventory tracking, order processing, packing, invoice preparation, and shipping.

Although automated warehouses may cost as much as $10 million, they can provide major savings for high-volume distributors such as grocery chains. They can "read" computerized store orders, choose the correct number of cases, and move them in the desired sequence to loading docks. These warehouses reduce labor costs, worker injuries, pilferage, fires, and breakage; they also assist in inventory control.

Location Factors

A major decision each company faces concerns the number and location of its storage facilities. The two general factors involved are (1) warehousing and materials-handling costs and (2) delivery costs from warehouse to customer.

THE COMPETITIVE EDGE

Wal-Mart Stores

The dream began back in 1962 when Bentonville, Arkansas, native Sam Walton converted his 16 Ben Franklin variety stores into a then new concept called *dollar stores,* which brought discount store merchandising and pricing practices into midwestern towns too small to attract larger competitors such as Kmart and J. C. Penney. By 1989 Walton was a billionaire, and his 1,100-plus chain of Wal-Mart Stores and Sam's Warehouse Club discount outlets was making the retail giants tremble. Even though Wal-Mart operated in fewer than 30 states, it ranked number 2 among mass merchandising discount chains, number 4 among mass merchandisers, and number 7 among all retailers. Annual sales growth of 30 percent was expected through 1990. Discount competitors such as Target Stores, Rose's, Venture, and Zayre prepared for an industry shakeout as Wal-Mart marketers increased their share of the retail market in the South, Midwest, and Southwest.

What are the keys to Wal-Mart's success? Walton and his associates cite good management, excellent customer service, low prices, and efficiency. Good management and customer service involve intangible hard-to-define qualities. But Wal-Mart's low prices and efficiency can be traced to a tangible ingredient: warehouses.

Warehouses are not the stuff of dramatic business success tales—indeed, in today's economy, warehouses often are unprofitable. But not for Wal-Mart. Walton went to work converting a competitive weakness into a major competitive advantage: "We were in the boondocks. We didn't have distributors falling over themselves to serve us like our competitors did in larger towns. Our

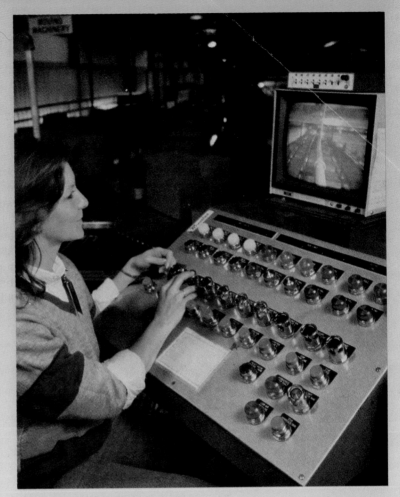

only alternative was to build our own warehouses so we could buy in volume at attractive prices and store the merchandise."

So Walton began to build warehouses, and it paid off in a big way. All Wal-Mart retail stores are clustered within 200 miles of a distribution center, enabling the firm to develop a just-in-time delivery system before that concept became fashionable. Order processing is handled by a satellite communications network that provides computerized linkages between the retailers and their distribution centers. Wal-Mart trucks deliver goods within 36 to 48 hours of

ordering. They also often pick up merchandise from vendors on the way back to the warehouse, a practice known as *backhauling.* Wal-Mart's 65 percent backhauling rate significantly cuts physical distribution costs.

The photo illustrates the computerized inventory systems designed to improve speed of handling and accuracy and to create other cost efficiencies. These processes have reduced the worker hours required to distribute goods from warehouse to retail store by 60 percent.

Wal-Mart isn't standing still. In 1988, the firm's Sam's Warehouse

Club passed Price Company as the nation's largest discount warehouse club. Its entry into deep-discount drugstores has been successful thus far, and the number of units is being expanded. Tests are in process to determine the feasibility of Hypermarket USA, a 220,000-plus-square-foot combination supermarket and general merchandise center. All of these new ventures are designed to capitalize on Wal-Mart's hub-and-spoke distribution center approach. At 3 percent of sales, the firm's distribution costs amount to only about half those of most retail chains. That kind of cost saving has brought this small-town retail operation into the big cities and made its founder a billionaire.

Sources: Walton quotation from Howard Rudnitsky, "Play It Again, Sam," *Forbes* (August 10, 1987), p. 48. See also *Wal-Mart Stores 1987 Annual Report,* pp. 9–10), and "The Second 100," *Advertising Age* (November 23, 1987), pp. S-48, S-49. *Photo source:* Courtesy of Wal-Mart Stores, Incorporated.

The first types of costs are subject to economies of scale; therefore, on a per-unit basis they decrease as volume increases. Delivery costs, on the other hand, rise as the distance from the warehouse location to the customer increases.

The specific location of the firm's warehouses presents a complicated problem. Factors that must be considered include (1) local, county, and state taxes; (2) local, county, and state laws and regulations; (3) availability of a trained labor force; (4) police and fire protection; (5) access to the various transport modes; (6) community attitude toward the proposed warehouses; and (7) cost and availability of public utilities, such as electricity and natural gas.

Inventory Control Systems

Inventory control is a major component of the physical distribution system. Current estimates of inventory holding costs are about 25 percent per year. This means that $1,000 of inventory held for a single year costs the company $250. Inventory costs include storage facilities, insurance, taxes, handling costs, opportunity costs for funds invested in inventory, depreciation, and possible obsolescence of the goods.

Inventory control analysts have developed a number of techniques for helping the physical distribution manager effectively control inventory. The most basic is the **economic order quantity (EOQ) model.** This technique emphasizes a cost trade-off between two fundamental inventory costs: inventory carrying costs, which increase with the addition of more inventory, and order processing costs, which decrease as the quantity ordered increases. As Figure 15.8 indicates, these two cost items are traded off to determine the optimal order quantity for each product. Here the EOQ point is the one at which total cost is minimized. By placing orders for this amount as needed, firms can minimize their inventory costs.

economic order quantity (EOQ) model
Technique for determining the optimal order quantity for each product. Optimal point is determined by balancing the costs of holding inventory and the costs involved in placing orders.

The Just-in-Time System

A new approach to inventory control, borrowed from the Japanese, is rapidly gaining acceptance in the United States. Known as the **just-in-time (JIT) inventory system,** it involves minimizing inventory at each production facility. Manufacturers prefer this system because it greatly reduces their inventory carrying costs. Often parts arrive the same day they are used in the production

just-in-time (JIT) inventory system
Inventory control system designed to minimize inventory at production plants.

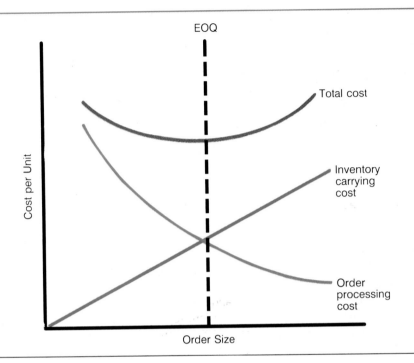

Figure 15.8
Determining the Economic
Order Quantity

process. Just-in-time inventory control requires precise delivery schedules with heavy emphasis on coordination between the purchaser's traffic department and carriers to ensure timely delivery. The seller also must have efficient personnel to ensure that products arrive as scheduled. In order to ensure its customers timely delivery schedules, Dana Corporation, a major supplier to the automobile industry, is relocating production plants close to its major customers.[14]

Reducing inventory investment requires closer relationships between the purchasing firm and its suppliers. Multiple suppliers are frequently utilized in the United States both to encourage price competition and to provide alternative supply sources should a labor dispute, fire, or plant closing interrupt shipments. In contrast, a single supplier for each production input is typical for Japanese companies. For example, Toyota uses 250 suppliers while General Motors has 4,000.[15]

The just-in-time system is particularly effective with products that have relatively few variations. Consequently, heavy users of this approach, such as Toyota, offer a number of "luxury" features on their cars as standard equipment. U.S. auto manufacturers, which previously charged extra for such options, are beginning to duplicate the Japanese approach by offering fewer options and many more standard features.

Order Processing

Like customer service standards, order processing is a quasi-logistics function. The physical distribution manager is concerned with order processing because it directly affects the firm's ability to meet its customer service standards. If its order processing system is inefficient, the company may have to compensate by using costly, premium transportation or increasing the number of field warehouses in all major markets.

Order processing typically consists of four major activities: (1) a credit check; (2) recording the sale, such as crediting a sales representative's commission account; (3) making the appropriate accounting entries; and (4) locating the item, shipping, and adjusting inventory records. An item that is not available for shipment is known as a **stockout.** This occurrence requires the order processing unit to advise the customer of the situation and the contemplated action.

Technological innovations such as increased use of the Universal Product Code are contributing to greater efficiency in order processing. Although well behind pioneers in the grocery and automobile supply industries, Levi Strauss is following dozens of apparel manufacturers by stitching the black-line code onto its jeans and then using elaborate software services to track them through the marketing channel. The results have been dramatic: Some retailers have reported that the new LeviLink system has reduced the time between order and receipt of the shipment from 40 to 12 days. Although Levi Strauss marketers did not begin using the UPC until 1985, by 1988 25 percent of all orders were being received in the form of automatic electronic purchase orders.[16]

Protective Packaging and Materials Handling

All of the activities associated with moving products within the manufacturer's plants, warehouses, and transportation company terminals comprise the **materials-handling** component of physical distribution. These activities must be thoroughly coordinated for both intracompany and intercompany activities. The efficiency of plants and warehouses depends on an effective system.

Two important innovations in the area of materials handling have been developed. One is known as **unitizing**—combining as many packages as possible into one load, preferably on a pallet (a platform, generally made of wood, on which products are transported). Unitizing can be accomplished by using steel bands to hold the unit in place or by shrink packaging. A shrink package is constructed by placing a sheet of plastic over the unit and then heating it. As the plastic cools it shrinks, enabling it to hold the individual packages together securely. Unitizing is advantageous because it requires little labor per package, promotes rapid movement, and minimizes damage and pilferage.

The second innovation is **containerization**—the combining of several unitized loads. The container is typically a big box, 8 feet high, 8 feet wide, and 10, 20, 30, or 40 feet long. Such a container facilitates intertransport mode changes. A container of oil rig parts, for example, can be loaded in Tulsa and trucked to Kansas City, placed on a high-speed, run-through train to New York City, and then placed on a ship to Saudi Arabia.

Containerization also markedly reduces the time involved in loading and unloading ships. Container ships often can be unloaded in fewer than 24 hours—a task that otherwise could take up to 2 weeks. In-transit damage is also reduced, because individual packages are not handled en route to the purchaser.

stockout
Inventory item that is unavailable for shipment or sale.

materials handling
All activities involved in moving products within a manufacturer's plants, warehouses, and transportation company terminals.

unitizing
Process of combining as many packages as possible into one load, preferably on a pallet, in order to expedite product movement and reduce damage and pilferage.

containerization
Process of combining several unitized loads of products into a single load to facilitate intertransport changes in transportation modes.

Figure 15.9

Importance of Information in International Physical Distribution

If you're here, how in the world do you   run your shipping business over here?

To stay on top in the shipping industry, you've got to stay on top of your markets.

But how do you do that when your company is based in California, and your business is in places like Kobe, Hong Kong and Kuala Lumpur?

For American President Companies, a major transportation corporation, the choice was either to move their shipping subsidiary (American President Lines) closer to Asia, or to move information faster. They asked IBM to help.

Working together, IBM and American President Companies (APC) built an enterprise-wide telecommunications network, using satellites, IBM computers, and ROLM voice and data switching technology. IBM NetView™ software centralized management of the system which includes offices across the globe.

With IBM service and support, APC can count on around-the-clock access to information from anywhere in their network. So they have more flexibility in ship deployment, truck and train scheduling, all of which cut cargo transportation time.

Moreover, APC uses the IBM Information Network to extend the same system-wide data to customers. Companies doing business with APC can use their own personal computers to track merchandise movements and pinpoint delivery dates, reducing warehouse and inventory costs.

Recently, APC increased their share of the Pacific Basin market, thanks in part to IBM telecommunications.

With help from IBM, APC's ship has come in—right on schedule. **IBM**

Source: Courtesy of International Business Machines Corporation.

International Physical Distribution

The United States has experienced rapid growth in international trade since World War II. Over the past decade, the dollar value of U.S. exports has tripled and imports have grown even faster. This growth has placed new responsibilities on physical distribution departments.

Months of intensive cooperative efforts between IBM and American President Lines made it possible for the California-based transporter to continue its operations from the U.S. mainland. As the advertisement shown in Figure 15.9 points out, most of American President Lines' cargo shipping business comes from markets in the Pacific Basin. IBM's custom-designed telecommunications network provides the shipper and its clients with round-the-clock information on merchandise movements, ship deployments, and delivery dates, thus reducing warehouse and inventory costs.

A major problem facing international marketers is the flood of paperwork involved in exporting products. More than 100 different international trade documents representing over 1,000 separate forms must be completed for each international shipment. The result is that an average export shipment requires approximately 36 employee hours for documentation and 27 employee hours for importing a shipment. Paperwork alone equals 7 percent of the total value of U.S. international trade. Many physical distribution departments are too small to employ international specialists. They subcontract the work to *foreign freight forwarders* — wholesaling intermediaries that specialize in physical distribution outside the United States.

A major impetus to exporting has been the advent of containerization and container ships. One shipping company currently has container ships that can make a round trip between New York, Bremerhaven, and Rotterdam in 14 days. Only four days are needed for crossing the Atlantic and another six days for three port calls. This speed allows U.S. exporters to provide competitive delivery schedules for European markets.

Summary of Chapter Objectives

1. Explain the role of physical distribution in an effective marketing strategy. The goal of a physical distribution department is to produce a specified level of customer service while minimizing the costs involved in physically moving and storing the product from its production point to its ultimate purchase.

2. Identify and compare the major components of a physical distribution system. Physical distribution involves a broad range of activities concerned with efficient movement of finished products from the end of the production line to the consumer. As a system, physical distribution consists of six elements: (1) customer service, (2) transportation, (3) inventory control, (4) protective packaging and materials handling, (5) order processing, and (6) warehousing. These elements are interrelated and must be balanced in order to have a smoothly functioning distribution system and avoid suboptimization. The physical distribution department is one of the classic examples of the systems approach to business problems.

3. Outline the suboptimization problem in physical distribution. *Suboptimization* refers to a situation in which each manager of a physical distribution activity attempts to minimize his or her costs, resulting in a negative impact on other physical distribution activities. The objective of the physical distribution function is to focus on *total* distribution costs to minimize the degree of suboptimization.

4. Explain the impact of transportation deregulation on physical distribution activities. Deregulation has had a profound effect on transportation in recent years. Many transporters now are free to develop unique solutions to shippers' needs. Deregulation has been particularly important for motor carriers, railroads, and air carriers.

5. Compare the major transportation alternatives on the basis of factors such as speed, dependability, cost, frequency of shipments, availability in different locations, and flexibility in handling products. Railroads rank high on flexibility in handling products and availability in different locations; average on speed, dependability in meeting schedules, and cost; and low on frequency of shipments. Motor carriers are relatively high in cost but are ranked high on speed, dependability, shipment frequency, and availability in different locations. Water carriers balance their slow speed, low shipment frequency, and limited availability with very low costs. The special nature of pipelines makes them rank relatively low on availability, flexibility, and speed but also low in cost. Air transportation is high in cost but offers very fast and dependable delivery schedules.

Key Terms

physical distribution
system
suboptimization
customer service standards
class rates
commodity rate
storage warehouse

distribution warehouse
economic order quantity (EOQ) model
just-in-time (JIT) inventory system
stockout
materials handling
unitizing
containerization

Review Questions

1. Why was physical distribution one of the last areas in most companies to be carefully studied and improved?
2. Outline the basic reasons for the increased attention to physical distribution management.
3. What are the basic objectives of physical distribution?
4. Explain the role of customer service standards in the physical distribution system.
5. What factors should be considered in locating a new distribution warehouse?
6. Who should be ultimately responsible for determining the level of customer service standards? Explain.
7. Outline the basic strengths and weaknesses of each mode of transport. Describe the relative importance of each mode in terms of ton-miles.
8. Under what circumstances are freight forwarders used?
9. Identify the major forms of intermodal coordination, and give an example of a product for which each is likely to be used.
10. Explain the advantages of and potential problems in the just-in-time system of inventory control.

Discussion Questions

1. Suggest the most appropriate method of transportation for each of the following products, and defend your choices:
   a. Iron ore
   b. Dash detergent
   c. Heavy earth-moving equipment
   d. Crude oil
   e. Orchids
   f. Lumber
2. Comment on the following statement: "The popularity of physical distribution management is a fad; ten years from now it will be considered a relatively unimportant function of the firm."

3. Explain why the study of physical distribution is one of the classic examples of the systems approach to business problems.

4. Which mode of transportation do you believe will experience the greatest ton-mile percentage change during the 1990s? Why?

5. Discuss the basic cost factors involved in the EOQ model. Does the basic EOQ model consider all relevant costs? Explain.

VIDEO CASE 15

Arrowhead Drinking Water Co.

Bottled water got a big boost in the late 1970s when the importers of Perrier launched a $4 million advertising campaign in the United States promoting their sparkling spring water as an alternative to soft drinks and alcoholic beverages. The campaign spoke to a receptive audience — a growing number of health-conscious and fitness-minded Americans concerned about water pollution and purity, and showing a preference for low-calorie, alcohol-free beverages.

The advertising blitz not only helped Perrier become the market leader in U.S. bottled water sales; it also fueled an explosive growth in the industry, as other bottled water marketers began aggressively promoting their mineral water, club soda, seltzer, and sparkling water. Americans responded by buying bottled water in record numbers. Per-capita consumption grew from 1.5 gallons in 1976 to 5.7 gallons in 1986.

Today the $1.7 billion bottled water market is the fastest growing segment of the beverage business. According to the Beverage Marketing Corporation, bottled water sales grew 15 percent each year from 1983 to 1986, and are expected to continue growing at an annual rate of 10 percent through 1991. The bottled water business in the United States is highly regionalized, but the market's growth during the past decade has attracted competitors such as PepsiCo and other national soft-drink, beer, and spirits marketers. Perrier, eager to maintain its market leadership and increase its market share, acquired Arrowhead Drinking Water Co. from Beatrice Foods in 1987. The acquisition not only doubled Perrier's market share to 21 percent, it also broadened the firm's presence in the nonsparkling water market.

Arrowhead, based in Monterey Park, California, is a major regional distributor of jug water. Jug water is marketed primarily as a substitute for tap water through two channels: through supermarkets in 1- and 2.5-gallon containers, and delivered directly to consumers in 5-gallon bottles for their water coolers. Though jug water lacks the sparkle of its specialty counterparts, it accounts for the lion's share — 77 percent — of all U.S. bottled water sales. In 1985, Arrowhead entered the sparkling water market by introducing Arrowhead Springs Sparkling Water in 1.5-liter bottles and six-packs of 10-ounce bottles. A year later, the company extended the line by adding Ozarka Sparkling Water.

Perrier's marketing success in the United States can be attributed to its promotional efforts, but Arrowhead's accomplishments as a bottled water marketer are tied mainly to a superior product and an efficient distribution system that brings mountain spring water to customers' homes and offices and to supermarkets in Arizona, California, Hawaii, and Nevada.

Arrowhead's beginnings date to the early 1800s when David Smith built a health spa at Arrowhead Springs. Visitors flocked there to bathe in — and drink — the supposedly restorative mineral water. As customer demand for the drinking water increased, Smith began piping water down the mountainside and, in 1905, started bottling it in the basement of the spa's hotel and shipping it to customers.

Today, Arrowhead gathers water from seven springs in the San Bernardino Mountains. From these sources, water flows through 7-mile pipelines to storage reservoirs, where it is loaded by gravity within 25 minutes into 64,000-gallon-capacity tanker trucks that transport it to Arrowhead's bottling plant. The tankers operate 24 hours a day, seven days a week. While alternative methods such as railroad and pipeline have been tried, trucks have proven to be the most efficient way to transport the water supply needed to satisfy Arrowhead's customer demand.

At the bottling plant, water is pumped through several filtration stages to produce three different products: spring, distilled, and fluoridated water. In a computer-controlled bottling room, sanitized bottles are rapidly filled and capped. Five-gallon bottles are individually crated, while smaller containers are packed in boxes. Boxes and crates are unitized to ensure that forklift operators can move them safely and efficiently from the production line to the warehouse or delivery yard.

Arrowhead generates most of its sales from the delivery of 5-gallon water bottles directly to consumers. Satisfying these customers is the firm's top priority, and Arrowhead's route salespeople do more than deliver water. They are responsible for soliciting new business and completely servicing existing accounts. They control their own truck inventory and make daily adjustments to accommodate last-minute customer requests, collect money, update orders, and balance their books. Route salespeople receive support from telephone operators in the order processing department who answer customer inquiries, transmit called-in orders, and set up delivery schedules. Because deliveries are scheduled at 14-day intervals, route salespeople must ensure that each delivery will satisfy a two-week demand. "The route salesperson is really the backbone of the company," says Larry Fried, director of marketing. "If it weren't for the route salespeople, Arrowhead wouldn't even exist. They're the most important part of the company."

Since home delivery involves high transportation and labor costs, it takes up a large part of Arrowhead's expense budget. To contain delivery costs, Arrowhead marketers chose a different approach for grocery-store customers. Rather than investing in a fleet of delivery trucks, Arrowhead offers the grocery trade a freight allowance as an incentive for retailers to pick up products at Arrowhead's warehouse.

To compete profitably with other bottled water companies and municipal water systems and yet maintain its high level of customer service, Arrowhead marketers strive for operating efficiency in inventory control, materials handling, packaging, and warehousing. Marketers plan for inventory needs by preparing detailed 1-, 5-, and 10-year forecasts of consumer demand, which enable them to estimate the type of water and number of bottles that will be needed. These estimates assist planners in the purchase of bottles, containers, boxes, crates, and other operating equipment and supplies, and in determining future warehousing needs.

Arrowhead marketers balance their large capital investment expenses by maintaining a minimum inventory of 5-gallon bottles. Bill Lindop, manager of production operations, states that the inventory plan operates on the principle of one day for empty bottles to be filled, one day for full bottles on the route trucks to be delivered, and a quarter to a half day for bottles on hand as backup. To the extent possible, bottles are taken directly from the production line and loaded on delivery trucks to avoid double handling.

Because the production process for the bottled water sold to supermarkets is slower than that for the 5-gallon bottles, these products are warehoused to ensure that enough is available when the retailers need them. To balance production output with retail demand, Arrowhead marketers try to maintain a three- to four-day supply of 1- and 2.5-gallon bottles and several weeks' supply of sparkling water. They move inventory on a first-in, first-out basis to keep the product as fresh as possible on supermarket shelves. They also encourage retailers to keep their own backroom inventories of high-volume drinking water to meet customer demand.

As Arrowhead's distribution requirements have increased through the years, so have their costs for loading and unloading delivery trucks — a process that originally required route salespeople to stay with their trucks during the one to one and a half hours of loading. To reduce loading expenses, Arrowhead marketers asked their engineers to develop a more cost-efficient system. They designed a straddle trailer that moves hundreds of bottles at one time. "With the straddle trailer, it's a 15-minute turnaround time," says Lindop, "so you're saving between an hour and an hour and 15 minutes, not only of the drivers' time, but the capital investment on the equipment that you can keep on the road, which is about $150,000 worth of equipment."

In making packaging decisions, Arrowhead marketers consider production-line efficiency as well as the rate of product turnover. All aspects of marketing home-delivered bottled water are geared to the 5-gallon size — the industry standard since the turn of the century. Changes in bottle size would involve millions of dollars of new production equipment. Without changing the size, Arrowhead has significantly improved 5-gallon productivity by changing from a 14-pound glass bottle to a 3-pound polycarbonate bottle. With the lighter bottle, route salespeople carry one ton less a day in weight and have fewer lifting-related injuries, while delivery trucks get much better gas mileage.

When Arrowhead introduced its sparkling water, marketers decided to package the 1.5-liter plastic bottles in eight-bottle cases, even though the industry standard for sparkling water in glass bottles was 12 per case. Their decision, which took into account the advice of industry suppliers and other experts, was based on providing the best distribution economies throughout the system.

Sources: Beverage Marketing Corp., *1987 Annual Industry Survey;* Marcy Magiera, "Bottled Waters Spring Up," *Advertising Age* (September 21, 1987), pp. 24, 83; and "Water, Water Everywhere," *Consumer Reports* (January 1987), pp. 42–47.

Questions

1. Arrowhead marketers use multiple distribution channels in reaching the firm's customers. Draw a diagram of each channel used and label each part.

2. Relate each of the components of the physical distribution system to the way that Arrowhead provides mountain spring water to customers.

3. What are Arrowhead's physical distribution objectives? Identify several possible sources for suboptimization to occur and explain how the total-cost approach is used by Arrowhead marketers to avoid the occurrence of suboptimization.

4. Which transportation factors discussed in the chapter might have affected Arrowhead's decision to switch from the use of railroad cars to trucks in transporting water from its source to the bottling plant?

5. Which of Arrowhead's marketing decisions have improved the effectiveness and efficiency of the firm's physical distribution system?

COMPUTER APPLICATIONS

The physical distribution manager must balance two types of costs involved in inventory: (1) inventory holding costs, which increase with the addition of more inventory, and (2) order costs, which decrease as the quantity ordered increases. The *economic order quantity (EOQ)* model is a particularly useful quantitative technique for determining the order size that will most closely balance these two types of costs. It is described in more detail on pages 520 to 521.

The following formula is used to determine the economic order quantity:

$$EOQ = \sqrt{\frac{2RS}{IC}},$$

where

EOQ = economic order quantity (in units)

R = annual usage rate

S = cost of placing an order

I = annual inventory carrying costs expressed as a percentage

C = item's cost per unit (the "unit" may consist of a single item or a prepackaged box containing a dozen items, a gross, or even more)

In the above formula, R is an estimate based on the demand forecast for the item; S is calculated from the firm's cost records; and I is an estimate based on the costs of such items as handling, insurance, interest, storage, depreciation, and taxes. Since the item's per-unit cost may vary over time, C is also likely to be an estimate. The EOQ can be determined by inserting specific data into the formula. Consider, for example, the following:

$$R = 6,000$$
$$S = \$8.50$$
$$I = 15\%$$
$$C = \$14.50$$
$$EOQ = \sqrt{\frac{(2)(6,000)(8.50)}{(14.50)(.15)}}$$
$$= 216.56$$

The calculation often results in a fractional quantity that must be rounded to the next whole number to determine the economic order quantity. Thus, the EOQ in the above example would be rounded to 217 units.

Although the exact EOQ calculation has been determined at 217 units, other factors may have to be considered. For instance, suppliers may place additional constraints on the ordering firm. In some cases, orders may be limited to even dozens or multiples of 100. The economic order quantity must be adjusted to match such constraints.

Directions: Use menu item 13 titled "Economic Order Quantity (EOQ)" to solve the following problems.

Problem 1   Appliance Mart of Salisbury, Maryland, sells 160 refrigerators annually. The store pays an average of $300 for each unit, and each order costs

$25 to place. The annual inventory carrying cost is 10 percent. What is the appropriate EOQ for Appliance Mart?

Problem 2　An Erie, Pennsylvania, retailer sells about 220 dozen of a certain brand of men's shirts each year. The wholesale cost is $145 per dozen. The retailer tries to keep the inventory as low as possible because of the 26 percent annual carrying cost. Each order costs the store $30 to place. Calculate the EOQ for this retailer.

Problem 3　A souvenir shop in Myrtle Beach, South Carolina, pays 12 cents for each of the 30,000 postcards it sells annually. Inventory carrying costs are a modest 5 percent, and placing an order costs only $5. Calculate this retailer's EOQ.

Problem 4　The owner of a Bridgeport, Connecticut, sporting goods retail store wants to calculate the EOQ for a certain line of tennis racquets. The racquets cost the store $20 and have an average inventory carrying cost of 25 percent. Each order costs $25. The store sells 600 of these racquets each year.
a. Determine the economic order quantity for the tennis racquets.
b. Suggest the most appropriate order size if the manufacturer insists that orders be placed in multiples of 10.

Problem 5　A Birmingham, Alabama, motorcycle shop has an order placement cost of $50 for its $75 (wholesale cost) helmets. Its average annual inventory carrying cost is 15 percent. The shop sells 250 helmets each year.
a. Determine the EOQ for the motorcycle helmets.
b. Determine the most appropriate order size if the shop's supplier decides to require that all orders be placed in multiples of one dozen.

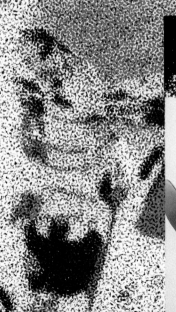

Promotional Strategy

Photo source: Courtesy of Anheuser-Busch Companies, Inc.

16

Introduction to Promotion

Chapter Objectives

1. To explain the relationship of promotional strategy to the process of communication.

2. To list the objectives of promotion.

3. To explain the concept of the promotional mix and its relationship to the marketing mix.

4. To identify the primary determinants of a promotional mix.

5. To contrast the two major alternative promotional strategies.

6. To compare the primary methods of developing a promotional budget.

7. To defend promotion against common public criticisms.

I f tennis players were given a word association test, the name "Prince" would most likely evoke a response of "racquet," for Prince Manufacturing is widely recognized as a leading marketer of premium tennis racquets. But Prince also markets a line of tennis apparel and footwear, a fact not as well known as the firm's management would like it to be. Prince marketers decided that a unique promotional program was needed to heighten consumer awareness of its apparel and footwear while continuing strong racquet awareness. Prince devised a series of three promotions. Objectives were threefold: to increase the visibility of Prince's apparel and shoes at pro shops and sporting goods stores, to encourage players to continue to use demonstrator racquets at stores and to continue strong sell through exposure of Prince tennis products.

Winners of the first "Dream Match" promotion received a trip to the U.S. Open in New York City. During the trip, they also participated in a doubles match against Prince's tennis spokespeople Stan Smith and Gabriela Sabatini. Before filling out an entry form, contestants had to either try out a Prince racquet or try on Prince clothing or shoes. The Dream Match could be called a smashing success, with a response rate of 3.4 percent based on the estimated number of exposures. In most cases, a response rate of 1 percent is considered a promotional success.

In the second promotional contest, "Dress for a Winning Season," entrants again had to try on Prince clothing. But this time they were required to state on the entry form why they would or would not buy Prince apparel. To increase store traffic, Prince marketers had every participating pro shop or sporting goods store pick a winner to receive a prize of Prince clothing and shoes. Prince

marketers were able to convince additional distributors to carry the apparel line during the second promotional period using the argument that a winner in every store would bring in more customers.

The last leg of the campaign courted the "pro" in every player. Called "Picture Yourself as a Prince Pro," the promotion offered tennis players free action posters of themselves in Prince clothing and holding their Prince racquet. To receive the poster premium illustrated in the photo, customers had to purchase $150 of Prince merchandise. Posters were made from photos taken by the pro shop dealers. One pro shop set up a Hall of Fame display of members' posters in a hallway between the tennis clubhouse and pro shop— just the sort of publicity firms encourage. Not only does each poster represent $150 in purchased merchandise; the display is a type of continuing free publicity that helps stretch promotional dollars.[1]

Photo source: Courtesy of Prince Manufacturing, Inc., P.O. Box 2031, Princeton, NJ 08540.

Chapter Overview

Thus far we have examined three of the four broad variables of the marketing mix. In Part 7, we analyze the fourth marketing mix variable—promotion. This chapter introduces promotion and briefly describes the elements comprising a firm's promotional mix—personal and nonpersonal selling—and the factors that determine the optimal mix. Then it identifies the objectives of promotion and describes the importance of developing promotional budgets and measuring the effectiveness of promotions. Finally, the chapter discusses the importance of the business, economic, and social aspects of promotion. Chapter 17 discusses advertising, sales promotion, and the other nonpersonal selling elements of the promotional mix. Chapter 18 completes this section by focusing on personal selling.

A good place to begin the discussion of promotion is by defining the term. **Promotion** is the function of informing, persuading, and influencing the consumer's purchase decision. Figure 16.1 depicts the relationship between the firm's promotional strategy and the other elements of the overall marketing strategy in achieving organizational objectives and producing utility for the consumers who comprise the firm's target market.

The marketing manager sets the goals and objectives of the firm's promotional strategy in accordance with overall organizational objectives and the goals of the marketing organization. Based on these objectives, the various elements of the strategy—personal selling, advertising, sales promotion, publicity, and public relations—are formulated into a coordinated promotional plan. This becomes an integral part of the total marketing strategy for reaching selected consumer segments. The feedback mechanism, including marketing research and field reports, completes the system by identifying any deviations from the plan and suggesting modifications for improvement.

Promotional strategy is closely related to the process of communication. A standard definition of *communication* is the transmission of a message from a sender to a receiver. **Marketing communications,** then, are those messages that deal with buyer-seller relationships. Marketing communication is a broader concept than promotional strategy, because it includes word-of-mouth advertising and other forms of unsystematic communication. A planned promotional strategy, however, is certainly the most important part of marketing communications.

promotion
Function of informing, persuading, and influencing the consumer's purchase decision.

marketing communications
Transmission from a sender to a receiver of messages dealing with buyer-seller relationships.

The Communications Process

Figure 16.2 shows a general communications process and its application to promotional strategy. The *sender* is the source of the communications system, since he or she seeks to convey a *message* (a communication of information, advice, or request) to a *receiver* (the recipient of the communication). The message must accomplish three tasks in order to be effective:

1. It must gain the receiver's attention.
2. It must be understood by both receiver and sender.
3. It must stimulate the receiver's needs and suggest an appropriate method of satisfying them.

Figure 16.1
How Promotion Fits into the Total Marketing Mix

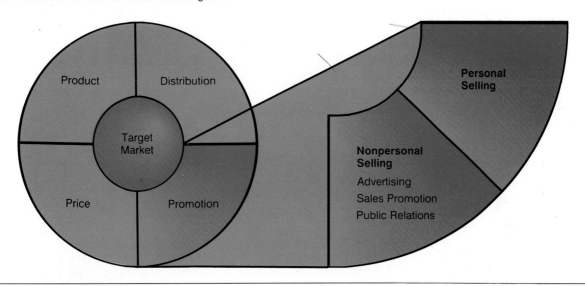

Source: Based on an idea suggested by Professor James H. Kennedy of Navarro College.

The three tasks are related to the **AIDA concept** *(attention-interest-desire-action)* proposed by E. K. Strong over 60 years ago as an explanation of the steps an individual must go through before making a purchase decision. First, the potential consumer's attention must be gained. Then the promotional message seeks to arouse interest in the good or service. The next stage is to stimulate desire by convincing the would-be buyer of the product's ability to satisfy his or her needs. Finally, the sales presentation or advertisement attempts to produce action, in the form of a purchase or a more favorable attitude, that may lead to future purchases.

AIDA concept
Acronym for *attention-interest-desire-action,* the traditional explanation of the steps an individual must take prior to making a purchase decision.

The message must be *encoded,* or translated into understandable terms, and transmitted through a communications medium. *Decoding* is the receiver's interpretation of the message. The receiver's response, known as *feedback,* completes the system. Throughout the process, *noise* can interfere with the transmission of the message and reduce its effectiveness.

The marketing manager is the sender in the system, as shown in Figure 16.2. The message is encoded in the form of sales presentations, advertising, displays, or publicity releases. The *transfer mechanism* for delivering the message may be a salesperson, a public relations channel, or an advertising medium. The decoding step involves the consumer's interpretation of the sender's message. This is often the most troublesome aspect of marketing communications, because consumers do not always interpret a promotional message in the same way the sender does. Since receivers are likely to decode messages according to their own frames of reference or experiences, the sender must be careful to ensure that the message is encoded correctly so that it will match the frame of reference of the target audience.

Figure 16.2
Relating Promotion to the Communications Process

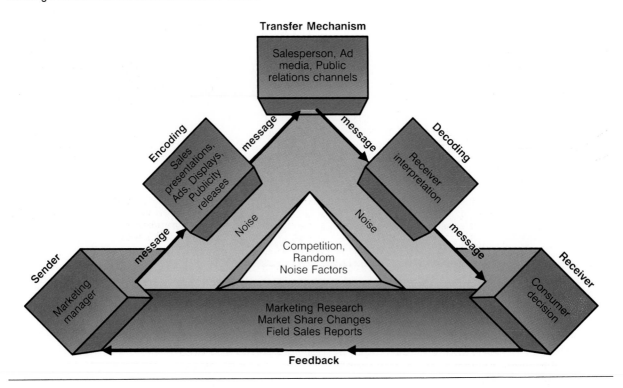

Feedback is the receiver's response to the message. It may take the form of attitude change, purchase, or nonpurchase. In some instances, firms use promotion to create a favorable attitude toward their new products or services. Such attitude changes may result in future purchases. Yogurt makers, for example, are using television advertising in an effort to change the attitudes of nonpurchasers, including many who perceive yogurt as a spoiled-milk product. The millions of Americans who consume almost 1 billion pounds of yogurt each year view the product as a healthy, convenient food. But between 30 and 40 percent of the U.S. population has never tasted yogurt. According to a recent study of foods people dislike most, yogurt ranked third after lima beans and liver. The television advertising campaign is designed to let consumers see, feel, and taste yogurt through the actor's experience and hopefully entice non-users to try the product.[2] In other instances, the objective of the promotional communication may be to stimulate consumer purchases. Such purchases indicate positive responses to the firm, its product/service offerings, its distribution channels, its prices, and its promotion. Even nonpurchases may serve as feedback to the sender. Failure to purchase may result from ineffective communication in which the message was not believed or not remembered. Alternatively, the message may have failed to persuade the receiver that the firm's products or services are superior to its competitors'. Feedback can be obtained from techniques such as marketing research studies and field sales reports.

Table 16.1
Examples of Marketing Communications

Type of Promotion	Sender	Encoding	Transfer Mechanism	Decoding by Receiver	Feedback
Personal selling	Sharp business products	Sales presentation on new model of office copier	Sharp sales representative	Office manager and employees in local firm discuss Sharp sales presentation and those of competing suppliers	Order placed for Sharp copier
Two-dollars-off coupon (sales promotion)	Wendy's hamburgers	Wendy's marketing department and advertising agency	Coupon insert in Sunday newspaper	Newspaper reader sees coupon for hamburger and saves it	Hamburgers purchased by consumers using coupon
Television advertising	Walt Disney Enterprises	Advertisement for a new, "G"-rated animated movie is developed by Disney's advertising agency	Network television during programs with high percentage of viewers under 12 years old	Children see ad and ask parents to take them; parents see ad and decide to take children	Movie tickets purchased

Noise represents interference at some stage in the communications process. It may result from such factors as transmission of competitive promotional messages over the same communications channel, misinterpretation of a sales presentation or advertising message, receipt of the promotional message by the wrong person, or random noise factors such as people conversing during a television commercial or leaving the room. When Sunlight liquid detergent was introduced with the promotional theme "containing real lemon juice," Sunlight marketers were shocked to discover that some consumers who received trial samples mistook the detergent for lemon juice. A few product misusers were even hospitalized.

In some instances, the noise produced by misinterpretations of faulty communications results in amusing examples of miscommunications. Here are two classified advertisements that have appeared in newspapers:[3]

FOR SALE
1969 Cadillac Hearse. Body
in good condition.

FOR SALE
Large Great Dane.
Registered pedigree. Will eat
anything. Especially fond of
children.

Table 16.1 illustrates the steps in the communications process with several examples of promotional messages. Although the types of promotion may vary from a highly personalized sales presentation to such nonpersonal promotions as television advertising and two-dollars-off coupons, each goes through every stage in the communications model.

Objectives of Promotion

Determining the precise objectives of promotion has always been a perplexing problem for management. What specific tasks should promotion accomplish? The answer to this question seems to be as varied as the sources one consults. Generally, however, the following are considered objectives of promotion: (1) to provide information, (2) to increase demand, (3) to differentiate the product, (4) to accentuate the product's value, and (5) to stabilize sales.

Providing Information

The traditional function of promotion was to inform the market about the availability of a particular product or service. Indeed, a large part of current promotional efforts is still directed at providing product information for potential customers. For example, the typical newspaper advertisement for a university or college extension course program emphasizes informative features, such as the availability, time, and location of different courses.

Firms also use promotion to give information about their company. The advertisement in Figure 16.3 was the first in a national advertising campaign launched by Primerica to introduce its new name to the business community. The ad explains why Primerica changed its name from American Can Company and presents other pertinent information about the firm, including a listing of its lesser-known marketing activities in financial services and specialty retailing, its New York Stock Exchange symbol, and how to correctly pronounce its new name.

Stimulating Demand

The primary objective of most promotional efforts is to increase the demand for a specific brand of product or service. Successful promotion can shift demand, resulting in increased sales without having to reduce prices. To stimulate consumer demand for catfish, the Catfish Institute designed a $2 million promotional campaign consisting of print advertisements and a public relations program. In the United States, per capita consumption of catfish is less than one pound a year compared to 70 pounds of poultry. Moreover, 75 percent of all catfish consumption occurs in 12 states in the Deep South. The Institute hopes its promotional efforts overcome this heavy regional skew in consumption patterns and will prompt poultry buyers to purchase catfish. Targeted to an upscale, health-conscious audience, the "Mississippi Prime" advertisement in Figure 16.4 touts the benefits of catfish as a low-calorie food that is quick and easy to prepare and includes an offer for a catfish recipe book. Other advertisements contain directly competitive headlines such as "Think of It as Chicken That Doesn't Cluck." Part of the Institute's attempt to boost catfish demand involves

Figure 16.3
Using Advertising to Inform

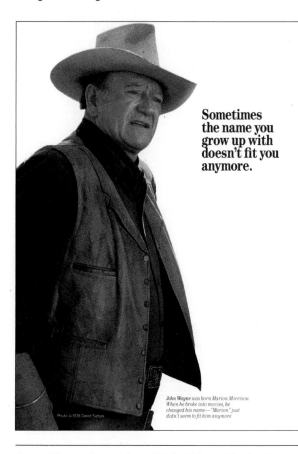

Sometimes
the name you
grow up with
doesn't fit you
anymore.

John Wayne was born Marion Morrison.
When he broke into movies, he
changed his name—"Marion" just
didn't seem to fit him anymore.

That's why
American Can
has changed
its name
to Primerica.

When we redirected American Can Company out of manufacturing and into financial services and specialty retailing, our name just didn't fit us any longer. Which is why we sold it along with our packaging business last year.

After all, it doesn't make much sense to go on calling yourself American Can when you no longer make cans.

Primerica (pronounced pry-MER-i-ca) is our new name. It provides a link to our proud heritage, yet gives us flexibility to enter new businesses in the future. It also better suits what we have become.

We are the country's number one underwriter of individual life insurance. One of the largest originators of home mortgages. And one of the nation's top managers of mutual funds and pension assets.

We're also the largest retailer of recorded music and audio/video products in the U.S. And one of the country's largest direct mail marketers.

Over the past six years, as we redirected the company, our shareholders have been rewarded with substantial increases in the value of their stock. From a low of 25¾ in 1982, our common stock price hit an all-time high of 107 in early 1987, prior to a two-for-one stock split.

We're Primerica. A company with prime growth prospects and the resources to fund that growth. A name to be reckoned with. NYSE symbol: PA.

PRIMERICA

Primerica Corporation, Greenwich, Connecticut 06830

Financial Services: American Capital Management & Research, Inc.; Berg Enterprises, Inc.; Insurance Marketing Corp. of America (a co-venture); Mass. Indemnity and Life Ins. Co.; Margarethen & Co., Inc.; National Benefit Life Ins. Co.; PennCorp Financial, Inc.; Penn Life Ins. Co.; RCM Capital Management (a partnership); Satellite Conference Network, Inc.; Transport Life Ins. Co.; Triad Life Ins. Corp.; Voyager Group, Inc. **Specialty Retailing:** Current, Inc.; Dunham's Athleisure Corp.; Figi's, Inc.; Fingerhut Companies, Inc.; Michigan Bulb Co.; The Musicland Group, Inc.

Primerica is a service mark and a trademark of Primerica Corporation.

Source: Photograph copyright © 1978 David Sutton. Reprinted with permission of David Sutton, Wayne Enterprises, and Primerica Corporation. Agency: Marquardt & Roche, Incorporated.

dispelling consumer stereotypes of catfish as an unappealing scavenger fish. To this end, the advertisements explain how Mississippi Prime are farm raised, cultivated in clean ponds, and fed "a gourmet diet of natural grains and proteins."[4]

Differentiating the Product

A frequent objective of the firm's promotional effort is *product differentiation*. Homogeneous demand means consumers regard the firm's output as virtually identical to its competitors' products. In these cases, the individual firm has almost no control over marketing variables such as price. A differentiated demand schedule, in contrast, permits more flexibility in marketing strategy, such as price changes. For example, the high quality and distinctiveness of Cross pens are widely advertised, which has enabled Cross's marketers to ask for and obtain a price 100 times those of some disposable pens.

Figure 16.4
Advertisement Designed to Stimulate Consumer Demand

Source: Courtesy of The Catfish Institute.

Accentuating the Product's Value

Promotion can point out greater ownership utility to buyers, thereby accentuating the product's value. The good or service might then be able to command a higher price in the marketplace. For example, status-oriented advertising may allow a retail clothing store such as Banana Republic to command higher prices for its products than other retail competitors. The demand curve—a schedule of the amounts of a product or service that a firm expects consumers to purchase at different prices—facing a prestige store may be less responsive to price differences than that of a competitor without a quality reputation.

Stabilizing Sales

For the typical firm, sales are not uniform throughout the year. Sales fluctuations may be caused by cyclical, seasonal, or irregular demand. Stabilizing these variations is often an objective of the firm's promotional strategy. Coffee sales, for example, follow a seasonal pattern, with purchases and consumption increasing during the winter months. To stimulate summer sales of the Sanka brand of decaffeinated coffee, General Foods has created advertisements that include a recipe for making instant iced coffee, promoting it as a refreshing, caffeine-free summer beverage.

The Promotional Mix

Like the marketing mix, the **promotional mix** involves the proper blending of numerous variables to satisfy the needs of the firm's target market and achieve organizational objectives. While the marketing mix is comprised of product, pricing, promotion, and distribution elements, the promotional mix is a subset of the overall marketing mix. With the promotional mix, the marketing manager attempts to achieve the optimal blending of various promotional elements to attain promotional objectives. The components of the promotional mix are personal selling and nonpersonal selling, including advertising, sales promotion, and public relations.

Personal selling, advertising, and sales promotion are the most significant elements, because they usually account for the bulk of a firm's promotional expenditures. However, all factors contribute to efficient marketing communications. A detailed discussion of each of these elements is presented in the following chapters. Here we will simply set the framework for the discussion of promotion.

promotional mix
Blending of personal selling and nonpersonal selling (including advertising, sales promotion, and public relations) by marketers in an attempt to achieve promotional objectives.

Personal Selling

Personal selling may be defined as a seller's promotional presentation conducted on a person-to-person basis with the buyer. It is a direct, face-to-face form of promotion.

Selling was the original form of promotion. Today an estimated 6 million people in the United States are employed in personal selling.

personal selling
Interpersonal influence process involving a seller's promotional presentation conducted on a person-to-person basis with the prospective buyer.

Nonpersonal Selling

Nonpersonal selling includes advertising, sales promotion, and public relations. Advertising and sales promotion are usually regarded as the most important forms of nonpersonal selling.

Advertising may be defined as paid, nonpersonal communications through various media by business firms, nonprofit organizations, and individuals that are in some way identified in the advertising message and hope to inform or persuade members of a particular audience.[5] Advertising involves the mass media, such as newspapers, television, radio, magazines, and billboards. Businesses have come to realize the tremendous potential of this form of promotion, and in recent decades advertising has become increasingly important in marketing. Mass consumption and geographically dispersed markets make advertising particularly appropriate for products that rely on sending the same promotional message to large audiences.

advertising
Paid, nonpersonal communication through various media by business firms, nonprofit organizations, and individuals that are in some way identified in the advertising message and hope to inform or persuade members of a particular audience.

Figure 16.5
Advertising a Sales Promotion

Source: Courtesy of Artemide Inc./Guido Buratto, Vice President Marketing–Creative Director.

sales promotion
Marketing activities other than personal selling, advertising, and publicity that stimulate consumer purchasing and dealer effectiveness; includes displays, trade shows and expositions, demonstrations, and various nonrecurrent selling efforts.

Sales promotion consists of marketing activities other than personal selling, advertising, and publicity that stimulate consumer purchasing and dealer effectiveness. These include displays, trade shows and expositions, product demonstrations, and various nonrecurrent selling efforts used on an irregular basis. Sales promotion is a short-term incentive and is usually combined with other forms of advertising to emphasize, assist, supplement, or otherwise support the objectives of the promotional program.

Marketers often use advertising to communicate sales promotions to consumers. Artemide, Inc., the New York–based table and desk lamp marketer, ran the ad shown in Figure 16.5 in *Metropolitan Home* magazine to announce a sales promotion for its famous Tizio lamp. Readers who found the lamp hidden in the intricate illustration were eligible for a $25 rebate on its purchase price. Such advertisements not only add excitement to the promotion; they also give marketers the opportunity to present product information. The ad for the Tizio promotion, for example, begins with a description of the lamp and its design origins.

public relations
Firm's communications and relationships with its various publics.

Public relations is a firm's communications and relationships with its various publics. These publics include customers, suppliers, stockholders, employees, the government, the general public, and the society in which the organi-

Table 16.2
Comparing Alternative
Promotional Techniques

Type of Promotion	Cost	Advantages	Disadvantages
Personal			
Personal selling	Expensive per contact	Permits flexible presentation and gains immediate response	Costs more than all other forms per contact; difficult to attract qualified salespeople
Nonpersonal			
Advertising	Relatively inexpensive per contact	Appropriate in reaching mass audiences; allows expressiveness and control over message	Considerable waste; difficult to demonstrate product; difficult to close sales; difficult to measure results
Sales promotion	Can be costly	Gains attention and has immediate effect	Easy for others to imitate
Public relations	Relatively inexpensive; publicity is free	Has high degree of believability	Not as easily controlled as other forms

zation operates. Public relations programs can be either formal or informal. The critical point is that every organization, whether or not it has a formally organized program, must be concerned about its public relations.

Publicity is an important part of an effective public relations effort. It can be defined as the nonpersonal stimulation of demand for a product, service, person, cause, or organization by placing significant news about it in a published medium or by obtaining favorable presentation of it through radio, television, or the stage that is not paid for by an identified sponsor. Compared to personal selling, advertising, and even sales promotion, expenditures for public relations are usually low in most firms. Since they don't pay for it, companies have less control over the publication by the press or electronic media of good or bad company news. For this reason, a consumer may find this type of news source more believable than if the information were disseminated directly by the company.

As Table 16.2 indicates, each type of promotion has both advantages and shortcomings. Although personal selling entails a relatively high per-contact cost, there is less wasted effort than in nonpersonal forms of promotion such as advertising. Personal selling often is more flexible than the other forms because the salesperson can tailor the sales message to meet the unique needs—or objections—of each potential customer.

On the other hand, advertising is an effective means of reaching mass audiences with the marketer's message. Sales promotion techniques are effective in gaining attention, and public relations efforts such as publicity frequently have

publicity
Stimulation of demand by disseminating commercially significant news or obtaining favorable media presentation not paid for by an identified sponsor.

Anheuser-Busch

Growth in the American beer industry is only in the one percent range. This is a disturbing trend for most breweries—but not for Anheuser-Busch, the nation's largest. Anheuser-Busch sold twice as much beer last year as it did a decade ago, stretching its market share to 40 percent—more than Stroh's and Miller, its two largest competitors, combined.

The beer marketing picture vastly differed back in 1975, when August Busch III became chairman of the company that his great-grandfather turned into an industry giant. Miller's hops were bringing that firm to the point where Miller marketers spoke of becoming number one in the industry. Busch, then 37, was not about to let that happen.

Part of Miller's success in the early 1970s came from its humorous promotional messages featuring retired sports personalities. Busch did Miller one better, implementing a strategy of "total marketing." Today Anheuser-Busch's marketing prowess is the envy of the beer industry. The firm doesn't just advertise—it targets markets with astonishing precision, aiming commercials at blacks, whites, Hispanics, blue-collar workers, white-collar workers, gray-collar workers, and residents of particular states, and creating different promotions for different seasons. The company also goes grass roots within its 210 designated market areas; it sponsors softball teams in small towns, promotes sporting events, sends its famous Clydesdales to parades—anything to spread the name and enhance its image.

Since most beer drinkers watch sports, August Busch decided that sports would be the foundation of his firm's advertising and promotional efforts. The company has exclusive advertising contracts with 23 of the 26 major league baseball teams, 18 of the 28 NFL teams, 300 college sports teams, and a dominant percentage of NBA, NHL, and U.S.

pro soccer teams. It sponsors the Bud Light Iron Man Triathlon, the Busch Clash (NASCAR) and boxing matches. It even has an exclusive advertising contract with the all-sports ESPN cable channel.

Another facet of total marketing is a consistent message. "This Bud's For You" has been a company slogan for nearly a decade (1979), and "Head for the Mountains" has hallmarked Busch beer for even longer (1978).

Sponsoring sports events and teams and creating catchy slogans help the firm's marketers ensure that customers will continue buying its products. But Anheuser-Busch also knows how to give its wholesalers the right push. It is a strong, aggressive channel captain, demanding brand loyalty and innovative promotions from its wholesalers. But it also ingratiates them, usually picking up

half the cost of some key local promotions, making top executives accessible, involving them in marketing strategy, and sponsoring courses to help them polish selling techniques. It also rewards wholesalers handsomely through perks such as extravagant conventions every three years.

Total marketing brought Anheuser-Busch back to supremacy in the beer industry, but unflagging attention to quality is another factor in its success formula. Most of its major competitors have given product quality short shrift at some point in the last decade, which has hurt their images—and sales totals. As Busch heads into the 1990s, its growth goal is clear: a 50 percent market share.

Source: Patricia Sellers, "How Busch Wins in a Doggy Market," *Fortune* (June 22, 1987), pp. 99–111. *Photo source:* Courtesy of Anheuser-Busch, Incorporated.

a high degree of believability compared to other promotional techniques. The task confronting the marketer is to determine the appropriate blend of each technique in marketing the firm's products and services.

Developing an Optimal Promotional Mix

The blending of advertising, personal selling, sales promotion, and public relations to achieve marketing objectives is the promotional mix. Since quantitative measures for determining the effectiveness of each mix component in a given market segment are not available, the choice of a proper mix of promotional elements is one of the most difficult tasks facing the marketing manager. Factors affecting the promotional mix are (1) the nature of the market, (2) the nature of the product, (3) the stage in the product life cycle, (4) price, and (5) funds available for promotion.

Nature of the Market

The marketer's target audience has a major impact on the type of promotion to be used. In cases in which there are a limited number of buyers, personal selling may prove highly effective. However, markets characterized by a large number of potential customers scattered over a sizable geographical area may make the cost of contact by personal salespeople prohibitive. In such instances, advertising may be used extensively. The type of customer also affects the promotional mix. A target market made up of industrial purchasers or retail and wholesale buyers is more likely to be served by firms that rely heavily on personal selling than is a target market consisting of ultimate consumers.

Nature of the Product

A second important factor in determining an effective promotional mix is the product itself. Highly standardized products with minimal servicing requirements are less likely to depend on personal selling than are custom products that are technically complex and/or require frequent servicing. Consumer goods are more likely to rely heavily on advertising than are industrial goods.

Promotional mixes vary within each product category. For example, installations typically involve heavy reliance on personal selling compared to the marketing of operating supplies. In contrast, the marketing mix for convenience goods is likely to involve more emphasis on manufacturer advertising and less on personal selling. On the other hand, personal selling plays an important role in the marketing of shopping goods, and both personal and nonpersonal selling are important in the marketing of specialty goods. A personal-selling emphasis is also likely to be more effective in the marketing of products involving trade-ins.

Stage in the Product Life Cycle

The promotional mix must be tailored to the product's stage in the product life cycle. In the introductory stage, heavy emphasis is placed on personal selling to inform the marketplace of the merits of the new product or service. Salespeo-

Figure 16.6
Creative Promotion on a Small Budget

Source: Courtesy of Pos-A-Traction Industries, Inc., J. R. Krech, Promotion Director.

ple contact marketing intermediaries to secure interest in and commitment to handling the offering. Trade shows and exhibitions are frequently used to inform and educate prospective dealers and ultimate consumers. Advertising at this stage is mostly informative, and sales promotion techniques, such as product samples and cents-off coupons, are designed to influence consumer attitudes and stimulate initial purchases.

As the product or service moves into the growth and maturity stages, advertising becomes relatively more important in persuading consumers to make purchases. Personal-selling efforts continue to be directed at marketing intermediaries in an attempt to expand distribution. As more competitors enter the marketplace, advertising begins to stress product differences to persuade consumers to purchase the firm's brand. Reminder advertisements begin to appear in the maturity and early decline stages.

Price

The price of the good or service is the fourth factor that affects the choice of a promotional mix. Advertising is the dominant promotional mix component for low-unit-value products due to the high per-contact costs in personal selling. The cost of an industrial sales call, for example, is estimated at almost $200. As a result, it has become unprofitable to promote lower-value products and services through personal selling. Advertising, in contrast, permits a low promotional expenditure per sales unit because it reaches mass audiences. For low-value consumer products, such as chewing gum, soft drinks, and snack foods, advertising is the most feasible means of promotion.

Table 16.3
Factors Influencing Choice of Promotional Mix

		Emphasis	
	Factor	**Personal Selling**	**Advertising**
Nature of the Market	Number of buyers	Limited number	Large number
	Geographic concentration	Concentrated	Dispersed
	Type of customer	Industrial purchaser	Ultimate consumer
Nature of the Product	Complexity	Custom-made, complex	Standardized
	Service requirements	Considerable	Minimal
	Type of good	Industrial	Consumer
	Use of trade-ins	Trade-ins common	Trade-ins uncommon
Stage in the Product Life Cycle		Introductory and early growth stages	Latter part of growth stages and maturity and early decline stages
Price		High unit value	Low unit value

Funds Available for Promotion

A real barrier to implementing any promotional strategy is the size of the promotional budget. A single 30-second television commercial on the most recent Super Bowl telecasts cost the advertiser $600,000! Although the message may be received by millions of viewers and the cost per contact is relatively low, such an expenditure exceeds the entire promotional budget of thousands of firms. For many new or small firms, the cost of mass advertising is prohibitive, and they are forced to seek less efficient but cheaper methods. Neighborhood retailers may not be able to advertise in metropolitan newspapers or on local radio and television stations. They may choose to concentrate their promotional budgets on a well-trained group of retail salespeople and devote a smaller amount of advertising dollars on a Yellow Pages listing in the telephone directory, periodic advertisements in a neighborhood weekly newspaper, store window signs, and in-store displays. Pos-A-Traction Industries, a small Compton, California–based manufacturer of high-performance tires, does not have the promotional budget with which to compete with Goodyear and Firestone. To reach its target audience, Pos-A-Traction relies on display posters, such as the one in Figure 16.6, at local car dealers and tire outlets that handle its product line.

Table 16.3 summarizes the factors that influence the determination of an appropriate promotional mix.

Promotional Strategy: Pull or Push

Essentially marketers may use two promotional alternatives: a pulling strategy and a pushing strategy.

A **pulling strategy** is a promotional effort by the seller to stimulate final-user demand, which then exerts pressure on the distribution channel. When

pulling strategy
Promotional effort by a seller to stimulate demand by final users, who will then exert pressure on the distribution channel to carry the good or service.

Figure 16.7

Use of a Pulling Strategy to
Stimulate Consumer Demand

WE SATURATE THE MARKET AS WELL
AS WE SATURATE LAWNS.

To keep Greensweep moving off the shelf, we keep commercials running on television.
And we back up our television advertising with magazine and newspaper ads, too. So not only is Greensweep easy to use,
it's easy to see. For more information, contact Tru Quigley at 1-800-537-3370. (In Ohio call 1-800-472-3220.)

Source: Courtesy of Greensweep Appliances

marketing intermediaries stock a large number of competing products and exhibit little interest in any one of them, a pulling strategy may be necessary for
motivating them to handle the product. In such instances, this strategy is implemented with the objective of building consumer demand so that consumers will
request the product when they go to retail stores.

The successful pulling strategy by lawn care products marketer Greensweep, illustrated in the advertisement in Figure 16.7, demonstrates the application of this approach. Here Greensweep marketers are warning retail channel
members that their extensive consumer advertising—including television, magazine, and newspaper promotions—will bring customers to their stores requesting Greensweep products. Personal selling by the manufacturer is limited
largely to contacting intermediaries, providing requested information about the
product, and taking orders. Since most retailers want to stimulate repeat purchases by satisfied customers, the promotional efforts of manufacturers, such
as Greensweep, that result in shopper requests for the product will usually succeed in getting the item on the retailers' shelves.

Advertising and sales promotion are the most commonly used elements of
promotion in a pulling strategy. Two sales promotion techniques—sponsoring
of special events and unusual sampling settings—are becoming popular with
food marketers as means of gaining consumer support. While many food marketers set up sampling displays inside stores, some are turning to out-of-store

Photo source: Courtesy of H&R Block, Incorporated.

During the recent tax seasons, H&R Block, the nation's largest tax preparation service, has increased its emphasis on pretransactional promotion to help alleviate taxpayer confusion resulting from passage of the Tax Reform Act of 1986. It launched its first national network advertising, in which company president Henry Block addressed taxpayer questions and concerns. Corporate affair representatives appeared on television and radio talk shows and gave newspaper and magazine interviews throughout the country. These public relations efforts helped build an image of the company's tax expertise in the public's mind.

promotions. New York Seltzer marketers, for example, have distributed samples of their beverage at dentist conventions, garlic festivals, and sailing races. Atlantis Dairy Products sponsored some 50 special events at which it used mobile sampling centers to promote its Bon Lait brand of *fromâge frais*—a yogurtlike blend of cheese and fruit popular in European markets. When Atlantis launched its new market entry in Southern California, many retailers were reluctant to stock the product due to their lack of familiarity with *fromâge frais*. But the consumer promotions worked. According to Atlantis' marketing manager, "Being able to show retailers crowds of people eating the product really helped to get shelf space."[6]

In contrast, a **pushing strategy** relies more heavily on personal selling. Here the objective is promoting the product to the members of the marketing channel rather than to the final user. This can be done through cooperative advertising allowances, trade discounts, personal selling efforts by the firm's sales force, and other dealer supports. Such a strategy is designed to gain marketing success for the firm's products by motivating representatives of wholesalers and/or retailers to spend extra time and effort promoting the products to customers.

While pulling and pushing strategies are presented here as alternative methods, it is unlikely that many companies depend entirely on either one. Most firms use a combination of the two methods. The primarily pulling strategy employed for Greensweep lawn care products illustrated in Figure 16.7 was ac-

pushing strategy
Promotional effort by a seller to members of the marketing channel to stimulate personal selling of the good or service.

companied by promotion aimed at marketing intermediaries and direct retailer contacts by the manufacturer's sales representatives.

Timing is another factor to consider in developing a promotional strategy. The relative importance of advertising and selling changes during the various phases of the purchase process. During the pretransactional period (prior to the actual sale), advertising usually is more important than personal selling. It is often argued that one of the primary advantages of a successful advertising program is that it assists the salesperson in approaching the prospect. Selling becomes more important than advertising during the transactional phase of the process. In most situations, personal selling is the actual mechanism for closing the sale. In the posttransactional stage, advertising regains primacy in the promotional effort. It affirms the customer's decision to buy a particular good or service and reminds him or her of the product's favorable qualities in an attempt to reduce any cognitive dissonance that might occur.

Budgeting for Promotional Strategy

Promotional budgets may differ not only in amount but in composition. Industrial firms generally invest a larger proportion of their budgets for personal selling than for advertising, while the reverse is usually true of most producers of consumer goods.

Evidence suggests that sales initially lag behind promotion for structural reasons—filling up retail shelves, low initial production, and lack of buyer knowledge. This produces a threshold effect whereby there may be few sales but substantial initial investment in promotion. A second phase might produce returns (sales) proportionate to a given promotional expenditure; this would be the most predictable range. Finally, the area of diminishing returns is reached when an increase in promotional spending fails to produce a corresponding increase in sales.

For example, an initial expenditure of $40,000 may result in the sale of 100,000 product units for a consumer goods manufacturer. An additional $10,000 expenditure may generate sales of 30,000 more units and another $10,000 sales of an additional 35,000 units. The cumulative effect of the expenditures and repeat sales will have resulted in increasing returns from the promotional outlays. However, as the advertising budget moves from $60,000 to $70,000, the marginal productivity of the additional expenditure may fall to 28,000 units. At some later point, the return may actually become zero or negative as competition intensifies, markets become saturated, and less effective advertising media are employed.

To test the thesis that a saturation point for promotion exists, Anheuser-Busch marketers once quadrupled their advertising budget in several markets. After three months, the company's distributors demanded an advertising cut. Many claimed that beer consumers were coming into their stores demanding, "Give me anything *but* Bud."

The ideal method of allocating a promotional budget is to increase the budget until the cost of each additional increment equals the additional incremental revenue received. In other words, the most effective allocation procedure is to increase promotional expenditures until each dollar of promotional expense is matched by an additional dollar of profit. This procedure—referred

Method	Description	Example
Percentage of sales	Promotional budget is set as a specified percentage of either past or forecasted sales.	"Last year we spent $10,500 on promotion and had sales of $420,000. Next year we expect sales to grow to $480,000, and we are allocating $12,000 for promotion."
Fixed sum per unit	Promotional budget is set on the basis of a predetermined dollar amount of each unit sold or produced.	"Our forecast calls for sales of 14,000 units, and we allocate promotion at the rate of $65 per unit."
Meeting competition	Promotional budget is set to match competitors' promotional outlays on either an absolute or a relative basis.	"Promotional outlays average 4 percent of sales in our industry."
Task-objective	Once marketers determine their specific promotional objectives, the amount (and type) of promotional spending needed to achieve them is determined.	"By the end of next year, we want 75 percent of the area high school students to be aware of our new, highly automated fast-food prototype outlet. How many promotional dollars will it take, and how should they be spent?"

Table 16.4
Promotional Budget Determination

to in Chapter 10 as *marginal analysis*—results in maximization of the input's productivity. The difficulty arises in identifying the optimal point, which requires a precise balancing of marginal expenses for promotion and the resulting marginal receipts.

Traditional methods for creating a promotional budget are percentage of sales, fixed sum per unit, meeting the competition, and task-objective. Each method is briefly examined in Table 16.4.

The **percentage-of-sales method** is perhaps the most common way of establishing promotional budgets. The percentage can be based on either past (such as the previous year) or forecasted (estimated current year) sales. While this plan is appealing in its simplicity, it is not an effective way to achieve basic promotional objectives. Arbitrary percentage allocations, whether applied to historical or future sales figures, fail to provide the required flexibility. Further, such reasoning is circular, since the promotional allocation depends on sales rather than vice versa, as it should. Consider, for example, the implications of a decline in sales, an occurrence that would force the marketer to further curtail the firm's promotional outlays.

The **fixed-sum-per-unit method** differs from percentage of sales in only one respect: It applies a predetermined allocation to each sales or production unit. This can also be based on either historical or forecasted figures. Producers of high-value, consumer durable goods, such as automobiles, often use this budgeting method.

Another traditional approach is simply to match competitors' outlays—in other words, meet competition—on either an absolute or a relative basis. However, this kind of approach usually leads to a status quo situation with each company retaining its percentage of total sales. Meeting the competition's

percentage-of-sales method
Promotional budget allocation method in which the funds allocated for promotion during a given time period are based on a specified percentage of either past or forecasted sales.

fixed-sum-per-unit method
Promotional budget allocation method in which promotional expenditures are a predetermined dollar amount for each sales or production unit.

task-objective method
Promotional budget allocation method in which a firm defines its goals and then determines the amount of promotional spending needed for achieving them.

budget does not necessarily pertain to promotional objectives and, therefore, seems inappropriate for most contemporary marketing programs.

The **task-objective method** of developing a promotional budget is based on a sound evaluation of the firm's promotional objectives and, as a result, is better attuned to modern marketing practices. It involves two sequential steps:

1. The firm's marketers must *define the realistic communication goals* they want the promotional mix to achieve; for example, a 25 percent increase in brand awareness or a 10 percent rise in the number of consumers who realize that the product has certain specific, differentiating features. The key is to specify in quantitative terms the objectives to be attained. These in turn become an integral part of the promotional plan.

2. Marketers must *determine the amount (as well as type) of promotional activity required for achieving each objective that has been set.* Combined, these units become the firm's promotional budget.

A crucial assumption underlies the task-objective approach—that the productivity of each promotional dollar is measurable. That is why the objectives must be carefully chosen, quantified, and accomplished through promotional efforts. Generally an objective such as "We wish to achieve a 5 percent increase in sales" is a marketing objective, because a sale is a culmination of the effects of *all* elements of the marketing mix. Therefore, an appropriate promotional objective might be "to make 30 percent of the target market aware of the one-hour optical service concept."

While promotional budgeting is always difficult, recent research studies and more frequent use of computer-based models have made it less of a problem than it used to be.

Measuring the Effectiveness of Promotion

It is widely recognized that part of a firm's promotional effort is ineffective. John Wanamaker, a successful nineteenth-century retailer, observed: "I know half the money I spend on advertising is wasted, but I can never find out which half."

Measuring the effectiveness of promotional expenditures has become an extremely important research issue, particularly among advertisers. Studies aimed at this measurement dilemma face several major obstacles, one of them being the difficulty of isolating the effect of the promotional variable.

Most marketers would prefer to use a *direct-sales-results test* to measure the effectiveness of promotion. Such an approach would reveal the specific impact on sales revenues for each dollar of promotional spending. This type of technique has never been possible, however, due to the marketer's inability to control for other variables operating in the marketplace. A firm may experience $20 million in additional sales following a new, $1.5 million advertising campaign, but the success may have resulted from price increases of competing products rather than from the advertising outlays.

Because of the difficulty of isolating the effects of promotion from the other marketing elements and outside environmental variables, many marketers have simply abandoned all attempts at measurement. Others, however, turn to indirect evaluation. These researchers concentrate on the factors that are quantifiable, such as *recall* (how much is remembered about specific products or advertisements) and *readership* (size and composition of the audience). The basic

FOCUS ON ETHICS

"Your Free Prize Is Waiting for You to Claim . . . "

The above headline is increasingly appearing in the mailboxes of America. Marketers of resort home-sites, condominiums, and time-sharing operations have discovered that the timeless lure of "something for nothing" compels the general public to visit these operations. While most consumers recognize that fortunes in prizes won't follow receipt of computer-generated cards and letters, enough people respond to the prospect of receiving a "no-strings-attached" automobile, fur coat, or savings bond to make giveaways one of the most widely used promotional techniques in resort land and time-share condo marketing.

What does the consumer receive in exchange for a visit to the sales site and attendance at a 30-minute-to-1-hour, frequently high-pressure sales presentation? One Texas couple visited a time-share condominium being marketed by Resort Vacations International in response to a free portable television offer. After touring the facility and listening to the sales presentation, they paid a $79.95 "handling, processing, and insurance" fee to qualify for their prize, which would then be mailed to their home. The set they received was hardly what they had envisioned: a 5-inch portable model that runs on 10 size D batteries (not included) that need to be replaced after every three hours of continuous viewing.

The same company offered a Dallas woman the chance to receive either a new Mercedes-Benz or an all-terrain vehicle as a prize for touring an East Texas resort. After making a few calls to determine that any new Mercedes would retail for at least $25,000 and that ATVs sell for $1,000 and up, she decided to accept the offer. Once her tour of the facility was completed, she learned that she did not win the Mercedes but would receive the ATV if she paid the handling fee. Then she saw her prize: The so-called "all-terrain vehicle" turned out to be a four-wheeled lawn chair that can be converted to a cart.

Complaints about these seemingly unethical practices prompted several consumers to inquire about their legality. As a result, the Texas attorney general's office began an investigation of Resort Vacations International for possible deceptive trade practices.

The firm defends its practices. Says Charlotte Jones, customer relations manager, the so-called all-terrain vehicle "is a vehicle. It's a four-wheeled cart you can take anywhere—to the beach, to the pool. It may not be motorized but [the letter] didn't say it was motorized." Although she admitted that the firm did not give away its grand prize offer of a new car during the two previous years, she explained that the person who had received the winning letter each year never claimed the prize.

Source: Jones quotation from Carmella M. Padilla, "It's a . . . a . . . a . . . All-Terrain Vehicle, Yeah, That's It, That's the Ticket," *The Wall Street Journal* (July 17, 1987), p. 17.

problem is the difficulty of relating these variables to sales—for example, does extensive ad readership lead to increased sales?

Frequently used assessment methods for determining promotional effectiveness include sales inquiries and research studies aimed at determining changes in consumer attitudes toward the product and/or improvement in public knowledge and awareness. General Foods marketers recently developed a unique approach to consumer sales inquiries for its Ronzoni pasta products by offering free membership in its newly formed Sono Buoni Club. Club members were promised coupons, a newsletter, cook-offs, and other premiums. The benefits for General Foods were an extensive database indicating who uses Ronzoni pasta products and the ability to encourage brand loyalty through coupons and continued contacts.[7]

The technological innovation that promises to revolutionize evaluations of consumer promotions is the use of scanner sales data. One of the features of Information Resources, Inc.'s recently unveiled PromotionScan service is to provide clients with information on the best promotional mix for a given product for various retail outlets. The data collected from consumer purchases of UPC-coded products allow marketers to determine the effectiveness of newspaper feature ads, in-store displays, and coupon redemptions by correlating their use with consumer sales on a market-by-market basis. Early research studies of what one marketer calls "the electron microscope of marketing" have shed light on the different ways in which consumers respond to promotions and the impact of their responses on a promotion's profitability. Consumers can be categorized by shopping behavior as those who:

☐ Are not promotion sensitive

☐ Buy only sale brands

☐ Are loyal to the sale brand and stockpile products

☐ Buy a sale brand they would not normally buy

Once marketers have determined the type of consumer who is attracted to a promotion, they can more closely evaluate the effectiveness of specific promotions.[8]

The Value of Promotion

Promotion has often been the target of criticism. Common complaints are:

☐ "Promotion contributes nothing to society."

☐ "Most advertisements and sales presentations insult my intelligence."

☐ "Promotion 'forces' consumers to buy products they cannot afford and do not need."

☐ "Advertising and selling are economic wastes."

☐ "Salespersons and advertisers are usually unethical."

Consumers, public officials, and marketers agree that too many of these complaints are true.[9] Some salespeople do use unethical sales tactics. Some product advertising indeed is directed at consumer groups that can least afford the particular item. Many television commercials do contribute to the growing problem of cultural pollution.

While promotion can certainly be criticized on many counts, it is important to remember that promotion plays a crucial role in modern society. This point is best understood by examining the importance of promotion at the social, business, and economic levels.

Social Importance

Criticisms such as "most promotional messages are tasteless" and "promotion contributes nothing to society" sometimes ignore the fact that no commonly accepted set of standards or priorities exist within our social framework. We live in a varied economy characterized by consumer segments with differing needs, wants, and aspirations. What is tasteless to one group may be quite appealing to another. Promotional strategy faces an "averaging" problem that escapes many of its critics. The one generally accepted standard in a market society is freedom of choice for the consumer. Consumer buying decisions eventually determine what is acceptable practice in the marketplace.

Figure 16.8
Promotion Addressing a Social Concern

Source: Courtesy of Center for Attitudinal Healing.

Promotion has become an important factor in the campaigns to achieve socially oriented objectives, such as stopping smoking, family planning, physical fitness, and elimination of drug abuse. Highly publicized incidents of public ostracism of schoolchildren who carried the AIDS virus as a result of AIDS-infected mothers or blood transfusions prompted the California-based Center for Attitudinal Healing to design the poster shown in Figure 16.8. The promotion, combined with news releases emphasizing the fact that the virus cannot be transmitted through casual contact, is designed to combat the ignorance and psychological damage that result from this misinformation.

Promotion performs an informative and educational task that makes it crucial to the functioning of modern society. As with everything else in life, what is important is *how* promotion is used rather than whether it is used.

Business Importance

Promotional strategy has become increasingly important to both large and small business enterprises. The long-term increase in funds spent on promotion is well documented and certainly attests to management's faith in the ability of promotional efforts to produce attitude changes, brand loyalty, and additional sales. It is difficult to conceive of an enterprise that would not attempt to promote its product or service in some manner. Most modern institutions simply cannot survive in the long run without promotion. Business must communicate with its publics.

Nonbusiness enterprises also recognize the importance of promotional efforts. The U.S. government spends about $300 million a year on advertising and ranks twenty-sixth among all U.S. advertisers. The Canadian government is the leading advertiser in Canada, promoting many concepts and programs. Religious organizations have acknowledged the importance of promoting what they do. Even labor organizations have used promotional channels to make their viewpoints known to the public at large.

Economic Importance

Promotion has assumed a degree of economic importance if for no other reason than it provides employment for thousands of people. More important, however, effective promotion has allowed society to derive benefits not otherwise available. For example, the criticism that promotion costs too much isolates an individual expense item and fails to consider the possible beneficial effect of promotion on other categories of expenditures.

Promotional strategies that increase the number of units sold permit economies in the production process, thereby lowering the production costs associated with each unit of output. Lower consumer prices in turn make these products available to more people. Similarly, researchers have found that advertising subsidizes the informational content of newspapers and the broadcast media.[10] In short, promotion pays for many of the enjoyable entertainment and educational aspects of contemporary life as well as lowering product costs.

Summary of Chapter Objectives

1. Explain the relationship of promotional strategy to the process of communication. Communication is the transmission of a message from a sender (or source) to a receiver (or recipient). Marketing communications are those messages that deal with buyer-seller relationships. Promotional strategy focuses on the appropriate blending of the promotional mix elements—personal and nonpersonal selling—to inform, persuade, and remind present and potential customers and to achieve overall objectives. *Marketing communications* is a broader term than *promotional strategy*, because it includes other forms of communication. A planned promotional strategy, however, is certainly the most important part of marketing communications.

2. List the objectives of promotion. The five basic objectives of promotion are to provide information, stimulate demand, differentiate the product, accentuate the product's value, and stabilize sales.

3. Explain the concept of the promotional mix and its relationship to the marketing mix. The promotional mix, like the marketing mix, involves the proper blending of numerous variables in order to satisfy the needs of the firm's target market and achieve organizational objectives. While the marketing mix is comprised of product, pricing, promotion, and distribution elements, the promotional mix is a subset of the overall marketing mix. In the case of the promotional mix, the marketing manager attempts to achieve the optimal blending of personal and nonpersonal selling to attain promotional objectives.

4. Identify the primary determinants of a promotional mix. Developing an effective promotional mix is complex. The elements of promotion are related to the type and value of the product or service being promoted, the nature of the market, the stage of the product life cycle, and the funds available for promotion as well as to the timing of the promotional effort. Personal selling is used primarily for industrial goods and services, for higher-value items, and during the transactional phase of the purchase decision process. Advertising, in contrast, is used mainly for consumer goods and services, for lower-value items, during the later stages of the product life cycle, and during the pretransactional and posttransactional phases.

5. Contrast the two major alternative promotional strategies. A pushing strategy relies heavily on personal selling and attempts to promote the product to the members of the marketing channel rather than to the final user. A pulling strategy concentrates on stimulating final-user demand, primarily in the mass media through advertising and sales promotion.

6. Compare the primary methods of developing a promotional budget. The percentage-of-sales method bases the promotional budget on a percentage of either past or forecasted sales. The fixed-sum-per-unit method uses a predetermined allocation for each sales or production unit; this can be done on either a historical or forecasted basis. The approach of meeting competitors' promotional expenses can be used on either an absolute or percentage basis. The task-objective approach first defines realistic goals for the promotional effort and then determines the amount and type of promotional activity required for achieving each objective.

7. Defend promotion against common public criticisms. Criticisms of promotion range from lack of social contribution to unethical promotional practices. Marketers acknowledge that many of the criticisms are justified, but they also point out the considerable contributions promotion makes via its business, economic, and social roles.

Key Terms

promotion
marketing communications
AIDA concept
promotional mix
personal selling
advertising
sales promotion

public relations
publicity
pulling strategy
pushing strategy
percentage-of-sales method
fixed-sum-per-unit method
task-objective method

Review Questions

1. Relate the steps in the communications process to promotional strategy.

2. Explain the concept of the promotional mix and its relationship to the marketing mix.

3. Identify the major determinants of a promotional mix, and describe how they affect the selection of an appropriate blending of promotional techniques.

4. Compare the five basic objectives of promotion. Cite specific examples.

5. Explain the concept and causes of noise in marketing communications.

6. Under what circumstances should a pushing strategy be used in promotion? When would a pulling strategy be effective?

7. Relate the AIDA concept to the marketing communications process.

8. Identify and briefly explain the alternative methods of developing a promotional budget.

9. How should a firm attempt to measure the effectiveness of its promotional efforts?

10. Identify the major public criticisms of promotion. Prepare a defense for each criticism.

Discussion Questions

1. "Perhaps the most critical promotional question facing the marketing manager concerns when to use each component of promotion." Comment on this statement. Relate your response to the good's classification, product value, marketing channels, price, and timing of the promotional effort.

2. What mix of promotional variables would you use for each of the following?
- **a.** Champion spark plugs
- **b.** Weedeater lawn edgers
- **c.** Management consulting service
- **d.** Industrial drilling equipment
- **e.** Women's sportswear
- **f.** Customized business forms

3. Develop a hypothetical promotion budget for the following firms. Ignore dollar amounts by using percentage allocations for the various promotional variables (such as 30 percent for personal selling, 60 percent for advertising, and 10 percent for public relations).
- **a.** National Car Rental
- **b.** Ramada Inn
- **c.** Manufacturer of industrial chemicals
- **d.** Allstate Insurance Company

4. Should doctors, dentists, and lawyers be prohibited from promoting their services through such media as direct mail and newspaper advertisements? How do these professionals currently promote their services?

5. When paperback book sales suffered a downturn, several of the major publishers adopted new promotional strategies. One firm began using 30-cents-off coupons to promote its romance series. Another company, on the other hand, established a returns policy that rewarded dealers with high sales. The new policy also contained penalties to discourage low volume by retail book outlets. Relate these promotional strategies to the material discussed in the chapter.

Apple Computer, Inc.

"I've always believed that marketing must begin with a great product. So now, wouldn't you like to see one? Ladies and gentlemen, inside this small, handsome case rests one of the great visions of our company — the Apple IIc."

With those words, John Sculley, president and chief executive officer of Apple Computer, Inc., introduced the company's newest personal computer to 4,000 dealers, industry analysts, and members of the press during a product roll-out extravaganza in San Francisco back in 1984. The big, splashy event, complete with rock music and laser lights, was Apple's way of generating excitement for its new product. "We think we can put on great events," says Del Yocam, executive vice-president, "and so we like the idea of capturing individuals' entire attention — their focus whether it's for a day or a period of time. It helps them concentrate on Apple, whether it's the Macintosh group or the Apple II group, it is Apple. They feel a part of the family."

Event marketing — expensive, unconventional promotions in advertising, sales promotion, and personal selling — and innovative product design have helped Apple stay afloat in the high-risk personal computer market. Apple co-founders Steven Jobs and Steven Wozniak, who designed the first Apple personal computer in 1976, are credited with developing this multibillion dollar market. Apple sales grew rapidly during the late 1970s and early 1980s. But by 1983, the company was in trouble, losing market share to IBM, who entered the personal computer market in 1981. Two years later, IBM dominated the market, driving out many large and small competitors and causing others to reposition their products as IBM-compatibles.

Apple intended to survive the shakedown. In 1983, John Sculley was recruited from PepsiCo to bring professional management to Apple, consistency to its product line, and order to its marketing efforts. Under Sculley's direction, Apple changed its entire product line in 100 days, increased its advertising budget of $15 million in 1983 to $100 million in 1984, and embarked on an attention-getting promotional campaign. Sculley says, "We couldn't have taken that big risk of changing our products and gone with technology that was radically different from where IBM and the rest of the industry were headed unless we had the boldness and voice of big events."

Sculley's promotional plan of staging big events was based on an assessment of Apple's products and the industry. In the early 1980s, the personal computer industry was in its infancy. The products were expensive, in the introductory stage of the product life cycle, and embodied high technology that most people did not understand. Sculley believed that advertising for personal computers was ineffective because it was filled with high-tech jargon that baffled almost everyone other than computer experts. He planned to increase Apple sales by using big events that would differentiate Apple from other computer companies and communicate a single message to consumers and retailers: Apple was a winning company with vision and bold products.

Event marketing for the Apple IIc included consumer advertising that would bring customers into retail stores and the dramatic sales event for dealers that would help stimulate product interest among channel members. Dealers invited to Apple's product roll-out received intensive product training and a large dose of Apple hype to get them excited about selling the product. In promoting the Apple IIc to consumers, Apple marketers faced the considerable problem of how to communicate the small, compact computer's tremendous power, which was impossible to explain simply in a 30-second commercial. To show the computer's

17

Advertising, Sales Promotion, and Public Relations

Chapter Objectives

1. To explain the current status and historical development of advertising, sales promotion, and public relations.

2. To identify the major types of advertising.

3. To list and discuss the major advertising media.

4. To explain how advertising effectiveness is determined.

5. To outline the organization of the advertising function.

6. To describe the process of creating an advertisement.

7. To identify the principal methods of sales promotion.

8. To explain the role of public relations and publicity in an organization's promotional strategy.

A lthough the product life cycle concept, introduced in Chapter 8, cannot stipulate the precise number of years that will pass before a good or service enters the inevitable decline stage, most readers would agree that the days of a product first introduced in 1853 surely would be numbered. But don't try to tell that to the marketing people at Levi Strauss & Company.

Since Bavarian immigrant Levi Strauss fashioned the first pair of trousers from tent canvas back in 1853 (he called them by their lot number, 501; the California gold miners who bought them called them "Levi's pants" or just "Levi's"), they have joined such products as Coca-Cola and cowboy movies as distinctly American. Levi's jeans are defined in Webster's, enshrined in the Louvre, and displayed in the Americana collection at the Smithsonian Institution.

Product improvements have been made periodically over the past century, beginning with a fabric change to a tough, French cotton that became known as *denim.* Indigo blue dye and copper rivets were added in 1873. Gradually, Levi 501 jeans became an integral component of everyday work attire. Then, in the 1950s, James Dean and Marlon Brando made them a symbol of nonconformity in *Rebel Without a Cause* and *The Wild One.* This image carried over into the rebellious 1960s and early 1970s.

In the 1980s, designer jeans erupted in the marketplace. Levi Strauss & Co. marketers faced a key decision: Move to compete more directly with fashion jeans, or emphasize the marketing of basic jeans in keeping with the company motto, "Quality never goes out of style." Industry sales data revealing a 5 percent decline in sales of all jeans since the peak year of 1981 helped convince Levi Strauss & Co. marketers to return to basics—but in the

most creative way possible. Thus was born the Levi's 501 Blues promotional campaign.

And what a campaign! Since its initial launch in 1984, over $100 million has been spent to deliver the key message, "Levi's 501 jeans give you a uniquely personal fit." The award-winning ads use lively, original music to show real-life urban street scenes of people just being themselves. The music ranges from blues to bluegrass and often features well-known artists such as Jerry Garcia of the Grateful Dead, Robert Cray, Jesse Colin Young, and Leon Redbone. Prospective musicians get a letter with three stipulations: Mention Levi's 501 jeans, "shrink-to-fit," and "button-fly," all key characteristics of the product. Otherwise, Steve Neely, executive producer of the firm's advertising agency, Foote, Cone & Belding, simply urges them to "have fun and do something most clients wouldn't buy. . . . But no jingles. I want to hang up the phone when I hear that word."[1]

The messages are aimed at a target audience consisting of men, women, and children age 12 to 24. To reach them, advertising is concentrated on prime-time network television, MTV, network radio, and magazines. In addition, publicity releases on the product's success are generating news coverage and newspaper and magazine articles; the Levi's Campus Public Relations Challenge produced a national competition among 25 universities; and point-of-sale materials in the form of posters, buttons, banners, and dressing room and pocket-sized fit guides augment the Levi's 501 jeans message.

But the key to Levi's marketing success has been the advertising. As one business writer put it,

What's different about this advertising is that it's so natural. It's America—people with style and humor, and not the canned, cutesy images we've grown used to. In its own effortless way, it's patriotism.

And that's a strong way to sell Levi's—after all, they're natural America, too.[2]

Today the brand is firmly entrenched as the best-selling jeans in the world. In some countries, Levi's 501 jeans are a treasured black market commodity, sometimes selling for twice the American price. Even more amazing has been the growth in sales of the world's original jeans:

Since the Levi's 501 Blues campaign began in 1984, sales have more than doubled.

Photo source: Courtesy of Levi's 501 Blues, Levi Strauss & Company, San Francisco, CA.

Chapter Overview

As Chapter 16 explained, promotion consists of both personal and nonpersonal elements. This chapter examines the nonpersonal elements of promotion: advertising, sales promotion, and public relations. These components play critical roles in the promotional mixes of thousands of organizations.

For many organizations, including Levi Strauss & Company, advertising represents the most important type of nonpersonal promotion. This chapter examines advertising objectives, the importance of planning for advertising, and the different types of advertisements and media choices. It discusses both retail advertising and manufacturer (national) advertising and examines alternative methods of assessing an advertisement's effectiveness. Finally, the chapter discusses sales promotion and public relations, including publicity.

Advertising

If you sought to be the next member of the U.S. Senate, you would have to communicate with every possible voter in your state. If you developed new computer software and went into business to market it, your chances of success would be slim without informing and persuading students, businesspeople, and other potential customers of the usefulness of your offering. In these situations you would discover, as have countless others, the need to use advertising to communicate to buyers. As defined in Chapter 16, **advertising** is paid, nonpersonal communication through various media and by business firms, nonprofit organizations, and individuals who are in some way identified in the advertising message and hope to inform or persuade members of a particular audience.

advertising
Paid, nonpersonal communication through various media by business firms, nonprofit organizations, and individuals who are identified in the advertising message and hope to inform or persuade members of a particular audience.

Today's widespread markets make advertising an important part of business. Since the end of World War II, advertising and related expenditures have risen faster than the gross national product and most other economic indicators. Furthermore, about 200,000 workers are employed in advertising.

The nation's leading advertisers—Procter & Gamble, Philip Morris, and Sears—spend more than $1 billion a year on advertising. The total annual expenditure for advertising in the United States exceeds $100 billion, or approximately $420 for every man, woman, and child.

Advertising expenditures vary among industries and companies. Cosmetic companies often are cited as examples of firms that spend a high percentage of their funds on advertising and promotion. Chicago-based Pansophic Systems, Inc., studied 5,500 firms and calculated their average advertising expenditures as a percentage of sales. Estimates for selected industries are given in Figure 17.1. As shown in the figure, wide differences exist among industries.

Figure 17.1

Estimated Average Advertising Expenditures as Percentage of Sales in 10 Industries

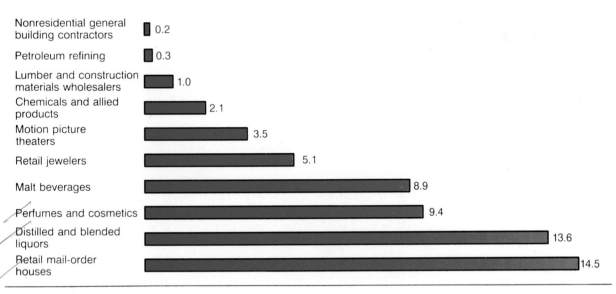

Industry	Percentage
Nonresidential general building contractors	0.2
Petroleum refining	0.3
Lumber and construction materials wholesalers	1.0
Chemicals and allied products	2.1
Motion picture theaters	3.5
Retail jewelers	5.1
Malt beverages	8.9
Perfumes and cosmetics	9.4
Distilled and blended liquors	13.6
Retail mail-order houses	14.5

Source: Pansophic Systems, Inc.

Advertising spending can range from .2 percent in an industry such as nonresidential general building contracting to more than 14 percent of sales in the retail mail-order house industry.

Evolution of Advertising

It is likely that some form of advertising has existed since the development of the exchange process. Most early advertising was vocal. Criers and hawkers sold various products, made public announcements, and chanted advertising slogans such as this:

One-a-penny, two-a-penny, hot-cross buns
One-a-penny, two for tuppence, hot-cross buns.

Criers were common in colonial America. The cry "Rags! Any rags? Any wool rags?" filled the streets of Philadelphia in the 1700s. Signs were also used in early advertising. Most used symbolism in their identification of products or services. In Rome, a goat signified a dairy, a mule driving a mill implied a bakery, and a boy being whipped suggested a school.

Later the development of the printing press greatly expanded advertising's capabilities. A 1710 advertisement in the *Spectator* billed one dentifrice as "The Incomparable Powder for cleaning Teeth, which has given great satisfaction to most of the Nobility and Gentry in England." Colonial newspapers such as Benjamin Franklin's *Gazette* also featured advertising—in fact, many newspapers carried it on their front pages. Most of these advertisements would be called "classified ads" today. A few national advertisers, such as Lorillard, a producer of tobacco products, also began to use newspaper advertising in the late 1700s.

Figure 17.2

Advertising Products of
Questionable Value in the
Nineteenth Century

Volney Palmer organized the first advertising agency in the United States
in 1841. George P. Rowell was another advertising pioneer. Originally advertising agencies simply sold ad space; services such as advertising research, copywriting, and planning came later. In the early 1900s, Claude C. Hopkins used a
large-scale consumer survey on home-baked beans before launching a campaign for Van Camp's Pork and Beans. Hopkins claimed that home-baked
beans were difficult to digest and suggested that consumers try Van Camp's.
He advocated the use of "reason-why copy" to persuade people to buy the
product.

Some early advertising promoted products of questionable value, such as
patent medicines. An example is the advertisement in Figure 17.2 promoting
Pratt's Healing Ointment "for man and beast." As a result, a reform movement
in advertising developed during the early 1900s, and some newspapers began
to screen their advertisements. *Saturday Evening Post* publisher Cyrus Curtis
began rejecting certain types of advertising, such as medical copy that claimed
cures and advertisements for alcoholic beverages. In 1911, the forerunner of
the American Advertising Federation drew up a code of improved advertising.

One identifying feature of advertising in the twentieth century is its concern
for researching its target markets. Originally advertising research dealt primarily
with media selection and the product. Then advertisers became increasingly
concerned with determining the appropriate *demographics*—characteristics
such as the ages, sex, and income levels of potential buyers. Understanding
consumer behavior is now an important aspect of advertising strategy. Behavioral influences in purchase decisions, often called *psychographics,* can be
useful in describing potential markets for advertising appeals. As discussed in

Chapter 7, these influences include factors such as life-style and personal attitudes. Increased information about consumer psychographics has led to improved advertising decisions.

The emergence of the marketing concept, with its emphasis on a companywide consumer orientation, expanded the role of advertising as marketing communications assumed greater importance in business. Today the average American is exposed to 2,000 advertising images a day.[3] Advertising provides an efficient, inexpensive, and fast method of reaching the much-sought-after consumer. It currently rivals sales promotion and personal selling in extent of use. Advertising has become a key ingredient in the effective implementation of the marketing concept.

Advertising Objectives

Traditionally advertising objectives were stated in terms of direct sales goals. A more realistic approach, however, is to view advertising as having communications objectives that seek to inform, persuade, and remind potential customers of the product. Advertising attempts to condition the consumer to adopt a favorable viewpoint toward the promotional message. The goal is to improve the likelihood that the customer will buy a particular product or service. In this sense, advertising illustrates the close relationship between marketing communications and promotional strategy.

Recent findings have confirmed the ability of effective advertising to enhance consumer perceptions of quality in a good or service. The results of these quality perceptions are stronger customer loyalty, more repeat purchases, and less vulnerability to price wars. In addition, perceived superiority pays off in the ability to raise prices without losing market share.[4]

Where personal selling is the primary component of a firm's marketing mix, advertising may be used in a support role—to assist salespeople. Much of Avon's advertising is aimed at assisting the neighborhood salesperson by strengthening the image of Avon, its products, and its salespeople.

Translating Advertising Objectives into Advertising Plans

Advertising planning begins with the marketing objectives and strategies derived from the firm's overall objectives. These general marketing objectives and strategies are the basis for marketing communications objectives and strategies. Effective research is essential for both marketing and advertising planning. The results of the research allow management to make strategic decisions that are translated into tactical areas such as budgeting, copywriting, scheduling, and media selection. Posttests are used to measure the effectiveness of advertising and form the basis for feedback concerning needs for possible adjustment. The elements of advertising planning are shown in Figure 17.3.

There is a real need for following a sequential process in advertising decisions. Novice advertisers often are overly concerned with the technical aspects of advertisement construction and ignore the more basic steps, such as market analysis. The type of advertisement to be used in a particular situation is largely related to the planning phase of this process.

Figure 17.3
Elements of Advertising Planning

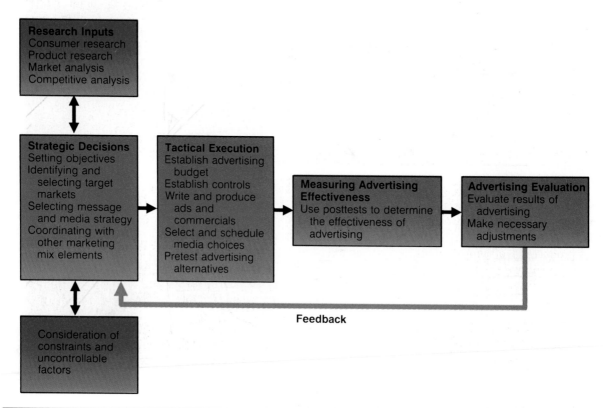

Source: Adapted from S. Watson Dunn and Arnold M. Barban, *Advertising: Its Role in Modern Marketing*, 6th ed. (Hinsdale, Ill.: Dryden Press, 1986), p. 240.

Positioning

positioning
Developing a marketing strategy aimed at a particular market segment and designed to achieve a desired position in the prospective buyer's mind.

One of the most widely discussed strategies in advertising is the concept of **positioning**—developing a marketing strategy aimed at a particular market segment and designed to achieve a desired position in the prospective buyer's mind. Marketers use a positioning strategy to distinguish their good or service from the competition. While advertising experts continue to debate its effectiveness and origin, positioning has been used by hundreds of firms since its inception a little over a decade ago. The strategy is applied primarily to products that are not leaders in their particular industries. Apparently these products are more successful if their advertising concentrates on specific "positions" in consumers' minds.

As Professors David A. Aaker and J. Gary Shansby point out, a variety of positioning strategies are available to the advertiser. An object can be positioned by:

1. Attributes (*Crest is a cavity fighter.*)

2. Price/quality (*Sears is a value store.*)

3. Competitors ("*Avis is only number two in rent-a-cars, so why go with us? We try harder.*")

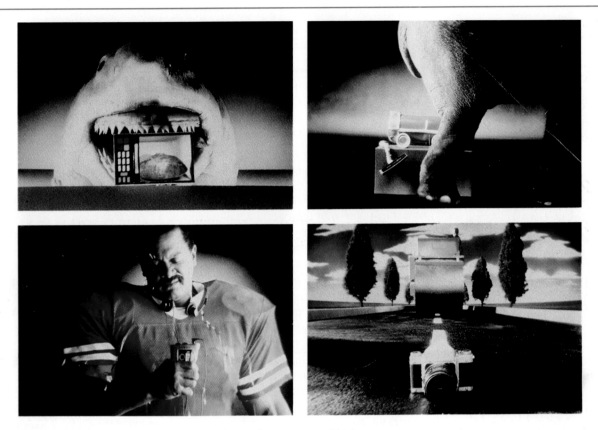

To distinguish itself from competitors, Mita Copier marketers use a positioning strategy that emphasizes the firm's focus on marketing only one product line. Scenes from one of Mita's television commercials that show competitors' products being crushed and devoured help communicate Mita's position as a one-product specialist to its target audience.

Photo source: Courtesy of Mita Copystar America/HDM Advertising.

4. Application *("Raid kills bugs dead.")*

5. Product user *(Miller is for the blue-collar, heavy beer drinker.)*

6. Product class *(Carnation Instant Breakfast is a breakfast food.)*

A common positioning technique is to position some aspect of the firm's marketing mix against the leading competitors. Advertising for Mita Copiers, for example, is designed to position the firm as a nondiversified company that markets only one product line, unlike leading competitors that sell a host of products—ranging from cameras and stereos to vacuum cleaners—in addition to copiers. One television commercial in Mita's campaign attacks competitors' diversified-product approach by "destroying" their products: A steamroller crushes a camera, an elephant sits on a vacuum cleaner, a shark devours a microwave oven, and a football player smashes a radio. The music accompanying these scenes of annihilation reinforces the visual: "We don't make cameras like they do, we don't make stereos like they do. . . . Just copiers. . . ."

The song, an adaptation of a popular 1967 hit, is remembered by and appeals to Mita's target market of businesspeople age 35 to 50.[5]

Success in positioning requires a careful, well-researched plan:

The selection of a positioning strategy involves identifying competitors, relevant attributes, competitor positions, and market segments. Research-based approaches can help in each of these steps by providing conceptualization even if the subjective judgments of managers are used to provide the actual input information to the position decision.[6]

Types of Advertising

Two broad types of advertisements exist: product and institutional. **Product advertising** deals with the nonpersonal selling of a particular good or service. It is the type that comes to the average person's mind when he or she thinks about advertisements. **Institutional advertising,** in contrast, is concerned with promoting a concept, an idea, a philosophy, or the goodwill of an industry, company, organization, person, geographic location, or government agency. It is a broader term than *corporate advertising,* which is typically limited to nonproduct advertising sponsored by profit-seeking firms. Institutional advertising is often closely related to the public relations function of the enterprise.

Advertising can be subdivided into three categories, depending on the primary objective of the message: informative, persuasive, and reminder. **Informative advertising** seeks to develop initial demand for a product, service, organization, person, place, idea, or cause. It tends to characterize the promotion of any new market entry because the objective often is simply to announce its availability. Informative advertising is used in the introductory stage of the product life cycle.

Persuasive advertising attempts to develop demand for a product, service, organization, person, place, idea, or cause. It is a competitive type of promotion used in the growth stage and early in the maturity stage of the product life cycle.

Reminder advertising strives to reinforce previous promotional activity by keeping the name of the product, service, organization, person, place, idea, or cause before the public. It is used in the latter part of the maturity stage as well as throughout the decline stage of the product life cycle. The Walt Disney World magazine advertisement in Figure 17.4 uses an emotional appeal to remind readers about the firm's recreational facilities.

Advocacy Advertising

One form of persuasive institutional advertising whose use has increased during the past decade is advocacy advertising. **Advocacy advertising,** sometimes referred to as *cause advertising,* can be defined as any kind of paid public communication or message, from an identified source and in a conventional advertising medium, that presents information or a point of view bearing on a publicly recognized, controversial issue. Such advertising is designed to influence public opinion, affect current and pending legislation, and gain a following.

Advocacy advertising, described in the discussion of idea marketing in Chapter 1, has been effectively utilized by nonprofit organizations such as Mothers Against Drunk Driving (MADD), Planned Parenthood, the National Rifle Association, and "right-to-life" antiabortion groups. In recent years, profit-seek-

product advertising
Nonpersonal selling of a good or service.

institutional advertising
Promoting a concept, an idea, a philosophy, or the goodwill of an industry, company, organization, place, person, or government agency.

informative advertising
Promotion that seeks to announce the availability of and develop initial demand for a product, service, organization, person, place, idea, or cause.

persuasive advertising
Competitive promotion that seeks to develop demand for a product, service, organization, person, place, idea, or cause.

reminder advertising
Promotion that seeks to reinforce previous promotional activity by keeping the name of the product, service, organization, person, place, idea, or cause in front of the public.

advocacy advertising
Paid public communication or message that presents information on a point of view bearing on a publicly recognized, controversial issue.

Figure 17.4
Reminder Advertising

A place in your heart.

Walt Disney World®

Call (305) 828-8181 for the 32-page Disney Vacation Guide.

Source: © The Walt Disney Company. Used with permission.

ing companies (particularly energy and resource firms and banks and other financial institutions) with a stake in some issue have turned to advocacy advertising. Among the firms that have used advocacy advertising to take aggressive
positions on particular issues and convince the public of their viewpoints are
Mobil Oil and Bethlehem Steel.

Media Selection

One of the most important decisions in developing an advertising strategy is the
media to be used for transmitting the firm's message. A mistake at this point
can cost a company literally millions of dollars in ineffective advertising. The
advertising media the marketer selects must be capable of accomplishing the
communications objectives of informing, persuading, and reminding potential
customers of the product, service, person, or idea.

Research should identify the target market to determine its size and characteristics and then match the target with the audience and the effectiveness of

the available media. The objective is to achieve adequate media coverage without advertising beyond the identifiable limits of the potential market. Finally, alternative costs should be compared to determine the best possible media purchase.

The various advertising media are compared on the bases of their shares of overall advertising expenditures as well as their major strengths and weaknesses in Table 17.1.[7] *Broadcast media* include television and radio; newspapers, magazines, outdoor advertising, and direct mail represent the major types of *print media*. As Table 17.1 reveals, newspapers and television are the leading advertising media, and radio, magazines, and outdoor advertising rank at the bottom. Since 1950 newspapers, radio, and magazines have experienced declines in their market shares, while television has grown tremendously.

Television

Even though only 29 cents of every advertising dollar is spent in the broadcast media of television and radio, the television medium contains so many characteristics favorable to effective advertising that it has grown to the point where it rivals newspapers as the dominant advertising medium. Although television ranks second to newspapers, with a 22 percent share of overall advertising revenues, the relative attractiveness of the two media differs in local and national markets. Most newspaper advertising revenues come from local advertisers. In contrast, television is the dominant medium for national advertising.

Television advertising can be divided into four categories: network, national, local, and cable. Columbia Broadcasting System, National Broadcasting Company, and American Broadcasting Company are the three major national networks. Their programs usually account for a substantial portion of total television advertising expenditures. A national "spot" is nonnetwork broadcasting used by a general advertiser. Local advertising spots, used primarily by retailers, consist of locally developed and sponsored commercials. Cable television is a rapidly growing medium, currently serving more than 42 million people in 48 percent of U.S. households. Total cable advertising revenues were $948 million in 1987. Procter & Gamble, Philip Morris, and Anheuser-Busch were the largest cable advertisers.

Television advertising offers the advantages of impact, mass coverage, repetition, flexibility, and prestige. Its disadvantages include loss of control of the promotional message to the telecaster (who can influence its impact), high costs, high mortality rates for commercials, some public distrust, and lack of selectivity in the ability of specific television programs to reach precisely-defined target market consumers without considerable wasted coverage.

Radio

Advertisers who use radio can also be classified as network, national, and local. Radio accounts for about 7 percent of total advertising revenue and 10 percent of local expenditures. Its advantages are immediacy (studies show most people regard radio as the best source for up-to-date news), low cost, flexibility, practical and low-cost audience selection, and mobility. Its disadvantages include fragmentation (Boise, Idaho, for example, has a population of 100,000 and 20 radio stations), the temporary nature of messages, and less research information than for television.

Table 17.1
Advertising Media Alternatives

Media	Percentage of Total Advertising Expenditures[a]	Advantages	Disadvantages
Broadcast Media			
Television	22%	Great impact Mass coverage Repetition Flexibility Prestige	Temporary nature of message High cost High mortality rate for commercials Evidence of public lack of selectivity
Radio	7	Immediacy Low cost Practical audience selection Mobility	Fragmentation Temporary nature of message Little research information
Print Media			
Newspapers	29	Flexibility Community prestige Intensive coverage Reader control of exposure Coordination with national advertising Merchandising service	Short life span Hasty reading Relatively poor reproduction
Direct mail	16	Selectivity Intense coverage Speed Flexibility of format Complete information Personalization	High per-person cost Dependency on quality of mailing list Consumer resistance
Magazines	6	Selectivity Quality reproduction Long life Prestige associated with some magazines Extra services offered by some publications	Lack of flexibility
Outdoor advertising	1	Communication of quick and simple ideas Repetition Ability to promote products available for sale locally	Brevity of message Public concern over aesthetics

[a]An additional 19 percent is spent on a variety of miscellaneous advertising media, including transit advertising, point-of-purchase displays, cinema advertising, directories, and regional farm papers.

Source: Based on S. Watson Dunn and Arnold M. Barban, *Advertising: Its Role in Modern Marketing,* 6th ed. (Hinsdale, Ill.: Dryden Press, 1986), pp. 572–685. Relative shares of total advertising expenditures from *Statistical Abstract of the United States* (Washington, D.C.: Government Printing Office, 1987), p. 538.

Newspapers

Newspaper advertising continues to dominate local markets. It accounts for 29 percent of total advertising revenues. Newspapers' primary advantages are flexibility (advertising can be varied from one locality to the next), community prestige (newspapers have a deep impact on their communities), intensive coverage (in most locations, 90 percent of the homes can be reached with a single newspaper), reader control of exposure to the advertising message (unlike with electronic media, readers can refer back to newspapers), coordination with national advertising, and merchandising services (such as promotional and research support). The disadvantages are a short life span, hasty reading (the typical reader spends only 20 to 30 minutes reading the newspaper), and relatively poor reproduction.

Magazines

Magazines, which are divided into three basic categories—consumer, farm, and business publications—account for about 6 percent of national advertising, 45 percent of which appears in weekly magazines. The primary advantages of magazine advertising are their selectivity in reaching precise target markets, quality reproduction, long life, the prestige associated with some magazines, and the extra services many publications offer. The primary disadvantage is that magazines lack the flexibility of newspapers, radio, and television.

Reader's Digest is the nation's leading magazine in terms of annual paid subscriptions, with 18 million. Other leading magazines include *TV Guide, National Geographic, Modern Maturity,* and women's magazines such as *Better Homes & Gardens, Family Circle,* and *Woman's Day.*

Direct Mail

Sales letters, postcards, leaflets, folders, broadsides (which are larger than folders), booklets, catalogs, and house organs (periodical publications issued by organizations) are forms of direct-mail advertising. The advantages of direct mail are selectivity, intensive coverage, speed, format flexibility, completeness of information, and personalization of each mailing piece. Disadvantages of direct mail are its high cost per reader, its dependence on the quality of mailing lists, and some consumers' resistance to it.

Consumer objections to receipt of unsolicited direct mail led the Direct Mail/Marketing Association to establish its Mail Preference Service in 1971. This consumer service sends name-removal forms to people who do not wish to receive direct-mail advertising. It also provides add-on forms for those who like to receive a lot of mail. Approximately 16 percent of total advertising is spent on direct mail.

Outdoor Advertising

Posters (commonly called *billboards*), painted bulletins or displays (such as those that appear on the walls of buildings), and electric spectaculars (large, illuminated, and sometimes animated signs and displays) make up the outdoor-advertising medium. This form of advertising has the advantages of ready com-

THE COMPETITIVE EDGE

Rolling Stone

The year 1989 marked the twenty-second year that the *Stone* had rolled. Over that period, the magazine has grown from a modest monthly production with 24 pages and black-and-white pictures to a 100-page biweekly filled with wild color and award-winning writers and photographers. It now attracts more than 1 million readers per issue, most of whom have forgotten the 1960s motto "Never trust anyone over 30." After all, most current subscribers who read the magazine at its birth are over 40 now, and readership studies show that *Rolling Stone* has one of the most affluent reader bases in the nation.

But prior to its recent success, *Rolling Stone* had an image problem. Too many potential advertisers were shying away because they saw the magazine as a cult publication targeted to an audience with sandals, long hair, and precious little income. At the magazine's headquarters, the assignment was clear: Reposition *Rolling Stone* in potential advertisers' minds to inform them that it had changed with the times and so had its readers. But repositioning is a difficult undertaking. In what later proved a brilliant decision, the magazine's marketers brought in the Fallon McElligott advertising agency to address the issue creatively.

The accompanying advertisement illustrates the campaign's direct attack on the image issue. Other ads feature the words "perception" and "reality" emblazoned over contrasting pictures, such as a keg of beer on one side and a lineup of 12 brands of ice-cold premium beers on the other. In short, they address the misconception of the typical *Rolling Stone* reader as someone going nowhere in life versus the "real" reader, who is a financially successful participant in the American Dream, and force readers to question their current perceptions.

Beneath the pictures, a paragraph of pithy prose offers statistics meant to impress advertisers with the market potential of any ad appearing in *Rolling Stone*. The *Rolling Stone* ads are featured in publications devoted to business, marketing, and advertising, and they reach the magazine's target market of potential advertisers. These advertisers have been introduced to a communications vehicle capable of delivering their commercial messages to an established market segment of well-educated, successful individuals with average incomes approaching $30,000 a year—and they have jumped at the opportunity.

Thanks to its carefully conceived,

brilliantly executed ads, *Rolling Stone's* advertising revenues rank it as the third most rapidly growing magazine in the United States. A quick perusal of a current issue reveals advertising for such high-price, high-fashion products as automobiles, fashion items, alcoholic beverages, and personal grooming aids (the last category increased by 126 percent in a single year). The repositioning victory has been sweet for the advertising agency as well. Among the many awards won by Fallon McElligott is *Nation's Business* grand prize as the "Best Business Advertising" campaign. The rewards for *Rolling Stone* are greatly enhanced revenues resulting from a changed image. So rolls the stone.

Sources: Statistical data provided by *Rolling Stone* press release, August 24, 1987. See also Martha L. Finny, "The Winning Edge," *Nation's Business* (April 24, 1987), pp. 41–43. *Photo source:* From *Rolling Stone* 1986 by Straight Arrow Publishers, Inc. © 1986. All Rights Reserved. Reprinted by Permission.

Figure 17.5
Effective Use of Outdoor Advertising

Celebrate the San Diego Zoo's 70th birthday.

Source: Courtesy of San Diego Zoo; Phillips-Ramsey, Advertising Agency.

munication of quick and simple ideas, repetition, and the ability to promote products that are available for sale locally. Outdoor advertising is particularly effective in metropolitan and other high-traffic areas. Its disadvantages are the brevity of its messages and public concern over aesthetics. The Highway Beautification Act of 1965, for example, regulates outdoor advertising near interstate highways. This medium accounts for approximately 1 percent of all advertising.

Figure 17.5 shows an award-winning outdoor advertisement for the San Diego Zoo. The series of three billboards were placed one-quarter of a mile apart in the style of the famous Burma Shave consecutive signs.

Media Scheduling

Once the advertiser has selected the media that best match its advertising objectives and promotional budget, attention shifts to **media scheduling**—the timing and sequencing of advertisements. A variety of factors influence this decision as well. Sales patterns, repurchase cycles, and competitive activities are the most important variables.

media scheduling
Timing and sequencing of
advertisements.

Seasonal sales patterns are common in many industries. For example, an airline might reduce advertising during peak travel periods and boost its media schedule during low travel months (see the discussion of promotion as a variable for stabilizing sales in Chapter 16). Repurchase cycles may also play a role in media scheduling—the shorter the repurchase cycle, the more likely it is that the media schedule will be consistent throughout the year. Competitive activity is still another influence on media scheduling. For instance, a small firm may elect to avoid advertising during periods of heavy competitive advertising.

Hypothetical Media Schedule

Figure 17.6 shows a hypothetical media schedule for the introduction of a new automobile designed to appeal primarily to male buyers. The model is introduced in November with a direct-mail piece offering recipients test drives. It is supported by extensive outdoor and transit advertising during a three-month introductory period and is featured in the firm's commercials shown during a Christmas television special early in December.

This particular manufacturer also advertises in selected network shows throughout the year, as well as on football and baseball telecasts. The manufacturer is also an extensive user of magazines. Since women are expected to purchase 20 percent of the total number of models sold, one women's publication is used every month and two national magazines on an alternating basis: one for the first two weekly issues and the second for the last two weeks each month. Finally, newspapers are used for cooperative advertising, in which the manufacturer and dealer share the advertising costs.

Organization of the Advertising Function

Although the ultimate responsibility for advertising decision making often rests with top marketing management, the organization of the advertising function varies among companies. A producer of a technical industrial product may be served by one person within the company whose primary task is writing copy for submission to trade publications. A consumer goods company, on the other hand, may have a large department staffed with advertising specialists.

The advertising function is usually organized as a staff department reporting to the vice-president (or director) of marketing. The director of advertising is an executive position that heads the functional activity of advertising. The individual in this position must be not only a skilled and experienced advertiser but an effective communicator within the organization. The success of a firm's promotional strategy depends on the advertising director's willingness and ability to communicate both vertically and horizontally. The major tasks typically organized under advertising include advertising research, design, copywriting, media analysis, and, in some cases, sales promotion.

Figure 17.6
Hypothetical Media Schedule for a New Auto Model

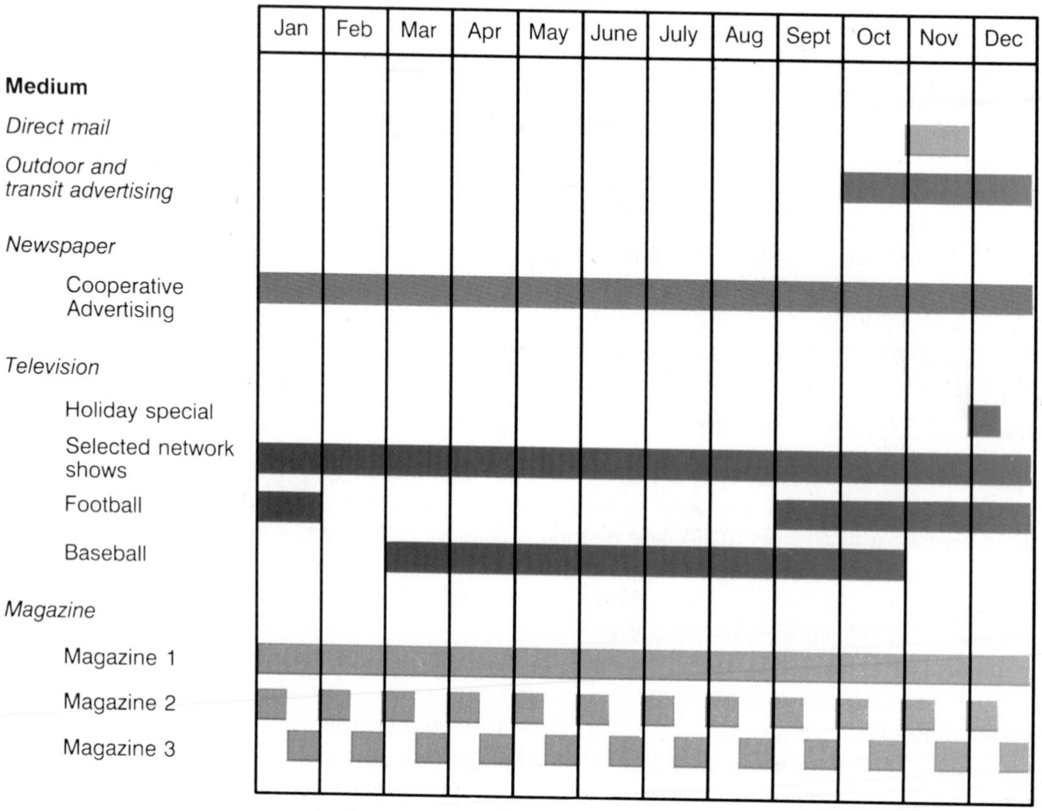
Jan
Feb
Mar
Apr
May
June
July
Aug
Sept
Oct
Nov
Dec
Medium
Direct mail
Outdoor and transit advertising
Newspaper
Cooperative Advertising
Television
Holiday special
Selected network shows
Football
Baseball
Magazine
Magazine 1
Magazine 2
Magazine 3

Advertising Agencies

advertising agency
Marketing specialist firm used to assist advertisers in planning and implementing advertising programs.

Many major advertisers use one of the nearly 10,000 independent advertising agencies in the United States. An **advertising agency** is a marketing specialist firm that assists advertisers in planning and preparing advertisements.

There are several reasons why most large advertisers use agencies for at least a portion of their advertising. Agencies typically are staffed with highly qualified specialists who provide a degree of creativity and objectivity that is difficult to sustain in a corporate advertising department. In some cases, they also reduce the cost of advertising because the advertiser can avoid many of the fixed expenses associated with maintaining an internal advertising department. Finally, since agencies are typically compensated by the media used (usually in the form of a 15 percent discount based on advertising expenditures), their services are available at little cost. However, effective use of an advertising agency requires a close relationship between the advertiser and the agency.

Figure 17.7 shows the organization chart for a large advertising agency. While the titles may vary among agencies, the major operational functions may

Figure 17.7
Advertising Agency Organization Chart

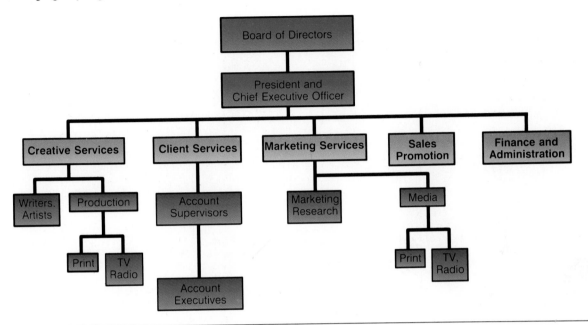

be classified as creative services, client services (account management), marketing services in the form of media services and marketing research, and sales promotion. The top U.S. advertising agencies ranked by worldwide billings are Young & Rubicam, Saatchi & Saatchi Advertising, Backer Spielvogel Bates, BBDO Worldwide, Ogilvy & Mather Worldwide, and McCann-Erickson Worldwide. Each has worldwide billings of over $3.4 billion.[8]

Creating an Advertisement

The final step in the advertising process—the development and preparation of an advertisement—should flow logically from the promotional theme selected. It should be a complementary part of the marketing mix and its role in the total marketing strategy carefully determined. Major factors to consider when preparing an advertisement are its creativity, its continuity with past advertisements, and possibly its association with other company products.

What should an advertisement accomplish? Regardless of the chosen target, an advertisement should (1) gain attention and interest, (2) inform and/or persuade and (3) eventually lead to buying action.

Gaining attention should be productive; that is, it should instill some recall of the product or service. Consider Gillette Company, which once had a chimpanzee shave a man's face in a commercial. After testing the commercial in two cities, one Gillette spokesperson lamented, "Lots of people remembered the chimp, but hardly anyone remembered our product. There was fantastic interest in the monkey, but no payoff for Gillette."[9] The advertisement gained

Figure 17.8

Elements of a Typical Advertisement: A) Headline; B) Illustration;
C) Body Copy; and D) Signature

Source: Courtesy of American Isuzu Motors Inc. Agency: Della Femina, Travisano.

the audience's attention, but it failed to lead to buying action. An advertisement that fails to gain and hold the receiver's attention is ineffective.

An advertisement should also inform and/or persuade. For example, insurance advertisements are informative—they typically specify the policy's features—and they are persuasive—they may use testimonials in attempting to persuade prospective purchasers.

Stimulating buying action is often difficult because an advertisement cannot actually close a sale. Nevertheless, if the ad gains attention and informs or persuades, it is probably well worthwhile. Too many advertisers fail to suggest how the receiver can purchase a product if he or she so desires. This is a shortcoming that should be eliminated.

The humorous Isuzu advertisement in Figure 17.8 identifies the four major elements of a print advertisement: headline, illustration, body copy, and signature. Headlines and illustrations (photographs, drawings, or other artwork) should work together to generate interest and attention. Body copy serves to inform, persuade, and stimulate buying action. The signature, which may in-

Figure 17.9
A Comparative Advertising Strategy

Source: Courtesy of U.S. News & World Report/Saatchi & Saatchi DES Compton, 1987.

clude company name, address, phone number, slogan, trademark, or product photo, names the sponsoring organization. An ad may also have a subhead—a heading subordinate to the main headline that either links the main headline to the body copy or subdivides sections of the body copy.

The creation of each advertisement in a campaign, such as the Isuzu ad illustrated in Figure 17.8, is an evolutionary process that begins with an idea and ultimately results in a finished product in the form of print and electronic media advertising. The idea itself must first be converted into a thought sketch, a tangible summary of the intended message. The next step involves refinement of the thought sketch into a rough layout. Continued refinements of the rough layout eventually produce the final version of the advertisement that is ready to print or record.

Comparative Advertising

Comparative advertising is an advertising strategy in which the firm's advertising messages make direct promotional comparisons with leading competitive brands. An example is the advertisement in Figure 17.9, in which *U.S. News &*

comparative advertising
Nonpersonal-selling efforts that make direct promotional comparisons with leading competitive brands.

World Report compares itself with other leading news magazines. Directed at potential business advertisers, the ad positions the magazine as one that caters to readers who prefer news coverage of substantial issues. That position is reinforced by the ad's illustrations: the *U.S. News & World Report* cover deals with a serious subject—education—while the covers of competitors' magazines feature rock stars, actors, and actresses.

A comparative advertising strategy is best employed by firms whose products and services do not lead their markets. Most market leaders do not acknowledge in their advertising that competitive products even exist. Procter & Gamble and General Foods, for example, traditionally have devoted little of their huge promotional budgets to comparative advertising. But many firms use it extensively. An estimated 23 percent of all radio and television commercials make comparisons with competitive products. Here are some examples:

☐   Scope mouthwash prevents "medicine breath," but Listerine is never mentioned.

☑   Minute Maid lemonade is better than the "no-lemon lemonade," a reference to General Foods' Country Time brand.

☑   Suave antiperspirant will keep you just as dry as Ban Ultra Dry does, and for a lot less.

☑   Nationwide, more Coca-Cola drinkers prefer the taste of Pepsi.

Marketers who contemplate using comparative advertising in their promotional strategies should take care to ensure that they can substantiate their claims. Comparative advertising has the potential to produce lawsuits.

Advertising experts disagree on the long-term effects of comparative advertising. The likely conclusion is that comparative advertising is a useful strategy in a limited number of circumstances.

Celebrity Testimonials: Advantages and Disadvantages

In attempting to improve the effectiveness of their advertising, a number of marketers utilize celebrities to present their advertising messages. Well-known examples include Michael Jackson and Michael J. Fox for Pepsi-Cola, model Cheryl Tiegs for Cover Girl makeup and Sears sportswear, Chris Evert for Rolex watches, actress Cybill Shepherd for the Beef Industry Council, ice skater Peggy Fleming for the National Pork Producers Council, singer Kenny Rogers for Dole pineapple and other products, and basketball star Michael Jordan for Nike.

The primary advantage of using big-name personalities is that they may improve product recognition in a promotional environment filled with hundreds of competing 15- and 30-second commercials. (Advertisers use the term *clutter* to describe this situation.) In order for this technique to succeed, the celebrity must be a credible source of information for the item being promoted. Bill Cosby dressed up as an ice cream vendor to promote Jello-O Pudding Pops is an effective spokesperson. He was equally convincing when he discussed quality and integrity in advertising for Ford Motor Company. But when E. F. Hutton advertisers abandoned their 14-year campaign "When E. F. Hutton talks, people listen" and began featuring Cosby, the ads bombed. Similarly, actor John

Sports sponsorship can be an effective promotional tool when the selected event fits the target market and is integrated with other elements of the promotional strategy. CPC International's cholesterol-free Mazola corn oil reaches its target audience of health-conscious consumers by being the official sponsor of the U.S. race-walking team. Both the product and the event are associated with general fitness and a healthy diet.

Photo source: Kelly-Mooney Photography. Courtesy of Mazola Corn Oil, Best Foods Division of CPC International Incorporated.

Houseman proved a memorable and highly effective spokesperson for brokerage firm Smith Barney, delivering the message that they "make money the old-fashioned way: they earn it." However, his appearances in television ads promoting Big Macs and french fries met with incredulity. As Chiat/Day advertising agency head, Jay Chiat, put it, "I can't imagine John Houseman ever having been in a McDonald's."[10] Celebrity advertisements are ineffective when there is no apparent relationship between the celebrity and the advertised product or service.

Millions of Americans are currently very sports and celebrity oriented. Therefore, there is opportunity for firms to profitably sponsor athletes or sporting events. However, such promotions should be clear adjuncts to existing promotional programs. There are several principles that corporate sponsors should consider before getting involved. First, they must be selective and specific. A target market should be pinpointed and a sport or celebrity carefully matched to that target and objective. Second, they should follow sports interest trends carefully; too often firms get involved without assessing the trend's strength. Third, they must be original and look for a special focus. Is it possible to come up with a unique concept? Fourth, they should analyze the results in both the short and long terms. Sponsorship is a business decision that should pay off in profits.[11]

FOCUS ON ETHICS

Should Billboards Be Banned?

Marketers of such controversial products as tobacco and liquor have faced increased restrictions on their promotional strategy alternatives. Some media, such as radio and television, ban them entirely. A growing number of magazines are limiting or banning entirely advertising for some of these products. Not surprisingly, these marketers have turned to alternative media. One of the most important is outdoor advertising. A sizable portion of revenues in the $1.28 billion outdoor advertising industry is generated from billboards promoting cigarettes and alcoholic beverages.

But many people regard billboards as major contributors to visual pollution. Anyone who views a city street or highway completely cluttered with signs and billboards can't help but wonder whether more restrictions, or perhaps even an outright ban, should be imposed.

During Lyndon Johnson's administration, the nation's First Lady led the charge for environmentalists

in a major antibillboard campaign that resulted in the passage of the Highway Beautification Act of 1965. A primary objective of the law was total elimination of billboards on federal highways. However, a loophole allowing them to remain in commercial and industrial areas has, in practice, neutralized the law. Moreover, the final version of the original bill required federal and state governments to pay for billboard removal.

In 1986, a coalition of environmentalists and fiscal conservatives, including the National Taxpayers Union, tried to change that. As Jill Lancelot, NTU's director of congressional affairs, pointed out, the act "is the only federal law we know of that pays polluters to stop polluting." Although bills proposed by Washington senator Slade Gorton and Vermont senator Robert Stafford were endorsed by President Reagan, they failed to be enacted into law.

Outdoor-advertising executives defend their signs and accuse politi-

cians of hypocrisy on the issue. "A politician complains that we put up ugly signs," says Jim McLaughlin, managing partner of Turner Outdoor Advertising in Atlanta. "But when he's running for office, we're the first place he calls for advertising space."

Environmentalists have achieved most of their victories at the state and local levels. By 1988, four states and several cities (mostly resort communities but also major cities such as Houston, which, buried under a mountain of 7,000 billboards, banned new ones in 1980) had enacted new restrictions on billboards. But whether local victories will be extended to other states or even to federal restrictions is open to debate.

Sources: Lancelot and McLaughlin quotations from Craig C. Carter, "Billboard Foes Are on a Tear-'em-Down Tear," *Fortune* (July 21, 1986), p. 88. See also Ronald Alsop, "Billboard Firms Lure New Ads as Tobacco, Liquor Sales Slide," *The Wall Street Journal* (May 7, 1987), p. 29, and Lisa Phillips, "Marketers Look to New Medium," *Advertising Age* (June 8, 1987), p. S2.

Retail Advertising

retail advertising
Nonpersonal selling by stores that offer goods or services directly to the consuming public.

Retail advertising is all advertising by stores that sell goods or services directly to the consuming public. While it accounts for a sizable portion of total annual advertising expenditures, retail advertising varies widely in its effectiveness. One study showed that consumers are often suspicious of retail price advertisements. Source, message, and shopping experience seem to affect consumer attitudes toward these advertisements.[12]

The basic problem is that retail stores often treat advertising as a secondary activity. Except for some retail giants, they rarely use advertising agencies. Instead, store managers are usually given the responsibility of advertising along with their normal functions. The basic step in correcting this deficiency is to give one individual both the responsibility and the authority for developing an effective retail advertising program.

cooperative advertising
Sharing of advertising costs between the retailer and the manufacturer of the good or service.

Cooperative Advertising   The sharing of advertising costs between the retailer and the manufacturer or wholesaler is called **cooperative advertising.** For example, Ocean Pacific Sportswear may pay 50 percent of the cost of a retail store's newspaper advertisement featuring its product lines.

Cooperative advertising resulted from the media's practice of offering lower rates to local advertisers than to national ones. Later cooperative advertising was seen as a way to improve dealer relations. From the retailer's viewpoint, it permits a store to secure advertising that it otherwise would not get.

Assessing the Effectiveness of an Advertisement

Because advertising represents a major expenditure for many firms, it is imperative to determine whether a chosen campaign is accomplishing its promotional objectives. Advertisers are well aware of the number of advertising messages to which consumers are exposed daily and their ability to practice *selective perception* by simply screening them out. Novel forms of advertising, such as inserting ads in videocassettes and cinema advertising, are aimed at increasing the likelihood that the messages will be seen and heard. The recent barrage of three-dimensional pop-up ads for Disney World, Dodge trucks, and Honeywell computers in magazines are designed to stand out—and be remembered. Coca-Cola advertisers had similar objectives in mind in 1988 when they distributed special 3-D viewing glasses through 250,000 outlets where the products are sold so that viewers could catch the world's first three-dimensional commercial on network television. Absolut vodka marketers even inserted musical microchips in some of their two-page magazine ads so that the ads would play songs when readers turned to them.[13]

The objective of these novel approaches is to enhance the likelihood that the advertisement message will be received and remembered. However, determining whether an advertising message has achieved its intended objective is one of the most difficult undertakings in marketing. Assessment of advertising effectiveness consists of two primary elements: pretesting and posttesting.

Pretesting

Pretesting is the assessment of an advertisement's effectiveness before it is actually used. It includes a variety of evaluative methods. To test magazine advertisements, the Batten, Barton, Durstine & Osborn ad agency cuts ads out of advance copies of magazines and then "strips in" the ads it wants to test. Interviewers later check the impact of the advertisements on readers who receive free copies of the revised magazine.

Another ad agency, McCann-Erickson, uses a *sales conviction test* to evaluate magazine advertisements. Interviewers ask heavy users of a particular item to pick one of two alternative advertisements that would convince them to purchase it.

Potential radio and television advertisements often are screened by consumers who sit in a studio and press two buttons, one for a positive reaction to the commercial and the other for a negative reaction. Sometimes proposed ad copy is printed on a postcard that also offers a free product; the number of cards returned is viewed as an indication of the copy's effectiveness. *Blind product tests* are also often used. In these tests, people are asked to select unidentified products on the basis of available advertising copy. Mechanical means of assessing how people read advertising copy are yet another method.

pretesting
Assessment of an advertisement's effectiveness before it is actually used.

One mechanical test uses a hidden eye camera to photograph how people read ads. The results help determine headline placement and advertising copy length.

Posttesting

posttesting
Assessment of an advertisement's effectiveness after it has been used.

Posttesting is the assessment of advertising copy after it has been used. Pretesting generally is a more desirable testing method than posttesting because of its potential cost savings. However, posttesting can be helpful in planning future advertisements and in adjusting current advertising programs.

In one of the most popular posttests, the *Starch Readership Report,* interviewers ask people who have read selected magazines whether they have read various ads in them. A copy of the magazine is used as an interviewing aid, and each interviewer starts at a different point in the magazine. For larger ads, respondents are also asked about specifics, such as headlines and copy. Figure 17.10 shows an advertisement for Jif peanut butter with the actual Starch scores. All such *readership,* or *recognition, tests* assume that future sales are related to advertising readership.

Unaided recall tests are another method of posttesting advertisements. Here respondents are not given copies of the magazine but must recall the ads from memory. Interviewers for the Gallup and Robinson marketing research firms require people to prove they have read a magazine by recalling one or more of its feature articles. The people who remember particular articles are given cards with the names of products advertised in the issue. They then list the ads they remember and explain what they recall about them. Finally, the respondents are asked about their potential purchase of the product. A readership test concludes the Gallup and Robinson interview. Burke Research Corporation uses telephone interviews the day after a commercial has aired on television to test brand recognition and the advertisement's effectiveness. Another unaided recall test is Ad Watch, a joint project of *Advertising Age* magazine and SRI Research Center. It measures ad awareness by polling consumers by telephone, asking them to name the advertisement that first comes to mind of all the ads they have seen, heard, or read in the past 30 days.

Inquiry tests are another popular form of posttest. Advertisements sometimes offer a gift—generally a sample of the product—to people who respond to them. The number of inquiries relative to the advertisement's cost is used as a measure of its effectiveness.

Split runs allow advertisers to test two or more ads at the same time. Although they have traditionally been used in newspapers and magazines, split runs are frequently used with cable television systems to test the effectiveness of TV ads. With this method, the cable TV audiences or a publication's subscribers are divided in two: Half would view advertisement A and the other half would view advertisement B. The relative effectiveness of the alternatives is then determined through inquiries or recall and recognition tests.

Regardless of the exact method used, marketers must realize that pretesting and posttesting are expensive and, as a result, they must plan to use them as effectively as possible.

Figure 17.10
Magazine Advertisement with Starch Scores

The "Ad-As-A-Whole" label indicates the percentage of readers interviewed who "Noted" the ad in the issue, "Associated" it with a specific advertiser or product, and "Read Most" (more than 50%) of the ad copy. This label summarizes the ad's total readership.

This "Read %" label indicates the percentage of readers interviewed who read the headline.

The "Signature %" label indicates the percentage of readers who saw the logo or signature.

The "Seen %" label indicates the percentage of readers interviewed who saw the illustration.

The "Read Some %" label indicates the percentage of readers interviewed who read some or all of the body copy.

Source: Courtesy of Starch INRA Hooper, Inc.

Sales Promotion

Although sometimes mistakenly relegated to a secondary role in a firm's overall promotional strategy, the second type of nonpersonal selling actually surpasses advertising in terms of promotional dollar outlays. **Sales promotion** may be defined as those marketing activities, other than personal selling, advertising, and publicity, that enhance consumer purchasing and dealer effectiveness. Over $100 billion is spent each year on such sales promotion activities as displays, trade shows and exhibitions, demonstrations, and various nonrecurrent promotional efforts.[14]

Although sales promotion techniques traditionally were viewed as a supplement to other elements of the firm's promotional mix, today they are an integral part of many marketing plans. Frequent-flier programs have enabled airlines to build a base of loyal customers where none existed before. Magazines entice new subscribers with novel premiums. Sweepstakes and contests have long been staples for direct marketers. Packaged goods marketers use an array of coupons, game cards, in-store displays, and contests.[15] Rather than reduce the price of several unsold Oldsmobile Toronados to encourage their sale, Mystic, Connecticut, auto marketer Tom Quirk offered a special promotion: Buy a Toronado, get a free Yugo. All of the Toronados in stock were sold within a month.[16]

Sales promotion techniques may be used by all members of a marketing channel: manufacturers, wholesalers, and retailers. When retailer Marshall Field opened a new department store in San Antonio, Texas, it promoted the store's merchandise and encouraged potential customers to apply for a credit card by sending 7,500 local residents a videocassette that also showed such city landmarks as the Alamo. To reach its target market, Field sent the video only to VCR owners with high incomes. As an incentive to watch the video, Field ran a contest offering a chance to win a $1,000 gift certificate to those who could identify the city landmarks shown in the video.[17]

Sales promotion activities typically are targeted at specific markets. For example, a manufacturer such as Texize Corporation might use trial sample mailings of a new spot remover to consumers and a sales contest for wholesalers and retailers that handle the product.

Marketers using sales promotion can choose from various methods—point-of-purchase advertising; specialty advertising; trade shows; samples, coupons, and premiums; contests; and trading stamps. More than one option may be used in a single promotional strategy, but probably no promotional strategy has ever used all of them in a single program. While they are not mutually exclusive, promotions generally are employed on a selective basis.

Point-of-Purchase Advertising

Point-of-purchase advertising refers to displays and other promotions located near the site of the actual buying decision. The in-store promotion of consumer goods is a common example. Such advertising may be useful in supplementing a theme developed in another area of promotional strategy. A life-size display of a celebrity used in television advertising is a very effective in-store display. Another example is the familiar L'eggs store displays; pantyhose packaged in plastic "eggs" completely altered marketing practices in this industry.

Specialty Advertising

Specialty advertising is a sales promotion technique that utilizes useful articles carrying the advertiser's name, address, and advertising message to reach target consumers. The origin of specialty advertising has been traced to the

Middle Ages, when wooden pegs bearing artisans' names were given to prospects to be driven into their walls and serve as a convenient place on which to hang armor.

By 1989, specialty advertising had grown to a $3-billion-a-year business. Wearables, including T-shirts, baseball caps, and jackets, are the most popular products, followed by writing instruments. Other popular forms of contemporary advertising specialties that carry the sponsoring firm's name include desk and business accessories, calendars, and glassware/ceramics.

Advertising specialties help reinforce previous or future advertising and sales messages. A study by Gould/Pace University in New York found the use of advertising specialties generates a greater response to direct mail and three times the dollar volume of sales of those produced by direct mail alone.[18]

Trade Shows

To influence channel members and resellers in the distribution channel, it has become common for sellers to participate in *trade shows*. These shows are often organized by an industry's trade association and may be part of the association's annual meeting or convention. Vendors serving the industry are invited to the show to display and demonstrate their products for the association's membership. The National Restaurant Association, for example, holds the annual National Restaurant/Hotel-Motel Show in Chicago each May. In 1987, the show attracted more than 100,000 attendees from all 50 states and 70 countries and almost 2,000 exhibitors.

Shows are also used to reach the ultimate consumer. Home and recreation shows, for instance, allow businesses to display and demonstrate home care, recreation, and other consumer products to entire communities.

Samples, Coupons, and Premiums

The distribution of samples, coupons, and premiums is probably the best-known sales promotion technique. *Sampling* is the free distribution of a product in an attempt to obtain future sales. Price Choppers, a chain of 58 discount supermarkets, increased its sales of Canfield's Diet Chocolate Fudge soda from 80 to 250 cases per week after it ran a five-week sampling promotion.[19] Samples may be distributed on a door-to-door basis, by mail, via demonstrations, or by inclusion in packages containing other products. Sampling is especially useful in promoting new or unusual products.

A *coupon* offers a discount—usually some specified price reduction—on the next purchase of a product or service. Coupons are redeemable at retail outlets that receive a handling fee from the manufacturer. Mail, magazine, newspaper, and package insertions are the standard methods of distributing coupons.[20]

Premiums are items given free or at a reduced cost with the purchase of another product. They have proven effective in motivating consumers to try new products or different brands. Premiums should have some relationship with the purchased item. For example, the service department of an auto dealership might offer its customers ice scrapers. Similarly, the premium offer of a raisin bank, shown in Figure 17.11, resembles the hip dancing raisins popularized by the television advertising campaign of the California Raisin Advisory Board. Such premiums are also used to elicit direct-mail purchases. The value of premium giveaways runs into billions of dollars each year.

Figure 17.11
Example of a Premium Offer

Source: Courtesy of Sun•Maid Raisin Growers of California.

Contests

Firms often sponsor contests to introduce new products and services and to attract additional customers. Contests, sweepstakes, and games offer substantial prizes in the form of cash or merchandise as inducements to potential customers.

In recent years, a number of court rulings and legal restrictions have limited the use of contests. As a result, firms contemplating using this promotional technique should engage the services of a specialist.

Trading Stamps

A sales promotion technique similar to premiums is *trading stamps*. Customers receive trading stamps with their purchases in various retail establishments. The stamps can be saved and exchanged for gifts, usually at special redemption centers operated by the trading-stamp company. The degree to which the consumer benefits by trading stamps depends on the relative values of the goods offered.

Although the trading-stamp industry was founded by Sperry & Hutchison in 1896, the height of their popularity as a sales promotion tool occurred in 1969, when some 400 stamp companies operated and nearly three-quarters of all groceries and supermarkets, and hundreds of retail gas stations issued them. Since then, their U.S. market has declined more than 50 percent, and only three major companies — Sperry & Hutchison, Quality Stamp, and Gold Stamp — remain. The extent of their usage seems to depend on such factors as relative price levels, location of redemption centers, and legal restrictions.

Public Relations

In Chapter 16, **public relations** was defined as the firm's communications and relationships with various publics, including customers, employees, stockholders, suppliers, government, and the society in which it operates. Public relations efforts date back to 1889, when George Westinghouse hired two people to publicize the advantages of alternating current to counter arguments for direct-current electricity.

Public relations is an efficient indirect communications channel for promoting products, although its objectives typically are broader than those of other components of promotional strategy. It is concerned with the prestige and image of all parts of the organization. Anheuser-Busch marketers, for example, use advertisements to promote the sale of their beer products. However, to enhance its image as a company concerned about alcohol abuse and driving while intoxicated, the firm has developed a number of public relations programs. One program, Training and Intervention Procedures by Servers of Alcohol (TIPS), is aimed at educating retailers. Another program, ALERT Cab, is a taxi program developed for use by wholesalers, retailers, and cab companies during the holiday season; it offers patrons of public drinking establishments free taxi rides home. Other examples of nonmarketing-oriented public relations objectives include a company's attempt to gain favorable public opinion during a long strike and an open letter to Congress published in a newspaper during congressional debate on a bill affecting a particular industry. Although the public relations departments of some companies are not part of the marketing divisions, their activities invariably have an impact on promotional strategy.

Public relations is a $2-billion-a-year industry employing 157,000 people in both the nonprofit and profit-oriented sectors. Some 1,800 public relations firms currently operate in the United States, including the largest, Hill & Knowlton, with almost 2,000 employees. Of these, the top 50 firms have billings of over $2 million. In addition, there are thousands of smaller firms and one-person operations.

Public relations is considered to be in a period of major growth as a result of increased environmental pressure for better communication between industry and the public. Many top executives are becoming involved, as illustrated by Lee Iacocca's efforts to publicize the need for increased competitiveness on the part of U.S. firms. A survey of chief executives concluded that nearly 40 percent spend 25 to 50 percent of their working days engaged in public relations activities.[21]

public relations
Firm's communications and relationships with its various publics.

Publicity

The aspect of public relations that is most directly related to promoting a firm's products or services is publicity. **Publicity** can be defined as the nonpersonal stimulation of demand for a product, service, place, idea, person, or organization by placing significant news about it in a print or broadcast medium without having to pay for the time or space. Members Only, a marketer of men's outerwear, received favorable publicity for its unique anti-drug abuse program. For 15 months, the company used all of its advertising budget on television commercials, magazine and newspaper ads, billboards, and posters designed to discourage drug abuse. The program so impressed New York Governor Mario Cuomo that he held a press conference to honor Members Only for its campaign and showed two of the firm's commercials. Reporters and media personnel attending the conference reported the news nationally and locally, resulting in coverage worth an estimated $6 million.[22]

Since publicity is designed to familiarize the general public with the characteristics, services, and advantages of a product, service, place, idea, person, or organization, it is an informational activity of public relations. While its associated costs are minimal compared to those of other forms of promotion, publicity is not entirely cost free. Publicity related expenses include the costs of employing marketing personnel assigned to create and submit publicity releases, printing and mailing costs, and other related expense items.

Some publicity is used to promote a company's image or viewpoint, but a significant amount provides information about products, particularly new ones. Because many consumers accept information in a news story more readily than they do that in an advertisement, publicity releases are often sent to media editors for possible inclusion in news stories. In some cases, the information in a publicity release about a new product or service provides valuable assistance for a television, newspaper, or magazine writer and eventually is broadcast or published.

Publicity releases are sometimes used to fill voids in a publication and at other times are used in regular features. In either case, publicity releases are a valuable supplement to advertising.

Today public relations must be considered an integral part of promotional strategy even though its basic objectives extend far beyond the attempt to influence the purchase of a particular good or service. Public relations programs— especially publicity—make a significant contribution to the achievement of promotional goals.

Summary of Chapter Objectives

1. Explain the current status and historical development of advertising, sales promotion, and public relations. Some forms of the nonpersonal-selling elements of promotion have probably existed since the beginnings of the exchange process. The origins of advertising, for instance, can be traced to the vocal chants of criers and hawkers. Symbolic signs were an early form of sales promotion. Today these promotional elements enjoy professional status and are vital aspects of most for-profit and nonprofit organizations.

2. Identify the major types of advertising. Advertising may be divided into two broad categories. Product advertising involves the nonpersonal selling of a good or service. Institutional advertising is the nonpersonal promotion of a concept, idea, philosophy, or goodwill of an industry, company, organization, person, geographic area, or government agency. Each of these types can be further subdivided into informative, persuasive, and reminder-oriented product or institutional advertising.

3. List and discuss the major advertising media. A variety of media exist for the advertiser: broadcast media, such as television and radio, and print media, including newspapers, magazines, outdoor advertising, and direct mail, along with assorted alternative media ranging from transit advertising to ads placed in videocassettes. Each type possesses its own distinct advantages and disadvantages. Newspapers are the dominant local medium, while television is the most significant national advertising medium.

4. Explain how advertising effectiveness is determined. The effectiveness of advertising can be measured by both pretesting and posttesting. Pretesting is the assessment of an ad's effectiveness before it is actually used. It includes such methods as sales conviction tests and blind product tests. Posttesting is the assessment of the advertisement's effectiveness after it has been used. Commonly used posttests include readership tests, unaided recall tests, inquiry tests, and split runs.

5. Outline the organization of the advertising function. Within a firm, the advertising department is usually a staff group that reports to a vice-president (or director) of marketing. Advertising departments typically include the following capabilities: research, art and design, copywriting, and media analysis. In many instances, they also include a sales promotion function. Many advertisers use independent advertising agencies to provide the creativity and objectivity that might be missing in their own organizations and to reduce advertising costs. Such marketing specialist firms are typically divided into the functions of creative services, account management, research, and promotional services.

6. Describe the process of creating an advertisement. Effective advertisements must accomplish the following: (1) gain attention and interest; (2) inform, persuade, and/or remind; and (3) eventually lead to buying action. An advertisement evolves from initial ideas to a thought sketch, which is then converted into a rough layout. The layout is further refined until the final version of the advertisement is ready to print or record.

7. Identify the principal methods of sales promotion. Expenditures for sales promotion exceed total spending on advertising each year. A variety of methods are used, including (1) point-of-purchase advertising (in-store displays), (2) specialty advertising (giveaway items bearing the advertiser's name), (3) trade shows (large-scale product demonstrations), (4) samples (product giveaways), (5) coupons (one-time price reductions), (6) premiums (gift items given with a product purchase), (7) contests, and (8) trading stamps.

8. Explain the role of public relations and publicity in an organization's promotional strategy. Public relations consists of the firm's communications and relationships with its various publics, including customers, employees, stockholders, suppliers, government, and the society in which it operates. Publicity, the aspect of public relations that is most closely linked to promotional strategy, is the dissemination of newsworthy information about a product or organization. This information activity of public relations is frequently used in new-product introductions.

Key Terms

advertising
positioning
product advertising
institutional advertising
informative advertising
persuasive advertising
reminder advertising
advocacy advertising
media scheduling
advertising agency

comparative advertising
retail advertising
cooperative advertising
pretesting
posttesting
sales promotion
point-of-purchase advertising
specialty advertising
public relations
publicity

Review Questions

1. Explain the wide variation in advertising expenditures as a percentage of sales in the industries shown in Figure 17.1.

2. Describe the primary objectives of advertising. Offer a local example of an advertising campaign, and explain how the campaign seeks to accomplish specific objectives.

3. Give a specific example of each of the six basic types of advertising.

4. Discuss the relationship between advertising and the product life cycle.

5. What are the major advantages and disadvantages associated with using each of the advertising media? Give examples of advertisers most likely to use each medium.

6. Under what circumstances are celebrity spokespersons in advertising likely to be effective? Suggest recent examples of effective and ineffective use of spokespersons in advertisements.

7. Why is retail advertising so important today? Relate cooperative advertising to the discussion of alternative promotional strategies in Chapter 16.

8. Discuss the organization of the advertising function. Consider all the major activities associated with advertising.

9. Distinguish between advertising and sales promotion. Explain the principal methods of sales promotion, and give an example of each.

10. Describe the public relations component of a firm's promotional mix. Do you agree with the statement that publicity is free advertising?

Discussion Questions

1. Develop a sales promotion program for each of the following. Justify your choice of each sales promotion method employed.
   a. Independent insurance agent
   b. Retail furniture store
   c. Interior decorator
   d. Local radio station

2. Present an argument favoring the use of comparative advertising by a marketer who is currently preparing an advertising plan. Make any assumptions necessary.

3. Review the changes in the relative importance of the various advertising media during the past 40 years that are mentioned in the chapter. Suggest likely explanations for these changes.

4. Over half of the 50 states currently have government-operated lotteries. Suggest a promotional plan for marketing lottery tickets with particular emphasis on nonpersonal-selling aspects of the promotional mix.

5. Choose a candidate who ran for political office during the most recent election. Assume that you were in charge of advertising for this person's campaign. Develop an advertising strategy for your candidate. Select a campaign theme and the media to be employed. Finally, design an advertisement for the candidate.

VIDEO CASE 17

Chiat/Day

Advertising agencies such as Chiat/Day are referred to in marketing texts as *facilitating agencies.* Like transportation and warehousing firms, financial institutions and insurance companies, and marketing research firms, they provide specialized assistance to producers, wholesalers, and/or retailers in marketing their goods and services. In addition to providing specialized marketing assistance for their clients, advertising agencies are also engaged in marketing within their own industry. They must compete with other agencies in marketing their expertise to attract new clients and retain current ones.

The blend of clients served by the advertising agency is often critical in its marketing efforts. For example, the agency handling the Ford Motor Company account is extremely unlikely to attract such direct competitors as General Motors or Chrysler to its client list. In some cases, client losses can occur due to advertisements created for another client in an entirely different industry. In 1988 Saatchi & Saatchi DFS Compton, the world's largest advertising agency, created a TV commercial for Northwest Airlines showing passengers applauding the airline's in-flight smoking ban. Another Saatchi DFS client, RJR Nabisco, Inc., interpreted the ad as evidence of disloyalty and fired the agency, taking its $80 million account that included such products as cookie market leaders Oreo and Chips Ahoy!, Bubble Yum and CareFree gums, and Life Savers roll candy to another agency. A former RJR Nabisco executive summed up the move: "It's a case of 'You're either with us or against us.' "

Chiat (pronounced SHY-at)/Day has accumulated a number of satisfied clients in its brief existence. When it was created back in 1968 through the merger of two small Los Angeles agencies, total billings amounted to about $8.6 million. Today it ranks among the 25 largest agencies in the world with $350 million in billings in 1987. (Gross income, amounting to 15 percent of total billings, came to $52.5 million). A major factor in the firm's growth is its reputation as a cauldron of creativity, one whose maverick behavior raised eyebrows, won awards — and produced results.

A glance at Chiat/Day's history shows why it's a maverick; it seems a given for a firm that got its start during a Dodgers baseball game. Even the agency's first attempts to branch out of its initial business, technical advertising, were unorthodox. Chiat/Day decided to pursue consumer-product accounts, and it devised its own ad campaign to assist. The ads featured the headline, "Who Says Chiat/Day Doesn't Do Technical Advertising?", causing readers to infer that the technical advertising specialist actually spent much of its efforts in other market niches.

Such audacious tactics paid off, as the firm drew consumer-goods companies, including some of Honda's first U.S. automotive ads. Among the other companies Chiat/Day has represented over the past 10 years are Yamaha USA, Nike, Pioneer, Apple, Porsche, Nissan, National Car Rental, Reebok, Pizza Hut, and Royal Caribbean Cruises. Innovative approaches to advertising keep the firm growing and expanding, but to date it has managed to maintain the creativity associated with smaller firms.

Part of the reason behind its consistent creativity is its association with clients who share the same sort of corporate creed: believe in what you do. "We definitely are more inspired to do work for a firm that believes in advertising," said Greg Helm, general manager of the agency's Los Angeles office. "Our goal is to be the best agency in the world."

The Chiat/Day organizational structure differs somewhat from those of most ad agencies. At the top is the president, and beneath this position are two offices: creative services and the general manager. Creative services breaks down into the same form as the agency organizational structure shown on page 583, and the general manager is in charge of three departments: account management, finance and administration, and media. However, the general manager also supervises an account planning department, a department not found in most U.S. agencies. "We have no research department," said Helm. "Instead, we use an account planner."

Chiat/Day's efforts to attract the Porsche account provides insight into the work of the account planner. Where most firms would have involved a number of different departments in this endeavor, C/D assigned a single research and strategy specialist (the account planner) to the account. This individual was responsible both for conducting needed research on the account and for ensuring that the research was properly used, a practice that CEO Jay Chiat borrowed from the British agency Boase Massimi & Pollitt. "Account planners devote their energies to understanding the market — they're focused on relevance to the consumer," said Helm. "Once [they've] decided on what's relevant, 'creative' goes to work."

The account planner also acts as a sort of ombudsman between the client and Chiat/Day's creative department. For the Porsche account, the planner discovered that previous Porsche advertising had not lived up to the firm's image. He then tried to direct the creative services staff to develop an advertising campaign that would focus on Porsche's desire to offer the ultimate in performance. Two possible ads were devised based on this theme. The first one, which attempted to put the viewer behind the wheel of a Porsche, failed to impress the client. The second featured Porsche's chairman frowning unhappily at the car, emphasizing the firm's commitment to offering unmatched performance. This one sold the client.

"The other significant difference between our structure and that of most ad agencies is that we have departments, but we physically dissolve them in the office, so that people are grouped by client," said Helm.

Chiat/Day's willingness to depart from convention has resulted in the creation of some famous and controversial ads. Perhaps its best-known, and most controversial, was the "1984" ad created for the introduction of the Apple

Macintosh computer. The minute-long commercial, based on George Orwell's novel, aired during the 1984 Super Bowl and prompted at least one newscaster to say, "Well, the game wasn't much, but did you see that commercial?"

Following a popular Chiat/Day style, the Macintosh ad mentioned Apple only in passing. C/D has created similar ads for Nike, and they, too, gave little emphasis to the company name. The highly visible Nike billboards featured, among others, Michael Jordan, Carl Lewis, and Michael Cooper, athletes whose Nike shoes send them beyond the billboard's bounds. Still, run in conjunction with striking TV ads, they were followed by Nike sales increases as high as 30 percent in some areas.

In 1987, the firm landed the $150 million Nissan account, the single largest account opened in a number of years. One of the elements in the C/D approach that most impressed Nissan decision makers was Jay Chiat's insistence that his team work closely with Nissan's marketers during the development process, long before the account had been won.

The firm is now expanding into fields that complement its advertising business. Most large ad agencies offer their clientele "below the line" services, such as direct marketing and public relations, and Chiat/Day has made moves in recent years to follow suit. In 1987, it acquired Bright & Associates, a design and marketing consultant, and Jessica Dee Communications, a public relations and marketing firm. In 1988, C/D created Perkins/Butler to specialize in direct marketing. It continued to negotiate for the possible purchase of a sales promotion firm.

The expansion is part of C/D's efforts to provide comprehensive marketing services for its clients and to enhance revenues. As CEO Jay Chiat puts it, "As margins get tighter and tighter, in order to be viable financially, it's important that you have other income streams."

Despite the awards and generally effective advertising results, Chiat/Day, like every other agency, loses accounts. It's all a part of the business for an ad agency: Porsche left when C/D won the Nissan account, Nike left when it slashed its advertising budget and C/D went after Reebok, and Apple left when another agency won a "shoot-out" competition. Other current clients of the agency include California Cooler, Eveready, Sunbeam Appliance, and Arrow shirts.

Sources: RJR Nabisco quotation from Christine Donahue and Dottie Enrico, "'You Are Either With Us or Against Us,'" *Adweek's Marketing Week* (April 11, 1988), p. 4. Greg Helm quotations from telephone interview (April 4, 1988). See also "Chiat/Day," *Advertising Age* (March 30, 1988), p. 36; Jon Lafayette, "Chiat/Day Expands Holdings," *Advertising Age* (February 29, 1988), p. 12; Brian Lowry, "Nike Trails Apple Out Chiat Door," *Business Week* (October 19, 1987), pp. 70–71; Geoffrey Colvin, "Long Hours + Bad Pay = Great Ads," *Fortune* (July 23, 1984), pp. 77–79; and Betsy Gilbert, "Apple Drives Off with Unusual Handling," *Advertising Age* (May 2, 1985), p. 18.

Questions

1. Draw an organization chart for Chiat/Day and label each part.

2. Why would a marketer such as Porsche or Nike go to an advertising agency rather than relying on company personnel?

3. Explain the perceived benefits of the account planning department concept. What potential problems exist for agencies who use this approach?

4. What kind of ad might Chiat/Day create for itself today? What headline or headlines might be used? Who would its audience be? What medium would it be most likely to choose?

COMPUTER APPLICATIONS

Since advertising frequently represents a substantial portion of total marketing costs, marketers are continually seeking more efficient methods of achieving their promotional objectives. Advertisers not only seek to communicate with and persuade prospective customers; they also want to accomplish this at the lowest possible cost. In evaluating alternative advertising media, marketers attempt to match the characteristics of their target market customers with the audiences for radio and television programs, newspapers, magazines, and so on. But the advertising costs of specific media vary greatly according to such factors as market coverage, size or length of the advertisement, and location of the advertising message. Consequently, some common denominator with which to compare available alternatives is needed.

One commonly used method for comparing alternative vehicles within a single advertising medium is the *cost-per-thousand* criterion. Since *M* is the Roman numeral for 1,000, "cost per thousand" is frequently abbreviated *CPM*. For magazines, the following formula is used:

$$\text{Cost Per Thousand (CPM)} = \frac{\text{Magazine Page Cost} \times 1,000}{\text{Circulation}}.$$

For radio or television, the CPM formula is modified as follows:

$$\text{Cost Per Thousand (CPM)} = \frac{\text{Cost of Commercial} \times 1,000}{\text{Circulation}}.$$

Since circulation and program audience data are available from independent research sources, CPM calculations can easily be made and updated regularly. Circulation data for magazines are available from research specialists such as Standard Rate & Data Service. Program audience data for television and radio can be obtained from firms such as A. C. Nielsen or Arbitron.

Assume that *Modern Maturity* magazine has a circulation of 8 million and charges $75,000 for a one-page, full-color advertisement. Its CPM could be calculated as follows:

$$\text{CPM} = \frac{\$75,000 \times 1,000}{8,000,000} = \frac{75,000,000}{8,000,000} = \$9.375.$$

In addition to the basic CPM calculation, a potential advertiser may be able to more precisely evaluate different advertising vehicles by focusing solely on the percentage of the magazine's readers, radio program's listeners, or television program's viewers who match the demographic and geographic profiles of the firm's target market. The denominator in the CPM formulation would be changed to include only the target market members in the advertising medium's audience. If the advertiser feels that only one-eighth of the total circulation of *Modern Maturity* matches the precise profiles of the firm's target market, the CPM calculation will be made as follows:

$$\text{CPM} = \frac{\text{Advertisement Cost} \times 1,000}{\text{Number of Target Market Members in Audience}} = \frac{75,000,000}{1,000,000} = \$75.$$

However, CPM is of little use in comparing different *types* of advertising media: "You can't compare a CPM figure for a page in *Reader's Digest* with a CPM for a

30-second commercial . . . because there's no basis for comparing the value of a magazine ad to the value of a TV commercial. The communications approaches are totally different, as are audience attention and involvement."[23] Nevertheless, such comparisons may be extremely useful in evaluating alternative vehicles within a single advertising medium.

Once the advertiser has established a common denominator for making such comparisons, it can make qualitative judgments about the leading candidates' relative merits. One author suggests four factors that should be considered before deciding where to place the advertisements:

First, the measure should be adjusted for *audience quality*. For a baby lotion advertisement, a magazine read by one million young mothers would have an exposure value of one million, but if read by one million old men would have a zero exposure value. Second, the exposure value should be adjusted for the *audience attention probability*. Readers of *Vogue*, for example, pay more attention to ads than readers of *Newsweek*. Third, the exposure value should be adjusted for the *editorial quality* (prestige and believability) that one magazine [or broadcast program] might have over another. Fourth, the exposure value should be adjusted for the magazine's [or broadcaster's] *ad placement policies and extra services*.[24]

Directions: Use menu item 15 titled "Advertising Evaluations" to solve each of the following problems.

Problem 1   Cynthia Faulkner is in charge of placing advertisements for Long Island–based National Consumer Goods, Inc. She is currently in the process of comparing seven major magazines. The cost of a one-page, four-color advertisement is shown below. Which magazine has the lowest CPM? Which has the lowest CPM for male readers? For female readers?

Magazine	Four-Color Page Rate	Total Readers	Male Readers	Female Readers
Amazing World	$62,750	12,375,000	3,473,000	8,902,000
Weekly Facts	80,675	10,335,000	5,575,000	4,760,000
Sunday Digest	53,175	7,300,000	4,220,000	3,080,000
52	82,400	19,940,000	8,790,000	11,150,000
SportWeek	45,550	5,365,000	4,045,000	1,320,000
Viewer	70,775	8,180,000	4,645,000	3,535,000
Contemporary Homes	70,000	16,650,000	7,590,000	9,060,000

Problem 2   After comparing the readership profiles of the seven magazines discussed in Problem 1, Cynthia Faulkner has developed the following estimates of the percentages of male and female readers for each magazine who match the profile of National's target market customers:

Magazine	Readers in Target Market	
	Male Readers	Female Readers
Viewer	1,750,000	1,800,000
Contemporary Homes	1,900,000	1,600,000
Amazing World	1,000,000	800,000
Weekly Facts	2,200,000	3,700,000
Sunday Digest	1,350,000	225,000
SportWeek	1,200,000	900,000
52	1,900,000	2,300,000

a. Which magazine has the lowest CPM for male readers who match National's target market profile? Which has the highest CPM?
b. Which magazine has the lowest CPM for female readers who match National's target market profile? Which has the highest CPM?

Problem 3 Vicky Ballow is senior branch manager for the snacks division of Best Treats of Richmond, Virginia. She is in the process of narrowing the number of magazines under consideration for next year's advertising campaign and has prepared the following table for eight magazines whose readership appears to best match the characteristics of Best Treats' target market. Ballow has also included her estimate of the percentage of each magazine's readers who precisely match the demographic characteristics of her firm's market.

Magazine	Four-Color Page Rate	Total Readers	Estimated Number of Magazine Readers Matching Best Treats' Market Profile
21st Century Homes	$11,500	1,800,000	520,000
Elan	17,500	2,200,000	440,000
Family	13,000	1,900,000	380,000
Gotham Lady	36,000	8,500,000	850,000
Happy Home	28,000	5,700,000	800,000
Modern Homemaker	7,500	900,000	250,000
Single Parent	34,500	8,000,000	450,000
Suburban Garden	26,000	4,900,000	100,000

a. Which magazine has the lowest CPM if total readers are considered? Which has the highest CPM?
b. Which magazine has the lowest CPM if only target market readers are considered? Which has the highest CPM?

Problem 4 Dave Putnam is brand manager for LongDrive golf balls, one of more than 50 brand names produced and marketed by Bluegrass Sporting Goods Company of Louisville, Kentucky. Putnam has analyzed six likely magazines for use in advertising the LongDrive brand. He has collected the following data:

Magazine	Black-and-White Page Rate	Total Readers	College Graduates	Managerial, Administrative
SportView	$18,800	1,900,000	700,000	1,100,000
Modern Golf	13,500	1,000,000	300,000	500,000
Links	16,300	2,600,000	400,000	1,300,000
Golf Tips	9,750	600,000	200,000	300,000
18 Holes	38,200	4,000,000	800,000	900,000
Golf Pro	12,960	2,200,000	400,000	600,000

a. Which magazine has the lowest overall CPM? Which is most expensive in terms of overall CPM?
b. If Putnam defines his target market as consisting of only college graduates, which magazine will offer him the lowest CPM?
c. If Putnam decides to focus solely on persons holding managerial or administrative positions, which magazine will allow him to reach his target at the lowest CPM? Which will be the most expensive in terms of CPM?

Problem 5 Joe Ed Anderson is in charge of advertising for Cajun Video Rentals in New Orleans. He is targeting his advertising message at persons aged 18 to 49 in the New Orleans metropolitan area and plans to use radio during morning and afternoon drive times. He has assembled the following data on four radio stations that offer the programming blend designed to attract his target market listeners:

Radio Station	Cost of 30-Second Commercial	Total Audience	Listeners Age 18–34	Listeners Age 35–49
WZED	$100	25,000	6,500	6,000
WZZZ	90	28,000	5,600	7,000
WNEL	220	42,000	16,800	12,600
WBBB	250	70,000	21,000	17,500

a. Which radio station has the lowest overall CPM? Which is the most expensive in terms of overall CPM?

b. Which station has the lowest CPM for listeners between the ages of 18 and 34? Which is the most expensive for this age category?

c. Which would reach Anderson's targeted customers at the lowest CPM?

18 Personal Selling and Sales Management

Chapter Objectives

1. To explain the factors affecting the relative importance of personal selling in the promotional mix.

2. To contrast field selling, over-the-counter selling, and telemarketing.

3. To identify the three basic sales tasks.

4. To outline the steps in the sales process.

5. To describe sales management's boundary-spanning role.

6. To list the functions of sales management.

B y 1989, one U.S. resident in twelve was of Hispanic descent. In addition, Census Bureau reports show that the Hispanic population is growing five times faster than the non-Hispanic segment. Such statistics are music to the ears of marketers at Goya Foods, the family-owned Secaucus, New Jersey, company that is the nation's largest purveyor of Hispanic foods. Goya, whose origins trace back to 1936, accounts for almost 65 percent of total sales to Hispanics in the food categories in which it competes. Its product lines consist of more than 700 products, ranging from staples such as rice, black beans, and flour to spicy *sofrito* and *racaito* sauces.

With sales and profits growing at an annual rate of 12 percent, Goya marketers realized that it was just a matter of time before one of the multibillion-dollar food giants discovered their market segment. The move came in 1987, when Campbell Soup Company introduced its Hispanic food line under the Casera brand name on the U.S. mainland. The name, acquired when Campbell purchased a Puerto Rican food company, has already been used on 50 products, with more on the way.

While Goya marketers have a healthy respect for the distribution strength and advertising dollars of their giant competitor, they also know that Goya products enjoy intense brand loyalty from both shoppers and retail stores. A major factor in creating and maintaining this loyalty is Goya's personal selling strategy.

Campbell and the other food giants market their products through wholesale distributors. Their strategies for introducing new product lines typically consist of heavy consumer advertising and sales promotion to build awareness coupled with large price discounts to wholesalers. Goya marketers follow a different path. Their secret for long-term retailer and customer satisfaction is the Goya Spanish-speaking sales force that serves both large retailers and the *bodegas,* the Hispanic mom-and-pop stores that were the firm's original customers. These direct and continuous contacts between retailer and producer ensure prompt response to retailer needs as well as quick resolution of problems. In addition, they represent an invaluable source of retailer and customer feedback for Goya. The firm's sales representatives also work with each retail buyer to tailor the Goya product mix to the taste preferences of local households. Various items in Goya's line are designed to appeal specifically to the diverse tastes of consumers of Mexican, Puerto Rican, Venezuelan, and Cuban origin. Finally, the sales representatives consistently follow the company policy of giving the same price breaks to both small stores and supermarkets. Owner-operators of the small stores know this and demonstrate their loyalty with regular reorders.

The product-customer match has been a good one, as Goya market share figures show. Instead of spreading the Goya products throughout the store, retailers frequently stock as many as 100 different Goya items together in one aisle. As one Florida retailer notes, "They've earned the shelf space, and they've earned the support."[1]

Photo source: Courtesy of Heartland Food Warehouse, Malden, Massachusetts.

Chapter Overview

Chapters 16 and 17 focus on the concept of promotion, the promotional mix, and the use of advertising and other nonpersonal promotion in achieving marketing objectives. This chapter examines the second major variable of the promotional mix: personal selling.

Table 18.1

Factors Affecting the Importance of Personal Selling in the Promotional Mix

Variable	Factors Increasing the Relative Importance of Personal Selling	Factors Increasing the Relative Importance of Advertising
Consumer	Geographically concentrated	Geographically dispersed
	Relatively few in number	Relatively large in number
Product	Expensive	Inexpensive
	Technically complex	Simple to understand
	Custom made	Standardized
	Requires special handling	Does not require special handling
	Frequently involves trade-ins	Does not involve trade-ins
Price	Relatively high	Relatively low
Channels	Relatively short	Relatively long

personal selling
Interpersonal influence process involving a seller's promotional presentation conducted on a person-to-person basis with the buyer.

Personal selling was defined in Chapter 16 as an interpersonal influence process. Specifically it involves a seller's promotional presentations conducted on a person-to-person basis with the buyer. It is an inherent function of any enterprise. Accounting, engineering, personnel, production, and other organizational activities are useless unless the firm's product or service matches the need of a client or customer. The 8 million salespeople currently employed full-time in the United States testify to selling's importance in the late 1980s. While the average firm's advertising expenses may represent from 1 to 3 percent of total sales, selling expenses are likely to equal 10 to 15 percent. Approximately one cent of every Avon Products sales dollar is spent on advertising. But Avon's personal-selling expenses amount to 40 percent of total sales. In many firms, personal selling is the single largest marketing expense.

As Chapter 16 pointed out, personal selling is likely to be the primary component of a firm's promotional mix when consumers are geographically concentrated; when orders are large; when the products or services are expensive, are technically complex, and require special handling; when trade-ins are involved; when channels are short; and when the number of potential customers is relatively small. Table 18.1 summarizes the factors that influence the importance of personal selling in the overall promotional mix.

How Personal Selling Evolved

Selling has been a standard business activity for thousands of years. The earliest peddlers were traders who had some type of ownership interest in the goods they sold after manufacturing or importing them. In many cases, these people viewed selling as a secondary activity.

Selling later became a separate function. The peddlers of the eighteenth century sold to the farmers and settlers of the vast North American continent. In the nineteenth century, salespeople called _drummers_ sold to both consumers and marketing intermediaries. These early sellers sometimes used questionable sales practices and techniques and earned undesirable reputations for themselves and their firms. Some of these negative stereotypes persist today. To some people, the term *salesperson* conjures up unpleasant visions of Arthur Miller's antihero Willy Loman in *Death of a Salesman:*

You don't understand: Willy was a salesman. . . . He don't put a bolt to a nut. He don't tell you the law or give you medicine. He's a man way out there in the blue, riding on a smile and a shoeshine. And when they start not smiling back — that's an earthquake.[2]

But selling is far different from what it was in its early years. Far from the fast-talking, joke-telling, back-slapping caricatures in some novels and comic strips, today's salesperson is a professional. He or she is a problem solver, armed with product knowledge and typically seeking mutually beneficial relationships with clients on a regular basis over an extended period. The old stereotype of the salesperson has been replaced with the realization that personal selling is a vital, vibrant, dynamic process. With the increased emphasis on productivity resulting from domestic and foreign competition, personal selling is taking on a more prominent role in the corporate marketing mix. Salespeople must be able to communicate the subtle advantages of their firms' products and services over competitors'. Mergers and acquisitions and a host of new products and promotions have expanded the scope and complexity of many selling jobs.[3] Even the way in which salespeople perform their jobs is changing as selling enters the age of automation. More and more firms are equipping their salespeople with personal computers, printers, and cellular phones.

Personal selling is an attractive career choice for today's college and university students. Approximately 60 percent of all marketing graduates choose sales as their first marketing position. Job prospects in selling are also attractive. The Bureau of Labor Statistics projects that jobs in selling and marketing occupations that require a college degree will grow the most rapidly of all occupations for the remainder of the twentieth century.[4]

Finally, a sales background provides visibility for the individual and serves as an excellent route to the top of the corporate hierarchy. Giant corporations such as Englehard, Fluor, Honeywell, JP Stevens, MCA, Reebok International, Union Camp, and Xerox are all headed by executives who began their careers in sales.

The Three Selling Environments

The personal-selling process may occur in a variety of environments. **Field selling** involves sales calls to customers at their homes or businesses. Some situations, such as in-home sales of encyclopedias and insurance or industrial sales of major computer installations, involve considerable creative selling. In other cases, such as calling on already established customers in such industries as food, textiles, or wholesaling, processing of customer orders is the chief selling task.

In the rapidly changing banking industry, financial deregulation, bank mergers, and the emergence of regional banks have resulted in unprecedented competition among financial institutions. Even retail giants Sears and Kmart and some supermarket chains have joined the competitive battle by offering loans and financial services to their customers. The impact of these changes is evi-

field selling
Sales presentations made at prospective customers' homes or businesses on a face-to-face basis.

Figure 18.1

Private Banking: Personal Selling Services to Affluent Customers

Source: Courtesy of Citicorp/Penchina, Selkowitz Inc., Advertising Agency.

dent in new, marketing-oriented thinking as financial institutions have begun to practice market segmentation and market banking services in the same way that firms in other industries market their products. Wells Fargo's commercial lending sales force makes direct calls on presidents and chief financial officers of midsize companies, selling them on the merits of their bank. They are compensated with a modest salary plus commissions that can exceed the pay of top bank executives.[5] Citibank marketers offer private banking services to affluent clients, a highly profitable customer segment described in Figure 18.1. Citibank's private bankers frequently operate as field salespersons by delivering bank services directly to their clients' homes or offices.

The second approach, **over-the-counter selling**, typically describes selling in retail locations. Customers take the initiative to come to the seller's location — sometimes in response to direct mail or personal letters of invitation from store personnel or to take advantage of advertised sales, special events, or the introduction of new product lines. This type of selling typically involves providing product information and arranging for completion of the sales transaction.

Both field selling and over-the-counter selling sometimes utilize the telephone in such activities as prospecting for new customers and following up with existing accounts. The telephone is also the basis for a third approach to personal selling — telemarketing. **Telemarketing** refers to a sales approach con-

---

over-the-counter selling
Personal selling conducted in retail and some wholesale locations in which customers come to the seller's place of business.

telemarketing
Promotional presentation involving the use of the telephone on an outbound basis by salespeople or an inbound basis by customers who initiate calls to obtain information and place orders.

ducted entirely by telephone. It can be classified as either outbound or inbound. *Outbound telemarketing* involves a sales force that uses only the telephone to contact customers. This approach is designed to reduce the substantial costs entailed in making personal visits to customers' homes or businesses. *Inbound telemarketing* typically involves a toll-free 800 number that customers can call to obtain information and make purchases. This form of selling provides maximum convenience for customers who initiate the sales process.

Sales Tasks

The sales job has evolved into a professional occupation. Today's salesperson is more concerned with helping customers select the correct products for meeting their needs than with simply selling whatever is available. Professional salespeople advise and assist customers in their purchase decisions. Where repeat purchases are common, the salesperson must be certain that the buyer's purchases are in his or her best interest; otherwise, no future sales will be made. The seller's interests are tied to the buyer's in a symbiotic relationship.

Not all selling activities are alike. While all sales activities assist the customer in some manner, the exact tasks that are performed vary from one position to another.[6] Three basic sales tasks can be identified: (1) order processing, (2) creative selling, and (3) missionary sales. These tasks form the basis for a sales classification system.

It should be observed, however, that most sales personnel do not fall into a single category. Instead, salespersons often perform all three tasks to a certain extent. A sales engineer for a computer firm may be doing 50 percent missionary sales, 45 percent creative selling, and 5 percent order processing. Most selling jobs, however, are classified on the basis of the primary selling task performed.

Order Processing

Order processing, which can involve both field selling and telemarketing, is most often typified by selling at the wholesale and retail levels. For instance, a Pepsi-Cola route salesperson who performs this task must take the following steps:

order processing
Selling at the wholesale and retail levels; specifically, identifying customer needs, pointing them out to customers, and completing orders.

1. *Identify customer needs.* The route salesperson determines that a store that normally carries an inventory of 40 cases has only 7 cases left in stock.
2. *Point out the need to the customer.* The route salesperson informs the store manager of the inventory situation.
3. *Complete (write up) the order.* The store manager acknowledges the situation. The driver unloads 33 cases, and the manager signs the delivery slip.

Order processing is part of most selling positions. It becomes the primary task in situations in which needs can be readily identified and are acknowledged by the customer. Even in such instances, however, salespersons whose primary responsibility involves order processing will devote some time to seeking to convince their wholesale or retail customers to carry more complete inventories of their firms' products or handle additional product lines. They also are

Hoffmann-LaRoche's prescription pharmaceuticals are sold directly to about 500 wholesalers nationwide that distribute the products to hospitals, pharmacies, and chain stores. The drug manufacturer's sales representatives perform missionary sales tasks by explaining product benefits, risks, side effects, and treatment to physicians and other health care professionals.

likely to try to motivate purchasers to feature some of their firms' products, increase the amount of shelf space devoted to their products, and improve product location in the stores.

Creative Selling

creative selling
Personal selling involving situations in which a considerable degree of analytical decision making on the buyer's part results in the need for skillful proposals of solutions for the customer's needs.

When a considerable amount of analytical decision making is involved in purchasing a product or service, the salesperson must use **creative selling** techniques to solicit an order. A senior sales manager at IBM recently booked a seat on a flight to Boston so that he would sit beside a Harvard University professor in charge of a $2 million contract to purchase laptop computers. The sales manager spent most of the flight listening, but he won the contract. "In the past, IBM salespeople had an attitude of 'take it or leave it,'" says Jomen M. Hammett, Pillsbury's vice-president for information management. "Now, they're willing to spend more time understanding our needs."[7]

New products often require a high degree of creative selling. The salesperson must first identify the customer's problems and needs and then propose a

THE COMPETITIVE EDGE

Hewlett-Packard Portable PLUS Laptops

Stress frequently enters the professional salesperson's day. As a one-person representative of the firm to a potential client, the salesperson is expected to provide technical expertise; be knowledgeable about the prospect's business operations, customers, and problems; and supply detailed information on almost every aspect of his or her firm. The professional salesperson must be a problem solver for the client and a source of all information with which to answer the questions posed by the various participants in the purchase process. All too often, however, the salesperson simply can't answer the questions being asked and must spend time on the telephone or — even worse — drive back to the office and then make a return visit to the customer. Thus can ensue an infinite cycle of questions-and-answers. But with the introduction of the portable, or laptop, computer, somebody somewhere realized that this innovation would permit salespeople to take their offices with them.

Hewlett-Packard, a major high-technology force that markets its own laptops, decided to conduct a test to learn whether HP sales representatives armed with laptops would have a competitive edge in the field. Initial results were so encouraging (27 percent more of the salesperson's day spent with customers, 10 percent more sales, and three times the productivity level of the HP control group that did not use laptops) that HP's marketing leaders decided to invest an estimated $6 million to $8 million outfitting its en-tire sales force with the Portable PLUS.

Armed with the laptop, the HP salesperson can quickly retrieve account histories and track the status of orders. Order entries and sales call schedules are automated; specialized software makes letter writing and direct mail targeted at specific prospects or existing accounts a simple matter; paperwork is reduced; and the network of laptops expedites communications among sales representatives and with sales management. Each HP sales representative has the *Lotus 1-2-3®* spreadsheet program, which helps analyze product sales, spot developing trends, and maintain customer purchase and payment records.

The new technology has turned the HP sales force into the envy of the industry. HP district manager Marc Duane believes that one of the laptop's major contributions is enhanced sales force morale: "The portable has generated a great deal of enthusiasm, confidence, and professionalism. The reps are now more creative . . . more team-minded . . . and feel more professional about addressing customer needs."

Other companies are following HP's lead by equipping their own sales forces with laptops. Back in 1986, one out of every six laptops shipped was destined for a salesperson. By 1990, one in three will be used to improve the sales representative's capabilities.

Sources: Quotation in paragraph four from Thayer Taylor, "Hewlett-Packard Gives Sales Reps a Competitive Edge," *Sales and Marketing Management* (February 1987), pp. 36, 37. See also Jonathan B. Levine, "If Only Willy Loman Had Used a Laptop," *Business Week* (October 2, 1987), p. 137; "Have Laptop, Will Sell," *Sales and Marketing Management* (October 1986), p. 26; and Thayer C. Taylor, "S&MM's Survey Results," *Sales and Marketing Management* (May 1987), pp. 50–53. *Photo source:* Courtesy of Hewlett-Packard Company.

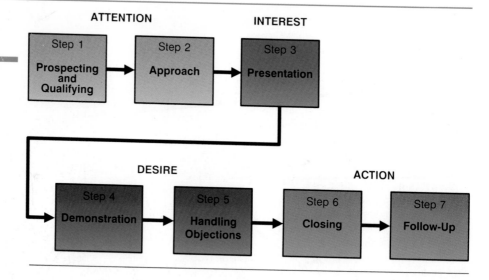

Figure 18.2
The AIDA Concept and the Personal Selling Process

ATTENTION

INTEREST

Step 1
Prospecting and Qualifying

Step 2
Approach

Step 3
Presentation

DESIRE

ACTION

Step 4
Demonstration

Step 5
Handling Objections

Step 6
Closing

Step 7
Follow-Up

solution, in the form of the product or service being offered, with which to solve the problems and fill the needs. Creative selling, which may occur in telemarketing, over-the-counter selling, and field selling, may be the most demanding of the three tasks.

Missionary Sales

missionary sales
Indirect type of selling in which specialized salespeople promote the firm's goodwill, often by assisting customers in product use.

Missionary sales are an indirect type of selling: Salespeople sell the firm's goodwill and provide their customers with technical or operational assistance. For example, a toiletries company salesperson may call on retailers to check on special promotions and overall stock movement, even though a wholesaler is used to take orders and deliver merchandise. The medical detail salesperson seeks to persuade doctors, the indirect customers, to specify the pharmaceutical company's product brand in prescriptions. However, the company's actual sales ultimately are made through a wholesaler or directly to the pharmacists who fill prescriptions.

Missionary sales may involve both field selling and telemarketing. In recent years, technical and operational assistance, such as that provided by a systems specialist, also have become a critical part of missionary selling.

The Sales Process

What are the steps involved in selling? While the terminology may vary, most authorities agree on the following sequence: (1) prospecting and qualifying, (2) approach, (3) presentation, (4) demonstration, (5) handling objections, (6) closing, and (7) follow-up.

As Figure 18.2 indicates, the steps in the personal selling process follow the attention-interest-desire-action (AIDA) concept discussed in Chapter 16. Once a sales prospect has been qualified, an attempt is made to secure his or

Figure 18.3
Use of Advertising to Identify Sales Prospects

Source: Courtesy of Barnstead/Thermolyne Corporation.

her attention. The presentation and demonstration steps are designed to generate interest and desire. Successful handling of buyer objections should arouse further desire. Action occurs at the close of the sale.

Prospecting and Qualifying

Prospecting, the identification of potential customers, is difficult work involving many hours of diligent effort. Prospects may come from many sources: previous customers, friends and neighbors, other vendors, nonsales employees in the firm, suppliers, and social and professional contacts. While a firm may emphasize personal selling as the primary component of its overall promotional strategy, advertising may be effective in identifying prospective customers. The advertisement in Figure 18.3 is designed to motivate purchasers of water purification systems to contact Boston-based Barnstead Industrial Products for additional information. A Barnstead sales representative will contact each respondent to discuss the firm's water purification requirements and Barnstead's capabilities.

prospecting
Personal-selling function of identifying potential customers.

New sales personnel may find prospecting frustrating, because there is usually no immediate payback. But without prospecting, there are no future sales. For example, in the marketing of various types of adhesive tapes for industrial use, a representative of a tape manufacturing company — perhaps a manufacturers' agent — must seek out potential users of these products. Prospecting is a continuous process because of the inevitable loss of some customers over time as well as the emergence of new potential customers or first-time prospects. Many sales management experts consider prospecting as the very essence of the sales process.

qualifying
Determining that a prospect has the needs, income, and purchase authority necessary for being a potential customer.

Qualifying — determining that the prospect really is a potential customer — is another important sales task. Not all prospects are qualified to become customers. Qualified customers are those with both the money and the authority to make purchase decisions. A person with an annual income of $25,000 may wish to own a $200,000 house, but his or her ability to actually become a customer is questionable. Similarly, a parent with six children may strongly desire a two-seater sports car, but this would probably be an impractical purchase as the sole family vehicle. Both direct mail and telephone communications are utilized in prospecting and setting up appointments with prospective customers.

Approach

approach
Salesperson's initial contact with a prospective customer.

precall planning
Use of information collected during the prospecting and qualifying stages of the sales process and during previous contacts with the prospect to tailor the approach and presentation to match the customer's needs.

Once the salesperson has identified a qualified prospect, he or she collects all available relevant information and plans an **approach** — the salesperson's initial contact with the prospective customer. Collecting information prior to the initial contact is invaluable for telemarketers and field salespeople.

This information-gathering component of personal selling makes **precall planning** possible. Salespeople who have gathered relevant information about their clients are prepared for the opening discussions that may ultimately result in a purchase. Effective precall planning permits the salesperson to make an initial contact armed with knowledge about the client's purchasing habits; his or her attitudes, activities, and opinions; and commonalities between the salesperson and the client.

Precall planning is used less frequently by retail salespeople, but they can compensate by asking leading questions to learn more about the prospect's purchase preferences. Industrial marketers have far more data available, and they should make use of it before scheduling the first sales contact.

Presentation

presentation
Describing a product's major features and relating them to a customer's problems or needs.

When the salesperson gives the sales message to a prospective customer, he or she makes a **presentation.** The seller describes the product's major features, points out its strengths, and concludes by citing illustrative successes. The seller's objective is to talk about the product or service in terms meaningful to the buyer — benefits rather than technical specifications. Thus, the presentation is the stage in which the salesperson relates product features to customer needs.

The presentation should be clear and concise, and it should emphasize the positive. In an attempt to increase its significant share of the $1.5 billion retail market for sheet-vinyl floor covering, marketers at Mannington Mills decided to assist retail salespeople by including an electronic pattern/color selector as part of in-store displays. The Mannington computerized selection aid emits beeps to attract the attention of shoppers in the store. After it has been activated by the customer's pushing the "Go" button, it asks eight questions about such factors as room decor, color preference, and the volume of foot traffic. It then "digests" the customer's answers and displays style numbers of between three and ten appropriate Mannington patterns. The salesperson and the customer are spared the task of searching through almost 300 samples of Mannington vinyl flooring in the surrounding display. The computer aid has proven more than satisfactory to both retail managers and Mannington marketers, who are competing with larger manufacturers such as Armstrong World Industries and Congoleum Corporation. Many stores have increased their sales of the Mannington line from 100 to 400 percent since obtaining the electronic unit. The pattern and color purchased by the customer are almost always from among the computer's recommended choices, because the program is based on in-depth input from professional home decorators.

The traditional approach to sales presentations, the canned approach, originally was developed by John H. Patterson of National Cash Register Company during the late 1800s. The **canned approach** is a memorized sales talk used to ensure uniform coverage of the points management deems important. While canned presentations are still used in such areas as door-to-door *cold canvassing* — making unsolicited sales calls on a random group of people — most sales forces have long since abandoned them. Flexible presentations are nearly always needed to match the unique circumstances of each purchase decision. Proper planning, of course, is an important part of tailoring a presentation to each prospective customer.

canned approach
Memorized sales talk used to ensure uniform coverage of the selling points that management has deemed important.

Demonstration

One important advantage of personal selling over most advertising is its ability to actually demonstrate the product or service to the potential buyer. As the advertisement in Figure 18.4 illustrates, creative print illustrations and television commercials are sometimes capable of simulating a product demonstration. In this example, the ad's courageous copywriter, David Abbott, had so much faith in Volvo's sturdy construction that he literally laid down his life as a test of the Swedish automaker's claims by sliding himself under a Volvo suspended from a cable hooked to the car's roof.

But a static magazine advertisement or even a quasi-demonstration of a product in action on a television screen is a far cry from the real thing. A demonstration ride in a new automobile, on the other hand, allows the prospect to become involved in the presentation. It awakens customer interest in a way that no amount of verbal presentation can. Demonstrations supplement, support, and reinforce what the sales representative has already told the prospect.

The key to a convincing demonstration is planning. A unique demonstration is likely to gain a customer's attention and be remembered. Consequently, it must be well planned and executed if a favorable impression is to be made. The salesperson should check and recheck all aspects of the demonstration prior to its delivery.

Figure 18.4
Demonstration: A Critical Step in Consumer Decision Making

Source: Courtesy of Volvo Concessionaires, U.K.

Handling Objections

A vital part of selling involves handling objections. *Objections* are expressions of sales resistance by the prospect. It is reasonable to expect a customer to say, "Well, I really should check with my spouse" or "Perhaps I'll stop back next week" or "I like everything except the color." Objections typically involve the product's features, its price, and services to be provided by the selling firm.

The professional salesperson uses each objection as a cue for providing additional information for the prospect. In most cases, an objection such as "I don't like the color of the interior" is really the prospect's way of asking what other choices or product features are available. A customer's question reveals an interest in the product and gives the seller an opportunity to expand a presentation by supplying additional information. For instance, testimonials from satisfied customers may be effective in responding to product objections. Also, providing a copy of the warranty and the dealer's service contract may resolve the buyer's doubts about product service.

Closing

The moment of truth in selling is the **closing** — the point at which the salesperson asks the prospect for an order. A sales representative should not hesitate during the closing. If he or she has made an effective presentation based on applying the product to the customer's needs, the closing should be the natural conclusion.

A surprising number of sales personnel find it difficult to actually ask for an order. To be effective, they must overcome this difficulty. Commonly-used methods of closing a sale include the following:

1. The *"If-I-can-show-you . . . "* technique first identifies the prospect's major concern in purchasing the product or service and then offers convincing evidence of the offering's ability to resolve it. ("If I can show you how the new heating system will reduce your energy costs by 25 percent, would you be willing to let us install it?")

2. The *alternative-decision technique* poses choices for the prospect where either alternative is favorable to the salesperson. ("Will you take this sweater or that one?")

3. The *SRO (standing-room-only) technique* warns the prospect that a sales agreement should be concluded now because the product may not be available later or an important feature, such as price, will soon be changed.

4. *Silence* can be used as a closing technique, since a discontinuance of a sales presentation forces the prospect to take some type of action (either positive or negative).

5. An *extra-inducement close* offers special incentives designed to motivate a favorable buyer response. Extra inducements may include quantity discounts, special servicing arrangements, or layaway options.

closing
Point in personal selling at which the salesperson asks the customer to make a purchase decision.

Follow-up

The word *close* can be misleading, since the point at which the prospect accepts the seller's offer is where much of the real work of selling begins. In the competitive sales environment of the late 1980s, the successful salesperson seeks to ensure that today's customers will be future purchasers.

The postsales activities that often determine whether a person will become a repeat customer constitute the sales **follow-up.** To the maximum extent possible, the sales representative should contact customers to find out whether they are satisfied with their purchases. This step allows the salesperson to psychologically reinforce the customer's original decision to buy. It gives the seller an opportunity to correct any sources of discontent with the purchase as well as to secure important market information and make additional sales. Automobile dealers often keep elaborate records of their previous customers so that they can promote new models to individuals who already have shown a willingness to buy from them. One successful travel agency never fails to telephone customers upon their return from a trip. Proper follow-up is a logical part of the selling sequence.

Marketers at Sears complement the follow-up activities of their store sales representatives with advertising aimed at emphasizing the service capabilities that are a key component in the purchase of Sears products. The Sears service

follow-up
Postsales activities that often determine whether an individual who has made a recent purchase will become a repeat customer.

Figure 18.5
Postsales Service at Sears

Source: Courtesy of Sears, Roebuck and Company.

network of 15,000 technicians and 12,000 service trucks is described in the advertisement in Figure 18.5.

Effective follow-up also means that the salesperson should conduct a critical review of every call made by asking "What was it that allowed me to close that sale?" or "What caused me to lose that sale?" Such continuous review results in significant sales dividends.

Managing the Sales Effort

sales management
Activities of planning, organizing, staffing, motivating, compensating, and evaluating and controlling a sales force to ensure its effectiveness.

boundary-spanning role
Role performed by a sales manager in linking the sales force to other elements of the organization's internal and external environments.

The overall direction and control of the personal-selling effort is in the hands of **sales management,** which is organized on a hierarchical basis. For example, in a typical geographical sales structure, a district or divisional sales manager might report to a regional or zone manager, and these people, in turn, may report to a national sales manager or vice-president of sales.

Sales managers perform what is known as a **boundary-spanning role;** that is, they link the sales force to other elements of the internal and external environments. The internal organizational environment consists of top management, other functional areas in the firm, and other internal information sources.

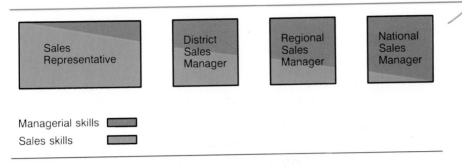

Managerial skills
Sales skills

The external environment includes trade groups, competitors, customers, suppliers, and regulatory agencies.

The sales manager's job requires a unique blend of administrative and sales skills, depending on the specific level in the sales hierarchy. Sales skills are very important for first-level sales managers, since these managers must train and directly lead the sales force. But as one rises in the sales management structure, more managerial skills and fewer sales skills are required for performing the job. This concept is illustrated in Figure 18.6.

Sales management is the administrative channel for sales personnel; it links individual salespersons to general management. The sales manager performs seven basic managerial functions: (1) recruitment and selection, (2) training, (3) organization, (4) supervision, (5) motivation, (6) compensation, and (7) evaluation and control.

Recruitment and Selection

The initial step in building an effective sales force is recruiting and selecting qualified personnel. Sources of new salespeople include colleges and universities, trade and business schools, sales and nonsales personnel in other firms, and the firm's current nonsales employees.

Not all of these sources are equally productive. One problem area involves the reluctance of some high school guidance counselors to promote the advantages of a selling career to students. But in fact, a successful sales career offers satisfaction in all five areas that a person generally considers when deciding on a profession:

1. *Opportunity for advancement.* Studies have shown that successful sales representatives advance rapidly in most companies. Advancement can come either from within the sales organization or laterally to a more responsible position in some other functional area of the firm.

2. *High earnings.* The earnings of successful salespersons compare favorably with those of successful people in other professions. As Figure 18.7 indicates, the average top-level industrial products salesperson earns more than $44,000 per year.

3. *Personal satisfaction.* One derives satisfaction in sales from achieving success in a competitive environment and helping customers satisfy their wants and needs.

Figure 18.7
Average Annual Compensation for Salespeople

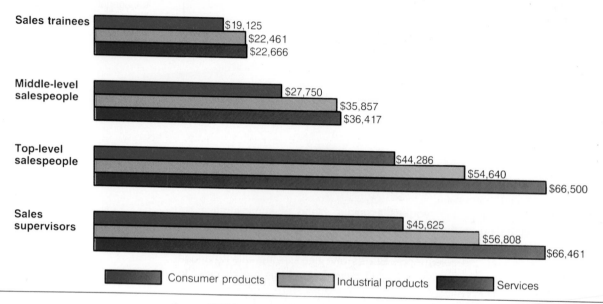

Sales trainees	$19,125 / $22,461 / $22,666
Middle-level salespeople	$27,750 / $35,857 / $36,417
Top-level salespeople	$44,286 / $54,640 / $66,500
Sales supervisors	$45,625 / $56,808 / $66,461

Consumer products   Industrial products   Services

Source: "1987 Survey of Selling Costs," *Sales and Marketing Management* (February 16, 1987), p. 56.

4. *Security.* Contrary to what many students believe, selling provides a high degree of job security. Experience has shown that economic downturns affect personnel in sales less than they do people in most other employment areas. In addition, there is a continuing need for good sales personnel.

5. *Independence and variety.* Salespersons most often operate as "independent" businesspeople or as managers of sales territories. Their work is quite varied and provides an opportunity for involvement in numerous business functions.

The careful selection of salespeople is important for two reasons. First, the selection process involves substantial amounts of money and management time. Second, selection mistakes are detrimental to customer relations and sales force performance as well as costly to correct.

A seven-step process typically is used in selecting sales personnel: application, screening interview, in-depth interview, testing, reference checks, physical examination, and analysis and hiring decision. An application screening is followed by an initial interview. If there is sufficient interest, an in-depth interview is conducted. Next, the company may use testing in its selection procedure, including aptitude, intelligence, interest, knowledge, and/or personality tests. Then references are checked to ensure that job candidates have represented themselves accurately. A physical examination is usually included before the final analysis and hiring decision.

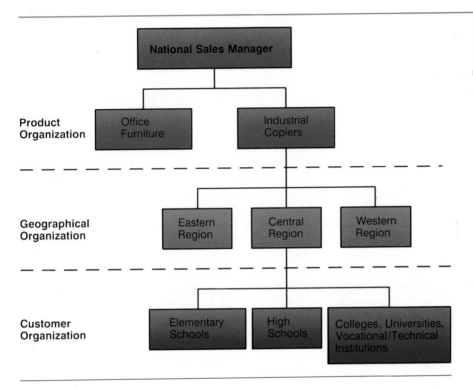

Figure 18.8
Basic Approaches to
Organizing the Sales Force

Training

In order to shape new sales recruits into an efficient sales organization, management must conduct an effective training program. The principal methods used in sales training are lectures, role playing, and on-the-job training.

Ongoing sales training is also important for veteran salespeople. Much of this type of training is conducted by sales managers in an informal manner. A standard format is for the sales manager to travel with a field sales representative periodically and then compose a critique of the person's work. Sales meetings are another important part of training for experienced personnel.

Organization

Sales managers are responsible for the organization of the field sales force. General organizational alignments, which are usually made by top marketing management, may be based on geography, products, types of customers, or some combination of these factors. Figure 18.8 presents simplified organizational charts illustrating each of these alignments.

A product sales organization would have specialized sales forces for each major category of the firm's products. This approach is common among industrial product companies such as Alcoa which market large numbers of similar but separate products that are very technical or of a complex nature and are sold through different marketing channels. A customer organization would use different sales forces for each major type of customer served. For example, Bell

Telephone has systems salespeople specializing in 26 different markets, such as the oil companies. A Bell salesperson assigned to the Texaco account will become extremely knowledgeable about the oil industry and about Texaco's communication system needs.[8]

The final approach, geographical specialization, is a widely used approach for firms marketing similar products throughout a large territory. For example, Textron Chemical, which primarily sells industrial chemicals used in plastics manufacturing, is organized along geographic lines, with an eastern division, central division, and western division. Multinational corporations may have different sales divisions in different continents, with a European division, a North American division, and a Far Eastern division, among others. Geographical organization may also be combined with other organizational methods, such as customer or product.

The individual sales manager also has the task of organizing the sales territories within his or her area of responsibility. Factors such as sales potential, strengths and weaknesses of available personnel, and workloads are considered in territory allocation decisions. The workload method of sales force allocation is described in the Computer Applications at the end of the chapter.

Supervision

A source of constant debate among sales managers is the supervision of the sales force. It is impossible to pinpoint the exact amount of supervision that is correct in each situation, since this varies with the individuals involved and the environments in which they operate. However, the concept of the span of control can be used in reaching some generalizations. In this instance, the *span of control* refers to the number of sales representatives who report to the first level of sales management. The optimal span of control is affected by such factors as complexity of work activities being performed, ability of the individual sales manager, degree of interdependence among individual salespersons, and the extent of training each salesperson receives. Johnson, Kurtz, and Scheuing suggest a 6-to-1 ratio as the optimal span of control for first-level sales managers supervising technical or industrial salespeople. In contrast, they suggest a 12-to-1 ratio if the sales representatives are calling on wholesale and retail accounts.[9]

Motivation

The sales manager's responsibility for motivating the sales force cannot be taken lightly. Because the sales process is a problem-solving one, it often leads to considerable mental pressures and frustrations. Often sales are achieved only after repeated calls on customers and may, especially with new customers and complex technical products, occur over long periods. Motivation of salespeople usually takes the form of debriefings, information sharing, and both psychological and financial encouragement. Appeals to emotional needs, such as ego needs, recognition, and peer acceptance, are examples of psychological encouragement. Monetary rewards and fringe benefits, such as club memberships and sales contest awards, are types of financial incentives.

Ameritech, a Huntington Beach, California, copier dealership, motivates its sales force by giving salespeople who earn at least $40,000 in commissions the

Providing financial incentives and satisfying emotional needs are important aspects of motivating salespeople. Sales managers at Glenfed, Inc., a financial and real estate services corporation, recognize salespersons' achievements with salary incentives, awards, and rallies such as this "Sell-A-Bration" on the Queen Mary in Long Beach, California.

Photo source: Courtesy of Glendale Federal Savings/photography, Scott Slobodian.

choice of a luxury car — a Jaguar, Porsche, Mercedes, or BMW. Those who do not reach the $40,000 mark receive no car at all. The incentive works especially well in California. Ameritech chief executive Tom Barry says, "People out here are in love with their automobiles. And with our freeway system, you spend a lot of time in your car." So far, 13 of the company's 52 salespeople have earned a car, including the youngest person in the sales force—a 23-year-old who chose a Porsche.[10]

Compensation

Because monetary rewards are an important factor in motivating subordinates, compensating sales personnel is a critical matter for managers. Basically, sales compensation can be based on a straight salary plan, a commission plan, or some combination of these.

A **commission** is a payment tied directly to the sales or profits that a salesperson achieves. For example, a sales representative might receive a 5 percent commission on all sales up to a specified quota and 7 percent on sales beyond that point. While commissions provide a maximum selling incentive, they may cause some sales force members to shortchange nonselling activities, such as completing sales reports, delivering sales promotion materials, and normal account servicing. A **salary** is a fixed payment made periodically to an employee. For example, a firm that has decided to use salaries rather than commissions might pay a salesperson a set amount every week.

commission
Incentive compensation directly related to the sales or profits achieved by a salesperson.

salary
Fixed compensation payments made periodically to an employee.

There are both benefits and disadvantages in using predetermined salaries to compensate management and sales personnel. A straight salary plan gives management more control over how sales personnel allocate their efforts, but it reduces the incentive to expand sales. As a result, many firms use compensation programs that combine features of both salary and commission plans. When the Broadway retail store chain in Southern California added a system of sales commissions ranging from 5 percent to 9.5 percent (depending on the items being sold) to a base salary, management discovered that star salespeople increased sales in their individual departments by as much as 20 percent.[11] According to a recent survey of compensation practices, most firms offer a salary-plus-bonus plan (46 percent) or a salary-plus-commission program (46 percent). A small percentage pay salary only (4 percent) or commission only (4 percent).[12]

Evaluation and Control

Perhaps the most difficult tasks required of sales managers are evaluation and control. The basic problems are setting standards and choosing instruments with which to measure sales performance. Sales volume, profitability, and investment return are the usual means of evaluating sales effectiveness. They typically involve the use of a **sales quota**—a specified sales or profit target that a salesperson is expected to achieve. For example, a particular sales representative might be expected to sell $300,000 in territory 414 during a given year. In many cases, the quota is tied to the compensation system.

sales quota
Level of expected sales for a territory, product, customer, or salesperson against which actual results are compared.

Regardless of the key elements in the evaluation program, the sales manager must follow a formal system of decision rules. The purpose of such a system is to supply information to the sales manager for action. What the sales manager needs to know are the answers to three general questions.

First, what are the rankings of the salesperson's performance relative to the predetermined standards? In making this comparison, full consideration should be given to the effect of uncontrollable variables on sales performance. Preferably, each adjusted ranking should be stated in terms of a percentage of the standard. This simplifies evaluation and facilitates converting the various rankings into a single, composite index of performance.

Second, what are the salesperson's strong points? One way to answer this question is to list areas of the salesperson's performance in which he or she has surpassed the respective standard. Another way is to categorize a salesperson's strong points in three areas of the work environment:

1. *Task,* or the person's technical ability. This is manifested in knowledge of the product (end uses), customer, and company, as well as selling skills.
2. *Process,* or the sequence of work flow. This pertains to the actual sales transaction—the salesperson's application of technical ability and interaction with customers. Personal observation frequently is used for measuring process performance. Other measures are sales calls and expense reports.
3. *Goal,* or the end results or output of sales performance. Usually this aspect of the salesperson's work environment is stated in terms of sales volume and profits.

Third, what are the weaknesses or negatives in the salesperson's performance? These should be categorized to the same degree as the salesperson's

Figure 18.9
Performance Evaluation
Summary

Name: *Chris Steinmetz*

Territory: *Southern California*

Time Period Covered: *1st Quarter 1989*

Salesperson's Ability

Strong Points *Has extensive product knowledge, knows end uses*

Keeps up to date on company pricing policies

Weaknesses *Does not have in-depth knowledge of customer requirements*

Selling Proficiency

Strong Points *Exceeded by 20 percent the standard for sales/calls*

Exceeded by 12 percent the standard for sales calls/day

Exceeded by 8 percent the standard for invoice lines/order

Weaknesses *Overspending of expense monies (14 percent)*

Overaggressive in selling tactics

Sales Results

Strong Points *Exceeded sales quota by 3 percent*

Exceeded new account quota by 6 percent

Weaknesses *Turnover of customers amounted to 5 percent*

Repeated delay in report submission

Source: Adapted from H. Robert Dodge, *Field Sales Management* (Dallas, Tex.: Business Publications, 1973), pp. 337–338.

strong points. An evaluation summary for a hypothetical salesperson appears in Figure 18.9.

In making the evaluation summary, the sales manager should follow a set procedure:

1. Each aspect of sales performance for which a standard exists should be measured separately. This helps prevent the halo effect, whereby the rating given on one factor is carried over to other performance variables.

2. Each salesperson should be judged on the basis of actual sales performance rather than potential ability. This emphasizes the importance of rankings in the evaluation.

3. Each salesperson should be judged on the basis of sales performance for the entire period under consideration rather than for particular incidents. As the rater, the sales manager should avoid reliance on isolated examples of the salesperson's success or failure.

4. Each salesperson's evaluation should be reviewed for completeness and evidence of possible bias. Ideally this review would be made by the sales manager's immediate superior.

While the evaluation step includes both revision and correction, the sales manager must focus his or her attention on correction. This translates into ad-

FOCUS ON ETHICS

The Unethical Sales Presentation

Evaluation and control of the sales force is one of the most demanding tasks faced by today's sales managers. When the product they represent is controversial, control can become a critical consideration.

All-terrain vehicles (ATVs) have come under increasing fire because of their tendency to tip over and fall on the rider, causing injury or death. The Consumer Product Safety Commission estimates that 7,000 ATV injuries a month send riders to hospital emergency rooms. Since 1982, ATV accidents have caused an average of 15 deaths per month, almost 40 percent of them children.

In 1987, ATV makers settled a federal lawsuit by agreeing to withdraw from the market all three-wheel models, which are regarded as the most dangerous. They also agreed to continue installing warning labels on four-wheel ATVs concerning proper use and providing driver training for new purchasers. In addition, they promised to refrain from marketing techniques targeted at children under 16, although no age restrictions for riding exist.

One highly publicized instance of questionable personal-selling tactics appeared on "60 Minutes." Motorcycle authority Randy Nelson was sent to buy a Honda ATV for his twin nine-year-old boys. The dealer, located in Yuma, Arizona, tried to sell him an adult vehicle. The presentation went something like this:

Dealer: And right now, their size, this vehicle is just right. Or if . . . you think these guys are going to get really good at, and they really like it, maybe you'll go to the 200.
Nelson: What's the biggest, the one that you'd think that they'd be okay on? 250?
Dealer: Yes.
Nelson: I see this says no passengers. Can these guys ride together or no?
Dealer: Sure.
Nelson: It's okay?
Dealer: They all say that. Now big guys like this now are big enough to carry you on it, two adults.
Nelson: Okay. Yeah, they're almost ten, so they're . . .
Dealer: (cuts in) But they're recommended for one for safety reasons, okay?
Nelson: Okay.
Dealer: But you can ride two on it.
Nelson: Okay . . .

What can a firm do to protect itself from such violations of store and manufacturer policies by its salespeople? One possibility is to borrow a practice from the airline industry and have the manufacturer's employees make "secret shopper" visits to retail outlets to evaluate sales presentations and customer service. Incentive programs could be devised in the form of bonus awards to dealers and individual salespeople for exceptional performance and sanctions against those who violate company policies. If violations have been flagrant or repeated, the manufacturer can even revoke the franchise or other distribution agreement.

Other monitoring methods are possible. The bottom line is that all marketers — at both the manufacturer and retail levels — must find some way to ensure that their policies are followed, particularly those that are critical to corporate integrity.

Sources: Nelson and dealer conversation from "The Most Dangerous Vehicle?" episode from "60 Minutes" (April 12, 1987). See also Lee Byrd, "Manufacturers Agree to Stop Selling ATVs," *The Mobile Register* (December 31, 1987), p. 7A; Daniel B. Moskowitz, "Why ATVs Could Land in a Heap of Trouble," *Business Week* (November 30, 1987), p. 38; and Joseph P. Shapiro, "Crossing Swords over Consumer Safety," *U.S. News & World Report* (October 26, 1987), p. 28.

justing actual performance to predetermined standards. Corrective action, with its obviously negative connotations, typically poses a substantial challenge for the sales manager.

Summary of Chapter Objectives

1. Explain the factors affecting the relative importance of personal selling in the promotional mix. Personal selling is likely to be relatively more important in the following instances: (1) when consumers are concentrated geographically and relatively small in number; (2) when the products or services are expensive, are technically complex, require special handling, or typically involve trade-ins; (3) when channels are relatively short; and (4) when the price of the product or service is relatively high.

2. Contrast field selling, over-the-counter selling, and telemarketing. Field selling involves sales calls to customers at their homes or businesses for the purpose of providing demonstrations or information about the product or service. Over-the-counter (retail) selling involves providing product information and arranging for completion of the sales transaction to customers at the retail location. Telemarketing is used to reduce the substantial cost involved in maintaining a sales force for making personal calls at customers' homes or businesses. It involves personal selling conducted entirely by telephone, either outbound (when salespeople contact customers) or inbound (when customers call to obtain information and make purchases).

3. Identify the three basic sales tasks. Order processing is basically the routine handling of an order; it characterizes a sales setting in which the need is made known to and is acknowledged by the customer. Creative selling is persuasion aimed at making the prospect see the value of the good or service being presented. Missionary sales are indirect selling, such as making goodwill-type calls and providing technical or operational assistance.

4. Outline the steps in the sales process. The basic steps in the sales process are prospecting and qualifying, approach, presentation, demonstration, handling objections, closing, and follow-up.

5. Describe sales management's boundary-spanning role. Sales managers link the sales force to other aspects of the internal and external environments. The internal environment consists of top management, other functional units in the firm, such as advertising, and other internal information sources. The external environment includes trade groups, customers, competitors, suppliers, and regulatory agencies.

6. List the functions of sales management. Sales management involves seven basic functions: recruitment and selection, training, organization, supervision, motivation, compensation, and evaluation and control.

Key Terms

personal selling
field selling
over-the-counter selling
telemarketing
order processing
creative selling
missionary sales
prospecting
qualifying
approach

precall planning
presentation
canned approach
closing
follow-up
sales management
boundary-spanning role
commission
salary
sales quota

Review Questions

1. How does personal selling differ among the three major selling environments? Give examples of local firms that operate in each environment.

2. Explain the AIDA concept and its relationship to the steps in the personal-selling process.

3. Cite two local examples of each of the three basic sales tasks.

4. Under what conditions is the canned approach to selling likely to be used? What are the major problems with this method?

5. Discuss the benefits of a sales career.

6. What roles do flight crews play in an airline's promotional efforts?

7. How does retail selling differ from field selling?

8. Give an example of each function performed by sales managers in an organization.

9. Compare the alternative sales compensation plans. Point out the advantages and disadvantages of each.

10. Explain how a sales manager's problems and areas of emphasis might change in dealing with each of the following:
   a. Telephone salespeople
   b. Over-the-counter retail salespeople
   c. Field sales representatives
   d. Missionary salespeople

Discussion Questions

1. As marketing vice-president of a large paper company, you are asked to address a group of university students about selling as a career. List the five most important points you would make in your speech.

2. Explain and offer examples of how the following factors affect the decision to emphasize personal selling or advertising:
   a. Geographic market concentration
   b. Length of marketing channels
   c. Degree of product technical complexity
   d. Price
   e. Number of customers
   f. Prevalence of trade-ins

3. What sales tasks are involved in selling the following products?
   a. IBM office equipment
   b. United Way (to an employee group)
   c. Arby's fast-food restaurant
   d. Ed's Used Cars
   e. Cleaning compounds for use in plant maintenance

4. How would you describe the job of each of the following salespersons?
   a. Salesperson in a retail record store
   b. Century 21 real estate sales representative
   c. Route driver for Frito-Lay snack foods (sells and delivers to local food retailers)
   d. Sales engineer for Wang computers.

5. Suppose that you are the local sales manager for the telephone company's Yellow Pages and you employ six representatives who call on local firms to solicit advertising space sales. What type of compensation system would you use? How would you suggest that these sales personnel be evaluated?

VIDEO CASE 18

Lipton & Lawry's

Top management at Lipton & Lawry's raves about the firm's sales force. After all, the L&L sales organization is largely responsible for generating annual sales of more than $1.3 billion for the Unilever subsidiary and maintaining market shares of more than 80 percent for several L&L products. Admittedly, the strong consumer franchise enjoyed by such buyer favorites as Lipton's teas and dried soups, Lawry's blended seasonings, and Wishbone salad dressings is a decided advantage, but the marketing leadership at Lipton & Lawry's works hard to ensure that its salespeople are well-prepared to meet customer needs.

Newly-hired field sales personnel must complete a rigorous 27-week training program. The first week of training is spent orienting the new sales representatives, giving them a broad understanding of L&L and the markets it serves. The second week takes them into the field to observe experienced salespeople in action. This is followed by another week of specialized training sessions on selling skills, including three days where they engage in simulated selling situations. Their performances are recorded on videotape and critiqued by experienced sales representatives who conduct the training activities. The next 24 weeks constitute a period of gradually increased responsibility for the trainees. During this period they accompany various L&L sales representatives in calling on established accounts and prospects. At the end of six months, the new sales representatives attend a week-long L&L national training seminar. Here they work on fine-tuning their sales and customer-service skills.

The training program is heavily weighted toward time spent in the field with experienced sales representatives. The approach is a logical one, since the L&L salespeople spend most of their workdays there, representing the company to the retail merchants they call on.

Periodic sales meetings are a fact of life for today's professional salesperson, but poorly planned or unnecessary meetings are blamed as timewasters by the sales forces of many firms. This is not the case at Lipton & Lawry's. "We never have a sales meeting unless there is a reason to have a meeting," says Frank Cleveland, L&L's Los Angeles district sales manager. "The two primary reasons you have sales meetings are, one, to discuss the work plan and the strategies that surround it, and the other reason would be due to motivation: challenging people and showing them how they can accomplish the things that need to be accomplished if the programs we have are properly implemented."

Such programs may involve heavy increases in seasonal advertising, special in-store promotions, use of recipe giveaways, and coupons. To make certain that the sales force believes in the products it represents, members of the L&L sales organization frequently travel to company headquarters, where they participate in blind taste tests of new products. Such participation is useful in involving them in the product development process, providing conviction about product strengths, and supplying them with information about the strengths and weaknesses of competing brands.

Each sales representative is responsible for selling the entire Lipton & Lawry's product line — approximately 250 items — ranging from seasoning salts to taco shells. The L&L sales organization is divided into four regions: West, Midwest, East, and South. Within each region are four or five districts, which are in turn divided into business units.

At the national level, the national sales manager is responsible for direct sales to grocery chains, such as Kroger's, Safeway, and A&P. (Separate divisions are used to market the L&L lines to company buyers for mass merchandisers and drug store chains.)

Each sales unit is staffed by a business manager who calls on the major accounts located in its geographic area, and a retail unit manager who oversees between 6 and 10 of the approximately 35 salespersons in each district. Some units also have senior sales representatives who are responsible for calling on smaller chain-store accounts located in the unit's territory. Each district also has a district sales administrator to handle computer-related activities and a district sales trainer, who is responsible for coordinating training activities for newly-hired salespeople and continuing training activities for experienced sales reps.

L&L sales representatives are compensated on a straight salary basis. However, they can earn bonuses of up to an additional 25 percent of their base salaries, depending on total sales in the district. Merchandisers, approximately 10 in each district, receive hourly wages, but they can also earn bonuses of up to 10 percent of their annual wages depending on district sales.

Selling at Lipton & Lawry's is a two-phase operation. First, the national sales manager and the various unit business managers must sell the product to headquarters buyers of various food chain retailers. Then the retail sales force takes over to meet the needs of the individual stores.

L&L salespeople frequently work in two-person teams consisting of the sales representative and a merchandiser. The latter's responsibilities consist of replacing the physical stock on store shelves, setting up special cardboard displays (known as shippers) of L&L products, and checking inventory, thereby saving the store manager both time and labor costs. Both the merchandiser and the salesperson are trained to spot display opportunities for L&L brands within the store.

The unit retail sales manager performs a number of functions, including sales assistance, motivation, and performance evaluation. Several days will be spent in the field with each sales representative over a three-month period, during which the unit sales manager will assist the salesperson in making difficult sales, handling problems, and conducting on-the-spot performance reviews through what L&L calls *curbstone review*. Such reviews take place immediately following a sales call and consist of a summarization by the manager of positive components of the sales call and suggestions for improvement. The intent, of course, is to aid the sales professional in becoming even more effective. As district sales manager Frank Cleveland points out, "If you're with us a year or 15 years, you're still always learning and growing."

Techniques such as the taste tests and curbstone reviews are intended to enhance motivation. Financial rewards such as the potential bonus are also used. Sales awards are also part of the salesperson motivation formula, and L&L marketers give them on national, regional, district, and business unit levels. All phases of the sales representative's job—selling, merchandising, and customer service—are evaluated in choosing the award winners. Suzanne Valker, a senior sales representative who has won the salesperson of the year award, summed up her goal as a Lipton & Lawry's salesperson, "You want to help the customer."

Questions

1. Draw the Lipton & Lawry's, Inc. sales organization chart. Evaluate the basis used for aligning the L&L sales organization. Why do you feel that one of the other alternative bases for sales force organization was not used?

2. Categorize the L&L salesperson on the following bases described in Chapter 18: (a) personal selling environment and (b) sales tasks. What contributions might result from adding telemarketing to the current use of salespeople?

3. Evaluate the L&L compensation method for its salespeople. Would the use of sales commissions be warranted for this company?

4. Describe the functions performed by the L&L district sales manager and give an example from the case of each function. Propose a performance evaluation method based on the text discussion of sales tasks, process, and goals using the performance evaluation summary shown in the chapter.

COMPUTER APPLICATIONS

Although a quality sales force may represent the difference between marketing success and failure, the salaries and direct expenses needed for supporting a field sales force may be the largest single component of total marketing expenses. Consequently, one important marketing decision involves determining the optimal number of salespersons. This decision often is made by using the *workload* method. It consists of the following steps:[13]

1. *Classify the firm's customers into categories.* Because customers vary greatly in terms of sales, servicing costs, and profitability, they should be divided into categories. One writer estimates that the top 15 percent of a firm's customers will account for 65 percent of its sales, the next 20 percent for 20 percent, and the remaining 65 percent for only 15 percent.[14] The first group might be labeled *type A accounts,* the second *type B accounts,* and the third *type C accounts.* A firm with 5,200 accounts might categorize them as follows:

> 800 type A accounts (high sales, high profitability)
> 1,400 type B accounts (medium sales, moderate profitability)
> 3,000 type C accounts (low sales, low profitability)

2. *Specify the desired number of annual calls for each account type and the average length of each call.* These specifications can be based on analyses of sales call reports submitted by the field sales force. In addition, they are likely to involve the judgment and experience of sales management. Suppose that sales management decides on weekly contacts for type A accounts, biweekly contacts for type B accounts, and monthly contacts for type C accounts. In addition, the desired length of an average sales call is set at 40 minutes for A, 30 minutes for B, and 20 minutes for C. Finally, an additional 10 percent is included for emergency or other unplanned calls in each account category. The number of hours required for each type of account is calculated in Table 1.

Table 1
Determination of Total Number of Hours Required for Sales Calls for Each Type of Account

Type of Account	Number of Contacts per Year	×	Minutes per Sales Call	=	Time Required for Planned Calls	+	Time Required for Unplanned/ Emergency Calls[a]	=	Total Minutes	=	Total Hours
A	52		40		2,080		208		2,288		38.13
B	26		30		780		78		858		14.30
C	12		20		240		24		262		4.40

[a]Estimated by management at 10 percent of total time required for planned calls.

3. *Calculate the total hours required for contacting all accounts.* This step is accomplished by multiplying the total number of hours required for servicing each account type by the number of customers in each category. In this example, the calculation would be:

> 800 type A accounts × 38.13 hours = 30,504 hours
> 1,400 type B accounts × 14.30 hours = 20,020 hours
> 3,000 type C accounts × 4.40 hours = 13,200 hours
>
> Total = 63,724 hours

4. *Calculate the time available for each salesperson.* This step is accomplished by multiplying the number of hours the typical salesperson works each week by the average number of weeks worked per year. If the typical salesperson works 40 hours per week for 46 weeks, the average number of hours per year is 1,840 (40 × 46).

5. *Allocate each salesperson's time to assigned tasks.* A considerable percentage of the typical salesperson's time is spent on activities other than calling on established accounts, such as traveling between accounts. In addition, the typical representative is responsible for such nonselling activities as preparing reports and attending sales meetings. Finally, the salesperson may devote additional time to contacting potential customers. For example, the salesperson working an average of 1,840 hours per year may divide his or her hours as shown in Table 2.

Activity	Percentage of Available Time	Number of Hours per Year
Sales/service calls on established accounts	40%	736
Sales calls on potential accounts	10	184
Travel	30	552
Other nonselling activities	20	368
Total	100%	1,840 hours

Table 2
Allocation of Salesperson's Time to Assigned Tasks

6. *Determine the required number of salespersons.* The final step can be accomplished by dividing the total number of hours required for servicing all accounts by the average number of hours each salesperson devotes to sales and servicing established accounts. The formula is:

$$\text{Required Number of Salespersons} = \frac{\text{Total Number of Hours Required for Servicing Accounts}}{\text{Total Number of Hours Each Salesperson Devotes to Calling on Established Accounts}}$$

$$= \frac{63,724 \text{ hours}}{736 \text{ hours}}$$

$$= 86.6 \text{ or } 87 \text{ salespersons.}$$

Directions: Use menu item 16 titled "Sales Force Size Determination" to solve each of the following problems.

Problem 1   Gwen Finney is a Tampa-based manufacturer's agent in the clothing industry. Over the years, the number of salespersons in her organization has grown along with the number of her firm's retail accounts. Finney divides her 3,500 retail store accounts as follows: 525 type A, 700 type B, and 2,275 type C. She expects each type A account to be contacted once a month and the sales call to last 60 minutes. Type B accounts should be contacted every other month, with the average call lasting 45 minutes. The less profitable type C accounts should be contacted once in the spring, summer, autumn, and winter, with each call lasting an average of 40 minutes. Unplanned/emergency calls add another 5 percent to the total. Finney estimates that her average sales representative works 40 hours each week and 45 weeks each year. Approximately 40 percent of a sales representative's time is spent contacting established accounts, 30 percent on potential accounts, 15 percent on travel, and 15 percent on nonselling activities. How many salespersons does Finney need for covering her market?

Problem 2   John Brodski is vice-president of sales at Ohio-based Springfield Industrial Supplies. Brodski uses three classifications for his firm's 1,600 accounts: 220 type A firms, 580 type B firms, and 800 type C firms. He estimates that type A accounts should be called on 26 times per year and types B and C 20 and 15 times per year, respectively. The length of time for each sales call should be 30 minutes for type A and type B accounts and 15 minutes for type C accounts. Another 15 percent is to be added to each type of account for unplanned/ emergency calls. The typical Springfield Industrial Supplies sales representative works a 40-hour week for 48 weeks each year and devotes 50 percent of his or her time calling on established accounts, 20 percent on potential accounts, 20 percent on travel, and 10 percent on nonselling activities. How many salespersons should Brodski have in his department?

Problem 3   Lynn Victor's sales force calls on 4,000 beauty shops and hairstyling salons throughout Missouri, Kansas, Oklahoma, and Nebraska from her Tulsa headquarters. She estimates that she currently has 800 type A accounts for her firm's beauty supplies, 1,000 type B accounts, and 2,200 type C accounts. Each type A account is contacted every other week for 30 minutes per call, type B accounts are contacted monthly for 30 minutes per call, and type C accounts are contacted every other month for 20 minutes per call. An additional 10 percent of the time involved in contacting established accounts is included for unplanned/ emergency calls. Victor's sales representatives work 48 weeks per year with an average workweek of 40 hours. Each sales representative spends approximately 40 percent of his or her time contacting established accounts, 15 percent on potential accounts, 30 percent on travel, and 15 percent on nonselling activities.
a. How many sales representatives should Victor employ to service her accounts?
b. What effect would reducing the number of weeks worked per year from 48 to 45 have on the size of her sales force?
c. What effect would increasing the amount of time spent on a type C account sales call from 20 to 30 minutes and increasing the number of contacts from 6 to 12 have on the size of Victor's sales force?

Problem 4   Len Gordon is sales manager for a Providence-based industrial distributor. Gordon categorizes 100 of his 600 accounts as type A, 125 as type B, and 375 as type C. Type A accounts are contacted every other week and type B and C accounts once a month. Average sales calls last 30 minutes for type A and B accounts and 20 minutes for type C accounts. An additional 15 percent of the time involved in contacting each account is included for unplanned/emergency calls. Gordon's sales representatives work 40-hour weeks for an average of 47 weeks each year. Gordon estimates that they spend 35 percent of their time on actual sales calls on established accounts, 20 percent on potential accounts, 15 percent on travel, and 30 percent on nonselling activities.
a. How many sales representatives does Gordon need for servicing his accounts?
b. Gordon is considering several methods of reducing sales expenses. Since type C accounts generate smaller sales and profits than do types A and B, he is contemplating reducing the number of contacts from 12 to 6 and lowering the average sales call time from 20 to 15 minutes. What effect would these changes have on the number of sales representatives required?
c. One of Gordon's senior sales representatives has argued that the percentage of time spent on sales calls on established accounts could be increased from 35 to

50 percent by reducing the frequency and amount of reports and other paperwork each salesperson must prepare. Assuming the sales representative is correct, what effect would this change have on the number of sales representatives needed for servicing the firm's accounts?

Problem 5   Tomas Sanchez has gradually increased the market coverage of his Fort Worth–based wholesaling firm; currently it serves retail accounts throughout Texas. His type A accounts represent 15 percent (165) of the firm's 1,100 accounts. Another 25 percent (275) of his accounts are categorized as type B and the remaining 60 percent (660) as type C. Type A accounts are contacted weekly, type B accounts biweekly, and type C accounts monthly. The average length of sales calls for each account type is 40 minutes, 30 minutes, and 20 minutes, respectively. An additional 10 percent is added to the time spent on each type of account as a result of unplanned/emergency calls. Sanchez's sales representatives work 40-hour weeks for an average of 46 weeks each year and spend approximately 35 percent of their time contacting established accounts, 25 percent on potential accounts, 20 percent on travel, and 20 percent on nonselling activities.
a. How many salespersons should Sanchez employ?
b. Sanchez is considering increasing the number of sales calls on type C retail customers from 12 to 24 in order to stimulate additional sales. What impact would this have on the number of salespersons he needs?
c. Rather than attempting to stimulate purchases by type C customers, Sanchez is considering using his current sales force to contact prospective customers. To accomplish this, he would have to reallocate the current usage of time by his sales force. He estimates that he would have to reduce the time spent on established accounts from 35 to 25 percent. What impact would this change have on the number of salespersons needed?

PART

8

Marketing in Special Settings

Photo source: Adam Woolfitt/Woodfin Camp.

19

Global Dimensions of Marketing

Chapter Objectives

1. To describe the importance of international marketing from the perspectives of the individual firm and the nation.

2. To relate marketing environment variables to international marketing.

3. To identify the various methods of entering international markets.

4. To differentiate between a global marketing strategy and a multinational marketing strategy.

5. To describe the alternative product/promotional strategies used in international marketing.

6. To explain the attractiveness of the United States as a target market for foreign marketers.

U. S. marketers who wish to expand their geographic operations to Japan face a number of seemingly insurmountable hurdles, among them cultural differences, distribution snafus, and business practices that radically differ from those of Western countries. Those willing to meet the challenge are advised to proceed with patience, perseverance, and flexibility—virtues that eventually can help build big profits in a nation whose economy is second only to the United States'.

When Ore-Ida Foods, a subsidiary of H. J. Heinz Company, decided to crack the Japanese market in the early 1980s, it not only faced the usual barriers to marketing in Japan; it also was up against selling a product—frozen potatoes—historically not part of the Japanese diet. At the time, demand for frozen potatoes in Japan was only 3 percent of that in the United States. Today Ore-Ida potatoes are stocked in about 11,000 Japanese stores, and the company has joined the ranks of the more than 3,000 U.S. firms that have learned how to market effectively to the Japanese.

Part of Ore-Ida's success stems from its decision to tailor its product to fit the Japanese market. The company reduced the size of its package to accommodate the small freezers in Japanese households. To get its product on store shelves, Ore-Ida made a distribution arrangement with Japan's Mitsubishi Corporation, coupled with a dedicated Ore-Ida sales force.

Ore-Ida's next challenge was to persuade Japanese consumers to buy frozen potatoes. Unlike Americans, the Japanese dislike hard-sell advertising approaches that focus on product benefits and testimonials; rather, they expect ads to entertain

them. To promote Ore-Ida potatoes, the firm's Japanese advertising agency, Dai-Ichi Kikaku, came up with the idea of using a cute cartoon character. Ore-Ida initially resisted the idea as too gimmicky, but the agency convinced the company that such characters are big hits with Japanese consumers. It even cited the Tokyo police, whose mascot is a floppy-eared mouse called Peepokun.

Thus was born Mr. Ore-Ida, an Idaho potato with a whimsical face and decked out in a red-white-and-blue farmer's cap and overalls flaunting a stars-and-stripes emblem— an outfit that gives the product a decidedly American cachet. Research showed that Mr. Ore-Ida increased brand awareness to 64 percent of Tokyo homemakers and 92 percent of children.[1]

Photo source: Ore-Ida Foods.

Chapter Overview

Increasing numbers of U.S. organizations are crossing national boundaries in search of markets and profits. For many of these firms, the international marketplace generates a sizable portion of total revenues and profits. Johnson & Johnson receives 43 percent of its total revenue and 90 percent of its net income from abroad. Gillette, NCR, Eastman Kodak, Coca-Cola, and Dow Chemical derive more than 40 percent of their annual earnings from international operations.

Overseas sales are also important to many U.S. service firms. American Express earns about 20 percent of its profits from operations abroad. More than half of Manpower's revenue comes from temporary-help operations in 31 foreign countries. Software firms such as Lotus Development, Microsoft, and Ashton-Tate get between 20 and 40 percent of revenues from foreign sales. The Chase Manhattan Bank advertisement in Figure 19.1 illustrates that organization's involvement in global marketing. With operations in more than 100 countries, Chase receives 46 percent of its revenues and 20 percent of its profits from foreign operations.

Just as some firms depend on foreign sales, others rely on purchasing raw materials for use in their domestic manufacturing operations. A furniture company's purchase of South American mahogany is an example.

Components of a firm's international product line may be acquired through foreign purchases. Although Sony Corporation of Japan is one of the world's leading innovators in developing sophisticated electronic equipment ranging from digital audiotape recorders and high-quality TV sets to compact receivers and disk-based storage devices, the firm's marketers recognize that software is typically more profitable than hardware. In 1988, it agreed to pay CBS $2 billion for CBS Records, whose contract roster of performers includes such international recording stars as Bruce Springsteen, Bob Dylan, Michael Jackson, Barbra Streisand, and Willie Nelson. These artists will continue to produce software products to complement the sale of Sony's entire product line.

International marketing is valuable to the individual firm for other reasons. In some instances, the company discovers significant product innovations being offered by competitors in foreign markets. These improved offerings may be adapted for the firm's product line currently being offered in its home country, thereby providing a way to generate profitable new-product ideas. Another reason is that the global marketer may be able to meet foreign competition abroad before the latter infringes on home markets. After Japan's Makita Electric Works succeeded in capturing a 20 percent market share for professional tools in Europe over a three-year period by offering a highly standardized, low-priced product line, Black & Decker responded with a crash program designed to cut costs and tighten quality control to match the Japanese firm's retail prices. These corrective measures prevented Makita from expanding its European successes to the United States.

Foreign marketers, in turn, are becoming increasingly attracted to the huge U.S. market. Foreign product invasions are no longer limited to such industries as automobiles, electronics, and steel. Americans buy tires from Canada, jewelry boxes from Taiwan, golf balls from South Korea, vitamin C from West Germany, and Gouda cheese from the Netherlands.

International trade is vital to a nation and its marketers for several reasons. It expands the market and makes production and distribution economies feasi-

Figure 19.1
Chase Manhattan Bank: An International Service Marketer

Source: Courtesy of Chase Manhattan Bank.

ble. It also means more jobs at home: Each billion dollars of exports supports about 25,000 jobs.

Foreign trade can be divided into **exporting**—selling goods and services abroad—and **importing**—purchasing foreign goods and raw materials. Major U.S. exports include transportation equipment, electrical and electronic equipment, specialty chemicals, computers, semiconductors, drugs, and food and related products. Although U.S. marketers may never make a significant comeback in such mass-manufactured commodities as textiles, shoes, consumer electronics, and machine tools, the more complex the product, the more likely American marketers will enjoy a significant competitive advantage over foreign competitors. U.S. firms account for 40 percent of the world market share for semiconductors, two-thirds of the worldwide personal computer market, and 90 percent of all jet engines sold. In addition, U.S. firms remain the leading force in health care, entertainment, and financial services.[2]

The foreign products Americans most often purchase include transportation equipment, electrical and electronic equipment, machinery, primary metals, petroleum and coal products, and apparel and other mill products. While the United States trades hundreds of thousands of products with many countries,

exporting
Marketing of goods and services in foreign countries.

importing
Purchasing of foreign products and raw materials.

Table 19.1
Successful U.S. Exporters of
Products and Services

Company	Exports as a Percentage of Total Sales
Boeing	45%
MGM/UA Communications	38
Advanced Micro Devices	37
Pittston	36
Teradyne	34
Computervision	30
Caterpillar	28
Universal Leaf Tobacco	26
Cray Research	24
McDonnell Douglas	22

Source: Data from Standard & Poor's Compustat Services, Inc.; reported in *Business Week* (November 16, 1987), p. 169.

its major trading partners are Canada, Japan, Mexico, the United Kingdom, and West Germany.

Although the United States is the world's second largest exporter and largest importer, foreign trade is less critical to it than to many other nations. In fact, U.S. exports account for a modest 4.9 percent of the nation's gross national product. In contrast, exports comprise 13 percent of Japan's GNP, 27 percent of Canada's and West Germany's GNP, and 55 percent of the Netherlands' GNP. The leading U.S. firms in volume of export sales are General Motors, Boeing, Ford, General Electric, and IBM. Table 19.1 lists the most successful U.S. exporters in terms of exports as a percentage of total sales.

Since the marketing functions of buying, selling, transporting, storing, standardization/grading, financing, risk taking, and obtaining market information must be performed regardless of whether the market is domestic or global, a question arises about the wisdom of treating international marketing as a distinct subject. After all, international marketing is marketing—that is, the firm performs the same functions and has the same objectives. Although international marketing requires implementation of marketing strategies consisting of identification of target markets, analyses of environmental influences, and development of marketing mixes, both similarities and differences between international and domestic marketing exist. This chapter examines the characteristics of the international marketplace, environmental influences on international marketing, and the development of an international marketing mix. It also discusses the sequence of steps that most firms use in entering the international marketplace.

The International Marketplace

Many U.S. firms never venture outside their domestic markets; they feel they do not have to because the U.S. market is huge. Even today only about 10 percent of domestic manufacturing firms export their products and only 250 of these account for 80 percent of all U.S. exports.[3] Those that do venture abroad find the international marketplace far different from the domestic one. Market

Photo source: Costa Manos/Magnum.

With a population over the 1 billion mark, China represents a huge market for many U.S. firms. Corning Glass Works has designed and built a television-bulb glass manufacturing plant in the People's Republic of China as part of its expanded marketing involvement in Asia. The Pacific Rim nations, which comprise the world's fastest-growing economic region, offer great potential for Corning and other international marketers.

sizes, buyer behavior, and marketing practices all vary, meaning that international marketers must carefully evaluate all market segments in which they expect to compete.

Market Size

In 1865 the world population was recorded at 1 billion. By 1989 it exceeded 5 billion, and forecasters predict that it will reach 6 billion by the year 2000—just 13 years after the 5 billion mark was reached.

The United States has attained one of the highest standards of living in world history, but its population size is insignificant when compared with the rest of the world. The U.S. population is dwarfed by those of countries such as India and China. While one-fifth of the world's population lives in China, only one-twentieth resides in the United States.

A prime ingredient of market size is population growth. Every day the world's population increases by about 200,000 people; hence, it is expected to be 8.2 billion by 2025. A review of these projections produces some important contrasts. Average birthrates are dropping, but death rates are declining even more rapidly. In the next 25 years, the population of more developed countries is expected to rise from 1.2 billion to only 1.4 billion and that of less developed countries from 4 billion to 6.8 billion. Nearly 80 percent of the population in 2025 will live in less developed nations.

The world marketplace is increasingly an urban marketplace. By the year 2000, almost one of every two of the world's inhabitants will live in large cities. These cities are also growing in size: 39 of them currently have a population of

5 million or more. Mexico City, whose population of 18 million ranks it as the world's largest city, is expected to grow to 26.3 million by the year 2000. Increased urbanization will expand the need for transportation, housing, machinery, and services.

The increased size and growing urbanization of the international marketplace does not mean that all foreign markets will offer the same market potential. Income differences, for instance, vitally affect any nation's market potential. India has a population of 830 million, but its per capita income of $150 is very low. Canada's population of 27 million, on the other hand, is only a small fraction of India's, but its per capita income is about $10,000.

Another factor influencing market potential is the stage of a nation's economic development. In *subsistence economies,* in which most people engage in agriculture and per capita income is low, few opportunities for international trade exist. In *newly industrialized countries,* such as Brazil and South Korea, an increase in manufacturing creates more demand for consumer goods and industrial goods such as high-technology equipment. As countries become more developed, they give rise to an increasingly affluent and educated middle class, creating a need for more leisure goods and services ranging from child care to financial. The *industrial nations*—the United States, Japan, France, Great Britain, and West Germany—trade manufactured goods and services among themselves and export to less developed countries. With their large middle classes and high per capita incomes, industrial nations constitute attractive opportunities for international marketers. Luxury goods, such as the expensive Louis Vuitton luggage promoted in the advertisement in Figure 19.2, are targeted at affluent consumers in industrialized countries. While affluent households exist in every nation, their concentration in industrial nations makes effective marketing programs implemented in these countries pay off in sales and profits.

Buyer Behavior

Buyer behavior differs among countries and often among different market segments within each nation. Therefore, marketers should carefully study each market before implementing a marketing strategy. In marketing corn flakes and other ready-to-eat breakfast cereals in France, Kellogg Company marketers use advertising and packaging instructions to overcome certain ingrained consumer habits. Kellogg's marketing research has shown that French breakfast eaters prefer a croissant, but about one-third of the adult population skips breakfast entirely. Only a small percentage of French adults eat cereal, and of those, 40 percent pour warm milk over it. To persuade the French to try an American-style, cold-cereal breakfast, Kellogg includes step-by-step instructions on packages that explain how to prepare a bowl of cereal and stress the use of cold milk. Television commercials reinforce the idea of using cold milk. They show milk being poured from a transparent glass pitcher, which the French customarily use for cold milk, rather than the opaque porcelain jug from which the French pour hot milk into their morning cup of café au lait.[4]

Marketers must also be careful to make their marketing strategies comply with local customs, tastes, and living conditions. In some cases, even the product itself must be modified. Remington Products, Inc., for example, offers different styles of its electric shavers for overseas markets. In Great Britain, where few bathrooms have electric outlets, Remington markets a battery-powered

Figure 19.2

Marketing to Affluent Consumers in Industrialized Nations

Source: Courtesy Louis Vuitton.

shaver. For Japanese consumers, Remington has redesigned its product to accommodate smaller hands.[5]

Different buying patterns mean that marketing executives should do considerable research before entering a foreign market. Sometimes the research can be done by the marketer's own organization or a U.S.-based research firm. In other cases, a foreign-based marketing research organization is needed. Foreign research firms are often innovative. For example, Audits, Ltd., of Great Britain pioneered the field of home audits of package goods. The British firm provided its respondents with special trash containers rather than relying on diaries of purchases. It then studied discarded packages to determine consumer buying patterns.[6]

The Environment for International Marketing

Various environmental factors can influence international marketing strategy. Marketers should be as aware of economic, social/cultural, and political/legal influences in foreign markets as they are of those in domestic ones.

Economic Factors

A nation's size, per capita income, and stage of economic development determine its feasibility as a candidate for international business expansion. Nations with low per capita incomes may be poor markets for expensive industrial machinery but good ones for agricultural hand tools. These nations cannot afford the technical equipment an industrialized society needs. Wealthier countries may be prime markets for the products of many U.S. industries, particularly those involving consumer goods and advanced industrial products.

Another economic factor that marketers must consider is a country's infrastructure. **Infrastructure** refers to a nation's communication systems (television, radio, print media, telephone services), transportation networks (paved roads, railroads, airports), and energy facilities (power plants, gas and electric utilities). An inadequate infrastructure may constrain marketers' plans to manufacture, advertise, and distribute products and services. Infrastructures must be evaluated even when considering an international venture in an industrialized nation. For example, to ensure access to its new theme park outside Paris, Disney managers requested that the French government build subway extensions to the park and add new highway interchanges.[7]

Changes in exchange rates can also complicate international marketing. An **exchange rate** is the price of one nation's currency in terms of other countries' currencies. From 1980 to 1985, the U.S. dollar was strong compared to other currencies; in 1985, for example, $1 could be exchanged for 3.3 German deutschemarks or about 240 Japanese yen. During this period, West German and Japanese consumers and industrial buyers considered U.S. products relatively expensive, while American shoppers thought foreign goods were attractively priced. Overseas sales of many U.S. exporters suffered during this period; some firms even withdrew from certain export markets due to lack of sales and profits. By 1988, the dollar had declined significantly against these and other currencies in the face of huge balance of trade deficits and world concerns over the possibility of recession. For example, during one period the dollar declined to 1.6 deutschemarks and 120 yen. The impact of these fluctuations was all too evident to U.S. travelers, who discovered that it took twice as many dollars to purchase the same products and services in West Germany and Japan as it had only three years before. But the exchange rate fluctuations helped ease the balance-of-trade problem, because they resulted in less expensive U.S. products for West German and Japanese shoppers and higher prices for products imported from these countries for U.S. buyers.

infrastructure
A nation's communication systems (television, radio, print media, telephone services), transportation networks (paved roads, railroads, airports), and energy facilities (power plants, gas and electric utilities).

exchange rates
Price of one nation's currency in terms of other countries' currencies.

Social/Cultural Factors

Before entering a foreign market, firms must study all aspects of a nation's culture, including language, education, social values, and religious attitudes. In India, where many women still cover their bodies from head to toe, Western-style advertisements showing women clad in swimsuits or jeans have offended religious fundamentalists and women's rights advocates. As a result, the Indian Parliament has proposed a law that, if passed, would carry a fine of $7,000 and a prison sentence of up to five years for advertisers who "indecently" portray women.[8]

Because languages frequently differ in international markets, firms must take pains to ensure that their communications are correctly translated and con-

THE COMPETITIVE EDGE

American Family Life Assurance Company

Marketing the right product at the right time, in the right place, and in the right way has earned an American firm the distinction of being one of the most successful companies—domestic or foreign—doing business in Japan. Those achievements are attributed to John Amos, founder and chief marketer of American Family Life Assurance Company of Columbus, Georgia. In 1970, Amos decided to take his product—cancer insurance—to Japan. Today American Family Life is Japan's largest writer of cancer policies, insuring about 14 percent of Japan's 120 million people and receiving two-thirds of its revenues from Japan.

One important factor in the timing of American Family's entry in Japan was the Japanese government's decision to open its insurance market to foreign firms. The government stipulated, however, that foreign competitors could enter the market only by offering a type of insurance not provided by Japanese firms. At the time, American Family's product was new to Japan, as no domestic firm sold cancer insurance.

But even with the right product, American Family's success didn't come overnight. As Amos points out, "You've got to be patient as Job and figure out how to do things the Japanese way." Amos was patient: He waited four years after filing an application with the Japanese government before being allowed to sell the first policy in 1975.

About the time that American Family began offering its unique insurance in Japan, Japanese health officials released a report citing cancer as the major cause of death in Japan. Cancer-related deaths—1 out of every 4.2 deaths—had moved ahead of both strokes and heart disease. The announcement was a boon to American Family's sales. While Amos expected to sell 15,000 policies the first year, the final tally came to 250,000. Sales have mushroomed each year since. American Family is now one of the 20 largest insurers in Japan.

Why are the Japanese more receptive to cancer insurance than people in the United States? The answer lies in the nations' medical systems. Unlike the United States, Japan has a socialized medical system that does not offer complete coverage for prolonged and expensive medical treatment. Thus, the Japanese are big buyers of supplemental coverage from private firms.

But Amos didn't stop at supplying an innovative product that consumers want and need. He also devised a unique way to market it—a plan especially suited to Japan's features of lifetime employment and low employee turnover. Instead of selling insurance the way most Japanese firms do—using part-time salespeople for door-to-door sales—American Family formed an all-Japanese sales force, consisting mainly of retired workers, that markets group policies directly to large corporations such as Nippon Steel and Hitachi. Because premiums are paid through payroll deductions, American Family does not incur the costs of processing bills.

American Family is looking to fill other Japanese market niches. Paul Otake, president of the firm's Japan branch, emphasizes: "We have to keep one hand on the rudder, which is the present, and the other sketching a map for the future." Part of Japan's future is the task of providing for an ever growing older population; by 2000, one-fifth of Japan's population will be 60 or older. In its attempt to be a future provider, American Family now offers dementia insurance—a policy intended to supplement Japanese pension plans.

Sources: Amos and Otake quotes from Kenneth F. Englade, "Getting a Piece of the Japanese Pie," *American Way* (April 1, 1987), pp. 46–48, 50–53. See also "Patient Insurer," *Forbes* (January 11, 1988), p. 154. *Photo source:* Courtesy of American Family Life Assurance Company of Columbus.

vey the intended meanings. A classic example of an international miscommunication is PepsiCo's theme "Come Alive with Pepsi," which in German translates as "Come Alive Out of the Grave."

U.S. products sometimes face consumer resistance abroad. American automobiles, for example, traditionally have been rejected by European drivers, who complain of poor styling, low gasoline mileage, and inferior handling. But Detroit's new, smaller cars are making modest inroads into European markets. This reversal suggests that it is not always possible to determine the precise impact of cultural, economic, or societal factors prior to entering a foreign market. For centuries Japanese tea drinkers have preferred natural tea, but Boston Tea Company's blended, spiced, and herbal teas now sell well in Japan.

Political/Legal Factors

Political factors greatly influence international marketing. Political turmoil in the Philippines, Lebanon, Nicaragua, El Salvador, and Iran suggests how volatile this factor can be in international markets. Sometimes political unrest results in acts of violence, such as destruction of a firm's property. The Managua, Nicaragua, paint factory of H. B. Fuller Company, a U.S. manufacturer of paints, adhesives, and coatings, was burned to the ground by a group of Sandinista revolutionaries. Fuller's main competitor in Managua is a nationalized firm.[9]

Many U.S. firms have set up internal political risk assessment (PRA) units or turned to outside consulting services to evaluate the political risks of the marketplaces in which they operate. Sometimes marketing strategies must be adjusted to reflect the new situation. For example, when Colgate-Palmolive introduced Irish Spring in England, it marketed the soap as Nordic Spring.

Many nations try to achieve political objectives through international business activities. Japan, for instance, has openly encouraged involvement in international marketing because much of its economy depends on overseas sales.

Legal requirements complicate world marketing. A law in France prohibits comparative advertising. Indonesia has banned commercial advertisements from its single television channel; it feared that such advertisements would cause people living in rural areas—80 percent of the nation's population—to envy city dwellers. All commercials in the United Kingdom and Australia must be cleared in advance. In the Netherlands, ads for candy must show a toothbrush. Some nations have local content laws specifying the portion of a product that must come from domestic sources. Other governments require that package and labeling information be provided in local languages. These examples suggest that managers involved in international marketing must be well versed in legislation affecting their specific industries.

The legal environment for U.S. firms operating abroad can be divided into three dimensions: (1) U.S. law, (2) international law, and (3) legal requirements of host nations. International law can be found in the treaties, conventions, and agreements that exist among nations. The United States has many **friendship, commerce, and navigation (FCN) treaties**—agreements that deal with many aspects of commercial relations with other countries, such as the right to conduct business in the treaty partner's domestic market. Other international business agreements concern worldwide standards for various products, patents, trademarks, reciprocal tax treaties, export control, international air travel, and

friendship, commerce, and navigation (FCN) treaties International agreements that deal with many aspects of commercial relations among nations.

Photo source: Courtesy of Ford Motor Company.

Political conflicts among host nations have influenced the international marketing activities of U.S. firms. Arab nations, for example, have boycotted the products of several U.S. firms with investments in Israel. In 1966, an Arab boycott was placed on the Ford Motor Company. With the lifting of the boycott almost 20 years later, Ford has returned to the region and has appointed dealerships in many Arab nations, including the Arabian Motors Group in Kuwait.

international communication. The International Monetary Fund lends foreign exchange to nations that require it in order to conduct international trade. These agreements facilitate the whole process of world marketing.

The legal requirements of host nations affect foreign marketers. For example, some nations limit foreign ownership in their business sectors. International marketers generally recognize the importance of obeying the laws and regulations of the countries within which they operate. Even the slightest violations of these legal requirements would set back the future of international trade.

International marketing is subject to various trade regulations, tax laws, and import/export requirements. One of the best-known U.S. laws is the Webb-Pomerene Export Trade Act (1918), which exempts from antitrust laws various combinations of U.S. firms acting together to develop foreign markets. Its intent is to give U.S. industry economic power equal to that possessed by cartels, the monopolistic organizations of foreign firms. Companies operating under the Webb-Pomerene Act cannot reduce competition within the United States or use "unfair methods of competition." Generally, Webb-Pomerene associations have been insignificant in the growth of U.S. trade.

Other legislation that has had a major impact on international marketing is the Foreign Corrupt Practices Act of 1977, which makes it illegal to bribe a foreign official in an attempt to solicit new or repeat sales abroad. The act also mandates that adequate accounting controls be installed to monitor internal compliance. Violations can result in a $1 million fine for the firm and a $10,000 fine and five years' imprisonment for the individuals involved. This law has been controversial, mainly because it fails to clearly define what constitutes bribery. Efforts to amend the law to include more specific statements of prohibited practices are in progress.

tariff
Tax levied against imported products.

General Agreement on Tariffs and Trade (GATT)
International trade agreement that has helped reduce world tariffs.

import quota
Trade restriction that limits the number of units of certain products that can enter a country for resale.

embargo
Complete ban on the import of specified products.

exchange control
Method used to regulate the privilege of international trade among importing organizations by controlling access to foreign currencies.

dumping
Controversial practice of selling a product in a foreign market at a price lower than that it receives in the producer's domestic market.

Trade Barriers Assorted trade barriers also affect global marketing. These barriers are most commonly implemented through **tariffs**—taxes levied against imported products. Some tariffs are based on a set tax per pound, gallon, or unit; others are calculated according to the imported product's value.

Tariffs can be classified as either revenue or protective tariffs. *Revenue tariffs* are designed to raise funds for the importing government. Most early U.S. government revenue came from this source. *Protective tariffs,* which are usually higher than revenue tariffs, are designed to raise the retail price of an imported product to match or exceed that of a similar domestic product. In 1983, Harley-Davidson Motor Company requested that the International Trade Commission impose a protective tariff on large-size motorcycles imported from Japan. At the time, Japanese imports from Honda, Yamaha, Kawasaki, and Suzuki held 86 percent of the U.S. market while Harley's share had dropped from 21 percent in 1978 to 12 percent in 1983 and the firm was facing bankruptcy. The special tariff was set up on a sliding scale, adding 45 percent to the cost of Japanese imports in 1983 and gradually reducing the tariff to 10 percent in 1988. During that period, Harley implemented productivity improvements that made its products more competitive with imports. By 1986, Harley had regained 19 percent of the market and a year later asked the government to end the special protection.[10]

In the past, it was believed that a country should protect its infant industries by using tariffs to keep out foreign-made products. Some foreign goods did enter, but the high tariff payments made domestic products competitive in price. Recently it has been argued that tariffs should be raised to protect employment and profits in domestic U.S. industries.

Since 1947, the **General Agreement on Tariffs and Trade (GATT)**, an international trade accord, has sponsored eight major tariff negotiations that have reduced worldwide tariff levels. The latest series of conferences, called the *Uruguay Round,* was begun in 1986 to discuss stabilization of currencies and prevention of protectionist legislation.

Still other forms of trade restrictions exist. **Import quotas** limit the number of units of products in certain categories that can be imported. They seek to protect domestic industry and employment and to preserve foreign exchange. The ultimate quota is the **embargo**—a complete ban on the import of certain products. In the past, the United States has prohibited the import of products from some Communist countries. It has also used export quotas; in 1986, for example, President Reagan banned trade with Libya.

Foreign trade can also be regulated by exchange control through a central bank or government agency. **Exchange control** means that firms that gain foreign exchange by exporting must sell this exchange to the central bank or other agency and importers must buy foreign exchange from the same organization. The exchange control authority can then allocate, expand, or restrict foreign exchange according to existing national policy.

Dumping: A Contemporary Marketing Problem The practice of selling a product in a foreign market at a price lower than that it commands in the producer's domestic market is called **dumping.** It is often argued that foreign governments give substantial export support to their own companies. Such support may permit these firms to extend their export markets by offering lower prices abroad.

FOCUS ON ETHICS

Buy American?

Survey findings reveal that as many as 90 percent of American consumers prefer U.S.-made goods to imported ones. According to John A. McConville, director of merchandise at retailing giant J. C. Penney, whether a product is made in the United States "makes a significant amount of difference to a high percentage of consumers in industrial sectors of the country. Now it's spreading to other areas." This desire to "buy American" is being reflected in the merchandise and promotions of Penney, Wal-Mart, and other U.S. retailers that are highlighting American-made goods in their stores and catalogs.

Part of the reason for the increased preference for American goods is consumer awareness of the large number of jobs being lost to foreign competition, particularly in such industries as textiles and shoes, steel, and automobiles. This explains why the "buy American" campaigns were used early—and successfully—in hard-hit industrial areas. The patriotic appeals have hit a responsive chord throughout the United States. Consumers generally like feeling that they can help maintain the nation's global competitiveness with their product choices, provided that they need not sacrifice reasonable prices and quality levels.

Marketers recognize the presence of these purchase motivations and are doing their best to link U.S. products to U.S. customers. But are the goods touted as "made in the USA" really domestic products, or is their claim tenuous? Take the textile industry, one of those hit hardest by foreign competition. Textile marketers sponsored a three-year, $40 million advertising campaign using the theme "Crafted with Pride in the USA." Meanwhile, Bugle Boy Industries is wrapping itself in the flag with its successful line of Bugle Boy USA pants—made entirely in Asia.

Then there's the automobile industry. Although choosing between a Honda 626 and a Chevy Nova appears to be a simple matter for a patriotic car buyer seeking to support the domestic auto industry, the choice is likely to be misleading because two-thirds of both cars' components are purchased from foreign suppliers. All of the Big Three U.S. automakers import vehicles from abroad, and their domestically built cars and trucks sometimes contain a high proportion of foreign-made parts. To further complicate matters, a growing number of Japanese auto companies have begun producing cars and light trucks in the United States. In one case, General Motors Corporation and Toyota use the same California plant for production. After listening to the advertising of competing U.S. automakers, many consumers would give Chrysler their "buy American" awards based on its campaign "The Pride is Back." Interestingly, however, one Chrysler product in nine—from the Japanese-made Colt to the Canadian-made minivan—is imported. This proportion is far higher than those of GM (3.4 percent) and Ford (0.7 percent).

A similar situation exists with computers. Many computers supposedly "made in the USA" are built entirely of imported parts and subassemblies, with only their final assembly performed in the United States.

In all of these cases, the problems facing shoppers who wish to support U.S.-built products is a lack of knowledge. Distinguishing between an American-made good and one that is largely or wholly foreign requires unbiased sources of product information, such as the data provided in *Consumer Reports* and similar publications. Such product reports typically include data on the country of origin as well as product quality. Amid the current torrent of "Buy American" promotions, the old consumer adage *caveat emptor* still applies.

Sources: McConville quotation from Kenneth Dreyfack, "Draping Old Glory Around Just about Everything," *Business Week* (October 27, 1986), p. 66. See also Jason Zweig, "Buy American—and Win," *Forbes* (July 13, 1987), p. 14.

Products that have been dumped on U.S. markets can be subject to additional import tariffs to bring their prices in line with those of domestically produced products. For instance, a 32 percent dumping duty was assessed against five Japanese steel sellers. In response to Japan's dumping of semiconductor chips below cost, President Reagan threatened to set new, stiff tariffs at 100 percent if Japan did not stop the dumping. The tariffs would be imposed not only on the chips but on consumer electronics and other Japanese exports.[11]

foreign licensing
Agreement in which a domestic firm permits a foreign company to either produce or distribute the firm's goods in the foreign country or gives it the right to utilize the firm's trademark, patent, or processes in a specified geographical area.

Foreign licensing is an agreement in which a firm permits a foreign company to produce and distribute its merchandise or use its trademark, patent, or processes in a specified geographical area. Hasbro, for example, has licensing agreements with firms in Japan and Latin America to locally manufacture, distribute, and market Hasbro toys. Licensing offers several advantages over exporting, including availability of local marketing information and distribution channels and protection from various legal barriers. Because licensing does not require a capital outlay, it is an attractive entry method for many firms, especially small ones.

A firm that maintains a separate marketing or selling operation in a foreign country is involved in *overseas marketing*. Examples are foreign sales offices and overseas marketing subsidiaries. The product may be produced by domestic factories, foreign licensees, or contract manufacturers, but the company always directly controls foreign sales.

Foreign production and foreign marketing, the ultimate degree of company involvement in the international market arena, may be performed in one of the following ways:

1. The firm may set up its own production and marketing operation in the foreign country. Baxter Travenol Laboratories, Inc., a U.S. supplier of health care products, services, and systems, operates manufacturing plants in 21 countries, a strategy that gives it a competitive advantage in penetrating overseas markets.[15]

2. The firm may acquire an existing firm in the country in which it wants to do business. In an effort to expand its operations in the United States, Cadbury Schweppes PLC of Great Britain, maker of candy and soft drinks, acquired the Canada Dry and Sunkist labels.

3. The firm may form a **joint venture,** in which it shares the risks, costs, and management of the foreign operation with one or more partners who are usually nationals of the host country.

joint venture
Agreement in which a firm shares the risks, costs, and management of a foreign operation with one or more partners who are usually citizens of the host country.

In recent years, several U.S. firms have formed joint ventures in China and the Soviet Union. Kentucky Fried Chicken International opened the first fast-food restaurant in China through a joint venture with Beijing Travel and Tourism Corporation and Beijing Corporation of Animal Products Processing Industry and Commerce.[16] Top management of the U.S. firm Combustion Engineering has set up a joint venture with the Soviet Ministry of Oil Refining and Petrochemical Industry to manufacture oil and petrochemical controls and help manage the modernization of Soviet refineries and plants.[17] A joint venture company formed by U.S.-based Welch Foods and its Japanese partner, Welch Foods of Japan Limited, promotes Welch's juices to upscale Japanese consumers through advertisements such as the one in Figure 19.4. In the ad copy, a mother describes her son's lively nature and explains how Welch's all-natural juices, with no sugar or additives, benefit his general health.

The Multinational Corporation

World marketing often is closely associated with multinational firms. For example, Switzerland's Nestlé now operates in more than 50 national markets, with 140,000 employees and over 280 plants. Sales total approximately $13.3 billion. Nestlé obtains 40 percent of its revenue from Europe, 28 percent from Third World nations, and the remainder primarily from the United States and Japan.[18]

Figure 19.4
Marketing Welch's Juices in
Japan by Joint Venture

Source: © 1987 Welch Foods, Concord, Mass. and Welch Foods of Japan Limited. Agency: Nihon Keiszisha
Advertising, Tokyo.

A **multinational corporation** is a firm with significant operations and mar-
keting activities outside its home country. Examples of multinationals include
General Electric, Siemens, and Mitsubishi in the heavy electrical equipment in-
dustry; Caterpillar and Komatsu in large construction equipment; and Timex,
Seiko, and Citizen in watches. The 10 largest U.S. multinationals are listed in
Table 19.2.

The worldwide operations of Hewlett-Packard illustrate how a firm can operate effectively in dozens of different nations. The California-based electronics
company sells nearly as much abroad as it does in the United States. How does
Hewlett-Packard do it? The company encourages its European subsidiaries to
run autonomously with European management and to use local technical talent
for producing export products. Hewlett-Packard's German subsidiary has been
particularly successful, deriving more than half of its revenues from non-Ger-
man markets. Some German executives now manage Hewlett-Packard operations in California.[19]

Changing Attitudes toward Multinationals   One would expect India to
worry about foreign-based multinationals operating within its borders after the
Bhopal chemical leak disaster. But on the contrary, the nation's policy under
Prime Minister Rajiv Gandhi is to seek greater foreign investment. Gandhi has

multinational corporation
Firm with significant operations
and marketing activities outside
its home country.

Figure 19.6
Alternative International Product and Promotional Strategies

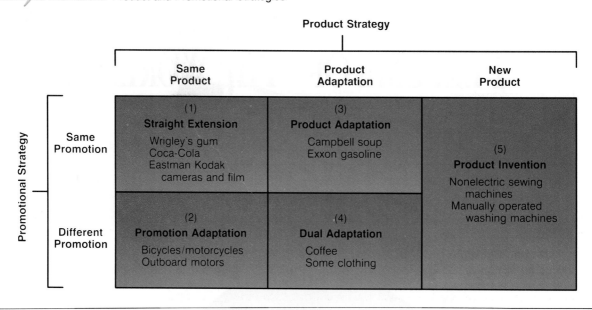

Source: Adapted from Warren Keagan, *Multinational Marketing Management* (Englewood Cliffs, N.J.: Prentice-Hall, 1984), pp. 317–322.

straight extension
International product/promotional strategy whereby the same product marketed in the home market is introduced in the foreign market using the same promotional strategy.

product adaptation
International product/promotional strategy wherein product modifications are made for the foreign market, but the same promotional strategy is used.

promotional adaptation
International product/promotional strategy in which the same product is introduced in a foreign market with a unique promotional strategy for the new market.

dual adaptation
International product/promotional strategy in which modifications of both product and promotional strategies are employed in the foreign market.

Product and Promotional Strategies

International marketers can choose from five alternative strategies in selecting the most appropriate product/promotion strategy for a specific foreign market. As Figure 19.6 indicates, the strategies center on whether to extend a domestic product and promotional strategy into international markets or adapt one or both to meet the target market's unique requirements.

The one-product/one-message **straight extension** strategy is typical for firms employing a global marketing strategy, such as PepsiCo and Benetton. This strategy permits economies of scale in production and marketing and a universally recognized product for consumers traveling from country to country.

Other strategies call for **product adaptation, promotion adaptation,** or both. While products such as bicycles, motorcycles, and outboard motors are primarily recreational vehicles in the United States, they may represent important transportation modes in other nations. Consequently, the promotional message may be adapted even if the product remains unchanged. In contrast, a promotional theme such as Exxon's "Put a Tiger in Your Tank" may be successfully used in dozens of nations even though Exxon gasoline is reformulated to meet varying weather conditions and engine specifications in different countries. In still other instances, both the product and the promotional message may require a **dual adaptation** to meet the unique needs of specific international markets. Coffee marketers such as Nescafé develop different blends and promotional campaigns to match consumer preferences in different countries.

The final strategy alternative is **product invention.** In this case, the firm may decide to develop an entirely different product to take advantage of unique foreign market opportunities. For example, to match dissimilar foreign needs in developing nations, an appliance manufacturer might introduce a hand-powered washing machine even though such products have been obsolete in industrialized countries for many years.

product invention
In international marketing, the development of an entirely different product combined with a new promotional strategy to take advantage of unique foreign opportunities.

Distribution Strategy

Distribution is a vital aspect of overseas marketing. Proper channels must be set up and extensive physical distribution problems handled. Transportation systems and warehousing facilities may be unavailable or of poor quality. International marketers must adapt promptly and efficiently to these situations if they are to profit from overseas sales.

Distribution decisions involve a two-step sequence. First, the firm must decide on a method of entering the foreign market. Second, it must determine how to distribute the product within the foreign market once it has chosen an appropriate entry channel.

Distribution decisions are based on many factors, including the nature of the firm's products, consumer tastes and buying habits, and market competition. These considerations affected Anheuser-Busch's distribution strategy when it decided to market Budweiser beer in Europe. Europeans are eager buyers of many American products, but not beer. They prefer their own brews and consider American beer weak and flavorless. For these reasons, American brewers have not attempted to sell their beer in Europe. Anheuser-Busch marketers, however, have decided to try, largely because the potential market for European beer sales is four times that of the United States.

Because the British are considered the most discriminating beer drinkers, Anheuser-Busch marketers chose Great Britain as their first European target market. The company hoped that British acceptance of Budweiser would pave the way for marketing in other European countries. Most British pubs are owned by one of Britain's major breweries or operated under a franchise agreement. Anheuser-Busch signed a licensing agreement with Watney, Mann, and Truman, the country's largest brewer. Under the agreement, Budweiser is made at Watney's brewery and distributed throughout Watney's system of 5,000 pubs. This distribution approach enables Anheuser-Busch to reach a large part of the beer-drinking market and is an important element in helping the company attain its goal of making Budweiser the best-selling brand in Great Britain by the late 1990s.[23]

Pricing Strategy

Pricing in foreign markets can be a critical ingredient in overall marketing strategy. Pricing practices in overseas markets are subject to considerable competitive, economic, political, and legal constraints. International marketers must thoroughly understand these requirements if they are to succeed.

A pricing strategy that works in the United States does not always succeed abroad. Procter & Gamble marketers learned that lesson when they used a penetration pricing strategy to introduce Cheer laundry detergent in Japan.

Cheer's discounted price alienated wholesalers — which are vital links in Japan's distribution system — because it reduced their profit margins. The small neighborhood retailers, where nearly one-third of Japanese consumers buy laundry detergent, are also averse to price-cutting policies, because they make less money on discounted goods. Unlike in the United States and Europe, in Japan penetration pricing frequently devalues a product's reputation in the eyes of consumers as well as marketing intermediaries. Moreover, it is difficult for firms to raise prices after the products have been sold at discount prices.[24]

An important development in pricing strategy for international marketing has been the emergence of commodity marketing organizations that seek to control prices through collective action. The Organization of Petroleum Exporting Countries (OPEC) is the best example of these collective export organizations, but many others exist.

Countertrade   In a growing number of nations, the only way a marketer can gain access to foreign markets is through **countertrade** — a form of exporting whereby products and services are bartered rather than sold for cash. Countertrade enables less developed nations that lack the foreign currency with which to pay for goods and services they want or need from exporting countries to secure them by using an alternative form of payment. Such requirements are also used in some industrialized nations as a means of controlling balance-of-trade problems. A typical example of a countertrade transaction is an agreement that PepsiCo marketers recently made with the Soviet Union. In order to set up soft-drink manufacturing plants in that country, PepsiCo agreed to import Soviet vodka and other products in the United States.

Countertrade comprises an estimated 25 percent of all world trade. Some 100,000 U.S. firms engage in countertrade. About 90 U.S. firms, including Sears, Citicorp, and General Electric, have set up special departments to handle countertrade transactions.[25]

countertrade
Form of exporting whereby products and services are bartered rather than sold for cash.

The United States as a Market for International Marketers

The United States is an inviting target for foreign marketers. It has a large population, high levels of discretionary income, political stability, an attitude generally favorable to foreign investment, and economic ills that are relatively controlled.

Foreign-owned assets in the United States total more than $1 trillion and are growing by over $100 billion a year. The retailing industry has been a recent target market of foreign companies. U.S. retailers that are owned in full or in part by an overseas firm include A&P (Germany), Grand Union (France), Allied Stores (Canada), Fed Mart (Germany), Bi-Lo (Netherlands), Kohl (United Kingdom), Federated Department Stores (Canada), and Winn's Stores (Germany).

Some consumers have shown a preference for foreign over domestic products. Foreign sports cars, English china, and French wine all hold sizable shares of the U.S. market. Some foreign products, such as Porsche sports cars, sell in the United States because of their quality image. Others, such as minicars like the Excel from South Korea and the Yugo from Yugoslavia, sell on the basis of price advantage over domestic competition.

U.S. marketers must expect to face substantial foreign competition in the years ahead both at home and abroad. The United States' high level of buying power will likely continue to attract foreign firms to enter the U.S. market, and the reduction of trade barriers and expanded international marketing appear to be long-run trends. U.S. marketers no longer have the choice of whether to compete with foreign firms. Their continued long-term success greatly depends on their ability to compete.

Summary of Chapter Objectives

1. Describe the importance of international marketing from the perspectives of the individual firm and the nation. Global marketing is important to many U.S. firms. Some, like Boeing and MGM/UA Communications depend on foreign markets for more than one-third of their revenues. Others rely on imports as a source of raw materials and component parts. But foreign trade is less important to the United States than it is to other nations. Less than 5 percent of the U.S. gross national product is from exports. In other countries, the percentage may be considerably higher.

2. Relate marketing environment variables to international marketing. Buyer behavior varies significantly from country to country. Environmental factors can influence buyer behavior and thus international marketing strategy. Cultural, economic, and social factors may hinder international marketing efforts, as may assorted trade restrictions and political/legal factors.

3. Identify the various methods of entering international markets. Several levels of involvement in world marketing are possible, including indirect or direct exporting, foreign licensing, overseas marketing, and foreign production and marketing. The world's largest firms are usually multinational in their orientation. Such companies operate in more than one country and view the world as their market.

4. Differentiate between a global marketing strategy and a multinational marketing strategy. Some firms use a global marketing strategy, in which they apply their domestic marketing strategies directly in foreign markets with little or no modifications. Marketers of products such as Coca-Cola feel that tastes are sufficiently homogeneous to ensure the successful use of their existing marketing strategies throughout the world. In contrast, most firms employ a multinational marketing strategy in marketing outside their home countries. In such instances, they employ different marketing programs to match the characteristics and requirements of buyers in each foreign market.

5. Describe the alternative product/promotional strategies used in international marketing. Alternative product/promotional strategies for international markets include (1) straight extensions, whereby the same product is introduced in the foreign market using the same promotional strategy as in the home market; (2) promotional adaptation, in which the same product is introduced with a unique promotional strategy designed for the specific market; (3) product adaptation, wherein product modifications are made but the same promotional strategy is used; (4) dual adaptation, in which modifications of both product and promotional strategies are employed; and (5) product invention, whereby the firm decides to develop an entirely different product and combine it with a new promotional strategy to take advantage of unique foreign opportunities.

6. Explain the attractiveness of the United States as a target market for foreign marketers. A number of factors contribute to the attractiveness of the U.S. market to foreign firms: its large population, high levels of discretionary income, political stability, general acceptance of foreign investment, and relatively controlled economic ills. Recent declines in the value of the dollar relative to foreign currencies have also attracted many foreign marketers.

Key Terms

exporting	dumping
importing	foreign licensing
infrastructure	joint venture
exchange rates	multinational corporation
friendship, commerce, and navigation (FCN) treaties	global marketing strategy
	multinational marketing strategy
tariff	straight extension
General Agreement on Tariffs and Trade (GATT)	product adaptation
	promotional adaptation
import quota	dual adaptation
embargo	product invention
exchange control	countertrade

Review Questions

1. Why is international marketing important to U.S. firms? To the U.S. economy?

2. Describe the world's growing economic interdependence. What types of products are most often marketed abroad by U.S. firms? What are the leading U.S. imports?

3. Outline the major variables in the world marketing environment. Explain how trade restrictions may be used to either restrict or stimulate international marketing activities.

4. Explain the international marketing practice of dumping. Why does dumping sometimes occur?

5. The Dutch swapped beads, trinkets, and cloth with native Americans in exchange for Manhattan. What international marketing concept described in this chapter does this business deal illustrate? Discuss.

6. Explain the provisions of the Foreign Corrupt Practices Act.

7. Outline the stages of participation in the global marketplace. How will current world population trends affect participation in international marketing by U.S. firms?

8. Outline the basic premises behind the operation of a multinational corporation. Why do you think the term has a negative connotation in some economies? Discuss the changing attitudes toward multinationals.

9. Differentiate between a global marketing strategy and a multinational marketing strategy. In what ways is the international marketing mix most likely to differ from a marketing mix used in the domestic country?

10. Explain the impact of countertrade on a firm's international marketing operations.

Discussion Questions

1. Give a local example of each of the five product and promotional strategy alternatives available to international marketers.

2. Relate specific environmental considerations to each of the following aspects of a firm's international marketing mix:
   a. Brands and warranties   **d.** Discounts to intermediaries
   b. Advertising   **e.** Use of comparative advertising
   c. Distribution channels

3. Give a hypothetical or actual example of a firm operating at each of the following levels of international marketing:
   a. Indirect exporting   **d.** Overseas marketing
   b. Direct exporting   **e.** Foreign production and marketing
   c. Foreign licensing

4. American-made clothing now carries a "made in the USA." label. This fact has been heavily advertised in recent years through general advertising campaigns and by retailers such as Wal-Mart. Relate the congressionally mandated labeling requirement to specific concepts discussed in this chapter.

5. Some people argue that foreign investment in the United States should be limited. Would you agree with a plan that would limit such investment by foreign firms or individuals in a particular firm to some specified amount? Explain.

VIDEO CASE 19

Fluor Corp.

In a shrinking world experiencing increased competition by globally-oriented companies, it was inevitable that both U.S. and foreign marketers would shift their focus to the People's Republic of China. Not only is China the home of over 1 billion people, it is also rapidly changing from an abacus technology to a computer one. China's decision in the 1970s to modernize its economy opened the doors to foreign firms. Government leaders realized that outside expertise would be needed to help the nation improve its infrastructure, beef up its technology, increase productivity, and boost exports.

Even though trade between the United States and China officially began in 1972, it was more dreams than dollars until the 1980s. Not surprisingly, China's neighbor, Japan, was the first to build a strong presence in the Chinese economy during the 1970s, and Japanese brand names such as Hitachi, Seiko, and Toshiba are well-established today. In fact, Japan is China's leading trade partner.

U.S. firms and American brand names have become a common sight on the Chinese mainland in the late 1980s, however. A visitor to Chairman Mao's mausoleum in Beijing's Tiananmen Square has only to look across the square to spot the 500-seat Kentucky Fried Chicken fast-food restaurant. PepsiCo Inc. and the Coca-Cola Co. are engaged in their Chinese version of the cola wars, even though both firms have had to invest heavily in trucks and refrigerators for retailers. By 1988, American–Chinese trade had exceeded the $10 billion mark.

20 Marketing of Services

Chapter Objectives

1. To distinguish between goods and services.

2. To explain the importance of the service sector.

3. To identify the characteristics of services.

4. To discuss buyer behavior as it relates to services.

5. To outline the evaluation of marketing in service firms.

Judi Nevonen awoke to both a personal and a business problem. An assistant vice-president of First Bank System in Minneapolis, Nevonen was scheduled to speak at a bank management training session, but her 18-month-old son had come down with an ear infection that would keep him out of his usual day-care center.

Nevonen resolved the problem by calling a unique service firm, Chicken Soup. A nurse answered Nevonen's call and assessed the youngster's illness. Following this, the toddler was booked into Chicken Soup's "Sniffles Room," a unit designed to deal with minor respiratory ailments. Nevonen gave her presentation at work, assured that her son was getting the personalized attention he needed that day.

Chicken Soup, which clearly saved the day at the Nevonen household, is one of a growing number of new service firms targeted at working parents. The rising number of working women has created a need for services such as day care for sick children. According to the U.S. Bureau of Labor Statistics, mothers of infants and toddlers comprise one of the most rapidly growing segments of the labor force. Today 51 percent of women with children under 3 are in the labor force — up from 42 percent in 1980.

Day-care centers that cater specifically to sick children fill a need unmet by traditional facilities. Licensing regulations in most states prohibit regular day-care centers from accepting sick youngsters. That leaves a working parent with basically two alternatives — staying home from work to care for the child or finding a friend or family member to help out.

Facilities such as Chicken Soup not only provide a solution to working parents' personal/business dilem-

mas; they also appeal to — and in some cases are even supported by — employers. To curb absenteeism and offer an attractive benefit for prospective employees, some firms subsidize their employees' use of day-care centers for sick children. For example, under a standing arrangement with Chicken Soup, Judi Nevonen's employer paid $30 of the $40 fee for her child's care.[1]

Photo source: Courtesy of Chicken Soup.

Chapter Overview

Marketers typically approach the development of marketing programs for both goods and services in the same manner. Such programs begin with an investigation, analysis, and selection of a particular target market and continue with the development of a marketing mix designed to satisfy that segment. But while tangible goods and intangible services are both designed to satisfy consumer wants and needs, their marketing entails significant differences. This chapter examines the similarities and differences between marketing programs for goods and services.

Services are difficult to define, and it is hard to distinguish between certain kinds of goods and services. Personal services, such as hairstyling and dry cleaning, are easily recognizable as services rather than tangible goods, but they represent only a small part of the total service industry.

Figure 20.1
The Goods-Services
Continuum

Pure Goods   Pure Services

Some firms offer a combination of goods and services. Rent-A-Center rents television sets and applies the rental payments toward their eventual purchase.[2] It provides both a service (rental) and a good (the television set, when title is ultimately transferred to the customer). Similarly, Wackenhut Corporation, a protection specialist, markets alarms and closed-circuit televisions (goods) in addition to uniformed guards and trained dogs (services). An optometrist may provide both eye examinations (services) and sell contact lenses and eyeglasses (goods). Some services represent an integral part of the marketing of physical goods. For example, an IBM sales representative may emphasize the firm's service capabilities at minimizing machine downtime.

The above examples suggest that some method of clarifying the definition of services is needed.

What Are Services?

goods-services continuum
Method of visualizing the differences and similarities between goods and services.

One method of defining services is the use of a product spectrum, which shows that most products have both goods and services components. Figure 20.1 presents a **goods-services continuum** — a method for visualizing the differences and similarities between goods and services.[3] A dress is a pure good, although the store's alteration service may be sold along with it or included in the total price. Most banking services are pure services, but some banks also sell products such as financial planning guides.

In the middle range of the continuum are products with both goods and services components. For example, the satisfaction that results from dining at an exclusive restaurant is derived not only from the food and drink but from the services rendered by the establishment's personnel.

services
Intangible tasks that satisfy consumer and industrial user needs when efficiently developed and distributed to chosen market segments.

It is impossible to describe all the services available to consumer and industrial purchasers, but a general definition can be offered: **Services** are intangible tasks that satisfy consumer and industrial user needs when efficiently developed and distributed to chosen market segments.

The Importance of the Service Sector

Consumer expenditures for services have increased considerably during the past decade. Ranging from such necessities as electric power and medical care to such luxuries as foreign travel, backpacking guides, ski resorts, and tennis

Figure 20.2
Growth of the Service Sector

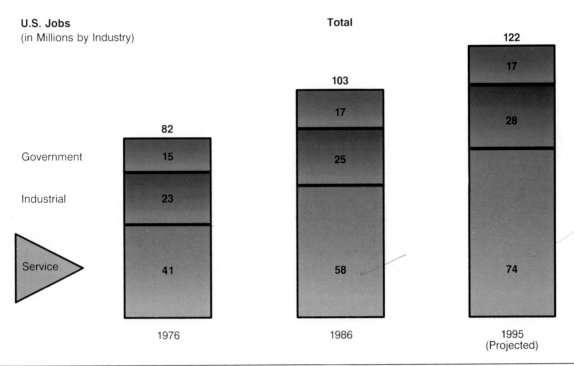

schools, services now account for over 52 percent of the average consumer's total expenditures.[4]

Over three-quarters of all new jobs in the United States over the past decade have been in the service sector. Virtually all of the gains in female employment have come from this sector. Figure 20.2 indicates that the trend in service job creation will continue to 1995.

It is interesting to note that despite the export problems facing the United States (described in Chapter 19), services are a bright spot in U.S. international trade. Services now account for about 25 percent of all U.S. exports.

For most consumer and business firms, marketing is emerging as a significant activity for two reasons. First, the growth potential of the service market represents a vast marketing opportunity. Second, increased competition is forcing traditional service industries to emphasize marketing in order to be able to compete in the marketplace.

Characteristics of Services

The preceding discussion suggests that services are varied and complex.[5] Following are the five key features of services that have major marketing implications:

1. Services are intangible.
2. Services are inseparable from the service provider.
3. Services are perishable.
4. Standardization of services is difficult.
5. Buyers often are involved in the development and distribution of services.

Each of these service characteristics is discussed in the following sections.

Intangibility

Services do not have tangible features that appeal to consumers' senses of sight, hearing, smell, taste, and touch. Therefore, they are difficult to demonstrate at trade shows, to display in retail stores, to illustrate in magazine advertisements, and to sample. Consequently, personal selling and advertising must show the benefits of using the service. For example, an insurance agent can discuss the peace of mind derived from adequate home and automobile insurance. To this end, an Allstate television commercial shows a home that is restored after a major fire.

Inseparability

In consumers' minds, those who provide the service *are* the service. Consumer perceptions of the service marketer become their perceptions of the service itself. Recognizing this relationship, the U.S. Postal Service recently began offering Dale Carnegie self-development courses to employees in several cities.[6]

Buyers often are unable to judge the quality of a service prior to purchase. Because of this, the service vendor's reputation is frequently a key factor in the buying decision. Since consumers essentially are buying a promise, the service marketer must attempt to help them perceive the service in tangible terms. Institutional or corporate advertising that promotes the firm's image helps to accomplish this objective. Consumers often judge the quality of financial institutions on the basis of an intangible concept — strength. In corporate advertisements such as the one in Figure 20.3, Chemical Bank promotes its image as a sound financial institution by defining its strengths in terms of the capital and managerial assets of hard work, financial skill, and sound judgment.

Hartford Insurance marketers have used a stag in their corporate advertising since the 1860s. During the 1970s, the stag personalized Hartford Insurance in advertisements that showed the animal looking through windows of homes and even helping schoolchildren board a bus. But in 1981, Hartford decided to promote specific types of insurance and thus discontinued using the stag in advertising. Later marketing research indicated that when consumers were asked to name insurance companies, Hartford's name recognition had decreased from 14 to 7 percent. By 1987, the stag had reappeared in corporate ads to help promote the firm's personalized services.[7]

Perishability

The utility of most services is short-lived; therefore, unlike manufactured products, they cannot be produced ahead of time and stored in inventory for periods of peak demand. Vacant seats on an airplane, unsold symphony tickets, idle

Figure 20.3
Advertisement Promoting a Firm's Image

Source: Copyright 1987 Chemical Bank, New York.

aerobics instructors, and unused electrical generating capacity represent economic losses that can never be recovered. Sometimes, however, facilities that are idled during slack periods must be tolerated so that the firm will have sufficient capacity for peak periods.

Industries such as electric and natural gas utilities, resort hotels, telephone companies, and airlines all face the problem of perishability. Some service firms are able to overcome this problem with off-peak pricing. Vacation resorts feature high- and low-season prices, telephone companies grant reduced rates on evenings and weekends, and baseball teams offer lower-priced general admission seats.

Difficulty of Standardization

It is often impossible to standardize offerings among sellers of the same service or even to ensure consistency of quality in the services provided by a single seller. Rent-A-Mom, a firm that provides child-care services as well as a full line of domestic services for individuals and families, approaches the standardization problem by charging an hourly rate for the various types of services offered. Care services for children and the elderly are billed at the current basic rate, housecleaning at a higher figure, and specialized baby nursing care at a still higher rate. Extra services are considered add-ons and are charged at rates different than those for the basic service.

Buyer Involvement

The consumer often plays a major role in the marketing and production of services. The hairstylist's customer may describe the desired look and make suggestions at several stages of the styling process. Clients of tax preparation firms supply relevant information and frequently work closely with the tax specialist. Restaurant customers may put together their entire meals at a well-stocked soup-and-salad bar. Although buyer specifications also play a role in the creation of major products such as installations, the interaction of buyer and seller at both the production and distribution stages is a common feature of services.

Types of Consumer and Industrial Services

Service firms can serve consumer markets, industrial markets, or both. For example, ServiceMaster's more than 3,000 franchises provide cleaning services for both consumer and business markets. Literally thousands of services are available to consumer and industrial users. In some instances, they are provided by specialized machinery with almost no personal assistance, such as automated car washes. In other cases, they are performed by skilled professionals with little reliance on specialized equipment, such as accountants and management consultants.

Figure 20.4 illustrates a means of classifying services according to two factors: the extent of reliance on equipment in providing the service and the degree of skill possessed by the people who perform it. Thus, the initial classification is based on whether the service is equipment or people based. A movie theater is an equipment-based service, while legal services, obviously, are people based. The second level of classification is based on the skill levels of the performance. Equipment-based services can be classified as automated, monitored by relatively unskilled workers, or operated by skilled workers. Similarly, people-based services can be provided by unskilled workers, skilled workers, or professionals.

Buyer Behavior

Chapters 5 and 6 discussed elements of consumer and organizational buyer behavior. Many similarities exist between buyer behavior for goods and for services, but there are some important differences. These may be grouped into three categories: attitudes, needs and motives, and purchase behavior. Usually, the personal element of services is the key to the consumer's decision as to which services to purchase.[8]

Service marketers are sometimes perceived as being more personal, friendly, and cooperative than goods marketers. These and other distinctive personal elements often differentiate service marketers from goods marketers and thus offer service providers unique marketing opportunities.

Figure 20.4
Types of Service Businesses

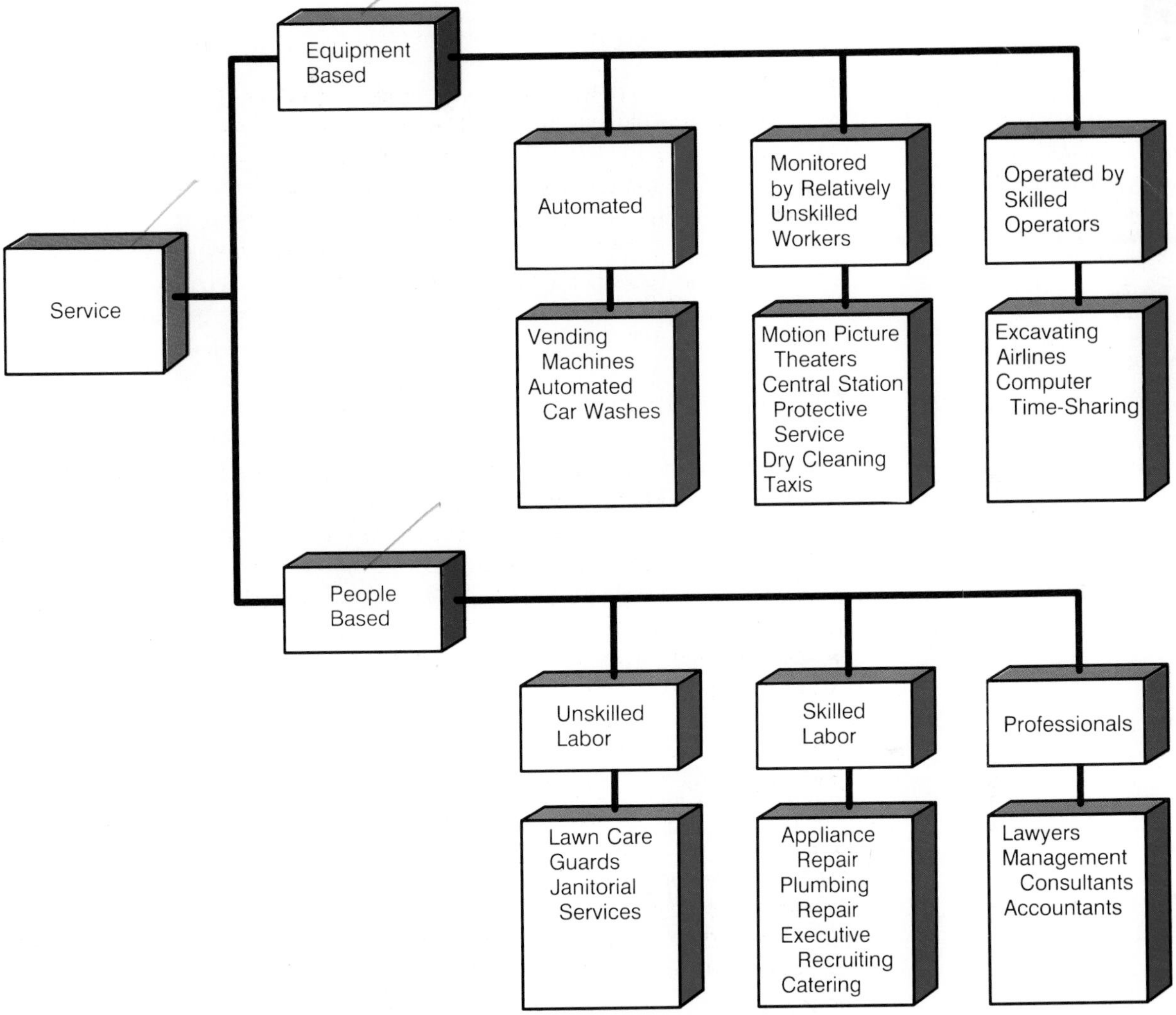

Source: Reprinted by permission of the *Harvard Business Review.* An exhibit from "Strategy Is Different in Service Business" by Dan R. E. Thomas (July-August 1978). Copyright ©1978 by the President and Fellows of Harvard College; all rights reserved.

Attitudes

As mentioned earlier, consumer attitudes directly influence buying decisions. Attitudes seem to be especially important in service marketing because of the intangible nature of services. This intangibility tends to make buyers rely on

Service marketers have the opportunity to satisfy consumers' needs for personal attention. Providing in-terminal transportation for airline passengers is one way that US-Air's special assistance representatives give personal attention to the elderly, the young, and other passengers with special needs.

Photo source: © 1986 Mike Mitchell for USAir Group, Incorporated.

subjective impressions of the service and its seller. Reliance on subjective impressions is less apparent in the purchase of tangible goods.

There are two important distinctions between goods and services: Services are perceived as being more personal than goods, and consumers sometimes are less satisfied with service purchases. Dissatisfaction with the personal elements of a service, such as an unfriendly flight attendant or an impolite bank teller, is often the seed of a negative attitude toward the entire service.

Needs and Motives

A comparison of needs and buying motives for goods and services suggests that similarities predominate. Essentially the same types of needs are satisfied whether a person buys the materials for do-it-yourself home repair or hires a service firm to perform that task. Although service needs have increased in importance, they often can be satisfied with new or modified goods as well as with services. For example, fast-food restaurants satisfy consumers' desire for quick, convenient meals but the same need can be fulfilled with microwave ovens and the development of better-tasting microwavable food products.

One need that services marketers should be able to satisfy better than goods marketers is the consumer's desire for personal attention. By appealing to this need, the hairstylist, banker, or insurance agent provides a form of satisfaction that the seller of a good cannot easily match. The desire for personal attention is often the dominant need satisfied by a service.

Consider the 11 Centennial Suites at Chicago's Michael Reese Hospital and Medical Center. For an extra $40 to $95 a day over the private-room rate, patients get a mauve-carpeted room with fresh flowers, velour robes, fruit baskets, stocked refrigerators, and full-size bathrooms complete with toothbrushes and toiletries. In addition to the regular complement of physicians and nurses, a Centennial Suite patient is served by a concierge who does everything from delivering the morning paper to arranging for bedside secretarial services. To round out the Centennial Suite service, patients select meals from a complete menu and are served by a white-jacketed waiter.[9]

Purchase Behavior

Research suggests that differences between goods and services are most noticeable in the area of purchase behavior. Selection decisions for tangible goods normally are more concerned with the question of whether to purchase, while services selection decisions emphasize proper timing and the selection of a source.[10] This suggests several distinctions between purchase behavior for goods and services: The degree of prepurchase planning may differ, influences on the buyer may vary, and the buyer may be more personally involved in a service purchase.

Consumers are more influenced by interpersonal determinants — friends, family members, neighbors, and salespeople — when buying services than when buying goods. The intangibility of services makes it difficult for buyers to judge quality and value and to inspect or sample a service prior to its purchase. Consequently, service buyers may depend more on the experiences and observations of others. This suggests two principal implications for services marketing. First, greater emphasis must be placed on developing professional relationships between service suppliers and their customers. Second, promotional efforts must be aimed at exploiting word-of-mouth promotion.

Evolution of the Marketing Function in the Service Sector

Although spending for services has increased substantially in recent years, the development of marketing as a major business activity has come slowly to most service industries. This is largely due to what Theodore Levitt calls *marketing myopia,* a topic discussed in Chapter 1.[11] Levitt proposes that top executives in many industries fail to recognize the scope of their businesses; thus, future growth is endangered because management is product rather than customer oriented. Levitt specifically cites certain service industries as examples, namely, the dry cleaning, motion picture, railroad, and electric utilities industries. For instance, the film studio president who defines the firm's activities as "making movies" instead of "marketing entertainment" suffers from marketing myopia according to Levitt.

Since Levitt's pioneering article, recognition of marketing's importance in service firms has grown substantially. Some early marketing efforts have taken dubious twists. Consider the brochure put out by a Providence, Rhode Island, law firm. It featured two nude women in a bathtub with the caption "Like a bathtub, trial lawyers have to fill up on the facts and the law of a case. . . ."[12]

But most marketing efforts by service firms take more traditional avenues. For example, many banks have instituted personal banking departments for customers who maintain large account balances or loan volumes. Banks offer these customers services ranging from personal financial counseling to separate offices in which they can conduct their banking business. Many hospitals that in the past did little to promote their services have come to accept marketing as the ticket to survival in a competitive environment characterized by an average bed occupancy rate of only 50 percent. In fact, hospitals now spend over $1 billion on marketing, approximately 45 percent of which goes to advertising.[13]

Environments for Service Firms

In many ways, the economic, social/cultural, political/legal, technological, and competitive forces exert the same types of pressures on service firms as they do on goods producers. However, certain features of these environments must be highlighted for the marketing of services.

Economic Environment

The growth of consumer expenditures for services has been accompanied by further expansion of business and government services to keep pace with the increasing complexity of the American economy. The sharp increase in spending for services and the development of service industries as the major employer of labor have been among the most significant economic trends in the post–World War II economy. Most explanations of this trend are predicated on the changes associated with a maturing economy and the by-products of rapid economic growth.

A theory developed by economist Colin Clark describes the growth of service industries.[14] In the first (and most primitive) stage, the vast majority of an economy's population is engaged in farming, hunting, fishing, and forestry. As the society becomes more advanced, the emphasis shifts from an agrarian economy to one based on manufacturing activities. The final (and most advanced) stage occurs when the majority of labor is engaged in **tertiary industries**—those involved in the production of services.

tertiary industry
Business that specializes in the production of services.

Many people associate service industries with low skill and poor pay. But the transformation described by Clark and witnessed in states such as Massachusetts does not support this conclusion. Many service-sector jobs, such as those in the computer software industry, provide skilled jobs at commensurate pay. For instance, Massachusetts is frequently cited as a state that has completed the shift from a manufacturing-based to a service-based economy. It is worth noting that Massachusetts' per capita income increased from 6 to 16 percent over the U.S. average during the past decade.[15]

Technological advances, population shifts, and changes in consumer needs have contributed to increased spending for consumer services. The evolution of science and technology has altered productivity trends, and higher productivity in the manufacturing industries has brought about the shift of workers to service industries. Technological advances have helped create a higher stan-

THE COMPETITIVE EDGE

Moto Photo Inc.

One-hour film processing now accounts for 25 percent of the photo processing industry, up from 2 percent in 1985. Experts expect this segment to increase to 50 percent of the total market by the 1990s. This type of market growth naturally attracts a lot of competitors.

Moto Photo Inc. of Dayton, Ohio, a franchise chain of 161 photo processing outlets, has attempted to gain a competitive edge with a series of service retailing innovations. For instance, the firm offers a variety of photographic and video services within individual stores. In addition to one-hour film developing, Moto Photo offers a one-hour portrait studio, a video studio in which a customer can prepare a video message in just 30 minutes, one-hour photo enlargements, posters, and custom framing as well as a line of photographic supplies.

The one-hour portrait studio is unique. Moto Photo allows customers to design their own backdrops rather than use the ones photographers provide. Customers can watch their portrait orders being processed and make any needed changes. Michael Adler, Moto Photo's president, comments: "The craftsman and consumer are dealing directly with each other. This allows for a certain creative interaction to take place." It also gives the customer time to examine

the photographic supplies Moto Photo carries.

Moto Photo retailers use a variety of methods to reach the one-hour film developing market. The Moto Photo Club is a plan that offers three free rolls of film and a 25 percent discount on developing for an annual fee of $20. Other marketing tactics include giving free teddy bears to new mothers who become customers, offering free baby books to expectant parents, and providing vacationers with travel diaries.

All of these services are continually evaluated. Greg Lechner, Moto Photo's vice-president of marketing, notes: "We're very market research driven." Focus group interviews and telephone surveys of Moto Photo customers and noncustomers are conducted twice a year.

One thing is certain: Moto Photo has gained a competitive edge and it shows up on the bottom line. The firm's franchises average $250,000 in annual sales volume compared to $190,000 for the typical independent film processor.

Source: "Extra Service Provides Niche for Film Processor," *Marketing News* (March 13, 1987), p. 26. *Photo source:* Courtesy of Moto Photo Incorporated.

dard of living for the average person, who currently spends a larger portion of his or her increased discretionary income for services. In addition, population changes, particularly increased urbanization, have widened the demand for personal and public services. Changes in consumer needs, such as an increased demand for convenience, have led to greater spending for consumer services. As a result, the prices of many services have risen rapidly. In contrast, the excess capacity in many goods industries have held the prices of their tangible outputs in check.[16]

Even more marked than the growth of consumer expenditures for services has been the increased spending for business services. The servicing of business has become very profitable. Companies in this field range from suppliers of temporary help to highly specialized management consultation services. Two reasons exist for the rapid growth of business services. First, business service firms frequently are able to perform a specialized function more cheaply than the purchasing company can by itself. Enterprises that provide maintenance, cleaning, and protection services to office buildings and industrial plants are common examples. Second, many companies are unable to perform certain specialized services themselves. Marketing research studies, for example, often require outside specialists.

Social/Cultural Environment

The social/cultural environment has a significant impact on the marketing of services. Consumers are offered a wide array of services; some are accepted, and others are rejected. Consumer preferences also shift over time. For instance, the increased use of counselors and consultants has affected many aspects of modern personal, family, and work lives. A few years ago, some of these services were not even available, let alone influential. Now there are even leisure consultants to advise consumers on what to do with their spare time.

Some services are truly unique to today's social/cultural environment. The Apology Service in Bethel, Ohio, offers to make third-party apologies to people for a $6 fee. Its owner reports that clients range from husbands to daughters-in-law.[17]

A variety of social/cultural trends are relevant to the increased marketing of services. For example, there is evidence that the American consumer's tastes are shifting to a preference for services as status symbols. Travel, culture, health and beauty, and higher education have partially replaced durable goods as status symbols in many consumers' minds. Other trends include a growing emphasis on security, which has widened the market for insurance and investment services, and greater concern for health, which has led to an increased demand for health clubs and medical services.

Animal Health Insurance Agency reflects a unique aspect of this trend. Health insurance has always been a big business — for people, that is. Now Animal Health Insurance Agency marketers seek to cash in on the huge sums spent on animal health care by providing health insurance policies for pets. The Connecticut-based agency began offering health and accident policies for pets in late 1986, with the first one going to Benji, the canine movie star. For annual premiums ranging from $36 to $89, consumers can get $1,000 to $2,500 in coverage for veterinary care, not including neutering/spaying, cosmetic enhancements, or euthanasia. Estimating that Americans spend $4.6 billion on their pets' health, the firm's marketers felt they had identified a strategic window. Thus far they have been more than satisfied with the response their policies have received.[18]

Political/Legal Environment

Service businesses are more closely regulated than most other forms of private enterprise. Nearly all service firms are subject to government regulation in addition to the usual taxes, antitrust legislation, and restrictions on promotion and

FOCUS ON ETHICS

Utility's Wildlife Protection Benefits Its Bottom Line

Ever hear of a utility using the Endangered Species Act to fight off regulators? A mind-boggling thought — but not quite so surprising when you look at Florida Power & Light's environmental record.

In the 1970s, many utilities ran into trouble with environmental groups, especially in their efforts to build nuclear power plants. Some fought the environmentalists, but others, like FP&L, decided that constant fighting was too expensive and began to take environmental considerations into account. FP&L did so well that it has received a corporate award from the Florida Audubon Society for its programs to protect endangered species.

Utilities are large landholders, which means they are more likely than most firms to come into contact with animals. In addition, they must build power plants and transmission lines, which increases their geographical spread—and contacts with wildlife—still further. Since utilities operate in a highly regulated environment, in which environmental regulations are a fixture, they have come to terms with these restrictions more rapidly than most firms. Florida

Power & Light's contact with wildlife is especially frequent because Florida is home to so many kinds of plants and animals, including 50 on the federal list of endangered species and 500 on a state list of threatened species.

Environmental awareness first came to FP&L in 1972, when it was building its Turkey Point nuclear plant. The company had planned to dump the plant's cooling water into Biscayne Bay, but environmentalists convinced regulators that a system of canals was needed for cooling the water. As a side effect, the 168-mile canal system became a home for crocodiles (one of only three sites in the country with breeding populations), manatees, sea turtles, and other creatures. As Charles Lee, senior vice-president of the Florida Audubon Society, says, "They got smart and realized that if they brought some good environmental scientists on board, they would be in a much better position to watch their own operations." The scientists, including chief ecologist Ross Wilcox, lobby company officials to better accommodate wildlife, help restore swampland, and conduct censuses

of endangered species on company property. The information is invaluable whenever the firm has to go to regulators. "This is all driven by good business. When I call up an agency and say I need a permit to do something, I don't walk in with two strikes against me," says Wilcox. "All you need is for a major project not to be tied up in litigation for a couple of months, with interest charges and so on, and the crocodile project has paid for itself."

The case of the Endangered Species Act involved the manatee. The Environmental Protection Agency wanted FP&L to change its warm-water discharge from its Fort Myers plant because it was harming fish larvae in the Orange River. But the company was able to produce data showing that the warmth of the discharge made it the largest gathering spot in Florida for the endangered manatee. As a result, the EPA agreed not to require the change — which, incidentally, would have cost millions of dollars.

Source: Eric Morgenthaler, "Ecology Effort: A Florida Utility Wins Naturalists' Praise for Guarding Wildlife," *The Wall Street Journal* (May 7, 1987), pp. 1, 19.

price discrimination. For example, a bus company must have the approval of the local public service commission before adding or dropping a route, and a hairstylist must comply with state licensing requirements.

Service marketers must recognize the impact of government regulation on their competitive strategies. Regulation affects the marketing of services in three significant ways:

1. It generally reduces the range of competition; if competition remains, its intensity usually increases.

2. It reduces a marketer's array of options and introduces certain rigidities into the marketing process.

3. Because the decisions of the regulatory agency are binding, part of the marketing decision-making process must be aimed at predicting the agency's actions.[19]

Many service industries are regulated at the national level by government agencies such as the Federal Power Commission, the Federal Trade Commission, the Federal Communications Commission, and the Securities and Exchange Commission. Other service industries, such as insurance and real estate, traditionally are regulated at state and local levels. In addition, many personal and business services are restricted at state and local levels by special fees or taxes and certification or licensing requirements. Often included in this category are members of the legal and medical professions, funeral directors, accountants, and engineers.

Technological Environment

productivity
Output produced by each worker.

Historically, two-thirds of the economic growth in the United States has resulted from increases in **productivity** — the output produced by each worker. In the past, technological developments accounted for significant increases in productivity. Cyrus H. McCormick was able to almost triple the output of the average wheat farmer. Henry Ford's innovations made it possible to reduce the average cost of a car by 50 percent. How are increases in productivity accomplished in a service economy?

Theodore Levitt argues that service marketers should assume a "manufacturing attitude." "Instead of expecting service workers to improve results by greater exertion of animal energy, managers must see what kinds of organizations, incentives, technology, and skills could improve overall productivity."[20]

Levitt cites McDonald's as the ultimate example of how service can be industrialized:

Each variety of McDonald's hamburger is in a color-coded wrapper. Parking lots are sprinkled with brightly painted, omnivorous trash cans that even the most chronic litterer finds difficult to ignore. A special scoop has been devised for french fries so that each customer will believe he is getting an over-flowing portion, while actually receiving a uniform ration. Employee discretion is eliminated; everything is organized so that nothing can go wrong.[21]

The manufacturing approach Levitt suggests is evident at Salt Lake City's LDS Hospital. There elective surgery patients are first interviewed by a computer named HELP, which takes the person's medical history and asks the appropriate follow-up questions without human assistance.[22] Similarly, robots are now used in various service industries ranging from surveillance of prisons and other buildings to Help-Mate, which serves meals to hospital patients.[23]

Services will be a major growth sector of the U.S. economy during the coming decade. It is likely that consumers will spend more for services and significant employment gains will evolve in this area. But these advances can be achieved only if service industries improve their productivity records. This will most likely occur through improved marketing.

Competitive Environment

The competitive environment for services represents a paradox: For many service industries, competition comes not from other services but from goods manufacturers or from government services. Internal competition is almost nonexistent in some service industries. Price competition often is limited in such

Service marketers can improve their operating efficiency by adapting technological developments to their specific needs. The Bayside Exposition Center in Boston uses a Denning Mobile Robotics' surveillance vehicle, shown here in multiple exposure, to provide building security. The robotic "security guard" can see 130 feet in the dark.

Photo source: © John Madere 1987.

services as communication, legal, and medical services. Moreover, many important service producers such as hospitals, educational institutions, and religious and welfare agencies are nonprofit organizations. Finally, many service industries are difficult to enter; many require a major financial investment or special education or training; and many may be restricted by government regulations.

Competition from Goods   Direct competition between goods and services is inevitable, because competing goods and services often provide the same basic satisfactions. Consumers may satisfy their service requirements by substituting goods. Competition has increased as manufacturers, recognizing consumers' changing needs, have built services and added conveniences into their products. For example, continuous-cleaning ovens, frost-free refrigerators, and textured-surface appliances have reduced the need for domestic employees, and videocassette recorders compete with motion pictures and other forms of entertainment. Consumers often have a choice between goods and services that perform the same general functions.

Competition from Retailers and Manufacturers   The entry of retailers and manufacturers into consumer and service markets also has intensified competition for the service dollar. Large retailers provide such services as optical centers, insurance, dental offices, legal services, and automobile repairs. Sears has led the trend toward diversifying into services with its entry into insurance (Allstate Insurance), real estate (Coldwell Banker), and investments (Dean Witter Reynolds Inc.). Sears and other large retailers recognize that mass merchandising of consumer services is both possible and profitable.

Competition from Government   Many services are provided by government. Some services can be provided only by government agencies, but others compete with privately produced goods and services. For example, the U.S. Postal Service's Express Mail competes with Federal Express, Airborne, UPS, and other next-day delivery services.

The consumption of some government services is mandatory, such as social security. Current public debates concern how to pay for such services and which level of government is responsible for providing them.

The Marketing Mix for Service Firms

Like goods marketers, service marketers begin by identifying their target markets. The Forethought Group, a marketer of pre-need funerals, defines its target market as people age 60 to 65. Women at Large, a health spa franchise for large women, targets females in the 175-to-250 pound weight range.[24]

Service marketers can use either geographic, demographic, psychographic, or benefit segmentation to identify their target markets. As with goods markets, demographic segmentation is the most commonly used segmentation variable. The AARP/Prudential advertisement in Figure 20.5 illustrates demographic segmentation based on age.

Satisfying buyers' service needs also requires developing an effective marketing mix. Service policies and pricing, distribution, and promotional strategies must be combined into an integrated marketing program. The following sections briefly describe the marketing mix for service firms.

Service Policies

Like tangible goods, services may be classified according to their intended use. All services are either consumer services or industrial services. Even when the same service (telephone, gas, or electric services, for example) is sold to both consumer and organizational buyers, the service firm often maintains separate marketing groups for each customer segment.

Consumer services may be classified as convenience, shopping, and specialty services. Dry cleaning, shoe repair, and similar personal services commonly are purchased on a convenience basis. Automobile repairs and insurance are typically shopping services; they usually involve some shopping effort in comparing price and quality. Specialty services usually include professional services, such as financial, legal, and medical assistance.

Some service firms have diversified their offerings or combined with other service marketers in an attempt to boost sales. For example, Marine Midland's MasterCard gives users credit on Continental and Eastern Airlines' frequent-flyer program. Similarly, First Chicago's Visa card gives its users credit on United Airlines' frequent-flyer program.

The intangible nature of services means that many marketing strategies used with tangible goods are of little or no use. For example, packaging and labeling decisions are very limited; service marketers are rarely able to use packages as promotional tools. In addition, the use of sampling as a means of introducing a new service to the market is limited. Marketers of such services as racquetball clubs and cable television frequently offer trial periods without

Figure 20.5
Demographic Segmentation in
Service Marketing

charge or at greatly reduced rates to move potential customers through the
stages of the adoption process and convert them to regular patrons.

Pricing Strategy

Pricing practices in service industries do not substantially differ from those in
goods industries. In developing a pricing strategy, the service marketer must
consider the demand for the service; production, marketing, and administrative
costs; and the influence of competition. However, price competition has been
limited for many services; for instance, the prices charged by most utilities are
closely regulated by federal, state, and local government agencies. Many other
service firms, such as advertising agencies, adopt a traditional pricing structure
that is followed within their respective industries.

The prices of many highly sought-after services have risen rapidly in recent years. In fact, with the exception of food and energy, the prices of services have risen approximately 80 percent more than the prices of goods over the past 20 years.[25]

Price negotiation is an important part of many professional service transactions. Consumer services that sometimes involve price negotiation include auto repairs, physical-fitness programs, and financial, legal, or medical assistance. Specialized business services, such as equipment rental, marketing research, insurance, and maintenance and protection services, are also sometimes priced through direct negotiation. Many firms use variable pricing to overcome the problems associated with the perishable nature of services. For example, airlines offer discounted fares on many highly competitive routes.

Distribution Strategy

The distribution channels for services, which are also discussed in Chapter 12, are shown in Figure 20.6. Generally, service channels are simpler and more direct than those for products. This is largely due to the intangibility of services. The service marketer is less concerned with storage, transportation, and inventory control and typically employs shorter channels of distribution. Another consideration is the need for continuing personal relationships between performers and users of many services. Consumers will remain clients of the same insurance agents, banks, or travel agents if they are reasonably satisfied. Similarly, firms often retain public accounting firms and lawyers on a relatively permanent basis.

Any marketing intermediaries used by service firms are usually agents or brokers. In the travel industry, for instance, retail agents often sell vacation packages developed by travel brokers. These packages typically combine travel, hotel, and restaurant services.

Promotional Strategy

The marketing strategy for services includes a promotional mix consisting of the most appropriate blends of personal and nonpersonal selling to inform, persuade, and/or remind individuals or business firms that represent the service provider's target market. The intangible nature of services adds to the challenges of developing an effective promotional strategy.

A frequently-used promotional strategy is to "tangibilize" the service by linking it to concrete images. The insurance industry provides numerous examples of this approach:

- "You're in good *hands* with Allstate."
- "I've got a piece of the *rock.*" (Prudential)
- "Under the Traveler's *umbrella.*"
- "The Kemper *cavalry.*"
- "The Nationwide *blanket* of protection."

Other service marketers make their offerings seem more tangible by personalizing them through advertising featuring employees or celebrities. In recent years, American Express advertisements have featured well-known personali-

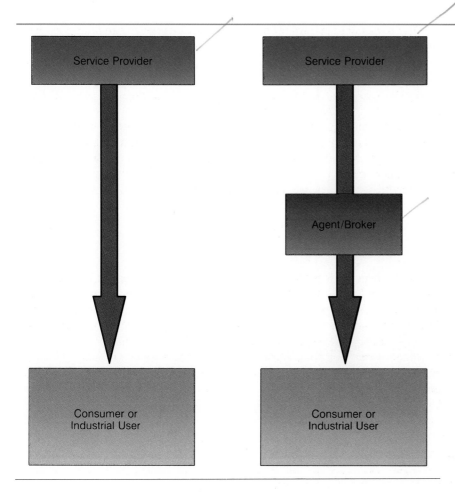

Figure 20.6
Distribution Channels for
Services

ties who are also cardholders. An example of this highly regarded campaign is shown in Figure 20.7.

A second strategy is to attempt to create a favorable image for the service or service company. Among the most commonly used themes by service organizations are efficiency, progressiveness, status, and friendliness.

A third strategy shows the tangible benefits of purchasing an intangible service. For instance, a local bank shows a retired small-business owner relaxing in Florida thanks to a retirement account she established years ago. These and many similar themes help buyers relate to the benefits of the particular service that they otherwise would be unable to visualize.

The desire of many service buyers for a personal relationship with a service provider increases the importance of personal selling. Life insurance marketing provides a good illustration of the key role of the sales representative. Because insurance is a confusing, complex subject for the average buyer, the salesperson must be a professional financial advisor and develop a close, personal relationship with the client. Insurance companies and other service firms must develop a well-trained, highly motivated sales force for providing the high-quality, personalized service that customers require.

Figure 20.7
Use of Celebrities in the Promotion of a Service

Source: Reprinted by permission of American Express Travel Related Services Company, Inc.

Because services are intangible, their sales promotion is difficult. Possibilities for sampling, demonstration, and physical display are limited, and service firms typically do not use premiums or contests. Publicity is also important for many services, especially for entertainment and sports events. Television and radio reports, newspaper articles, and magazine features inform the public of these events and stimulate interest. Contributions to charitable causes, employee services to nonprofit organizations, sponsorship of public events, and similar activities are also publicized to influence the public's opinion of the service firm.[26]

Summary of Chapter Objectives

1. Distinguish between goods and services. Services can be defined as intangible tasks that satisfy consumer and industrial user needs when efficiently developed and distributed to chosen market segments. Although tangible goods and intangible services are similar in that both provide consumer benefits, they differ significantly in their marketing.

2. Explain the importance of the service sector. Almost 52 percent of all personal consumption spending is used for the purchase of services. The service sector also accounts for over 75 percent of all new jobs in the U.S. economy and 25 percent of the nation's exports.

3. Identify the characteristics of services. Five key elements of services have marketing implications: Services are intangible; services are inseparable from the provider; services are perishable; standardization of services is difficult; and buyers often are involved in the development and distribution of services.

4. Discuss buyer behavior as it relates to services. Important aspects of buyer behavior are different for services than for goods. These differences may be grouped into three categories: attitudes, needs and motives, and purchase behavior.

5. Outline the evolution of marketing in service firms. Although service industries have grown substantially, their development of effective marketing programs has been slow. Theodore Levitt attributes much of this problem to what he calls *marketing myopia*. Since Levitt's pioneering work, however, most service firms have adopted marketing.

Key Terms

goods-services continuum
services
tertiary industry
productivity

Review Questions

1. Explain why services are difficult to define.
2. How is a goods-services continuum useful in defining services?
3. Explain the status of the service sector with respect to personal consumption expenditures, employment, and international trade.
4. Why is marketing becoming more important to service firms?
5. Identify the key features of services, and explain how each affects the marketing of services.
6. Explain the classification of services on the bases of reliance on equipment and relative skills of service personnel.
7. How does Levitt's marketing-myopia thesis relate to service industries?
8. What is the status of the marketing concept in service industries?
9. Explain how Colin Clark's concept describes the growth of service industries.
10. Cite the major differences in the marketing strategies of firms that produce goods and those that produce services.

Discussion Questions

1. Prepare a brief report on the marketing activities conducted by a local health care practitioner such as a hospital, health maintenance organization (HMO), medical or dental practice, or laboratory. What generalizations can be made from your study?

2. Describe the last service you purchased. What was your impression of the way in which the service was marketed? How could the firm's marketing effort have been improved?

3. Outline a marketing mix for the following service firms:
   a. Local radio station
   b. Independent insurance agency
   c. Janitorial service
   d. Funeral home

4. Holiday Inns once used the slogan "The best surprise is no surprise" to stress its efforts at providing service of consistently reliable quality. What is your opinion of Holiday Inns' approach to the consistency problem faced by various service providers?

5. Prepare a brief report on the competitive environment in the overnight package delivery business. Draw some generalizations about marketing in service firms for discussion in class.

VIDEO CASE 20

Azure Seas

Cruising is big business. Cruise ships carried 3.5 million passengers in 1988, up 500,000 from the previous year. Since 1980, annual passenger growth has averaged 14 percent. Furthermore, research has shown that 30 to 50 million Americans are interested in taking a cruise, including 90 percent of the 10 million people who had previously done so.

What explains the popularity of cruising? Kirk Lanterman, chairman of the Cruise Lines International Association, puts it this way: "Cruising is hot. It's a vacation experience that offers surprising value and affordability and, at the same time, provides the type of luxurious pampering and attention that you might find only in the most expensive and exclusive resorts around the world."

While the growth of cruising over the past decade is impressive, cruise line executives note that 95 percent of all Americans have not sailed. This statistic suggests a tremendous market potential for the industry. As a result, cruise lines have been adding ships and berths since 1980. Some 40 new cruise ships have been introduced during the decade. Ten new vessels with 8,000 berths were added in 1988 alone. A total of 31,000 new berths have been added to the industry's capacity since the start of the decade. In addition to the new vessels, 43 older ships have been refurbished during this period.

One of these refurbished ships was the Azure Seas, which operates out of Los Angeles. The Azure Seas was purchased by Western Cruise Lines (now known as Admiral Cruises, Inc.) for $30 million and refurbished at a cost of an additional $7 million. The 604-foot long, 78-foot wide vessel has 9 decks and can reach a top speed of 20 knots. The Azure Seas carries over 300 passengers who are served by a crew of 300 to 350.

The company planned to introduce a new concept to West Coast cruising — the short, three- to four-day cruise. The Azure Seas would sail from Los Angeles to Ensenada, Mexico with varying intermediate stops. The ship's 1988 sailing schedule is shown below.

Three-Night Friday Cruise

Depart:	Los Angeles	Friday	7:45 p.m.
Arrive:	Catalina Island	Saturday	9:00 a.m.
Depart:	Catalina Island	Saturday	3:30 p.m.
Arrive:	Ensenada	Sunday	9:00 a.m.
Depart:	Ensenada	Sunday	6:30 p.m.
Arrive:	Los Angeles	Monday	8:00 a.m.

Four-Night Monday Cruise

Depart:	Los Angeles	Monday	4:45 p.m.
Arrive:	San Diego	Tuesday	9:00 a.m.
Depart:	San Diego	Tuesday	3:30 p.m.
Arrive:	Catalina Island	Wednesday	9:00 a.m.
Depart:	Catalina Island	Wednesday	3:30 p.m.
Arrive:	Ensenada	Thursday	9:00 a.m.
Depart:	Ensenada	Thursday	6:30 p.m.
Arrive:	Los Angeles	Friday	8:00 a.m.

Western's management was quite familiar with the short cruise concept. Western's sister company, Eastern Cruise Lines (now also called Admiral Cruises), had long operated short cruises on the East Coast. As Alex Currie, Western's general manager, remarked: "We thought we were the short cruise experts." However, things were different on the West Coast and the firm had to adapt its service strategy to succeed. Short cruises were sold in the East as a recreational and resort experience, but that idea did not work with West Coast (predominantly California) consumers who were accustomed to such resort areas as Malibu and Tahoe. Management's strategy had to be different for the West Coast market.

Western decided to test market its short cruise concept with area travel agents who would market the cruises. The emphasis was on an affordable, total cruise experience. The travel agents were receptive to the concept and the Azure Seas venture was launched with extensive advertising in the travel sections of newspapers.

The target market was called the "Golden Core" by Western executives and was defined as the Los Angeles metropolitan area. Western soon discovered that 70 percent of its passengers came from the so-called Golden Core, and 70 percent of these were first-time cruisers. So, the biggest market segment for the Azure Seas was first-time cruisers from Los Angeles, making up about half of all passengers. Western Cruise Lines also used newspaper advertising throughout an 11-state western region. As part of its effort, Western offered a sea-jet program that included air fare to Los Angeles.

While Western's marketing strategy was well planned, the firm encountered some problems a few years later. The Azure Seas' bottom line had not met expectations the previous quarter and fall bookings were also running behind schedule. Furthermore, marketing research revealed that only 4 percent of Los

Angeles area travelers recognized the name "Azure Seas." By contrast, Princess Line had an 80 to 90 percent recognition factor. Western's management attributed this difference to the popular "Love Boat" television series, which featured a Princess vessel. The question facing Western's executives was how to better use their $1 million advertising budget to overcome these problems.

In a meeting with its advertising agency, Western's management decided to conduct a two-week test of television advertising as an alternative to traditional newspaper advertising. The television commercials, which were used only in the Los Angeles area, stressed affordability, food, and service. The results of the experiment were impressive. Revenues jumped 40 percent. Still, management decided to play it cautious. The company cut the commercials after the initial trial run to see what would happen. The result was that sales declined. When television advertising was reintroduced, sales went up. In fact, during one period, sales actually rose an astounding 80 percent. In addition, a new marketing research study showed that public awareness of the Azure Seas shot up from 4 percent to 13 percent.

The advertising experience of the Azure Seas has been duplicated by other cruise lines. As Ken Istel, a Miami advertising account executive, put it: "You can't fill 10,000 beds a week running ads in newspapers." Other firms have demonstrated that Western's emphasis on price advertising was also on target. When its competitor, Carnival Cruise Lines, first ran television commercials, it did not specify prices until marketing research discovered that potential consumers thought the cruise was expensive. When low prices were highlighted, Carnival's sales increased.

Sources: "1988 Shapes Up As Biggest Ever For New Cruise Ships," *Seattle Times* (January 23–24, 1988), p. 8 (special Travel Show section: Data Source: Cruise Lines International Association); *Supercruise,* 1988 Admiral Seas brochure; "Cruises: TV is Becoming the Industry Medium of Choice." *Adweek* (September 14, 1987), p. F.P.38; and Gail DeGeorge, "Carnival Cruise Lines is Making Waves," *Business Week* (July 6, 1987), p. 34.

Questions

1. How would you place a cruise on the goods-services continuum?
2. What type of segmentation strategy was demonstrated in this video case?
3. How did market segmentation help Western Cruise Lines' marketers?
4. How did Western Cruise Lines attempt to influence the consumer behavior of potential buyers?

COMPUTER APPLICATIONS

In the previous chapter, five of the sixteen analytical techniques introduced earlier were used to aid decisions and to solve problems affecting international marketers. The focus of this chapter is on the marketing of services in both the for-profit and nonprofit sectors. Accordingly, the analytical techniques focus on problems and decisions affecting companies and nonprofit organizations ranging from a financial planning service and a resort to a fund-raising organization and a recycling center. The following problems illustrate the marketing issues facing a diverse array of service firms and the applicability of these analytical techniques for nonprofit organizations as well as profit-seeking service marketers.

Directions: Use menu item 8 titled "Return on Investment" to solve Problems 1 and 2. Use menu item 3 titled "Sales Forecasting" to solve Problem 3. Use menu item 16 titled "Sales Force Size Determination" to solve Problem 4. Use menu item 2 titled "Decision Tree Analysis" to solve Problem 5.

Problem 1   A major New York hotel and entertainment chain is considering buying a highly successful West Virginia lodge and vacation facility for $50 million. The West Virginia property currently produces a $15 million profit on annual revenues of $60 million. Review the discussion of return on investment (ROI) on page 292, then use menu item 8 titled "Return on Investment" to determine the ROI if this West Virginia resort is purchased.

Problem 2   Lewis & Burns, a Long Beach, California, certified public accounting practice, is considering offering a new financial planning service. The partners believe they will generate $225,000 in professional fees and an annual net profit of $75,000. However, the new service will require purchasing $40,000 in software and an addition to the office costing $72,500. Review the discussion of return on investment (ROI) on page 292, then use menu item 8 titled "Return on Investment" to determine the ROI of the proposed new service.

Problem 3   Annual operations of the Heart Fund of Urbana, Illinois, are funded entirely from contributions from area residents and businesses. A substantial portion of these contributions results from an annual telethon conducted by a local television station. The Heart Fund board of directors bases the annual operating budget on estimated contributions. Contributions for the past eight years are shown below:

Year 1	$ 370,000
Year 2	650,000
Year 3	880,000
Year 4	1,200,000
Year 5	1,600,000
Year 6	2,100,000
Year 7	2,750,000
Year 8	3,500,000

Review the discussion of sales forecasting using trend extension on page 116. Then use menu item 3 titled "Sales Forecasting" to forecast Heart Fund contributions for next year.

Problem 4   Gladys McFarland, director of the Florida office of the Mothers' March Against Muscular Dystrophy, is attempting to use more scientific techniques in determining the number of collectors needed for the annual fund drive.

McFarland has labeled several neighborhoods containing 30,000 of the 220,000 Miami households as Type A (high-contribution households); another group of neighborhoods containing 60,000 households as Type B (moderate-contribution households); and a third group of neighborhoods containing 130,000 households as Type C (low-contribution households). A Mothers' March volunteer collector will personally contact each household once during the eight-week fund drive. A stamped, addressed contribution envelope will be left if no one is home. McFarland estimates the desired length of an average contact at 15 minutes for Type A households, 10 minutes for Type B households, and 5 minutes for Type C households. All contacts by Mothers' March collectors will be planned contacts. She also estimates that the average volunteer collector will work 10 hours per week for the eight-week period. Each volunteer will spend 40 percent of available time in calling on specifically designated accounts, 30 percent on travel, and the remaining 30 percent on nonselling activities (training and reports).

Review the discussion of the workload method for determining the required sales force size on pages 636 and 637. Then use menu item 16 titled "Sales Force Size Determination" to specify the number of collectors needed in Miami by the Mothers' March Against Muscular Dystrophy.

Problem 5   Rose Stout, manager of the Los Angeles Recycling Center, has been pleased that recent publicity emphasizing the importance of recycling has greatly increased the amount of materials brought to the center. In fact, she is giving serious consideration to adding two suburban locations in addition to the main center. She estimates a 60 percent likelihood of high growth in the sale of materials for recycling over the next year and a 40 percent chance of moderate growth. Although the expenses associated with operating the proposed new recycling locations would reduce her profits earned on a per-pound basis, the added convenience is certain to generate additional recyclable materials. Stout summarized her two alternatives as follows:

A. Continuing operating at one central location
   1. A high-growth environment will result in 25,000 pounds of materials and generate profits of $.10 per pound.
   2. A moderate-growth environment will result in 15,000 pounds of materials and profits of $.06 per pound.
B. Open two suburban locations
   1. A high-growth environment will result in 40,000 pounds of materials and generate profits of $.06 per pound.
   2. A moderate-growth environment will result in 24,000 pounds of materials and profits of $.01 per pound.

Review the discussion of decision tree analysis on page 79. Then use menu item 2 titled "Decision Tree Analysis" to recommend a course of action for the Los Angeles Recycling Center. Would your recommendation change if the likelihood of high growth were increased to 80 percent?

Appendix
Careers in Marketing

College students select marketing as their career field for a variety of reasons.[1] Here are what some California marketing students have said about their career choice:

I like change and you get that in marketing. You have all sorts of options and you have to decide which is the best option and go out and do it. It's like an adventure. (California State Polytechnic University, *Pomona*)

I wanted to do something that was creative and filled people's needs. (University of Southern California)

You get to bring your own individual touch to the field, especially sales. (Cal Poly)

I like to be creative and I love working with people. In marketing, you can do both. (USC)[2]

A marketing career is also excellent preparation for top management. Korn/Ferry International, an executive search firm, recently surveyed 1,362 leading executives about the most desirable background for someone aspiring to top management. Marketing/sales was identified by 34 percent of the respondents, followed by finance/accounting (25 percent) and general management (24 percent). These results are in marked contrast to a Korn/Ferry survey done eight years earlier when finance was picked as the most desirable background area.[3]

The obvious question is: How does one go about getting a job in marketing? Sometimes it takes considerable creativity on the student's part. Consider the case of David Brickley, who wanted to get a job with an advertising agency. Brickley used the advertisement in Figure 1 to differentiate himself in the fiercely competitive advertising job market. Brickley's strategy worked — he was hired by Hal Riney & Partners of San Francisco.[4]

This appendix focuses on the following aspects of careers in marketing:

1. The kinds of positions available and the responsibilities attached to each
2. The career ladder for the various functional areas within marketing
3. Marketing employment trends and opportunities
4. Marketing employment status of women and minorities.

"BOY HERE NEEDS A JOB."

Father always expected a lot. Like when he decided I was going to be "sumbuddy big n' famous, who's gonna kick ass n' save the world," he wasn't about to grow old waiting. He got old anyway. And I got a job—in advertising. Six years later, as an art director, I realized that I was just guessing how good ads are really done. And that wasn't good enough. So I left work to finish school at Art Center. Although moves like that never impressed father— a man still waiting for me to be king of the whole planet—you may feel differently. If you have a world that needs saving, and need an art director who is used to great expectations, call (818) 356-7504. I promise never to ride my Harley indoors and I'll remember to keep my knuckles off the floor.

David Brickley
Not just another big baby

David Brickley, who had worked as an art director in advertising for six years, left his job to go back to college and get a degree in communication design. But knowing that agencies want people with training as well as a college degree, Brickley created this poster as a direct marketing tool to position himself as a seasoned art director. He sent the poster only to advertising agencies for which he wanted to work, targeting people within agencies who were responsible for hiring creative talent. His targeted self-promotion landed him a job with Hal Riney & Partners, one of the fastest-growing and most respected advertising agencies in the country.

Photo source: Courtesy of David Brickley.

Marketing Positions

Marketing is the single largest employer in the U.S. civilian labor force. Students intending to pursue a marketing career may be bewildered at the range of employment opportunities in the field. How can they find their way through the maze of marketing occupations and concentrate on the ones that best match their interests and talents? The starting point is an understanding of the different positions and the duties each requires.

The precise nature of the various marketing jobs differs among organizations and industries. Marketing tasks may be undertaken in-house by company marketing personnel or subcontracted to outside sources. Indeed, a large number of agencies are available for supporting in-house marketing efforts, including advertising agencies, public relations firms, and marketing research companies. Marketing employment can be found in a variety of organizations:

manufacturing firms, nonprofit organizations, distributive enterprises such as retailers and wholesalers, service suppliers, and research agencies.

All of these organizations offer managerial positions in marketing. The specific duties of the positions vary with the organization's size, the nature of its
business, and the extent to which marketing operations are departmentalized
or centralized. Marketing management jobs generally require the individual to
assist in formulating the organization's marketing policies and to plan, organize,
coordinate, and control marketing operations and resources. Some typical marketing management positions and their responsibilities are described below.
(Specific titles of positions may vary among companies.)

Chief Marketing Executive   The chief marketing executive oversees all
marketing activities and is ultimately responsible for the success of the marketing function. All other marketers report through channels to this person.

Marketing Research Director   The marketing research director determines the organization's marketing research needs and plans and directs the
various stages of its marketing research projects. These stages include problem
definition, research design, data collection, analysis, and interpretation of results. On the basis of this research, the director helps formulate marketing policy and strategies pertinent to each marketing variable.

Product Manager   The product manager is in charge of marketing operations for a particular type of product, such as clothing, building materials, and
appliances. This person also assumes responsibility for some or all of the marketing executive's functions, but only as they pertain to specific products.

Brand Manager   The brand manager performs functions similar to those of
the product manager, but only with regard to a specific brand.

Sales Manager   The person responsible for managing the sales force is the
sales manager. Some of the manager's specific duties are establishing sales
territories; deploying the sales force; recruiting, hiring, and training salespeople;
and setting sales quotas.

Advertising Manager   The advertising manager plans and arranges for promotion of the company's products or services. Among this person's duties are
formulating advertising policy, selecting advertising agencies, evaluating creative promotional ideas, and setting the advertising budget.

Public Relations Officer   The public relations officer directs all the activities that project and maintain a favorable image for the organization. This person arranges press conferences, exhibitions, news releases, and the like.

Purchasing or Procurement Manager   The purchasing or procurement
manager controls all the activities involved in acquiring merchandise, equipment, and materials for the organization.

Retail Buyer   The retail buyer is responsible for purchasing merchandise
from various sources — manufacturers, wholesalers, and importers, among
others — for resale through retail outlets.

Wholesale Buyer   The wholesale buyer purchases products from manufacturers, importers, and others for resale through wholesale outlets. This buyer's duties are similar to the retail buyer's but within the specific context of wholesale distribution.

Physical Distribution Manager   The trend for firms to consolidate physical distribution activities under a single managerial hierarchy has significantly increased the importance of the physical distribution manager. This person is involved with activities such as transportation, warehousing, inventory control, order processing, and materials handling.

Preparing for a Marketing Career

What are the requirements for obtaining a marketing job? At which positions do marketing careers typically begin? What is the usual sequence of progression to the top spots in marketing management?

The starting point is a sound education. Of course, college course work does not guarantee entry into any career field. But the more one knows about business, careers, employment trends, and the like, the better prepared he or she will be when entering the labor force. In fact, business administration is now the most popular major on most American campuses.

The Marketing Career Ladder

The career ladder to top marketing management involves a series of marketing positions.[5] These positions require varying amounts of education, but a college degree is becoming increasingly necessary, and for some positions an M.B.A. or some specialized technical degree is essential. Opportunities for work abound both in-house and in firms that supply marketing services to other organizations, such as direct-mail companies and advertising agencies. Opportunities for marketers exist in as many firms as there are industries — in today's business environment, all firms must effectively market their goods and services in order to survive.

Following are some of the positions that aspiring marketers might hold at some point in their careers. Most companies will not offer all of these positions, and some combine positions. For example, a small firm or in-house operation probably can make do with a single copywriter who performs duties that a large firm would assign to an assistant or senior copywriter.

Sales   Every business has to sell something. The people responsible for this activity go by a variety of titles, such as sales representative, account executive, or bank loan officer. Traditionally, sales positions have been equivalent to marketing one on one. Today there is less emphasis on face-to-face selling to consumers as direct-mail and telemarketing campaigns become more widespread. However, sales representatives still go into the field to deal directly with industrial buyers, distributors, and other corporate and individual users. Sales can be a career in itself or a starting point for moving on to other kinds of marketing jobs, since working directly with a product gives the salesperson firsthand opportunities to see how it might best be marketed.

Marketing Research   Research can make the difference between a successful product or promotion and a failure. In most marketing research organizations, "researcher" is an entry-level position, for either moving on in research or expanding into another part of the marketing field. Marketing research departments operate as microcosms of the corporate hierarchy: A project manager oversees the research process, an account executive solicits business and keeps the research focused on the client's needs, a project director directs the research along the appropriate avenues, and a marketing research specialist does the actual work.

Product Management   The position of product or brand manager is a common one at firms that sell consumer goods, such as Procter & Gamble (which originated the brand manager position) and Johnson & Johnson, but not among other types of organizations. The major firms tend to employ teams of product managers composed of an associate and assistant product manager as well as a product manager, a group manager who oversees several teams, and a division head above the group managers. The product management team essentially operates as a self-contained marketing department; thus, each team member performs extensive marketing duties.

Advertising   The major advertising firms employ people in every marketing position, from the direct-sales functions of the account executive to the public relations expert. Yet no one walks out of college into a position of account executive or art director or even copywriter unless a firm is extremely small and the individual performed well as an intern somewhere. In advertising, a hierarchy exists at every position — assistant and associate copywriters, art directors, and media buyers toil to become full-fledged copywriters, art directors, and media buyers. People in "name" positions, such as account executive, art director, copywriter, sales promotion manager, and specialty ad distributor, have two, three, or four steps to go before reaching the top level.

Nonprofit Organizations   Increasing numbers of nonprofit institutions are employing marketing directors to help them solicit grants and contributions or to attract more people to see exhibits, hear performances, and the like. There is no real hierarchy in the field, and responsibilities vary widely among nonprofit groups.

Retailing   Retail operations employ sales personnel, buyers, and operations people. A store manager directs the retail outlet's overall operation.

Physical Distribution   While often overlooked by people seeking jobs in marketing, physical distribution is an essential segment of the marketing process. This field offers an extensive number of positions — from customer service to inventory control — all of which require independence of thought and the ability to coordinate effectively.

Marketing Occupation	Recent Employment	Projected Employment Growth through 1995		Table 1
Buyers, retail and wholesale trade	299,000	AFA		Employment Projections for Selected Marketing Positions through 1995
Insurance agents and brokers	371,000	MMSTA		
Manufacturers' sales workers	547,000	MSTA		
Public relations workers	95,000	MFTA		
Purchasing agents	189,000	AFA		
Real estate agents and brokers	363,000	AFA		
Reservation agents and ticket clerks	109,000	MMSTA		
Retail trade sales workers	4,000,000	AFA		
Securities sales workers	81,000	MFTA		
Wholesale trade sales workers	1,200,000	FTA		

Key: MFTA = much faster than average; FTA = faster than average; AFA = about as fast as average; MSTA = more slowly than average; MMSTA = much more slowly than average.

Source: U.S. Department of Labor, Bureau of Labor Statistics, *Occupational Outlook Handbook, 1986–1987 Edition* (Washington, D.C.: Government Printing Office, April 1986), pp 50–52, 208, 253–267, 289.

Trends and Opportunities

Table 1 reports the Bureau of Labor Statistics employment projections through 1995 for selected marketing occupations. Some sales positions are forecasted to do particularly well during this period.

Marketing Salaries

In a recent year, Irving Rousso, vice-president of sales and merchandising at Russ Togs, earned $1,256,500 (including a $781,500 bonus). Dozens of other marketing executives earned six-figure incomes; for instance, Victoria Brown, senior vice-president of sales and marketing at Timeplex, a New Jersey data communications equipment manufacturer, earned $237,000.[6] These examples illustrate the income potential of marketing careers. But perhaps a more pertinent concern from the student's viewpoint is the beginning salary levels in marketing. During 1987, most marketing and sales graduates were hired within a range of approximately $20,000 to $23,000.[7]

Status of Women and Minorities in Marketing

Advertising, marketing research, and retailing are marketing occupations in which women traditionally have held jobs. Women often enter marketing by way of retail sales, where they outnumber men by a ratio of more than two to one, as shown in Table 2. Women also account for a high percentage of total employees in real estate sales.

Although there have been gains in women's employment in recent years, an earnings gap between men and women employees still exists. The average

NOTES

Chapter 1

1. Fattal quotation in Ellen Paris, "California Chic," *Forbes* (September 23, 1985), p. 203. See also "A Shady Business," *Newsweek* (May 11, 1987), p. 61; "Hot Promotion Tool Helps Drivers Keep Their Cool," *Marketing News* (May 22, 1987), p. 18; and "Using Consumer Demand to Persuade Buyers," *Sales and Marketing Management* (August 1986), pp. 60–61.

2. Peter F. Drucker, *The Practice of Management* (New York: Harper & Row, 1954), p. 37.

3. Joseph P. Guiltinan and Gordon W. Paul, *Marketing Management* (New York: McGraw-Hill, 1985), pp. 3–4.

4. "AMA Board Approves New Marketing Definition," *Marketing News* (March 1, 1985), p. 1.

5. Wroe Alderson, *Marketing Behavior and Executive Action* (Homewood, Ill.: Irwin, 1957), p. 292.

6. Robert J. Keith, "The Marketing Revolution," *Journal of Marketing* (January 1960), p. 36.

7. The company's experience is described in Chester M. Woolworth, "So We Made a Better Mousetrap," *The President's Forum* (Fall 1962), pp. 26–27.

8. Keith, "The Marketing Revolution," p. 38.

9. Theodore Levitt, *Innovations in Marketing* (New York: McGraw-Hill, 1962), p. 7.

10. General Electric Company, *Annual Report,* 1952, p. 21.

11. Janet Novack, "A Close Call," *Forbes* (January 26, 1987), p. 38.

12. Theodore Levitt, "Marketing Myopia," *Harvard Business Review* (July-August 1960), pp. 45–56. See also Irving D. Canton, " 'Marketing Myopia' Revisited," *Marketing News* (March 13, 1987), pp. 1, 23.

13. Philip Kotler and Sidney J. Levy, "Broadening the Concept of Marketing," *Journal of Marketing* (January 1969), pp. 10–15.

14. David J. Luck, "Broadening the Concept of Marketing—Too Far," *Journal of Marketing* (July 1969), pp. 53–55.

15. This interesting series of exchanges appears in the *Journal of the Academy of Marketing Science* (Summer 1979). See Gene R. Laczniak and Donald A. Michie, "The Social Disorder of the Broadened Concept of Marketing," pp. 214–232; Sidney J. Levy and Philip Kotler, "Toward a Broader Concept of Marketing's Role in Social Order," pp. 232–239; and Laczniak and Michie, "Broadening Marketing and Social Order: A Reply," p. 239–242.

16. Katrine Ames, "Beverly in Bloom," *Savvy* (May 1987), pp. 33–35, 80.

17. Jay Finegan, "Tax Advantages," *Inc.* (August 1987), p. 23.

18. "Selling of Self," *Marketing News* (August 14, 1987), pp. 4, 11.

19. For a detailed discussion on the use of computerized market research in political marketing, see Brad Edmondson, "The Political Sell," *American Demographics* (November 1986), pp. 26–27, 63–66.

20. Thomas D. Brandt, "Babbitt Tries to Sharpen His Profile," *Insight* (March 2, 1987), p. 26.

21. Ford S. Worthy, "Booming American Cities," *Fortune* (August 17, 1987), pp. 34–35.

22. Susan Sewell, "Cancer Society Says Cover Up or Face Consequences," *Adweek* (April 15, 1986), p. 8.

23. Jim Osterman, "The Trinitarians Are Looking for a Few Good Men," *Adweek* (April 15, 1986), p. 8.

24. Philip Kotler, *Marketing for Nonprofit Organizations* (Englewood Cliffs, N.J.: Prentice-Hall, 1982), p. 9.

25. Stephan Wilkinson, "Selling Condoms to Women," *Working Woman* (October 1985), p. 68. See also Louis E. Boone and David L. Kurtz, "AIDS and the Marketing of Condoms," *Health Marketing Quarterly* (Winter 1988).

26. "Solution for Soggy Cereal," *Time* (July 27, 1987), p. 70.

27. "New Mousetrap Kills Without Mess," *Marketing Week* (October 19, 1987), p. 8.

28. Senator Bradley quoted in Robert E. Taylor, "Entrance Fees at U.S. Parks Stir Controversy," *The Wall Street Journal* (June 9, 1987), p. 35.

29. Michael Hiestand, "White Castle Off to Market, Again," *Adweek* (March 16, 1987), p. 1.

30. "P&G Pours Firepower into Dishwasher Wars for Liquid Cascade's Attack," *Chicago Tribune* (February 16, 1987), sec. 4, p. 7.

31. Tom Jenkins, "Winning Customers with a Newsletter," *Sales and Marketing Management* (May 1987), p. 85.

32. *3M Report to Shareholders* (First Quarter, 1987), p. 3.

Chapter 2

1. Quotations in paragraphs 2 and 7 are from Laurie Hays, "DuPont's Difficulties in Selling Kevlar Show Hurdles of Innovations," *The Wall Street Journal* (September 29, 1987), pp. 1, 23. See also "What's Causing the Scratches in DuPont's Teflon," *Business Week* (December 8, 1986), pp. 60–61; and Lee Smith, "A Miracle in Search of a Market," *Fortune* (December 1, 1980), pp. 92–94.

2. Among the marketing texts that treat the marketing environment as consisting of uncontrollable variables are E. J. McCarthy and William D. Perreault, Jr., *Basic Marketing* (Homewood, Ill.: Irwin, 1987), Chapter 4, and Joel Evans and Barry Berman, *Marketing* (New York: Macmillan, 1987), p. 37.

3. S. M. Scherer, *Industrial Market Structure and Economic Performance* (Chicago: Rand McNally, 1980), p. 470.

4. Robert Johnson, "Quaker Oats to Sell Line to Kraft, Inc.," *The Wall Street Journal* (May 29, 1987), p. 2.

5. "Plastic Hits Steel in Auto Industry," *Sales and Marketing Management* (February 3, 1986), p. 25.

6. Gulf & Western Corporation, *Annual Report,* 1985, p. 6.

7. Patrick Houston, "Multifoods Is Ditching Its 'Mishmash of Little Businesses,' " *Business Week* (September 22, 1986), p. 34.

8. Cynthia Mitchell, "How Kimberly-Clark Wraps Its Bottom Line in Disposable Huggies," *The Wall Street Journal* (July 23, 1987), pp. 1, 20.

9. "Florida Enacts 'Do Not Call' Law," *Marketing News* (July 31, 1987), p. 9.

10. Christine Dugas and Paula Dwyer, "Deceptive Ads: The FTC's Laissez-Faire Approach Is Backfiring," *Business Week* (December 2, 1986), p. 136.

11. Robert Taylor, "Velsicol Agrees with EPA to Halt Sales of Anti-Termite Chemicals Pending Test," *The Wall Street Journal* (August 12, 1987), p. 20.

12. Michael Allen, "Florida's New Tax on Services Begins; Some Foresee a 'Nightmare' to Enforce," *The Wall Street Journal* (July 7, 1987), p. 9; Alex Taylor III, "Why Florida Faces Tax Rebellion," *Fortune* (July 6, 1987), pp. 82–83; and "Firms Pull TV Ads to Protest Florida Law," *Insight* (July 27, 1987), p. 46.

13. "Turkey and Trimmings," *Time* (November 30, 1987), p. 15. See also Robb Deigh, "Dairy's Endangered Sacred Cow," *Insight* (July 20, 1987), p. 22.

14. "The Consumer's Role: Large and Worrisome," *The Wall Street Journal* (August 10, 1987), p. 1.

15. Susan Dillingham, "A Generic Decline," *Insight* (May 4, 1987), p. 44.

16. Michael Oneal, "A Retailored Hartmarx Still Needs Some Altering," *Business Week* (March 9, 1987), p. 109.

17. "The Consumer's Role: Large and Worrisome," *The Wall Street Journal* (August 10, 1987), p. 1.

18. *The Story of Chewing Gum and the Wm. Wrigley Jr. Company.*

19. David B. Wolfe, "The Ageless Market," *American Demographics* (July 1987), p. 27.

20. Stephen Kreider Yoder, "Superconductivity Electrifies Japan, Inc.," *The Wall Street Journal* (August 12, 1987), p. 6.

21. For more information on superconductivity research and potential applications, see John W. Wilson and Otis Port, "Our Life Has Changed," *Business Week* (April 6, 1987), pp. 94–100.

22. "U.S. Gunmaker Back on Target," *Chicago Tribune* (July 12, 1987), sec. 7, p. 10A.

23. Security Pacific Corporation, *Annual Report,* 1986, p. 6.

24. Karen Berney, "Customizing for Customer Service," *Nation's Business* (March 1986), pp. 61–62.

25. Mimi Bluestone and Evert Clark, "These Maps Can Almost Read People's Minds," *Business Week* (May 11, 1987), pp. 138–139.

26. Martha Farnsworth Riche, "Computer Mapping Takes Center Stage," *American Demographics* (June 1986), pp. 26, 28–29.

27. *Statistical Abstract of the United States: 1987* (Washington, D.C.: U.S. Government Printing Office, 1986), p. 565.

28. "The Top Companies in 1986 R&D Spending," *Business Week* (June 22, 1987), p. 140.

29. Jeffrey Trachtenberg, "It's Become Part of Our Culture," *Forbes* (May 5, 1987), pp. 134–135.

30. Joe Schwartz, "Hispanic Opportunities," *American Demographics* (May 1987), p. 56.

31. David W. Cravens and Gerald G. Hills, "Consumerism: A Perspective for Business," *Business Horizons* (August 1970), p. 21.

32. Michael Oneal, "Anheuser-Busch: The Scandal May Be Small Beer After All," *Business Week* (May 11, 1987), p. 72.

33. "ATA Unit Monitors Legislation," *Marketing News* (July 31, 1987), p. 9.

34. *Rebuttal to Some Unfounded Assertions about Advertising* (New York: American Advertising Foundation, 1967), p. 13.

35. See Steven N. Brenner and Earl A. Mollander, "Is the Ethics of Business Changing?" *Harvard Business Review* (January-February 1977), pp. 61–62, and Jeffrey Sonnenfeld and Paul R. Lawrence, "Why Do Companies Succumb to Price Fixing?" *Harvard Business Review* (July-August 1978), pp. 145–157.

36. James F. Engel and Roger D. Blackwell, *Consumer Behavior,* 4th ed. (Hinsdale, Ill.: Dryden Press, 1982), p. 668.

37. Terri Thompson and Mimi Bluestone, "Garbage: It Isn't the Other Guy's Problem Anymore," *Business Week* (May 25, 1987), p. 154.

38. Fred Langan, "New Plastic Could Help Roadside Litter Do a Better Vanishing Act," *Christian Science Monitor* (May 5, 1987), p. 22.

Chapter 3

1. "Why Kodak is Starting to Click Again," *Business Week* (February 23, 1987), p. 134.

2. Alfred D. Chandler, *Strategy and Structure* (Cambridge, Mass.: MIT Press, 1962), p. 13. See also Paul F. Anderson, "Marketing, Strategic Planning, and the Theory of the Firm," *Journal of Marketing* (Spring 1982), pp. 15–26.

3. Coca-Cola Company, *Annual Report,* 1985, 1986.

4. "Strategic Planning Should Occupy 30 to 50 Percent of CEO's Time: Schanck," *Marketing News* (June 1, 1979), p. 1.

5. Sara E. Moran, "General Mills Going Back to the Basics," *Advertising Age* (April 1, 1985), p. 92.

6. Ronald Alsop, "Don Rickles and Devilish Kid Bring Dull Carpet Ads to Life," *The Wall Street Journal* (July 9, 1987), p. 29.

7. Brenton R. Schlender and Michael Waldholz, "Genentech's Missteps and FDA Policy Shift Led to TPA Setback," *The Wall Street Journal* (June 6, 1987), pp. 1, 16. See also Joan Hamilton, "Birth of A Blockbuster: How Genentech Delivered the Goods," *Business Week* (November 30, 1987), pp. 138–142.

8. Derek F. Abell, "Strategic Windows," *Journal of Marketing* (July 1978), pp. 21–26. See also John K. Ryans, Jr., and William L. Shanklin, *Strategic Planning: Concepts and Implementation* (New York: Random House, 1985), p. 11.

9. This strategy has also been called *product differentiation.* See Wendell R. Smith, "Product Differentiation and Market Segmentation as Alternative Marketing Strategies," *Journal of Marketing* (July 1956), pp. 3–8. The terms *undifferentiated marketing, differentiated marketing,* and *concentrated marketing* were suggested by Philip Kotler. See his *Marketing Management* (Englewood Cliffs, N.J.: Prentice-Hall, 1984), pp. 267–271.

10. WD-40 Company, *Annual Report,* 1985, and other product literature.

11. "International Newsletter," *Sales and Marketing Management* (April 1987), p. 86.

12. Paula Span, "Have Idea, Will Travel," *Savvy* (January 1987), pp. 24, 26, 76.

13. Frederick A. Brodie, "Collapse of Diesel Car Market Leaves Many Firms Sputtering in Its Wake," *The Wall Street Journal* (July 11, 1984), p. 17.

14. Laurie Freeman, "Minnetonka Abandons Mass Market," *Advertising Age* (May 18, 1987), p. 75.

15. Lester A. Neidell, *Strategic Marketing Management* (Tulsa, Okla.: PennWell Books, 1983), p. 92.

16. Thomas More, "Old-Line Industry Shapes Up," *Fortune* (April 27, 1987), p. 26.

17. Philippe Haspeslagh, "Portfolio Planning: Uses and Limitations," *Harvard Business Review* (January-February 1982), pp. 58–73.

18. Harold Geneen, *Managing* (New York: Doubleday, 1984), p. 27.

19. Quoted in Arthur R. Roolman, "Why Corporations Hate the Future," *MBA* (November 1975), p. 37.

20. Ely S. Lurin, "Audit Determines the Weak Link in the Marketing Chain," *Marketing News* (September 12, 1986), pp. 35, 37.

21. Ed Roseman, "An Audit Can Make the 'Accurate' Difference," *Product Marketing* (August 1979), pp. 24–25.

22. Douglas J. Dalrymple, *Sales Forecasting Practices* (Bloomington, Ind.: Indiana University School of Business Working Paper, 1985), p. 28.

23. Daniel Akst, "Disney Plans Large-Scale Expansion Into Retailing Starting Next Spring," *The Wall Street Journal* (December 23, 1987), p. 18; and Marcy Magiera, "Disney Tries Retailing," *Advertising Age* (June 1, 1987), p. 80.

24. Appendix text is adapted from Stephen K. Keiser, Robert E. Stevens, and Lynn J. Loudenback, *Contemporary Marketing Study Guide,* Fifth Edition (Hinsdale, Ill.: The Dryden Press, 1986), pp. 482–487. A more detailed discussion of marketing plans can be found in David S. Hopkins, *The Marketing Plan* (New York: The Conference Board, 1981), and W. Douglas Johnstone, *Planning for Corporate Growth: The Annual Marketing Plan* (Washington, D.C.: Direct Selling Association, n.d.).

Chapter 4

1. "Safeway Stores Double as Research Lab," *Marketing News* (August 28, 1987), p. 56.

2. Correspondence from Leonard Berry, then AMA president (May 4, 1987).

3. "Include Marketing Research in Every Level of Corporate Strategic Planning," *Marketing News* (September 18, 1981), sec. 2, p. 8.

4. Jeffrey A. Trachtenberg, "Beyond the Hidden Persuaders," *Forbes* (March 23, 1987), p. 135.

5. Eric Scigliano, "Research Hinges on Human Factors," *Monthly* (October 1981), p. 9.

6. Toni Mack, "Let the Computer Do It," *Forbes* (August 10, 1987), p. 94.

7. *The Wall Street Journal* (May 29, 1986), p. 1.

8. "Marketing Research Needs Right Organization People to Fulfill Its Strategic Planning Potential," *Marketing News* (September 18, 1981), sec. 1, p. 14.

9. Jack J. Honomichl, "Top 46 Companies' Growth Is Partly Illusion," *Advertising Age* (May 11, 1987), p. S-1.

10. The classification and definitions of marketing research companies are based on William G. Zikmund, *Exploring Marketing Research,* 2d ed. (Hinsdale, Ill.: Dryden Press, 1986), pp. 35–39.

11. Amanda Bennett, "Once a Tool of Retail Marketers, Focus Groups Gain Wider Usage," *The Wall Street Journal* (June 3, 1986), p. 31.

12. Mary Abbott, "Cut-Price Message vs. 'Free' Offer," *Advertising Age* (February 2, 1987), p. 44.

13. "Marketing Research Needs Right Organization People."

14. Trachtenberg, "Beyond the Hidden Persuaders," pp. 135, 138.

15. "Let a Data Base Get You the Facts," *Changing Times* (October 1981), pp. 47, 49.

16. "1990 Census Update," *American Demographics* (June 1986), p. 13.

17. Mimi Bluestone and Evert Clark, "These Maps Can Almost Read People's Minds," *Business Week* (May 11, 1987), p. 138.

18. Ronald Alsop, " 'People Watchers' Seek Clues to Consumers' True Behavior," *The Wall Street Journal* (September 4, 1986), p. 29.

19. Eugene Carlson, "Census Debate: Is an Estimate More Accurate Than a Count?" *The Wall Street Journal* (August 4, 1987), p. 35, and "1990 Census Update."

20. "Side-Lines," *The Chronicle of Higher Education* (August 6, 1986), p. 31.

21. Selwyn Feinstein, "Computers Replacing Interviewers for Personnel and Marketing Tasks," *The Wall Street Journal* (October 9, 1986), p. 37.

22. Debbie Seaman, "Simple Messages for Simple Way to Message," *Adweek* (August 3, 1987), p. 22.

23. Bennett, "Once a Tool of Retail Marketers."

24. Cathy Reiner, "Seattle-Area Pop Drinkers to Test Decaffeinated Pepsi," *The Seattle Times* (August 3, 1982), p. E4.

25. "Great Ideas In Marketing: Decision Support Systems." Reprinted from *Marketing News.* Copyright ©1986 by the American Marketing Association.

26. Steven P. Galante, "Urban Entrepreneurs Tutored in How to Read Market Cues," *The Wall Street Journal* (August 10, 1987), p. 25.

Chapter 5

1. Betty Marton, "How Sweet It Is, Again," *Adweek* (April 6, 1987), pp. H.M. 22, H.M. 24.

2. This definition is adapted from James F. Engel, Roger D. Blackwell, and Paul W. Miniard, *Consumer Behavior,* 5th ed. (Hinsdale, Ill.: Dryden Press, 1986), p. 9.

3. Kurt Lewin, *Field Theory in Social Science* (New York: Harper & Row, 1951), p. 62. See also C. Glenn Walters, "Consumer Behavior: An Appraisal," *Journal of the Academy of Marketing Science* (Fall 1979), pp. 237–284.

4. Joshua Hyatt, "Bad Translations Turn Ads from Mild to Spicy," *INC.* (November 1986), p. 18.

5. Engel, Blackwell, and Miniard, *Consumer Behavior,* p. 362.

6. For a more complete discussion of other American core values and their influence on consumer behavior, see Leon Schiffman and Leslie Kanuk, *Consumer Behavior,* 3rd ed. (Englewood Cliffs, N.J.: Prentice-Hall, 1987), pp. 491–504.

7. The discussion of the baby boom generation is adapted from Connie Lauerman, "Where Have All the Flower Children Gone?" *Florida* (November 8, 1981), pp. 6–7.

8. *The Ethan Allen Report: The Status and Future of the American Family* is profiled in Joe Schwartz, "Family Traditions," *American Demographics* (March 1987), p. 58.

9. "Learning How to Please the Baffling Japanese," *Fortune* (October 5, 1981), p. 122.

10. David A. Ricks, "How to Avoid Business Blunders Abroad," *Business* (April–June 1984), pp. 3–12.

11. "Italian-American Anger Scuttles Al Capone Ads," *Insight* (September 21, 1987), p. 47.

12. "Profile of Tomorrow's New U.S.," *U.S. News & World Report* (November 24, 1986), p. 32.

13. William O'Hare, "Blacks and Whites: One Market or Two?" *American Demographics* (March 1987), pp. 44–48.

14. The Conference Board report is cited in "Blacks and Whites."

15. Alphonzia Wellington, "Traditional Brand Loyalty," *Advertising Age* (May 18, 1981), sec. 2, p. 52.

16. Thomas Exter, "How Many Hispanics?" *American Demographics* (May 1987), p. 38.

17. Ed Fitch, "Marketing to Hispanics," *Advertising Age* (February 9, 1987), p. S-1.

18. The *1987 U.S. Hispanic Market Study* by Strategy Research Corporation is profiled in Joe Schwartz, "Hispanic Opportunities," *American Demographics* (May 1987) pp. 56, 58–59.

19. Joel Kotkin, "Selling to the New America," *INC.* (July 1987), pp. 45–46.

20. Ibid., p. 45.

21. Ibid., p. 46.

22. Ibid., p. 47.

23. S. E. Asch, "Effects of Group Pressure upon the Modification and Distortion of Judgments," in *Readings in Social Psychology,* ed. E. E. MacCoby et al. (New York: Holt, Rinehart and Winston, 1956), pp. 174–183.

24. Richard P. Coleman, "The Significance of Social Stratification in Selling" and "Retrospective Comment," *Classics in Consumer Behavior,* ed. Louis E. Boone (New York: Macmillan, 1984), pp. 288–302, and Richard P. Coleman and Lee Rainwater, *Social Standing in America: New Dimensions of Class* (New York: Basic Books, 1978).

25. Charles M. Schaninger, "Social Class versus Income Revisited: An Empirical Investigation," *Journal of Marketing Research* (May 1981), pp. 192–208.

26. See Danny N. Bellenger and Elizabeth C. Hirschman, "Identifying Opinion Leaders by Self-Report," in *Contemporary Marketing Thought,* ed. Barnett A. Greenberg and Danny N. Bellenger (Chicago: American Marketing Association, 1977), pp. 341–344.

27. Elihu Katz and Paul F. Lazarsfeld, *Personal Influence* (New York: Free Press, 1956), p. 32.

28. "Caddy Strikes Back," *American Demographics* (August 1987), pp. 22–23.

29. U.S. Department of Commerce, Bureau of the Census, *Households, Families, Marital Status, and Living Arrangements: March 1986* (Washington, D.C.: U.S. Government Printing Office, 1986), p. 1.

30. Bill Abrams, "TV Ad Shows Struggles to Replace Bygone Images of Today's Mother," *The Wall Street Journal* (October 5, 1984), p. 35.

31. Engel, Blackwell, and Miniard, *Consumer Behavior,* pp. 274–277.

32. From a study conducted by Teen-Age Research Unlimited, cited in "$100 a Month," *American Demographics* (June 1986), pp. 11–12.

33. From the *Teenage Attitudinal Study,* cited in Selina Guber, "The Teenage Mind," *American Demographics* (August 1987), pp. 42–44.

34. Mark N. Dodosh, "Widely Ignored Teen Market Has a Lot of Spending Power," *The Wall Street Journal* (June 17, 1982), p. 23; Richard Kreisman, "Teens' Role Grows in Family's Grocery Purchases," *Advertising Age* (May 17, 1982), p. 28; and an advertisement in *Seventeen* magazine that appears in *Advertising Age* (May 3, 1982), p. 33.

35. A. H. Maslow, *Motivation and Personality* (New York: Harper & Row, 1954).

36. Ronald Alsop, "To Snare Shoppers, Companies Test Talking, Scented Displays," *The Wall Street Journal* (June 12, 1986), p. 31.

37. Anita Busch, "No Nonsense about Rolls-Royce Ad," *Advertising Age* (August 10, 1987), p. S-28.

38. Henry Assael, *Consumer Behavior and Marketing Action* (Boston: Kent, 1984), p. 124.

39. See J. Steven Kelly and Barbara M. Kessler, "Subliminal Seduction: Fact or Fantasy," in *Proceedings of the Southern Marketing Association* (November 1978), pp. 112–114; and Joel Saegert, "Another Look at Subliminal Perception," *Journal of Advertising Research* (February 1979), pp. 55–57.

40. Ronald Alsop, "Agencies Scrutinize Their Ads for Psychological Symbolism," *The Wall Street Journal* (June 11, 1987), p. 27.

41. Susan Dillingham, "Inaudible Messages Making a Noise," *Insight* (September 14, 1987), pp. 44–45.

42. This example draws heavily from Ralph King, Jr., "Autodom's Persistent Bad Image," *Forbes* (August 24, 1986), p. 124.

43. This section is based on Michael L. Rothschild and William C. Gaidis, "Behavioral Learning Theory: Its Relevance to Marketing and Promotions," *Journal of Marketing* (Spring 1981), pp. 70–78.

44. John Koten, "For Kellogg, the Hardest Part Is Getting People Out of Bed," *The Wall Street Journal* (May 27, 1982), p. 27.

45. B. M. Campbell, "The Existence of Evoked Set and Determinants of Its Magnitude in Brand Choice Behavior," in *Buyer Behavior and Empirical Foundations,* ed. John A. Howard and Lonnie Ostrom (New York: Knopf, 1973), pp. 243–244.

46. Engel, Blackwell, and Miniard, *Consumer Behavior,* p. 95.

47. These categories were originally suggested in John A. Howard, *Marketing Management: Analysis and Planning* (Homewood, Ill.: Irwin, 1963). This discussion is based on Donald R. Lehmann, William L. Moore, and Terry Elrod, "The Development of Distinct Choice Process Segments over Time: A Stochastic Modeling Approach," *Journal of Marketing* (Spring 1982), pp. 48–50.

Chapter 6

1. Adapted and reprinted from Lawrence Kilman, "Copy Machines Taken For Granted, But Have Changed The Way We Work," *Mobile Press Register* (January 12, 1986), p. 50. Reprinted by permission of The Associated Press.

2. *Statistical Abstract of the United States* (Washington, D.C.: U.S. Government Printing Office, 1987), p. 724.

3. "Survey of Industrial & Commercial Buying Power," *Sales and Marketing Management* (April 27, 1987), p. 26.

4. Todd Mason and Geoff Lewis, "Tandy Finds a Cold, Hard World Outside the Radio Shack," *Business Week* (August 31, 1987), pp. 68, 70.

5. The development of the new type of pole and the problems involved in its adoption are described in Arch G. Woodside, "Marketing Anatomy of Buying Process Can Help Improve Industrial Strategy," *Marketing News* (May 1, 1981), sec. 2, p. 11.

6. This discussion follows Michael D. Hutt and Thomas W. Speh, *Industrial Marketing Management,* 2d ed. (Hinsdale, Ill.: Dryden Press, 1985), pp. 65–69.

7. Ibid., pp. 97–105.

8. Adapted from Frederick E. Webster, Jr., and Yoram Wind, *Organizational Buying Behavior* (Englewood Cliffs, N.J.: Prentice-Hall, 1972), pp. 77–80. This adaptation is reprinted from Hutt and Speh, *Industrial Marketing Management,* p. 193. Used by permission of Prentice-Hall, Inc., and CBS College Publishing.

9. This section is based on Manoj K. Agarwal, Philip C. Burger, and Alladi Venkatesh, "Industrial Consumer Behavior: Toward an Improved Model," in *Developments in Marketing Science,* ed. Venkatakrishna V. Bellur, Thomas R. Baird, Paul T. Hertz, Roger L. Jenkins, Jay D. Lindquist, and Stephen W. Miller (Miami Beach: Academy of Marketing Science, 1981), pp. 68–73.

10. Winston Williams, "Bidders and Congress Join in the Fray," *The New York Times* (May 12, 1985), sec. 3, p. 9.

11. "Out of the Maze," *Sales and Marketing Management* (April 9, 1979). Material updated by the GSA.

12. See Warren H. Suss, "How to Sell to Uncle Sam," *Harvard Business Review* (November-December 1984), pp. 136–144.

13. Ibid., pp. 44–46, 48, 50, 52.

14. Ibid., pp. 46, 48, 50, 52.

15. "GSA and Life Cycle Costing: A Formula for Success," *Government Executive* (April 1984).

16. "Concentrating on Concentration," *Sales and Marketing Management* (January 1987), p. 10.

Chapter 7

1. The Stinnett quote is from Anthony Bianco, "Marketing's New Look," *Business Week* (January 26, 1987), pp. 64–69; Larry Carpenter, "How to Market to Regions," *American Demographics* (November 1987), pp. 44–45; Christine Donahue, "Campbell Soup May Restructure in Favor of Regional Marketing," *Adweek's Marketing Week* (May 4, 1987), pp. 1, 8; and Judann Dagnoli, "Local Move: GF Prepares Regional Plan with Promo $," *Advertising Age* (February 9, 1987), pp. 3, 76.

2. Philip Kotler, *Marketing Management,* 6th ed. (Englewood Cliffs, N.J.: Prentice-Hall, 1988), p. 298.

3. Based on "Managing Consumer Change," a presentation made by Gordon W. Green, Jr., Assistant Chief, Population Division, U.S. Bureau of the Census (February 12–14, 1986), as cited in *Lifestyles and Economic Well-Being in the United States,* American Demographics Institute, p. 7.

4. John Kasarda, Michael D. Irwin, and Holly L. Hughes, "The South Is Still Rising," *American Demographics* (June 1986), p. 34.

5. National Planning Association projections as reported in "Population Profile," *The Wall Street Journal* (August 28, 1986).

6. *Lifestyles and Economic Well-Being,* p. 3.

7. "Americans Don't Move As Often, Report Says," *Journal-American* (March 5, 1984), p. A5. (AP story.)

8. Patricia Sellers, "How Busch Won in a Doggy Market," *Fortune* (June 22, 1987), p. 100.

9. Peter Oberlink, "Regional Marketing Starts Taking Hold," *Adweek* (April 6, 1987), p. H.M. 38.

10. Kenneth Runyon, *Consumer Behavior,* 2d ed. (Columbus, Ohio: Merrill, 1980), p. 35.

11. Peter Oberlink, "What a Team!" *Adweek* (February 2, 1987), pp. C.R. 8, 9.

12. Paul Witteman, "In the Driver's Seat," *Savvy* (October 1987), pp. 42–45.

13. Patrick E. Murphy and William A. Staples, "A Modernized Family Life Cycle," *Journal of Consumer Research* (June 1979), p. 16.

14. These examples are from an earlier life cycle study. See William D. Wells and George Gubar, "Life Cycle Concept in Marketing Research," *Journal of Marketing Research* (November 1966), p. 362. See also Frederick W. Derrick and Alane K. Lehfeld, "The Family Life Cycle: An Alternative Approach," *Journal of Consumer Research* (September 1980), pp. 214–217.

15. "Spending by Men and Women," *The Wall Street Journal* (June 1, 1987), p. 22.

16. See *News,* U.S. Department of Labor, Bureau of Labor Statistics, Washington, D.C. (December 19, 1984), Table 2.

17. Barbara Everitt Bryant, "Built for Excitement," *American Demographics* (March 1987), pp. 38–42, and Alan L. Otten, "This Is for the Person Who Enjoys Being Reduced to a Stereotype," *The Wall Street Journal* (June 23, 1986), p. 25.

18. "Reading the Buyer's Mind," *U.S. News & World Report* (March 16, 1987), p. 59.

19. See "Lifestyle Research: A Lot of Hype versus Little Performance," *Marketing News* (May 14, 1982), sec. 2, p. 5.

20. Tim Schriner, "Who Plays California's Lottery," *American Demographics* (June 1986), p. 52.

21. Harriet C. Johnson, "New Programs Reward Frequent Buyers," *USA Today* (August 21, 1987), p. 5B.

22. "Photon's Space-Age Demographics," *Sales and Marketing Management* (July 1987) pp. 28–29.

23. Daniel Yankelovich, "New Criteria for Market Segmentation," *Harvard Business Review* (March-April 1964), pp. 83–90.

24. Alfred E. Goldman, "Market Segmentation Analysis Tells What to Say to Whom," *Marketing News* (January 22, 1982), sec. 1, p. 10.

25. Ronald Alsop, "The Shame of Smelly Clothes Makes Lever Detergent a Hit," *The Wall Street Journal* (July 2, 1987), p. 21.

26. Myron Magnet, "How to Compete With IBM," *Fortune* (February 6, 1984), p. 58.

27. Stuart Gannes, "The Riches in Market Niches," *Fortune* (April 27, 1987), p. 228.

28. Ibid., pp. 227–228.

29. This section is adapted from M. Dale Beckman, David L. Kurtz, and Louis E. Boone, *Foundations of Marketing*, 3rd ed. (Toronto: Holt, Rinehart and Winston of Canada, 1985), pp. 121–124. The materials were originally prepared by Professor J. D. Forbes of the University of British Columbia and are reprinted by permission of the authors and publisher.

30. "Small Clothes Are Selling Big," *Business Week* (November 16, 1981), pp. 152, 156.

31. Jennifer Alter, "Toothbrush Makers' Lament: Who Notices?" *Advertising Age* (October 4, 1982), p. 66.

32. Philip Kotler and Ravi Singh, "Basic Marketing Strategy for Winning Your Marketing War," *Marketing Times* (November-December 1982), pp. 23–24.

33. David Kiley, "Chrysler Hits Bulls-Eye with Special Incentive Aimed at Local Markets," *Marketing Week* (September 21, 1987), pp. 1, 4.

34. Jennifer Lawrence, "Squeeze Play," *Advertising Age* (September 14, 1987), p. 36.

Chapter 8

1. "The Case of the Glue That Didn't Stick Right," *Training* (February 1985), p. 38; "The 'Blunders' Making Millions for 3M," *Business Week* (July 18, 1984), p. 118; and "Post-it Notes Click Thanks to Entrepreneurial Spirit," *Marketing News* (August 31, 1984), p. 21.

2. This three-way classification of consumer goods was first proposed by Melvin T. Copeland. See his *Principles of Merchandising* (New York: McGraw-Hill, 1924), Chapters 2–4.

3. Laurie Petersen, "Study Confirms Impulse Buying on Rise," *Promote* (October 12, 1987), p. 6.

4. A similar classification scheme has been proposed by Leo Aspinwall, who considers five product characteristics in classifying consumer goods: replacement rate, gross margin (the difference between cost and selling price), adjustment (the necessary changes made in a good to satisfy the consumer's precise needs), time of consumption (the time interval during which the product provides satisfaction), and length of consumer search time. See Leo V. Aspinwall, "The Characteristics of Goods Theory," in *Four Marketing Theories* (Boulder Colo.: Bureau of Business Research, University of Colorado, 1961).

5. Amy Dunkin, "Maxwell House Serves Up a Yuppie Brew," *Business Week* (March 2, 1987), p. 62.

6. "Pumping Up," *American Demographics* (July 1987).

7. An excellent discussion of the management of firms with mature products is in Robert C. Bennett and Robert G. Cooper, "The Product Life Cycle Trap," *Business Horizons* (September-October 1984), pp. 7–16.

8. See William Lazer, Mushtaq Lugmani, and Zahir Quraeshi, "Product Rejuvenation Strategies," *Business Horizons* (November-December 1984), pp. 21–28, and E. Stewart DeBruicker and Gregory L. Summe, "Make Sure Your Customers Keep Coming Back," *Harvard Business Review* (January-February 1985), pp. 92–98.

9. Julie Liesse Erickson, "Turkey's Holiday-Only Image Plucked," *Advertising Age* (October 13, 1986), p. S-24.

10. Arthur Bragg, "Back to the Future," *Sales and Marketing Management* (November 1986), p. 62.

11. *Report of the Annual Meeting*, Kraft, Inc. (First Quarter, 1987), p. 3.

12. Bragg, "Back to the Future," p. 62.

13. Everett M. Rogers and F. Floyd Shoemaker, *Communication of Innovation* (New York: Free Press, 1971), pp. 135–157.

14. Van Wallach, "Cereals Dish Up Instant Gratification in Cash," *Advertising Age* (April 27, 1987), p. S-16.

15. Cynthia F. Mitchell, "How Kimberly-Clark Wraps Its Bottom Line in Disposable Huggies," *The Wall Street Journal* (July 23, 1987), pp. 1, 25.

16. For a more thorough discussion of the speed of the adoption process, see Rogers and Shoemaker, *Communication of Innovations*, pp. 135–157.

17. These factors are suggested in J. Fred Weston and Eugene F. Brigham, *Essentials of Managerial Finance*, 8th ed. (Hinsdale, Ill.: Dryden Press, 1988).

Chapter 9

1. PepsiCo, Inc., *1986 Annual Report*, pp. 8–10, and Jennifer Lawrence, "Testing Juices Up Slice's Performance," *Advertising Age* (August 24, 1987), pp. S-2–S-5.

2. "Name Game," *Time* (August 31, 1981), p. 42.

3. Ronald Alsop, "For More Men, Old Gray Hair Ain't What It Appears to Be," *The Wall Street Journal* (July 30, 1987), p. 25.

4. Amy Borrus, "How Sony Keeps the Copycats Scampering," *Business Week* (June 1, 1987), p. 69.

5. *1985 Annual Report, Aluminum's Centennial: Reynolds' Role*, Reynolds Metals Company, pp. 1–13.

6. Alex Taylor III, "Why the Bounce at Rubbermaid?" *Fortune* (April 13, 1987), pp. 77–78.

7. "The Chrysler Guidebook to Creative Packaging," *Fortune* (June 22, 1987), p. 39.

8. Howard Rudnitakey, "Snap Judgments Can Be Wrong," *Forbes* (April 12, 1982).

9. Anna R. Field, "Why the Hardware Giants Are Hustling into Software," *Business Week* (July 27, 1987), pp. 53–54.

10. Ellen Paris, "To Catch a Thief," *Forbes* (August 24, 1987), p. 92.

11. Eileen Norris, "Product Hopes Tied to Cities with the 'Right Stuff,'" *Advertising Age* (February 20, 1984), p. M-10.

12. These alternative strategies were first suggested in H. Igor Ansoff, "Strategies for Diversification," *Harvard Business Review* (September-October 1957), pp. 113–124.

13. "Selling Smells," *Fortune* (March 16, 1987), p. 14.

14. Trish Hall, "Miller Seeks to Regain Niche as Envy of Beer Industry," *The Wall Street Journal* (December 3, 1986), p. 6.

15. Kathleen Deveny, "Maytag's New Girth Will Test Its Marketing Muscle," *Business Week* (February 16, 1987), p. 68.

16. Nancy Giges, "Colgate Sets 2nd New Product Unit," *Advertising Age* (February 9, 1987), p. 12.

17. Jacob M. Duker and Michael V. Laric, "The Product Manager: No Longer on Trial," in *The Changing Marketing Environment: New Theories and Applications*, ed. Kenneth Bernhardt, Ira Dolich, Michael Etzel, William Kehoe, Thomas Kinnear, William Perrault, Jr., and Kenneth Roering (Chicago: American Marketing Association, 1981), pp. 93–96, and Peter S. Howsam and G. David Hughes, "Product Management System Suffers from Insufficient Experience, Poor Communication," *Marketing News* (June 26, 1981), sec. 2, p. 8.

18. Susan Voyles, "Calls Help Companies Give Us What We Want," *USA Today* (May 21, 1987), p. 7B.

19. Christopher S. Eklund, "How Black & Decker Got Back in the Black," *Business Week* (July 13, 1987), pp. 86, 90.

20. Lois Therrieu, "Has Hasbro Become King of the Toymakers," *Business Week* (September 22, 1986), p. 90.

21. Bro Uttal, "Speeding New Ideas to Market," *Fortune* (March 2, 1987), p. 64.

22. "Copycat Stuff? Hardly!" *Business Week* (September 13, 1987), p. 112.

23. Ronald Alsop, "Companies Get on Fast Track to Roll Out Hot New Brands," *The Wall Street Journal* (July 10, 1986), p. 27.

24. B. G. Yonovich, "Competition Jumps the Gun," *Advertising Age* (February 9, 1981), p. S-18.

25. Robert England, "As Ford Constellation Rises, Taurus Is the Brightest Star," *Insight* (July 13, 1987), p. 15, and Uttal, "Speeding New Ideas to Market," pp. 62–63.

26. Alan L. Unikel, "Imitation Might be Flattering, But Beware of Trademark Infringement," *Marketing News* (September 11, 1987), pp. 20–21.

27. Susan Dillingham, "Brand Name Produce," *Insight* (February 23, 1987), p. 48.

28. Laurie Freeman, "IH Reincarnated as Navistar," *Advertising Age* (January 13, 1986), p. 61.

29. Ronald Alsop, "Firms Create Unique Names, But Are They Pronounceable?" *The Wall Street Journal* (April 2, 1987), p. 31.

30. Unikel, "Imitation Might be Flattering," p. 21.

31. John Koten, "Mixing with Coke over Trademarks Is Always a Fizzle," *The Wall Street Journal* (March 9, 1978). For a thorough discussion of the brand name decision, see James U. McNeal and Linda M. Zeren, "Brand Name Selection for Consumer Products," *MSU Business Topics* (Spring 1981), pp. 35–39.

32. Bill Whalen, "Product Pirates," *Insight* (February 16, 1987), p. 31; Maggie Jackson, "Japan Moves against Counterfeiting of Products," *The Times-Picayune* (July 6, 1986), pp. C-2, C-3; and Reginald Rhein, Jr., "Patent Pirates May Soon Be Walking the Plank," *Business Week* (June 15, 1987), pp. 62–63.

33. Meir Statman and Tyzoon T. Tyebjee, "Trademarks, Patents, and Innovation in the Ethical Drug Industry," *Journal of Marketing* (Summer 1986), pp. 71–81.

34. Bill Abrams, "Brand Loyalty Rises Slightly, But Increase Could be Fluke," *The Wall Street Journal* (February 7, 1982), p. 21.

35. Bill Abrams, "Shoppers Are Often Confused by All the Competing Brands," *The Wall Street Journal* (April 22, 1982), p. 33.

36. Julie Franz, "Ten Years May Be Generic Lifetime," *Advertising Age* (March 23, 1987), p. 76.

37. John Koten, "Why Do Hot Dogs Come in Packs of 10 and Buns in 8s or 12s?" *The Wall Street Journal* (September 21, 1984), p. 1.

38. "Packaging Linked to Ad's Effect," *Advertising Age* (May 3, 1982), p. 63.

39. Sonja Steptol, "Drug Company Giving Capsules Another Chance," *The Wall Street Journal* (July 31, 1986), p. 27.

40. Bill Abrams and David P. Garino, "Package Gains Stature as Visual Competition Grows," *The Wall Street Journal* (August 6, 1981).

41. Phyllis Furman, "Redesign Puts Old Packages in a New Light," *Advertising Age* (May 4, 1987), p. S-20.

42. John Wall, "State-of-the-Mart Product Packages," *Insight* (January 19, 1987), p. 62.

43. Nancy Youman, "Seagram's Golden Wine Cooler, Last Year's New Arrival, Is This Year's Hottest Brand," *Adweek* (August 3, 1987), p. M.R.C. 29.

44. National Confectioners Association of the United States.

45. Betsey Sharkey, "Budget Gourmet's Downscale Look (and Its Upscale Taste) Whetted Consumers' Appetites," *Adweek* (August 3, 1987), p. M.R.C. 30.

46. "Shift to Metrics Moving Ahead in Millimeters," *U.S. News & World Report* (June 7, 1982), p. 77.

47. Len Strazewski, "Wands Trace Path from Store to Shelf," *Advertising Age* (August 24, 1987), pp. S-11–S-12.

48. Karen Lowry Miller, "Seaweed for Breakfast: Courting Japanese Travelers," *Puget Sound Business Journal* (August 3, 1987), pp. 1, 15.

49. John Hillkirk, "Domino's Service No Game," *USA Today* (July 21, 1987), p. 7B.

50. Joseph P. Kahn, "Caddy Shack," *INC.* (May 1987), p. 80.

51. Stephen Battaglio, "GE Makes Bold Service Move," *Adweek's Marketing Week* (March 16, 1987), pp. 1, 6, and Stephen Battaglio, "GE's Guarantee Sparks Flurry of Me-Too's in Appliance Industry," *Adweek's Marketing Week* (July 13, 1987), pp. 1, 5.

52. "Taking Offense at Breakfast," *Time* (October 26, 1987), p. 116.

Chapter 10

1. Payson quote from Richard W. Walker, "Van Gogh's *Irises:* How Much?" *Art In America* (November 1987), p. 25. See also "Going, Going, Van Gone," *Time* (November 23, 1987), p. 57, and Miriam Horn, "Marketing Masterpieces Department-Store Style," *U.S. News & World Report* (November 23, 1987), p. 56.

2. Lisa Phillips, "Seiko's Expensive Lines Wind Up with More Ads," *Advertising Age* (February 11, 1985), p. 4.

3. Abridged and adapted from *Marketing Today,* Third Edition, by David J. Schwartz, copyright © 1981 by Harcourt Brace Jovanovich, Inc. Reprinted by permission of the publisher.

4. Kenneth C. Schneider and James C. Johnson, "Marketing Managers and the Robinson-Patman Act: How Large Is the Fog Factor?" in *1985 AMA Educators Proceedings,* ed. Robert F. Lusch et al. (Chicago: American Marketing Association, 1985), pp. 317–323.

5. Anthony D. Greco, "State Regulation of Fluid Milk," *Northwest Business Review* (Fall 1983), pp. 28–33.

6. The current status of resale price maintenance is discussed in Mary Jane Sheffert and Debra L. Scammon, "Resale Price Maintenance: Is It Safe to Suggest Retail Prices?" *Journal of Marketing* (Fall 1985), pp. 82–91.

7. Jon G. Udell, "How Important Is Pricing in Competitive Strategy?" *Journal of Marketing* (January 1964), pp. 44–48.

8. Louis E. Boone and David L. Kurtz, *Pricing Objectives and Practices in American Industry: A Research Report.* All rights reserved. These findings are consistent with those of Professor Robert A. Robicheaux. See "How Important Is Pricing in Competitive Strategy? Circa 1975," in *Proceedings of the Southern Marketing Association,* ed. Henry W. Nash and Donald Robin (Atlanta: Southern Marketing Association, 1976), pp. 55–57.

9. Research by Professor Saeed Samiee ranked "satisfactory return on investment" first among a similar list of objectives. Samiee correctly points out the difficulties in making the meeting competition objective operational. See "Pricing in Marketing Strategies of U.S.- and Foreign-Based Companies," *Journal of Business Research,* 15 (1987), pp. 17–30.

10. Lois Therrien, "Pet Food Moves Upscale—and Profits Fatten," *Business Week* (June 15, 1987), pp. 80, 82.

11. Robert A. Lynn, *Price Policies and Marketing Management* (Homewood, Ill.: Irwin, 1967), p. 99. See also Stuart U. Rich, "Price Leadership in the Paper Industry," *Industrial Marketing Management* (April 1983), p. 101.

12. Robert D. Buzzell and Frederick D. Wiersema, "Successful Share Building Strategies," *Harvard Business Review* (January-February 1981), pp. 135–144.

13. These pricing objectives are suggested in Philip Kotler, *Marketing for Nonprofit Organizations* (Englewood Cliffs, N.J.: Prentice-Hall, 1982), pp. 306–309.

14. Allen Dodds Frank, "Dear Pharmacist," *Forbes* (June 16, 1986), p. 50.

15. Data for the home building example are adapted from Carol Nanninga, "Constructing a Price," *Bellevue Journal-American* (June 24, 1984), p. G1.

16. Theodore E. Wentz, "Realism in Pricing Analysis," *Journal of Marketing* April 1966, p. 26.

Chapter 11

1. Cost and profit estimates are reported in Joseph Hooper, "Anatomy of a Sticker Price," *Esquire* (October 1987), pp. 168–169. See also Kevin Gudridge, "Subaru Focuses on Low-Price Cars," *Advertising Age* (November 2, 1987), p. 46.

2. "PC Marketing: Is Service All That Crucial?" *Sales and Marketing Management* (January 1987), p. 26. See also Gerald J. Tellis, "Beyond the Many Faces of Price: An Integration of Pricing Strategies," *Journal of Marketing* (October 1986), pp. 146–160.

3. "Polaroid Will Boost Prices on Two Cameras, Film Pack," *The Wall Street Journal* (May 15, 1986), p. 12.

4. Louis E. Boone and David L. Kurtz, *Pricing Objectives and Practices in American Industry: A Research Report.* All rights reserved.

5. See James B. Wilcox, Roy D. Howell, Paul Kusdrall, and Robert Britney, "Price Quantity Discounts: Some Implications for Buyers and Sellers," *Journal of Marketing* (July 1987), pp. 60–70.

6. "Secrets Behind the Specials," *Fortune* (July 11, 1983), p. 94.

7. Michael Hiestand, "Selling Healthcare With Rebates," *Marketing Week* (April 20, 1987), p. 1.

8. "Who Uses Rebates?" *Promote* (July 13, 1987), p. 9.

9. Valerie A. Zeithaml, "Consumer Response to In-Store Price Information Environments," *Journal of Consumer Research* (March 1982), pp. 357–369.

10. J. Edward Russo, "The Value of Unit Price Information," *Journal of Marketing Research* (May 1977), pp. 193–201. See also David A. Aaker and Gary T. Ford, "Unit Pricing Ten Years Later: A Replication," *Journal of Marketing* (Winter 1983), pp. 118–122.

11. Robert A. Mamis, "Take It Off, Take Most of It Off," *INC.* (June 1987), p. 10.

12. Walter J. Primeax, Jr., "The Effect of Consumer Knowledge and Bargaining Strength on Final Selling Price: A Case Study," *Journal of Business* (October 1970), pp. 419–426, and James R. Krum, "Variable Pricing as a Promotional Tool," *Business* (November-December 1977), pp. 47–50.

13. Raymond Serafin, "Saab Ads Blast Off with Aircraft Link," *Advertising Age* (November 9, 1987), p. 70.

14. Bernie Faust, William Gorman, Eric Oesterle, and Larry Buchta, "Effective Retail Pricing Policy," *Purdue Retailer* (Lafayette, Ind.: Department of Agricultural Economics, Purdue University, 1963), p. 2.

15. Karl A. Shilliff, "Determinants of Consumer Price Sensitivity for Selected Supermarket Products: An Empirical Investigation," *Akron Business & Economic Review* (Spring 1975), pp. 26–32.

16. J. Douglass McConnell, "An Experimental Examination of the Price-Quality Relationship," *Journal of Business* (October 1968), pp. 439–444. See also two articles in the May 1980 issue of the *Journal of Marketing Research:* Peter C. Riesz, "A Major Price-Perceived Quality Study Re-Examined," pp. 259–262, and J. Douglass McConnell, "Comment on a Major Price-Perceived Quality and Study Re-Examined," pp. 263–264.

17. Rustan Kosenko and Don Rahtz, "Buyer Market Price Knowledge Influence on Acceptable Price Range and Price Limits," in *Advances in Consumer Research,* ed. Michael J. Houston (Association for Consumer Research, 1987), and Anthony D. Cox, "New Evidence Concerning Consumer Price Limits," in *Advances in Consumer Research,* ed. Richard Lutz (Association for Consumer Research, 1986), pp. 268–271.

18. *Market Spotlight* (Edmonton, Alberta: Alberta Department of Consumer and Corporate Affairs, March 1979).

19. Robert G. Eccles, "Control with Fairness in Transfer Pricing," *Harvard Business Review* (November-December 1983), pp. 149–161.

Chapter 12

1. "Broad Price, Product Mix Just What Docktor Ordered," *Marketing News* (December 19, 1986), p. 7.

2. "Doctors Get OK to Sell Drugs," *Sales and Marketing Management* (February 1987), pp. 19–20.

3. These functions were originally described by Wroe Alderson, "Factors Governing the Development of Marketing Channels," in *Marketing Channels for Manufactured Products,* ed. Richard M. Clewitt (Homewood, Ill.: Irwin, 1954), pp. 5–22.

4. Kenny Hannon, "Party Animal," *Forbes* (November 16, 1987), pp. 262, 266, 270.

5. "Brushing Up at Fuller," *Newsweek* (September 7, 1987), p. 44, and "Fuller Brush to Open 2 Stores," *Chicago Tribune* (July 26, 1987), sec. 7, p. 9C.

6. "Business Bulletin," *The Wall Street Journal* (August 6, 1987), p. 1.

7. "Kodak 'Stands Tall' With Consumers While Demarketing Instant Photo Line," *Marketing News* (January 31, 1987), p. 1, and "Coping with 16.5 Million Headaches," *Fortune* (March 3, 1987), p. 38.

8. These bases were identified in John R. P. French, Jr., and Bertram Raven, "The Bases of Social Power," in *Group Dynamics: Research*

and Theory, 2d ed., ed. Darwin Cartwright and Alvin Zandler (Evanston, Ill.: Row, Putnam, 1960), pp. 607–623. The list originally came from Darwin Cartwright, ed., *Studies in Social Power* (Ann Arbor, Mich.: University of Michigan, 1959), pp. 612–613.

9. David Kiley, "Lever in a Lather over Shelf Space," *Adweek's Marketing Week* (November 2, 1987), pp. 1, 6.

10. The discussion of brand hostaging is based on Keith M. Jones, "Held Hostage by the Trade?" *Advertising Age* (April 26, 1987), p. 18.

11. Dan Wascoe, Jr., "Bottles to Honor Carew Fell Flatter Than Day-Old Coke," *Star Tribune* (September 14, 1987), p. 3M.

12. Raymond Serafin, "Cadillac, Dealers Project Opposites," *Advertising Age* (May 4, 1987), p. 12.

13. Paul B. Carroll, "IBM Is Becoming More Dealer-Friendly," *The Wall Street Journal* (May 8, 1987), p. 6.

14. Paul A. Allen, "Why Distributors Sue Manufacturers," *INC.* (November 1981), p. 157.

15. "Gas-Pumpers Revolt," *Forbes* (September 9, 1985), p. 8.

16. Janice Castro, "Franchising Fever," *Time* (August 31, 1987), pp. 36–38.

17. Harriet C. Johnson, "USA Franchise Sales Gallop in '86," *USA Today* (January 19, 1987), p. 6B, and Castro, "Franchising Fever," p. 36.

18. Stephen Koepp, "Big Mac Strikes Back," *Time* (April 13, 1987), p. 58.

19. Ellen Paris, "Franchising—Hope or Hype?" *Forbes* (December 15, 1986), p. 42.

20. Peter Matega, " 'The Marketing Nightmare': Product Recalls Are Serious, but Damage Can Be Minimized," *Marketing News* (May 8, 1987), p. 28.

Chapter 13

1. Matt O'Connor, "Surprise of a Market Has Grainger Growing," *Chicago Tribune* (July 12, 1987), sec. 7, p. 1.

2. Steven P. Galante, "Distributors Switch Strategies to Survive Coming Shakeout," *The Wall Street Journal* (July 20, 1987), p. 25.

3. Ibid., p. 25.

4. Marilyn Wellemeyer, "Middlemen of Metal," *Fortune* (March 1977), pp. 163–165.

5. Galante, "Distributors Switch Strategies."

6. James R. Moore, "Wholesaling: Structural Changes and Manufacturers' Perceptions," in *Foundations of Marketing Channels,* ed. Arch G. Woodside, J. Taylor Sims, Dale M. Lewison, and Ian F. Wilkinson (Austin, Tex.: Austin Press, 1978), pp. 118–131.

7. Louis P. Bucklin, *Competition and Evolution in the Distributive Trades* (Englewood Cliffs, N.J.: Prentice-Hall, 1972), p. 214.

8. "Surveys Find Trade Shows Cost-Effective, Productive," *Marketing News* (October 3, 1980), p. 4. See also Steven Kelly and James M. Comer, "Trade Show Exhibiting: A Managerial Perspective," in *Evolving Marketing Thought for 1980,* ed. John H. Summey and Ronald D. Taylor (Southern Marketing Association, 1980), pp. 11–13.

9. Chicago Mart Center, *The Mart Center Fact Sheet.*

10. Manufacturers' Agents National Association, *MANA's 1983 Survey of Sales Commissions.*

11. Madhav Kacker, "Wholesaling Ignored Despite Modernization," *Marketing News* (February 14, 1986), p. 35.

Chapter 14

1. Eloise Salhoz, "The Corporate Clothiers," *Savvy* (May 1987), pp. 44–47, 91.

2. For a complete discussion of the wheel of retailing hypothesis, see Stanley C. Hollander, "The Wheel of Retailing," *Journal of Marketing* (July 1960), pp. 37–42.

3. Pier 1, Inc., *1985 Annual Report,* p. 4.

4. "Business Bulletin," *The Wall Street Journal* (May 7, 1987), p. 1, and Arthur Bragg, "Will the Department Store Survive?" *Sales and Marketing Management* (April 1986), pp. 60–64.

5. Steve Weiner and Ellen Paris, "Food as Fashion," *Forbes* (September 7, 1987), pp. 106–107.

6. Lois Therrien, "Birth of a Salesman: How Video Is Revving Up Retailing," *Business Week* (September 7, 1987), p. 109.

7. Patricia Strnad, "Kmart Dangles Lure for Affluent Shopper," *Advertising Age* (August 24, 1987), p. 12.

8. Dayton Hudson Corporation, *1985 Annual Report,* p. 9, and *1986 Annual Report,* p. 4.

9. John S. DeMott, "The Store That Runs on a Wrench," *Time* (July 27, 1987), p. 54.

10. Jonathan Dahl, "Sad but True: No Place Is Safe from Fast Food," *The Wall Street Journal* (May 15, 1986), p. 31.

11. "94 Percent of Americans Visit Shopping Malls Each Month," *The Evening Journal* (June 17, 1987), p. C-1.

12. Roger Lowenstein, "Regional-Mall Developers Try New Tactics as Market Shrinks," *The Wall Street Journal* (September 2, 1987), p. 25, and Ann Hagedorn, "Turning the Shopping Mall Upside Down," *The Wall Street Journal* (May 29, 1987), p. 21.

13. Michael Oneal, "Sears: Trimming the Worst of the Corporate Fat," *Business Week* (March 16, 1987), p. 39.

14. Sally F. Robbins, "Retailers of Casual Fashions Turn Up the Volume," *Advertising Age* (February 2, 1987), p. S-10, and Maureen McFadden, "College Media Lead to Deep Pockets on Campus," *Advertising Age* (February 2, 1987), p. S-2.

15. Maggie Malone, "Classic Furniture Carves Out New Retailing Niche," *Adweek's Marketing Week* (November 9, 1987), p. 60.

16. Joan O'C. Hamilton and Amy Dunkin, "Why Rivals Are Quaking as Nordstrom Heads East," *Business Week* (June 15, 1987), pp. 99–100.

17. Sallie Hook, "All the Retail World's a Stage," *Marketing News* (July 31, 1987), p. 16.

18. Scott Kilman, "Retailers Change Their Stores and Goods, Looking to Cash in on New Buying Habits," *The Wall Street Journal* (September 8, 1986), p. 31.

19. Diane Schneidman, "Visual Aura, 'Kinetics' Help Stabilize Store Image," *Marketing News* (October 23, 1987), p. 4.

20. Betsy Morris, "As a Favored Pastime, Shopping Ranks High with Most Americans," *The Wall Street Journal* (July 30, 1987), pp. 1, 13.

21. This section is adapted from Louis P. Bucklin, "Retail Strategy and the Classification of Consumer Goods," *Journal of Marketing* (January 1963), pp. 50–55, published by the American Marketing Association.

22. Lori Kesler, "St. Louis' Diebergs Serves More Than the Usual Fare," *Advertising Age* (May 4, 1987), pp. S-4, S-6.

23. "Smart Shopping," *Fortune* (May 11, 1987), p. 9.

24. *The Wall Street Journal* (May 7, 1987), p. 1.

25. See Jack G. Kaikati, "Don't Discount Off-Price Retailers," *Harvard Business Review* (May-June 1986), pp. 85–92.

26. Russell Mitchell, "How Comp-U-Card Hooks Home Shoppers," *Business Week* (May 18, 1987), pp. 73–74.

27. Maggie McComas, "Catalogue Fallout," *Fortune* (January 20, 1986), pp. 63–64, and "Catalogues for Sale," *Fortune* (July 6, 1987), p. 9.

28. This discussion of home shopping is based on Judann Dagnoli, "Merger Trend Hits TV Home Shopping," *Advertising Age* (January 26, 1987), pp. 1, 68; Sydney P. Fresdberg, "Home Shopping Shakeout Forces Survivors to Find Fresh Approach," *The Wall Street Journal* (November 4, 1987), p. 33; and Mark Ivey, Mary J. Pitzer, Kenneth Dreylock, and Mark N. Vamos, "Home Shopping," *Business Week* (December 14, 1986), pp. 62–64, 68–69.

29. Donald R. Kutz, "The Big Store," *Esquire* (September 1987), p. 109.

30. These examples are from Lynn Asinof, "Briefs," *The Wall Street Journal* (August 6, 1987), p. 1; Raymond Serafin, "Kmart Shows More Interest in Banking," *Advertising Age* (January 6, 1986), p. 40; David Kiley, "Dry Goods Muscle into Supermarkets," *Adweek's Marketing Week* (June 15, 1987), pp. 1, 6; and Lisa Gubernick, "Stores for Our Times," *Forbes* (November 3, 1986), p. 42.

31. Bragg, "Will the Department Store Survive?" pp. 62–63.

32. "Brave New Shopping," *Newsweek* (June 15, 1987), p. 67.

33. "Work and Sweat," *Time* (November 16, 1987), p. 94.

Chapter 15

1. Quotation in paragraph three from Peter Petre, "How to Keep Customers Happy Captives," *Fortune* (September 2, 1985), p. 4. See also Hal Lancaster, "American Hospital's Marketing Program Places Company Atop a Troubled Industry," *The Wall Street Journal* (August 24, 1984), p. 1, and Anne B. Pillsbury, "The Hard-Selling Supplier to the Sick," *Fortune* (July 26, 1982), pp. 56–61.

2. National Council of Physical Distribution Management, *Measuring and Improving Productivity in Physical Distribution: 1984,* p. 7.

3. Bro Uttal, "Companies That Serve You Best," *Fortune* (December 7, 1987), p. 112.

4. James C. Johnson and Donald F. Wood, *Contemporary Physical Distribution* (New York: Macmillan, 1986).

5. Warren Rose, *Logistics Management* (Dubuque, Iowa: Wm. C. Brown, 1979), p. 4.

6. Uttal, "Companies That Serve You Best," p. 104.

7. Robert E. Sabath, "How Much Service Do Customers Really Want?" *Business Horizons* (April 1978), pp. 26–32. See also Thomas E. Schuster, "A Breeze in the Face," *Harvard Business Review* (November-December 1987), p. 40.

8. Jeremy Main, "Toward Service Without a Snarl," *Fortune* (March 23, 1981), p. 61.

9. Bill Saporito, "A Smart Cookie at Pepperidge," *Fortune* (December 22, 1986), p. 74.

10. The deregulation issue is discussed in Donald F. Wood and James C. Johnson, *Contemporary Transportation* (New York: Macmillan, 1988), Chapters 3–5.

11. *1983 Consolidated Freightways Annual Report.*

12. "Pininfarina Heads for the U.S. in a Caddy," *Business Week* (February 9, 1987), pp. 58–59.

13. James Cook, "If It Isn't Profitable, Don't Do It," *Forbes* (November 30, 1987), p. 54.

14. See Steven P. Galante, "Distributors Bow to Demands of 'Just-in-Time' Delivery," *The Wall Street Journal* (June 30, 1986), p. 27.

15. Brian C. Kullman and Robert W. Haessler, "Kanban, American Style," *Annual Proceedings of the NCPDM* (1984), p. 105. See also Charles R. O'Neal, "Devise New Marketing Strategies to Serve 'JIT' Producers," *Marketing News* (September 14, 1984), pp. 20–21.

16. "How Levi Strauss Is Getting the Lead Out of Its Pipeline," *Business Week* (December 21, 1987), p. 92.

Chapter 16

1. Laurie Petersen, "Prince Courts the Fashionable Set," *Marketing Week* (November 16, 1987), p. 18.

2. Kim Carter, "Growing Yogurt Culture Warms Sales," *Advertising Age* (October 13, 1986), pp. S35–S36.

3. Reported in John W. Hardy and E. Dee Hubbard, "Internal Reporting Guidelines: Their Coverage in Cost Accounting Texts," *Accounting Review* (October 1976), p. 917.

4. Michael Hiestand, "Catfish in Fresh Move to Hook Upscale Market," *Adweek's Marketing Week* (April 4, 1988), pp. 5, 10.

5. S. Watson Dunn and Arnold M. Barban, *Advertising: Its Role in Modern Marketing* (Hinsdale, Ill.: Dryden Press, 1989).

6. Michael Hiestand, "Been to Any Garlic Festivals Lately?" *Adweek* (August 3, 1987), p. 43.

7. "Notebook: A Review of Current Promotions," *Marketing Week* (May 11, 1987), p. 8.

8. B. G. Yovovich, "Scanner Research May Revolutionize the Approach to Consumer Promotions," *Marketing Week* (May 11, 1987), pp. 6–7.

9. Richard W. Pollay, "The Distorted Mirror: Reflections on the Unintended Consequences of Advertising," *Journal of Marketing* (April 1986), pp. 18–36.

10. Francis X. Callahan, "Does Advertising Subsidize Information?" *Journal of Advertising Research* (August 1978), pp. 19–22. See also Morris B. Holbrook, "Mirror, Mirror on the Wall, What's Unfair in the Reflections on Advertising?" *Journal of Marketing* (July 1987), pp. 95–103.

Chapter 17

1. Levi Strauss & Company news release, July 1987.

2. Barbara Lippert, "Levi's 501s Keep Singin' the Blues, and That Ain't Bad," *Adweek* (July 1, 1985), p. 27.

3. Edward Giltenan, "Confronting the Negatives," *Forbes* (April 27, 1987), p. 83.

4. Sarah Stiansen, "Ogilvy Study: Advertising Works," *Marketing Week* (December 14, 1987), p. 2.

5. Debbie Seaman, "HCM Trashes the Place for Mita Copiers," *Adweek* (March 23, 1987), p. 30.

6. David A. Aaker and J. Gary Shansby, "Positioning Your Product," *Business Horizons* (May-June 1982), p. 62.

7. The following discussion of various advertising media is adapted from S. Watson Dunn and Arnold M. Barban, *Advertising: Its Role in Modern Marketing,* 6th ed. (Hinsdale, Ill.: Dryden Press, 1986), pp. 512–591.

8. R. Craig Endicott, "U.S. Ad Income Dips 4.690," *Advertising Age* (March 30, 1988), p. 1.

9. William M. Carley, "Gillette Co. Struggles as Its Rivals Slice at Fat Profit Margin," *The Wall Street Journal* (February 2, 1972), p. 1.

10. Christy Marshall, " 'It Seemed Like a Good Idea at the Time,' " *Forbes* (December 28, 1987), pp. 98–99.

11. "Nothing Sells Like Sports," *Business Week* (August 31, 1987), pp. 48–53, and J. Max Robins, "Choosing the Right Event," *Adweek* (November 17, 1987), pp. 7–8.

12. Joseph N. Fry and Gordon H. McDougall, "Consumer Appraisal of Retail Price Advertisements," *Journal of Marketing* (July 1974), pp. 64–67.

13. Patricia Winters, "Coke Pops First 3-D Spot," *Advertising Age* (January 11, 1988), pp. 1, 58; Amy Dunkin, "Print Ads That Make You Stop, Look—and Listen," *Business Week* (November 23, 1987), p. 38, and Annetta Miller, "The Escalating Ads Race," *Newsweek* (December 7, 1987), p. 65.

14. Joe Agnew, "Burgeoning Sales Promotion Spending to Top $100 Billion," *Marketing News* (May 22, 1987), pp. 8, 14.

15. Paul L. Edwards, "Sales Promotion Comes into Its Own," *Advertising Age* (July 28, 1986), p. 65.

16. Timothy K. Smith, "Buy One Car, Get One Free: Marketers Experiment with Freebies on Grand Scale," *The Wall Street Journal* (March 16, 1987), p. 27.

17. Ronald Alsop, "Car Advertisers Switch Gears to Find Out If Modesty Sells," *The Wall Street Journal* (October 30, 1986), p. 35.

18. Nancy Bishop, "Specialty Advertising Embarks on Second Century," *Marketing Week* (January 4, 1988), p. 32.

19. Alix M. Freedman, "Use of Free Product Samples Wins New Favor as Sales Tool," *The Wall Street Journal* (August 26, 1986), p. 17.

20. Kapil Bawa and Robert W. Shoemaker, "The Coupon-Prone Consumer: Some Findings Based on Purchase Behavior Across Product Classes," *Journal of Marketing* (October 1987), pp. 99–110.

21. Alvin P. Sanoff, "Image Makers Worry about Their Own Images," *U.S. News & World Report* (August 13, 1979), pp. 57–59.

22. Ronnie Telzer, "Celebrities Join Anti-Drug Campaign," *Advertising Age* (April 27, 1987), p. S25.

23. Harold W. Berkman and Christopher Gilson, *Advertising*: *Concepts and Strategies* (New York: Random House, 1987), p. 231.

24. Phillip Kotler, *Marketing Management* (Englewood Cliffs, N.J.: Prentice-Hall, 1988), p. 633.

Chapter 18

1. Frank McCoy, "Goya: A Lot More than Black Beans and Sofrito," *Business Week* (December 7, 1987), pp. 137–138.

2. Arthur Miller, *Death of a Salesman* (New York: Viking, 1949).

3. Mark Blessington, "Winning the Sales Pay Battle," *Sales and Marketing Management* (February 16, 1987), p. 20.

4. "Job Market for College Graduates," *Occupational Outlook Quarterly* (Summer 1986), p. 7.

5. Al Urbanski, "Wells Fargo's Sales Force Tames the Wild West," *Sales and Marketing Management* (January 1987), pp. 38–41.

6. See William C. Moncrief III, "Selling Activity and Sales Position Taxonomies for Industrial Salesforces," *Journal of Marketing Research* (August 1986), pp. 261–270.

7. "How IBM Is Fighting Back," *Business Week* (November 17, 1986), p. 56.

8. Charles Futrell, *Sales Management* (Hinsdale, Ill.: Dryden Press, 1988), p. 137.

9. Eugene M. Johnson, David L. Kurtz, and Eberhard Scheuing, *Sales Management* (New York: McGraw-Hill, 1986).

0. "The Best Fleet in Town," *Sales and Marketing Management* (April 1987), p. 61.

11. "Commissions Catch On at Department Stores," *Marketing Week* (February 1, 1988), p. 5.

12. A. S. Hansen, Inc., *Sales Compensation Survey 1986,* as reported in *Sales and Marketing Management* (February 16, 1987), p. 57.

13. The workload method was first described in Walter J. Talley, Jr., "How to Design Sales Territories," *Journal of Marketing* (January 1961), pp. 7–13. The steps are described in Douglas J. Dalrymple, *Sales Management* (New York: Wiley, 1988), pp. 477–478, and Gilbert A. Churchill, Jr. Neil M. Ford, and Orville C. Walker, Jr., *Sales Force Management* (Homewood, Ill,: Irwin, 1985), pp. 181–183.

14. Porter Henry, "The Important Few — The Unimportant Many," *1980 Portfolio of Sales and Marketing Plans* (New York: Sales and Marketing Management, 1980), pp. 34–37.

Chapter 19

1. Kenneth F. Englade, "Getting a Piece of the Japanese Pie," *American Way* (April 1, 1987), pp. 50–51, and Damon Darlin, "Blind Luck, Cartoon Help a U.S. Firm Sell Frozen Potato Products to Japanese," *The Wall Street Journal* (May 27, 1987), p. 26.

2. "Taking on the World," *Time* (October 19, 1987), p. 46.

3. Sharon Nelton, "Doing Business Overseas," *Working Woman* (March 1984), p. 129.

4. Philip Revzin, "While Americans Take to Croissants, Kellogg Pushes Cornflakes on France," *The Wall Street Journal* (November 11, 1986), p. 40.

5. Christopher Elias, "A New Razor-Sharp Approach to Old-Fashioned Capitalism," *Insight* (January 12, 1987), p. 42.

6. Ralph Z. Sorenson II, "U.S. Marketers Can Learn from European Innovators," *Harvard Business Review* (September-October 1972), p. 97.

7. Larry Armstrong, "Disneyland Abroad: Today Tokyo, Tomorrow the World," *Business Week* (March 9, 1987), pp. 68–69.

8. Sheila Tefft, "India's Bill Could Jail Advertisers," *Advertising Age* (May 4, 1987), p. 77.

9. Mary Pitzer, "Most U.S. Companies Are Innocents Abroad," *Business Week* (November 16, 1987), pp. 168–169.

10. Beth Bogart, "Harley-Davidson Trades Restrictions for Profits," *Advertising Age* (August 10, 1987), p. S-27.

11. Robert H. Bork, Jr., " 'New Protectionism' to Fit the Times," *U.S. News & World Report* (April 6, 1987), p. 44.

12. Edith Terry, Bill Javetski, Steven J. Dryden, and John Pearson, "A Free-Trade Milestone," *Business Week* (October 19, 1987), pp. 52–53.

13. Michael Allen, "The Foreign Connection," *The Wall Street Journal,* (May 15, 1987), p. 16D.

Notes   **N11**

14. Barbara Bradley, "U.S. Exporters Must Learn to Ask the Right Questions," *The Christian Science Monitor* (June 5, 1987), p. 22.
15. Baxter Travenol Laboratories, Inc., *1986 Annual Report,* p. 19.
16. Lynne Curry, "Chinese Gobble Kentucky Fried," *Advertising Age* (November 9, 1987), p. 57.
17. Resa W. King and Peter Galuszka, "The Twain Are Meeting—and Cutting Deals," *Business Week* (December 7, 1987), p. 88.
18. Information provided by Nestlé (June 4, 1984).
19. "Hewlett-Packard's Buffer Against Recession," *Business Week* (July 7, 1980), p. 32.
20. Nicholas D. Kristof, "Curbs Give Way to Welcome for Multinational Companies," *The New York Times* (May 11, 1985), pp. 1, 33.
21. John Marcom, Jr., "Cable and Satellites Are Opening Europe to TV Commercials," *The Wall Street Journal* (December 22, 1987), p. 1. See also Gerald M. Hampton and Erwin Buske, "The Global Marketing Perspective," in *Advances in International Marketing,* ed. S. Tamer Cavusgil (Greenwich, Conn.: JAI Press, 1987), pp. 259–277.
22. Julie Skur Hill and Joseph Winski, "Goodbye Global Ads," *Advertising Age* (November 16, 1987), pp. 22, 36.
23. Jeffrey Ferry, "A Tussle Is Brewing," *Northwest* (April 1987), pp. 54–60.
24. Andrew Tanzer, "They Didn't Listen to Anybody," *Forbes* (December 15, 1986), pp. 168–169.
25. Lynn G. Reiling, "Countertrade Revives 'Dead Goods,' " *Marketing News* (August 29, 1986), p. 1.

Chapter 20
1. Sharron Hannon, "RX for Working Parents," *Savvy* (November 1987), p. 36; U.S. Department of Labor, press release number 86–345, August 20, 1986.
2. David Henry, "Lender of Last Resort," *Forbes* (May 18, 1987), pp. 73, 75.
3. The concept of a goods-services continuum is suggested in G. Lynn Shostack, "Breaking Free from Product Marketing," *Journal of Marketing* (April 1977), p. 77. See also John M. Rathmell, "What Is Meant by Services," *Journal of Marketing* (October 1980), pp. 32–36.
4. Bruce Bartlett, "Is U.S. Industry Collapsing All Around Us?" *The Wall Street Journal* (May 8, 1987), p. 21; U.S. Bureau of the Census, *Statistical Abstract of the United States: 1987,* 107th ed. (Washington, D.C.: Government Printing Office, 1986), p. 428; James L. Heskett, "Thank Heaven for the Service Sector," *Business Week* (January 26, 1987), p. 22; and Alan Murray, "Services Equal 25% of Exports, U.S. Study Says," *The Wall Street Journal* (July 2, 1987), p. 9.
5. An interesting article on the complexities of services is Valerie A. Ziethaml, A. Parasuraman, and Leonard L. Berry, "Problems and Strategies in Service Marketing," *Journal of Marketing* (Spring 1985), pp. 33–46.
6. Jeanne Sodeller, "Postal Service Seeks to Dispel Bad Image," *The Wall Street Journal* (May 27, 1987), p. 6.
7. Ronald Alsop, "Financial Services Rediscover Merits of Familiar Ad Symbols," *The Wall Street Journal* (May 14, 1987).
8. This section is based on Eugene M. Johnson, "Are Goods and Services Different? An Exercise in Marketing Theory" (D.B.A. dissertation, Washington University), pp. 83–205. See also Leonard L. Berry, "Services Marketing Is Different," *Business* (May-June 1980), pp. 24–29: Joseph L. Orsini, "Strategic Implications of Differences between Goods and Services: An Empirical Analysis of Information Source Importance," in Stephen H. Achtenhagen, ed., *Proceedings of the 1982 Conference of the Western Marketing Educators,* pp. 61–62; and Duane L. Davis and Robert M. Cosenza, "Identifying Search Prone Segments in the Service Sector: A Test of Taxonometric Research," in Vinay Kothari, Danny R. Arnold, James Cavusgil, Jay D. Lindquist, Jay Nathan, and Stan Reid, eds., *Developments in Marketing Science* (*Proceedings of the Sixth Annual Conference of the Academy of Marketing Science, Las Vegas, 1982*), pp. 301–305.
9. Paul Galloway, "Hospital Chic," *Chicago Tribune* (November 3, 1986), sec. 5, pp. 1, 3.
10. Sidney P. Feldman and Merline C. Spencer, "The Effect of Personal Influence in the Selection of Consumer Services," in *Marketing and Economic Development,* ed. Peter D. Bennett, (Chicago: American Marketing Association, 1967), p. 440.
11. Theodore Levitt, "Marketing Myopia," *Harvard Business Review* (July-August 1961), pp. 45–56.
12. Patricia Bellew Gray, "More Lawyers Reluctantly Adopt Strange New Practice—Marketing," *The Wall Street Journal* (January 30, 1987), p. 25.
13. Pamela Sherrod, "Hospitals, HMOs Still Scrambling to Keep the Lid on Costs," *Chicago Tribune* (January 19, 1987), sec. 4, p. 18.
14. Colin Clark, *The Conditions of Economic Progress,* 3d. ed. (London: Macmillan, 1957), pp. 490–491.
15. David L. Birch, "No Respect," *INC.* (May 1987), pp. 22, 24.
16. Rose Gutfeld, "The Prices of Services, Unlike Those of Goods, Keep Rising Strongly," *The Wall Street Journal* (September 11, 1986), p. 1.
17. "Sorry Service," *Insight* (April 20, 1987), p. 55.
18. John Anderson, "Coverage for Cat-astrophic Illness," *Chicago Tribune* (January 28, 1987), p. D.1.
19. Blaine Cook, "Analyzing Markets for Service," in *Handbook of Modern Marketing,* ed. Victor P. Buell (New York: McGraw-Hill, 1970), pp. 2–44.
20. "The Big Mac Theory of Economic Progress," *Forbes* (April 15, 1977), p. 137. See also Theodore Levitt, "The Industrialization of Service," *Harvard Business Review* (September-October 1976), pp. 63–75.
21. Levitt, "Industrialization of Service," p. 70.
22. William D. Marbach, Jennet Conant, and Mary Hager, "Doctor Digital, We Presume," *Newsweek* (May 20, 1985), p. 83.
23. Gene Bylinsky, "Invasion of the Service Robots," *Fortune* (September 14, 1987), pp. 81–82, 84–86, 88.
24. These examples are from David Elsner, "Funerals Before Their Time," *Chicago Tribune* (July 5, 1987), sec. 7, pp. 1, 5, and Karen Dilgmueller, "A Spa Where Full Figures Fit In," *Insight* (June 22, 1987), p. 40.
25. Joan Berger, "In the Service Sector, Nothing Is 'Free' Anymore," *Business Week* (June 8, 1987), p. 144.
26. The use of promotions in service industries is discussed in Christopher H. Lovelock and John A. Quelch, "Consumer Promotions in Service Marketing," *Business Horizons* (May-June 1983), pp. 66–75.

Appendix
1. The authors would like to thank Dinoo Vanier and Michael Fitzgerald for their contribution to this appendix.
2. These quotes are from Liz Murphy, "Tomorrow's Marketers Speak Out," *Sales and Marketing Management* (July 1986), pp. 58, 61.
3. "Marketing Newsletter," *Sales and Marketing Management* (February 1987), p. 27.
4. Betsy Spethman, Lawro Low, Jo Beth McDaniel, and Marie Spadoni, "How to Join the Ad World," *Advertising Age* (November 16, 1987).
5. This section is partly based on David Rosenthal and Michael A. Powell, *Careers in Marketing* (Englewood Cliffs, N.J.: Prentice Hall, 1984).
6. Al Urbanski, "Are You Keeping Up with Your Peers?" *Sales and Marketing Management* (October 1987), pp. 50–56.
7. Data from College Placement Council Survey, Formal Report No. 3 (July 1987).

accelerator principle The disproportionate impact that changes in consumer demand have on industrial market demand (p. 213)

accessory equipment Capital items, usually less expensive and shorter-lived than installations, such as typewriters, hand tools, and adding machines (p. 276)

administered marketing system Vertical marketing system in which channel coordination is achieved through the exercise of power by a dominant channel member (p. 429)

adoption process Series of stages in the consumer decision process regarding a new product, including awareness, interest, evaluation, trial, and rejection or adoption (p. 285)

advertising Paid, nonpersonal communication through various media by business firms, nonprofit organizations, and individuals who are identified in the advertising message and hope to inform or persuade members of a particular audience (pp. 543, 570)

advertising agency Marketing specialist firm used to assist advertisers in planning and implementing advertising programs (p. 584)

advocacy advertising Paid public communication or message that presents information on a point of view bearing on a publicly recognized, controversial issue (p. 576)

affective component (of attitude) Feelings or emotional reactions (p. 184)

agents Marketing intermediaries who perform wholesaling functions but do not take title to the goods handled (p. 415)

agents and brokers Independent wholesaling intermediaries that may or may not take possession of goods but never take title to them (p. 453)

AIDA concept Acronym for *attention-interest-desire-action,* the traditional explanation of the steps an individual must take prior to making a purchase decision (p. 537)

AIO statements Collection of statements in a psychographic study to reflect the respondents' activities, interests, and opinions (p. 246)

approach Salesperson's initial contact with a prospective customer (p. 618)

Asch phenomenon Occurrence first documented by psychologist S. E. Asch that illustrates the effect of a reference group on individual decision making (p. 170)

aspirational group Subcategory of a reference group where the individual desires to be associated with a group (p. 172)

atmospherics Combination of physical store characteristics and amenities provided by the retailer that results in developing a retail image and attracting customers (p. 480)

attitudes One's enduring favorable or unfavorable evaluations, emotional feelings, or pro or con action tendencies (p. 184)

auction house Establishment that brings buyers and sellers together in one location for the purpose of permitting buyers to examine merchandise before purchase (p. 453)

basing point system System for handling transportation costs used in some industries during the early twentieth century in which the buyer's costs include the factory price plus freight charges from the basing point city nearest the buyer (p. 387)

BCG matrix *See* market share/market growth matrix.

behavioral component (of attitude) Tendencies to act in a certain manner (p. 184)

benefit segmentation Dividing a population into homogeneous groups on the basis of benefits consumers expect to derive from a product or service (p. 249)

bids Written sales proposals from vendors (p. 221)

bottom line Business jargon referring to the overall profitability measure of performance (p. 19)

boundary-spanning role Role performed by a sales manager in linking the sales force to other elements of the organization's internal and external environments (p. 622)

brand Name, term, sign, symbol, design, or some combination of these used to identify the products of one firm and differentiate them from competitive offerings (p. 312)

brand extension Decision to use a popular brand name for a new-product entry in an unrelated product category (p. 315)

brand hostaging Situation in which a retailer demands trade promotion funds from a manufacturer in exchange for shelf space (p. 420)

brand insistence Stage of brand acceptance at which the consumer will accept no alternatives and will search extensively for the product or service. Also known as *brand requirement* (p. 315)

brand name Part of the brand consisting of words or letters that comprise a name used to identify and distinguish the firm's offerings from those of competitors' (p. 312)

brand preference Stage of brand acceptance at which the consumer will select one brand over competitive offerings based on previous experience with it (p. 315)

brand recognition Stage of brand acceptance at which the consumer is aware of the existence of a brand but does not prefer it to competing brands (p. 315)

break-bulk center Facility at which large shipments are divided into many smaller ones and delivered to individual customers in the area, in the interest of reducing transportation expenses (p. 518)

breakeven analysis Pricing technique used to determine the number of products or services that must be sold at a specified price in order to generate sufficient revenue to cover total cost (p. 360)

broadening concept Expanded view of marketing as a generic function to be performed by both profit-seeking and nonprofit organizations (p. 14)

broker Agent wholesaling intermediary that does not take title to or possession of goods and whose primary function is to bring buyers and sellers together (p. 453)

buyers Those who have the formal authority to select a supplier and implement the procedures for securing the product (p. 219)

buyer's market Marketplace characterized by an abundance of goods and/or services (p. 10)

buying center Participants in an organizational buying action (p. 218)

canned approach Memorized sales talk used to ensure uniform coverage of the selling points that management has deemed important (p. 619)

cannibalizing Refers to a product that takes sales from another offering in a product line (p. 296)

capital items Long-lived business assets that must be depreciated over time (p. 213)

cash-and-carry wholesaler Limited-function merchant wholesaler that performs most wholesaling functions except financing and delivery (p. 451)

cash discount Price reduction offered to a consumer, industrial user, or marketing intermediary in return for prompt payment of a bill (p. 383)

catalog retailer Retail merchant who operates from a showroom displaying samples of the product line. Customers place orders for displayed products or items in the store's catalog, and these orders are filled from a warehouse, usually on the store premises (p. 489)

Celler-Kefauver Antimerger Act (1950) Federal legislation amending the Clayton Act to include restrictions on the purchase of assets, where such purchase would decrease competition. Previously, only "acquiring the stock" of another firm was prohibited if it lessened competition (p. 48) *See also* Clayton Act.

census Collection of data from all possible sources in a population or universe (p. 144)

chain store Group of retail stores that are centrally owned and managed and handle essentially the same product lines (p. 492)

channel captain Dominant and controlling member of a marketing channel (p. 418)

class rate Standard transportation rate established for shipping various commodities (p. 509)

Clayton Act (1914) Federal statute that strengthened antitrust legislation by restricting such practices as price discrimination, exclusive dealing, tying contracts, and interlocking boards of directors (p. 48)

closed sales territory Restricted geographical selling region specified by a manufacturer for its distributors (p. 427)

closing Point in personal selling at which the salesperson asks the customer to make a purchase decision (p. 621)

closure The human tendency to produce a complete picture (p. 181)

cluster sample Probability sample in which geographical areas or clusters are selected and all of or a sample within them become respondents (p. 145)

cocooning The current trend that emphasizes greater consciousness of convenience and household comforts (p. 244)

coercive power The threat of economic punishment (p. 418)

cognitions An individual's knowledge, beliefs, and attitudes about certain events (p. 192)

cognitive dissonance Postpurchase anxiety that results when an imbalance exists among an individual's cognitions (knowledge, beliefs, and attitudes) (p. 192)

commercial goods Industrial products not directly used in producing other goods (p. 234)

commission Incentive compensation directly related to the sales or profits achieved by a salesperson (p. 627)

commission merchant Agent wholesaling intermediary that takes possession of goods when they are shipped to a central market for sale, acts as the producer's agent, and collects an agreed-upon fee at the time of sale (p. 453)

commodity rate Special transportation rate granted by carriers to shippers as a reward for either regular use or large-quantity shipments (p. 509)

common carrier Freight transporters that offer shipping service to the public at large (p. 510)

Common Market In international marketing, a format for multinational economic integration involving a customs union and continuing efforts to standardize trade regulations of all governments. *See also* customs unions. (p. 656)

community shopping center A group of 15 to 50 retail stores, often including a branch of a department store as the primary tenant. This type of center typically serves 20,000 to 100,000 persons within a radius of a few miles (p. 477)

comparative advertising Nonpersonal-selling efforts that make direct promotional comparisons with leading competitive brands (p. 587)

competitive bidding Process in which potential suppliers submit price quotations to a buyer for a proposed purchase or contract (p. 393)

competitive environment Interactive process that occurs in the marketplace among marketers of directly competitive products, marketers of products that can be substituted for one another, and marketers competing for the consumer's purchasing power (p. 43)

competitive pricing strategy Pricing strategy designed to de-emphasize price as a competitive variable by pricing a product or service at the general level of comparable offerings (p. 382)

component parts and materials Finished industrial goods that actually become part of the final product. Also known as *fabricated parts and materials* (p. 276)

concentrated marketing Marketing strategy that directs all of a firm's marketing resources toward serving a small segment of the total market (p. 96)

concept testing Measuring consumer attitudes and perceptions of a product idea prior to its actual development (p. 306)

Consolidated Metropolitan Statistical Area (CMSA) Major population concentration, including the 25 or so urban giants (p. 238)

consumer behavior All the acts of individuals in obtaining, using, and disposing of economic goods and services, including the decision processes that precede and determine these acts (p. 162)

consumer goods Products purchased by the ultimate consumer for personal use (p. 234)

Consumer Goods Pricing Act (1975) Federal legislation that halted all interstate usage of resale price maintenance agreements (p. 342)

consumer innovator First purchaser of a new product or service (p. 285)

Consumer Product Safety Act (1972) Federal statute that set up the Consumer Product Safety Commission to specify safety standards for most consumer products (p. 49)

consumerism Social force within the environment designed to aid and protect the consumer by exerting legal, moral, and economic pressures on business and government (p. 64)

consumer orientation Business philosophy incorporating the marketing concept of first determining unmet consumer needs and then designing a system for satisfying them (p. 10)

consumer rights As stated by President Kennedy in 1962, the consumer's right to choose freely, to be informed, to be heard, and to be safe (p. 64)

containerization Process of combining several unitized loads of products into a single load to facilitate intertransport changes in transportation modes (p. 522)

contract carriers Freight transporters who are contracted to certain firms and operate exclusively for a particular industry (p. 510)

contractual marketing system Vertical marketing system in which channel coordination is achieved through the exercise of power by a dominant channel member (p. 429)

convenience goods Products that consumers want to purchase frequently, immediately, and with a minimum of effort (p. 271)

convenience retailer One who sells to the ultimate consumer and focuses chiefly on a central location, long store hours, rapid checkout, and adequate parking facilities (p. 483)

convenience sample Nonprobability sample based on the selection of readily available respondents (p. 145)

cooperative advertising Sharing of advertising costs between the retailer and the manufacturer of the good or service (p. 590)

corporate advertising Form of institutional advertising consisting of nonproduct advertising sponsored by profit-seeking firms (p. 576)

corporate marketing system Vertical marketing system in which there is single ownership of each stage of the marketing channel (p. 428)

corrective advertising Policy of the Federal Trade Commission, under which companies found to have used deceptive promotional messages are required to correct their earlier claims with new messages (p. 50)

cost-plus pricing In pricing strategy, the practice of adding a percentage or specified dollar amount (markup) to the base cost of a product or service to cover unassigned costs and to provide a profit (p. 358)

cost trade-offs Concept in physical distribution whereby some functional areas of the firm will experience cost increases while others will have cost reductions, but the result will be that total physical distribution costs will be minimized (p. 506)

countertrade Form of exporting whereby products and services are bartered rather than sold for cash (p. 664)

coupons Sales promotional tool in which a specially marked slip of paper entitles the bearer to a discount on the purchase of a particular product (p. 593)

creative selling Personal selling involving situations in which a considerable degree of analytical decision making on the buyer's part results in the need for skillful proposals of solutions for the customer's needs (p. 614)

cue Any object existing in the environment that determines the nature of the response to a drive (p. 187)

culture Complex of values, ideas, attitudes, and other meaningful symbols that help people communicate, interpret, and evaluate as members of society (p. 164)

customary prices In pricing strategy, the traditional prices that customers expect to pay for certain products and services (p. 350)

customer service Manner in which marketers treat their customers (p. 323)

customer service standards Quality of service that a firm's customers will receive (p. 506)

customs union In international marketing, a format for multinational economic integration that sets up a free trade area for member nations and a uniform tariff for nonmember nations (p. 656)

data Statistics, opinions, facts, or predictions categorized on some basis for storage and retrieval (p. 147)

database Collection of data that are retrievable through a computer (p. 137)

deciders Those who actually make the buying decision (p. 218)

decision support system (DSS) An interactive, single-source computer storage and retrieval system that incorporates company and commercial data (p. 148)

decoding In marketing communications, the receiver's interpretation of a message (p. 537)

Delphi technique Qualitative sales forecasting method that involves several rounds of anonymous forecasts and ends when a consensus of the participants is reached (p. 106)

demand Schedule of the amounts of a firm's product or service that consumers will purchase at different prices during a specified time period (p. 352)

demarketing Process of reducing consumer demand for a product or service to a level that the firm can supply (p. 55)

demographic segmentation Dividing a population into homogeneous groups based on characteristics such as age, sex, and income level (p. 239)

demographics Characteristics such as age, sex, and income level of potential buyers (p. 572)

department store Large retail firm that handles a variety of merchandise, including clothing, household goods, appliances, and furniture (p. 486)

depreciation The accounting concept of charging a portion of a capital item as a deduction against the company's annual revenue for purposes of determining its net income (p. 213)

derived demand Demand for an industrial product that is linked to demand for a consumer good (p. 210)

differentiated marketing Marketing strategy employed by organizations that produce numerous products or services and use different marketing mixes designed to satisfy numerous market segments (p. 95)

diffusion process Acceptance of new products and services by the members of a community or social system (p. 285)

DINKs Marketing jargon for couples described as dual income, no kids (p. 244)

direct communication flow Communication channel in which information flows from mass media to the general population (p. 173)

direct exporting In international marketing, the activities of a firm that has made a commitment to seek export business (p. 657)

direct marketing Direct communication, other than personal sales contacts, between buyer and seller (p. 412)

direct-sales-results test Technique for measuring the effectiveness of promotional expenditures by ascertaining the increase in revenue per dollar spent (p. 554)

direct selling Direct sales contact between buyer and seller (p. 412)

discount house Store that charges lower-than-normal prices but may not offer many typical retail services such as credit, sales assistance, and home delivery (p. 488)

dissociative group Reference group with which a person does not want to be identified (p. 172)

distribution channel Entity consisting of marketing institutions and their interrelationships responsible for the physical and title flow of goods and services from producer to consumer or industrial user (p. 408)

distribution strategy Element of marketing decision making comprising activities and marketing institutions involved in getting the right product or service to the firm's customers (p. 24)

distribution warehouse Facility designed to assemble and then redistribute products to facilitate rapid movement of products to purchasers (p. 518)

drive Strong stimulus that impels action (p. 187)

drop shipper Limited-function merchant wholesaler that receives orders from customers and forwards them to producers, which ship directly to the customers (p. 452)

dual distribution Network in which a firm uses more than one distribution channel to reach its target market (p. 415)

dumping Controversial practice of selling a product in a foreign market at a price lower than that it receives in the producer's domestic market (p. 654)

economic environment Factors that influence consumer buying power and marketing strategies, including stage of the business cycle, inflation, unemployment, resource availability, and income (p. 52)

economic order quantity (EOQ) model Technique for determining the optimal order quantity for each product; optimal point is determined by balancing the costs of holding inventory and costs involved in placing orders (p. 520)

elasticity Measure of responsiveness of purchasers and suppliers to a change in price (p. 354)

embargo Complete ban on the import of specified products (p. 654)

encoding In marketing communications, the translation of a message into understandable terms and its transmittal through a communication medium (p. 537)

end-use application segmentation Dividing an industrial market into homogeneous groups on the basis of precisely how different industrial purchasers will use the product (p. 253)

Engel's laws Three general statements on spending behavior: As a family's income increases, (1) a smaller percentage of income goes for food; (2) the percentage spent on household operations, housing, and clothing remains constant; and (3) the percentage spent on other items increases (p. 245)

environmental forecasting Broad-based economic forecasting that focuses on the impact of external factors on the firm's markets (p. 109)

environmental management Attainment of organizational objectives by predicting and influencing the competitive, political/legal, economic, technological, and social/cultural environments (p. 42)

Environmental Protection Act (1970) Federal legislation establishing the Environmental Protection Agency and giving it the power to deal with pollution issues (p. 49)

EOQ model *See* economic order quantity model

Equal Credit Opportunity Act (1975–1977) Federal legislation banning discrimination in lending practices based on sex, marital status, race, national origin, religion, age, or receipt of payments from a public assistance program (p. 49)

escalator clause In industrial pricing, component of a bid that allows the seller to adjust the final price based on changes in the costs of the product's ingredients between the placement of the order and the completion of construction or delivery of the product (p. 394)

ethics *See* marketing ethics.

evaluative criteria In consumer decision making, features considered in a consumer's choice of alternatives (p. 191)

evoked set In consumer decision making, number of brands that a consumer actually considers before making a purchase decision (p. 191)

exchange control Method used to regulate the privilege of international trade among importing organizations by controlling access to foreign currencies (p. 654)

exchange process Process by which two or more parties give something of value to each other to satisfy perceived needs (p. 7)

exchange rates Price of one nation's currency in terms of other countries' currencies (p. 650)

exclusive-dealing agreement Arrangement between a manufacturer and a marketing intermediary that prohibits the intermediary from handling competing product lines (p. 427)

exclusive distribution Policy in which a firm grants exclusive rights to a wholesaler or retailer to sell in a particular geographical area (p. 426)

expense item Industrial products and services that are used within a short period of time (p. 213)

experiment Scientific investigation in which a researcher controls or manipulates a test group and compares these results with those of a group that did not receive the controls or manipulations (p. 143)

expert power Channel power that is based on knowledge (p. 418)

exploratory research Process of discussing a marketing problem with informed sources within the firm as well as outside sources such as wholesalers, retailers, and customers and examining secondary sources of information (p. 132)

exponential smoothing Quantitative forecasting technique that assigns weights to historical sales data, giving greater weight to the most recent data (p. 109)

exporting Marketing of goods and services in foreign countries (p. 645)

extended problem solving Situations in which a new brand is difficult to categorize or evaluate (p. 194)

external data In marketing research, the type of secondary data that comes from sources outside a firm (p. 137)

facilitating agency Institution, such as an insurance company, bank, or transportation company, that provides specialized assistance for channel members in moving products from producer to consumer (p. 417)

fads Fashions with abbreviated life cycles such as disco, punk, and new wave music (p. 280)

Fair Credit Reporting Act (1970) Federal legislation providing for individuals' access to credit reports about them and the opportunity to change information that is incorrect (p. 49)

Fair Debt Collection Practices Act (1978) Federal legislation prohibiting harassing, deceptive, or unfair collection practices by debt-collecting agencies (p. 49)

Fair Packaging and Labeling Act (1967) Federal statute requiring disclosure of product identity, name and address of the manufacturer or distributor, and information on the quality of the contents (p. 49)

fair-trade laws Statutes enacted in most states that permitted manufacturers to stipulate a minimum retail price for a product (p. 342)

family brand Name used for several related products, such as the Johnson & Johnson line of baby care products (p. 316)

family life cycle Process of family formation and dissolution that includes five major stages: (1) young single, (2) young married without children, (3) other young, (4) middle-age, and (5) older (p. 242)

fashions Currently popular products that tend to follow recurring life cycles (p. 280)

Federal Trade Commission Act (1914) Federal legislation that prohibited unfair methods of competition and established the Federal Trade Commission to oversee the various laws dealing with business (p. 48)

feedback In marketing communications, the receiver's response to a message (p. 537)

field selling Sales presentations made at prospective customers' homes or businesses on a face-to-face basis (p. 611)

fixed-sum-per-unit method Promotional budget allocation method in which promotional expenditures are a predetermined dollar amount for each sales or production unit (p. 553)

Flammable Fabrics Act (1953) Federal legislation prohibiting the interstate sale of flammable fabrics (p. 48)

flanker brands New products introduced into markets in which the firm already has established positions in an attempt to increase overall market share (p. 301)

FOB plant "Free on board" price quotation that does not include shipping charges and for which the buyer is responsible; also called *FOB origin* (p. 386)

focus group interview Information-gathering procedure in marketing research that typically brings eight to twelve individuals together in one location to discuss a given subject (p. 142)

follow-up Postsales activities that often determine whether an individual who has made a recent purchase will become a repeat customer (p. 621)

Food, Drug, and Cosmetic Act (1938) Federal legislation strengthening the Pure Food and Drug Act to prohibit the adulteration and misbranding of food, drugs, and cosmetics (p. 48)

foreign freight forwarders Transportation intermediaries who consolidate international shipments in order to reduce global transportation costs (p. 524)

foreign licensing Agreement in which a domestic firm permits a foreign company to either produce or distribute the firm's goods in the foreign country or gives it the right to utilize the firm's trademark, patent, or processes in a specified geographical area (p. 658)

form utility Want-satisfying power created by the conversion of raw materials into finished products (p. 4)

franchise Contractual arrangement in which a wholesaler or retail dealer (the franchisee) agrees to meet the operating requirements of a manufacturer or other franchisor (p. 430)

free trade area In international marketing, economic integration between participating nations, without any tariff or trade restrictions (p. 656)

freight absorption System for handling transportation costs under which the buyer may deduct shipping expenses from the cost of the goods (p. 387)

freight forwarders Transportation intermediaries who consolidate shipments to reduce shipping costs for their customers (p. 516)

friendship, commerce, and navigation (FCN) treaties International agreements that deal with many aspects of commercial relations among nations (p. 652)

full-cost pricing Pricing procedure in which all costs are considered in setting a price, allowing the firm to recover all of its costs and realize a profit (p. 359)

full-service research supplier An organization that contracts with a client to conduct a complete marketing research project (p. 129)

functional accounts Income statement expense categories representing the purpose for which an expenditure is made (p. 134)

Fur Products Labeling Act (1951) Federal statute requiring that the name of the animal from which a fur garment was derived be identified (p. 48)

General Agreement on Tariffs and Trade (GATT) International trade agreement that has helped reduce world tariffs (p. 654)

general merchandise retailer Establishment carrying a wide variety of product lines, all of which are stocked in some depth (p. 486)

generic name Brand name that has become a generally descriptive term for a product (p. 314)

generic product Food or household item characterized by a plain label, little or no advertising, and no brand name (p. 318)

geographic segmentation Dividing a population into homogeneous groups on the basis of location (p. 236)

global marketing strategy Standardized marketing mix with minimal modifications that a firm uses in all of its foreign markets (p. 662)

goods-services continuum Method of visualizing the differences and similarities between goods and services (p. 676)

home shopping Use of cable television to merchandise products via telephone order (p. 490)

homogeneous goods Goods the consumer views as essentially the same (p. 273)

hypermarket Giant mass merchandisers of soft goods and groceries that operate on a low-price, self-service basis (p. 488)

hypothesis Tentative explanation about some specific event; statement about the relationship among variables, including clear implications for testing it (p. 135)

iceberg principle Theory suggesting that collected data in summary form often obscure important evaluative information (p. 134)

idea marketing Identification and marketing of a cause to chosen consumer segments (p. 17)

importing Purchasing of foreign products and raw materials (p. 645)

import quota Trade restriction that limits the number of units of certain products that can enter a country for resale (p. 654)

impulse goods Products for which the consumer spends little time in conscious deliberation prior to making a purchase decision (p. 272)

incremental-cost pricing Pricing procedure in which only the costs directly attributable to a specific output are considered in setting a price (p. 360)

indirect exporting Activities of a firm that takes a passive level of involvement in international marketing (p. 657)

individual brand Strategy of giving an item in a product line its own brand name rather than identifying it by a single family brand name used for all products in the line (p. 316)

individual factors Characteristics of the individual, including not only sensory processes but experiences with similar items and basic motivations and expectations (p. 180)

individual offerings Primary component of a product mix consisting of single products (p. 296)

industrial distributor Wholesaling marketing intermediary that operates in the industrial goods market and typically handles small accessory equipment and operating supplies (pp. 276, 414)

industrial goods Products purchased for use directly or indirectly in the production of other goods for resale (p. 234)

industrial (producer) market Component of the organizational market consisting of individuals and firms that acquire goods and services to be used, directly or indirectly, to produce other goods and services (p. 204)

inflation Rising price level that results in reduced purchasing power for the consumer (p. 55)

informal investigation Exploratory marketing research interviews with informed persons outside the firm (p. 132)

information Data relevant to the marketing manager in making decisions (p. 147)

informative advertising Promotion that seeks to announce the availability of and develop initial demand for a product, service, organization, person, place, idea, or cause (p. 576)

infrastructure A nation's communication systems (television, radio, print media, telephone services), transportation networks (paved roads, railroads, airports), and energy facilities (power plants, gas and electric utilities) (p. 650)

installations Major capital items, such as new factories and heavy machinery, that typically are expensive and relatively long-lived (p. 275)

institutional advertising Promoting a concept, an idea, a philosophy, or the goodwill of an industry, company, organization, place, person, or government agency (p. 576)

intensive distribution Policy in which a manufacturer of a convenience good attempts to saturate the market with the product (p. 425)

internal secondary data In marketing research, the type of information that is found in records of sales, product performances, sales force activities, and marketing costs (p. 137)

joint demand Demand for an industrial good as related to the demand for another industrial good that is necessary for the use of the first item (p. 210)

joint venture Agreement in which a firm shares the risks, costs, and management of a foreign operation with one or more partners who are usually citizens of the host country (p. 658)

jury of executive opinion Qualitative sales forecasting method that combines and averages the future business and sales expectations of executives from functional areas such as finance, production, marketing, and purchasing (p. 106)

just-in-time (JIT) inventory system Inventory control system designed to minimize inventory at production plants. Also called *Kan-ban* inventory system (p. 520)

Kefauver-Harris Drug Amendments (1962) Amendments to the Pure Food and Drug Act requiring generic labeling of drugs and a summary of adverse side effects (p. 48)

label Descriptive part of a product's package, listing brand name or symbol, name and address of manufacturer or distributor, ingredients, size or quantity of product, and/or recommended uses, directions, or serving suggestions (p. 322)

Lanham Act (1946) Federal statute providing for federal registration of all trademarks and requiring that registered trademarks not contain words in general use. Such *generic words* are descriptive of a particular type of product, such as "automobile" or "suntan lotion," and thus cannot be given trademark protection (p. 314)

learning Changes in behavior, immediate or expected, that occur as a result of experience (p. 187)

legitimate power The power derived from an organizational structure (p. 418)

life-cycle costing Determining the cost of using a product over its lifetime rather than just the initial bid price (p. 222)

life-style The way people decide to live their lives, including family, job, social activities, and consumer decisions (p. 246)

limited-line store Retail establishment that offers a large assortment of one-product lines or just a few related product lines (p. 484)

limited problem solving A situation in which a consumer has set evaluative criteria but encounters a new, unknown brand (p. 193)

limited-service research supplier A firm that specializes in a limited number of marketing research activities (p. 129)

line extension New product that is closely related to other products in the firm's existing product line (p. 297)

list price Established price normally quoted to potential buyers (p. 383)

logistics *See* physical distribution.

loss leader Product offered to consumers at less than cost to attract them to retail stores in the hope that they will buy other merchandise at regular prices (p. 390)

Magnuson-Moss Warranty Act (1975) Federal statute authorizing the Federal Trade Commission to develop regulations on warranty practices (p. 325)

mail-order wholesaler Limited-function merchant wholesaler that utilizes catalogs instead of a sales force to contact customers in an attempt to reduce operating expenses (p. 452)

make-bulk center Facility at which several small shipments are consolidated into a large shipment and delivered to a central destination in an attempt to reduce transportation costs (p. 518)

mall intercepts Marketing research interviews conducted in shopping centers (p. 142)

manufacturers' agent Agent wholesaling intermediary who represents a number of manufacturers of related but non-competing products and receives a commission based on a specified percentage of sales (p. 453)

manufacturer's (national) brand Brand name owned by a manufacturer or other producer (p. 317)

manufacturer's representative Agent wholesaling intermediary that acts as an independent sales force in contacting buyers (p. 415)

markdown Amount by which the retailer reduces the original selling price of a product (p. 476)

market Group of people who possess purchasing power and the authority and willingness to purchase (p. 234)

market development strategy A product strategy that concentrates on finding new markets for existing products (p. 300)

marketing Process of planning and executing the conception, pricing, promotion, and distribution of ideas, goods, and services to create exchanges that will satisfy individual and organizational objectives (pp. 5, 86)

marketing audit Thorough, objective evaluation of an organization's marketing philosophy, goals, policies, tactics, practices, and results (p. 104)

marketing communications Transmission from a sender to a receiver of messages dealing with buyer-seller relationships (p. 536)

marketing channels Route taken by a product or service and/or title to the product or service as it moves from producer to final purchaser; includes producer, consumer or industrial user, and any marketing intermediaries involved in the channel (p. 445)

marketing concept Companywide consumer orientation with the objective of achieving long-run success (p. 11)

marketing cost analysis Evaluation of such items as selling costs, billing, and advertising to determine the profitability of particular customers, territories, or product lines (p. 134)

marketing ethics Marketers' standards of conduct and moral values (p. 65)

marketing information system (MIS) Planned, computer-based system designed to provide managers with a continuous flow of information relevant to their specific decision areas (p. 147)

marketing intermediary Business firm, either wholesale or retail, that operates between the producer of goods and the consumer or industrial user; sometimes called *middleman* (p. 408)

marketing mix Blending the four strategy elements of marketing decision making — product, pricing, distribution, and promotion — to satisfy chosen consumer segments (p. 22)

marketing myopia Term coined by Theodore Levitt in his argument that executives in many industries fail to recognize the broad scope of their businesses; according to Levitt, future growth is endangered because these executives lack a marketing orientation (p. 13)

marketing planning Process of anticipating the future and determining the courses of action necessary for achieving marketing objectives (p. 86)

marketing research Systematic gathering, recording, and analysis of data about problems and opportunities relating to the marketing of goods and services, persons, places, ideas, and organizations (p. 126)

marketing strategy Overall company program for selecting a particular target market and then satisfying target consumers through a blending of the marketing mix elements (p. 93)

market price Price a consumer or marketing intermediary actually pays for a product or service after subtracting any discounts, allowances, or rebates from the list price (p. 383)

market segmentation Process of dividing the total market into several relatively homogeneous groups with similar product or service interests based on such factors as demographic or psychographic characteristics, geographic location, or perceived product benefits (p. 235)

market share/market growth matrix Matrix developed by the Boston Consulting Group that enables a firm to classify its products and services in terms of the industry growth rate and its market share relative to competitive products. The four segments are stars, cash cows, question marks, and dogs (p. 101)

market share objective Pricing objective linked to achieving and maintaining a stated percentage of the market for a firm's product or service (p. 347)

market test Quantitative forecasting technique in which a new product, price, promotional campaign, or other marketing variable is introduced in a relatively small test market location in order to assess consumer reactions under realistic market conditions (p. 107)

markup In pricing strategy, amount added to the cost of an item to determine its selling price (p. 474)

mass merchandiser Store that stocks a wider line of goods than does a department store but usually does not offer the same depth of assortment (p. 488)

materials handling All activities involved in moving products within a manufacturer's plants, warehouses, and transportation company terminals (p. 522)

media scheduling Timing and sequencing of advertisements (p. 583)

membership group Type of reference group in which the reference group members are members of a formal group such as a country club, church group, or other organization (p. 172)

merchandise mart Permanent exhibition facility in which manufacturers rent showrooms to display products for visiting retail and wholesale buyers, designers, and architects (p. 449)

merchant wholesaler Wholesaling intermediary that takes title to the goods it handles (p. 450)

Metropolitan Statistical Area (MSA) Large, free-standing area for which detailed marketing-related data are collected by the Bureau of the Census (p. 238)

middleman *See* marketing intermediary.

Miller-Tydings Resale Price Maintenance Act (1937) Federal legislation that exempted interstate fair trade contracts from compliance with antitrust requirements (p. 342)

missionary sales Indirect type of selling in which specialized salespeople promote the firm's goodwill, often by assisting customers in product use (p. 616)

modified breakeven analysis Pricing technique used to evaluate consumer demand by comparing the number of products or services that must be sold at a variety of prices in order to cover total cost with estimates of expected sales at the various prices (p. 363)

modified rebuy Situation in which purchasers are willing to reevaluate available options in a repurchase of the same product or service (p. 217)

monopolistic competition Market structure involving a heterogeneous product and product differentiation among competing suppliers, allowing the marketer some degree of control over prices (p. 353)

monopoly Market structure involving only one seller of a product or service for which no close substitutes exist (p. 353)

motive Inner state that directs a person toward the goal of satisfying a felt need (p. 178)

MRO items Supplies for an industrial firm, categorized as maintenance items, repair items, or operating supplies (p. 278)

multinational corporation Firm with significant operations and marketing activities outside its home country (p. 659)

multinational marketing strategy Application of market segmentation to foreign markets by tailoring the firm's marketing mix to match specific target markets in each nation (p. 663)

multistep communication flow Communication channel in which information flows from mass media to opinion leader and then on to other opinion leaders before being disseminated to the general population (p. 173)

national brand *See* manufacturer's brand.

natural accounts Expense categories traditionally listed on an organization's income statement. An example is salary expenses (p. 134)

need Lack of something useful; a discrepancy between a desired state and the actual state (p. 178)

neighborhood shopping center Geographical cluster of stores, usually consisting of a supermarket and about 5 to 15 smaller stores. The center provides convenient shopping for 5,000 to 15,000 shoppers in its vicinity (p. 477)

new-task buying First-time or unique purchase situations that require considerable effort on the decision makers' part (p. 218)

noise In marketing communications, interference in a transmitted message (p. 537)

nonprobability sample Arbitrary sample in which most standard statistical tests cannot be applied to the collected data (p. 145)

nonprofit organization Firm whose primary objective is something other than the return of a profit to its owners (p. 15)

odd pricing Pricing policy based on the belief that a price with an uncommon last digit is more appealing than a round figure, such as $9.99 rather than $10 (p. 388)

off-price retailer Retailer that sells designer labels or well-known brand name clothing at less than typical retail prices (p. 488)

oligopoly Market structure involving relatively few sellers and barriers to new competitors due to high start-up costs (p. 353)

opinion leader Individual in a group who serves as an information source for other group members (p. 173)

order processing Selling at the wholesale and retail levels; specifically, identifying customer needs, pointing them out to customers, and completing orders (p. 613)

operating supplies *See* MRO items.

organizational market Marketplace made up of producers, trade industries (wholesalers and retailers), institutions, and governments at the federal, state, and local levels (p. 204)

organization marketing Marketing by mutual benefit organizations, service organizations, and government organizations that seek to influence others to accept their goals, receive their services, or contribute to them in some way (p. 18)

outlet mall Shopping center consisting entirely of off-price retailers (p. 488)

overseas marketing In international marketing, a firm's maintenance of a separate selling operation in a foreign country (p. 658)

over-the-counter selling Personal selling conducted in retail and some wholesale locations in which customers come to the seller's place of business (p. 612)

ownership A classification of wholesaling intermediary on the basis of whether they are independent, manufacturer-owned, or retailer-owned (p. 446)

ownership utility Want-satisfying power created by marketers when title to a product is transferred to the customer at the time of purchase. Also known as *possession utility* (p. 409)

party selling Retail distribution strategy under which a company's representative makes a presentation of the product(s) in a party setting. Orders are taken and the host or hostess receives a commission or gift based on the amount of sales (p. 489)

penetration pricing strategy Pricing strategy involving the use of a relatively low entry price as compared with competitive offerings; based on the theory that this initial low price will help secure market acceptance (p. 380)

percentage-of-sales method Promotional budget allocation method in which the funds allocated for promotion during a given time period are based on a specified percentage of either past or forecasted sales (p. 553)

perception Manner in which an individual interprets a stimulus; the often highly subjective meaning that one attributes to an incoming stimulus or message (p. 180)

perceptual screen Perceptual filter through which messages must pass to be consciously perceived (p. 180)

personal selling Interpersonal influence process involving a seller's promotional presentation conducted on a person-to-person basis with the prospective buyer (pp. 543, 610)

person marketing Marketing efforts designed to cultivate the attention, interest, and preference of a target market toward a person (typically a political candidate or celebrity) (p. 15)

persuasive advertising Competitive promotion that seeks to develop demand for a product, service, organization, person, place, idea, or cause (p. 576)

phased development A traditional method for developing new products which follows a sequential pattern whereby products are developed in an orderly series of steps (p. 309)

physical distribution Broad range of activities concerned with efficient movement of finished products from the end of the production line to the consumer; includes customer service, transportation, inventory control, packaging and materials handling, order processing, and warehousing (p. 502)

place marketing Marketing efforts to attract people and organizations to a particular geographical area (p. 16)

place utility Want-satisfying power created by marketers who have products available where consumers want to buy them (p. 409)

planned shopping center Group of retail stores planned, coordinated, and marketed as a unit to shoppers in a geographic trade area (p. 476)

planning Process of anticipating the future and determining the courses of action necessary for achieving organizational objectives (p. 86)

point-of-purchase advertising Displays and other promotions located near the site of the actual buying decision (p. 594)

political/legal environment Component of the marketing environment consisting of laws and interpretations of laws that require firms to operate under competitive conditions and to protect consumer rights (p. 47)

population (universe) Total group that the researcher wants to study (p. 144)

positioning Developing a marketing strategy aimed at a particular market segment and designed to achieve a desired position in the prospective buyer's mind (p. 574)

POSLSQ Acronym for unmarried persons of the opposite sex living together in the same quarters; U.S. Census Bureau designation of a household format whose numbers are increasing (p. 244)

possession utility *See* ownership utility.

posttesting Assessment of an advertisement's effectiveness after it has been used (p. 592)

precall planning Use of information collected during the prospecting and qualifying stages of the sales process and during previous contacts with the prospect to tailor the approach and presentation to match the customer's needs (p. 618)

premiums Items given free or at low costs with the purchase of a specified good or service (p. 595)

presentation Describing a product's major features and relating them to a customer's problems or needs (p. 618)

pretesting Assessment of an advertisement's effectiveness before it is actually used (p. 591)

price Exchange value of a good or service (p. 340)

price flexibility Pricing policy permitting variable prices for products and services (p. 389)

price lining *See* product line pricing.

pricing policy General guidelines based on pricing objectives and intended for use in specific pricing decisions (p. 388)

pricing strategy Element of marketing decision making that deals with the methods of setting profitable and justifiable exchange values for goods and services (p. 24)

primary data Information or statistics collected for the first time during a marketing research study (p. 137)

Primary Metropolitan Statistical Area (PMSA) Major urban area within a CMSA (p. 238)

private brand Brand name owned by a wholesaler or retailer (p. 317)

private carriers Freight transporters who operate only for a particular firm and cannot solicit business from others (p. 511)

probability sample Sample in which every member of the population has an equal chance of being selected (p. 144)

producers Component of the organizational market consisting of industrial customers who purchase goods and services for the production of other goods and services (p. 204)

product Bundle of physical, service, and symbolic attributes designed to enhance consumer want satisfaction (p. 271)

product advertising Nonpersonal selling of a good or service (p. 576)

product development strategy A product strategy based on the introduction of new products into identifiable or established markets (p. 300)

product diversification strategy A product strategy employing the development of new products for new markets (p. 301)

product improvement strategy A product strategy that relies on a modification of the product offering (p. 300)

production orientation Business philosophy stressing efficiency in producing a quality product; attitude toward marketing is "a good product will sell itself" (p. 8)

productivity Output produced by each worker (p. 688)

product liability Concept that manufacturers and marketers are responsible for injuries and damages caused by their products (p. 326)

product life cycle Four stages through which a successful product passes—introduction, growth, maturity, and decline (p. 278)

product line Various related goods offered by a firm (p. 296)

product line pricing Practice of marketing different lines of merchandise at a limited number of prices (p. 390)

product manager Individual in a manufacturing firm assigned a product or product line and given complete responsibility for determining objectives and establishing marketing strategies (p. 302)

product mix Assortment of product lines and individual offerings available from a marketer (p. 296)

product positioning Consumer's perception of a product's attributes, use, quality, and advantages and disadvantages (p. 300)

product segmentation Dividing an industrial market into homogeneous groups on the basis of product specifications identified by industrial buyers (p. 252)

product strategy Element of marketing decision making comprising activities involved in developing the right product or service for the firm's customers; involves package design, branding, trademarks, warranties, product life cycles, and new-product development (p. 23)

profit center Any part of an organization to which revenue and controllable costs can be assigned (p. 395)

Profit Impact of Market Strategies (PIMS) project Major research study that discovered a strong positive relationship between a firm's market share and its return on investment (p. 347)

profit maximization In pricing strategy, point at which the additional revenue gained by increasing the price of a product equals the increase in total cost (p. 345)

promotion Function of informing, persuading, and influencing the consumer's purchase decision (p. 536)

promotional allowance Advertising or sales promotion funds provided by a manufacturer to other channel members in an attempt to integrate promotional strategy within the channel (p. 385)

promotional mix Blending of personal selling and nonpersonal selling (including advertising, sales promotion, and public relations) by marketers in an attempt to achieve promotional objectives (p. 543)

promotional pricing Pricing policy in which a lower-than-normal price is used as a temporary ingredient in a firm's marketing strategy (p. 390)

promotional strategy Element of marketing decision making that involves appropriate blending of personal selling, advertising, and sales promotion for use in communicating with and seeking to persuade potential customers (p. 25)

prospecting Personal-selling function of identifying potential customers (p. 617)

psychographics Behavioral profiles developed from analyses of buyer activities, opinions, interests, and life-styles that may be used to segment consumer markets (p. 572)

psychographic segmentation Dividing a population into homogeneous groups on the basis of behavioral and life-style profiles developed by analyzing consumer activities, opinions, and interests (p. 246)

psychological pricing Pricing policy based on the belief that certain prices or price ranges are more appealing than others to buyers (p. 386)

Public Health Cigarette Smoking Act (1971) Federal legislation restricting tobacco advertising on radio and television (p. 49)

publicity Stimulation of demand for a product, service, place, idea, person, or organization by disseminating commercially significant news or obtaining favorable media presentation not paid for by the sponsor (pp. 545, 598)

public relations Firm's communications and relationships with its various publics (pp. 544, 595)

public warehouse Independently owned storage facility that stores and ships products for a rental fee (p. 447)

pulling strategy Promotional effort by a seller to stimulate demand by final users, who will then exert pressure on the distribution channel to carry the product or service, thereby "pulling" it through the marketing channel (p. 549)

pure competition Market structure characterized by homogeneous products in which there are so many buyers and sellers that none has a significant influence on price (p. 352)

Pure Food and Drug Act (1906) Federal legislation that prohibits the adulteration and misbranding of foods and drugs in interstate commerce (p. 48)

pushing strategy Promotional effort by a seller to members of the marketing channel to stimulate personal selling of the good or service, thereby "pushing" it through the marketing channel (p. 551)

qualifying Determining that a prospect has the needs, income, and purchase authority necessary for being a potential customer (p. 618)

quantity discount Price reduction granted for a large-volume purchase (p. 385)

quota *See* sales quota.

quota sample Nonprobability sample that is divided such that different segments or groups are represented in the total sample (p. 145)

rack jobber Full-function merchant that markets specialized lines of merchandise to retail stores and provides the services of merchandising and arrangement, pricing, maintenance, and stocking of display racks (p. 451)

raw materials Industrial goods, such as farm products (wheat, cotton, soybeans) and natural products (coal, lumber, iron ore), used in producing final products (p. 276)

rebate Refund for a portion of the purchase price, usually granted by the product's manufacturer (p. 385)

reciprocity Highly controversial practice of extending purchasing preference to suppliers who are also customers (p. 221)

reference group Group with which an individual identifies to the point where it dictates a standard of behavior for him or her (p. 171)

referent power Power derived from an agreement among channel members as to what is in their mutual best interests (p. 418)

regional shopping center Largest type of a planned cluster of retail stores, usually involving one or more major department stores and as many as 200 other stores. A center of this size typically is located in an area with at least 250,000 people within 30 minutes driving time of the center (p. 478)

reinforcement Reduction in drive that results from an appropriate response (p. 187)

reminder advertising Promotion that seeks to reinforce previous promotional activity by keeping the name of the product, service, organization, person, place, idea, or cause in front of the public (p. 576)

research design Series of advanced decisions that, when taken together, comprise a master plan or a model for conducting marketing research (p. 136)

response Individual's reaction to cues and drives (p. 187)

retail advertising Nonpersonal selling by stores that offer goods or services directly to the consuming public (p. 590)

retail cooperative A wholesaling operation established by a group of retailers to help them better compete in the marketplace (p. 429)

retailer One who sells products or services to the ultimate consumer and not for resale (p. 409)

retail image Consumers' perception of the store and the shopping experience it provides (p. 470)

retailing All activities involved in the sale of products and services to the ultimate consumer (p. 468)

reverse channel Path goods follow from consumer back to manufacturer (p. 416)

reverse reciprocity The practice of extending supply privileges to firms that provide needed supplies (p. 221)

reward power A situation whereby a channel member can offer some type of reward to another member (p. 418)

Robinson-Patman Act (1936) Federal legislation prohibiting price discrimination that is not based on a cost differential; also prohibits selling at an unreasonably low price to eliminate competition (p. 341)

roles Behavior that members of a group expect of individuals who hold a specific position within it (p. 170)

routinized response behavior Purchases made on the basis of a preferred brand or selection from a limited group of acceptable brands (p. 193)

salary Fixed compensation payments made periodically to an employee (p. 627)

sales analysis In-depth evaluation of a firm's sales (p. 133)

sales branch Establishment maintained by a manufacturer that serves as a warehouse for a particular sales territory, thereby duplicating the services of independent wholesalers; carries inventory and processes orders to customers from available stock (p. 447)

sales force composite Qualitative sales forecasting method in which sales estimates are based on the combined estimates of the firm's sales force (p. 106)

sales forecast Estimate of company sales for a specified future period (p. 104)

sales management Activities of planning, organizing, staffing, motivating, compensating, and evaluating and controlling a sales force to ensure its effectiveness (p. 622)

sales maximization Practice of setting the lowest acceptable profit level as a minimum and then seeking to enlarge sales within this framework. Under this policy, marketers believe that increased sales are more important than immediate high profits in the long run (p. 346)

sales office Manufacturer's establishment that serves as a regional office for salespeople but does not carry inventory (p. 448)

sales orientation Business philosophy assuming that consumers will resist purchasing nonessential products and services; attitude toward marketing is that creative advertising and personal selling are required in order to overcome consumer resistance and convince them to buy (p. 9)

sales promotion Marketing activities other than personal selling, advertising, and publicity, that stimulate consumer purchasing and dealer effectiveness; includes displays, trade shows and expositions, demonstrations, and various nonrecurrent selling efforts (pp. 544, 593)

sales quota Level of expected sales for a territory, product, customer, or salesperson against which actual results are compared (p. 134)

sample A representative group (p. 595)

samples Products that are distributed at no cost to consumers in an attempt to obtain future sales (p. 595)

scrambled merchandising Retailing practice of carrying dissimilar product lines in an attempt to generate additional sales volume (p. 493)

secondary data Previously published data (p. 137)

selective distribution Policy in which a firm chooses only a limited number of retailers to handle its product line (p. 426)

selective perception Idea that consumers "perceive by exception"; they are consciously aware of only those incoming stimuli they wish to perceive (p. 180)

self-concept Mental conception of one's self, comprised of the real self, self-image, looking-glass self, and ideal self (p. 189)

seller's market Marketplace characterized by a shortage of goods and/or services (p. 10)

selling agent Agent wholesaling intermediary responsible for the total marketing program of a firm's product line (p. 453)

selling up Retail sales technique of convincing a customer to buy a higher-priced item than he or she originally intended (p. 480)

services Intangible tasks that satisfy consumer and industrial user needs when efficiently developed and distributed to chosen market segments (p. 676)

shaping Process of applying a series of rewards and reinforcements so that more complex behavior can evolve over time (p. 187)

Sherman Antitrust Act (1890) Federal antitrust legislation that prohibits restraint of trade and monopolization and subjects violators to civil suits as well as to criminal prosecution (p. 48)

shopping goods Products purchased only after the consumer has made comparisons of competing goods in competing stores on such bases as price, quality, style, and color. Can be classified as either *homogeneous* (consumer views them as essentially the same) or *heterogeneous* (consumer sees significant differences in quality and style) (p. 272)

shopping store Establishment at which customers typically compare prices, assortments, and quality levels with those of competing outlets before making a purchase decision (p. 483)

simple random sample Basic type of probability sample in which every item in the relevant universe has an equal opportunity to be selected (p. 144)

situation analysis The internal data collection stage of marketing research (p. 132)

skimming pricing strategy Pricing strategy involving the use of a high price relative to competitive offerings (p. 377)

social class Relatively permanent divisions of a society into which individuals or families are categorized on the basis of prestige and community status (p. 172)

social/cultural environment Component of the marketing environment consisting of the relationship between the marketer and society and its culture (p. 60)

social responsibility Marketing philosophies, policies, procedures, and actions that have the enhancement of society's welfare as a primary objective (p. 69)

specialty advertising Sales promotion technique that involves the use of articles such as key rings, calendars, and ballpoint pens that bear the advertiser's name, address, and advertising message (p. 594)

specialty goods Products with unique characteristics that cause the buyer to prize them and make a special effort to obtain them (p. 274)

specifications Written description of a product or service needed by a firm; prospective bidders use this description first to determine whether they can manufacture the product or deliver the service and then to prepare bids (p. 221)

spreadsheet analysis Marketing planning tool that uses a decision-oriented computer program designed to answer "what-if" questions by analyzing different groups of data provided by the manager (p. 103)

SSWD Refers to single, separated, widowed, or divorced people; a term applied to single-person households, an emerging market segment (p. 244)

Standard Industrial Classification (SIC) Numerical system developed by the U.S. government that subdivides the industrial marketplace into detailed market segments (p. 208)

status Relative position of any individual in a group (p. 170)

stimulus factors Characteristics of the physical object such as size, color, weight, or shape (p. 180)

stockout Inventory item that is unavailable for shipment or sale (p. 522)

storage warehouse Traditional warehouse in which products are stored prior to shipment (p. 518)

straight rebuy Recurring purchase decision in which an item that has performed satisfactorily is purchased again by a customer (p. 217)

strategic business unit (SBU) Related product groupings of businesses within a multiproduct firm with specific managers, resources, objectives, and competitors; structured for optimal planning purposes (p. 100)

strategic planning Process of determining an organization's primary objectives, allocating funds, and then proceeding with a course of action designed to achieve those objectives (p. 86)

strategic window Limited periods during which the "fit" between the key requirements of a market and the particular competencies of a firm is optimal (p. 91)

stratified sample Probability sample that is constructed so that randomly selected subsamples of different groups are represented in the total sample (p. 144)

subculture Subgroup of a culture with its own distinct mode of behavior (p. 166)

subliminal perception Receipt of information at a subconscious level (p. 182)

suboptimization Condition in which individual objectives are achieved at the expense of broader organizational objectives (p. 505)

suggestion selling Form of retail selling that attempts to broaden the customer's original purchase with related items, special promotions, and holiday or seasonal merchandise (p. 480)

supermarket Large-scale departmentalized retail store offering a variety of food products and various nonfood items. It typically operates on a self-service basis and emphasizes low prices and adequate parking (p. 485)

supplies Regular expense items necessary in the firm's daily operation but not part of the final product (p. 277)

supply Schedule of the amounts of a product or service that a firm will offer for sale at different prices during a specified time period (p. 352)

survey of buyer intentions Qualitative sales forecasting method in which sample groups of present and potential customers are surveyed concerning their purchase intentions (p. 106)

syndicated service An organization that provides a standardized set of data to customers on a regular basis (p. 129)

system Organized group of components linked according to a plan for achieving specific objectives (p. 504)

tactical planning Implementation of activities specified in the strategic plan that are necessary in the achievement of the firm's objectives (p. 87)

target market Group of people toward whom a firm markets its goods, services, or ideas with a strategy designed to satisfy their specific needs and preferences (p. 20)

target market decision analysis Evaluation of potential market segments by dividing the overall market into homogeneous groups; cross-classifications may be based on variables such as type of market, geographic location, frequency of use, or demographic characteristics (p. 256)

target return objectives Short-run or long-run pricing objectives of achieving a specified return on either sales or investment (p. 346)

tariff Tax levied against imported products (p. 654)

task-objective method Promotional budget allocation method in which a firm defines its goals and then determines the amount of promotional spending needed for achieving them (p. 554)

technological environment Applications to marketing of knowledge based on discoveries in science, inventions, and innovations (p. 57)

telemarketing Promotional presentation involving the use of the telephone on an outbound basis by salespeople or an inbound basis by customers who initiate calls to obtain information and place orders (p. 612)

tertiary industry Industry whose firms specialize in the production of services (p. 684)

test marketing Process of selecting a specific city or television coverage area considered reasonably typical of a new total market and introducing the product with a marketing campaign in this area (p. 308)

time utility Want-satisfying power created by marketers having products available when consumers want to buy them (p. 409)

title flows A term that refers to how title passes from the manufacturer to the wholesaling intermediary (p. 446)

trade discount Payment to a channel member or buyer for performing marketing functions; also known as a *functional discount* (p. 384)

trade fair Periodic show at which manufacturers in a particular industry display wares for visiting retail and wholesale buyers (p. 448)

trade-in Credit allowance given for an old item when a customer purchases a new item (p. 385)

trade industries Component of the organizational market composed of retailers or wholesalers that purchase goods for resale to others (p. 204)

trademark Brand that has been given legally protected status exclusive to its owner (p. 312)

trading stamps Sales promotion technique involving special stamps that are given as a purchase premium in some retail establishments and can be collected and redeemed for cash or gifts at special redemption centers operated by the trading stamp company (p. 596)

transfer mechanism In marketing communications, the means of delivering a message (p. 537)

transfer price Cost assessed when a product is moved from one profit center in a firm to another (p. 395)

trend analysis Quantitative sales forecasting method in which estimates of future sales are determined through statistical analyses of historical sales patterns (p. 107)

truck wholesaler Limited-function merchant wholesaler that markets perishable food items; also called *truck jobber* (p. 452)

truth-in-lending act (1968) Federal legislation requiring disclosure of the annual interest rates on loans and credit purchases; formally known as Title I of the Consumer Credit Protection Act (1968) (p. 49)

two-step process of communication Communication channel in which information flows from mass media to opinion leaders to the general population (p. 173)

tying agreement Arrangement between a marketing intermediary and a manufacturer that requires the intermediary to carry the manufacturer's full product line in exchange for an exclusive dealership (p. 427)

undifferentiated marketing Marketing strategy employed by organizations that produce only one product or service and market it to all customers using a single marketing mix (p. 93)

unfair-trade laws State laws requiring sellers to maintain minimum prices for comparable merchandise (p. 342)

uniform delivered price System for handling transportation costs under which all buyers are quoted the same price, including transportation expenses (p. 387)

unitizing Process of combining as many packages as possible into one load, preferably on a pallet, in order to expedite product movement and reduce damage and pilferage (p. 522)

unit pricing Pricing policy in which prices are stated in terms of a recognized unit of measurement or a standard numerical count (p. 389)

unit trains Time- and money-saving service provided by railroads to large-volume customers, in which a train is loaded with the shipments of only one company and transports solely for that customer (p. 512)

Universal Product Code (UPC) Special code on packages read by optical scanners (p. 322)

users Those who control the information to be reviewed by other buying center members (p. 218)

utility Want-satisfying power of a product or service (p. 4)

value added by manufacturing Difference between the price charged for a manufactured good and the cost of the raw materials and other inputs (p. 206)

value analysis Systematic study of the components of a purchase to determine the most cost-effective way to acquire the item (p. 215)

variety store A retail firm that offers an extensive range and assortment of low-priced merchandise (p. 486)

vendor analysis Assessment of a supplier's performance in areas such as price, back orders, timely delivery, and attention to special requests (p. 215)

venture team Organizational strategy for identifying and developing new-product areas by combining the management resources of technological innovation, capital, management, and marketing expertise (p. 303)

vertical marketing system (VMS) Preplanned distribution channel organized to be cost effective and achieve improved distribution efficiency (p. 428)

warehouse club A no-frills, cash-and-carry outlet (p. 488)

warranty Guarantee to the buyer that the manufacturer will replace a product or refund its purchase price if the product proves defective during a specified time period (p. 325)

Webb-Pomerene Export Trade Act (1918) Federal legislation that excludes voluntary export trade associations from restrictions of the Sherman Act, but only in their foreign dealings (p. 653)

Wheeler-Lea Act (1938) Federal statute amending the FTC Act so as to ban deceptive or unfair business practices per se (p. 48)

wheel of retailing Hypothesis stating that new types of retailers gain a competitive foothold by offering lower prices through reduction or elimination of services; once established, they add more services, gradually raise their prices, and then become vulnerable to the emergence of a new, low-price retailer with minimum services (p. 469)

wholesaler Wholesaling intermediary that takes title to the goods it handles; also called *jobber* or *distributor* (p. 439)

wholesaler-sponsored voluntary chain A wholesaler organized chain of independent retail stores (p. 429)

wholesaling intermediary Broad term describing both wholesalers and agents and brokers that perform important wholesaling activities without taking title to the goods (p. 439)

Wool Products Labeling Act (1939) Federal legislation requiring that the kind and percentage of each type of wool in a product be identified (p. 48)

zone pricing System for handling transportation costs under which the market is divided into geographic regions and a different price is set in each region (p. 387)

NAME & COMPANY INDEX

SUBJECT INDEX

*Key terms and the page number(s) on which they are defined appear in boldface type.